Lecture Notes in Computer Science 1320

Edited by G. Goos, J. Hartmanis and J. van Leeuwen

Advisory Board: W. Brauer D. Gries J. Stoer

Springer

Berlin
Heidelberg
New York
Barcelona
Budapest
Hong Kong
London
Milan
Paris
Santa Clara
Singapore
Tokyo

Marios Mavronicolas
Philippas Tsigas (Eds.)

Distributed Algorithms

11th International Workshop, WDAG '97
Saarbrücken, Germany, September 24-26, 1997
Proceedings

Springer

Series Editors

Gerhard Goos, Karlsruhe University, Germany

Juris Hartmanis, Cornell University, NY, USA

Jan van Leeuwen, Utrecht University, The Netherlands

Volume Editors

Marios Mavronicolas
University of Cyprus, Department of Computer Science
Nicosia CY-1678, Cyprus
E-mail: mavronic@turing.cs.ucy.ac.cy

Philippas Tsigas
Max-Planck-Institut für Informatik
Im Stadtwald, D-66123 Saarbrücken, Germany
E-mail: tsigas@mpi-sb.mpg.de

Cataloging-in-Publication data applied for

Die Deutsche Bibliothek - CIP-Einheitsaufnahme

Distributed algorithms : 11th international workshop ; proceedings /
WDAG '97, Saarbrücken, Germany, September 24 - 26, 1997. Marios
Mavronicolas ; Philippas Tsigas (ed.). - Berlin ; Heidelberg ; New
York ; Barcelona ; Budapest ; Hong Kong ; London ; Milan ; Paris ;
Santa Clara ; Singapore ; Tokyo : Springer, 1997
   (Lecture notes in computer science ; Vol. 1320)
   ISBN 3-540-63575-0

CR Subject Classification (1991): F.2.2, C.2.2, D.1.3, F.1, C.2.4, D.4.4-5,
I.2.11

ISSN 0302-9743
ISBN 3-540-63575-0 Springer-Verlag Berlin Heidelberg New York

Typesetting: Camera-ready by author
SPIN 10545777   06/3142 – 5 4 3 2 1 0   Printed on acid-free paper

Preface

The International Workshop on Distributed Algorithms (WDAG) is intended
to provide an annual forum for researchers from both academia and industry
interested in distributed algorithms and their applications. The aim has been
to host presentations of new results and to identify important future research
directions.

This volume contains the 20 papers presented at the 11th International Workshop on Distributed Algorithms (WDAG'97), which was held September 24–26,
1997, in Saarbrücken, Germany. Opening the volume are two extended abstracts
based on the two keynote lectures delivered by Andreas Reuter (International
University in Germany, Germany) and Fred Schneider (Cornell University, USA)
at the workshop; following these is an invited paper in honor of the memory of
Anya Pogosyants, a former graduate student at the Theory of Distributed Systems research group in the Laboratory for Computer Science, MIT, USA, who
died in a car accident on December 15th, 1995, at the age of 26. A biographical note of Anya Pogosyants, written by Nancy Lynch, her academic advisor at
MIT, is also included in this volume.

The contributed papers were selected from 59 submissions, at a meeting
of the program committee held on June 9, 1997, at Tel Aviv University. The
papers were read and evaluated by the program committee members, with the
additional precious assistance of external reviewers. It is also expected that most
of these papers will appear in a more extended form in scientific journals in the
future. Selected contributed papers have been already invited to a special issue
of *Theoretical Computer Science*, guest edited by the
program committee Chair.

The program committee of WDAG'97 consisted of:

Y. Afek (Tel Aviv U.)	S. Chaudhuri (Iowa State U.)
V. Hadzilacos (U. Toronto)	M. Herlihy (Brown U.)
L. Kirousis (Patras U. and CTI)	K. Marzullo (UC San Diego)
M. Mavronicolas (U. Cyprus) - Chair	S. Moran (The Technion)
Y. Moses (The Weizmann Institute of Science)	R. Reischuk (U. Lübeck)
A. Schiper (EPFL)	M. Shapiro (INRIA)
P. Spirakis (Patras U. and CTI)	Ph. Tsigas (MPI) - CoChair
P. Vitányi (CWI)	M. Yung (CertCo-BTEC)

Partial funding for WDAG'97 was provided by the Max Planck Institut für
Informatik, Saarbrücken, and by the European Union ESPRIT LTR Project
on Algorithms and Complexity in Information Technology (ALCOM-IT). Their
kind sponsorship is gratefully acknowledged. Our sincere thanks go also to the
ESPRIT Network of Excellence CaberNet that supported the workshop by other
means.

We would like to warmly thank all the authors who submitted extended
abstracts for consideration, the invited speakers for joining us in Saarbrücken
and delivering the keynote lectures, and Roberto Segala (University of Bologna,

Italy) for giving the talk for the invited paper in honor of the memory of Anya Pogosyants. We wish to express our gratitude to all program committee members and to the external reviewers who assisted them.

We are deeply thankful to Kurt Mehlhorn, for his kind support of the workshop, and to the other people from the Max Planck Institut für Informatik, for taking excellent care of the local organization; in particular, we would like to thank Ralf Brockenauer, Bernd Färber, Jörg Herman, Marina Papatriantafilou, Christoph Storb, and Roxane Wetzel for all their time and effort they kindly offered for the workshop. Last but not least, we would like to thank Yehuda Afek for hosting the program committee meeting in Tel Aviv University in a superb way.

Continuation of the WDAG events is supervised by the WDAG Steering Committee, which, for 1997, consists of:

Ö. Babaoğlu (U. Bologna)	B. Charron-Bost (E. Polytechnique)
V. Hadzilacos (U. Toronto)	M. Mavronicolas (U. Cyprus)
M. Raynal (IRISA)	S. Toueg (Cornell U.) - *Chair*
	S. Zaks (The Technion) - *Vice Chair*

July 1997   Marios Mavronicolas & Philippas Tsigas
WDAG'97 Program Committee Chair & CoChair

External Reviewers

S. Agrotou
G. Alonso
E. Anceaume
H. Attiya
Ö. Babaoğlu
X. Blondel
C. Bouras
A. Bremler
A. Casimiro
B. Charron-Bost
J.-J. Codani
A. Cohen
S. Dolev
N. Dorta
B. Eduard
M. Eleftheriou
P. Fatourou
P. Ferreira
F. le Fessant
G. Florin
B. Folliot
C. Fournet
R. Friedman
E. Gafni
K. Genther
F. Greve
R. Guerraoui
K. Hadzis
S. Haldar
J. M. Hélary
T. Herman
A. Himaris
A. Israeli

A. Jakoby
S. Katz
A. Knapp
S. Kontogiannis
E. Kranakis
D. Krizanc
S. Kutten
D. Malkhi
M. Makpangou
B. Mamalis
M. Merritt
M. Moir
A. Montresor
G. Neiger
N. Papadakis
G. Papadopoulos
M. Papatriantafilou
G. Pentaris
G. Pierre
P. Psycharis
L. Rappoport
M. Raynal
M. Reiter
P. Robert
Y. Stamatiou
B. Tampakas
G. Taubenfeld
J. Träff
J. Tromp
P. Veríssimo
K. Vidyasankar
J. L. Welch
S. Zaks

Table of Contents

Keynote Lectures

Towards Fault-Tolerant and Secure Agentry 1
F. B. Schneider

Workflow Management: An Exercise in Distributed Computing 15
A. Reuter

Invited Paper in Memory of Anya Pogosyants

In Memory of Anya Pogosyants (Biographical Note) by N. Lynch 20

*Verification of the Randomized Consensus Algorithm of Aspnes and Herlihy:
A Case Study* 22
A. Pogosyants, R. Segala, N. Lynch

Contributed Papers

A Simple DFS-Based Algorithm for Linear Interval Routing 37
T. Eilam, S. Moran, S. Zaks

ATM Layouts with Bounded Hop Count and Congestion 52
M. Flammini, E. Nardelli, G. Proietti

Scheduling in Synchronous Networks and the Greedy Algorithm 66
K.-S. Lui, S. Zaks

*Rapid Convergence of a Local Load Balancing Algorithm for Asynchronous
Rings* 81
J. E. Gehrke, C. G. Plaxton, R. Rajaraman

Performing Tasks on Restartable Message-Passing Processors 96
B. S. Chlebus, R. De Prisco, A. A. Shvartsman

Revisiting the Paxos Algorithm 111
R. De Prisco, B. Lampson, N. Lynch

*Heartbeat: A Timeout-Free Failure Detector for Quiescent Reliable
Communication* 126
M. K. Aguilera, W. Chen, S. Toueg

Genuine Atomic Multicast 141
R. Guerraoui, A. Schiper

Low-Overhead Time-Triggered Group Membership 155
S. Katz, P. Lincoln, J. Rushby

Towards Fault-Tolerant and Secure Agentry*

Fred B. Schneider

Department of Computer Science
Cornell University
Ithaca, New York 14853
USA

Abstract. Processes that roam a network—*agents*—present new technical challenges. Two are discussed here. The first problem, which arises in connection with implementing fault-tolerant agents, concerns how a voter authenticates the agents comprising its electorate. The second is to characterize security policies that are enforceable as well as approaches for enforcing those policies.

1 Why Agents?

Concurrent programs are traditionally described in terms of *processes*, an abstraction that hides the identity of the processor doing the actual execution. This hiding allows processes to be implemented by time-multiplexing one or more identical processors, making the process abstraction well suited for concurrent programs—like operating systems and scientific codes—that will be executed on uniprocessors and multiprocessors.

It is unreasonable to suppose that the processors comprising even a modest-sized network would be identical. Moreover, a user's security authorizations are likely to differ from site to site in a network, so even were the network's processors identical, they would not necessarily behave in that way. An abstraction that hides processor identities is, therefore, not as suitable for programming networks. An *agent* is like a process except that, while running, an agent can specify and change the processor on which it is executed. Having the identity of processors be under program control is attractive for a variety of technical reasons:

Communications bandwidth can be conserved. An agent can move to a processor where data is stored, then filter or otherwise digest that raw data, and finally move on, carrying with it only some relevant subset of what it has read. This means that the computation can be moved to the data rather than paying a cost (in communications bandwidth) for moving the data to the computation.

---

* Supported in part by ARPA/RADC grant F30602-96-1-0317, NASA/ARPA grant NAG-2-893, and AFOSR grant F49620-94-1-0198. The views and conclusions contained herein are those of the author and should not be interpreted as necessarily representing the official policies or endorsements, either expressed or implied, of these organizations or the U.S. Government.

Efficient and flexible service interfaces become practical. An agent can move to the processor where a server is executing and invoke server opera- tions there using procedure calls. Since the overhead of invoking an operation is now low, the use of agents allows server interfaces having more-primitive operations. Sequences of these operations would be invoked to accomplish a task. In effect, the agent dynamically defines its own high-level server operations—high-level operations that can be both efficient and well suited for the task at hand.

Besides these technical benefits, agents also provide an attractive architecture for upgrading fielded systems with new software. Users of extensible software systems have less incentive to abandon that software, so software manufacturers regard extensibility as critical for preserving their customer bases. Today, it is not unusual for a web browser to download "helper applications" which enable working with new types of data, and much PC software is installed and upgraded by downloading files over the Internet. The logical next step is an architecture where performing an upgrade does not require an overt action by the user. Agents can support such an architecture.

Engineering and marketing justifications aside, agents also raise intriguing research questions. The agent abstraction extends the process abstraction by making processor identities explicit. At first, this might seem like little more than a cosmetic change. But it actually alters the computational model in fun- damental and scientifically interesting ways. For example, coordinating replicas of agents in order to implement fault-tolerance requires solving problems that do not arise when it is (only) processes that are being replicated. Another set of new challenges follows from the new forms of sharing and interaction that agents enable, because they are accompanied by new forms of abuse.

These two examples—fault-tolerance and security—are the subject of this paper. Specifically, some initial work on agent-replica coordination [10] is dis- cussed in section 2; see [11] for a somewhat expanded treatment. And, section 3 discusses new security work that was motivated by the agent abstraction.

2 Agent Fault-tolerance

An agent, roaming a network, is easily subverted by a processor that is faulty. The most challenging case is when no assumptions can be made about the behav- ior of faulty processors. Then, executing on a faulty processor might corrupt an agent's program and/or data in a manner that completely alters the agent's sub- sequent behavior. Moreover, a faulty processor can disrupt an agent's execution, even if that agent is never executed there, by taking actions that the processor attributes to that agent or by generating bogus agents that then interfere with the original agent.

Replication and voting can be used to mask the effects of executing an agent on a faulty processor. However, faulty processors that do not execute agents can confound a replica-management scheme—by spoofing and by casting bogus votes—unless votes are authenticated. This authentication can be implemented by hardware, as done in triple modular redundancy (TMR) [16], where each component that can vote has an independent and separate connection to the voter. But, in a network, there may well be no correspondence between the physical communications lines, the replicas, and the voter. Authentication of votes must be implemented in some other manner.

We describe execution of an agent in terms of a *trajectory*, the sequence of processors on which that agent is executed. Some terminology in connection with trajectories will be convenient: the ith processor in a trajectory is called the ith *stage*, the first processor in a trajectory is called the *source*, and the last processor in a trajectory is called the *destination*. (The destination often is the same as the source.) A trajectory can be depicted graphically, with nodes representing processors and edges representing movement of an agent from one processor to another. For example, in Figure 1, S is the source and D is the destination.

Fig. 1. A simple agent computation

The computation depicted in Figure 1 is not fault-tolerant. To tolerate faulty processors (other than the source and destination) in a trajectory, we require that the behavior of the agent at each processor be deterministic² and we replicate each stage except the source and destination:

– Each processor in stage i takes as its input the majority of the inputs that it receives from the replicas comprising stage $i-1$.

– Each processor in stage i sends its output to all of the processors that it determines comprise stage $i+1$.

The computation no longer involves a single agent; Figure 2 shows the trajectories of these agents.

Missing from this description is how the voters in stage i processors determine their *electorate*, the processors comprising stage $i-1$. Without this knowledge of electorates, a sufficiently large number of processors could behave as though they are in the penultimate stage and foist a majority of bogus agents on the destination. If agents carry a *privilege*, bogus agents can be detected and ignored

² This determinacy assumption can be relaxed somewhat without fundamentally affecting the solution.

by the destination. Two protocols for implementing such privileges are sketched in the following.

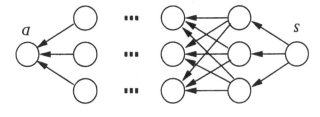

Fig. 2. Replicated-agent computation with voting

Protocols based on Shared Secrets

One implementation of the privilege employs a secret that is initially known only to the source and destination. It is necessary to defend against two attacks:

— A faulty processor that learns the secret might misuse it and direct a bogus agent to the destination.

— A faulty processor could destroy the secret (making it impossible for the computation to terminate).

To simplify the discussion, we start with a scheme that only prevents misuse of the secret by faulty processors. This scheme ensures that, provided a majority of agent replicas in each stage are executed by correct processors, only the source and destination can ever learn the secret.

Clearly, agent replicas cannot simply carry copies of the secret, since the secret could then be stolen by any faulty processor that executes a replica. It is tempting to circumvent this problem by the use of an (n,k) threshold secret sharing scheme [15] to share the secret embodying the privilege.[3] In a system where each stage has $2k-1$ processors, the source would create fragments of the secret using a $(2k-1,k)$ threshold scheme and send a different fragment to each of the processors in the next stage. Each of these processors would then forward its fragment to a different processor in the next stage, and so on. This protocol is flawed. Minorities in different stages can steal different subsets of the secret fragments. If together these minorities hold a majority of the secret fragments, then the faulty processors can collude to reconstruct the secret. One way to stop collusion between processors separated by a vote is to further divide the secret fragments after each stage. Here is the outline of a protocol based on this insight. For a system with $2k-1$ processors per stage:

[3] In an (n,k) *threshold scheme*, a secret is divided into n *fragments*, where possession of any k fragments will reveal the secret, but possession of fewer fragments reveals nothing.

- The source divides the secret into $2k-1$ fragments using a $(2k-1, k)$ threshold scheme and sends each fragment along with an agent to one of the processors in the next stage.

- A processor in stage i takes all the agents it receives from stage $i-1$, extracts the secret fragment in each, concatenates those fragments, and divides that into $2k-1$ fragments using a $(2k-1, k)$ threshold scheme. Each fragment is then sent along with the agent to a different processor in stage $i+1$.

- The destination uses the threshold scheme (backwards) to recover the original secret.

This protocol is immune to faulty processors that might misuse a secret, the first of the attacks described above. To address the second attack—the destruction of the secret by a faulty processor—it is necessary to replace the secret sharing scheme with verifiable secret sharing (VSS) [4]. VSS schemes enable correct reconstruction of a secret (or uniform discovery that no secret was distributed) even when processors, including the source, are faulty.

The protocols just described are inefficient, because secret sharing schemes require the aggregate size of the fragments to grow by a constant fraction. However, a protocol described in [11] that works with constant-size messages; it employs the same basic ideas as outlined above, but with proactive secret sharing [6].

Protocols based on Authentication Chains

A second scheme for implementing the privilege is based on pedigree: all processors are assumed to know a priori the identity of the source; agents carry (unforgeable) certificates describing their trajectories, and voters use that information in order to reject bogus agents.

Let $[A]_p$ denote a text A that has been cryptographically signed by processor p. A digital certificate $[(p : P) \leftarrow (q : Q)]_p$, called a forward, will accompany the agent that a processor p, a member of electorate P, sends to processor q, a member of electorate Q. Notice that if p is non-faulty, then p is the only processor[4] that can construct forward $[(p : P) \leftarrow (q : Q)]_p$; any processor can check the validity of such a certificate, though.

To simplify the exposition, assume that processors in distinct stages are disjoint and that the source initiates only this one agent computation. Let P_i be the set of processors comprising stage i. As above, we assume that a majority of the processors in each stage are non-faulty. The voter at a processor q in stage $i+1$ can select some agent that was sent by a non-faulty processor p of stage i if two things hold: (i) that voter knows its electorate P_i and (ii) processor q can authenticate the sender of each message that q receives. The selection would then be done by the voter as follows.

---

[4] Recall that we are assuming that faulty processors can collude. Therefore, a faulty processor can forge a forward on behalf of any other faulty processor.

- The voter uses sender-authentication to reject any agent that is not from a processor in electorate P_i—this foils attacks by faulty processors that are not in the previous stage.

  - Of those agents that remain, the voter selects any agent for which it has received $\lceil |P_i|/2 \rceil$ equivalent[5] replicas—this masks the effects of faulty processors from the previous stage.

Sender authentication can be implemented with digital signatures. Thus, all that remains is to describe a means for the voter at q to learn electorate P_i.

The processors in stage $i-1$ necessarily know what P_i is, because any agent executing on a stage $i-1$ processor is supposed to be sent to all processors in P_i (i.e. stage i). Therefore, P_i becomes available to p, to q, and to all processors in stage i and beyond, if each agent carries with it the forward $[(r:P_{i-1}) \leftarrow (p:P_i)]_r$, when sent by a processor r at stage $i-1$ to a processor p of stage i.

Processor q receives agents carrying these forwards from processors in P_i, but might also receive an arbitrary number of agents carrying other forwards due to the activities of faulty processors. If the bogus agents can be detected, then the voter at q can determine electorate P_i by discarding the bogus agents and taking the majority value for P_i in the remaining forwards.

The bogus agents can be detected if agents carry a sufficient number of forwards. Specifically, an agent will carry enough forwards so that a voter can check that the trajectory of the agent started at the source and passed through a sequence of stages, where a majority of the processors in each stage agreed on the electorate of the next stage and agreed on what agent to send to the processors in that stage. And these additional forwards would be carried by agents, provided that each voter augments the set of forwards associated with the agent it selects to be executed. The forwards of all agents in the majority are added by the voter to the set of forwards already being carried by the agent that is selected and executed. Faulty processors cannot produce an agent having such a set of forwards.

The protocol just developed is summarized below; notice that message size now grows linearly with the number of replicas and stages.

- Source processor p sends agents to each of the processors in P_2, the processors comprising stage 2. The agent that is sent to a processor q carries the forward $[(p:P_1) \leftarrow (q:P_2)]_p$.

  - The voter at each processor p of stage i:
    - receives agents from processors comprising stage $i-1$ (and perhaps from faulty processors elsewhere),
    - discards any agents that do not carry a suitable set of forwards. Such a set contains forwards to establish a trajectory that started at the source and

[5] Replicas of an agent are considered to be equivalent if they differ only in the sets of forwards they carry.

3 Security through Automata

Not only must agents be protected from attack by processors, but agents must be protected from attack by other agents. And, processors must also be protected from attack by malevolent agents. Section 2 concerns protecting against attacks by processors. In this section, we turn to the other piece of the problem—attacks by other agents.

A *security mechanism* prevents executions that, for one reason or another, have been deemed unacceptable. Typically, a security mechanism will work by truncating an execution that is about to violate the *security policy* being enforced. For example, the security policy might restrict what files users can access and a security mechanism for that policy would maintain information for each file and use that information to block file-access operations whose execution would not comply with the security policy.

With agents, new security policies become desirable—policies where the acceptability of an operation depends on past execution. For example, a policy might stipulate

Policy: No message is sent after reading any file.   (1)

as a way to prevent information from being leaked. Notice, the per-object permission bits that operating systems traditionally maintain would not suffice for enforcing this policy; historical information must be saved.

3.1 Characterizing Security Properties

Formally, a *security policy* is a set of executions. Acceptable executions are included in the set; unacceptable executions are not. The manner in which executions are represented[6] is not important, but the ways in which this set can be characterized is. As we shall see, a practical implementation for a security policy P exists if and only if the set P can be characterized in certain ways.

---

[6] Finite and infinite sequences of atomic actions, of program states, and of state/action sequences each can work.

---

passed through a sequence of stages, where a majority of the processors in each stage agreed on the next stage and agreed on what agent to send to the processors in that stage.

- determines whether a majority of the remaining agents are equivalent and, if so, augments that agent's set of forwards to include the forwards of all agents in the majority.

- When an agent is ready to move from a processor p to next stage $i+1$: for each processor q in the next stage, the forward $[(p : P_i) \leftarrow (q : P_{i+1})]_p$ is added to the set of forwards carried by that agent, and the agent is digitally signed and sent by p to q.

It seems reasonable to postulate that any mechanism for enforcing a security policy must work by analyzing the single execution in progress. This, because a mechanism's use of more than that execution would imply that the mechanism possessed the capability to analyze program text and determine whether some given instruction ever could execute. And such a capability cannot be programmed, given the undecidability of the halting problem [5].

In [1], a set of executions that can be defined by characterizing its elements individually is called a *property*. Using that terminology, we conclude that a security policy must be a property in order for an enforcement mechanism to exist. Discretionary access control [8] and mandatory access control [3] both are examples of security policies that are properties; prohibition of information flow, however, is not a property [9].[7]

Next, observe that a security mechanism, lacking the ability to predict the future, must be conservative about truncating execution. A mechanism for enforcing security policy $\mathcal{P}$ must prevent any partial execution σ, where $\sigma \notin \mathcal{P}$. This is because were σ permitted, the program being executed could terminate before σ is extended into an element of $\mathcal{P}$, and the mechanism would then have failed to enforce $\mathcal{P}$.

We can formalize this *conservatism* requirement for enforceability of security policies as follows. For σ a finite or infinite execution having i or more steps, and τ a finite execution, let:

$\sigma[..i]$ denote the prefix of σ involving its first i steps

$\sigma \tau$ denote execution σ followed by execution τ

Then, the conservatism requirement for a security policy is:

$$\sigma[..i] \notin \mathcal{P} \Rightarrow (\forall \tau : \sigma[..i]\, \tau \notin \mathcal{P}) \tag{2}$$

Properties $\mathcal{P}$ satisfying (2) are *safety* properties, the class of properties stipulating that no "bad thing" happens during an execution. Formally, a property S is defined to be a safety property if and only if it satisfies [7]

$$\sigma \notin S \Rightarrow (\exists i : (\forall \tau : \sigma[..i]\, \tau \notin S), \tag{3}$$

and this means that S is a safety property if S is characterized by a set of finite executions that are the prefix of no execution in S. Clearly, a property $\mathcal{P}$ satisfying (2) has such a set of finite prefixes—the set of prefixes $\sigma[..i] \notin \mathcal{P}$—so such a $\mathcal{P}$ is a safety property.

We have thus established that a security policy must be a safety property in order for an enforcement mechanism to exist. In the abstract, such an enforcement mechanism is a recognizer for the set of executions that is the security policy. The recognizer accepts exactly those executions that are in the policy.

---

[7] This means that mechanisms purporting to enforce information flow really enforce something different. Typically what they enforce is a property that (only) implies the absence of information flow by also ruling out some executions in which there is no information flow.

Recognizers for safety properties, then, must form the basis for all extant security policy enforcement mechanisms. Moreover, such recognizers must also be the basis for all new mechanisms, including mechanisms powerful enough to enforce security properties, like "no message is sent after a file is read," that previously have not been of concern.

3.2 Automata Specifications for Security Policies

A class of recognizers for safety properties was first defined (but not named) in [2]. Here, we shall refer to these recognizers as *security automata*. Security automata are similar to ordinary finite-state automata [5]. Both classes of automata involve a set of states and a transition relation such that reading an input symbol causes the automaton to make a transition from one state to another.[8] However, an ordinary finite-state automaton rejects a sequence of symbols if and only if that automaton does not make a transition into an accepting state upon reading the final symbol of the input. In a security automaton, all states are accepting states; the automaton rejects an input upon reading a symbol for which the automaton's current state has no transition defined. This acceptance criterion means that a security automaton can accept inputs that are infinite sequences as well as those that are finite sequences.

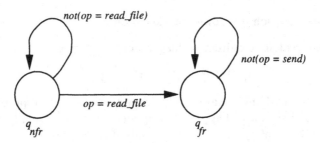

Fig. 3. No message sent after reading a file

As an example, Figure 3 depicts a security automaton that recognizes the above policy (1), which prohibits sends after file reads. The automaton's states are represented by the two nodes labeled q_{nfr} (for "no file read") and q_{fr} (for "file read"). In the figure, a transition between automaton state q_i and q_j is denoted by an edge linking node q_i to node q_j and labeled by *transition predicate* p_{ij}. The security automaton, upon reading an input symbol s when in automaton state q_i, changes to the state q_j for which transition predicate p_{ij} is satisfied by s.

---

[8] And, in both classes, non-deterministic automata are defined in terms of transition relations over sets of automaton states.

In Figure 3, the predicate labeling the transition from q_{nfr} to itself is satisfied by system execution steps that are not file read operations; the predicate labeling the transition from q_{nfr} to q_{fr} is satisfied by system execution steps that are file read operations. No transition is defined from q_{fr} for input symbols corresponding to message-send execution steps, so the security automaton rejects inputs in which a send operation follows a file read operation.

As a further demonstration of how security automata describe security policies, consider the two well-known and oft-implemented security policies:

Discretionary Access Control. This policy prohibits operations according to a system-maintained *access control matrix*. Specifically, given access control matrix A, a subject S is permitted to execute an operation $\Theta(Obj)$ involving object Obj only if $\Theta \in A[S, Obj]$ holds.

Mandatory Access Control. This policy prohibits the execution of operations according to a partially ordered set of *security labels* that are associated with the system's objects. The prohibitions prevent information flow from objects assigned high labels to objects assigned lower labels.

For example, a system's objects might be assigned labels from the set

$$\{\text{topsecret, secret, sensitive, unclassified}\}$$

ordered according to:

$$\text{topsecret} \succ \text{secret} \succ \text{sensitive} \succ \text{unclassified}$$

Suppose three types of system operations are supported—read, write, and upgrade. Then, a mandatory access control policy would restrict execution of these operations according to:

(i) a process with label p is permitted to execute a read naming a file with label F provided $p \succ F$ holds.

(ii) a process with label p is permitted to execute a write naming a file with label F provided $F \succ p$ holds.

(iii) an upgrade operation may be executed to change the label associated with an object from l to l' provided $l' \succ l$ holds.

Both discretionary access control and mandatory access control can be described using one-state security automata. The sole state has a transition to itself. For discretionary access control, the transition predicate associated with that transition is:

$$op = \Theta(Obj) \ \wedge \ \Theta \in A[S, Obj]$$

For mandatory access control, it is a predicate concerning security labels that formalizes rules (i)–(iii) above.

It should not be surprising that discretionary access control and mandatory access control can be described as security automata. By construction, security automata characterize security policies that might be enforceable. Security policies, like discretionary access control and mandatory access control, that have actually been implemented certainly are in that class.

3.3   Enforcing Policies Defined by Security Automata

How to enforce security policies—and not just how to specify them—is ultimately what is of interest. Therefore, we now turn attention to the enforcement question, describing a general implementation framework and discussing how various mechanisms in the literature can be seen as instances of that framework.

A security automaton can serve as an enforcement mechanism for some *target system* if the automaton can monitor and control the execution of that system. Each symbol (action or new state) that corresponds to the next step that the target system will take is sent to the automaton and serves as the next symbol of the automaton's input. If the automaton cannot make a transition on that input symbol, the target system is terminated; otherwise, the target system is allowed to perform that step and the automaton state is changed according to its transition predicates.

Two mechanisms are involved in this implementation approach:

Automaton Input Read: A mechanism to determine that an input symbol is being produced by the target system and then to forward that symbol to the security automaton.

Automaton Transition: A mechanism to determine whether the security automaton can make a transition on a given input and then to perform that transition.

The cost of these mechanisms determines the impact of using an enforcement mechanism built from them.

Hardware support often allows Automaton Input Read to be implemented in a way that has minimal impact on performance. For example, when the only inputs to the security automaton are the occurrences of system calls, then we can implement Automaton Input Read by using the hardware-trap mechanism that causes the transfer of control to an operating system routine whenever a system call is made. (The operating system then implements Automaton Transition.) Notice that, with this scheme, no enforcement overhead is incurred for executing other instructions, and since system calls are likely to be infrequent, the overall cost of enforcement is low. Moreover, security policies only involving system calls are rather common. The three security policies discussed in this paper— policy (1), discretionary access control, and mandatory access control—all are instances.

Most operating systems implement some form of memory protection. Memory protection is a security policy. It is a form of discretionary access control, where the operations are read, write, and execute, and the access control matrix tells which processes can access each region of memory. The usual implementation of memory protection employs hardware support: base/bounds registers or virtual memory. This can be seen as a hardware-supported implementation of Automaton Input Read in light of an optimization:

Automaton Input Read Optimization: An input symbol is not forwarded to the security automaton if the state of the automaton just after the transition would be the same as it was before the transition.

Legal memory references do not cause the memory protection security automaton to change state, and they are not forwarded to the automaton. Illegal memory references cause traps, and they are forwarded to the automaton.

Another enforcement mechanism that has recently attracted attention is *soft-ware fault isolation* (SFI), also known as "sandboxing" [17]. SFI implements memory protection, but without hardware assistance. Instead, a program is edited before it is executed, and only such edited programs are run. The edits insert instructions to test the values of operands, so that illegal memory references are caught before they are attempted.

Cast in our framework, the inserted instructions for SFI simply implement Automaton Input Read by implementing Automaton Transition in-line after each target system instruction that produces an input symbol. The security policy being enforced by SFI is specified by a one-state automaton. However, nothing would prevent a more complicated automaton from being used—say, a multi-state automaton having transition predicates that are richer than the simple bounds checks that comprise SFI. If the security automaton's transition predicates are sensitive to all state changes, in-line code for Automaton Transition might have to be inserted after every target system instruction. A decent optimizer, however, should be able to simplify this added code and eliminate the useless portions.[9]

Finally, there is no need for a run-time enforcement mechanism if the target system can be analyzed and proved not to violate the security policy of interest. This approach is employed for the same kinds of security policies that SFI addresses—policies specified by one-state security automata—with *proof carrying code* (PCC) [13]. In PCC, a proof is supplied along with a program, and this proof comes in a form that can be checked mechanically before running that program. The security policy will not be violated if, before the program is executed, the accompanying proof is checked and found to be correct. The original formulation of PCC required that proofs be constructed by hand. This restriction can be relaxed. For security policies specified by one-state security automata, [12] shows how a compiler can automatically produce PCC from programs written in high-level, type-safe programming languages.

To extend PCC for security policies that are specified by arbitrary security automata, a method is needed to extract proof obligations for establishing that a program satisfies the property specified by such an automaton. Such a method does exist—it was described in [2].

4   Concluding Remarks

This paper has touched on two problems that arise in connection with processes that can roam a network. Our purpose was to illustrate that this agent paradigm provides opportunities for rich scientific investigations.

---

[9] Úlfar Erlingsson of Cornell is currently implementing a system that does exactly this.

Of course, there is more to implementing fault-tolerant agents than a proto-col used by voters to authenticate agents comprising an electorate, the problem addressed in section 2. The agent replicas must also somehow find independent processors running the services they require, for example. In addition, the question of ensuring that replicas don't diverge must be addressed. Techniques developed for the state machine approach [14] may not be applicable in this setting, because replicas might execute different sets of requests or execute requests in different orders.

And, there is much work to be done with regard to enforcing security policies in systems of agents. Execution of an agent can span multiple processors. Information about where an agent has executed and what it has done—plausible inputs to a security policy—is not necessarily available to every processor on which the agent executes. The agent itself cannot be trusted to convey such information, nor can the other processors be trusted to furnish it. Perhaps cryptographic techniques will enable some of this information to be conveyed, but it is easy to show that some of an agent's trajectory can be hidden by certain forms of attack.

Acknowledgments

I am grateful to my past and current collaborators in the TACOMA (Tromso and Cornell Moving Agents) Project: Dag Johansen, Robbert van Renesse, Greg Morrisett, Úlfar Erlingsson, Yaron Minsky, Scott Stoller, and Lidong Zhou. Robbert's efforts have been instrumental in initiating all of the work described herein.

References

1. Alpern, B. and F.B. Schneider. Defining liveness. *Information Processing Letters* *21*, 4 (Oct. 1985), 181–185.

2. Alpern, B. and F.B. Schneider. Recognizing safety and liveness. *Distributed Computing 2* (1987), 117-126.

3. Bell, D.E. and L.J. La Padula. Secure computer systems: Mathematical foundations. Technical Report ESD-TR-73-278, Hanscom AFB, Bedford, Mass., Nov. 1973.

4. Ben-Or, M., S. Goldwasser, and A. Widgerson. Completeness theorems for non-cryptographic fault-tolerant distributed computation. *ACM Symposium on Theory of Computing*, 1988, 1-10.

5. Hopcroft, J. and J. Ullman. *Formal Languages and Their Relation to Automata.* Addison Wesley Publishing Company, Reading, Mass., 1969.

6. Jarecki, S. *Proactive Secret Sharing and Public Key Cryptosystems.* Master's thesis, MIT, Sept. 1995.

7. Lamport, L. Logical Foundation. In *Distributed Systems-Methods and Tools for Specification*, Lecture Notes in Computer Science, Vol 190. M. Paul and H.J. Siegert, eds. (1985), Springer-Verlag, New York.

8. Lampson, B. Protection. *Proceedings 5th Symposium on Information Sciences and Systems* (Princeton, New Jersey, March 1971), 437–443. Reprinted in *Operating System Review 8*, 1 (Jan. 1974), 18–24.

9. McLean, J. A general theory of composition for trace sets closed under selective interleaving functions. *Proceedings 1994 IEEE Computer Society Symposium on Research in Security and Privacy* (Oakland, Calif., May 1994), IEEE Computer Society, Calif., 79–93.

10. Minsky, Y., R. van Renesse, F.B. Schneider, and S.D. Stoller. Cryptographic support for fault-tolerant distributed computing. *Proc. of the Seventh ACM SIGOPS European Workshop "System Support for Worldwide Applications"* (Connemara, Ireland, Sept. 1996), ACM, New York, 109–114.

11. Minsky, Y. and F.B. Schneider. Agents with Integrity: Tolerating Malicious Hosts. In preparation.

12. Morrisett, G., D. Walker, and K. Crary. From ML to typed assembly language. In preparation.

13. Necula, G. Proof-carrying code. *Proceedings of the 24th Annual Symposium on Principles of Programming Languages* (Paris, France, Jan. 1997), ACM, New York, 106–119.

14. Schneider, F.B. Implementing fault-tolerant services using the state machine approach: A tutorial. *ACM Computing Surveys 22*, 4 (Dec. 1990), 299–319.

15. Shamir, A. How to share a secret. *CACM 22*, 11 (Nov. 1979), 612–613.

16. Siewiorek, D.P. and R.S. Swarz. *The Theory and Practice of Reliable System Design*. Digital Press, Bedford, Mass. 1982.

17. Wahbe, R., S. Lucco, T.E. Anderson, and S. L. Graham. Efficient Software-Based Fault Isolation. *Proceeding of the Fourteenth ACM Symposium on Operating Systems Principles* (Asheville, North Carolina, Dec. 1993), ACM, New York, 202–216.

Workflow Management - An Exercise in Distributed Computing

Andreas Reuter

International University in Germany GmbH Stuttgart i.Gr.

1. Introduction

The report on the 1996 NSF Workshop on Workflow and Process Automation in Information Systems [1] begins with the following statement: "An interdisciplinary research community needs to address challenging issues raised by applying workflow management technology in information systems." This certainly is a correct observation, but it also is slighty misleading: One might conclude that workflow management technology in itself is well understood and it is the application that needs further investigation. When reading the report, though, it becomes clear that this is not what the authors want to imply. The point is that in all areas where workflow technology can be applied, the characteristics of the applications influence the technical solutions in complex ways. At the same time, the new possibilities opened up by wokflow technology change the ways applications are structured and processes are defined. Therefore, the whole problem is a moving target, and the challenge is to make it a goal--oriented movement rather than something resembling Brownian motion.

For the reasons mentioned there is indeed a strong need to proceed in an interdisciplinary fashion. But at the heart of the matter lies the necessity to build a distributed computing platform that is flexible, robust, scaleable, extensible - and yet can guarantee strict formal consistency constraints. In the following, we will exemplify and discuss some of the most challenging problems in that area. The discussion is mostly based on the ConTract model [2] that was developed in the author´s research group over the last seven years.

2. Research Issues in Workflow and Process Automation

The workshop report quoted above contains an extensive list of current research issues: Definition and Modeling; Representation, Languages and Meta-Modeling; Analysis, Testing, Verification and Evaluation; Simulation; Prototyping and Performance Support; Administration; Interoperation and Integration; Target Support; Monitoring and Measurement; Visualization; History Capture and Replay; Fault Detection, Error Handling and Repair; Evolution.

The authors have left out security and configuration management, which are research issues, too, but if you add these, it becomes obvious that the list comprises just about everything one has to investigate about software in general. This is not meant to be a trivial observation; workflow management is - among other things - a very complex programming problem. And it differs from traditional software issues in many ways. For example: Classical programming languages and environments are (mostly as an implicit assumption) geared towards programs organized into modules that execute within milliseconds up a few seconds. In workflow, we have to do with executions that "live" for months, maybe years. It should be at least intuitively clear that the programming primitives that work on one end of the lifetime scale do not necessarily work at a point that is eight orders of magnitude away. So workflow and process automation requires novel programming styles and appropriate run-time support; hence the long list above.

However, for the present paper we will not follow that menu of open issues; we will rather focus on a small number of structural problems that need to be solved before the corresponding programming constructs, recovery mechanisms, user interfaces etc. can be defined. In the talk, we will consider the following questions in some detail: What does fault tolerance mean in the context of workflow management? Long-lived executions require elaborate context management - how is it different form normal database applications? Are current techniques for distributed name resolution sufficient for workflow management? What are conceptual differences between static workflow and ad-hoc workflow? And finally: What is an appropriate notion of correctness in a workflow environment? This question will be investigated in the following section.

Note that currently many people believe that using URLs in some graphical programming environment gives them all the workflow they need; but also note that they may be wrong.

3. Formal Approaches to Consistency in Workflow

There is a well-established theory for reasoning about consistency of concurrent executions on shared state. It is based on ACID-transactions, and the fundamental criterion says that an interleaved execution of a set of transactions is correct if it is equivalent (in some sense) to a serial exection of the same transcations. Note that the equivalence to any serial schedule will do; this definition is not concerned with a specific outcome. The correctness of a serial execution is a built-in property of this consistency model.

This approach has proven to be very powerful and flexible; in particular, it allows to derive algorithms that automatically control parallel execution on shared state, thus presenting the application programmer with a single-user view of the system - which is a great advantage. The problem is that serializability is limited to shat transactions, i.e. units of computations that have a short lifetime and touch a small number of objects only. So from a workflow perspective, the model applies to the wrong end of the scale.

Nevertheless, there have been a number of quite promising attempts to generalize the notion of serializability such that the restrictions on size and duration of the computational units can be removed. The first observation these models are based on is quite simple: Upon first approximation a workflow instance can be viewed as an open nested transaction: Smaller steps inside the workflow commit their results, thus waiving the right to automatically roll back what they have done. They rather have to appoint a compensating transaction that is able to semantically repair what the original transaction has done in case the overall workflow execution should not be able to complete. The idea then is not to consider the serializability of atomic state transitions, but to reason about the interplay between the original transactions (which still have the ACID properties) and their compensating counterparts by modeling the effects on the shared state, i.e. the persistent data.

Serializability means that from each transaction´s perspective the data it has used do not change while the transaction runs. Clearly this cannot be carried over to lang-lived workflows. Therefore, the model presented in [3] assumes that rather than preventing the data from changing at all, one wants to preserve certain predicates on the data. The resulting notion of predicate serializability defines correctness by saying that an execution is serializable with respect to some predicate P if all reduced histories (this means you only look at the transactions touching data that are used in P) are serializable.

This approach is restrictive in the sense that it only considers which data elements are used in P. It might well be that a non-serializable schedule leaves P unchanged and thus fullfills the correctness criterion of the application, which is to preserve P. The work reported in [4] shows that one can define a different notion on generalized serializability, which treats all schedules as correct that preserve the invariant conditions among transactions. Those conditions, of course, are predicates on the database.

4. Conclusion

The example of what formal correctness of concurrent execution in a workflow environment could mean demonstrates at least two things: Solutions that work well in traditional settings with short-lived units of computation cannot simply be carried over to that problem domain. Second, there is no unique, general correctness criterion. It much depends on how the application perceives its data and the dependencies between them, so a practical solution may be a formal framework within which each specific appliction can define the type of correctness that is most appropriate. Defining such frameworks and finding ways of implementing them efficiently is one of the great challenges in workflow management technology.

5. References

[1]   Shet, A. et al.: Report from the NSF Workshop on Workflow and Process
        Automation in Information Systems, Athens, Georgia, May 8-10, 1996
        Technical Report UGA-CS-TR-96-003, Dept. of Computer Sc., University of
        Georgia, October 1996,
        available at: http://lsdis.cs.uga.edu/activities/NSF-workflow

[2]   Wächter, H., Reuter, A.: The ConTract Model, in: Elmagarmid, A.K. (ed.):
        Database Transaction Models, Morgan Kaufmann Publishers, San Mateo,
        1992.

[3]   Korth, H., Levy, E., Silberschatz, A.: A Formal Approach to Recovery by
        Compensating Transactions, in: Proc. of the 16th International Conference on
        Very Large Databases, 1990.

[4]   Reuter, A., Schneider, K., Schwenkreis, F.: ConTracts Revisited, in: Jajodia,
        S., Kerschberg, L. (eds.): Advanced Transaction Models and Architectures,
        Kluwer Verlag, 1997.

In Memory of Anya Pogosyants, by Nancy Lynch

Anya Pogosyants was a PhD student in my Theory of Distributed Systems research group at MIT, during 1994 and 1995. She died, along with her husband Igor Slobodkin, in an automobile accident on December 15, 1995, on an icy road in Vermont. The tragedy occurred while Anya and Igor were on their way to Lake Placid for a long-planned weekend of skiing.

Anya was born on March 31, 1969 in Moscow. She attended the famous School No. 57 for Mathematics in Moscow, and then completed a Master's degree in Computer Science from Moscow State University (receiving the prestigious Red Diploma). She and Igor married and emigrated to Boston in 1991 for graduate studies, she in computer science and he in physics and molecular biology.

Anya's research involved developing methods for algorithm verification amenable to machine checking. Her first research at MIT, with Steve Garland and John Guttag, involved developing decision procedures for the Larch Prover, an automatic theorem-prover developed at MIT. Her later work, in the Theory of Distributed Systems group, was in the area of verification of random-ized distributed algorithms. Together with Roberto Segala, she developed a methodology for formal analysis and verification of distributed algorithms that contain a mixture of probabilistic and nondeterministic choices. She developed a novel method for proving the correctness of probabilistic time bound statements. This method leads to formal proofs that allow partially automated verification. This research was presented at PODC '95.

At the time of her death, Anya was working on an ambitious, difficult project – a complete model, proof and time bound analysis of the Aspnes-Herlihy randomized consensus algorithm. Her idea was to break the algorithm down into logical components, prove properties of those components separately, then combine them using general theorems. Furthermore, the probabilistic reasoning was to be isolated to as small a part of the development as possible. Many new general theorems were needed for this, because this sort of work is quite new. She left this work in a half-completed state, but Roberto Segala (with some help from me) has carried it through to completion. This is the paper that appears in the following pages.

Anya was not only a brilliant research student. She was also a very kind, friendly, warm person. She was always cheerful and ready to help and encourage everybody. Besides her own outstanding research work, she helped many students, and even supervised an undergraduate research project.

All who know Anya miss her very much.

Verification of the Randomized Consensus Algorithm of Aspnes and Herlihy: A Case Study*

Anna Pogosyants[1]　　　　　Roberto Segala[2]　　　　　Nancy Lynch[1]

[1] Laboratory for Computer Science, MIT
[2] Dipartimento di Scienze dell'Informazione, Università di Bologna

Abstract. The Probabilistic I/O Automaton model of [11] is used as the basis for a formal presentation and proof of the randomized consensus algorithm of Aspnes and Herlihy. The algorithm is highly nontrivial and guarantees termination within expected polynomial time. The task of carrying out this proof has led us to develop several general proof techniques for probabilistic I/O automata. These include ways to combine expectations for different complexity measures, to compose expected complexity properties, to convert probabilistic claims to deterministic claims, to use abstraction mappings to prove probabilistic properties, and to apply random walk theory in a distributed computational setting.

1 Introduction

With the increasing complexity of distributed algorithms there is an increasing need for mathematical tools for analysis. Although there are several formalisms and tools for the analysis of ordinary distributed algorithms, there are not as many powerful tools for the analysis of randomization within distributed systems. This paper is part of a project that aims at developing the right math tools for proving properties of complicated randomized distributed algorithms and systems. The tools should be based on traditional probability theory, but at the same time should be tailored to the computational setting. Furthermore, the tools should have good facilities for modular reasoning due to the complexity of the systems to which they should be applied. The types of modularity we are looking for include parallel composition and abstraction mappings, but also anything else that decomposes the math analysis.

We develop our tools by analyzing complex algorithms of independent interest. In this paper we analyze the randomized consensus algorithm of Aspnes and Herlihy [3], which guarantees termination within expected polynomial time. The Aspnes-Herlihy algorithm is a rather complex algorithm. Processes move through a succession of asynchronous rounds, attempting to agree at each round. At each round, the agreement attempt involves a distributed random walk. The algorithm is hard to analyze because of its use of nontrivial results of probability theory (e.g., random walk theory), because of its complex setting, including asynchrony and both non-deterministic and probabilistic choice, and because of the interplay among several different sub-protocols.

* Supported by AFOSR-ONR contract F49620-94-1-0199, by ARPA contracts N00014-92-J-4033 and F19628-95-C-0118, and by NSF grant 9225124-CCR.

We formalize the Aspnes-Herlihy algorithm using probabilistic I/O automata [11]. In doing so, we decompose it formally into three subprotocols: one to carry out the agreement attempts, one to conduct the random walks, and one to implement a shared counter needed by the random walks. Properties of all three subprotocols are proved separately, and combined using general results about automaton composition. It turns out that most of the work involves proving non-probabilistic properties (invariants, simulation mappings, non-probabilistic progress properties, etc.). The probabilistic reasoning is isolated to a few small sections of the proof.

The task of carrying out this proof has led us to develop several general proof techniques for probabilistic I/O automata. These include ways to combine expectations for different complexity measures, to compose expected complexity properties, to convert probabilistic claims to deterministic claims, to use abstraction mappings to prove probabilistic properties, and to apply random walk theory in a distributed computational setting.

Previous work on verification of randomized distributed algorithms includes [8], where the randomized dining philosophers algorithm of [5] is shown to guarantee progress with probability 1, [6, 9], where the algorithm of [5] is shown to guarantee progress within expected constant time, and [1], where the randomized self-stabilizing minimum spanning tree algorithm of [2] is shown to guarantee stabilization within an expected time proportional to the diameter of a network. The analysis of [8] is based on converting a probabilistic property into a property of some of the computations of an algorithm (extreme fair computations); the analysis of [6, 9, 1] is based on part of the methodology used in this paper.

The paper is organized as follows. Section 2 presents the basic theoretical tools for our analysis; Section 3 presents the algorithm of Aspnes and Herlihy, describes the module that carries out the agreement attempts, and proves safety and liveness properties that do not depend on the details of the other modules; Section 5 builds the module that conducts the random walk and proves termination; Section 6 studies the expected time complexity of the algorithm; Section 7 gives some concluding remarks. In the presentation we focus mainly on the integration of probability with nondeterminism and we omit most of the analysis that does not involve probability.

2 Formal Model and Tools

2.1 Probabilistic I/O Automata

A *probability space* $\mathcal{P}$ is a triplet $(\Omega, \mathcal{F}, P)$ where Ω is a set, $\mathcal{F}$ is a collection of subsets of Ω that is closed under complement and countable union and such that $\Omega \in \mathcal{F}$, also called a σ-field, and P is a function from $\mathcal{F}$ to $[0, 1]$ such that $P[\Omega] = 1$ and such that for any collection $\{C_i\}_i$ of at most countably many pairwise disjoint elements of $\mathcal{F}$, $P[\cup_i C_i] = \sum_i P[C_i]$. A probability space $(\Omega, \mathcal{F}, P)$ is *discrete* if $\mathcal{F} = 2^\Omega$ and for each $C \subseteq \Omega$, $P[C] = \sum_{x \in C} P[\{x\}]$. For any arbitrary set X, let *Probs*(X) denote the set of discrete probability spaces $(\Omega, \mathcal{F}, P)$ where $\Omega \subseteq X$, and such that all the elements of Ω have a non-zero probability.

An *I/O automaton* A consists of five components: a set $States(A)$ of states; a non-empty set $Start(A) \subseteq States(A)$ of start states; an action signature $Sig(A) = (in(A), out(A), int(A))$, where $in(A)$, $out(A)$ and $int(A)$ are disjoint sets of input, output, and internal actions, respectively; a transition relation $Trans(A) \subseteq States(A) \times Actions(A) \times States(A)$, where $Actions(A)$ denotes the set $in(A) \cup out(A) \cup int(A)$, such that for each state s of $States(A)$ and each input action a of $in(A)$ there is a state s' such that $(s, a, s') \in Trans(A)$; a task partition $Tasks(A)$, which is an equivalence relation on $int(A) \cup out(A)$ that has at most countably many equivalence classes. The elements of $Trans(A)$ are called *transitions*, and A is said to be *input enabled*. An equivalence class of $Tasks(A)$ is called a *task* of A. A *probabilistic I/O automaton* M differs from an I/O automaton in its transition relation. That is, $Trans(M) \subseteq States(M) \times Actions(M) \times Probs(States(M))$. In the rest of the paper we refer to (probabilistic) I/O automata as (probabilistic) automata.

A state s of M is said to *enable* a transition if there is a transition $(s, a, \mathcal{P})$ in $Trans(M)$, and an action a is said to be enabled from s if s enables a transition with action a. An *execution fragment* of M is a sequence α of alternating states and actions of M starting with a state, and, if α is finite ending with a state, $\alpha = s_0 a_1 s_1 a_2 s_2 ...$, such that for each $i \geq 0$ there exists a transition $(s_i, a_{i+1}, \mathcal{P})$ of M such that $s_{i+1} \in \Omega$. Denote by $fstate(\alpha)$ the first state of α and, if α is finite, denote by $lstate(\alpha)$ the last state of α. An *execution* is an execution fragment whose first state is a start state. An execution fragment α is said to be *fair* iff the following conditions hold for every task T of M: 1) if α is finite then no action from T is enabled in $lstate(\alpha)$; 2) if α is infinite, then either actions from T occur infinitely many times in α, or α contains infinitely many occurrences of states from which no action from T is enabled. A state s of M is *reachable* if there exists a finite execution of M that ends in s. A finite execution fragment $\alpha_1 = s_0 a_1 s_1 \cdots a_n s_n$ of M and an execution fragment $\alpha_2 = s_n a_{n+1} s_{n+1} \cdots$ of M can be *concatenated*. The concatenation, written $\alpha_1 {}^\frown \alpha_2$, is the execution fragment $s_0 a_1 s_1 \cdots a_n s_n a_{n+1} s_{n+1} \cdots$. An execution fragment α_1 of M is a *prefix* of an execution fragment α_2 of M, written $\alpha_1 \leq \alpha_2$, iff either $\alpha_1 = \alpha_2$ or α_1 is finite and there exists an execution fragment α_1' of M such that $\alpha_2 = \alpha_1 {}^\frown \alpha_1'$.

An execution fragment of M is the result of resolving both the probabilistic and the nondeterministic choices of M. If only the nondeterministic choices are resolved, then we obtain a structure similar to a cycle-free Markov chain, which we call a *probabilistic execution fragment* of M. From the point of view of the study of algorithms, the nondeterminism is resolved by an *adversary* that chooses a transition to schedule based on the past history of the system. A probabilistic execution is the result of the action of some adversary. A probabilistic execution can be thought of as the result of unfolding the transition relation of a probabilistic automaton and then choosing one transition for each state of the unfolding. It has a structure similar to the structure of a probabilistic automaton, where the states are finite execution fragments of M. It is possible to define a probability space $\mathcal{P}_H = (\Omega_H, \mathcal{F}_H, P_H)$ associated with H. In particular Ω_H is a set of execution fragments of M, $\mathcal{F}_H$ is the smallest σ-field that contains the set of *cones* C_q, consisting of those elements of Ω_H having q as a prefix (let q denote a state of H), and the probability measure P_H is the unique extension of the probability measure defined on cones as follows:

$P_H[C_q]$ is the product of the probabilities of each transition of H leading to q. An *event E* of H is an element of $\mathcal{F}_H$. An event E is called *finitely satisfiable* if it can be expressed as a union of cones. A finitely satisfiable event can be represented by a set Θ of incomparable states of H. The event denoted by Θ is $\cup_{q \in \Theta} C_q$. We abuse notation by writing $P_H[\Theta]$ for $P_H[\cup_{q \in \Theta} C_q]$. We call a set of incomparable states of H a *cut* of H, and we say that a cut Θ is *full* if $P_H[\Theta] = 1$. An important event of $\mathcal{P}_H$ is the set of fair executions of Ω_H. We define a probabilistic execution fragment H to be fair if the set of fair execution fragments has probability 1 in $\mathcal{P}_H$.

Probabilistic automata can be composed in parallel. The states of the composition are the cross product of the states of the components. The composed probabilistic automata synchronize on their common actions and evolve independently on the others. Whenever a synchronization occurs, the state that is reached is obtained by choosing a state independently for each of the probabilistic automata involved. In a parallel composition the notion of *projection* is one of the main tools to support modular reasoning. A projection of an execution fragment α onto a component within a parallel composition is the contribution of the component to obtain α. Formally, let M be $M_1 \parallel M_2$, the parallel composition of M_1 and M_2, and let α be an execution fragment of M. The projection of α onto M_i, denoted by $\alpha \lceil M_i$, is the sequence obtained from α by replacing each state with its ith component and by removing all actions that are not actions of M_i together with their following state. It is the case that $\alpha \lceil M_i$ is an execution fragment of M_i. A similar construction is possible on probabilistic execution fragments. Here we just claim that $H \lceil M_i$ is a probabilistic execution fragment of M_i and that the probability space associated with $H \lceil M_i$ is the image space under projection of the probability space associated with H.

Proposition 1 [10]. *Let M be $M_1 \parallel M_2$, and let H be a probabilistic execution fragment of M. Let $i \in \{1, 2\}$. Then $\Omega_{H \lceil M_i} = \{\alpha \lceil M_i \mid \alpha \in \Omega_H\}$, and for each $\Theta \in \mathcal{F}_{H \lceil M_i}$, $P_{H \lceil M_i}[\Theta] = P_H[\{\alpha \in \Omega_H \mid \alpha \lceil M_i \in \Theta\}]$.*

2.2 Complexity Measures

A *complexity function* is a function from execution fragments of M to $\Re^{\geq 0}$. A *complexity measure* is a complexity function ϕ such that, for each pair α_1 and α_2 of execution fragments that can be concatenated, $max(\phi(\alpha_1), \phi(\alpha_2)) \leq \phi(\alpha_1 ⌢ \alpha_2) \leq \phi(\alpha_1) + \phi(\alpha_2)$. Informally, a complexity measure is a function that determines the complexity of an execution fragment. A complexity measure satisfies two natural requirements: the complexity of two tasks performed sequentially should not exceed the complexity of performing the two tasks separately and should be at least as large as the complexity of the more complex task.

Consider a probabilistic execution fragment H of M and a finitely satisfiable event Θ of $\mathcal{F}_H$. The elements of Θ represent the points where the property denoted by Θ is satisfied. Let ϕ be a complexity function. Then, define the expected complexity ϕ to reach Θ in H as

$$E_\phi[H, \Theta] \triangleq \begin{cases} \sum_{q \in \Theta} \phi(q) P_H[C_q] & \text{if } P_H[\Theta] = 1 \\ \infty & \text{otherwise.} \end{cases}$$

If several complexity measures are related by a linear inequality, then their expected values over a full cut are related by the same linear inequality. We use this result in the time analysis of the algorithm of Aspnes and Herlihy, where we express the time complexity of the protocol in terms of two other complexity measures.

Proposition 2. *Let Θ be a full cut of a probabilistic execution fragment H. Let ϕ, ϕ_1, ϕ_2 be complexity functions. and c_1, c_2 two constants such that, for each $\alpha \in \Theta$, $\phi(\alpha) \leq c_1 \phi_1(\alpha) + c_2 \phi_2(\alpha)$. Then $E_\phi[H, \Theta] \leq c_1 E_{\phi_1}[H, \Theta] + c_2 E_{\phi_2}[H, \Theta]$.*

Suppose now that within a computation it is possible to identify several phases, each one with its own complexity, and suppose that the complexity associated with each phase remains 0 until the phase starts. Suppose that the expected complexity of each phase is bounded by some constant c. If we know that the expected number of phases that start is bounded by k, then the expected complexity of the system is bounded by ck. The algorithm of Aspnes and Herlihy works in *rounds*, and at each round a special *coin flipping* protocol is run. The rounds can be seen as phases. The main difficulty is that several rounds may run concurrently.

Proposition 3. *Let M be a probabilistic automaton. Let $\phi_1, \phi_2, \phi_3, \ldots$ be a countable collection of complexity functions for M, and let ϕ' be a complexity function defined as $\phi'(\alpha) = \sum_{i \geq 0} \phi_i(\alpha)$. Let c be a constant, and suppose that for each fair probabilistic execution fragment H of M, each full cut Θ of H, and each $i > 0$, $E_{\phi_i}[H, \Theta] \leq c$.*

Let H be a probabilistic fair execution fragment of M, and let ϕ be a complexity measure for M. For each $i > 0$, let Θ_i be the set of minimal states q of H such that $\phi(q) \geq i$. Suppose that for each $q \in \Theta_i$, $\phi_i(q) = 0$, and that for each state q of H and each $i > \phi(q)$, $\phi_i(q) = 0$.

Then, for each full cut Θ of H, $E_{\phi'}[H, \Theta] \leq c E_\phi[H, \Theta]$.

Finally, to verify properties modularly it is useful to derive complexity properties of complex systems based on complexity properties of their components.

Proposition 4. *Let M be $M_1 \| M_2$, and let $i \in \{1, 2\}$. Let ϕ be a complexity function for M, and let ϕ_i be a complexity function for M_i. Suppose that for each finite execution fragment α of M, $\phi(\alpha) = \phi_i(\alpha \lceil M_i)$. Let c be a constant. Suppose that for each probabilistic execution fragment H of M_i and each full cut Θ of H, $E_{\phi_i}[H, \Theta] \leq c$. Then, for each probabilistic execution fragment H of M and each full cut Θ of H, $E_\phi[H, \Theta] \leq c$.*

2.3 Probabilistic Complexity Statements

A probabilistic complexity statement [9, 11] is a predicate that states whether all the fair probabilistic executions of a probabilistic automaton guarantee some reachability property within some complexity c with some minimum probability p. Probabilistic complexity statements essentially express partial progress properties of a probabilistic system. Such partial progress properties can then be used to derive upper bounds on the expected complexity for progress. Formally, $U \xrightarrow[p]{\phi \leq c} U'$ is a predicate that is true for M iff for each fair probabilistic execution fragment H of M that starts from a state of U, $P_H[e_{U',\phi(c)}(H)] \geq p$. where $e_{U',\phi(c)}(H)$ denotes the set of executions α of Ω_H with a prefix α' such that $\phi(\alpha') \leq c$ and $lstate(\alpha') \in U'$.

Denote by $U \Rightarrow U$ *unless* U' the predicate that is true for M iff for every execution fragment sas' of M, $s \in U - U' \Rightarrow s' \in U \cup U'$. Informally, $U \Rightarrow U$ *unless* U' means that, once a state from U is reached, M remains in U unless U' is reached. For each probabilistic execution fragment H of M, let $\Theta_{U'}(H)$ denote the set of minimal states of H where a state from U' is reached. The following theorem provides a way of computing the expected ϕ for reaching U'.

Proposition 5 [11]. *Let M be a probabilistic automaton and ϕ be a complexity measure. Suppose that for each execution fragment of M of the form sas', $\phi(sas') \leq 1$, that is, each transition of M increases ϕ by at most 1. Let U and U' be sets of states of M. Let H be a probabilistic execution fragment of M that starts from a state of U, and suppose that for each state q of H such that $lstate(q) \in U$ some transition is scheduled with probability 1. Suppose also that $U \xrightarrow[p]{\phi \leq c} U'$ and $U \Rightarrow U$ unless U'. Then, $E_\phi[H, \Theta_{U'}(H)] \leq (c+1)/p$.*

A useful technique to prove the validity of a probabilistic complexity statement $U \xrightarrow[p]{\phi \leq c} U'$ for a probabilistic automaton M is the following [9]: 1) choose a set of random draws that may occur within a probabilistic execution of M, and choose some of the possible outcomes; 2) show that, no matter how the nondeterminism is resolved, the chosen random draws give the chosen outcomes with some minimum probability p; 3) show that whenever the chosen random draws give the chosen outcome, a state from U' is reached within c units of complexity ϕ.

The first two steps can be carried out using the so-called *coin lemmas* [6, 9, 11], which provide rules to map a stochastic process onto a probabilistic execution and lower bounds on the probability of the mapped events based on the properties of the given stochastic process; the third step concerns non-probabilistic properties and can be carried out by means of any known technique for non-probabilistic systems. Coin lemmas are essentially a way of reducing the analysis of a probabilistic property to the analysis of an ordinary nondeterministic property.

2.4 Symmetric Random Walks for Probabilistic Automata

The correctness of the protocol of Aspnes and Herlihy is based on the theory of random walks [4]. That is. some parts of the protocol behave like a probabilistic process called random walk. The problem is to make sure that the protocol indeed behaves like a random walk. This is a point where intuition often fails, and therefore we need a proof technique that is sufficiently rigorous and simple to avoid mistakes.

Roughly speaking, a random walk is a process that describes the moves of a particle on the real line, where at each time the particle moves in one direction with probability p and in the opposite direction with probability $(1 - p)$. In this section we present a coin lemma for symmetric random walks. That is, $p = 1/2$.

Let M be a probabilistic automaton and let $Acts = \{flip_1, \ldots, flip_n\}$ be a subset of $Actions(M)$. Let $\mathbf{S} = \{(U_1^h, U_1^t), (U_2^h, U_2^t), \ldots, (U_n^h, U_n^t)\}$ be a set of pairs where for each $i, 1 \le i \le n$, U_i^h, U_i^t are disjoint subsets of $States(M)$ such that for every transition $(s, flip_i, \mathcal{P})$ with an action $flip_i$, $\Omega \subseteq U_i^h \cup U_i^t$, and $P[U_i^h] = P[U_i^t] = 1/2$. The actions from $Acts$ represent coin flips, and the sets of states U_i^h and U_i^t represent the two possible outcomes. Given a finite execution fragment α of M, let $Diff_{Acts,\mathbf{S}}(\alpha)$ denote the difference between the heads and the tails that occur in H. Let z, E, and T be natural numbers, and let $B < T$. The value of z denotes the starting point of the particle, while B and T denote $barriers$ in the real line. For each finite execution fragment α, let $z + Diff(\alpha)$ denote the position of the particle after the occurrence of α. For each probabilistic execution fragment H of M, let $\mathbf{Top}[B, T, z](H)$ be the set of executions α of Ω_H such that either the particle reaches the top barrier T before the bottom barrier B, or the total number of "flips" is finite and the particle reaches neither barrier. Define the symmetric event $\mathbf{Bot}[B, T, z](H)$, which is the same as $\mathbf{Top}$ except that the bottom barrier B should be reached before the top barrier T. Finally, define the event $\mathbf{Either}[B, T, z](H)$ as $\mathbf{Top}[B, T, z](H) \cup \mathbf{Bot}[B, T, z](H)$, which excludes those executions of M where infinitely many "flips" occur and the particle reaches neither barrier.

Proposition 6. *Let H be a probabilistic execution fragment of M, and let $B \le z \le T$. Then*

1. $P_H[\mathbf{Top}[B, T, z](H)] \ge (z - B)/(T - B)$.

2. $P_H[\mathbf{Bot}[B, T, z](H)] \ge (T - z)/(T - B)$.

3. $P_H[\mathbf{Either}[B, T, z](H)] = 1$.

We conclude with a result about the expected complexity of a random walk. Let $\phi_{Acts}(\alpha)$ be the complexity measure that counts the number of actions from $Acts$ that occur in α. Define $\phi_{Acts,B,T,z}$ to be the truncation of ϕ_{Acts} at the point where one of the barriers B and T is reached. Then we can prove an upper bound on the number of expected flip actions that occur before reaching one of the barriers.

Proposition 7. *Let H be a probabilistic execution fragment of M, and let Θ be a full cut of H. Let $B \le z \le T$. Then, $E_{\phi_{Acts,B,T,z}}[H, \Theta] \le -z^2 + (B + T)z - BT$.*

3 The Algorithm of Aspnes and Herlihy

3.1 Description of the Algorithm

The algorithm of Aspnes and Herlihy proceeds in rounds. Every process maintains a variable with two fields, *value* and *round*, that contain the process' current preferred value (0, 1 or $\bot$) and current round (a non-negative integer), respectively. We say that a process is at round r if its *round* field is equal to r. The variables (*value*, *round*) are multiple-reader single-writer. Each process starts with its *round* field initialized to 0 and its *value* field initialized to $\bot$.

After receiving the initial value to agree on, each process i executes the following loop. It first reads the (*value*, *round*) variables of all other processes in its local memory. We say that process i is a *leader* if according to its readings its own round is greater than or equal to the rounds of all other processes. We also say that a process i *observed* that another process j is a leader if according to i's readings the round of j is greater than or equal to the rounds of all other processes. If process i at round r discovers that it is a leader, and that all processes that are at rounds r and $r-1$ have the same value as i, then i breaks out of the loop and decides on its value. Otherwise, if all processes that i observed to be leaders have the same value v, then i sets its value to v, increments its round and proceeds to the next iteration of the loop. In the remaining case, (leaders that i observed do not agree), i sets its value to $\bot$ and scans again the processes. If once again the leaders observed by i do not agree, then i determines its new preferred value for the next round by invoking a coin flipping protocol. There is a separate coin flipping protocol for each round.

We represent the main part of the algorithm as an automaton AP (Agreement Protocol) and the coin flipping protocols as probabilistic automata CF_r (Coin Flipper), one for each round r. With this decomposition we can analyze several properties just on AP using ordinary techniques for non-probabilistic systems. Indeed, in this section we deal with AP only, and we leave the coin flippers unspecified.

The formal definition of AP is given in Table 1. Beside the shared variables *value*(i) and i), each process has a program counter pc, two arrays *values* and *rounds* containing the scans of the other processes, a set variable *obs* saying what processes have been observed, a variable *start* holding the initial preferred value, and two variables *decided*, and *stopped* stating whether the process has decided or failed. We explain some of the relevant predicates: *obs-leader*(j) is true if i observes that j is a leader; *obs-agree*(r, v) is true if the observations of all the processes whose round is at least r agree on v; *obs-leader-agree*(v) is true if i observes that the leaders agree on a value v; *obs-leader-value* is the value of one of the leaders observed by i. We say that a process is *active* if it is attempting to agree on a value. An active process becomes inactive either by deciding a value or by failing.

3.2 Safety Properties

Validity states that "if a process decides on a value, then this value is the initial value of some process". The proof of validity derives from a trivial invariant saying that no process will ever prefer a value different from its initial value if all processes have the same initial value. Agreement states that "any two processes that decide within an execution of the algorithm decide on the same value". The key idea of the proof of agreement is that if a process i that is at round r is "about to decide" on some value v, then every process that is at round r or higher has its value equal to v. Define *agree*(r, v) to be true if all the processes at round at least r prefer v.

Actions and transitions of process i.

input $init(v)_i$
    Eff: $start \leftarrow v$

output $start(v)_i$
    Pre: $pc = init \wedge start = v \neq \bot$
    Eff: $value(i) \leftarrow v$
        $round(i) \leftarrow 1$
        $obs \leftarrow \emptyset$
        $pc \leftarrow read1$

output $read1(k)_i$
    Pre: $pc = read1$
        $k \notin obs$
    Eff: $values[k] \leftarrow value(k)$
        $rounds[k] \leftarrow round(k)$
        $obs \leftarrow obs \cup \{k\}$
        if $obs = \{1, \ldots, n\}$ then $pc \leftarrow check1$

output $check1_i$
    Pre: $pc = check1$
    Eff: if $\exists_{v \in \{0,1\}} obs\text{-}agree(rounds[i] - 1, v) \wedge$
        $obs\text{-}leader(i)$ then
            $pc \leftarrow decide$
        elseif $\exists_{v \in \{0,1\}} obs\text{-}leader\text{-}agree(v)$ then
            $value(i) \leftarrow obs\text{-}leader\text{-}value$
            $round(i) \leftarrow rounds[i] + 1$
            $obs \leftarrow \emptyset$
            $pc \leftarrow read1$
        else
            $value(i) \leftarrow \bot$
            $obs \leftarrow \emptyset$
            $pc \leftarrow read2$

output $decide(v)_i$
    Pre: $pc = decide \wedge values[i] = v$
    Eff: $decided \leftarrow true$
        $pc \leftarrow nil$

output $read2(k)_i$
    Pre: $pc = read2$
        $k \notin obs$
    Eff: $values[k] \leftarrow value(k)$
        $rounds[k] \leftarrow round(k)$
        $obs \leftarrow obs \cup \{k\}$
        if $obs = \{1, \ldots, n\}$ then
            $pc \leftarrow check2$

output $check2_i$
    Pre: $pc = check2$
    Eff: if $\exists_{v \in \{0,1\}} obs\text{-}leader\text{-}agree(v)$ then
            $value(i) \leftarrow obs\text{-}leader\text{-}value$
            $round(i) \leftarrow rounds[i] + 1$
            $obs \leftarrow \emptyset$
            $pc \leftarrow read1$
        else
            $pc \leftarrow flip$

output $start\text{-}flip(r)_i$
    Pre: $pc = flip$
        $round(i) = r$
    Eff: $pc \leftarrow wait$

input $return\text{-}flip(v, r)_i$
    Eff: if $pc = wait \wedge round(i) = r$ then
            $value(i) \leftarrow v$
            $round(i) \leftarrow rounds[i] + 1$
            $obs \leftarrow \emptyset$
            $pc \leftarrow read1$

input $stop_i$
    Eff: $stopped \leftarrow true$
        $pc \leftarrow nil$

Tasks: The locally controlled actions of process i form a single task.

Table 1. The actions and transition relation of AP.

Invariant 4 *Given a reachable state of AP, let $v = value(i)$ and $r = round(i)$. Then $(obs\text{-}agree(r-1,v)_i \land obs\text{-}leader(i)_i \land obs_i = \{1,\dots,n\}) \Rightarrow agree(r,v)$.*

Invariant 4 is sufficient to prove agreement. The idea is that the premise of Invariant 4 is stable. In fact, if process i satisfies the premise of Invariant 4, then process i decides on value v, and thus the local state of process i does not change any more. The analysis of Invariant 4 follows standard methods for invariant proofs within ordinary nondeterministic systems, and is based on several other invariants. The main invariant, which we omit here, is expressed in a new style that we think is useful: it talks about the state of a process when it is in the middle of a scanning pass, and describes properties that would hold if the scanning pass is completed instantly.

4.1 Non-Probabilistic Progress Properties

Our next objective is to show that in the algorithm of Aspnes and Herlihy some decision is reached within some expected number of rounds. This property depends on the probabilistic properties of the coin flipping protocols. However, there are several progress properties of the algorithm that do not depend on any probabilistic assumption. In this section we study such properties. The advantage of this approach is that we can use most of the existing techniques for ordinary nondeterministic systems and confine probabilistic arguments to a limited section of the analysis.

For each round r, let CF_r denote the coin flipping protocol for round r. Define AH to be $AP \parallel (\parallel_{r \geq 1} CF_r)$. For each finite execution fragment α of AH, define the complexity measure $\phi_{MaxRound}(\alpha)$ as the difference between the maximum round numbers of the final and initial states of α. Define the following sets of states.

$\mathcal{R}$ the set of reachable states of AH such that there is an active process;
$\mathcal{D}$ the set of reachable states of AH such that there is no active process.

We show that, under some conditions on the coin flipping protocols, starting from any state of $\mathcal{R}$, a state from $\mathcal{D}$ is reached within some bounded number of rounds. We split the problem: first we show that, unless the algorithm terminates, the system reaches a point where one process just moved to a new maximum round; then, we show that from such an intermediate point the algorithm terminates. The proofs are based on simple invariants. Formally, for $v \in \{0,1\}$, define the following set of states.

$\mathcal{F}_v$ the set of states of $\mathcal{R}$ where there exists a round r and a process l such that $round(l) = r$, $value(l) = v$, $obs_l = \emptyset$, and for all processes $j \neq l$, $round(j) < r$.

Proposition 8. *If AH is in a state s of $\mathcal{R}$ and all invocations to the coin flippers on non-failing ports get a response, then a state from $\mathcal{F}_0 \cup \mathcal{F}_1 \cup \mathcal{D}$ is reached within one round.*

Proposition 9. *If AH is in a state s of $\mathcal{F}_v$, all invocations to the coin flippers on non-failing ports get a response, and all invocations to $CF_{s.max\text{-}round}$ get only response v, then a state from $\mathcal{D}$ is reached within two rounds.*

4.2 Probabilistic Progress Properties

Suppose that each coin flipping protocol CF_r satisfies the following properties.

C1 For each fair probabilistic execution fragment of CF_r that starts with a reachable state of CF_r, the probability that each invocation on a non-failing port gets a response is 1.

C2 For each fair probabilistic execution of CF_r, and each value $v \in \{0,1\}$, the probability that all invocations on a non-failing port get response v is at least p, $0 < p \leq 1$.

Proposition 10. *If each coin flipping protocol CF_r satisfies properties **C1** and **C2**, then in AH, starting from any state of $\mathcal{R}$ and under any fair scheduler, a state from $\mathcal{D}$ is reached within $O(1/p)$ expected rounds.*

Proof. We first derive the statement $\mathcal{R} \xrightarrow[p]{\phi_{MaxRound} \leq 3} \mathcal{D}$ from two intermediate statements $\mathcal{R} \xrightarrow[1]{\phi_{MaxRound} \leq 1} \mathcal{F}_0 \cup \mathcal{F}_1 \cup \mathcal{D}$ and $\mathcal{F}_v \xrightarrow[p]{\phi_{MaxRound} \leq 2} \mathcal{D}$, $v \in \{0,1\}$. The proofs of the intermediate statements rely on Propositions 8 and 9 and on **C1** and **C2**. Since in AH $\mathcal{R}$ is not left unless a state from $\mathcal{D}$ is reached, since each transition of AH increases $\phi_{MaxRound}$ by at most 1, and since from fairness and **C1** some transition is scheduled with probability 1 from each state of $\mathcal{R}$, by Theorem 5 we derive that within expected $4/p$ rounds a state from $\mathcal{D}$ is reached under any fair scheduler.

5 The Atomic Coin Flipping Protocol

5.1 The Protocol

We build a coin flipping protocol that satisfies **C1** and **C2** with $p = (K-1)/2K$. The protocol is based on random walks. We define the protocol by letting a probabilistic automaton DCN_r (Distributed CoiN) interact with a non-probabilistic counter CT_r (CounTer), that is, $CF_r = DCN_r \parallel CT_r$. In this Section, DCN_r is distributed while CT_r is composed of n processes that receive requests from DCN_r and read/update a single shared variable. In Section 5.4 we discuss how to decentralize CT_r. Since the protocols for DCN_r and CT_r are the same for any round r, we drop the subscript r from our notation. In DCN each process flips a fair coin to decide whether to increment or decrement the shared counter. Then the process reads the current value of the shared counter by invoking CT, and if the value read is beyond the barrier $-Kn$ $(+Kn)$, where K is a fixed constant, then the process returns 0 (1). The specification of CT states that an increment or decrement operation always completes unless the corresponding process fails, while a read operation is guaranteed to complete only if increments and decrements eventually cease.

5.2   Non-Probabilistic Analysis

Let $Acts$ be $\{flip_1, \ldots, flip_n\}$, and let S be $\{(U_1^i, U_1^d), (U_2^i, U_2^d), \ldots, (U_n^i, U_n^d)\}$, where U_j^i is the set of states of CF where process j has just flipped inc ($fpc_j = inc$), and U_j^d is the set of states of CF where process j has just flipped dec ($fpc_j = dec$). Given a finite execution fragment α of CF, let $\phi_{inc}(\alpha)$ be the number of coin flips in α that give inc, and let $\phi_{dec}(\alpha)$ be the number of coin flips in α that give dec.

Lemma 11. *Let α be a fair execution of CF, such that $\alpha \in \mathbf{Top}[-(K-1)n, (K+1)n, 0](H)$ for some probabilistic execution H of CF. Then in α every invocation on a non-failing port gets response 1.*

The proof of Lemma 11 follows from simple invariant properties. The main idea is that the value of the shared counter remains beyond Kn once the barrier $(K+1)n$ is reached. A symmetric argument is valid for $\mathbf{Bottom}[-(K-1)n, (K+1)n, 0](H)$.

5.3   Probabilistic Analysis

We prove only **C2** by applying our coin lemma for random walks.

Proposition 12. *The coin flipper CF satisfies **C2** with $p = (K+1)/2K$. That is, fixed $v \in \{0, 1\}$, for each fair probabilistic execution of CF, with probability at least $(K-1)/2K$ each invocation to CF on a non-failing port returns value v.*

Proof. Assume that $v = 1$; the case for $v = 0$ is symmetric. Let H be a fair probabilistic execution of CF. If α is an execution of $\mathbf{Top}[-(K-1)n, (K+1)n, 0](H)$, then, by Lemma 11, every invocation to CF in α gets response 1. Furthermore, by Theorem 6, $P_H[\mathbf{Top}[-(K-1)n, (K+1)n, 0](H)] \geq (K-1)/2K$.

5.4   Implementation of the Shared Counter

It is possible to build a distributed implementation of CT that preserves **C1** and **C2**. The implementation, which we denote by DCT (Distributed CounTer), is presented in [3]. In the full paper we verify that DCT implements CT by exhibiting a *refinement mapping* [7] from DCT to CT. This part of the proof is simple and does not involve probability. Then we use the compositionality results of [11] to show that DCT can replace CT in AH.

5.5   Summing Up

In this section we paste together the results of the previous sections to derive an upper bound on the expected number of rounds for termination. In particular, if we know that there is at least one initialized process that does not fail, then we know that a decision is reached within constant many rounds.

Theorem 13. *Using either the counters CT or DCT, from each reachable state of AH, under any fair scheduler, a state of $\mathcal{D}$ is reached within a constant expected number of rounds.*

Proof. The coin flippers with the counters CT or DCT satisfy properties **C1** and **C2** with $p = (K-1)/2K$. By Proposition 10, AH guarantees that $\mathcal{D}$ is reached within at most $O(2K/(K-1))$ expected rounds.

6 Timing Analysis of the Algorithm

In this section we derive an upper bound on the time to reach $\mathcal{D}$ once all processes have some minimum speed. We achieve this result by studying the expected number of *inc* and *dec* events that occur within the coin flippers and then converting the new expected bound into a time bound.

We change slightly our formal model to handle time. Specifically, we add a component *.now* to the states of all our probabilistic I/O automata, and we add the set of positive real numbers to the input actions of all our probabilistic I/O automata. The *.now* component is a nonnegative real number and describes the current time of an automaton. At the beginning (i.e., in the start states) the current time is 0, and thus the *.now* component is 0. The occurrence of an action d, where d is a positive real number, increments the *.now* component by d and leaves the rest of the state unchanged. Thus, the occurrence of an action d models the fact that d time units are elapsing. The amount of time elapsed since the beginning of an execution is recorded in the *.now* component. Since time-passage actions must synchronize in a parallel composition context, parallel composition ensures that the *.now* components of the components are always equal. Thus, we can abuse notation and talk about the *.now* component of the composition of two automata while we refer to the *.now* component of one of the components. We define a new complexity measure $\phi_t(\alpha)$ as the difference between the *.now* components of the last and first states of α. Informally, ϕ_t measures the time that elapses during an execution. We say that an execution fragment α of a probabilistic automaton M is *well-timed* if each task does not remain enabled for more than one time unit without being performed.

We give some preliminary definitions. Let, for each $r > 0$, DCF_r (Distributed Coin Flipper) denote $DCN_r \| DCT_r$. Let DAH (Distributed Aspnes-Herlihy) denote $AP\|(\|_{r \geq 1} DCF_r)$. For an execution fragment α of DCF_r or of DAH, let $\phi_{flip,r}(\alpha)$ be the number of *flip* events of DCF_r that occur in α, and let $\phi_{id,r}(\alpha)$ be the number of *inc* and *dec* events of DCF_r that occur in α. For each execution fragment α of DAH let $\phi_{id}(\alpha)$ be the number of *inc* and *dec* events that occur in α.

We start with some non-probabilistic properties about the new complexity measures. The first result, Lemma 14, provides a linear upper bound on the time it takes for DAH to span a given number of rounds and to flip a given number of coins under the assumption of well-timedness. The next two results state basic properties of the coin flipping protocols. That is, once a barrier $\pm(K+1)n$ is reached, there are at most n other *flip* events, and within any execution fragment of DCF_r the difference between the *inc*, *dec* events and the *flip* events is at most n.

Lemma 14. *Let α be a well-timed execution fragment of DAH, and suppose that all the states of α, with the possible exception of lstate(α) are active, that is, are states of $\mathcal{R}$. Let $R = fstate(\alpha).max\text{-}round$. Then, $\phi_t(\alpha) \leq d_1 n^2 (\phi_{MaxRound}(\alpha) + R) + d_2 n \phi_{id}(\alpha) + d_3 n^2$ for some constants d_1, d_2, and d_3.*

Lemma 15. *Let $\alpha = \alpha_1 \frown \alpha_2$ be a finite execution of DCF_r, and suppose that $|Diff_{Acts,S}(\alpha_1)| \geq (K+1)n$. Then $\phi_{flip,r}(\alpha_2) \leq n$.*

Lemma 16. *Let α be a finite execution fragment of DCF_r. Then,*
$\phi_{id,r}(\alpha) \leq \phi_{flip,r}(\alpha) + n$.

We now deal with probabilistic properties. First, based on our results on random walks and on Lemma 15, we show in Lemma 17 an upper bound on the expected number of coin flips performed by a coin flipper. Then, in Lemma 18 we use Lemma 16 and our results about linear combinations of complexity measures to derive an upper bound on the expected number of increment and decrement operations performed by a coin flipper, and we use our compositionality result about complexity measures to show that the bound is preserved by parallel composition. Finally, in Lemma 19 we use our result about phases of computations to combine Theorem 13 with Lemma 18 and derive an upper bound on the expected number of *inc* and *dec* events performed by the algorithm.

Lemma 17. *Let H be a probabilistic execution fragment of DCF_r that starts from a reachable state, and let Θ be a full cut of H. Then $E_{\phi_{flip,r}}[H, \Theta] \leq (K+1)^2 n^2 + n$.*

Lemma 18. *Let H be a probabilistic execution fragment of DAH that starts from a reachable state, and let Θ be a full cut of H. Then $E_{\phi_{id,r}}[H, \Theta] \leq (K+1)^2 n^2 + 2n$.*

Lemma 19. *Let H be a probabilistic fair execution fragment of DAH with start state s, and let $R = s.max\text{-}round$. Suppose that s is reachable. Let Θ denote the set of minimal states of H where a state from $\mathcal{D}$ is reached. Then $E_{\phi_{id}}[H, \Theta] = O(Rn^2)$.*

The main result is just a pasting together of the results obtained so far. An immediate consequence on the algorithm of Aspnes and Herlihy is that, if we know that some initialized process does not fail and that the maximum round is 1, then a decision is reached within expected cubic time.

Theorem 20. *Let H be a probabilistic fair, well-timed execution fragment of DAH with a reachable start state s, and let $R = s.max\text{-}round$. Let Θ denote the set of minimal states of H where a state from $\mathcal{D}$ is reached. Then $E_{\phi_t}[H, \Theta] = O(Rn^3)$.*

Proof. By Lemma 14 and Proposition 2, $E_{\phi_t}[H, \Theta] \leq d_1 n^2 E_{\phi_{MaxRound}}[H, \Theta] + d_1 n^2 R + d_2 n E_{\phi_{id}}[H, \Theta] + d_3 n^2$. Thus, by Theorem 13 and Lemma 19, $E_{\phi_t}[H, \Theta] = O(Rn^3)$.

7 Concluding Remarks

In the full paper [10] the length of the analysis of the Aspnes-Herlihy algorithm is double the length of the original proof of Aspnes and Herlihy [3]. This shows that it is possible to prove formally and rigorously the correctness of a randomized distributed algorithm without using too much space. Furthermore, even though in the full paper we have proved all the results, a shorter high level analysis of a protocol using our tools is sufficient to increase considerably our confidence in the correctness of the protocol. The high level analysis provides a designer with a collection of simple properties to check so that the possible subtleties of randomization can be discovered.

References

1. S. Aggarwal. Time optimal self-stabilizing spanning tree algorithms. Technical Report MIT/LCS/TR-632, MIT Laboratory for Computer Science, 1994. Master's thesis.
2. S. Aggarwal and S. Kutten. Time optimal self stabilizing spanning tree algorithms. In R.K. Shyamasundar, editor, *13th International Conference on Foundations of Software Technology and Theoretical Computer Science*, volume 761 of *Lecture Notes in Computer Science*, pages 400–410, Bombay, India., December 1993. Springer-Verlag.
3. J. Aspnes and M.P. Herlihy. Fast randomized consensus using shared memory. *Journal of Algorithms*, 15(1):441–460, September 1990.
4. W. Feller. *An Introduction to Probability Theory and its Applications. Volume 1*. Jokn Wiley & Sons, Inc., 1950.
5. D. Lehmann and M. Rabin. On the advantage of free choice: a symmetric and fully distributed solution to the dining philosophers problem. In *Proceedings of the 8th Annual ACM Symposium on Principles of Programming Languages*, pages 133–138, January 1981.
6. N.A. Lynch, I. Saias, and R. Segala. Proving time bounds for randomized distributed algorithms. In *Proceedings of the 13th Annual ACM Symposium on Principles of Distributed Computing*, Los Angeles, CA, pages 314–323, 1994.
7. Nancy Lynch and Frits Vaandrager. Forward and backward simulations – Part II: Timing-based systems. *Information and Computation*, 121(2):214–233, September 1995.
8. A. Pnueli and L. Zuck. Verification of multiprocess probabilistic protocols. *Distributed Computing*, 1(1):53–72, 1986.
9. A. Pogosyants and R. Segala. Formal verification of timed properties of randomized distributed algorithms. In *Proceedings of the 14th Annual ACM Symposium on Principles of Distributed Computing*, Ottawa, Ontario, Canada, pages 174–183, August 1995.
10. A. Pogosyants, R. Segala, and N. Lynch. Verification of the randomized consensus algorithm of Aspnes and Herlihy: a case study. Technical Memo MIT/LCS/TM-555, MIT Laboratory for Computer Science, 1997.
11. R. Segala. *Modeling and Verification of Randomized Distributed Real-Time Systems*. PhD thesis, MIT, Dept. of Electrical Engineering and Computer Science, 1995. Also appears as technical report MIT/LCS/TR-676.

A Simple DFS-Based Algorithm for Linear Interval Routing

T. Eilam, S. Moran*, S. Zaks

Department of Computer Science
The Technion,
Haifa 32000, Israel
email: {eilam,moran,zaks}@cs.technion.ac.il

Abstract. Linear Interval Routing is a space-efficient routing method for point-to-point communication networks. It is a restricted variant of Interval Routing where the routing range associated with every link is represented by an interval with no wrap-around. It was noted in [BLT91] that not every network has a valid Linear Interval Labeling Scheme (LILS). A complete characterization of the networks that admit a valid LILS was presented in [FG94], together with an algorithm that generates a valid LILS in case one exists. We present a new algorithm that generates an LILS for every network that admits one. Our algorithm is based on a DFS spanning tree of the network, and is "in the spirit" of the algorithms for Interval Routing. Our algorithm has few advantages over the algorithm of [FG94]: it utilizes the well-known theory of DFS spanning trees and is thus simpler to understand and to implement, it uses all links of the network for routing (thus it better distributes the load), and it guarantees that some paths traversed by messages are shortest length paths.

1 Introduction

In a communication network, where communication between nodes is accomplished by sending and receiving messages, a routing algorithm is employed to ensure that every message will reach its destination. An *optimal* routing method routes every message to its destination in the shortest way. Usually optimal routing is achieved by keeping in each node a table with n entries and such that the i-th entry in the table determines the edge to be traversed by a message destined to node i. For large networks it is practical to consider routing methods in which less than $\Omega(n)$ space is used in each node, though such routing methods may not be optimal. The trade-off between space and efficiency was extensively studied in the past decade (see, e.g., [PU89, ABLP89, AP92, GP96a, GP96b]) and many *compact* routing methods were developed and analyzed (see, e.g.,[SK82, LT83, BLT90, BLT91, FGS93, FGNT95]).

---

* This reseaech was supported by the fund for promoting reseach in the Technion, and by the Bernard Elkin Chair in Computer Science.

A popular compact routing method is *Interval Routing* which was introduced in [SK82], discussed together with other compact routing methods in [LT83] and implemented on INMOS transputer C104 Router chips [I91]. Under Interval Routing the nodes are labeled with unique integers from the set $\{1, ..., n\}$, where n is the number of nodes in the network, and at each node, each of its adjacent edges is labeled with one interval of $\{1, ..., n\}$. Cyclic intervals (i.e., intervals that wrap-around over the end of the name segment) are allowed. Under such Interval Labeling Scheme (ILS), at each node i, messages destined to node j are sent on the unique edge that is labeled with an interval that contains j. A *valid* ILS of a network is an ILS under which every message will eventually arrive at its destination. A simple algorithm that generates a valid ILS for every network was presented in [SK82]. The algorithm is based on a BFS spanning tree of the network, it implies an upper bound of $2D$ on the length of a path a message traverses, where D is the diameter of the network, but it has the disadvantage that all routings are performed on a tree. [LT83] presented a different algorithm for ILS, based on a DFS spanning tree; though the algorithm does not imply any upper bound on the length of a path traversed by a message, it has the advantage that every link of the network is used for routing. In [R91] a lower bound of $1.5D + 0.5$ was proved for the maximal length of a path a message traverses under Interval Routing, and this bound was improved in [TL94] to $1.75D - 1$.

Linear Interval Routing ([BLT91]) is a restricted variant of Interval Routing which uses only linear intervals (i.e., intervals with wrap-around are not allowed). It is also the simplest form of Prefix Routing which is another compact routing method (introduced in [BLT90]). It was noted in [BLT91] that not every network has a valid Linear Interval Labeling Scheme (LILS). A complete characterization of the networks that admit a valid LILS was presented in [FG94], together with an algorithm that generates a valid LILS in case one exists. The algorithm in [FG94] is incremental in the sense that it starts by labeling a small sub-network and then in each iteration it labels an unlabeled path in the network until all nodes and edges are labeled. The algorithm does not imply any upper bound on the length of a path traversed by a message; indeed, the question of finding a non-trivial upper bound for Linear Interval Routing is still open. In [EMZ96] a lower bound of $\Omega(D^2)$ on the length of a path a message traverses in a network under a valid LILS was presented.

In this paper we present a new algorithm that generates an LILS for every network that admits one. Our algorithm is based on a DFS spanning tree of the network and thus is "in the spirit" of the algorithms for Interval Routing ([SK82, LT83]). In fact, by utilizing the special structure of networks which admit valid LILS, it accomplishes the same benefits as the algorithm in [LT83] for Interval Routing but it does not use wrap-around intervals. Our algorithm has the following advantages over the algorithm of [FG94]: (1) It utilizes the well-known theory of DFS spanning trees, and is thus simpler to understand and to implement, (2) it uses all links of the network (at least in one direction) for routing, thus it better distributes the load, and (3) it guarantees that some paths traversed by messages (which depend on the structure of the network and will be completely characterized) are shortest length paths.

In Section 2 we present the model, previous results and a precise description of the routing methods under discussion. In Section 3 we present the algorithm and analyze its correctness. Properties and extensions are discussed in Section 4. Most of the proofs are only briefly sketched or omitted in this Extended Abstract.

2 Preliminaries

We assume a point-to-point asynchronous communication network where processors communicate with their neighbors by exchanging messages along the communication links, which are bidirectional. The network topology is modeled by a (connected) undirected graph $G = (V, E)$, $|V| = n$, where the set V of nodes corresponds to the processors, and the set E of edges corresponds to the communication links connecting them. An edge e connecting u and v is denoted by $e = (u, v)$. For a node v, E_v denotes the set of edges adjacent to v.

Each message has a header that includes its destination. When a message arrives at an intermediate node then the edge on which it will continue is determined by a local routing decision function.

The routing methods under discussion involve a labeling of the nodes and edges of the graph. Each node is labeled with a unique integer in $N = \{1, ..., n\}$, termed *node number*, and at each node v, each of the edges in E_v is labeled with an *interval of N*, defined as follows.

Definition 1. An *interval of N* is one of the following:

1. A *linear interval* $\langle p, q \rangle = \{p, p+1, ...q\}$, where $p, q \in N$ and $p \leq q$.
2. A *wrap-around interval* $\langle p, q \rangle = \{p, p+1, ..., n, 1, ..., q\}$, where $p, q \in N$ and $p > q$.
3. The *null interval* $\langle \rangle$ which is the empty set.

We say that a node $u \in V$ is *contained* in an interval $\langle p, q \rangle$ if $u \in \langle p, q \rangle$. Note that the null interval does not contain any node.

Definition 2. An *interval labeling scheme* (ILS) $\mathcal{L}_G = (L, \{I_v\}_{v \in V})$ of a graph $G = (V, E)$ is defined by:

1. A one-to-one function $L : V \to N$ that labels the nodes of V.
2. A set of edge labeling functions $I_v : E_v \to I$, for every $v \in V$, where I is the set of all intervals of N, that satisfy the following properties for every $v \in V$:
   union property the union of all the intervals corresponding to the edges in E_v is equal to N or to $N - \{L(v)\}$.
   disjunction property the intervals $I_v(e_1)$ and $I_v(e_2)$ corresponding to any two edges $e_1, e_2 \in E_v$ are disjoint.

(In other words, the non-empty intervals associated with all the edges adjacent to any node v form a partition of N or of $N - \{L(v)\}$.)

For $e = (u, v)$ we will write $I_u(u, v)$ instead of $I_u((u, v))$.

For simplicity, from now on, given an ILS and a node u, we will not distinguish between the node u and its node number $L(u)$.

Two variants of interval labeling scheme are defined as follows.

Definition 3. A *linear interval labeling scheme* (LILS) $\mathcal{L}_G$ of a graph G is an interval labeling scheme in which all the intervals $I_v(e)$ - for every $v \in V$ and every $e \in E_v$ - are either linear or null.

Definition 4. A *strict-linear* interval labeling scheme (strict-LILS) $\mathcal{L}_G$ of a graph $G = (V, E)$ is a linear interval labeling scheme in which $v \notin I_v(e)$ for every $v \in V$ and every $e \in E_v$.

By a *labeling scheme* we mean ILS or any of its two variants. Given a graph with any labeling scheme, the routing of messages is performed as follows. If node u has a message destined to node v, $v \neq u$, then u will send the message on the *unique* edge e such that $v \in I_u(e)$. Obviously, if the labeling scheme is arbitrary, the routing cannot ensure that every message will eventually arrive at its destination; though a message from u to v cannot be stuck at any node, it still can cycle forever without getting to v. We thus introduce the following definition.

Definition 5. A *valid* labeling scheme of a graph is a labeling scheme that guarantees that every message will eventually arrive at its destination.

Given a valid labeling scheme $\mathcal{L}_G$ of G, and two nodes u and v, $Path_G(u, v, \mathcal{L}_G)$ denotes the path along which a message, destined to v, will traverse starting from u, under the labeling scheme $\mathcal{L}_G$. From the definitions it is clear that if the routing is done according to a valid labeling scheme, each message will follow a simple path (in which all nodes are distinct), which implies a trivial upper bound of $n - 1$ on the length of such paths. We denote by IRS (Interval Routing Scheme) a valid ILS and correspondingly LIRS and strict-LIRS. A precise characterization of the graphs that admit LIRS was given in [FG94]. To state it, we first need the following definition.

Definition 6. A *lithium graph* is a connected graph $G = (V, E)$, $V = V_0 \cup V_1 \cup V_2 \cup V_3$, such that the sets V_i are disjoint, $|V_1|, |V_2|, |V_3| \geq 2$ and there is a unique edge connecting V_0 with each of the V_i's, $i = 1, 2, 3$, and no edge between any two different V_i and V_j, $1 \leq i, j \leq 3$ (see Figure 1).

Theorem 7. ([FG94]) A (connected) graph G admits an LIRS iff G is not a lithium graph.

In order to define a general representation of a non-lithium graph we first define:

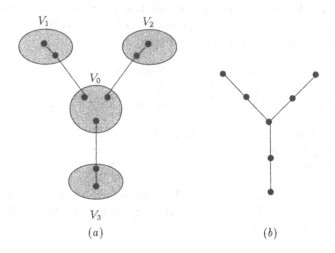

Fig. 1. (a) The general form of a lithium graph. (b) The simplest lithium graph.

Definition 8.

1. The *reduced graph* of a graph G, $R(G)$, is the graph obtained from G by removing all of its leaves and the edges adjacent to them (where a node v is a *leaf* if it has only one adjacent node, that is, $|E_v| = 1$).
2. A *2-edge-connected graph with leaves* is a graph G for which the reduced graph $R(G)$ is 2-edge-connected (a graph is 2-edge-connected if it does not contain any bridge, note that a graph that contains a single node is 2-edge-connected).

A non-lithium graph $G = (V, E)$ can be represented as a sequence $G_1, (v_1^2, v_2^1), G_2, (v_2^2, v_3^1), G_3, ..., (v_{n-1}^2, v_n^1), G_n, n \geq 1$, where $G_i = (V_i, E_i)$ is a 2-edge-connected graph with leaves (Definition 8), $v_1^2 \in V_1, v_n^1 \in V_n, v_i^1, v_i^2 \in V_i$ for every $1 < i < n$, $V = \cup_{i=1}^n V_i$, $E = \cup_{i=1}^n E_i \cup \cup_{i=1}^{n-1}\{(v_i^2, v_{i+1}^1)\}$ and each (v_i^2, v_{i+1}^1) is a bridge that connects G_i and G_{i+1}. The vertices $\{v_i^1, v_i^2\}_{1 \leq i \leq n}$ are termed *bridge points*. (See Figure 2.)

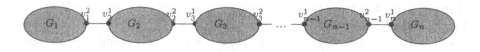

Fig. 2. A non-lithium graph. The G_is are 2-edge-connected graph with leaves and the v_i^js are the bridge points.

3 A Labeling Algorithm

3.1 Preliminaries

In this section we present a new algorithm, Algorithm Linear-Label, that generates an LIRS for every graph which admits one (i.e., for every connected non-lithium graph). Our algorithm, as the one of [FG94], does not imply any non-trivial upper bound for general non-lithium graphs (this question is still open), but it has the following advantages. First, it is based on a DFS-spanning tree of the graph, thus, it resembles the algorithms for IRS mentioned in Section 1 and is easier to understand and to implement. Second, it guarantees that the path that any message traverses between any two bridge points is a shortest length path (see Example 1). Last, it could be easily modified (as will be shown in the sequel) such that every link of the network (at least in one direction) will be used for routing.

Example 1. As an example consider the graph G depicted in Figure 3. Each G_i, $1 \leq i \leq n$, is a simple cycle of length n, with nodes $u_1^i, u_2^i, ..., u_n^i$, and an additional edge $(u_2^i, u_{n/2+1}^i)$. The edge $(u_{n/2}^i, u_1^{i+1})$ is the bridge that connects G_i and G_{i+1}. Under Algorithm Linear-Label a message between $s \in G_i$ and $t \in G_j$, $i < j$, will traverse a path of length at most $2n + 3(j - i - 1) + (j - i)$ (since the shortest length path between each u_1^i and $u_{n/2}^i$ is of length 3). The algorithm of [FG94] however, will route a messages between each u_1^i and $u_{n/2}^i$ on a cycle that contains both of the nodes. As a consequence, a message between s and t will traverse a path of length at least $n/2 \cdot (j - i - 1) + (j - i)$.

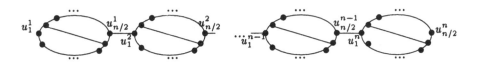

Fig. 3. An example.

Algorithm Linear-Label is based on the theory of DFS (Depth First Search) spanning trees. A DFS spanning tree of a graph is constructed by traversing the graph in a depth first style, backtracking only when there is no unvisited adjacent node. The DFS spanning tree T that is constructed throughout this traversal is a directed tree, rooted at the origin of the traversal. For any node x, we denote by T_x the sub-tree of T rooted at x. Each node in T_x including x is a *descendant* of x. Every node on the path from the root r to x except for x is an *ancestor* of x. Every node x (except for the root) has a predecessor $P_T(x)$ and every non-leaf node has a (non-empty) set of successors $S_T(x)$. A *frond* is an edge of the graph which is not an edge of the tree. A DFS spanning tree of a graph satisfies the property that any frond is an edge that connects a node with one of its ancestors in the tree. Additionally, it is well known (see, e.g., [E79]) that in a DFS spanning tree of a 2-edge-connected graph for every node x (except for the root) there is a frond which connect a descendant of x and an ancestor of it in the tree.

3.2   An Informal Description of Algorithm Linear-Label

We start by giving an informal description of Algorithm Linear Label in 2-edge-connected graphs. It is rather simple to generate an ILS (Interval Labeling Scheme) for any (undirected) graph G by using any spanning tree of G (such a scheme was presented in [SK82]). In order to label the nodes, we traverse the tree in a depth-first-style and label the nodes in a post-order fashion. Let T denote the resulted directed tree. For every node x, the labels of the nodes in T_x form a contiguous interval, and $L(x) > L(u)$ for every node u in T_x. The label $I_v(e)$ for an edge in E_v, for any node v, is defined as follows: if $e = (x, y)$, and y is a successor of x in T, then $I_x(e)$ is the interval of labels of nodes in T_y, otherwise, if y is the predecessor of x in T, then the interval $I_x(y)$ is the cyclic complement interval of the interval of labels of the nodes in T_x. The path a message traverses under such IRS is the unique path in the tree T between its source and its destination.

When considering LIRSs, cyclic intervals are not allowed. As a consequence, an interval of an edge from a node to its predecessor on the tree cannot contain both labels that are smaller than the labels of the nodes in T_x and labels that are larger than them. To avoid this problem we utilize the special structure of a non-lithium graphs which is a sequence of 2-edge-connected components (with leaves) connected by bridges. We first present a labeling algorithm for any 2-edge-connected graph (with leaves) and then generalize it to a labeling algorithm for any non-lithium graph (Section 3.4).

By Algorithm Linear-Label, a DFS spanning tree T of a 2-edge-connected graph G is found and each node x ($x \neq r$) is assigned a *back edge*, i.e., a frond between a descendant of x and an ancestor of it (note that since G is 2-edge-connected, such back edge exists for every node). A message from x to a node y in T_x will traverse the path in T from x to y. A message to a node y with $L(y) > L(x)$ will traverse the unique path in T from x to a common ancestor z of x and y, and then from z down to y. The interesting case is when x has a message destined to a node y that is not in the tree T_x (i.e., y is not a descendant of x) and such that $L(y) < L(x)$. In this case we use the back edges to go up the tree until a common ancestor of x and y is reached. More specifically, let $e = (u, v)$ be the back edge assigned to x; a message from x to y will traverse the path in T from x to u, then will continue on e to v, which is an ancestor of x. If v is an ancestor of y then we get to a previous case (and the message will continue down T towards y), otherwise, it will continue through another back edge (the back edge assigned to v) to an "upper" node in T, and so on, until an ancestor of y is reached. Note that the third case is the only one in which the path traversed by a message is not the unique path in the tree T.

There are two phases in Algorithm Linear-Label. In the first phase a DFS tree T is constructed and a back edge is assigned to every node. In the second phase we traverse the tree in a (specific) depth-first search and label the nodes (in a post-order fashion) and the edges. Specifically, consider any node x with a set of successors $y_1, ..., y_k$ and let $e = (u, v)$ be the back edge assigned to x in the first phase. If $u \neq x$ (that is, the back edge of x emanates from a successor u of x which is not equal to x) then assume that T_{y_i} is the sub-tree to which u belongs. Then the subtree T_{y_i} is traversed first and then all other subtrees T_{y_j}, $y_j \in S_T(x)$, are traversed in an arbitrary order. This traversal guarantees that the interval of labels of nodes in T_{y_i} is smaller then the interval of labels of nodes in any other sub-tree T_{y_j}, $y_j \in S_T(x)$. This property enables us to send both messages destined to nodes in T_{y_i} and messages destined to nodes not in T_x but with smaller labels, on the edge from x to y_i (towards the back-edge assigned to x) since the union of both sets of labels form a contiguous interval. If the back edge assigned to x emanates from x (that is, $u = x$), then there is no restriction on the order of the traversal of the subtrees T_{y_j}, $y_j \in S_T(x)$.

The formal code of Algorithm Linear-Label for any 2-edge-connected graph with leaves is presented in Section 3.3. The generalization of Algorithm Linear-Label to any non-lithium graph is in Section 3.4.

3.3 Labeling a 2-Edge-Connected Graph with Leaves

The input to Algorithm Linear-Label is a 2-edge-connected graph and the output is a strict-LIRS for it. Given a graph G, a strict-LIRS for it $\mathcal{L}_G$, and a graph G' such that $R(G') = G$ (see Definition 8) it is straightforward to generate an LIRS $L_{G'}$ for G' (see, [FG94]). Algorithm Linear-Label does not specify how to find back edges; however this task can be easily performed while doing the DFS traversal (see, e.g., [E79]).

Algorithm Linear-Label
Phase 1: Construct a DFS spanning tree T rooted at any node r of the graph G. Assign to every node x a back edge, $back(x)$, while keeping the following invariant.
INV: For every node x with $back(x) = (u, v)$ and for every node y on the path in T from x to u, $back(y) = back(x)$.

Phase 2:
A. Assigning labels to nodes
Traverse T in a depth first style; when a node x is reached for the first time,

1. If $x = r$ or $back(x) = (u, v)$ and $u = x$ then recursively traverse each T_y, $y \in S_T(x)$, in an arbitrary order.
   Otherwise ($back(x) = (u, v)$, $u \neq x$), let $y_1 \in S_T(x)$ be the successor of x such that u is a node in T_{y_1}. First recursively traverse T_{y_1} and then each T_z, $z \in S_T(x) - \{y_1\}$, in an arbitrary order.

2. Assign an integer $L(x)$ to x.
3. Integers are assigned in ascending order.

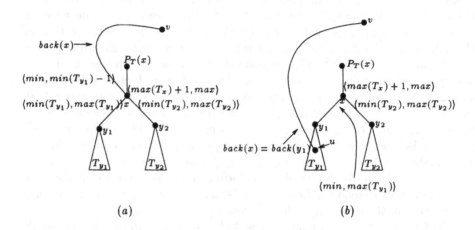

(a) (b)

Fig. 4. The labeling of the edges outgoing a node x where (a) $back(x)$ is an edge outgoing x (b) Otherwise $(back(x) = (u, v)$ and u is in $T_{y_1})$.

B. Assigning labels to edges

For a node $x \in V$ we denote by $max(T_x)$ and $min(T_x)$ the maximal and minimal label of a node in T_x (note that $max(T_x) = L(x)$).

Let $x \in V$ and let $y_1, ..., y_l$ be its successors in an ascending order (of their labeling). Let $back(x) = e = (u, v)$.

1. If $x = u$ then $I_x(e) = \langle min, min(T_x) - 1 \rangle$, $I_x(x, y_i) = \langle min(T_{y_i}), max(T_{y_i}) \rangle$ for each $1 \leq i \leq l$, $I_x(x, P_t(x)) = \langle max(T_x) + 1, max \rangle$ (see Figure 4(a)).
2. Otherwise $(x \neq u)$, the only difference in labeling in this case is: $I_x(x, y_1) = \langle min, max(T_{y_1}) \rangle$ (the back edge of x is not labeled yet) (see Figure 4(b)).

If the algorithm does not specify how to label an edge e at one of its end nodes u (that is, if $e = (u, v)$ is neither an edge of the tree nor the back edge assigned to node u) then $L_u(e) = \langle \rangle$ (the null interval).

Algorithm Linear-Label generates a strict-LIRS for any 2-edge-connected graph. As explained in [FG94], it is straightforward to generate from a strict-LIRS of any graph G, an LIRS for a graph G' whose reduced graph is equal to G (i.e., $R(G') = G$; Definition 8).

3.4 Labeling any Non-Lithium Graph

We now extend Algorithm Linear-Label to any non-lithium graph.

Consider a labeled DFS tree T. A node v is termed *a leftmost node* if every node u with label smaller than the label of v is a successor of v (that is, u is a node in the sub-tree T_v). Note that a back edge for a leftmost node in a DFS tree which was labeled by Algorithm Linear-Label is not needed (since the interval of nodes with labels smaller than $L(v)$ that are not in T_v is empty).

The structure of a non-lithium graph is a sequence of 2-edge-connected graphs (with leaves) connected by bridges. In a DFS spanning tree of the reduced graph of a non-lithium graph a back edge could be found to every node except for some of the bridge points. Therefore, the extension of Algorithm Linear-Label for non-lithium graphs will guarantee that every end-node of a bridge will be a left-most node in the tree (thus, a back edge for it is not needed).

Following is an informal description of the algorithm. Let $G = (V, E)$ be a non-lithium graph represented by the sequence of components $G_1, (v_1^2, v_2^1)$, $G_2, (v_2^2, v_3^1)$, $G_3, ..., (v_{n-1}^2, v_n^1), G_n$, where $G_i = (V_i, E_i)$ is a 2-edge-connected graph with leaves. We first find a strict-LIRS for the reduced graph of G, $R(G)$, and then transform it into an LIRS of G, as explained in Section 3.3. To simplify the notations, in the sequel G will stand for $R(G)$. In the first phase we traverse G in order to find a DFS spanning tree; for this, we first traverse a shortest length simple path P from the root - an arbitrary node $r \in V_n$ - to the node v_1^2 (such a path must pass through all the bridge points), then we continue to span G in a depth-first style arbitrarily. In this phase, we also assign a back edge to every node that is not on the path P. After a DFS spanning tree T is constructed, we traverse T in a depth-first style in order to label the nodes; when we reach a node $x \in P$ we first traverse recursively T_y, where $y \in S_T(x)$ is the successor of x in P, thus guaranteeing that all the nodes in P are leftmost nodes in the tree. Other nodes are treated as in the original algorithm.

Note that for the correctness of the algorithm the path P does not have to be a shortest length path. We construct P as a shortest length path in order to guarantee that the path that any message traverses between any two bridge points is a shortest length path (a property that will be analyzed in Section 4.1). The only difference between the two versions of Algorithm Linear-Label is that in the new version some nodes are not assigned a back edge. Note however that all such nodes are nodes in the path P, that is, leftmost nodes for which a back edge is not needed. The path P contains all the bridge points, thus for every node which is not contained in it, there exists a back edge.

Following is the formal code of Algorithm Linear-Label for any non-lithium graph together with an example.

Algorithm Linear-Label
Phase 1:
Start from any node r in G_n and construct a DFS spanning tree T of G; traverse first a shortest length path P between r and v_1^2 and then the rest of the graph. Assign to every node x that is not in the path P a back edge, $back(x)$, while keeping the following invariant.

$\mathcal{INV}$: For every node x with $back(x) = (u, v)$ and for every node y on the path in T from x to u, $back(y) = back(x)$.

Phase 2:
A. Assigning labels to nodes
Traverse T in a depth first style; when a node x is reached for the first time,

1. If x is a node in the path P then let $y_1 \in S_T(x)$ be its successor in the path P. Recursively traverse first T_{y_1} and then each T_z, $z \in S_T(x) - \{y_1\}$.
   Otherwise, let $back(x) = (u, v)$. If $u = x$ then recursively traverse each T_z, $z \in S_T(x)$, in an arbitrary order.
   Otherwise $(back(x) = (u, v), u \neq x)$, let $y_1 \in S_T(x)$ be the successor of x such that u is a node in T_{y_1}. Recursively traverse first T_{y_1} and then each T_z, $z \in S_T(x) - \{y_1\}$ (in an arbitrary order).
2. Assign an integer $L(x)$ to x.
3. Integers are assigned in ascending order.

B. Assigning labels to edges
For a node $x \in V$ we denote by $max(T_x)$ and $min(T_x)$ the maximal and minimal label of a node in T_x.
Let $x \in V$ and let $y_1, ..., y_l$ be its successors in an ascending order (of their labeling).
• If x is a node in the path P then $I_x(x, y_1) = \langle min, max(T_{y_1})\rangle$, $I_x(x, y_i) = \langle min(T_{y_i}), max(T_{y_i})\rangle$ for every $2 \leq i \leq l$, $I_x(x, P_t(x)) = \langle max(T_x) + 1, max\rangle$
Otherwise, let $back(x) = e = (u, v)$.
• If $u = x$ then $I_x(e) = \langle min, min(T_x) - 1\rangle$, $I_x(x, y_i) = \langle min(T_{y_i}), max(T_{y_i})\rangle$ for every $1 \leq i \leq l$, $I_x(x, P_t(x)) = \langle max(T_x) + 1, max\rangle$
• Otherwise $(x \neq u)$ the labeling of the edges in this case is similar to the first case.
If the algorithm does not specify how to label an edge e at one of its end nodes u (that is, if $e = (u, v)$ is neither an edge of the tree nor the back edge of Node u) then $L_u(e) = \langle \rangle$ (the null interval).

Example 2. Figure 5 is an example of a graph G that was labeled according to Algorithm Linear-Label (null intervals of edges are not marked). The graph G has three components which are 2-edge-connected graphs G_1, G_2 and G_3. We refer to the nodes in G by the integers assigned to them as labels. The edges $(6, 8)$ and $(15, 17)$ are the strong bridges that connect G_1 with G_2 and G_2 with G_3, respectively. Edges of the DFS spanning tree found by Algorithm Linear-Label are directed. A shortest length path P in T which passes through all the bridges is the path $\langle 21, 17, 15, 9, 8, 6\rangle$. Note that all the nodes in P are leftmost nodes. Consider for example the path a message from node 19 to node 2 will traverse. Since 19 is larger then 2 but node 2 is not a descendant of node 19, the message will go up the back edge of 19 to node 20. Still 2 is not a descendant of 20 thus the message go down to 18 and then up the back edge of node 20 (and 18) to node 21. Now 2 is a descendant of 21 thus the message will go down the tree to $17, 15, 9, 8, 6$ and 2. Note that the sub-path of this path between 17 and 6 is a shortest length path in G. A message from node 2 to node 19 will traverse the unique path on T between them. Again, the sub-path of this path between node 6 and node 17 is a shortest length path.

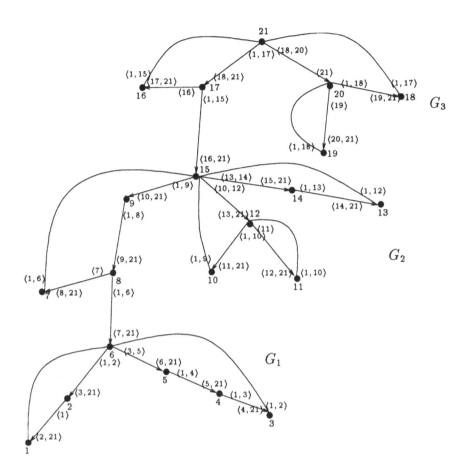

Fig. 5. A graph G together with an LILS for it, generated by Algorithm Linear-Label.

4 Properties and Extensions of Algorithm Linear-Label

4.1 Properties of the Algorithm

Let $s \in V_i$ and $t \in V_j$ be any two nodes in G_i and G_j, respectively, $i < j$. We show that the sub-path between the bridge points v_i^2 and v_j^1 of either of the paths $Path(s, t, \mathcal{L}_G)$ and $Path(t, s, \mathcal{L}_G)$, where $\mathcal{L}_G$ is the LILS generated by Algorithm Linear-Label, is a shortest length path.

The path P in the tree T (which was constructed by the algorithm) between its root r and the node v_i^2 is a shortest length path which passes through the nodes $r, v_n^1, v_{n-1}^2, ..., v_1^2$. By Algorithm Linear-Label, $L(t) > L(s)$ and thus a message from s to t will traverse the unique path between s and t in the tree T. Since the sub-path of this path between v_i^2 and v_j^1 is a sub-path of the shortest length path P, it is also a shortest length path. Now consider a message from t

to s. Since $L(t) > L(s)$ then if s is not in T_t, the message will traverse a path in G_j until an ancestor of s, x, is reached and then it will traverse the unique path on T between x and s, and, again, the sub-path between v_j^1 and v_i^2 is a shortest length path.

Algorithm Linear-Label could be easily modified so that every link of the network (at least in one direction) will be used for routing. This property is desirable since it implies a more balanced load on the links of the network. Consider an LIRS $\mathcal{L}_G$ generated by Algorithm Linear-Label, and a node $x \in V$. Let $Back(x) = \{(x, v_1), ..., (x, v_k)\}$ be the set of fronds in G w.r.t T from x to its ancestors. At most one of these edges could be the back edge, $back(x)$, assigned to x by Algorithm Linear-Label. Algorithm Linear-Label assigns a null interval to all other edges in $Back(x)$. We can thus distribute the load on the edge $(x, P_T(x))$ from x to its predecessor in T also between the edges in the set $Back'(x) = Back(x) - \{back(x)\}$. We will divide the interval $\langle max(T_x) + 1, max \rangle$ assigned to $(x, P_T(x))$ to $|Back'(x)|+1$ approximately equal subintervals $\langle max(T_x) + 1, n_1 \rangle, \langle n_1, n_2 \rangle, ..., \langle n_{k'-1}, max \rangle$ and assign every subinterval to a different edge in $Back'(x) \cup \{(x, p_T(x))\}$. It is easily seen that the algorithm remains correct after the modification although a message from node x to node y with larger label will not necessarily traverse the path on the tree T from x to y; the path on which the message will traverse up to a common ancestor may contain some fronds. Since every edge which is not an edge of T is of the form (x, v_i) where v_i is an ancestor of x, that is, the size of the interval initially assigned to $(x, P_T(x))$ is at least $|Back(x)'|+1$, then after the modification every edge is assigned a non-empty interval in at least one direction. We assume here that there are no multiple edges (that is, the graph is simple). Indeed, if the graph is not simple then any deterministic labeling algorithm cannot guarantee that each link will be used for routing since there could be more links than destinations.

4.2 Refinement of Algorithm Linear-Label for Subsets of Graphs

We show in this section how to refine Algorithm Linear-Label for a family of graphs which is a subset of the non-lithium graphs.

Consider a graph G such that the superstructure (defined in [E79]) of its reduced graph $R(G)$ is a line. These graphs can be decomposed in two levels; one level is by their 2-edge-connected components (as in the general case). A refined level is to further decompose every 2-edge-connected component to its 2-node-connected components. This decomposition could be represented as a sequence; $(G_1^1, t_1^1, G_1^2, t_1^2, ...t_1^{k_1-1}, G_1^{k_1}), (v_1^2, v_2^1), ..., (v_{r-1}^2, v_r^1), (G_r^1, t_r^1, ..., t_r^{k_r-1}, G_r^{k_r})$, where every G_i^j is the jth 2-node-connected component in the ith 2-edge-connected component, t_i^j is a separation node common to the 2-node-connected components G_i^j and G_i^{j+1}, and (v_i^2, v_{i+1}^1) is the bridge connecting two 2-edge-connected components. (The decomposition is demonstrated in Figure 6). Algorithm Linear-Label guarantees that a path traversed by any message between any two bridge points is a shortest length path. For this family of graphs we can refine Algorithm

Linear-Label so that it will guarantee the same property also for any two separation nodes $t_{i_1}^{j_1}$ and $t_{i_2}^{j_2}$ even if they are in the same 2-edge-connected component (that is, $i_1 = i_2$). For example, consider the nodes s and t in Figure 6. The refined algorithm will guarantee that the sub-path between the separation nodes t_1^1 and t_1^3 of either of the paths $Path(s, t, \mathcal{L}_G)$ and $Path(t, s, \mathcal{L}_G)$ is a shortest length path (although s and t are in the same 2-edge-connected component).

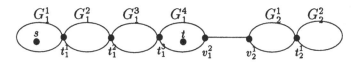

Fig. 6. A decomposition of a graph whose superstructure is a line. Every G_i^j is a 2-node-connected graph (with leaves)

The refinement of Algorithm Linear-Label in order for it to imply the stronger property for this family of graphs is as follows. When traversing the graph in the first phase in order to construct a DFS tree, we start in any node r in the last 2-node-connected component, $G_r^{k_r}$, (G_2^2 in Figure 6). We traverse first a shortest length path P from it to the separation node t_1^1 and then continue the DFS traversal arbitrarily. We label the nodes, as in the general case, such that all the nodes in the path P are leftmost nodes. It should be clear, by the same considerations as in the general case, that the stronger property is satisfied by this refined version of Algorithm Linear-Label.

It is interesting to note that the graphs for which this refinement could be applied (graph that satisfy that the superstructure of their reduced graph is a line) are all the graphs that are not *Petal graphs*. In [EMZ96], Petal graphs were introduced and a lower bound of the total$_2$-diameter (a quantity that can be as large as the square of the diameter) on the efficiency of Linear-Interval Routing was proved for all Petal graphs. Thus, the fact that the refinement of Algorithm Linear-Label applies to all non-petal graphs is not surprising.

References

[ABLP89] Awerbuch, B., Bar-Noy, A., Linial, N., Peleg, D.: Improved Routing Strategies with Succinct Tables. Journal of Algorithms, **11** (1990) 307–341.

[AP92] Awerbuch, B., Peled, D.: Routing with Polinomial Communication-Space Tradeoff. SIAM Journal on Discrete Math., **5** (1992) 151–162.

[BLT90] Bakker, E.M., van Leeuwen, J., Tan, R.B.: Prefix Routing Schemas in Dynamic Networks. Tech. Rep. RUU-CS-90-10, Dept. of Computer science, Utrecht University, Utrecht (1990), and, Computer Networks and ISDN Systems **26** (1993) 403–421.

[BLT91] Bakker, E.M., van Leeuwen, J., Tan, R.B.: Linear Interval Routing. Algorithms Review **2** (1991) 45–61.

[E79] Even, S.: Graph Algorithms. Computer Science Press, Inc., (1979).

[EMZ96] Eilam, T., Moran, S., Zaks, S.: Lower Bounds for Linear Interval Routing. Proc. 10th int. Workshop on Distributed Algorithms (WDAG) (1996) 191–205.

[FG94] Fraigniaud, P., Gavoille, C.: Interval Routing Schemes. Research Rep. 94-04, LIPS-ENS Lyon (1994).

[FGNT95] Flammini, M., Gambosi, G., Nanni, U., Tan, R.: Multi-Dimensional Interval Routing Scheme. Proc. 9th Int. Workshop on Distributed Algorithms (WDAG) (1995) 131–144.

[FGS93] Flammini, M., Gambosi, G., Salomone, S.: Boolean Routing. Proc. 7th Int. Workshop on Distributed Algorithms (WDAG) (1993) 219–233.

[FG96] Fraigniaud, P., Gavoille, C.: Local Memory Requirement of Universal Routing Schemes. Proc. 8th Annual ACM Symp. on Parallel Algorithms and Architecture (SPAA) (1996).

[GP96a] Gavoille, C., Perennes, S.: Memory Requirements for Routing in Distributed Networks. Proc. 15th Annual ACM Symp. on Principles of Distributed Computing (PODC) (1996) 125–133.

[GP96b] Gavoille, C., Perennes, S.,: Lower Bounds for Shortest Path Interval Routing. Proc. 3rd Colloq. on Structural Information and Communication Complexity (SIROCCO) (1996).

[I91] The T9000 Transputer Products Overview Manual, INMOS (1991).

[LT83] van Leeuwen, J., Tan, R.B.: Routing with Compact Routing Tables. Tech. Rep. RUU-CS-83-16, Dept. of Computer Science, Utrecht University (1983). Also as: Computer Networks with Compact Routing Tables. In: G. Rozenberg and A. Salomaa (Eds.) The book of L, Springer- Verlag, Berlin (1986) 298–307.

[LT86] van Leeuwen, J., Tan, R.B.: Computer Network with Compact Routing Tables. In: G. Rozenberg and A. Salomaa (Eds.), The Book of L., Springer-Verlag, Berlin (1986) 259–273.

[PU89] Peleg, D., Upfal, E.: A Trade-Off between Space and Efficiency of Routing Tables. Journal of the ACM **36** (1989) 510–530.

[R91] Ružička, P.: A Note on the Efficiency of an Interval Routing Algorithm. The Computer Journal **34** (1991) 475–476.

[SK82] Santoro, N., Khatib, R.: Routing Without Routing Tables. Tech. Rep. SCS-TR-6, School of Computer Science, Carleton University (1982). Also as: Labeling and Implicit Routing in Networks. The Computer Journal **28** (1) (1985) 5–8.

[TL94] Tse, S. S.H., Lau, F. C.M.: A Lower Bound for Interval Routing in General Networks. Networks **29** (1997) 49–53. Also as: Tech. Rep. TR-94-09, Department of Computer Science, University of Hong Kong (1994).

ATM Layouts with Bounded Hop Count and Congestion[*]

Michele Flammini[1,2], Enrico Nardelli[1,3] and Guido Proietti[1]

[1] Dipartimento di Matematica Pura ed Applicata, Università degli Studi di L'Aquila,
via Vetoio loc.Coppito, I-67100 L'Aquila, Italy.
E-mail: {flammini,nardelli,proietti}@univaq.it

[2] Project SLOOP I3S-CNRS/INRIA/Université de Nice–Sophia Antipolis,
930 route des Colles, F-06903 Sophia Antipolis Cedex, France

[3] Istituto di Analisi dei Sistemi ed Informatica, Consiglio Nazionale delle Ricerche
Viale Manzoni 30, I-00185 Roma, Italy

Abstract. In this paper we consider two new cost measures related to the communication overhead and the space requirements associated to virtual path layouts in ATM networks, that is the edge congestion and the node congestion. Informally, the edge congestion of a given edge e at an incident node u is defined as the number of VPs terminating or starting from e at u, while the node congestion of a node v is defined as the number of VPs having v as an endpoint. We investigate the problem of constructing virtual path layouts allowing to connect a specified root node to all the others in at most h hops and with maximum edge or node congestion c, for two given integers h and c. We first give tight results concerning the time complexity of the construction of such layouts for both the two congestion measures, that is we exactly determine all the tractable and intractable cases. Then, we provide some combinatorial bounds for arbitrary networks, together with optimal layouts for specific topologies such as chains, rings, grids and tori. Extensions to d-dimensional grids and tori with $d > 2$ are also discussed.

1 Introduction

The *Asynchronous Transfer Mode* (ATM for short) is the most popular networking paradigm for Broadband ISDN [11, 10, 13]. It transfers data in the form of small fixed-size *cells*, that are routed independently according to two routing fields at their header: the *virtual channel index* (VCI) and the *virtual path index* (VPI). At each intermediate switch, these fields serve as indices to two routing tables, and the routing is done in accordance to the predetermined information in the appropriate entries.

---

[*] Work supported by the EU TMR Research Training Grant N. ERBFMBICT960861, by the EU ESPRIT Long Term Research Project ALCOM-IT under contract N. 20244 and by the Italian MURST 40% project "Algoritmi, Modelli di Calcolo e Strutture Informative".

Routing in ATM is hierarchical in the sense that the VCI of a cell is ignored as long as its VPI is not null. Thus, given the graph underlying the network, it is possible to distinguish between the *virtual paths*, VPs for short, that are based on VPIs and are constituted by a sequence of successive edges or physical links, and *virtual channels* or VCs, that correspond to VCIs and are obtained by concatenating a given subset of VPs.

The VP layouts determined by the VPIs and VCIs entries can be evaluated with respect to different cost measures. In particular, a fundamental parameter is the *hop count*, which is given by the number of VPs which comprise the path of a VC and determines the efficiency of the setup of the VC (see, e.g., [2, 14, 15]). Another cost measure widely considered in the literature is the *load* of a physical edge, which is given by the number of virtual paths that share the edge. This number determines the size of the VP routing tables (see, e.g., [4]). Finally, the *stretch factor* is the ratio between the length of the path that a VC takes in the physical graph and the shortest possible path between its endpoints. This parameter controls the efficiency of the utilization of the network. For further details and technical justifications of the model for ATM networks see for instance [1, 9].

Some empirical results on the ATM layout problem have been given in [1, 12] and some more theoretical analysis in [9, 3, 7, 8, 5].

In particular, in [9] the computational complexity of determining the existence of a VP layout for a given network within a given maximum hop count and a given maximum load has been investigated and the authors have shown that this problem is NP-complete when there is no limit on the stretch factor. In [9] also some polynomial construction algorithms have been given for trees for the stretch factor equal to one, i.e. when the physical routed paths are shortest. These results have been extended in [5], where an exact characterization of the tractable and intractable cases has been given for shortest path layouts.

Concerning layout constructions for specific topologies, optimal and nearly optimal results for chains and trees have been provided in [9, 3, 8], while to the best of our knowledge no optimal results are known for other topologies like grids and tori.

In this paper we consider two new cost measures associated to virtual path layouts: the *edge congestion*, which is given by the number of VPs terminating or starting from a given edge at a given node, and the *node congestion*, that is the number of VPs having as an endpoint a given node. These cost measures take into account in a balanced (in case of edge congestion) or global (for node congestion) way the communication overhead at every given node. In fact, they are indicative of the number of accesses in the VC tables, as such tables are read at the end of the VPs. Moreover, these parameters influence directly the dimension of VC tables, as any VP which increases the congestion of an edge or of a node causes a number of entries in the corresponding VC table equal to the number of VCs such a VP belongs to.

As in [9] and [5], we will focus on layouts that enable the routing between all nodes and a single root node (rather than between any pair of nodes), under the assumption of a stretch factor equal to one, that is all the physical routed paths are the shortest. In fact, this restricted case can be seen as a building block for more complex routing problems and nevertheless its simplicity it has not been fully understood yet.

After showing some general combinatorial results holding for any network, we give tight results on the time complexity of constructing optimal rooted virtual path layouts. In fact, for the edge congestion case, we exactly establish the border between tractability and intractability, by determining the lowest (constant) values of h and c that make the problem computationally hard. Moreover, we give efficient construction algorithms for all the tractable cases. Analogous results are obtained for the node congestion case. We then provide some optimal layouts for specific networks, such as chains, rings, grids and tori. Extensions to d-dimensional grids and tori with $d > 2$ are also discussed.

The paper is organized as follows: In Section 2 we define the preliminary notation and definitions. In Section 3 we give some basic results for the considered cost measures. In Section 4 we provide the above-mentioned time complexity results. In Section 5 we present the optimal layouts for specific topologies and finally, in Section 6, we give some concluding remarks and list some open problems.

2   Preliminaries

We model the network as an undirected graph $G = (V, E)$, where nodes in V represent switches and edges in E are the point-to-point physical communication links.

Definition 1. A *rooted virtual path layout* (or simply layout) Ψ is a collection of paths in G, termed *virtual paths* (VPs for short), and a node $r \in V$, termed the *root* of the layout.

Definition 2. The *hop count* $\mathcal{H}(v)$ of a node $v \in V$ in a layout Ψ is the minimum number of VPs whose concatenation forms a shortest path in G from v to r. If no such VPs exist, define $\mathcal{H}(v) \equiv \infty$.

Definition 3. The *maximal hop count* of a layout Ψ is $\mathcal{H}_{\max}(\Psi) \equiv \max_{v \in V}\{\mathcal{H}(v)\}$.

Given $v \in V$, let us denote as $I(v)$ the set of the edges in E incident to v.

Definition 4. Given $v \in V$ and $e \in I(v)$, the *edge congestion* $\mathcal{E}(e, v)$ of the edge e with respect to v in a layout Ψ is the number of VPs $\psi \in \Psi$ that include e and have v as an endpoint.

Definition 5. The *maximal edge congestion* $\mathcal{E}_{\max}(\Psi)$ of a layout Ψ is $\max_{v \in V, e \in I(v)} \mathcal{E}(e, v)$.

A layout Ψ with $\mathcal{H}_{\max}(\Psi) \leq h$ and $\mathcal{E}_{\max}(\Psi) \leq c$ is called a $\langle h, c \rangle$-*edge layout*.

At each node of the network, a more global congestion measure can be considered which takes into account the total cost required at the node.

Definition 6. Given $v \in V$, the *node congestion* $\mathcal{N}(v)$ of v in a layout Ψ is the number of VPs $\psi \in \Psi$ such that v is an endpoint of ψ.

Definition 7. The *maximal node congestion* $\mathcal{N}_{\max}(\Psi)$ of a layout Ψ is $\max_{v \in V} \mathcal{N}(v)$.

A layout Ψ with $\mathcal{H}_{\max}(\Psi) \leq h$ and $\mathcal{N}_{\max}(\Psi) \leq c$ is called a $\langle h, c \rangle$-*node layout*.

Clearly, the hop count and the edge (or node) congestion are conflicting parameters, as in general a low hop count requires an high congestion and a low congestion causes a high hop count. Thus, a very natural problem arises in which one parameter is traded for the other. Moreover, once fixed two bounds h and c respectively on the hop count and on the edge (or node) congestion, in a parametric family of graphs it makes sense to consider the problem of determining the highest order graph that admits a layout respecting such bounds.

Definition 8. Let $\mathcal{G}$ be a family of graphs $\mathcal{G}$. For any two positive integers h and c, $E_{\mathcal{G}}(h, c)$ (resp. $N_{\mathcal{G}}(h, c)$) is defined as the maximum integer N such there exist an N-node graph in $\mathcal{G}$ with a $\langle h, c \rangle$-edge layout (resp. a $\langle h, c \rangle$-node layout).

For the sake of brevity, when clear from the context, we will denote $E_{\mathcal{G}}(h, c)$ and $N_{\mathcal{G}}(h, c)$ respectively as $E(h, c)$ and $N(h, c)$.

Notice that all the definitions above assume a stretch factor equal to one, i.e. all the physical routed paths are the shortest.

3 Basic results

In this section we give some basic results related to the new cost measures considered in the paper.

First of all, let us establish upper bounds on the number of nodes in graphs admitting $\langle h, c \rangle$-edge layouts or $\langle h, c \rangle$-node layouts.

Given a graph G with a specified root node r, we say that a non root node u has parameter d if it has exactly d edges $\{u, v_1\}, \ldots, \{u, v_d\}$ such that for each i, $1 \leq i \leq d$, u is on a shortest path from r to v_i. Informally, in the edge congestion case, the parameter of a node expresses its ability to reach other nodes, as it is equal to the number of edges that can be used to construct new VPs in any shortest path layout. Let the parameter of a family of graphs $\mathcal{G}$ be the maximum parameter of a non root node of a graph in $\mathcal{G}$.

Lemma 9. *Let $\mathcal{G}$ a family of the graphs with parameter d and such that every root r has degree at most d_r. Then $E(h, c) \leq 1 + c d_r \frac{(cd)^h - 1}{cd - 1}$.*

Proof. The lemma can be proved by observing that from the root node r in one hop it is possible to reach at most $c \cdot d_r$ nodes; each node with hop count 1 can then reach in another hop at most cd other nodes (for a total of $cd_r(cd)$ nodes), and this holds for every node with hop count at least 1, since the physical routed paths have to be the shortest and thus each node can use at most d outgoing edges to reach other nodes. Hence,

$$E(h,c) \leq 1 + cd_r + cd_r(cd) + cd_r(cd)^2 + \ldots + cd_r(cd)^{h-1} =$$

$$1 + cd_r \sum_{i=0}^{h-1}(cd)^i = 1 + cd_r \frac{(cd)^h - 1}{cd - 1}.$$

$\square$

Lemma 10. *For any family of graphs $\mathcal{G}$, $N(h,c) \leq \frac{c(c-1)^h - 2}{c-2}$.*

Proof. Starting from the root node r, in one hop it is possible to reach at most c nodes; each node with hop count 1 can then reach in another hop at most $c - 1$ other nodes, and this holds for every node with hop count at least 1, since the VP through which a node is reached contributes 1 to its node congestion. Thus,

$$N(h,c) \leq 1 + c + c(c-1) + c(c-1)^2 + \ldots + c(c-1)^{h-1} =$$

$$1 + c \sum_{i=0}^{h-1}(c-1)^i = 1 + c\frac{(c-1)^h - 1}{c-2} = \frac{c(c-1)^h - 2}{c-2}.$$

$\square$

We finally point out that in this context it does not make sense to consider layouts with unbounded physical routed lengths. In fact, optimal layout constructions for the node congestion case can be determined as follows. Consider any ordering of the nodes, except the root. Then, the root reaches through a VP in one hop the first c nodes, and iteratively in the order each reached node is assigned a VP to all the next $(c-1)$ unreached nodes, thus attaining the upper bound of Lemma 10, which holds also under the assumption of an unbounded stretch factor. In the edge congestion case the construction is slightly more complicated, since nodes have to be ordered non increasingly with respect to their degrees. Notice that, since to the purpose of minimizing the edge congestion VPs have not necessarily to correspond to simple physical paths, at every node the incident VPs can be equally distributed among its incident edges. Thus an optimal layout can be easily determined.

Optimal layouts can be easily found even in the gossip case in which, by respecting the bounds on the edge or node congestion, each node wants to reach every other node in at most a given number of hops. Here the construction becomes a pure combinatorial graph design problem. In fact, if the node congestion is bounded by c, there is a layout for a graph G within a given hop count h if and only if there exists a c-bounded degree graph with diameter h and at least the same number of nodes of G. Any embedding of such a graph on G gives the desired layout. A similar argument holds for the edge congestion, but here there is a layout respecting h and c if there exists a graph with the same number of nodes, diameter h and such that, if we denote as d_i the degree of node i in the initial graph G, the i-th node of the graph has degree at most $c \cdot d_i$.

4   Time complexity results

In this section we prove tight time complexity results for the problem of the construction of optimal layouts, by giving an exact characterization of all the tractable and intractable case. Some of the proofs are omitted in this extended abstract and will appear in the full version of the paper.

According to the previous sections, the following decision problem naturally arises.

Definition 11. $\langle h, c \rangle$-**edge layout Problem:**

INSTANCE: A network $G = (V, E)$ and a given root $r \in V$.
QUESTION: Is there a $\langle h, c \rangle$-edge layout for G with root r?

By using proof techniques like those in [5], surprisingly a very similar result holds for the edge congestion case.

Theorem 12. *The $\langle h, c \rangle$-edge layout problem is NP-complete for any h and c, except for the cases $h = 1$, any c and $h = 2, c = 1$.*

Suitable flow constructions prove the following theorem.

Theorem 13. *The $\langle h, c \rangle$-edge layout problem is polynomially solvable if $h = 1$ (any c) or $h = 2, c = 1$.*

Different results instead hold for the node congestion case. In fact, once fixed h and c, the problem of determining the existence of an $\langle h, c \rangle$-node layout for any graph G has a polynomial-time complexity, since from Lemma 10 we know that the number of nodes in G is $N(h, c) \leq \frac{c(c-1)^h - 2}{c-2}$, i.e. it is always bounded by a constant. Hence, it makes sense to consider different decision problems in which h or c are not constant, that is are part of the input of the instance.

Definition 14. $\langle h, \square \rangle$-**node layout Problem:**

INSTANCE: A network $G = (V, E)$, a given root $r \in V$ and a positive integer c.
QUESTION: Is there a $\langle h, c \rangle$-node layout for G with root r?

Definition 15. $\langle \Box, c \rangle$-**node layout Problem**:

INSTANCE: A network $G = (V, E)$, a given root $r \in V$ and a positive integer h.

QUESTION: Is there a $\langle h, c \rangle$-node layout for G with root r?

The following results can then be proved.

Theorem 16. *For $h \geq 2$ the $\langle h, \Box \rangle$-node layout problem is NP-complete.*

Proof. We first show that the $\langle 2, \Box \rangle$-node layout problem is NP-complete by providing a polynomial time transformation from the *Dominating Set* problem (DS) (known to be NP-complete; see [6]). In order to complete the proof, we then prove that if the $\langle h, \Box \rangle$-node layout problem is NP-complete, then also the $\langle h + 1, \Box \rangle$-node layout problem is NP-complete.

In the DS problem we have a universe set $U = \{u_1, \ldots, u_m\}$ of m elements, a family $\{A_1, \ldots, A_f\}$ of f subsets of U and an integer $k \leq f$; we want to decide if there exist k subsets $A_{j_1}, \ldots, A_{j_k}$ which cover U, i.e. such that $\bigcup_{i=1}^{k} A_{j_i} = U$.

Starting from an instance I_{DS} of DS, we construct a graph G that admits a $\langle 2, c \rangle$-node layout with $c = m$ if and only if I_{DS} admits a cover.

Let $G = (V, E)$, where $V = \{r\} \cup V_1 \cup V_2 \cup V_3 \cup V_4$ and $E = E_1 \cup E_2 \cup E_3 \cup E_4$, with:

$V_1 = \{v_a \mid a = 1, \ldots, m - k\}$,
$V_2 = \{q_b \mid b = 1, \ldots, m - (f - k) - 1\}$,
$V_3 = \{w_c \mid c = 1, \ldots, f\}$,
$V_4 = \{z_d \mid d = 1, \ldots, m\}$,
and
$E_1 = \{\{r, v_a\} \mid a = 1, \ldots, m - k\}$,
$E_2 = \{\{v_1, q_b\} \mid b = 1, \ldots, m - (f - k) - 1\}$,
$E_3 = \{\{v_1, w_c\} \mid c = 1, \ldots, f\}$,
$E_4 = \{\{w_c, z_d\} \mid u_d \in A_c\}$.

Informally, in the reduction graph each subset A_c corresponds to the subgraph induced by node w_c and all nodes z_d such that $u_d \in A_c$, which are all connected to w_c. The idea underlying our construction is that since at most k of the nodes w_c can be reached from r in one hop, if there are k dominating sets in I_{DS}, then all nodes of G can be reached from r in at most 2 hops.

Assume there are k dominating sets $A_{j_1}, \ldots, A_{j_k}$. We show that there exists a $\langle 2, c \rangle$-node layout for G. The VPs of Ψ are constituted by all edges in $E_1 \cup E_2 \cup E_3$, the edges $\{v_1, w_c\} \in E_3$ such that A_c is not one of the dominating sets, i.e. $c \neq j_i$, $i = 1, \ldots, k$, and finally the VPs $\langle r, v_1, w_{j_i} \rangle$ for $i = 1, \ldots, k$ (which correspond to the k dominating sets). By construction, $\mathcal{N}(v) \leq m = c$ for each node $v \in E$. In order to check that $\mathcal{H}_{\max}(\Psi) \leq 2$, it suffices to observe that all nodes $v_a \in V_1$ are reached in one hop, nodes $q_b \in V_2$ are reached in two hops, nodes $w_c \in V_3$ not corresponding to dominating sets are reached in two hops, nodes $w_{j_i} \in V_2$ corresponding to dominating sets are reached in one hop (through the VP $\langle r, v_1, w_{j_i} \rangle$), and as nodes $w_{j_1}, \ldots, w_{j_k}$ correspond to the k

dominating sets, all nodes $z_d \in V_4$ are reached in two hops, since every one of them is connected to at least one w_{j_i}.

It remains to show that if there are no k dominating sets, then no $\langle 2, c \rangle$-node layout Ψ for G exists. Consider any layout Ψ for G. Notice first that each of the edges $\{r, v_a\}$ must belong to Ψ, otherwise $\mathcal{H}(v_a) = \infty$. Similarly, since each node q_b must be reached through a shortest path, either the edge $\{v_1, q_b\}$ or the path $\langle r, v_1, q_b \rangle$ must be a VP of Ψ. Without loss of generality we can assume that the first case holds, as otherwise inserting $\{v_1, q_b\}$ in the set of the VPs of Ψ and replacing another VP starting from v_1 with a longer one directly from r, $\mathcal{H}(q_b) = 2$ and the hop count and node congestion of all the other nodes can only be decreased. Then, there are f nodes $w_c \in V_3$ to be reached along shortest paths and this can be done only through the remaining f VPs, of which k can start from the root and $f - k$ from v_1, yielding respectively hop count 1 and 2. Hence, no node in V_4 can be reached in two hops without exploiting a VP starting from a node $w_c \in V_3$. Let $w_{j_1}, \ldots, w_{j_k}$ be the k nodes in V_3 such that $\mathcal{H}(w_{j_i}) = 1$, $i = 1, \ldots, k$. Since there are no k dominating sets, then at least one node z_c is not connected to any of the nodes $w_{j_1}, \ldots, w_{j_k}$, and therefore $\mathcal{H}(z_c) \geq 3$.

In order to complete the proof, we now show that if the $\langle h, \square \rangle$-node layout problem is NP-complete, then also the $\langle h + 1, \square \rangle$-node layout problem is NP-complete.

This can be accomplished simply by observing that given the graph $G = (V, E)$ and the node congestion c corresponding to the instance of the $\langle h, \square \rangle$-node layout problem, the graph G' obtained by adding a new root node r' and connecting it to the old root r of G and to $c - 1$ additional new nodes has a $\langle h + 1, c \rangle$-node layout if and only if G has a $\langle h, c \rangle$-node layout. In fact, each of the new inserted edges in G' has to be a VP, so $\mathcal{H}(r) = 1$, and all the remaining VPs can only start from the old root r. $\qquad\square$

A graph $G = (V, E)$ admits a $\langle 1, c \rangle$-node layout if and only if $c \geq |V| - 1$, as from the root it is possible to reach with a VP at most c nodes and c nodes can always be reached along shortest paths by means of c VPs leaving the root. Thus the following theorem is trivially proved.

Theorem 17. *The $\langle 1, \square \rangle$-node layout problem is solvable in polynomial time.*

Let us now turn our attention to the second decision problem associated to the node congestion case, where c is a fixed constant and the hop count h belongs to the input of the instance.

Theorem 18. *For $c \geq 3$ the $\langle \square, c \rangle$-node layout problem is NP-complete.*

Theorem 19. *For $c \leq 2$ the $\langle \square, c \rangle$-node layout problem is solvable in polynomial time.*

All the polynomial time algorithms for the above tractable cases are constructive, that is they either find the proper layout (if it exists) or they return a negative answer.

A final interesting remark concerns the $\langle h, c \rangle$-edge layout problem. In fact, the same argument which leaded to the introduction of two different problems in the node congestion case, i.e. the constant upper bound on the total number of nodes in the graph, proves the following theorem.

Theorem 20. *Given any positive integer δ, the restriction of the $\langle h, c \rangle$-edge layout problem to the class of the graphs with maximum node degree δ is solvable in polynomial time.*

5   Results for specific topologies

In this section we give optimum layouts for specific topologies.

Let us consider first a chain or path of nodes with node set $V = \{1, \ldots N\}$ and edge set $E = \{\{i, i+1\} | 1 \leq i < N\}$. In order to give worst case estimations on the longest chain admitting a $\langle h, c \rangle$-edge or $\langle h, c \rangle$-node layout, we assume $r = 1$ as the root node.

Theorem 21. *Let $\mathcal{P}$ be the family of chain (or path) graphs. Then $E(h, c) = \frac{c^{h+1}-1}{c-1}$ and $N(h, c) = \frac{c(c-1)^h - 2}{c-2}$*

Proof. By Lemma 9 $E(h, c) \leq 1 + c\frac{c^h-1}{c-1} = \frac{c^{h+1}-1}{c-1}$ and by Lemma 10 $N(h, c) \leq \frac{c(c-1)^h - 2}{c-2}$.

The lower bound on $E(h, c)$ (resp. $N(h, c)$) follows by observing that from the root of any chain it is possible to reach the next c nodes in one hop, and from each node with hop count at least one again the first next unreached c nodes (resp. $c - 1$ nodes), thus yielding $E(h, c) \geq 1 + c + c^2 + \ldots + c^h = \frac{c^{h+1}-1}{c-1}$ and $N(h, c) \geq 1 + c + c(c-1) + \ldots + c(c-1)^{h-1} = \frac{c(c-1)^h - 2}{c-2}$. $\qquad\square$

A ring graph consists of a node set $V = \{0, \ldots, N-1\}$ and an edge set $E = \{\{i, (i+1)_{mod\,N}\} | 1 \leq i < N\}$. As a ring is node-symmetric, without loss of generality it is possible to choose any node as the root. By arguments similar those ones for chain graphs it is possible to prove the following theorem.

Theorem 22. *Let $\mathcal{R}$ be the family of ring graphs, then $E(h, c) = 2\frac{c^{h+1}-1}{c-1} - 1$ and $N(h, c) = \frac{c(c-1)^h - 2}{c-2}$ if c is even, otherwise $N(h, c) = 1 + \frac{(c-1)^{h+1}-1}{c-2}$.*

We now turn our attention to the 2-dimensional extensions of chains and rings, that is to grids and tori.

Given a square grid $G_{n \times n}$ of $N = n^2$ nodes, with node set $V = \{(i, j) | 1 \leq i \leq n, 1 \leq j \leq n\}$ and edge set $E = \{\{(i, j), (i+1, j)\} | 1 \leq i < n, 1 \leq j \leq n\} \cup \{\{(i, j), (i, j+1)\} | 1 \leq i \leq n, 1 \leq j < n\}$, again in order to give worst case estimations on the largest grid admitting a $\langle h, c \rangle$-edge or $\langle h, c \rangle$-node layout, we assume $r = (1, 1)$ as the root node.

For the case of edge congestion $c = 1$, as stated by the following theorem the dimension of the largest grid admitting a $\langle h, c \rangle$-edge layout is dominated by the maximum number of nodes reachable in h hops along the first row or column.

Theorem 23. *Let* $\mathcal{P}^2$ *be the family of square grid graphs, then* $E(h,1) = h^2$ *if* $h \leq 3$, *otherwise* $E(h,1) = (h+1)^2$.

Sketch of proof. By Lemma 9, taking $d_r = 2$ and $d = 2$, the maximum number of nodes reachable in h hops is $N \leq \frac{(2c)^{h+1}-1}{2c-1} = 2^{h+1} - 1$, which gives $E(h,1) \leq h^2$ for $h \leq 3$. Moreover, the maximum number of nodes along the first row or column reachable from the root in h hops is $h + 1$ (the root included), thus yielding $E(h,1) \leq (h+1)^2$ for $h > 3$. The layout attaining such bounds will be shown in the full paper. $\qquad\Box$

Theorem 24. *Let* $\mathcal{P}^2$ *be the family of square grid graphs. Then, for* $c \geq 4$, $E(h,c) = \lfloor\sqrt{N_{h,c}}\rfloor^2$, *where* $N_{h,c} = \frac{(2c)^{h+1}-1}{2c-1}$.

Proof. Again by Lemma 9 with $d_r = 2$ and $d = 2$, the maximum number of nodes reachable in h hops is $N_{h,c} \leq \frac{(2c)^{h+1}-1}{2c-1}$. Since every grid has a quadratic number of nodes, that is n^2 for a given integer $n \geq 1$, the upper bound on $E(h,c)$ derives directly by observing that $n = \lfloor\sqrt{N_{h,c}}\rfloor$ is the maximum integer such that $n^2 \leq N_{h,c}$.

In order to provide an optimal layout, given a square grid G with at least $N_{h,c}$ nodes, we define a gridoid G_h as the subgrid of G induced by nodes (i,j) with $i \leq \lfloor\sqrt{N_{h,c}}\rfloor$ and $j \leq \lfloor\sqrt{N_{h,c}}\rfloor$, i.e. the $\lfloor\sqrt{N_{h,c}}\rfloor \times \lfloor\sqrt{N_{h,c}}\rfloor$ subgrid induced by the first $\lfloor\sqrt{N_{h,c}}\rfloor$ rows and columns, plus the $N_{h,c} - \lfloor\sqrt{N_{h,c}}\rfloor^2$ nodes starting from node $(\lceil\sqrt{N_{h,c}}\rceil, 1)$, going toward node $(\lceil\sqrt{N_{h,c}}\rceil, \lceil\sqrt{N_{h,c}}\rceil)$ along row $\lceil\sqrt{N_{h,c}}\rceil$ and then eventually, if $N_{h,c} - \lfloor\sqrt{N_{h,c}}\rfloor^2 > \lceil\sqrt{N_{h,c}}\rceil$, up along column $\lceil\sqrt{N_{h,c}}\rceil$ taking nodes $(\lceil\sqrt{N_{h,c}}\rceil - 1, \lceil\sqrt{N_{h,c}}\rceil), (\lceil\sqrt{N_{h,c}}\rceil - 2, \lceil\sqrt{N_{h,c}}\rceil)$, and so on.

Let the order of G_h be $n_h = \lfloor\sqrt{N_{h,c}}\rfloor$, that is the number of rows or columns of the largest subgrid contained in G_h. We now show an incremental construction for layouts with edge congestion at most c such that, for any positive integer h, the subgraph induced by all the nodes with hop count at most h is G_h (see Figure 1). The theorem then follows by considering the restriction of the layout on the $n_h \times n_h$ subgrid of G_h containing $n_h^2 = E(h,c)$ nodes.

Clearly G_0 contains only the root $(1,1)$ and a $\langle 1, c\rangle$-edge layout for G_1 can be easily constructed by putting a suitable VP from the root to each node in G_1. Let us now show when $h \geq 1$ how to construct from a $\langle h, c\rangle$-edge layout for G_h a $\langle h+1, c\rangle$-edge layout for G_{h+1}. Notice that, for any node (i,j), all the nodes (i',j') with $i' \leq i$ and $j' \leq j$ belong to a shortest path from (i,j) to the root $(1,1)$. Then, we first have a set of *expanding* VPs that, for each row i (resp. column i) with $1 \leq i \leq n_h$, are between the nodes in row i (resp. column i) with hop count h (that is belonging to G_h but not to G_{h-1}) and the nodes in row i (resp. column i) belonging to $G_{h+1} - G_h$, so that each of them is reached in $h+1$ hops. All the remaining available VPs from the nodes in $G_h - G_{h-1}$ are used to reach the remaining not considered nodes (i,j) of $G_{h+1} - G_h$ with $i > n_h$ and $j > n_h$, i.e. in the right-down corner.

For any given row i (resp. column i) with $1 \leq i \leq n_h$, let d_h be the number of nodes in row i (resp. column i) belonging to $G_{h+1} - G_h$. Since each edge can

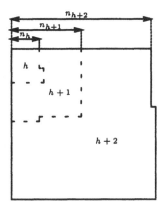

Fig. 1. The incremental layout for grids

have congestion at most c, in order to guarantee the correctness of the above incremental construction we have to prove that the $c \cdot d_h \geq d_{h+1}$.

By construction,

$$d_h \leq n_{h+1} - n_h + 1 = \lfloor \sqrt{N_{h+1,c}} \rfloor - \lfloor \sqrt{N_{h,c}} \rfloor + 1 \leq$$

$$\sqrt{\frac{(2c)^{h+2} - 1}{2c - 1}} - \sqrt{\frac{(2c)^{h+1} - 1}{2c - 1}} + 2 =$$

$$\sqrt{\frac{(2c)^{h+1}}{2c - 1}} \left(\sqrt{2c - \frac{1}{(2c)^{h+1}}} - \sqrt{1 - \frac{1}{(2c)^{h+1}}} \right) + 2 <$$

$$\sqrt{\frac{(2c)^{h+1}}{2c - 1}} \left(\sqrt{2c - \frac{1}{2c}} - \sqrt{1 - \frac{1}{2c}} \right) + 2 =$$

$$\sqrt{\frac{(2c)^{h+1}}{2c - 1}} \left(\sqrt{\frac{(2c - 1)(2c + 1)}{2c}} - \sqrt{\frac{2c - 1}{2c}} \right) + 2 =$$

$$\sqrt{(2c)^{h+1}} \left(\frac{\sqrt{2c + 1} - 1}{\sqrt{2c}} \right) + 2.$$

Similarly,

$$d_h \geq n_{h+1} - n_h - 1 = \lfloor \sqrt{N_{h+1,c}} \rfloor - \lfloor \sqrt{N_{h,c}} \rfloor - 1 \geq$$

$$\sqrt{\frac{(2c)^{h+2} - 1}{2c - 1}} - \sqrt{\frac{(2c)^{h+1} - 1}{2c - 1}} - 2 > \sqrt{(2c)^{h+1}} \left(\frac{\sqrt{2c} - 1}{\sqrt{2c - 1}} \right) - 2.$$

It is possible to verify that if $4 \le c \le 11$ and $h \ge 2$ and if $c \ge 12$, any h it is

$$cd_h > c\sqrt{(2c)^{h+1}}\left(\frac{\sqrt{2c}-1}{\sqrt{2c}-1}\right) - 2c \ge \sqrt{(2c)^{h+2}}\left(\frac{\sqrt{2c+1}-1}{\sqrt{2c}}\right) + 2 > d_{h+1}.$$

A case analysis shows that the construction works also for $4 \le c \le 11$ and $0 \le h < 2$. This completes the proof of the theorem. □

Consider now a square torus $T_{n \times n}$ of $N = n^2$ nodes. Similarly to grids, for edge congestion $c = 1$ we have the following theorem.

Theorem 25. Let $\mathcal{R}^2$ be the family of square torus graphs, then $E(h, 1) = (2h - 1)^2$ if $h \le 3$, otherwise $E(h, 1) = (2h + 1)^2$.

Theorem 26. Let $\mathcal{R}^2$ be the family of square torus graphs. Then, for $c \ge 4$, $E(h, c) = \lfloor \sqrt{N_{h,c}} \rfloor^2$, where $N_{h,c} = 4\left(\frac{(2c)^{h+1}-1}{2c-1} - \frac{c^{h+1}-2c^2+4c}{c-1}\right)$.

Sketch of proof. Since tori are node-symmetric, we can consider any node as the root. Unfortunately, Lemma 9 does not to give an exact estimation of the number of nodes reachable in h hops for any given h, since all the nodes in the same row or column of the root have parameter 3, that is can exploit 3 edges to reach the other nodes, while all the remaining ones have parameter 2.

A finer argument allows the exact estimation of $N_{h,c}$ in the claim and then, after defining like for grids a similar notion of toroid, the proof is similar to that of Theorem 24. The complete proof of the theorem will appear in the full paper. □

Tighter results can be determined for the node congestion case.

Theorem 27. Let $\mathcal{P}^2$ be the family of square grid graphs, then $N(h, c) = \lfloor \sqrt{\frac{c(c-1)^h - 2}{c-2}} \rfloor^2$.

Theorem 28. Let $\mathcal{R}^2$ be the family of square torus graphs, then $N(h, c) = \lfloor \sqrt{\frac{c(c-1)^h - 2}{c-2}} \rfloor^2$.

In the above two theorems the upper bound on $N(h, c)$ derives directly from Lemma 10, while matching layouts are constructed as in the edge congestion case by exploiting the gridoid and toroid methods. The formal proofs of these theorems will appear in the complete paper.

Before concluding the section, we remark that the gridoid and toroid methods can be easily extended to the d-dimensional case with $d > 2$, thus yielding corresponding optimal edge or node layouts for d-dimensional grids an tori. Even if we don't put separate claims, for c is suitably large in d-dimensional grids this yields $E(h, c) = \lfloor \left(\frac{(dc)^{h+1}-1}{dc-1}\right)^{\frac{1}{d}} \rfloor^d$ and $N(h, c) = \lfloor \left(\frac{c(c-1)^h - 2}{c-2}\right)^{\frac{1}{d}} \rfloor^d$, while $N(h, c) = \lfloor \left(\frac{c(c-1)^h - 2}{c-2}\right)^{\frac{1}{d}} \rfloor^d$ also for d-dimensional tori.

6 Conclusion and open problems

In this paper we have considered two new cost measures related to the communication overhead and the space requirements associated to virtual path layouts in ATM networks, that is the edge congestion and the node congestion.

All the provided time complexity results are tight, and the same holds for the layout constructions for specific topologies, except for the cases of an edge congestion $c = 2$ and $c = 3$ in grids and tori. We are very close to the determination of these layouts, but they are not incremental, that is the subset of the nodes with hop count at most equal to a given integer h in general does not form a gridoid or a toroid. In fact, it is possible to see that in these cases the incremental solution does not work, as there are values of h such that from the gridoid or toroid of the nodes with hop count at most h it is not possible to build the successive one corresponding to a hop count at most equal to $h + 1$. Similar considerations hold for the d-dimensional cases with $d > 2$.

An interesting issue to be pursued is the determination optimal path layouts for other network topologies. Moreover, it would be interesting to extend all these results to all-to-all layouts, where communication must be guaranteed between any two pair of nodes.

Another open question concerns the relationship between the congestion measures defined in this paper and the load parameter, that is the number of VPs that share a physical edge. For instance, as it can be easily verified, a load l implies an edge congestion $c \leq l$, but apart from this case it seems that there is no strong relationship between the different parameters.

Finally, while we have remarked that in this context it does not make sense to consider an unbounded stretch factor, a case worth to investigate is when the stretch factor is bounded by a given real number greater than one.

References

1. S. Ahn, R.P. Tsang, S.R. Tong, and D.H.C. Du. Virtual path layout design on ATM networks. In *INFOCOM'94*, pages 192–200, 1994.
2. J. Burgin and D. Dorman. Broadband ISDN resource management: The role of virtual paths. *IEEE Communicatons Magazine*, 29, 1991.
3. I. Cidon, O. Gerstel, and S. Zaks. A scalable approach to routing in ATM networks. In G. Tel and P.M.B. Vitányi, editors, *8th International Workshop on Distributed Algorithms (LNCS 857)*, pages 209–222, Terschelling, The Netherlands, October 1994. Submitted for publication in IEEE/ACM Trans. on Networking.
4. R. Cohen and A. Segall. Connection management and rerouting in ATM networks. In *INFOCOM'94*, pages 184–191, 1994.
5. T. Eilam, M. Flammini, and S. Zaks. A complete characterization of the path layout construction problem for ATM networks with given hop count and load. To appear in the *Proc. of the 24th International Colloquium on Automata, Languages and Programming (ICALP)*, 1997.
6. M.R. Garey and D.S. Johnson. *Computers and Intractability: A Guide to the Theory of NP-Completeness*. W.H. Freeman and Co., 1979.

7. O. Gerstel, I. Cidon, and S. Zaks. The layout of virtual paths in ATM networks. *IEEE/ACM Transactions on Networking*, 4(6):873–884, 1996.

8. O. Gerstel, A. Wool, and S. Zaks. Optimal layouts on a chain ATM network. In *3rd Annual European Symposium on Algorithms (ESA), (LNCS 979)*, Corfu, Greece, September 1995, pages 508-522. To appear in *Discrete Applied Mathematics*.

9. O. Gerstel and S. Zaks. The virtual path layout problem in fast networks. In *13th ACM Symp. on Principles of Distributed Computing*, pages 235–243, Los Angeles, USA, August 1994.

10. R. Händler and M.N. Huber. *Integrated Broadband Networks: an introduction to ATM-based networks*. Addison-Wesley, 1991.

11. ITU recommendation. I series (B-ISDN), Blue Book, November 1990.

12. F.Y.S. Lin and K.T. Cheng. Virtual path assignment and virtual circuit routing in ATM networks. In *GLOBCOM'93*, pages 436–441, 1993.

13. C. Partridge. *Gigabit Networking*. Addison Wesley, 1994.

14. K.I. Sato, S. Ohta, and I. Tokizawa. Broad-band ATM network architecture based on virtual paths. *IEEE Transactions on Communications*, 38(8):1212–1222, August 1990.

15. Y. Sato and K.I. Sato. Virtual path and link capacity design for ATM networks. *IEEE Journal of Selected Areas in Communications*, 9, 1991.

Scheduling in Synchronous Networks and the Greedy Algorithm

(Extended Abstract)

King-Shan Lui [1]   &   Shmuel Zaks [2]

Abstract. We study the greedy algorithm for delivering messages with
deadlines in synchronous networks. The processors have to determine a
feasible schedule, by which all messages will arrive at their destinations
and meet their deadlines. At each step a processor cannot send on any
of its outgoing links more messages than the capacity of that link. We
study bottleneck-free networks, in which the capacity of each edge outgoing any processor is at least the sum of the capacities of the edges
incoming it. For such networks, and in which there is at most one simple path connecting any pair of vertices, we determine a necessary and
sufficient condition for the initial configuration to have a feasible schedule, and prove that if this condition holds then the greedy algorithm,
that chooses at each step the most urgent messages (those with closest
deadlines), determines such a feasible schedule. We start with directed
chain networks with unit capacities, and modify the results to general
chains, directed rings, trees, and then for the general above-mentioned
class of networks. For bottleneck-free networks, in which the messages
between two processors have to follow only one of the paths connecting
them, the problem of deciding whether there exists a valid schedule is
NP-complete. For networks with a bottleneck and for half-duplex networks we show that no algorithm, that makes decisions based only on
local information, can solve the problem.

1 Introduction

This paper studies the scheduling issue on synchronous networks and the greedy
algorithm. Assume a synchronous network in which processors are holding messages, each with its own destination and deadline. At each step each processor
has to decide which of the messages it currently holds it will send, and on which
of its outgoing links. The processors have to determine a feasible schedule, by
which all messages will arrive at their destinations and meet their deadlines, and
such that at each step no processor will send on any outgoing link more messages
than the capacity of that link. A processor does not have any information about

---

[1] Department of Computer Science, University of California at Santa Barbara, CA,
U.S.A., email: `shan@cs.ucsb.edu`.
[2] Department of Computer Science, Technion, Haifa, Israel, email:
`zaks@cs.technion.ac.il`.

the messages that will pass it throughout the execution of the algorithm, and at each time unit it has to decide which messages to send by considering only the information in the messages it currently holds (namely, their destinations and deadlines).

This scheduling problem arises in several applications. Our problem originated from studies in ATM networks, but it is applicable for any synchronous network in which there are strict deadlines for messages to meet. Another application is in a factory production line, where certain products have to travel through several machines, and have to arrive at each machine by a known deadline. Each machine has a sending capacity, which is the number of products it can send in one time unit. Each product has to be scheduled so as to travel through the machines from its origin to its destination, through some predetermined route. The schedule has to be such that at each time unit no machine will send more products than its sending capacity. This production line can be viewed in a way similar to the message delivery problem, such that each machine knows only the products it currently holds, their destinations and deadlines, and it has to decide which products to send at each time unit so as to meet all deadlines; it can also be interpreted as managed by a central control (similar to other "classical" scheduling problems).

Though in general asynchronous networks, where messages can suffer finite but arbitrary delay (like the commonly-used message-passing model described in [4]) no such deadlines exist, in most networks deadlines do exist, usually employing certain timeout mechanisms. Our study of the problem was motivated by a similar scenario, of having a datagram service over ATM (see, e.g., [6]). In studies of networks, usually either link capacities are ignored, or synchrony is not assumed; ATM networks suggest a model in which both assumptions hold. Message delivery problems in networks, in various layers of communication, are often involving queuing theory problems (see [2]). Other scheduling problems in computer networks usually involve scheduling tasks on various machines or a variety of load balancing problems (for a comprehensive discussion, see, e.g., ([1, 3]). In all of these applications, the algorithms are sequential (even if eventually they are performed in parallel on various machines), or are done asynchronously (like some of the load balancing problems).

We study bottleneck-free networks, in which for each processor the capacity of each outgoing edge is at least the sum of the capacities of all of its incoming edges. For bottleneck-free networks with at most one simple path connecting any pair of vertices (termed uni-path networks), we determine a necessary and sufficient condition for the initial configuration to have a feasible schedule, and prove that if this condition holds then the greedy algorithm, that chooses at each step the most urgent messages (those with closest deadlines), determines such a feasible schedule. The proof of this last result follows from the conditions, developed, and not by transposing a feasible schedule to the greedy one (as done in [7]) in a step-by-step manner, as in usual proofs of correctness of greedy algorithms in many scheduling algorithms. We start with directed chain networks with unit capacities, and extend the results to general chains, directed rings, trees, and then to general bottleneck-free uni-path networks. We then focus on factors that make the problem difficult, which give rise to negative results. We show that (a) in networks with a bottleneck and in half-duplex networks no algorithm exists, that makes decisions based only on local information, and that (b) in networks which are not uni-path, and such that messages between two processors must follow only one predetermined path (as is the case in certain situations, like in certain ATM routing problems), the resulting decision problem is NP-complete.

The definitions and basic properties - in particular, the notion of virtual slacks - are presented in Section 2. In Section 3 we discuss chain networks with unit capacities, and present our basic results and proof techniques. The extension of the results to uni-path bottleneck-free networks is discussed in Section 4. The impossibility results for networks with bottlenecks and for half-duplex networks and the NP-complete result are presented in Section 5. Some of the proofs are only sketched in this Extended Abstract.

2 Preliminaries

2.1 Definitions

We first develop our technique for a chain network. For this case we consider a synchronous network, whose topology is a directed chain $\mathcal{N} = G(V, E)$, with $V = \{1, ..., N\}$ and $E = \{(i, i + 1) \mid i = 1, ... , N - 1\}$. Here, in this topology, we number the edge, or link, $(i, i + 1)$ as i. That is, the link between processor i and $i + 1$ is link i. There are messages at some processors, which have to be transmitted (to higher numbered ones) within given deadlines. A message sent by processor i at time t arrives at processor $i + 1$ before time $t + 1$. Each link has a capacity, and the number of messages that can be sent by each processor at any time unit is bounded by the capacity of its outgoing link. In this section all capacities are 1. We study scheduling algorithms that will determine, at each step, which messages have to be forwarded, and their goal will be to get all messages to their destinations on time.

Formally, we have a set of messages $\mathcal{M} = \{m_1, ..., m_k\}$, with $m_i = (p_i, d_i, s_i)$, where p_i is the position, d_i is the destination and s_i is the slack of the message. *Slack* is the delay that the message can still suffer so as to arrive at its destination within its deadline; namely, if m_i has to arrive by time t at d_i, its slack is $t - (d_i - p_i)$. Of special importance is the case where the slack is 0, which means that the message should be sent without any further delay.

At each time unit, processor i can send at most one message to processor $i + 1$, according to a *schedule* S. Formally, $S = \{S_t \mid t=0,1,2,...\}$, where $S_t \subset \{(i, j) \mid 1 \leq i < N \text{ and } 1 \leq j \leq k\}$. $(i, j) \in S_t$ means that processor i transmits message m_j at time t. Every schedule must terminate since in each step, some messages must advance one step. All the messages will either be delivered within their deadlines (in which case the algorithm terminates successfully), or otherwise at a certain step the algorithm will terminate unsuccessfully.

In the *greedy* algorithm for the transmission of the messages in such a network, at each time, each processor sends one of the most urgent message (a message is *most urgent* if its slack is smallest among all messages in the processor.

A *configuration* C_t is the arrangement of the set of messages $\mathcal{M}$ at time t. Formally, let $m_i(t) = (p_i^t, d_i, s_i^t)$, where p_i^t is the current position, d_i is the destination and s_i^t is the slack of the message at time t. Clearly, $p_i^0 = p_i$, $s_i^0 = s_i$ and thus $m_i(0) = m_i$. Then $C_t = \{m_i(t) \mid m_i \in \mathcal{M} \text{ and } p_i^t < d_i\}$. C_0 is the *initial* configuration. The message m_i t is undefined for t greater than the time when message m_i arrives. That is, p_i^t and s_i^t are undefined.

Given a schedule S and an initial configuration C_0, C_1 is obtained by sending messages in C_0 according to S_0. In general, the configuration C_t is obtained by sending messages in C_{t-1} according to S_{t-1}. Therefore, messages $m_i(t) = (p_i^t, d_i, s_i^t)$ are obtained by a certain schedule. A schedule for a given configuration is *admissible* if all messages meet their deadlines. A configuration is *admissible* if there exists an admissible schedule for it. It follows from definitions that if a configuration is admissible, then $s_i^0 \geq 0$ for every $i = 1, 2, ..., k$, and that if a schedule is admissible, then $s_i^t \geq 0$ for every i and t. Given a configuration and a schedule, we say that there is a *conflict* at time t in processor n if there is more than one message m_i for which $p_i^t = n$ and $s_i^t = 0$. Clearly, A schedule is admissible if and only if it has no conflicts.

Example 1. Suppose at time 0, in a directed chain $G(V, E)$ where $V = \{1,...,8\}$, we have a configuration $C_0 = \{m_1,...,m_7\}$ where $m_1 = (1,4,2)$, $m_2 = (3,5,4)$, $m_3 = (4,7,0)$, $m_4 = (5,6,1)$, $m_5 = (5,7,1)$, $m_6 = (6,7,0)$, $m_7 = (6,7,3)$. $m_1 = (1,4,2)$ means that the message m_1 is currently in processor 1 having destination 4 and slack 2; so, m_1 has to arrive before time 5. The configuration is depicted in Figure 1.a.

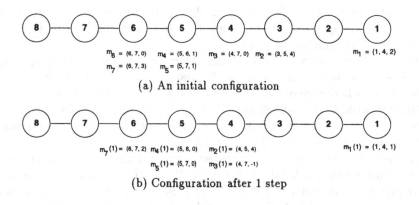

(a) An initial configuration

(b) Configuration after 1 step

Fig. 1. Chain network configurations for Example 1

Let $S_0 = \{(3,2), (6,6)\}$; thus processor 3 sends message 2 and processor 6 sends message 6 at time 0. As message 6 arrives at its destination, $C_1 = \{m_1$

(1), ..., m_5 (1), m_7 (1)} where m_1 (1) = (1,4,1), m_2 (1) = (4,5,4), m_3 (1) = (4,7,-1), m_4 (1) = (5,6,0), m_5 (1) = (5,7,0), m_7 (1) = (6,7,2). See Figure 1.b.

Note that the slacks of the messages sent are unchanged while all others are decreased by 1. The slack of m_3 becomes -1 which means that the message cannot be sent within its deadline.

□

2.2 Virtual Slack

Given a configuration and a schedule, we now extend the definition of a slack. The *virtual slack* $v_i^{t,n}$ of message m_i at time t is defined for processors n, $p_i^t \leq n < d_i$, by

$$v_i^{t,n} = s_i^t + (n - p_i^t). \tag{1}$$

(Intuitively, $v_i^{t,n}$ is defined to be the sum of s_i^t and the number of links that m_i should pass through when going from p_i^t to n.)

Note: While the slack s_i^t is defined only for the processor that is holding m_i at time t, the virtual slack of m_i is defined for all processors that the message should pass through. For processor n that is holding m_i at time t ($n = p_i^t$) the two definitions coincide; namely, $v_i^{t,n} = s_i^t$. Clearly, if a schedule is admissible, $v_i^{t,n} \geq 0$ for every i, t and n. It follows from the definitions that:

Lemma 1. *If a schedule is admissible, $v_i^{t,n} = 0$ if and only if message m_i is in processor n at time t with slack equals 0, for every i, t and n.*

Given a schedule, let $\mathcal{X}_j^{t,n} = \{m_i \mid v_i^{t,n} = j\}$ and $X_j^{t,n} = |\mathcal{X}_j^{t,n}|$. That is, $X_j^{t,n}$ is the number of messages with virtual slack j at time t for node n.

Example 2. In Example 1, the virtual slacks corresponding to processors 3 and 6 are $v_1^{0,3} = 4$, $v_2^{0,3} = 4$, $v_3^{0,6} = 2$, $v_5^{0,6} = 2$, $v_6^{0,6} = 0$, $v_7^{0,6} = 3$ (all the other virtual slacks for these processors are undefined).

Thus $X_4^{0,3} = 2$ and $X_j^{0,3} = 0$ for every $j \neq 4$, $X_0^{0,6} = 1$, $X_1^{0,6} = 0$, $X_2^{0,6} = 2$, $X_3^{0,6} = 1$ and $X_j^{0,6} = 0$ for every $j > 3$.

□

The virtual slacks play a major role in the discussion. The slack s_i^t measures the number of time units that the delivery of the message m_i can be delayed at time t. $(n - p_i^t)$ measures the number of steps the message needs to travel to processor n without decrementing the slack. Therefore, virtual slack $v_i^{t,n}$ measures the time limit before a message m_i must be sent by processor n.

Theorem 2. *Given an initial configuration and an admissible schedule, if message m_i has virtual slack $v_i^{t,n} \geq 0$ for processor n at time t, then it will be sent by processor n within the next $v_i^{t,n} + 1$ steps, for every i, t and n.*

Proof: Let $p = p_i^t$ and $n = p_i^t + k$ where $0 \leq k < d_i - p_i^t$. We prove the theorem by induction on k (for every i and t).

When $k = 0$, m_i is in $n = p$ at time t with virtual slack $v_i^{t,n} = s_i^t$. By the definition of a slack, the message will be sent by n within the next $v_i^{t,n} + 1$ steps.

Assume the theorem holds for $n = p + k$. We prove it for $n = p + k + 1$. By the inductive hypothesis, processor $n - 1$ will send m_i within the next $v_i^{t,n-1} + 1$ steps. $v_i^{t,n}$ is undefined if $d_i = n$. For $d_i > n$, processor n will send the message within the next $v_i^{t,n-1} + 2$ steps. But $v_i^{t,n-1} + 2 = s_i^t + (n - 1 - p_i^t) + 2 = s_i^t + (n - p_i^t) + 1 = v_i^{t,n} + 1$, as desired.

□

Example 3. Refer to Examples 1 and 2, we have $v_6^{0,6} = 0$ and $v_5^{0,6} = 2$. According to Theorem 2, in every admissible schedule, m_6 must be sent by processor 6 at time 0, and message m_5 must be sent by processor 6 at time 0,1 or 2. Note that if m_5 is sent by processor 5 at time 0, $m_5 (1) = (6,7,1)$; otherwise, $m_5 (1) = (5,7,0)$. If $m_5 (1) = (5,7,0)$, it must be sent by processor 5 at time 1 and so $m_5 (2) = (6,7,0)$. If $m_5 (1) = (6,7,1)$ and m_5 is not sent by processor 6 at time 1, $m_5 (2) = (6,7,0)$. In both cases m_5 must be sent by processor 6 at time 2. Thus, the message must be sent by processor 6 at time 0,1 or 2.

□

The next theorem shows that the virtual slacks corresponding to n are decreased by one after each step, as long as n does not send m_i (and are undefined after it sends m_i).

Theorem 3 (Virtual Slack Property). *Given an initial configuration and a schedule, if $p_i^t < n < d_i$ or $p_i^t = p_i^{t+1}$, $v_i^{t+1,n} = v_i^{t,n}$ - 1, for every n, t, and i.*

Sketch of Proof: If message m_i is in n and is sent at time t, then clearly $v_i^{t+1,n}$ is undefined. We thus have to consider the following three cases:

Case I: message m_i is in n but not sent; namely, $p_i^t = n$ and $p_i^{t+1} = n$.

$$v_i^{t+1,n} = s_i^{t+1} + (n - p_i^{t+1}) = s_i^t - 1 + (n - p_i^t) = v_i^{t,n} - 1.$$

In a similar way, we prove cases II and III below:

Case II: message m_i is not in n and not sent; namely, $p_i^t \neq n$ and $p_i^t = p_i^{t+1}$.

Case III: message m_i is not in n but is sent; namely, $p_i^t \neq n$ and $p_i^t = p_i^{t+1} - 1$.

□

Example 4. Refer to the configuration in Figure 1.a in Example 1, the defined virtual slacks corresponding to processor 6 are $v_3^{0,6} = 2$, $v_5^{0,6} = 2$, $v_6^{0,6} = 0$, $v_7^{0,7} = 3$. If at time 1, the configuration is as Figure 1.b. Since message 6 is sent by processor 6, the virtual slack $v_6^{1,6}$ becomes undefined. On the other hand, $v_3^{1,6} = 1$, $v_5^{1,6} = 1$ and $v_7^{1,7} = 2$ which follows what Theorem 3 suggests.

□

By Theorem 3, we have the following lemma.

Lemma 4. $X_{j+1}^{t,n} \geq X_j^{t+1,n}$ *for every* t, j *and* n, *with equality if and only if processor* n *does not send any message* m_i *with* $v_i^{t,n} = j+1$ *at time* t.

Sketch of Proof: By Theorem 3, each message m_i which is not sent with $v_i^{t,n} = j+1$ will have $v_i^{t+1,n} = j$. Therefore, $\mathcal{X}_{j+1}^{t,n} \supseteq \mathcal{X}_j^{t+1,n}$ and $X_{j+1}^{t,n} \geq X_j^{t+1,n}$. Since only the virtual slack for n of the message sent becomes undefined, the two sets are equal if and only if n does not send any message m_i with $v_i^{t,n} = j+1$ at time t.

$\square$

By Lemma 4, processor n sends $X_t^{l,n} - X_{t-1}^{l+1,n}$ messages m_i at time l with $v_i^{l,n} = t$. Similarly, processor n sends $X_{t-1}^{l+1,n} - X_{t-2}^{l+2,n}$ messages m_i at time $l+1$ with $v_i^{l,n} = t$. Combining the two, we know that processor n sends $X_t^{l,n} - X_{t-2}^{l+2,n}$ messages m_i with $v_i^{l,n} = t$ between time l and time $l+2$. By induction we prove the following lemma.

Lemma 5. *For every* t, n, k, *and* $0 < j \leq t$, *processor* n *sends exactly* $X_t^{k,n} - X_{t-j}^{k+j,n}$ *messages* m_i *with* $v_i^{k,n} = t$ *at times* $k, k+1, \ldots, k+j-1$.

3 Bottleneck-Free Chains with Unit Capacities

In this section we present our results for chains with unit capacities. We first present a necessary and sufficient condition for the admissibility of a schedule (Section 3.1). We then show (Section 3.2) a necessary and sufficient condition for the admissibility of a configuration, and show that if this condition holds, then the greedy algorithm determines a valid schedule.

3.1 A Necessary and Sufficient Condition for the Admissibility of a Schedule

Given a configuration and a schedule, we now develop a condition that will be equivalent to the validity of this schedule; namely, this condition will be necessary, and it also will guarantee that all messages meet their deadlines.

Recall that $X_0^{0,n}$ is the number of messages m_i with $v_i^{0,n} = 0$. It is obvious that this number of messages must be sent by processor n in an admissible schedule. At time 1, the virtual slack of the messages with $v_i^{0,n} = 1$ will become 0. Processor n has to send those messages at that time. $X_1^{0,n}$ measures that number of messages. This explains the intuition behind necessary condition, presented in the following theorem.

Theorem 6. *Given a configuration and an admissible schedule, processor* n *must send at least* $\sum_{j=0}^{t} X_j^{0,n}$ *messages before time* t, *for every* n *and* t.

Sketch of Proof: Let $X_j^{0,n} - X_0^{j,n} = x_j$. By Lemma 5, n sends x_j messages m_i, with $v_i^{0,n} = j$ before time j. Suppose each such message m_i is sent at time

t_i; hence $t_i < j$. Theorem 3 implies by induction that $v_i^{t_i,n} = v_i^{0,n} - t_i = j - t_i > 0$.

Let k_j be the number of messages with positive virtual slacks, $v_i^{0,n} > 0$, at time j in n sent at time j by n. Clearly, $k_j = 0$ or 1. Since $\sum_{j=0}^{t} x_j$ counts only the number of messages m_i with $0 \le v_i^{0,n} \le t$ and is sent with positive virtual slack for n, while $\sum_{j=0}^{t} k_j$ counts all the messages m_i sent with positive virtual slack for n, $\sum_{j=0}^{t} k_j \ge \sum_{j=0}^{t} x_j$.

At time t, there are $X_0^{t,n}$ messages with virtual slack 0 for processor n. By Lemma 1, these messages are in n with slacks 0 at time t, and, since the schedule is admissible, they must be sent at that time.

Therefore, by time t, n has already sent $\sum_{j=0}^{t} (X_0^{j,n} + k_j)$ messages. But,

$$\sum_{j=0}^{t}(X_0^{j,n} + k_j) = \sum_{j=0}^{t}X_0^{j,n} + \sum_{j=0}^{t}k_j \ge \sum_{j=0}^{t}X_0^{j,n} + \sum_{j=0}^{t}x_j =$$
$$\sum_{j=0}^{t}(X_0^{j,n} + x_j) = \sum_{j=0}^{t}X_j^{0,n},$$

which completes the proof.

$\square$

We now present the admissibility condition for a configuration, and prove its necessity. This condition will turn out to be also sufficient (see Theorem 10).

Theorem 7. *If a configuration is admissible, then*

$$\sum_{j=0}^{e}X_j^{0,n} \le e + 1 \quad \forall n, \forall e \ge 0 . \tag{2}$$

Proof: Assume to the contrary that there exists a node n and an $e \ge 0$ such that $\sum_{j=0}^{e}X_j^{0,n} > e+1$. Then, there are at least $e+2$ messages m_i with $v_i^{0,n} \le e$. By Theorem 6, n must send $e + 2$ messages by time e. In each time, only one message can be sent at node n. Therefore, by time e, n can send at most $e + 1$ messages, so the configuration is not admissible, a contradiction.

$\square$

For a given algorithm, we define a condition

$$\sum_{j=0}^{e}X_j^{t,n} \le e + 1 \quad \forall n, \forall t, \forall e \ge 0 . \tag{3}$$

We are now ready to present the admissibility condition for a schedule, as follows:

Theorem 8. *A schedule is admissible if and only if condition (3) is satisfied.*

Proof: If a schedule is admissible, the configuration after each step is admissible also. It is obvious from Theorem 7 that condition (3) is satisfied.

If condition (3) is satisfied, at each time there is at most one message with slack 0 in each processor. The schedule thus has no conflicts, and it is feasible.

$\square$

3.2 Admissibility of a Configuration and the Greedy Algorithm

We now turn to present the admissibility condition for a configuration, and to show that the greedy algorithm determines a valid schedule for an admissible configuration. Recall that in the greedy algorithm each processor sends at each time unit the most urgent message, unless it holds no message at that time . Our first main result follows:

Theorem 9. *If condition (2) is satisfied, then the greedy algorithm determines an admissible schedule.*

Sketch of Proof: Following Theorem 8, it suffices to prove (3). We prove (3) by induction on t.

For $t = 0$, (3) reduces to (2), and is thus satisfied.

Assume (3) holds for t, we prove it for $t + 1$.

For node n, let the message sent at time t be m_i and let $v_i^{t,n} = v$.

If $v = 0$, by (3), $X_0^{t,n} = 1$. All other messages m_i with $v_i^{t,n} > 0$ are not sent. By Lemma 4, $X_j^{t+1,n} = X_{j+1}^{t,n}$ for every $j \geq 0$. Hence,

$$\textstyle\sum_{j=0}^{e} X_j^{t+1,n} = \sum_{j=0}^{e} X_{j+1}^{t,n} = \sum_{j=1}^{e+1} X_j^{t,n} = \sum_{j=0}^{e+1} X_j^{t,n} - X_0^{t,n}$$

(by induction hypothesis) $\leq e + 2 - 1 = e + 1$.

If $v > 0$, it follows from Lemma 4 that

$$X_j^{t+1,n} = \begin{cases} X_{j+1}^{t,n} & \text{if } j + 1 \neq v \\ X_{j+1}^{t,n} - 1 & \text{if } j + 1 = v \end{cases}$$

If $e \geq v - 1$: $\sum_{j=0}^{e} X_j^{t+1,n} = \sum_{j=0}^{v-2} X_j^{t+1,n} + X_{v-1}^{t+1,n} + \sum_{j=v}^{e} X_j^{t+1,n}$
$= \sum_{j=0}^{v-2} X_{j+1}^{t,n} + X_v^{t,n} - 1 + \sum_{j=v}^{e} X_{j+1}^{t,n} = \sum_{j=1}^{e+1} X_j^{t,n} - 1.$

If $e < v - 1$: Since the algorithm sends the most urgent message in node n, there is no message in node n at $t + 1$ with virtual slack less than $v - 1$ which is also in node n at time t. All such messages are in processor $n - 1$ and before. For the same message m_i , if $d_i > n$, according to the definition of virtual slack, $v_i^{t,n} = v_i^{t,n-1} + 1$. Thus, for every $j \leq e$, $\mathcal{X}_j^{t+1,n} \subseteq \mathcal{X}_j^{t,n-1}$ and $X_j^{t+1,n} \leq X_j^{t,n-1}$. It follows by the induction hypothesis that

$$\textstyle\sum_{j=0}^{e} X_j^{t+1,n} \leq \sum_{j=0}^{e} X_j^{t,n-1} \leq e + 1 .$$

Here (3) is satisfied for $t + 1$, which thus completes the proof of the theorem.
□

Our second main result follows from Theorems 7 and 9:

Theorem 10. *A configuration is admissible if and only if condition (2) is satisfied.*

One conclusion from Theorems 9 and 10 is that in case there is a solution, the greedy algorithm determines it (see also [7], where this result is obtained by transposing a feasible schedule to the greedy one in a step-by-step manner, as in usual proofs of correctness of greedy algorithms in many scheduling algorithms).

4 Extensions to Uni-Path Bottleneck-Free Networks

We now extend the results of the previous chapter to uni-path bottleneck-free networks. In these networks there is a *capacity* associated with each link. We say that there is a *bottleneck* in a link outgoing processor n if the capacity of that link is less than the sum of the capacities of all the edges incoming n. A network is termed *bottleneck-free* if there is no bottleneck. The network is termed *uni-path* if there is at most one simple path between any pair of processors (directed trees - in particular, chains - and directed rings are examples for such networks).

To ease the presentation, we first extend the results to general chains (chains with general capacities), followed by directed rings, trees, and general uni-path network.

4.1 General Chain Networks

Let the capacity of the link $(i, i + 1)$ be $c_i \geq 1$. For each processor n, there is only one incoming link and one outgoing link. If there is no bottleneck, $c_i \leq c_{i+1}$ for all i.

Example 5. The network depicted in Figure 2.a, where $c_1 = c_2 = 2$, $c_3 = 3$, $c_4 = 4$, and $c_5 = c_6 = c_7 = 7$, is bottleneck-free.

The network depicted in Figure 2.b, where all the capacities are the same as in Figure 2.a except $c_4 = 2$, has a bottleneck in link $(4, 5)$. □

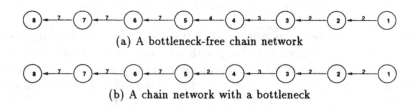

(a) A bottleneck-free chain network

(b) A chain network with a bottleneck

Fig. 2. General chain networks

We define virtual slacks as in Section 2.2. Theorems 2 - 3 are still valid. As the capacity of each link may be greater than 1, Theorems 7 - 10 have to be modified; Theorems 11, 12, 13 and 14 extend Theorems 7, 8, 9 and 10, respectively, as follows.

Theorem 11. *If a configuration in a bottleneck-free network is admissible, then*

$$\sum_{j=0}^{e} X_j^{0,n} \leq c_n(e + 1) \quad \forall n, \forall e \geq 0 . \tag{4}$$

Proof: Assume to the contrary that there exists a node n and an $e \geq 0$ such that $\sum_{j=0}^{e} X_j^{0,n} > c_n(e+1)$. Then, there are at least $c_n(e+1)+1$ messages m_i with $v_i^{0,n} \leq e$. By Theorem 6, n must send $c_n(e+1)+1$ messages by time e. At each time unit, at most c_n messages can be sent by node n. Therefore, by time e, n can send at most $c_n(e+1)$ messages, so the configuration is not admissible, a contradiction. □

We define the admissibility condition for a schedule as

$$\sum_{j=0}^{e} X_j^{t,n} \leq c_n(e+1) \quad \forall n, \forall t, \forall e \geq 0 . \tag{5}$$

By the same argument as in the proof in Theorem 8, we have

Theorem 12. *A schedule for a bottleneck-free network is admissible if and only if condition (5) is satisfied.*

We now prove that the greedy algorithm also works in a bottleneck-free chain network.

Theorem 13. *If condition (4) is satisfied, then the greedy algorithm determines an admissible schedule in a bottleneck-free chain network.*

Sketch of Proof: Following Theorem 12, it suffices to prove (5). The proof is by induction on t (similar to that of Theorem 9). Let processor n send i messages at time t. Among these messages, let v be the virtual slack of the message of largest slack. We consider two cases, $i = c_n$ and $i < c_n$.
Case I: $i = c_n$
  There are two cases, namely, $v = 0$ and $v > 0$.
  Case Ia): $v = 0$
  Since $i \leq X_0^{t,n} \leq c_n$ and $i = c_n$, $X_0^{t,n} = i$. All other messages m_i with $v_i^{t,n} > 0$ are not sent. By Lemma 4, $X_j^{t+1,n} = X_{j+1}^{t,n}$ for every $j \geq 0$. Hence,

$$\sum_{j=0}^{e} X_j^{t+1,n} = \sum_{j=0}^{e} X_{j+1}^{t,n} = \sum_{j=1}^{e+1} X_j^{t,n} = \sum_{j=0}^{e+1} X_j^{t,n} - X_0^{t,n}$$

(by induction hypothesis)

$$\leq c_n(e+2) - i = c_n(e+1).$$

  Case Ib): $v > 0$
  It follows from Lemma 4 that $X_j^{t+1,n} = X_{j+1}^{t,n}$ if $j \geq v$, and

$$\sum_{j=0}^{v-1} X_j^{t+1,n} = \sum_{j=0}^{v-1} X_{j+1}^{t,n} - c_n \leq \sum_{j=0}^{v} X_j^{t,n} - c_n .$$

When $e \geq v - 1$:

$$\sum_{j=0}^{e} X_j^{t+1,n} = \sum_{j=0}^{v-1} X_j^{t+1,n} + \sum_{j=v}^{e} X_j^{t+1,n} \leq \sum_{j=0}^{v} X_j^{t,n} - c_n + \sum_{j=v+1}^{e+1} X_j^{t,n}$$

$$\leq \sum_{j=0}^{e+1} X_j^{t,n} - c_n \text{ (by induction hypothesis)} \leq c_n(e+2) - c_n = c_n(e+1).$$

When $e < v - 1$: since the algorithm sends the most urgent messages in node n, for every $j \leq e$, $\mathcal{X}_j^{t+1,n} \subseteq \mathcal{X}_j^{t,n-1}$ and $X_j^{t+1,n} \leq X_j^{t,n-1}$. It follows that $\sum_{j=0}^{e} X_j^{t+1,n} \leq \sum_{j=0}^{e} X_j^{t,n-1}$ (by induction hypothesis) $\leq c_{n-1}(e+1)$ (by bottleneck-free assumption) $\leq c_n(e+1)$.

Case II: $i < c_n$

As node n sends all the messages at time t, all the messages with virtual slack at most e at time $t+1$ are in processor j, $j \leq n-1$, at time t. Thus, similarly, we have $\sum_{j=0}^{e} X_j^{t+1,n} \leq \sum_{j=0}^{e} X_j^{t,n-1}$ (by induction hypothesis) $\leq c_{n-1}(e+1)$ (by bottleneck-free assumption) $\leq c_n(e+1)$. Here (5) is satisfied for $t+1$, which thus completes the proof of the theorem. □

Theorem 11 and Theorem 13 imply the following theorem:

Theorem 14. *A configuration in a bottleneck-free chain network is admissible if and only if (4) is satisfied.*

4.2 Directed Ring Networks

In uniform directed rings, let the network be $\mathcal{N} = G(V, E)$, with $V = \{1, ..., N\}$ and $E = \{(i, i+1) \mid i = 1, ..., N-1\} \cup \{(N, 1)\}$. In order to have no bottleneck, all the capacities are the same. That is, $c_1 = c_2 = ... = c_N = c$. The virtual slack $v_i^{t,n}$ of message $m_i = (p_i, d_i, s_i)$ at time t for processor n, where m_i has to pass through n before getting to its destination, is defined as follows:

$$v_i^{t,n} = \begin{cases} s_i^t + (n - p_i^t) & \text{if } n \geq p_i^t \\ s_i^t + (n + N - p_i^t) & \text{if } n < p_i^t. \end{cases}$$

We show that all the theorems and lemmas still hold for this new definition, and it follows that

$$\sum_{j=0}^{e} X_j^{0,n} \leq c(e+1) \quad \forall n, \forall e \geq 0 \tag{6}$$

is a necessary and sufficient condition for a configuration to be admissible, and that the greedy algorithm determines a valid schedule for an admissible configuration.

4.3 Tree Networks

We now extend the results to networks whose underlying topology is a tree. We consider two cases.

1. The tree has one node v and a directed path from every other node to v. Note that for each processor, except for v, the capacity of the outgoing edge is greater than or equal to the sum of the capacities of all the incoming edges.
2. A directed tree (the tree is rooted at a certain node v; there is a directed path from v to every other node. Note that for each processor, except for v, the capacity of each of the outgoing edges is greater than or equal to the capacity of the incoming edge.

In case (1): in such networks, the virtual slack $v_i^{t,n}$ of message m_i at time t for processor n is defined only for those processors that m_i should pass through. Here, $v_i^{t,n} = s_i^t +$ height difference of n and p_i^t . All the properties of virtual slacks are still valid and the only difference is in the proof of Theorem 9. The case $v = 0$, and the case $v > 0$ and $e \geq v - 1$ follow the same proof. In the case where $v > 0$ and $e < v - 1$, let n' be a child of n. We have $\mathcal{X}_j^{t+1,n} \subseteq \cup_{n'} \mathcal{X}_j^{t,n'}$ and so $X_j^{t+1,n} \leq \sum_{n'} X_j^{t,n'}$. Then $\sum_{j=0}^{e} X_j^{t+1,n} \leq \sum_{j=0}^{e} (\sum_{n'} X_j^{t,n'}) \leq (\sum_{n'} c_{n'})(e+1) \leq c_n (e+1)$.

In case (2): for a link l directed out from processor n, we define the virtual slack $v_i^{t,l}$ of message m_i at time t for link l to be $s_i^t + \delta_i^{t,l}$ where $\delta_i^{t,l}$ is the number of links that m_i should pass through when going from p_i^t to n. It is clear that the virtual slacks for links also have the properties of the virtual slacks for processors. As there may be more than one link outgoing each processor, the inequalities in (4) and (5) should be satisfied for each link l, instead of for each n. That is, (5) should become

$$\sum_{j=0}^{e} X_j^{0,l} \leq c_l(e+1) \quad \forall l, \forall e \geq 0, \tag{7}$$

and (5) should be

$$\sum_{j=0}^{e} X_j^{t,l} \leq c_l(e+1) \quad \forall l, \forall t, \forall e \geq 0 . \tag{8}$$

4.4 General Networks

Following the proofs in Sections 4.1, 4.2 and 4.3, our characterization applies also to any bottleneck-free network in which there is at most one simple path between any two processors. In this case the virtual slacks for links can be defined unambiguously (like in the case of directed trees - see Section 4.3). All the properties concerning virtual slacks in the paper are still applicable. Following the arguments for directed trees, the bottleneck-free assumption ensures that the proof of Theorem 9 is also valid. Thus, an initial configuration is admissible if and only if (7) is satisfied, and in this case the greedy algorithm determines a feasible schedule.

5 Negative Results

We now show that easing some of our restrictions makes our problems either intractable or impossible. We first show (Section 5.1) that bottlenecks are real obstacles, in the sense that no algorithm (including the greedy algorithm) exists in these networks, that works correctly by making decisions based only on local information. This result is shown also for half-duplex networks, in which the communication lines can carry messages in each direction, but not simultaneously. We then discuss (Section 5.2) networks which are not uni-path, in which messages between two processors must follow only one predetermined route (as is the case in various situations, like in the ATM application from where our original problem stemmed). We show that the resulting decision problem is NP-complete.

5.1 Impossibility results

The impossibility of the validity of the greedy algorithm, in the presence of one bottleneck, is now discussed.

Theorem 15. *The greedy algorithm does not work in unidirectional chain networks with even a single bottleneck.*

Sketch of Proof: We present a chain network with a bottleneck from processor i to processor $i + 1$; that is, $c_i > c_{i+1}$. We present an initial configuration and showing that the greedy algorithm cannot send all the messages on time. Afterwards, we show that the configuration is in fact admissible by showing an admissible schedule. □

This impossibility result is even stronger; indeed, in the presence of even a unique bottleneck, no such algorithm exists, as shown in the following theorem.

Theorem 16. *Given a unidirectional chain network with a bottleneck, no algorithm, in which processors know only messages of their own, can solve the problem.*

Sketch of Proof: We present a chain network with a bottleneck from processor i to processor $i+1$; that is, $c_i > c_{i+1}$. Processor i is initially holding two messages, A and B. We show two scenarios: scenario S_1 where there is a solution if and only if message A is sent at time $t = 0$, and scenario S_2 in which there is a solution if and only if message B is sent at time $t = 0$. Clearly, in these two scenarios different messages are residing in processors j, $j < i$, but by our assumption processor i does not have this information. Given any algorithm, that is supposed to find an admissible schedule if one exists, we get to a contradiction: if processor i decides to send message A (B), then if the starting scenario is S_2 (S_1) then the algorithm cannot find a schedule (that would exist if the first message chosen would have been message B (A)). This proof is easily extended to any network with a bottleneck, and to scenarios when processors know only messages in their preceding k neighboring processors, for any constant k. □

In the next theorem, we show that knowing only information of local messages is also not enough for a processor to send messages correctly in a half-duplex chain with uniform capacities.

Theorem 17. *Given a half-duplex chain network with uniform capacities, no algorithm, in which processors know only messages of their own, can solve the problem.*

Sketch of Proof: Similar to the proof of Theorem 16. □

5.2 NP-Complete Result

It turns out that the difficulty of the problem lies not only in the fact that local decisions have to be made, as we have just shown, but it stems also from the fact that more than one route might be possible. If in this case the messages between two processors must follow only one path between them (as is the case in certain situations, like in certain ATM routing problems), then the resulting problem is now shown to be NP-complete, even when the network is bottleneck-free, and the processors have global information about the initial configuration.

Theorem 18. *Given a network $G = (V, E)$, with a given set of messages $m(i, j)$, $i, j \in V$, which have to be sent by processor i to processor j, such that each meets its given deadline and such that they all follow the same path and satisfy the capacity constraints, it is NP-complete to determine whether there is an admissible schedule for this configuration.*

Sketch of Proof: We show that the problem is NP-complete for a network, in which processor a is connected to processor b by two parallel lines, and b is connected to some other processors. The messages have to travel from a to all processors other than b, and they all have the same deadline. We use a reduction from a variant of the Partition problem (see [5]). □

References

1. J. Blazewicz, K. Ecker, G. Schmidt and J. Węglarz, *Scheduling in Computer and Manufacturing Systems*, Springer-Verlag, Heidelberg, 1993.
2. D. Bertsekas and R.G. Gallager, *Data Networks*, Prentice Hall, Englewood Cliffs, N.J., 1992.
3. T.L. Casavant and J.G. Kuhl, A taxonomy of scheduling in general-purpose distributed computer systems, in *Readings in Distributed Systems*, T. Casavant and M. Singhal (eds.), IEEE Computer Society Press, 1994, pp. 31-51.
4. R. G. Gallager, P. A. Humblet and P. M. Spira, A distributed algorithm for minimum spanning tree, *ACM Transactions on Programming Languages and Systems*, 5, 1, 1983, pp. 66-77.
5. M.R. Garey and D.S. Johnson, *Computers and Intractability: A Guide to the Theory of NP-Completeness*, W.H. Freeman and Co., San Francisco, CA, 1979.
6. O. Gerstel and S. Zaks, The Virtual Path Layout Problem in Fast Networks, *Proceedings of the 13th ACM Symposium on Principles of Distributed Computing (PODC)*, Los Angeles, CA, August 1994, pp. 235-243.
7. D. H. Ngok, Greedy Scheduling on Synchronous Chain Networks, M.Sc. Thesis, Department of Computer Science, Hong Kong University of Science and Technology, Hong Kong, February 1996; part of the results presented in
   D. H. Ngok and S. Zaks, On the Power of Local Information in Scheduling in Synchronous Networks, 3rd Int. Coll. on Structural Information and Communication Complexity, Siena, Italy, June 1996.
8. F. Wilder, *A guide to the TCP/IP protocol suite*, Artech House Telecommunications Library, Artech House, Boston, MA, 1993.

Rapid Convergence of a Local Load Balancing Algorithm for Asynchronous Rings

Johannes E. Gehrke [1,3]   C. Greg Plaxton [2,3]   Rajmohan Rajaraman [2,3]

Abstract. We consider the problem of load balancing in a ring network. We present an analysis of the following local algorithm. In each step, each node of the ring examines the number of tokens at its clockwise neighbor and sends a token to the neighbor if the neighbor has fewer tokens. We show that in a synchronous model, for any initial token distribution b, the algorithm converges to a completely balanced distribution within $4OPT(b) + n$ steps, where $OPT(b)$ is the time taken by the optimal centralized algorithm to balance b completely. Our main result is an analysis of the algorithm in an asynchronous model in which local computations and messages may be arbitrarily delayed, subject to the constraint that each message is eventually delivered and each computation is eventually performed. By generalizing our analysis for the synchronous model, we show that for any initial token distribution b, the algorithm converges to a completely balanced distribution within $8OPT(b) + 2n$ rounds, where a round is a minimal sequence of steps in which every component of the network is scheduled at least once. We also show that for every initial token distribution, the message complexity of the algorithm is asymptotically optimal among all algorithms that move tokens in the clockwise direction.

1 Introduction

An important problem in a distributed system is to balance the total workload over the processors. Such load balancing problems arise in a number of parallel and distributed applications including job scheduling in operating systems (e.g., see [12]), adaptive mesh partitioning (e.g., see [27]), and packet routing (e.g., see [22]). A natural approach towards load balancing is to have each node periodically poll the other nodes to which it is connected, and send some of its load to neighbors with lesser load. Indeed, such local balancing algorithms have been studied extensively on different models of computation (e.g., see [1, 8, 10]).

---

[1] Department of Computer Science, University of Wisconsin-Madison, Madison, WI 53706. Email: johannes@cs.wisc.edu.

[2] Department of Computer Science, University of Texas at Austin, Austin, TX 78712. Supported by the National Science Foundation under Grant No. CCR-9504145. Email: {rraj,plaxton}@cs.utexas.edu.

[3] Part of this work was done while the authors were visiting the University of Paderborn.

We address the static version of the load balancing problem: we assume that each processor has an initial collection of "tokens" (i.e., units of load), and that no tokens are created or destroyed while the tokens are being balanced. In each step, each node can communicate with each of its neighbors and send (resp., receive) at most one token along each of its incident edges. The problem is to design a distributed algorithm that converges to a balanced distribution quickly, where a distribution is said to be *balanced* if the difference between the number of tokens at any two nodes is at most one.

In this paper, we study static load balancing on a ring network. The ring network has been studied extensively in both theory and practice. Several problems arising in distributed computing have been addressed on the ring (see [5, 13, 14, 19] for a variety of examples). From a practical perspective, the ring is an essential component of several parallel and distributed architectures [17, 25].

Our main contribution is a tight analysis of a simple algorithm that is based on the local balancing approach. We show that this algorithm, which we denote by $\mathcal{A}$, converges to a balanced distribution in near-optimal time for *every* initial distribution on both *synchronous* and *asynchronous* rings. We are not aware of any other load balancing algorithm that has been shown to achieve such universal near-optimality with respect to a non-trivial family of networks (e.g., rings). All previous optimality results known for load balancing are worst-case results.

Our results. Let R be a ring network with the set $[n] = \{0, 1, \ldots, n-1\}$ of nodes and the set $\{(i, (i+1) \bmod n\}$ of edges. The local balancing algorithm $\mathcal{A}$ is defined as follows. In each step, for all i in $[n]$, node i sends a token to node $(i+1) \bmod n$ if and only if i has more tokens than $(i+1) \bmod n$. (See Section 2 for a message-passing implementation of $\mathcal{A}$.) We note that there is a single direction, say clockwise, in which all the token movements in $\mathcal{A}$ take place. We refer to algorithms that move tokens in the clockwise direction as *unidirectional* algorithms.

We first consider a synchronous model of computation in which: (i) in each step of the network, all of the nodes simultaneously perform one step of their computations, and (ii) each message sent during a step is delivered prior to the start of the subsequent step. We show that:

- The number of steps taken by $\mathcal{A}$ to balance any distribution b on a synchronous ring is at most $4OPT(b) + n$, where $OPT(b)$ is the time taken by an optimal centralized algorithm to balance b. The proof is given in Section 4.

We note that the optimal centralized algorithm need not be a unidirectional algorithm; that is, $OPT(b)$ is the time taken to balance b by the best algorithm among *all* algorithms that send and/or receive at most one token along each edge in each step. In fact, if $OPT(b)$ were instead defined as the time taken by an optimal centralized *unidirectional* algorithm to balance b, then the factor of 4 in the stated bound could be replaced by 2.

Our next result concerns an asynchronous model of computation, in which local computations may be performed at arbitrary speeds and messages may be delayed arbitrarily, subject to the constraint that each message is eventually delivered and each computation is eventually performed [18]. In order to measure time complexity in the asynchronous model, we define a *round* to be a minimal sequence of steps in which each component of the ring (i.e., each node or edge) is scheduled at least once. The time complexity of an algorithm is then defined as the maximum number of rounds taken over all possible schedulings of the components. (See Section 5 for a formal description of the asynchronous model.)

The above notion of time is based on the model proposed in [2] for shared memory systems. An analogous model for message-passing systems was studied in [4]. Moreover, the above models are equivalent to that proposed in [20], where the time complexity of an algorithm is defined to be the longest amount of elapsed real time from the start to the completion of the algorithm, assuming that the time delay between two steps of the same network component is at most one [2]. (The model proposed in [20] has been subsequently used in the study of several distributed computing problems [6, 7].)

We generalize our result for the synchronous model to the asynchronous model at the expense of a factor of 2; in particular, we show that:

- The number of rounds taken by $\mathcal{A}$ to balance any distribution b on an asynchronous ring is at most $8OPT(b) + 2n$. The proof is given in Section 5.

We remark that if $OPT(b)$ were instead defined as the time taken by an optimal centralized *unidirectional* algorithm for b, then the factor of 8 in the stated bound could be replaced by 4. We also show that in both the synchronous and asynchronous models, for every initial token distribution, the message complexity of $\mathcal{A}$ is asymptotically optimal among all unidirectional algorithms.

Previous and related work. A number of researchers have studied load balancing problems under different models of computation. These models can be classified on the basis of three characteristics: (i) centralized control (e.g., [21, 26]) versus distributed control (e.g., [8, 10]), (ii) uniform communication (e.g., [26]) versus fixed-connection network communication (e.g., [1, 11]), and (iii) unbounded edge capacity (e.g., [8, 10]) versus bounded edge capacity (e.g., [1, 15]) (the capacity of an edge is the maximum number of tokens it can transmit per step). In the discussion that follows, we restrict our attention to results for models of computation with the same basic characteristics as the model considered in the present paper, namely: distributed control, fixed-connection network communication, and bounded edge capacity.

Local algorithms restricted to particular networks have been studied on hypercubes [10, 24], meshes [16, 21], and expanders [22, 23]. All of these papers analyze the worst-case complexity of certain local algorithms. More recently, it has been shown that a simple local algorithm is optimal in the worst-case on arbitrary networks [15]. Application of the preceding result to the special case of the ring implies that if the initial imbalance (i.e., the difference between the maximum number of tokens at any node and the minimum number of tokens at any node) is Δ, then the local algorithm balances in $O(n\Delta)$ steps. While there exists a distribution with imbalance Δ for which any algorithm takes $\Omega(n\Delta)$ steps to balance, it is not the case that every distribution with imbalance Δ

requires $\Omega(n\Delta)$ steps to balance. In fact, it is easy to construct distributions with imbalance Δ that can be balanced in $O(\Delta)$ steps.

In recent work [3], asynchronous balancing algorithms on several networks including the ring have been studied. However, the results of [3] are geared towards establishing eventual convergence in the presence of dynamic network changes, while we are interested in determining the time to convergence for static load balancing. Also related is the result of [9], where a worst-case bound on the number of token migrations is given for a model in which tokens can be transferred between any two nodes.

Our result for the asynchronous model is similar in spirit to that of [7], in that our asynchronous algorithm is not obtained by using a general synchronizer [6] in conjunction with an algorithm optimized for a synchronous model. Instead, we show that $\mathcal{A}$ is directly implementable on asynchronous rings and hence avoids all of the overhead and complexity of a synchronizer while achieving near-optimal bounds.

2 The unidirectional algorithm $\mathcal{A}$

In this section, we give a message-passing implementation of the unidirectional algorithm $\mathcal{A}$ introduced in Section 1. Recall that the nodes of the ring are assigned unique labels from the set $[n]$. For convenience, we adopt the following notational convention: any arithmetic expression referring to a node is interpreted modulo n. For example, we will often refer to the neighbors of an arbitrary node i as node $i-1$ and node $i+1$, rather than node $(i-1) \bmod n$ and node $(i+1) \bmod n$.

In $\mathcal{A}$, each node i repeatedly communicates with node $i+1$ and sends a token to $i+1$ whenever the number of tokens at i exceeds that at $i+1$. In order to implement this balancing scheme efficiently, node i maintains three variables related to the number of tokens at $i+1$: (i) a count $x(i)$ of the number of tokens that i has sent to $i+1$ since the start of the algorithm, (ii) an estimate $y(i)$ of the number of tokens that $i+1$ has sent to $i+2$ since the start of the algorithm, and (iii) the number $z(i)$ of tokens initially at $i+1$. At a given point in the execution of the algorithm, let $w(i)$ denote the number of tokens at i. Thus, $w(i)$ equals $w_0(i)$ initially.

In $\mathcal{A}$, the nodes communicate with their neighbors using three types of messages: (i) *height*, a message that i sends to $i-1$ indicating the number of tokens at i, (ii) *update*, a message that i sends to $i-1$ indicating that i has sent a new token to $i+1$, and (iii) *token*, a message consisting of a token sent by i to $i+1$. In terms of these messages, the algorithm can be described as follows.

- In the initial step, i performs the following operations: (i) set $x(i)$ and $y(i)$ to zero and set $z(i)$ to ∞, and (ii) send a *height* message with value $w(i)$ to $i-1$.
- In each subsequent step, i performs the following operation. If $w(i) > z(i) + x(i) - y(i)$, then: (i) decrement $w(i)$ by 1, (ii) increment $x(i)$ by 1, (iii) send

a *token* message to $i + 1$, and (iv) send an *update* message to $i - 1$.
- On receipt of a *height* message, i sets $z(i)$ to the value of the message. On receipt of an *update* message, i increments $y(i)$.

3 Preliminaries

Let $\mathbf{Z}$ and $\mathbf{N}$ denote the integers and nonnegative integers. Let $V = \mathbf{Z}^n$ denote the set of n-tuples of integers. For any t in $\mathbf{N}$ and i in $[n]$, let w_t be such that $w_t(i)$ is the number of tokens at node i at the start of step t. (We number the steps from 0.) For any b in V, let $\mu(b) = \frac{1}{n} \sum_{i \in [n]} b(i)$ denote the average number of tokens in b. We say that the ring is *balanced* in step t if $w_t(i)$ is $\lfloor \mu(b) \rfloor$ or $\lceil \mu(b) \rceil$ for all i in $[n]$, where b is the initial distribution. For any subset S of $[n]$, let $w_t(S)$ denote the total number of tokens in S at the start of step t.

For any i and j in $[n]$, let $d(b, i, j)$ denote the total "imbalance" associated with the set of contiguous nodes obtained when going from node i to node j in the clockwise direction (i and j included). Formally, we have:

$$d(b, i, j) = \sum_{0 \leq k \leq (j-i) \bmod n} (b(i + k) - \mu(b)).$$

(In other words, if $i \leq j$, then $d(b, i, j)$ equals $\sum_{i \leq k \leq j} (b(k) - \mu(b))$; otherwise, $d(b, i, j)$ equals $[\sum_{j \leq k < n} (b(k) - \mu(b)) + \sum_{0 < k \leq i} (b(k) - \mu(b))]$.) Let $\ell(b)$ and $m(b)$ be two integers such that $d(b, \ell(b), m(b))$ is $\max_{i,j} d(b, i, j)$. Without loss of generality, we assume for the remainder of this paper that $\ell(b)$ is zero as we can relabel the nodes appropriately otherwise.

We now introduce the notion of *discrepancy*, which plays an important role in our analysis. The discrepancy of a distribution denotes the maximum imbalance among all sets of contiguous nodes of the ring. More formally, the discrepancy $D(b)$ of b is given by $d(b, 0, m(b))$. In Section 4.1, we show that $OPT(b)$ is at least $D(b)/2$ (Lemma 4.1).

In the remainder of this paper, we will be concerned with applying μ, d, and m, only with respect to the initial token distribution. Therefore, as a shorthand, we let μ, $d(i, j)$, and m, denote $\mu(w_0)$, $d(w_0, i, j)$, and $m(w_0)$, respectively.

4 Analysis for synchronous rings

In this section, we analyze $\mathcal{A}$ under the synchronous model of computation. For simplicity, we assume, in both this section as well as Section 5, that μ, the average number of tokens in the initial distribution, is an integer.

In the synchronous model, each node executes in a lock-step manner, and each message is transmitted in a single step. By the definitions of $x(i)$, $y(i)$, and $z(i)$, we obtain that the value of $z(i) + x(i) - y(i)$ at the start of step t equals $w_t(i + 1)$ for any $t > 0$. Therefore, each step of node i can be expressed as follows: if $w_t(i) > w_t(i + 1)$, then send a token to $i + 1$. For our analysis, it is helpful to consider a generalization of $\mathcal{A}$ given by Definition 4.2 below.

Definition 4.1 *We say that a step t of an algorithm is an **S-step**, where S is a subset of [n], if each node not in S is idle in step t and each node i in S performs the following operation: if $w_t(i) > w_t(i+1)$, then i sends a token to $i+1$.*

Definition 4.2 *A **partial algorithm** $\mathcal{B}$ is one in which each step is an S-step for some subset S of [n]. For any t in **N**, we let $\mathcal{B}(t)$ denote the set S such that step t of $\mathcal{B}$ is an S-step.*

It follows from Definitions 4.1 and 4.2 that $\mathcal{A}$ is a partial algorithm in which each step after step 0 is an [n]-step. We bound the running time of $\mathcal{A}$ by providing a general analysis that applies to all partial algorithms. Before proceeding to this analysis, which is given in Section 4.1, we present two additional definitions.

Given partial algorithms $\mathcal{B}$ and $\mathcal{C}$, we say that $\mathcal{B}$ *covers* (resp., *is covered by*) $\mathcal{C}$ if $\mathcal{B}(t)$ is a superset of (resp., subset of) $\mathcal{C}(t)$ for all t. Let $\mathcal{B}$ be a partial algorithm. For i in **N**, let r_i be defined as follows: r_0 is -1 and for all $i > 0$, r_i is the smallest integer greater than r_{i-1} such that $\cup_{r_{i-1} < j \leq r_i} \mathcal{B}(j) = [n]$. We define the *ith round* of $\mathcal{B}$ to be the sequence of steps in the interval $[r_i + 1, r_{i+1}]$.

4.1   Analysis of partial algorithms

While the number of tokens present at each node of the ring after any number of steps of $\mathcal{A}$ (or any other partial algorithm) is easy to calculate, the particular token distribution obtained does not directly provide a good barometer for the progress of the algorithm. For example, it is possible for the imbalance at some node (i.e., the difference between the number of tokens at the node and the average number of tokens) to initially increase with time. A simple approach to measure the progress of a load balancing algorithm is the following: (i) assign to each node a potential that grows with the imbalance at the node, and (ii) determine the rate at which the sum of the potentials of the nodes decreases with time. While this approach simplifies the worst-case analysis for general networks (see [15]), it appears to be inadequate for our purposes since information about the particular distribution of imbalance is lost.

By exploiting the simple structure of ring networks, we are able to capture the precise distribution of the imbalance of the network in a measure, referred to as the *prefix sum vector*, that also easily relates to the steps of a partial algorithm. For each t in **N**, let p_t be defined as follows:

$$p_t(i) = \sum_{0 \leq j \leq i} (w_t(j) - \mu) \text{ for all } i \text{ in } [n]. \tag{1}$$

(In other words, p_t is the n-tuple of the prefix sums of the difference between the number of tokens at each node at the start of step t and the average.) Given an initial token distribution $w_0 = b$, let $T(b)$ denote $\sum_{i \in [n]} p_0(i)$.

The following lemma gives a lower bound on the time complexity of any balancing algorithm and the number of token transmissions of any unidirectional balancing algorithm in terms of $D(b)$ and $T(b)$, respectively, where b is the initial token distribution. Recall that $D(b)$, which is formally defined in Section 3, is the discrepancy of b.

Lemma 4.1 *Any algorithm takes at least $D(b)/2$ steps to balance b. Any unidirectional algorithm incurs at least $T(b)$ token transmissions to balance b.*

Proof: Consider the set $S = \{i : 0 \le i \le m(b)\}$ of nodes. By definition, $w_0(S)$ is $D(b) + \mu|S|$. (Recall that $\ell(b)$ is 0.) If the ring is balanced in t steps, then for each node i in S, $w_t(i)$ is μ. Therefore, $w_t(S)$ is at most $\mu|S|$, and hence, at least $D(b)$ tokens are sent out of S in t steps. Since at most two tokens can be sent out of S per step, t is at least $D(b)/2$.

For each i in $[n]$, the number of token transmissions across edge $(i, i+1)$ required by any unidirectional algorithm is at least $p_0(i)$ since $p_0(i)$ is the excess number of tokens over the average in the interval $[0, i]$. Therefore, the total number of token transmissions needed by any unidirectional algorithm to balance b is at least $T(b)$. □

The remainder of this section is devoted to proving that the number of rounds taken by any partial algorithm to balance a distribution b is at most $2D(b)+n-1$. We begin by determining the effect of a step of a partial algorithm on the prefix sum vector. For this purpose, it is useful to define a partial order $\preceq$ on V as follows: $b \preceq c$ if and only if $b(i) \le c(i)$ for all i in $[n]$. For convenience, we use 0 to denote the n-tuple each of whose components is 0. Lemma 4.2 expresses a partial algorithm as a recurrence relation among the prefix sum vectors. The proof of Lemma 4.2 follows from Lemmas 4.3 and 4.5 below.

Lemma 4.2 *For any partial algorithm $\mathcal{B}$, we have: if i is in $\mathcal{B}(t)$ and $2p_t(i) > p_t(i-1) + p_t(i+1)$, then $p_{t+1}(i) = p_t(i) - 1$; otherwise, $p_{t+1}(i) = p_t(i)$.*

Lemma 4.3 *For any partial algorithm $\mathcal{B}$, if $0 \preceq p_t$, then: if i is in $\mathcal{B}(t)$ and $2p_t(i) > p_t(i-1) + p_t(i+1)$, then $p_{t+1}(i) = p_t(i) - 1$; otherwise, $p_{t+1}(i) = p_t(i)$.*

Proof: Since $0 \preceq p_t$, $p_t(0)$ is nonnegative, and hence $w_t(0)$ is at least μ. Moreover, by definition, $p_t(n-1)$ is 0. Since $p_t(n-2)$ is nonnegative, $w_t(n-1)$ is at most μ. Therefore, no token is sent from node $n-1$ to node 0. It follows that for each i in $[n]$, if node i sends a token to node $i+1$, then $p_{t+1}(i)$ is $p_t(i) - 1$; otherwise, $p_{t+1}(i)$ is $p_t(i)$. Node i sends a token to $i+1$ if and only if i is in $\mathcal{B}(t)$ and $p_t(i) - p_t(i-1)$ is greater than $p_t(i+1) - p_t(i)$. The desired claim follows. □

Lemma 4.4 *For any token distribution, we have $0 \preceq p_0$.*

Proof: The proof is by contradiction. Let i be the smallest nonnegative integer such that $p_0(i)$ is negative. From the definition of i, it follows that $d(i+1, m)$ equals $d(0, m) - d(0, i)$. Since $d(0, i) = p_0(i) < 0$, we obtain that $d(i+1, m)$ is greater than $d(0, m)$, which contradicts the definition of m. □

Lemma 4.5 *For any partial algorithm $\mathcal{B}$ and all t in $\mathbf{N}$, we have $0 \preceq p_t$.*

Proof: The proof is by induction on t. The base case follows from Lemma 4.4. The induction hypothesis is that $0 \preceq p_t$. For the induction step, we consider step t

and argue that $0 \preceq p_{t+1}$. By Lemma 4.3, we have: if $2p_t(i) > p_t(i-1) + p_t(i+1)$, then $p_{t+1}(i)$ is $p_t(i) - 1$; otherwise, $p_{t+1}(i)$ is $p_t(i)$. In either case, since $p_t(i)$ is nonnegative (by the induction hypothesis) and is an integer for all i, we obtain that $p_{t+1}(i)$ is nonnegative for all i, thus completing the induction step. $\square$

Lemma 4.6 shows that each step of a partial algorithm, when viewed as a function on the prefix sum vector, is monotonic with respect to $\preceq$.

Lemma 4.6 *Let S be an arbitrary subset of $[n]$. Let p and q denote the prefix sum vectors associated with token distributions b and c, respectively. Let p' and q' denote the prefix sum vectors associated with the token distributions obtained after performing an S-step on distributions b and c, respectively. If $p \preceq q$, then we have $p' \preceq q'$.*

Proof: Consider any i in $[n]$. If $p(i)$ is less than $q(i)$, then $p'(i) \leq q(i) - 1 \leq q'(i)$. Otherwise, we have $p(i) = q(i)$. By Lemma 4.2, if $q'(i)$ is $q(i) - 1$, then $2q(i) > q(i-1) + q(i+1)$. It then follows from the hypothesis of the lemma that $2p(i) > p(i-1) + p(i+1)$, which together with Lemma 4.2 implies that $p'(i)$ is $p(i) - 1$. Thus the desired claim holds. $\square$

Corollary 4.6.1 *Consider a partial algorithm $\mathcal{B}$. Let p_0 and q_0 denote the prefix sum vectors at the start of step 0 when the initial token distributions are b and c respectively. If $p_0 \preceq q_0$, then the number of rounds taken by $\mathcal{B}$ to balance b is at most that taken to balance c.* $\square$

Lemma 4.7 is used to prove Corollary 4.7.1 which states that if $\mathcal{B}$ covers $\mathcal{C}$, then $\mathcal{B}$ balances at least as quickly as $\mathcal{C}$.

Lemma 4.7 *Let $\mathcal{B}$ and $\mathcal{C}$ be two partial algorithm such that $\mathcal{B}$ covers $\mathcal{C}$. Given an initial token distribution, let p_t and q_t denote the prefix sum vectors at the start of step t of $\mathcal{B}$ and $\mathcal{C}$, respectively. Then, for each step t, $p_t \preceq q_t$.*

Proof: The proof is by induction on step t. The induction base is trivial since $p_0 = q_0$. For the induction hypothesis, we assume that $p_t \preceq q_t$. Consider step t of $\mathcal{B}$ and $\mathcal{C}$. Let $\mathcal{D}$ be a partial algorithm that is identical to $\mathcal{C}$ except that $\mathcal{D}(t) = \mathcal{B}(t)$. Let r represent the prefix sum vector obtained after step t of $\mathcal{D}$. Since $\mathcal{D}(t) \supset \mathcal{C}(t)$, it follows from Lemma 4.2 that $r \preceq q_{t+1}$. By Lemma 4.6 and the induction hypothesis, it follows that $p_{t+1} \preceq r$. By the transitivity of $\preceq$, it follows that $p_{t+1} \preceq q_{t+1}$. $\square$

Corollary 4.7.1 *Let $\mathcal{B}$ and $\mathcal{C}$ be two partial algorithm such that $\mathcal{B}$ covers $\mathcal{C}$. For any initial token distribution b, the number of rounds taken by $\mathcal{B}$ to balance b is at most that taken by $\mathcal{C}$.* $\square$

Given a nonnegative integer h, consider the set $U(h)$ of token distributions with discrepancy h. Let $P(h)$ denote the set of prefix sum vectors associated with the distributions in $U(h)$. It is easy to see that $f(h) = (2h, h, \ldots, h, 0)$ is the distribution whose prefix sum vector $g(h) = (h, h, \ldots, h, 0)$ is the unique least upper bound (with respect to $\preceq$) of $P(h)$. It thus follows from Corollary 4.6.1 that the number of rounds taken by a partial algorithm $\mathcal{B}$ to balance any distribution in $U(h)$ is at most the number of rounds taken by $\mathcal{B}$ to balance $f(h)$. We now place an upper bound on the number of rounds taken by any partial algorithm to balance $f(h)$.

Lemma 4.8 *For any nonnegative integer h, the number of rounds taken by any partial algorithm $\mathcal{B}$ to balance $f(h)$ is at most $2h + n - 1$.*

Proof: For any i, let the ith round of $\mathcal{B}$ consist of the steps $[r_i + 1, r_{i+1}]$. In order to establish the desired claim, we construct a partial algorithm $\mathcal{C}$ that is covered by $\mathcal{B}$. Since the rounds of $\mathcal{C}$ may differ from those of $\mathcal{B}$, to avoid ambiguity, we refer to $[r_i + 1, r_{i+1}]$ as interval i.

Given interval i and a node j, let $y_{i,j}$ be the smallest integer such that j is in $\mathcal{B}(y_{i,j})$. We now define $\mathcal{C}$ as follows. For each interval i, and each step t in interval i, node j is in $\mathcal{C}(t)$ if and only if: (i) t is $y_{i,j}$ and (ii) j equals $t - 2k$ for some $k \leq \min\{\lceil t/2 \rceil, h\}$ (i.e., j has the same parity as t). It follows directly from the definition that $\mathcal{C}$ is a partial algorithm and that $\mathcal{B}$ covers $\mathcal{C}$. We now show that $\mathcal{C}$ balances $f(h)$ before the start of interval $2h + n - 1$.

We mark the h excess tokens on node 0 with the labels 0 through $h - 1$ from the top. We show that during the execution of $\mathcal{C}$ the following property holds: at the start of interval t, if $i \leq \min\{\lceil t/2 \rceil, h\}$, token i is at node $\min\{t - 2i, n - 1\}$; otherwise, token i is at node 0. The proof is by induction on $t \leq 2h + n$. The induction base is trivial. For the induction hypothesis, we assume that the above statement holds at the start of interval t.

Consider interval t. By the definition of $\mathcal{C}$, if $t - j$ is even in interval t, then node j sends token $(t - j)/2$ to $j + 1$; otherwise, node j does not send any token. Thus, each node j sends at most one token to $j + 1$ in any interval. Furthermore, by the induction hypothesis, if $t - j$ is even then node j has token $(t - j)/2$ while node $j + 1$ has no marked token, thus completing the induction step.

By the aforementioned property, $\mathcal{C}$ balances $f(h)$ before the start of interval $2h + n - 1$. The lemma then follows by Corollary 4.7.1. $\qquad\Box$

The following lemma shows that $g(D(b))$ is an upper bound (with respect to $\preceq$) on the initial prefix sum vector of c.

Lemma 4.9 *For any initial token distribution b, we have $p_0 \preceq g(D(b))$.*

Proof: By the definition of D and p_0, for each i in $[n]$, $p_0(i)$ is at most $D(b)$. Moreover, since μ is an integer, $p_0(n-1)$ is zero. It thus follows from the definition of g that $p_0 \preceq g(D(b))$. $\qquad\Box$

The upper bound on the time complexity of a partial algorithm now follows from Corollary 4.6.1 and Lemma 4.9.

Lemma 4.10 *Given any initial token distribution b, the number of rounds taken by any partial algorithm to balance b is at most $2D(b) + n - 1$.*

Proof: By Lemma 4.9, $p_0 \preceq g(D(b))$. Therefore, by Corollary 4.6.1, the number of rounds taken to balance b is at most that taken to balance $f(D(b))$. By

Lemma 4.8, the number of rounds taken to balance $f(D(b))$ is at most $2D(b) + n - 1$. The desired claim follows. $\qquad\square$

We now place a bound on the number of token transmissions before balancing a distribution b. Whenever a node i sends a token in step t, we have $p_{t+1}(i) = p_t(i) - 1$. Therefore, the total number of token transmissions by any partial algorithm is exactly $T(b)$, which, by Lemma 4.1, is optimal with respect to all unidirectional algorithms.

Lemma 4.11 *Given an initial token distribution b, the number of token transmissions by any partial algorithm is $T(b)$.* $\qquad\square$

4.2 Complexity of $\mathcal{A}$

Every step of $\mathcal{A}$ after step 0 is an $[n]$-step. It thus follows from Lemma 4.10 that the number of steps taken to balance any distribution b with integral average is at most $2D(b) + n$.

We now consider the message complexity of $\mathcal{A}$. In step 0, n *height* messages are transmitted. The number of *update* messages transmitted is at most the total number of token transmissions since an *update* message is sent by a node i in step t only if i sends a token in step t. By Lemma 4.11, the number of token transmissions is at most $T(b)$. Hence the total number of message transmissions is at most $2T(b) + n$, proving the theorem below.

Theorem 1 *Consider the synchronous model of a ring network with n processors. If the initial token distribution is b, then the number of steps taken by $\mathcal{A}$ to balance b is at most $2D(b) + n$. The number of token transmissions and the number of message transmissions are $T(b)$ and $2T(b) + n$, respectively.* $\qquad\square$

5 Analysis for asynchronous rings

In this section, we analyze $\mathcal{A}$ under an asynchronous model of computation. We consider the ring network as consisting of $3n$ different components: n nodes given by the set $[n]$ and $2n$ directed edges given by the set $\{(i, i+1), (i, i-1)\}$. As defined in Section 2, each step of a node consists of sending a constant number of messages to its neighbors together with a small number of local operations. Each edge (i, j) is a directed channel that transmits messages from i to j in FIFO order. At any instant, there may be several messages in transit from i to j on edge (i, j). Each step of edge (i, j) consists of delivering the first message (if any) in FIFO order among the messages currently in transit from i to j.

We model asynchrony by means of an adversary $\mathcal{X}$ that schedules the components of the network over a sequence of steps. In step t, each component in a set $\mathcal{X}(t)$ of components chosen by the adversary executes its next step simultaneously. Given adversaries $\mathcal{X}_1$ and $\mathcal{X}_2$, we say that $\mathcal{X}_1$ is *weaker* (resp., *stronger*) than $\mathcal{X}_2$ if for all t, $\mathcal{X}_1(t)$ is a superset (resp., subset) of $\mathcal{X}_2(t)$. The notions of an adversary and that of weakness generalize the notions of a partial algorithm and that of covering defined in Section 4. Indeed, we establish our results for the asynchronous model by generalizing some of the claims of Section 4.

As mentioned above, when an edge is scheduled, the first message (if any) in FIFO order is delivered to the destination node. In the definition of $\mathcal{A}$, there are some operations that are performed at the node on receipt of a message. (An example of such an operation is the one that changes the value of $y(i)$ at node i on receipt of an *update* message.) Such operations may be executed either during the scheduling of the edge delivering the particular message or at the next scheduling of the destination node, as determined by the adversary.

Given an adversary, we define a *round* to consist of a minimal sequence of steps in which each component of the network is scheduled at least once by the adversary. The sequence of steps is partitioned into a sequence of non-overlapping rounds. The time complexity of an algorithm is defined to be maximum, over all adversaries, of the number of rounds taken to balance the ring. The message complexity of an algorithm is the maximum, over all adversaries, of the number of messages transmitted by the algorithm.

We now begin the analysis of $\mathcal{A}$ under the asynchronous model defined above. For any $t \geq 0$ and any i in $[n]$, let $u_t(i)$ denote the number of tokens in transit along edge $(i, i+1)$ at the start of step t. In analogy to Equation 1, we define two notions of prefix sums. For each t in $\mathbf{N}$, we define p_t and q_t as follows:

$$p_t(i) = \sum_{0 \leq j \leq i} (w_t(j) + u_t(j) - \mu) \text{ for all } i \text{ in } [n], \text{ and}$$

$$q_t(i) = p_t(i) - u_t(i) \text{ for all } i \text{ in } [n].$$

We refer to p_t and q_t as the *upper prefix sum vector* and the *lower prefix sum vector*, respectively. Let $\pi_t(i)$ denote the last step $t' < t$ such that a *height* or an *update* message sent by $i + 1$ in step t' is received by i in some step before step t. If no *height* or *update* message is received by i in any of the first t steps, we set $\pi_t(i)$ to -1. For convenience, we let $q_{-1}(i)$ equal ∞ for all i.

Lemmas 5.1, 5.2, 5.3, and 5.4 generalize Lemmas 4.3, 4.5, 4.2, and 4.6, respectively. The proofs of Lemmas 5.1 and 5.2 follow the same lines as the proofs of Lemmas 4.3 and 4.5, respectively. Due to space considerations, we omit these proofs in the present abstract.

Lemma 5.1 *Consider the execution of $\mathcal{A}$ against an adversary $\mathcal{X}$. Assume that $0 \preceq q_s$ for all $s \leq t$. If i is in $\mathcal{X}(t)$ and $2q_t(i) > p_t(i-1) + q_{\pi_t(i)}(i+1)$, then $q_{t+1}(i)$ is $q_t(i) - 1$; otherwise, $q_{t+1}(i)$ is $q_t(i)$.* $\square$

Lemma 5.2 *Given any adversary, $0 \preceq q_t$ and $0 \preceq p_t$ hold for all t in $\mathbf{N}$.* $\square$

Lemmas 5.1 and 5.2 together imply the following lemma.

Lemma 5.3 *Given any adversary $\mathcal{X}$, if i is in $\mathcal{X}(t)$ and $2q_t(i) > p_t(i-1) + q_{\pi_t(i)}(i+1)$, then $q_{t+1}(i)$ is $q_t(i) - 1$; otherwise, $q_{t+1}(i)$ is $q_t(i)$.* $\square$

Given a fixed initial distribution of tokens and two different adversaries, we now relate the prefix sum vectors obtained after t steps of $\mathcal{A}$ against the two adversaries. Lemma 5.4 states that both the upper and lower prefix sum vectors associated with the weaker adversary are lower bounds (with respect to $\preceq$) on the upper and lower prefix sum vectors associated with the stronger adversary.

Lemma 5.4 *Let $\mathcal{X}_1$ and $\mathcal{X}_2$ be two adversaries such that $\mathcal{X}_1$ is weaker than $\mathcal{X}_2$. Given an initial token distribution, let p_t^1 and q_t^1 denote the upper and lower prefix sum vectors at the start of step t of A against adversary $\mathcal{X}_1$, and let p_t^2 and q_t^2 denote the upper and lower prefix sum vectors at the start of step t of A against adversary $\mathcal{X}_2$. For each step t, we have $q_t^1 \preceq q_t^2$ and $p_t^1 \preceq p_t^2$.*

Proof: Let $\alpha_t(i)$ and $\beta_t(i)$ denote the value of $\pi_t(i)$ under adversaries $\mathcal{X}_1$ and $\mathcal{X}_2$, respectively. We prove by induction on t that: (i) $q_t^1 \preceq q_t^2$, (ii) $p_t^1 \preceq p_t^2$, and (iii) for all i, $q_{\alpha_t(i)}^1(i+1) \le q_{\beta_t(i)}^2(i+1)$. The induction base is trivial since $q_0^1 = q_0^2$ and $p_0^1 = p_0^2$ and $\alpha_t(i) = \beta_t(i) = -1$ for all i. For the induction hypothesis we assume that (i), (ii), and (iii) hold for all steps less than or equal to t.

We first show that $q_{t+1}^1 \preceq q_{t+1}^2$. Consider any i in $[n]$. If $q_t^1(i) < q_t^2(i)$, then $q_{t+1}^1(i) \le q_{t+1}^2(i)$. Otherwise, $q_t^1(i) = q_t^2(i)$. In this case, by Lemma 5.3, if $q_{t+1}^2 = q_t^2 - 1$, then $2q_t^2(i) > p_t^2(i-1) + q_s^2(i+1)$, where s equals $\beta_t(i)$. Let s' equal $\alpha_t(i)$. By the induction hypothesis, $q_{s'}^1(i+1) \le q_s^2(i+1)$. Since $q_t^1(i) = q_t^2(i)$, we thus obtain $2q_t^1(i) > p_t^1(i-1) + q_{s'}^1(i+1)$, which together with Lemma 5.3 implies that $q_{t+1}^1(i) = q_t^1(i) - 1$. Thus, we have $q_{t+1}^1 \preceq q_{t+1}^2$.

We next show that $p_{t+1}^1 \preceq p_{t+1}^2$. In order to prove that $p_{t+1}^1(i) \le p_{t+1}^2(i)$, we need only consider the case in which $(i, i+1)$ is in $\mathcal{X}_1(t)$, as otherwise the desired claim follows directly from the induction hypothesis. Accordingly, assume that $(i, i+1)$ is in $\mathcal{X}_1(t)$. Let $u_t^1(i)$ and $u_t^2(i)$ denote the values of $u_t(i)$ associated with adversaries $\mathcal{X}_1$ and $\mathcal{X}_2$, respectively. If $u_t^1(i)$ is positive, then $p_{t+1}^1(i) = p_t^1(i) - 1 \le p_t^2(i) - 1 \le p_{t+1}^2(i)$. Otherwise, we have $p_{t+1}^1(i) = p_t^1(i) = q_t^1(i)$, and $p_{t+1}^2(i) \ge p_t^2(i) - u_t^2(i) \ge q_t^2(i)$. Therefore, $p_{t+1}^1(i)$ is at most $p_{t+1}^2(i)$.

We now complete the induction step by showing that for all i, $q_{\alpha_{t+1}(i)}^1(i+1) \le q_{\beta_{t+1}(i)}^2(i+1)$. If $(i+1, i)$ is not in $\mathcal{X}_2(t)$, then $\alpha_{t+1}(i) \ge \alpha_t(i)$ and $\beta_{t+1}(i) = \beta_t(i)$, and hence the desired claim follows from the induction hypothesis and the fact that q_j^1 is nonincreasing as j increases. We now consider the case in which $(i+1, i)$ is in $\mathcal{X}_2(t)$. If $\alpha_{t+1}(i) \ne \alpha_t(i)$, then the desired claim holds since $q_{\alpha_{t+1}}^1(i+1) = q_{\alpha_t(i)}^1(i+1) - 1$, while $q_{\beta_{t+1}}^2(i+1) \ge q_{\beta_t(i)}^2(i+1) - 1$. Otherwise, either $\alpha_{t+1}(i) \ge \beta_{t+1}(i)$, or $q_{\alpha_{t+1}(i)}^1(i+1) = q_{\beta_{t+1}(i)}^2(i+1) \le q_{\beta_{t+1}(i)}^2(i+1)$. In either case, the desired claim follows from the induction hypothesis. $\square$

We are now ready to establish the main result for asynchronous rings.

Theorem 2 *The number of rounds taken by A to balance any initial token distribution b is at most $4D(b) + 2n - 2$. The number of token transmissions is at most $T(b)$ and the number of message transmissions is at most $2T(b) + n$.*

Proof: Given any adversary $\mathcal{X}_1$, we construct a stronger adversary $\mathcal{X}_2$ that schedules each component exactly once in each round, as follows: component α is in $\mathcal{X}_2(t)$ if and only if α is in $\mathcal{X}_1(t)$ and t is the first step in the current round such that α is in $\mathcal{X}_1(t)$. We next construct an adversary $\mathcal{X}_3$ that is stronger than $\mathcal{X}_2$ such that each round of $\mathcal{X}_3$ consists of scheduling the components in the following order: first all edges of the form $(i, i-1)$ in any order, then all the nodes in any order, and finally all edges of the form $(i, i+1)$ in any order.

By the definition of $\mathcal{X}_2$, the number of rounds taken by $\mathcal{A}$ against $\mathcal{X}_1$ is at most that taken by $\mathcal{A}$ against $\mathcal{X}_2$. By the definition of $\mathcal{X}_3$, the number of rounds taken by $\mathcal{A}$ against $\mathcal{X}_3$ equals the number taken by $\mathcal{A}$ in the synchronous model, which is at most $2D(b)+n$ by Theorem 1. Moreover, it is easy to see that $\mathcal{X}_3$ can be constructed such that for any t, the number of rounds completed at the start of step t of $\mathcal{X}_3$ is at least half the number completed at the start of step t of $\mathcal{X}_2$. It thus follows from Lemma 5.4 that for $\mathcal{A}$, the number of rounds taken against $\mathcal{X}_1$ is at most twice the number taken against $\mathcal{X}_3$. Thus, the number of rounds taken by $\mathcal{A}$ to balance any initial token distribution b is at most $4D(b)+2n$.

The bounds on the number of token and message transmissions follow as in the synchronous case. $\qquad\square$

6 Termination detection

Thus far, we have not given any mechanism for detecting termination. Fortunately, it is easy to modify our algorithm to efficiently detect termination. For instance, the following simple scheme results in only a constant factor blowup in the established time bounds. We create a dummy token that is initially at node 0. If a node i has the dummy token and if $w(i) = z(i) + x(i) - y(i)$, then i sends the dummy token to $i+1$. Let the height of the dummy token at any instant be defined as the number of tokens at the node holding the dummy token.

We detect termination on the basis of the following claim. The ring reaches a balanced state if and only if one of the following events occur: (i) the dummy token is passed around the n nodes of the ring without a change in its height, or (ii) a regular token (i.e., a non-dummy token) is passed around the n nodes of the ring. We now give a brief sketch of the proof of the preceding claim.

We first prove that if either event (i) or event (ii) occurs, then the ring is in a balanced state. If event (i) occurs, then the height of the dummy token remains the same through n transfers, implying that the ring is balanced. If event (ii) occurs, then a non-dummy token passes through the n nodes of the ring. Since the height of a token never increases, the height of the non-dummy token remains the same through n transfers. Therefore, the ring is balanced.

The proof of the other direction is easy. If the average number of tokens per node, μ, is an integer, then once the ring is balanced, the dummy token is passed around the ring without a change in the height. Thus, event (i) occurs. On the other hand, if μ is nonintegral, then once the ring is balanced, at least one token belonging to a node with $\lceil \mu \rceil$ tokens is passed around the n nodes of the ring. Thus, event (ii) occurs. Moreover, either event (i) or event (ii) occurs at most n steps (or rounds) after the ring is balanced and can be detected easily. Hence, the number of steps (resp., rounds) it takes for the algorithm to terminate is $O(n)$ more than the bound established in Theorem 1 (resp., Theorem 2).

7 Concluding remarks

In Sections 4 and 5, we obtained bounds on the time taken for $\mathcal{A}$ to converge to a balanced state. One unfortunate characteristic of the bounds is the additive linear term in the time complexity of $\mathcal{A}$ (see Theorems 1 and 2). We claim that such an additive linear term is unavoidable for any distributed algorithm. To observe this, consider two initial token distributions b and c that are defined as follows. In both distributions, node 0 has two tokens and every other node except node $\lfloor n/2 \rfloor$ has one token. In distribution b, $\lfloor n/2 \rfloor$ has zero tokens, while in c, $\lfloor n/2 \rfloor$ has one token. The optimal centralized algorithm for either distribution takes at most one step. However, any distributed algorithm takes at least linear time to terminate for at least one of the two distributions, since it takes linear time to distinguish between the two distributions.

Our model assumes that at most one token can be transmitted along any edge in any step. Our results can be easily generalized to models which allow more than one token, say c tokens, to be transmitted along an edge simultaneously. We can show that a suitable modification of $\mathcal{A}$ balances the ring to within $O(c)$ tokens in time which is optimal up to an additive $O(n)$ term.

Acknowledgments

A large part of this work was done while the authors were visiting the University of Paderborn, Germany. The authors would like to thank Friedhelm Meyer auf der Heide, Brigitte Oesterdiekhoff, and Rolf Wanka for their tremendous hospitality and several valuable discussions.

References

1. W. Aiello, B. Awerbuch, B. Maggs, and S. Rao. Approximate load balancing on dynamic and asynchronous networks. In *Proceedings of the 25th Annual ACM Symposium on Theory of Computing*, pages 632–641, May 1993.
2. E. Arjomandi, M. J. Fischer, and N. A. Lynch. Efficiency of synchronous versus asynchronous distributed systems. *Journal of the ACM*, 30:449–456, 1983.
3. A. Arora and M. Gouda. Load balancing: An exercise in constrained convergence. In J-M. Hélary and M. Raynal, editors, *Proceedings of the 9th International Workshop on Distributed Algorithms*, Lecture Notes in Computer Science, volume 972, pages 183–197. Springer-Verlag, 1995.
4. H. Attiya and M. Mavronicolas. Efficiency of semi-synchronous versus asynchronous networks. *Mathematical Systems Theory*, 27:547–571, 1994.
5. H. Attiya, M. Snir, and M. Warmuth. Computing on an anonymous ring. *Journal of the ACM*, 35:845–875, 1988.
6. B. Awerbuch. Complexity of network synchronization. *Journal of the ACM*, 32:804–823, 1985.
7. B. Awerbuch, L. Cowen, and M. Smith. Efficient asynchronous distributed symmetry breaking. In *Proceedings of the 26th Annual ACM Symposium on the Theory of Computing*, pages 214–223, 1994.

8. D. P. Bertsekas and J. N. Tsitsiklis. *Parallel and Distributed Computation: Numerical Methods*. Prentice-Hall, Englewood Cliffs, NJ, 1989.
9. E. Cohen. On the convergence span of greedy load balancing. *Information Processing Letters*, 52:181–182, 1994.
10. G. Cybenko. Dynamic load balancing for distributed memory multiprocessors. *Journal of Parallel and Distributed Computing*, 2:279–301, 1989.
11. X. Deng, H. N. Liu, L. Long, and B. Xiao. Competitive analysis of network load balancing. *Journal of Parallel and Distributed Computing*, 40:162–172, 1997.
12. D. Eager, D. Lazowska, and J. Zahorjan. Adaptive load sharing in homogeneous distributed systems. *IEEE Transactions on Software Engineering*, 12:662–675, 1986.
13. P. Fizzano, D. Karger, C. Stein, and J. Wein. Job scheduling in rings. In *Proceedings of the 6th Annual ACM Symposium on Parallel Algorithms and Architectures*, pages 210–219, June 1994.
14. G. Frederickson and N. Lynch. Electing a leader in a synchronous ring. *Journal of the ACM*, 34:98–115, 1987.
15. B. Ghosh, F. T. Leighton, B. M. Maggs, S. Muthukrishnan, C. G. Plaxton, R. Rajaraman, A. W. Richa, R. E. Tarjan, and D. Zuckerman. Tight analyses of two local load balancing algorithms. In *Proceedings of the 27th Annual ACM Symposium on Theory of Computing*, pages 548–558, May 1995.
16. A. Heirich and S. Taylor. A parabolic theory of load balance. Technical Report Caltech-CS-TR-93-22, Caltech Scalable Concurrent Computation Lab, March 1993.
17. D. Hutchinson. *Local Area Network Architectures*. Addison-Wesley, 1988.
18. L. Lamport and N. Lynch. Distributed computing: Models and methods. In J. van Leeuwen, editor, *Handbook of Theoretical Computer Science, Volume B: Formal Models and Semantics*, pages 1157–1199. Elsevier/MIT Press, 1990.
19. F. T. Leighton. *Introduction to Parallel Algorithms and Architectures: Arrays, Trees, and Hypercubes*. Morgan-Kaufmann, San Mateo, CA, 1991.
20. N. Lynch and M. Fisher. On describing the behavior and implementation of distributed systems. *Theoretical Computer Science*, 13:17–43, 1981.
21. F. Meyer auf der Heide, B. Oesterdiekhoff, and R. Wanka. Strongly adaptive token distribution. *Algorithmica*, 15:413–427, 1996.
22. D. Peleg and E. Upfal. The generalized packet routing problem. *Theoretical Computer Science*, 53:281–293, 1987.
23. D. Peleg and E. Upfal. The token distribution problem. *SIAM Journal on Computing*, 18:229–243, 1989.
24. C. G. Plaxton. Load balancing, selection, and sorting on the hypercube. In *Proceedings of the 1st Annual ACM Symposium on Parallel Algorithms and Architectures*, pages 64–73, June 1989.
25. A. Tanenbaum. *Computer Networks*. Prentice Hall, 1989.
26. A. N. Tantawi and D. Towsley. Optimal static load balancing in distributed computer systems. *Journal of the ACM*, 32:445–465, 1985.
27. R. D. Williams. Performance of dynamic load balancing algorithms for unstructured mesh calculations. *Concurrency: Practice and Experience*, 3:457–481, 1991.

Performing Tasks on Restartable
Message-Passing Processors[*]

Bogdan S. Chlebus[1] and Roberto De Prisco[2] and Alex A. Shvartsman[3]

[1] Instytut Informatyki, Uniwersytet Warszawski,
Banacha 2, 02-097 Warszawa, Poland.
chlebus@mimuw.edu.pl
[2] Laboratory for Computer Science, Massachusetts Institute of Technology,
545 Technology Square NE43-368, Cambridge, MA 02139, USA.
robdep@theory.lcs.mit.edu
[3] Department of Computer Science and Engineering, University of Connecticut,
191 Auditorium Road, U-155, Storrs, CT 06269, USA.
aas@eng2.uconn.edu

Abstract. This work presents new algorithms for the "Do-All" problem that consists of performing t tasks reliably in a message-passing synchronous system of p fault-prone processors. The algorithms are based on an aggressive coordination paradigm in which multiple coordinators may be active as the result of failures. The first algorithm is tolerant of $f < p$ stop-failures and it does not allow restarts. It has the available processor steps complexity $S = O((t + p \log p / \log \log p) \cdot \log f)$ and the message complexity $M = O(t + p \log p / \log \log p + f \cdot p)$. Unlike prior solutions, our algorithm uses redundant broadcasts when encountering failures and, for large f, it has better S complexity. This algorithm is used as the basis for another algorithm which tolerates any pattern of stop-failures *and restarts*. This new algorithm is the first solution for the Do-All problem that efficiently deals with processor restarts. Its available processor steps complexity is $S = O((t + p \log p + f) \cdot \min\{\log p, \log f\})$, and its message complexity is $M = O(t + p \cdot \log p + f \cdot p)$, where f is the number of failures.

1 Introduction

The problem of performing t tasks reliably and in parallel using p processors is one of the fundamental problems in distributed computation. This problem, which we call Do-All, was considered for the synchronous message-passing model

---

[*] This work was supported by the following contracts: ARPA N00014-92-J-4033 and F19628-95-C-0118, NSF 922124-CCR, ONR-AFOSR F49620-94-1-01997, and DFG-Graduiertenkolleg "Parallele Rechnernetzwerke in der Produktionstechnik" ME 872/4-1, DFG-SFB 376 "Massive Parallelität: Algorithmen, Entwurfsmethoden, Anwendungen". The research of the third author was substantially done at the Massachusetts Institute of Technology. The research of the first and the third authors was partly done while visiting Heinz Nixdorf Institut, Universität-GH Paderborn.

by Dwork, Halpern and Waarts in their pioneering work [2]. They developed several efficient algorithms for this problem in the setting where the processors are subject to fail-stop (or crash) failures and where the tasks can be performed using the *at-least-once* execution semantics (i.e., the tasks either are or can be made idempotent). In the setting of [2], the cost of local computation, whether performing low-level administrative tasks or idling, is considered to be negligible compared to the costs of performing each of the t tasks.

In solving Do-All, Dwork, Halpern and Waarts define the *effort* of an algorithm as the sum of the work complexity (i.e., the number of tasks executed, counting multiplicities) and message complexity (i.e., the number of messages used). This approach to efficiency does not account for any steps spent by processors waiting for messages or time-outs. This allows algorithm optimizations which keep the number of messages small, because processors can afford to wait to obtain sufficient information by not receiving messages in specific time intervals.

De Prisco, Mayer and Yung also consider the Do-All problem without processor restarts in their study [1]. Their goal is the development of fast and message-efficient algorithms. The work measure they consider is the available processor steps S (introduced by Kanellakis and Shvartsman [6]). This measure accounts for *all* steps taken by the processors, that is, the steps involved in performing the Do-All tasks and any other computation steps taken by the processors. Optimization of S leads to fast algorithms whose performance degrades gracefully with failures. The communication efficiency is gauged using the standard message complexity measure. The authors successfully pursue algorithmic efficiency in terms of what they call the *lexicographic optimization* of complexity measures. This means firstly achieving efficient work, then efficient communication complexity.

A similar approach to efficiency is pursued by Galil, Mayer and Yung [3] who also derive a very efficient Do-All solution for stop-failures.

Our contributions. In this paper we solve the Do-All problem in the setting where the p processors are subject to dynamic stop-failures *and restarts*. The complexity concerns in this paper follow the criteria established in [1]. We seek algorithmic efficiency with respect to both the work, expressed as available processor steps S, and the communication, expressed as the message complexity M. We want to minimize S, having M as small as possible.

We introduce an aggressive coordinator scheduling paradigm that allows multiple coordinators to be active concurrently. Because multiple coordinators are activated only in response to failures, our algorithms achieve efficiency in S and M.

It is not difficult to formulate trivial solutions to Do-All in which each processor performs each of the t tasks. Such solutions have work $\Omega(t \cdot (p+r))$, where r is the number of restarts, and they do not require any communication. Thus work-efficient solutions need to trade messages for work. Our solution is the first non-trivial efficient algorithm tolerant of stop-failures and restarts determined by the the worst-case omniscient adversary.

En route to the solution for restartable processors we introduce a new algorithm for the Do-All problem without restarts. This algorithm, that we call "algorithm AN" (Algorithm No-restart), is tolerant of $f < p$ stop-failures. It has available processor steps complexity[4] $S = O((t + p \log p / \log \log p) \cdot \log f)$ and message complexity $M = O(t + p \log p / \log \log p + f \cdot p)$.

Algorithm AN is the basis for our second algorithm, called "algorithm AR" (Algorithm with Restarts), which tolerates any number of stop-failures and restarts. Algorithm AR is the *first* such solution for the Do-All problem. Its available processor steps complexity is $S = O((t + p \log p + f) \cdot \min\{\log p, \log f\})$, and its message complexity is $M = O(t + p \cdot \log p + f \cdot p)$, where f is the number of failures.

Our algorithm AN is more efficient in terms of S than the algorithms of [1] and [3] when f, p and t are comparable; the algorithm also has efficient message complexity. Both algorithm AN and algorithm AR come within a $\log f$ (and $\log p$) factor of the lower bounds [6] for any algorithms that balance loads of surviving processors in each constant-time step. We achieve this by deploying an aggressive processor coordination strategy, in which more than one processor may assume the role of the *coordinator*, the processor whose responsibility is to ensure the progress of the computation. This approach is suggested by the observation that algorithms with only one coordinator cannot efficiently cope with restarts. Indeed the real advantage of this approach is that it can be naturally extended to deal with processor failures and restarts, with graceful deterioration of performance.

The improvements in S, however, come at a cost. Both of our algorithms assume reliable multicast [4]. Prior solutions do not make this assumption, although they do not solve the problem of processor restarts. The availability of reliable broadcast simplifies solutions for non-restartable processors, but dealing with processor restarts remains a challenge even when such broadcast is available. There are several reasons for considering solutions with reliable multicasts. First of all, in a distributed setting where processors cooperate closely, it becomes increasingly important to assume the ability to perform efficient and reliable broadcast or multicast. This assumption might not hold for extant WANs, but it is true for broadcast LANs (e.g., Ethernet and bypass rings). The availability of hardware-assisted broadcast makes the cost of using the broadcast communication comparable to the cost of sending a single point-to-point message. Note however that we are using a conservative cost measure which assumes that the cost of a multicast is proportional to the number of recipients. Secondly, by separating the concerns between the reliability of processors and the underlying communication medium, we are able to formulate solutions at a higher level of modularity so that one can take advantage of efficient reliable broadcast algorithms (cf. [4]) without altering the overall algorithmic approach. Lastly, our approach presents a new venue for optimizing Do-All solutions and for beating the $\Omega(t + (f + 1) \cdot p)$ lower bound of stage-checkpointing algorithms [1].

---

[4] All logarithms are to the base 2; the expression "log f" stands for 1 when $f < 2$ and $\log_2 f$ otherwise.

Review of prior work. Dwork, Halpern and Waarts [2] developed the first algorithms for the Do-All problem. One algorithm presented by the authors (protocol $\mathcal{B}$) has effort $O(t + p\sqrt{p})$, with work contributing the cost $O(t + p)$ towards the effort, and message complexity contributing the cost $O(p\sqrt{p})$. The running time of the algorithm is $O(t+p)$. Another algorithm in [2] (protocol $\mathcal{C}$) has effort $O(t + p\log p)$. This includes optimal work of $O(t + p)$, message complexity of $O(p\log p)$, and time $O(p^2(t + p)2^{t+p})$. Thus the reduction in message complexity is traded-off for a significant increase in time. The third algorithm (protocol $\mathcal{D}$) obtains work optimality and is designed for maximum speed-up, which is achieved with a more aggressive checkpointing strategy, thus trading-off time for messages. The message complexity is quadratic in p for the fault-free case, and in the presence of a failure pattern of $f < p$ failures, the message complexity degrades to $\Theta(f \cdot p^2)$.

De Prisco, Mayer and Yung [1] present an algorithm which has the available processor steps $O(t + (f + 1)p)$ and message complexity $O((f + 1)p)$. The available processor steps and communication efficiency approach requires keeping all the processors busy doing tasks, simultaneously controlling the amount of communication. De Prisco, Mayer and Yung were the first to report results on Do-All algorithms in the fail-stop case using this efficiency approach. To avoid the quadratic upper bound for S substantial processing slackness ($p \ll t$) is assumed. In [1] a lower bound of $\Omega(t + (f + 1)p)$ for algorithms that use the stage-checkpointing strategy is proved. However there are algorithmic strategies that have the potential of circumventing the quadratic bound. Consider the following scenarios. In the first scenario we have $t = o(p)$, $f > p/2$, and the algorithm assigns all tasks to every processor. Then $S = O(p \cdot t) = o(t + (f + 1) \cdot p)$, because $f \cdot p = \Theta(p^2)$. This naïve algorithm has a quadratic work performance for $p = O(t)$. In the second example assume that the three quantities p, t and f are of comparable magnitude. Consider the algorithm in which all the processors are coordinators, work is interleaved with communication, and the outstanding work is evenly allocated among the live processors based on their identifiers. The work allocation is done after each round of exchanging messages about which processors are still available and which tasks have been successfully performed. One can show that $S = O(p \cdot \log p/\log\log p)$. This bound is $o(t + (f + 1) \cdot p)$ for $f > p/2$ and $t = p$. Unfortunately the number of messages exchanged is more than quadratic, and can be $\Omega(p^2 \cdot \log p/\log\log p)$. These examples suggest a possibility of improvement of the bound $S = O(t + (f + 1)p)$, however the simple algorithms discussed above have either the available processor steps quadratic in p, or the number of messages more than quadratic in p in the case when p, t and f are of the same order. One interesting result of our paper is showing that an algorithm can be developed which has both the available processor steps which is always subquadratic, and the number of messages which is quadratic only for f comparable to p, even with restarts.

The algorithm in [1] is designed so that at each step there is at most one coordinator; if the current coordinator fails then the next available processor takes over, according to a time-out strategy. Having a single coordinator helps to bound the number of messages, but a drawback of such approach is that any protocol with at most one active coordinator is bound to have $S = \Omega(t + (f+1) \cdot p)$. Namely, consider the following behavior of the adversary: each coordinator is stopped immediately after it becomes one and before it sends any messages. This creates pauses of at least $O(1)$ steps, giving the $\Omega((f + 1) \cdot p)$ part. Eventually there remains only one processor which has to perform all the tasks, because it has never received any messages, this gives the remaining $\Omega(t)$ part. A related lower-bound argument for stage-checkpointing strategies is formally presented in [1]. Moreover, when processor restarts allowed, any algorithm that relies on a single coordinator for information gathering might not terminate (the adversary can always kill the current coordinator, keeping alive all the other processors so that no progress is made).

Another important algorithm was developed by Galil, Mayer and Yung [3]. Working in the context of Byzantine agreement with stop-failures (for which they establish a message-optimal solution), they improved the message complexity of [1] to $O(f \cdot p^\varepsilon + \min\{f + 1, \log p\}p)$, for any positive ε, while achieving the available processor steps complexity of $O(t + (f + 1) \cdot p)$.

The Do-All problem for the shared-memory model of computation, where it is called *Write-All*, was introduced and studied by Kanellakis and Shvartsman [6, 7]. Parallel computation using the iterated Do-All paradigm is the subject of several subsequent papers, most notably the work of Kedem, Palem and Spirakis [8], Martel, Park and Subramonian [11] and Kedem, Palem, Rabin and Raghunathan [9].

Kanellakis, Michailidis and Shvartsman [5] developed a technique for controlling redundant concurrent access to shared memory in algorithms with processor stop-failures. This is done with the help of a structure they call *processor priority tree*. In this work we use a similar structure in the qualitatively different message-passing setting. Furthermore, we are able to use our structure with restartable processors.

The structure of the rest of the paper is as follows. Section 2 contains definitions and gives a high-level view of the algorithms. Section 3 includes the presentation of algorithm AN with a proof of its correctness and analysis. Section 4 gives algorithm AR with correctness and analysis. The final Section 5 concludes with remarks and future work. The optional appendix contains proof sketches.

2 Definitions and algorithmic preliminaries

In this section we describe the model of distributed computation, the failure models, and we introduce the main ideas underlying our algorithms.

2.1 Model

We consider a distributed system consisting of a set $\mathcal{P}$ of p processors. Processors communicate only by message passing at the level of abstraction of the *network layer*, i.e., any processor can send messages to any other processor and the contents of messages are not corrupted. We assume that the set $\mathcal{P}$ is fixed and is known to all processors in $\mathcal{P}$. Processors have unique identifiers (PIDs) and the set of PIDs is totally ordered. The distributed system is synchronous and we assume that there is a global clock available to all the processors. Between each two consecutive clock ticks a processor takes a *step* during which the processor can receive messages, perform some local computation and send messages. For the sake of clarity of presentation we think of a step as further subdivided into three substeps: during the first one a processor receives messages sent to it during the previous step, during the second substep a processor performs some local computation, and during the third substep a processor may send some messages. We refer to these substeps as the *receive* substep, the *compute* substep and the *send* substep.

We define a *task* to be a computation that can be performed by any processor in unit time. Tasks are uniquely identified by their UIDs and the set of UIDs is totally ordered. Our distributed system has to perform t tasks with UIDs in the set $\mathcal{T}$ ($t = |\mathcal{T}|$). The tasks are *idempotent*, i.e., each can be performed using the *at-least-once* execution semantics. Initially, the set $\mathcal{T}$ of tasks is known to all the processors. A task can be performed during the compute substep together with some local computation.

We consider two processor failure models: the *fail-stop* model in which processors do not restart after a failure, and the *fail-stop/restart* model in which restarts are allowed. In either model any processors may stop at any moment during the computation. Such a processor does not receive any messages and does not perform any computation. In the fail-stop/restart model, a processor can restart at any point after a failure. Upon a restart the state of the restarted processor is reset to an initial state, but the processor is aware of the restart. Any messages sent to a processor prior to its restart are lost. We assume that during a single step a stopped processor can restart at most once (e.g., a processor can restart in response to a clock tick).

We define an execution to be a sequence of *steps* during which some number of processors, in parallel, perform their send, compute and send substeps. Given a particular finite execution we denote by f the number of actual failures and by r the number of actual restarts. For the fail-stop model we assume that at least one processor operational at any time, i.e., for any finite prefix of any execution we have $r = 0$ and that $f < p$. In the fail-stop/restart model it is possible to relax the assumption that there exists an infallible processor. The natural generalization of the condition $f < p$ is: for any finite prefix of any execution we have $f < r+p$, i.e., during each step there is at least one operational processor. However this condition turns out to be too weak because it allows for all information about progress to be lost. For example, consider the scenario in which half of the processors are alive initially, they perform some tasks, and then they all crash while the other half restarts. This can be repeated forever without any globally known progress. Thus we require a stronger condition which assumes that for any two consecutive "phases", where a phase is some small constant number of consecutive steps specific to an algorithm, there is at least one processor that is operational through the two phases. This condition rules out *thrashing* adversaries that repeatedly stop and restart processors in such a way that any progress made by the computation is lost (like in the above example).

We assume that reliable multicast [4] is available. With reliable multicast a processor q can send a message to any set $P \subseteq \mathcal{P}$ of processors in its send substep. All processors in P that are operational during the entire following receive substep receive the message sent by q.

Our goal is to execute the tasks in $\mathcal{T}$ efficiently, where the efficiency is measured in terms of the *available processor steps* S and the *communication complexity*. The available processor steps S is defined by the stipulation that any processor being operational during a time step contributes a unit to S. Formally, if p_i is the number of processors operational during step i then $S = \sum_{i=1}^{\delta} p_i$, where δ is the last step of the computation. The communication complexity M is the number of point-to-point messages sent by processors. Each message sent from a processor q_1 to processor q_2 (whether faulty or not) contributes a unit to M. During each step a processor can send at most one message to any of the other $p-1$ processors. We are not concerned with the size of messages; however, using bit-string set encoding, each message sent contains $O(\max\{t, p\})$ bits.

2.2 Overview of algorithmic techniques

Computation proceeds in a loop, which is repeated until all the tasks are done. An iteration of the loop is referred to as a *phase*. A phase consists of some constant number of consecutive steps (we use three steps for each phase). Because any phase consists of a constant number of steps, the available processor steps is $S = O(\sum_{\ell} p_{\ell})$, where p_{ℓ} is the number of processors taking at least one step in phase ℓ and the sum is over all phases of the execution of the algorithm.

Since we consider stop-failures, a processor can be in one of the following two states: *live*, when it is operational, or *stopped*, otherwise. For a given execution, the number f (resp. r) of failures (resp. restarts) is defined as the number of processor state changes from live to stopped (resp. from stopped to live). These state changes may occur at any point in the course of a phase. Throughout the rest of the paper we use the following terminology.

Definition 1. A processor is said to be:

- "available in phase ℓ", if it is alive at the beginning of the phase;
- "active in phase ℓ", if it is available in phase ℓ and sends all the messages it is supposed to send in phase ℓ;
- "restarted in phase ℓ" if it is not available in phase $\ell - 1$ but it is available in phase ℓ;
- "failed in phase ℓ" if it is available in phase ℓ but it is not available in phase $\ell + 1$.

This definition does not take into account the cases where a processor restarts and then fails shortly after the restart, without becoming available for the subsequent phase. We refer to such restarts as *false restarts*.

A processor can be a *coordinator* of a given phase. All available processor (including coordinators) are also *workers* in a given phase. Coordinators are responsible for recording progress, while workers respond to coordinators' inquiries and perform tasks in response to coordinators' requests. There may be multiple coordinators in a given phase.

Coordinator appointments. The number of processors which assume the coordinator role is determined by the *martingale principle*: if none of the expected coordinators survive through the entire phase, then the number of coordinators for the next phase is doubled. This guarantees that there can be $O(\log p)$ consecutive phases without active coordinators unless all processors stop. There are $\Theta(\log p)$ such phases only if the number of failures is $\Omega(p)$. Whenever at least one coordinator is active in a phase, the number of coordinators for the next phase is reduced to one. Allowing an exponential rate of growth in the number of coordinators seems to be an expensive strategy but we show that it is viable and efficient.

Local views. Processors assume the coordinator role based on their local knowledge. During the computation each processor w maintains a sequence $L_w = \langle q_1, q_2, ..., q_k \rangle$ of PIDs of potentially available processors. We call such list a *local view*, and we let $P_w = \{q_1, q_2, ..., q_k\}$ to be the set of PIDs in L_w. The PIDs in L_w are partitioned into *layers* consisting of consecutive PIDs: $L_w = \langle q_1, q_2, ..., q_k \rangle = \langle \Lambda^0, \Lambda^1, \Lambda^2, ..., \Lambda^{j_k} \rangle^5$. When $\Lambda^0 = \langle q_1 \rangle$ the layered structure can be visualized in terms of a complete binary tree rooted at processor q_1, where nodes are placed from left to right with respect to the linear order given by L_w; thus, in a tree-like layered structure, layer Λ^0 consists of processor q_1, layer Λ^i consists of 2^i consecutive processors starting at processor q_{2^i} and ending at processor $q_{2^{i+1}-1}$ (see Figure 1).

Layer Λ^0							5							
Layer Λ^1				17					12					
Layer Λ^2		14		1			16			7				
Layer Λ^3	15	9	10	11		3	13		4	8				
Layer Λ^4	6	2												

Fig. 1. An example showing the layered structure with processors $\langle 5, 17, 12, 14, 1, 16, 7, 15, 9, 10, 11, 3, 13, 4, 8, 6, 2 \rangle$.

The local view is used to implement the martingale principle of appointing coordinators as follows. Let $L_{\ell,w} = \langle \Lambda^0, \Lambda^1, \Lambda^2, ..., \Lambda^{j_k} \rangle$ be the local view of worker w at the beginning of phase ℓ. Then processor w expects processors in layer Λ^0 to act as coordinators in phase ℓ; in the case layer Λ^0 is not active in phase ℓ, then processor w expects layer Λ^1 to be active in phase $\ell+1$; in general processor w expects layer Λ^i to be active in phase $\ell+i$ if all previous layers Λ^j, $\ell \leq j < \ell+i$, were not active in phase $\ell+j$. The local view is updated at the end of each phase.

---

[5] For sequences $L = \langle e_1, ..., e_n \rangle$ and $K = \langle d_1, ..., d_m \rangle$ we define $\langle L, K \rangle$ to be the sequence $\langle e_1, ..., e_n, d_1, ..., d_m \rangle$.

Example. Let the local view of a worker w for phase ℓ be the one in Figure 1. Then a possible view for processor w for phase $\ell + 2$ is the one in Figure 2. Processor w view may get to this view in phase $\ell + 2$, if processor 5 is not active in phase ℓ and processors 17, 12 are not active in phase $\ell + 1$. Subsequently, the local view of processor w can be the one in Figure 3. Processor w may get to this view in phase $\ell + 4$ if, for example, processors 14, 1, 16, 7 are not active in phase $\ell + 2$ and in phase $\ell + 3$ processors 15, 9, 11, 3, 13, 4 are active, processors 8 and 10 are failed and processors 1 and 16 are restarted.

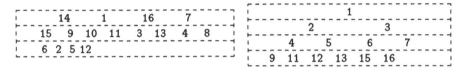

Fig. 2. The local view for phase $\ell + 2$.   **Fig. 3.** The local view for phase $\ell + 4$.

Allocating tasks and the load balancing rule. During the execution each processor w keeps its local information about the set D_w of units of tasks already performed, and the set P_w of live processors. Set D_w is always an underestimate of the set of tasks actually done and P_w is always an overestimate of the set of processors that are available. We denote by U_w the set of *unaccounted* tasks, i.e., whose done status is unknown to w. Sets U_w and D_w are related by $D_w = \mathcal{T} \setminus U_w$, where $\mathcal{T}$ is the set of all the tasks. Given a phase ℓ we use $P_{\ell,w}$, $U_{\ell,w}$ and $D_{\ell,w}$ to denote the values of the corresponding sets at the beginning of phase ℓ. Consider a phase ℓ and let w be a worker active in phase ℓ. Let i be the rank of processor w in the layered structure $L_{\ell,w}$. The *load balancing rule* tells worker w to execute the $(i \bmod |U_{\ell,w}|)^{th}$ unit of work.

Algorithm structure. At the beginning of phase ℓ processor w knows the local view $L_{\ell,w}$ (and thus the set $P_{\ell,w}$) and the set $U_{\ell,w}$ of unaccounted tasks (and thus the set $D_{\ell,w}$ of accounted tasks). Each processor performs one task according to the load balancing rule and attempts to report the execution of the task to any coordinator of phase ℓ. Any live coordinator c gathers reports from the workers, updates its information about $P_{\ell,c}$ and $U_{\ell,c}$ and broadcasts this new information causing local views to be reorganized. We will see that at the beginning of any phase ℓ all live processors have the same local view L_ℓ and the same set U_ℓ of unaccounted tasks and that accounted tasks have been actually executed. A new phase starts if U_ℓ is not empty.

3 No restarts – algorithm AN

In this section we define algorithm AN for the fail-stop model. Although solving Do-All using the machinery we assume is relatively easy, we develop algorithm AN as the basis for algorithm AR which solves the Do-All problem in the more general fail-stop/restart model.

Structure of a phase. A phase consists of 3 steps.

S1. The receive substep is not used. In the compute substep, any worker w performs a specific task u according to the load balancing rule. In the send substep the worker w sends a **report**(u) to any known coordinator.

S2. In the receive substep the coordinators gather **report** messages. For any coordinator c, let $u_c^1, ..., u_c^{k_c}$ be the set of task UIDs received. In the compute substep c sets $D_c \leftarrow D_c \cup \bigcup_{i=1}^{k_c}\{u_c^i\}$, and P_c to the set of worker PIDs from which c received **report** messages. In the send substep, coordinator c multicasts the message **summary**(D_c, P_c) to processors in P_c.

S3. During the receive substep **summary** messages are received by live processors. For any worker w, let $(D_w^1, P_w^1), ..., (D_w^{k_w}, P_w^{k_w})$ be the sets received in **summary** messages. In the compute step w sets $D_w \leftarrow D_w^i$ and $P_w \leftarrow P_w^i$ for an arbitrary $i \in \{1, ..., k_w\}$. The worker w also updates its local view L_w as described below. The send substep is not used.

Updating the local view. Initially (phase 0) the local view $L_{0,w}$ of any processor w is defined as the set of processors $\mathcal{P}$ structured in layers as a tree-like layered structure given in Section 2. Let us consider a generic phase ℓ and let the local view of processor w for phase ℓ be $L_{\ell,w} = \langle q_1, q_2, ..., q_k \rangle = \langle \Lambda^0, \Lambda^1, ..., \Lambda^{j_k} \rangle$. We distinguish two possible cases.

CASE 1. No coordinators are active in phase ℓ. Then the local view of processor w for phase $\ell + 1$ is $L_{\ell+1,w} = \langle \Lambda^1, ..., \Lambda^{j_k} \rangle$.

CASE 2. When at least one coordinator is active in phase ℓ, processor w receives messages from some coordinator in Λ^0. Processor w computes its set P_w as described in step S3 (we will see that all workers compute the same set P_w). The local view $L_{\ell+1,w}$ of w for phase $\ell + 1$ is the tree-like structure with processors in P_w ordered by their PIDs.

A generic phase is depicted in Figure 4 in Section 4 (for algorithm AN ignore the messages and steps of the restarted processors).

Correctness and efficiency. We first prove that algorithm AN correctly solves the Do-All problem. We start by showing that at the beginning of each phase every available processor has consistent knowledge of the ongoing computation. Then we prove safety (no live processor or undone task is forgotten) and progress properties (tasks execution) which imply the correctness of the algorithm.

Lemma 2 (AN:Consistency). *In any execution of algorithm* AN, *for any two processors* w, v *available in phase* ℓ, *we have that* $L_{\ell+1,w} = L_{\ell+1,v}$ *and that* $U_{\ell+1,w} = U_{\ell+1,v}$.

Because of the previous lemma, we can define $L_\ell = L_{\ell,w}$ for any w as the view at the beginning of phase ℓ, $P_\ell = P_{\ell,w}$ as the set of available processors, $D_\ell = D_{\ell,w}$ as the set of done tasks and $U_\ell = U_{\ell,w}$ as the set of unaccounted tasks at the beginning of phase ℓ.

Lemma 3 (AN:Safety1). *In any execution of algorithm* AN, *if a processor* w *is active in phase* $\ell - 1$ *then processor* w *belongs to* P_ℓ.

Lemma 4 (AN:Safety2). *In any execution of algorithm* AN, *if a task* u *has not been executed in phases* $1, 2, ..., \ell - 1$ *then* u *belongs to* U_ℓ.

We say that a phase ℓ is *attended* if at least one of the processor supposed to be coordinator according to the view L_ℓ is active during phase ℓ. Otherwise the phase is *unattended*.

Let us denote the set of all the attended phases by $A = \{\alpha_1, \alpha_2, ..., \alpha_\tau\}$, for $\alpha_1 < \alpha_2 < ... < \alpha_\tau$ and a given particular execution of algorithm AN. Let us denote by π_i the unattended phases in between the attended phases α_i and α_{i+1}. We refer to π_i as the ith (unattended) period; an unattended period can be empty. Hence the computation proceeds as follows: unattended period π_0, attended phase α_1, unattended period π_1, attended phase α_2, and so on. After the last attended phase α_τ, the algorithm terminates. Indeed since there are no other attended iterations it must be the case that there are no tasks left unaccounted after phase α_τ. We denote by p_i the cardinality of the set of available processors for phase i, i.e., $p_i = |P_i|$, and by u_i the cardinality of the set of unaccounted tasks for phase i, i.e., $u_i = |U_i|$. We let $u_1 = t$ and $u_{\tau+1} = 0$.

Lemma 5 (AN:Progress1). *In any execution of algorithm* AN, *for any attended phase ℓ we have that $u_\ell > u_{\ell+1}$.*

Lemma 6 (AN:Progress2). *In any execution of algorithm* AN, *any unattended period consists of at most $\log f$ phases.*

Theorem 7 (AN:Correctness). *In any execution of algorithm* AN *such that $f < p$, i.e., at least one processor survives, the algorithm terminates and all the units of work are performed.*

To assess S we consider separately all the attended phases and all the unattended phases of the execution. Let S_a be the part of S spent during all the attended phases and S_u be the part of S spent during all the unattended phases. Hence S is $S_a + S_u$.

The following lemma uses the construction by Martel [10, 6].

Lemma 8. *In any execution of algorithm* AN, *$S_a = O(t + p \log p / \log \log p)$.*

Lemma 9. *In any execution of algorithm* AN, *$S_u = O(S_a \cdot \log f)$.*

Theorem 10. *In any execution of algorithm* AN, *the available processor steps is $S = O(\log f \cdot (t + p \log p / \log \log p))$.*

Thus the work of algorithm AN is within a $\log f$ (and hence also $\log p$) factor of the lower bound of $\Omega(t + p \log p / \log \log p)$ [6] for any algorithm that performs tasks by balancing loads of surviving processors in each time step.

For each attended phase $\alpha_i \in A$, let d_i be some distinguished active coordinator, we refer to d_i as the *designated coordinator* of phase α_i. Let M_{d_i} be the number of messages sent or received in phase α_i by d_i. We denote by $M_d = \sum_{i=1}^\tau M_{d_i}$ the number of messages sent and received by the designated coordinators during all the attended phases. Let M_f be the number of all other messages, i.e., both the messages sent in unattended periods and the messages sent and received in attended phases by the non-designated coordinators.

Lemma 11. *In any execution of algorithm* AN, *$M_d = O(S_a)$.*

Lemma 12. *In any execution of algorithm* AN, *$M_f = O(f \cdot p)$.*

Theorem 13. *In any execution of algorithm* AN, *the number of messages sent is $M = O(t + p \log p / \log \log p + f \cdot p)$.*

4 Stop-failures and restarts – algorithm AR

In this section we describe algorithm AR which solves Do-All in the model of stop failures with restarts. This algorithm is obtained by modifying algorithm AN. The condition that the number of failures is $f < r+p$ provides the condition analogous to $f < p$ of the fail-stop model.

Algorithm AR is similar to algorithm AN; the difference is that there are added messages to handle the restart of processors. A stopped processor q may become live at any moment. At the moment of the restart, processor q has the initial information about the set $\mathcal{P}$ of processors and the set $\mathcal{T}$ of tasks but no information about the ongoing computation.

The steps S1, S2 and S3 in the phase in algorithm AR are similar to those of algorithm AN. After the restart, processor q broadcasts $\texttt{restart}(q)$ messages in the send substep of each step until it receives a response. Processors receiving such messages, ignore them if these messages are not received by a certain point within a phase. Thus we can imagine that a restarted processor q broadcasts a $\texttt{restart}(q)$ in step S1 of a phase ℓ. This message is then received by all the live and restarted processors of that phase, and, as we will see shortly, processor q is re-integrated in the view for the phase $\ell + 1$. Moreover processor q needs to be informed about the status of the ongoing computation. Hence all the processors who have been live since the start of S1 send an $\texttt{info}(U_\ell, L_\ell)$ to such q with the set U_ℓ of unaccounted tasks and the local view L_ℓ.

Structure of a phase ℓ. (See Figure 4.)

S1. The receive substep is not used. In the compute substep any worker w performs a specific task u according to the load balancing rule. In the send substep w sends a $\texttt{report}(u)$ to any known coordinator. Any restarted processor q broadcasts the $\texttt{restart}(q)$ message informing all live processors of its restart.

S2. In the receive step the coordinators gather $\texttt{report}$ messages and all live processors gather $\texttt{restart}$ messages. Let R be the set of processors that sent a $\texttt{restart}$ message. For any coordinator c, let $u_c^1, ..., u_c^k$ be the set of task UIDs received. In the compute substep c sets $D_c \leftarrow D_c \cup \bigcup_{i=1}^{k_c}\{u_c^i\}$ and P_c to be the set of workers from which c received $\texttt{report}$ messages. In the send substep, coordinator c multicasts the message $\texttt{summary}(D_c, P_c)$ to the available and restarted processors. Any available processor also sends the message $\texttt{info}(U_\ell, L_\ell)$ to processors in R.

S3. Restarted processors in R receive $\texttt{info}(U_\ell, L_\ell)$ messages. A restarted processor q sets $L_q \leftarrow L_\ell$ and $U_q \leftarrow U_\ell$. Let $(D_w^1, P_w^1), ..., (D_w^{k_w}, P_w^{k_w})$ be the sets received in $\texttt{summary}$ messages by processor w which received such messages. Processor w sets $D_w \leftarrow D_w^i$ and $P_w \leftarrow P_w^i$ for an arbitrary $i \in 1, ..., k$ and $U_w \leftarrow \mathcal{T} \setminus D_w$. Each processor w updates its local view L_w as described below. The send substep is not used.

Layered structure reorganization. Initially (phase 0) the local view $L_{0,w}$ of any processor w is defined as the set of processors $\mathcal{P}$ structured in layers as a tree-like layered structure given in Section 2. Let us consider a generic phase

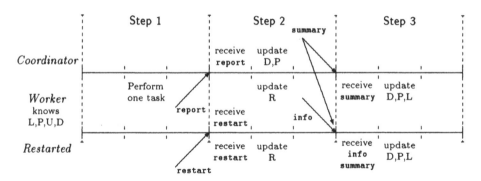

Fig. 4. A phase of algorithm AR (for algorithm AN ignore restarts).

ℓ and let the local view of processor w for phase ℓ be $L_{\ell,w} = \langle q_1, q_2, ..., q_k \rangle = \langle \Lambda^0, \Lambda^1, ..., \Lambda^{j_k} \rangle$. We distinguish three possible cases.

CASE 1. In phase ℓ no coordinator is active and no processor restarts. Then the algorithm proceeds exactly as in the no restart case: the local view of processor w for phase $\ell + 1$ is $L_{\ell+1,w} = \langle \Lambda^1, ..., \Lambda^{j_k} \rangle$.

CASE 2. In phase ℓ no coordinator is active but some processors restart. Let R^ℓ be the set of restarted processors who succeed in sending the **restart** messages. Let R' be the set of processors of R^ℓ that are not already in the local view $L_{\ell,w}$. Let $\langle R' \rangle$ be the processors in R' ordered according to their PIDs. The local view for the next phase is $L_{\ell+1,w} = \langle \Lambda^1, ..., \Lambda^{j_k} \rangle \oplus \langle R' \rangle$. The operator $\oplus$ places processors of R', in the order $\langle R' \rangle$, into the last layer Λ^{j_k} till this layer contains exactly the double of the processors of layer Λ^{j_k-1} and possibly adds a new layer Λ^{j_k+1} to accommodate the remaining processors of $\langle R' \rangle$. That is, newly restarted processors which are not yet in the view, are appended at the end of the old layered structure. Notice that restarted processors which receive **info** messages know the old view L_ℓ.

CASE 3. In phase ℓ there are both active coordinators and restarted processors. Since there are active coordinators, **summary** messages are received by available, live and restarted processors. Processor w sets P_w as described in step 3; moreover processor w knows the set R'. The new layered structure $L_{\ell+1,w}$ for the next phase consists of all the processors in $P_w \cup R'$, ordered according to their PIDs and the layered structure is the tree-like layered structure.

Correctness and efficiency. The proof of correctness is similar to that used for algorithm AN. The definitions of terms and of S_a, S_u, M_d and M_c carry over.

Lemma 14 (AR:Consistency). *In any execution of algorithm AR, for any two processors w, v available in phase ℓ, we have that $L_{\ell+1,w} = L_{\ell+1,v}$ and that $U_{\ell+1,w} = U_{\ell+1,v}$.*

Lemma 15 (AR:Safety1). *In any execution of algorithm AR, if a processor w is active or restarted in phase $\ell - 1$, then processor w belongs to P_ℓ.*

Lemma 16 (AR:Safety2). *In any execution of algorithm AR, if a task u has not been executed in phases $1, 2, ..., \ell - 1$ then u belongs to U_ℓ.*

Lemma 17 (AR:Progress1). *In any execution of algorithm* AR, *for any attended phase ℓ we have that $u_\ell > u_{\ell+1}$.*

Lemma 18 (AR:Progress2). *In any execution of algorithm* AR, *any unattended period consists of at most $\min\{\log p, \log f\}$ phases.*

Theorem 19 (AR:Correctness). *In any execution of algorithm* AR *such that $f < r + p$ with at least one processor active in any two consecutive phases the algorithm terminates and all the units of work are performed.*

We next analyze the performance of algorithm AR in terms of the available processor steps S used and the number M of messages sent.

Lemma 20. *In any execution of algorithm* AR, $S_a = O(t + p \log p + f)$.

Lemma 21. *In any execution of algorithm* AR, $S_u = O(S_a + f) \cdot \min\{\log p, \log f\})$.

Theorem 22. *For any execution of algorithm* AR, $S = O((t + p \log p + f) \cdot \min\{\log p, \log f\})$.

For each attended phase $\alpha_i \in A$, let d_i (designated coordinator) be some specific active coordinator, and M_{d_i} denote the number of messages sent or received in phase α_i by d_i, with the exception of the **restart** messages. $M_d = \sum_{i=1}^{\tau} M_{d_i}$ is the total number of such messages.

Lemma 23. *In any execution of algorithm* AR, $M_d = O(S_a)$.

The remaining messages are categorized into three groups. M_c is the number of messages sent by non designated coordinators during the attended phases plus the number of messages sent in response to such coordinators. M_w is the the number of messages sent by all workers to the expected coordinators during the unattended phases. M_r is the number of messages sent and received by processors that restart during the computation.

Lemma 24. *In any execution of algorithm* AR, $M_c + M_w + M_r = O(f \cdot p)$.

Theorem 25. *In any execution of algorithm* AN, $M = O(t + p \cdot \log p + p \cdot f)$.

5 Discussion

We have considered the Do-All problem of performing t tasks on a distributed system of p fault-prone synchronous processors. We presented the first algorithm for the model with processor failures and restarts. Previous algorithms accommodated only stop-failures. Prior algorithmic approaches relied on the single coordinator paradigm in which the coordinator is elected for the time during which the progress of the computation depends on it. However this approach is not effective in the general model with processor restarts: an omniscient adversary can always stop the single coordinator while keeping alive all other processors thus preventing any global progress. In this paper we have used a novel multi-coordinator paradigm in which the number of simultaneous coordinators increases exponentially in response to coordinator failures. This approach enables effective Do-All solutions that accommodate processor restarts. Moreover, when there are no restarts, the performance of the algorithm is comparable to that of any known algorithm.

The fault-prone processors in our algorithms use reliable communication. It can be shown, for example, that with minor modifications, our algorithms remain correct and efficient even if worker-to-coordinator multicasts are not reliable. However coordinators still need to use reliable broadcast. A worthwhile research direction is to design algorithms which use our aggressive coordinator paradigm and unreliable communication.

Acknowledgments: We thank Moti Yung for several discussions of processor restart issues and for encouraging this direction of research.

References

1. R. De Prisco, A. Mayer, and M. Yung, "Time-Optimal Message-Efficient Work Performance in the Presence of Faults," in *Proc. 13th ACM Symposium on Principles of Distributed Computing*, 1994, pp. 161–172.
2. C. Dwork, J. Halpern, O. Waarts, "Performing Work Efficiently in the Presence of Faults", to appear in *SIAM J. on Computing*, prelim. vers. appeared as Accomplishing Work in the Presence of Failures in *Proc. 11th ACM Symposium on Principles of Distributed Computing*, pp. 91-102, 1992.
3. Z. Galil, A. Mayer, and M. Yung, "Resolving Message Complexity of Byzantine Agreement and Beyond," in *Proc. 36th IEEE Symposium on Foundations of Computer Science*, 1995, pp. 724–733.
4. V. Hadzilacos and S. Toueg, "Fault-Tolerant Broadcasts and Related Problems," in *Distributed Systems*, 2nd Ed., S. Mullender, Ed., Addison-Wesley and ACM Press, 1993.
5. P.C. Kanellakis, D. Michailidis, A.A. Shvartsman, "Controlling Memory Access Concurrency in Efficient Fault-Tolerant Parallel Algorithms", *Nordic J. of Computing*, vol. 2, pp. 146-180, 1995 (prel. vers. in *WDAG-7*, pp. 99-114, 1993).
6. P.C. Kanellakis and A.A. Shvartsman, "Efficient Parallel Algorithms Can Be Made Robust," *Distributed Computing*, vol. 5, pp. 201–217, 1992; prel. version in *Proc. of the 8th ACM Symp. on Principles of Distributed Computing*, 1989, pp. 211–222.
7. P.C. Kanellakis and A.A. Shvartsman, *Fault-Tolerant Parallel Computation*, ISBN 0-7923-9922-6, Kluwer Academic Publishers, 1997.
8. Z.M. Kedem, K.V. Palem, and P. Spirakis, "Efficient Robust Parallel Computations," *Proc. 22nd ACM Symp. on Theory of Computing*, pp. 138-148, 1990.
9. Z.M. Kedem, K.V. Palem, M.O. Rabin, A. Raghunathan, "Efficient Program Transformations for Resilient Parallel Computation via Randomization," in *Proc. 24th ACM Symp. on Theory of Comp.*, pp. 306-318, 1992.
10. C. Martel, personal communication, March, 1991.
11. C. Martel, R. Subramonian, and A. Park, "Asynchronous PRAMs are (Almost) as Good as Synchronous PRAMs," in *Proc. 32d IEEE Symposium on Foundations of Computer Science*, pp. 590-599, 1990.

Revisiting the Paxos Algorithm

Roberto De Prisco*, Butler Lampson, Nancy Lynch

MIT Laboratory for Computer Science
545 Technology Square NE43, Cambridge, MA 02139, USA.

Abstract. This paper develops a new I/O automaton model called the Clock General Timed Automaton (Clock GTA) model. The Clock GTA is based on the General Timed Automaton (GTA) of Lynch and Vaandrager. The Clock GTA provides a systematic way of describing timing-based systems in which there is a notion of "normal" timing behavior, but that do not necessarily always exhibit this "normal" behavior. It can be used for practical time performance analysis based on the stabilization of the physical system.

We use the Clock GTA automaton to model, verify and analyze the PAXOS algorithm. The PAXOS algorithm is an efficient and highly fault-tolerant algorithm, devised by Lamport, for reaching consensus in a distributed system. Although it appears to be practical, it is not widely known or understood. This paper contains a new presentation of the PAXOS algorithm, based on a formal decomposition into several interacting components. It also contains a correctness proof and a time performance and fault-tolerance analysis.

Keywords: I/O automata models, formal verification, distributed consensus, partially synchronous systems, fault-tolerance

1 Introduction

I/O automata are simple state machines with transitions labelled with named actions. They are suitable for describing asynchronous and partially synchronous distributed systems. The general timed automaton (GTA) model, introduced by Lynch and Vaandrager [12, 13, 14], has formal mechanisms to represent the passage of time and is suitable for modelling partially synchronous distributed systems. In a partially synchronous distributed system, processes take actions within ℓ time and messages are delivered within d time, for given constants ℓ and d. However these time bounds hold when the system exhibits a "normal" timing behavior. Real distributed systems are subject to failures that may cause a temporary abnormal timing behavior. Hence the above mentioned bounds of ℓ and d can be occasionally violated (timing failures). In this paper we develop an I/O automaton model, called the *Clock GTA*, which provides a systematic way of describing both the normal and the abnormal timing behaviors of a distributed system. The model is intended to be used for performance and fault-tolerance

---

* Contact author. E-mail: robdep@theory.lcs.mit.edu

analysis of practical distributed systems based upon the stabilization of the system. We use the Clock GTA to formally describe and analyze the PAXOS algorithm, devised by Lamport [8] to solve the consensus problem.

Reaching consensus is a fundamental problem in distributed systems. Given a distributed system in which each process starts with an initial value, to solve a consensus problem means to give a distributed algorithm that enables each process to eventually output a value of the same type as the input values, in such a way that three conditions, called *agreement, validity* and *termination,* hold. There are different definitions of the problem depending on what these conditions require. Distributed consensus has been extensively studied. A good survey of early results is provided in [7]. We refer the reader to [11] for a more recent treatment of consensus problems.

Real distributed systems are often partially synchronous systems subject to process, channel and timing failures and process recoveries. Any practical consensus algorithm needs to consider the above practical setting. Moreover the basic safety properties must not be affected by the occurrence of failures. Also, the performance of the algorithm must be good when there are no failures, while when failures occur, it is reasonable to not expect efficiency.

The PAXOS algorithm meets these requirements. The model considered is a partially synchronous distributed system where each process has a direct communication channel with each other process. The failures allowed are timing failures, loss, duplication and reordering of messages, and process stopping failures. Process recoveries are considered; some stable storage is needed. PAXOS is guaranteed to work safely, that is, to satisfy agreement and validity, regardless of process, channel and timing failures and process recoveries. When the distributed system stabilizes, meaning that there are no failures, nor process recoveries, and a majority of the processes are not stopped, for a sufficiently long time, termination is also achieved and the performance of the algorithm is good. In [8] a variation of PAXOS that considers multiple concurrent runs of PAXOS for reaching consensus on a sequence of values is also presented. We call this variation the MULTIPAXOS algorithm[2]. PAXOS has good fault-tolerance properties and when the system is stable it combines those fault-tolerance properties with the performance of an efficient algorithm, so that it can be useful in practice. In the original paper [8], the PAXOS algorithm is described as the result of discoveries of archaeological studies of an ancient Greek civilization. That paper contains also a proof of correctness and a discussion of the performance analysis. The style used for the description of the algorithm often diverts the reader's attention. Because of this, we found the paper hard to understand and we suspect that others did as well. Indeed the PAXOS algorithm, even though it appears to be a practical and elegant algorithm, seems not widely known or understood.

---

[2] PAXOS is the name of the ancient civilization studied in [8]. The actual algorithm is called the "single-decree synod" protocol and its variation for multiple consensus is called the "multi-decree parliament" protocol. We use the name PAXOS for the single-decree protocol and the name MULTIPAXOS for the multi-decree parliament protocol.

This paper contains a new, detailed presentation of the PAXOS algorithm, based on a formal decomposition into several interacting components. It also contains a correctness proof and a time performance and fault-tolerance analysis. The MULTIPAXOS algorithm is also described together with an application to data replication. The formal framework used for the presentation is provided by the Clock GTA.

The correctness proof uses automaton composition and invariant assertion methods. Composition is useful for representing a system using separate components. We provide a modular presentation of the PAXOS algorithm, obtained by decomposing it into several components. Each one of these components copes with a specific aspect of the problem. The correctness of each piece is proved by means of invariants, i.e., properties of system states that are always true in an execution.

The time performance and fault-tolerance analysis is conditional on the stabilization of the system behavior starting from some point in an execution. Using the Clock GTA we prove that when the system stabilizes PAXOS reaches consensus in $24\ell + 10n\ell + 13d$ time and uses $10n$ messages, where n is the number of processes. This performance is for a worst-case scenario. We also discuss the MULTIPAXOS protocol and provide a data replication algorithm using MULTIPAXOS. With MULTIPAXOS the high availability of the replicated data is combined with high fault tolerance.

Related work. The consensus algorithms of Dwork et al. [5] and of Chandra and Toueg [2] bear some similarities with PAXOS. The algorithm of [5] also uses rounds conducted by a leader, but the rounds are conducted sequentially, whereas in PAXOS a leader can start a round at anytime and multiple leaders are allowed. The strategy used in each round by the algorithm of [5] is different from the one used by PAXOS. The time analysis provided in [5] is conditional on a "global stabilization time" after which process response times and message delivery times satisfy the time assumptions. This is similar to our stabilized analysis. A similar time analysis, applied to the problem of reliable group communication, can be found in [6].

The algorithm of Chandra and Toueg is based on the idea of an abstract failure detector. It turns out that failure detectors provide an abstract and modular way of incorporating partial synchrony assumptions in the model of computation. One of the algorithms in [2] uses the failure detector $\diamond S$ which incorporates the partial synchrony considered in this paper. That algorithm is based on the rotating coordinator paradigm and as PAXOS uses majorities to achieve consistency. The performances of the Toueg and Chandra algorithm and of the PAXOS algorithm seem to be comparable.

Both the Chandra and Toueg algorithm and the Dwork et al. algorithm consider a distributed setting that does not allow process restarts and channel failures (however the Chandra and Toueg algorithm can be modified to work with loss of messages). The PAXOS algorithm tolerates process restarts and channel failures; this makes PAXOS more suitable in practice.

MULTIPAXOS can be easily used to implement a data replication algorithm.

In [10, 15] Liskov and Oki provide a data replication algorithm. It incorporates ideas similar to the ones used in PAXOS.

PAXOS bears some similarities with the standard three-phase commit protocol [17]. However the standard commit protocol requires a fixed leader while PAXOS does not.

In [9] Lampson provides a brief overview of the PAXOS algorithm together with key ideas for proving the correctness of the algorithm.

Cristian's *timed asynchronous model* [3] is very similar to the distributed setting considered in this paper. Our Clock GTA provides a formal way of modelling the stability property of the timed asynchronous model.

In [16] Patt-Shamir introduces a special type of GTA used for the clock synchronization problem. Our Clock GTA automaton considers only the local time; our goal is to model good timing behavior starting from some point on and thus we do not require synchronization of the local clocks.

2 Models

Our formal framework is provided by I/O automata models. I/O automata models are simple type of state machines suitable for describing asynchronous and partially synchronous distributed systems. We use the general timed automaton (GTA), model (see [11], Section 23.2). We introduce a new type of GTA, called *Clock GTA*. We assume that the reader is familiar with the GTA model; briefly, it is a labelled transition system model that includes a time-passage action $\nu(t)$ that represents the passage of (real) time t.

2.1 The Clock GTA model

The Clock GTA model provides a systematic way of describing systems that may exhibit timing failures for portions of their executions, but may behave nicely for other portions. The ability to talk about such changing is crucial for realistic performance fault-tolerance analysis of practical algorithms.

A Clock GTA is a GTA with a special component included in the state; this special variable is called *Clock* and it assumes values in the set of real numbers. The purpose of *Clock* is to model the local clock of the process. The only actions that are allowed to modify *Clock* are the time-passage actions $\nu(t)$. When a time-passage action $\nu(t)$ is executed, the *Clock* is incremented by an amount of time $t' \geq 0$ independent of the amount t of time specified by the time-passage action. Since the occurrence of the time-passage action $\nu(t)$ represents the passage of (real) time by the amount t, by incrementing the local variable *Clock* by any amount t' we are able to model the passage of (local) time by the amount t'. As a special case, we have that $t' = t$; in this case the local clock of the process is running at the speed of real time.

In the following and in the rest of the paper, we use the notation $s.x$ to denote the value of state component x in state s.

Definition 1. A time-passage step $(s_{k-1}, \nu(t), s_k)$ of a Clock GTA is called *regular* if $s_k.Clock - s_{k-1}.Clock = t$; it is called *irregular* if it is not regular.

Definition 2. A timed execution fragment α of a Clock GTA is called *regular* if all the time-passage steps of α are regular. It is called *irregular* if it is not regular, i.e., if at least one of its time-passage steps is irregular.

2.2 The distributed setting

We consider a complete network of n processes communicating by exchange of messages in a partially synchronous setting. Each process of the system is uniquely identified by its identifier $i \in \mathcal{I}$, where $\mathcal{I}$ is a totally ordered finite set of n identifiers, known by all processes. Each process of the system has a local clock. Local clocks may run at different speeds (though in general we expect them to run at the same speed as real time). We assume that a local clock is available also for channels; though this may seem somewhat strange, it is just a formal way to express the fact that a channel is able to deliver a given message within a fixed amount of time, by relying on some timing mechanism (which we model with the local clock). We use Clock GT automata to model both processes and channels. We assume that processes take actions within ℓ time and that messages are delivered within d time, for given constants ℓ and d. A *timing failure* is a violation of these time bounds. A timing failure can be modelled with an irregular time-passage step.

Processes. We allow process stopping failures and recoveries and timing failures. To formally model process stops and recoveries we model process i with a Clock GTA that has a special state component called $Status_i$ and two input actions Stop$_i$ and Recover$_i$. The state variable $Status_i$ reflects the current condition of process i and can be either **stopped** or **alive**. It is updated by actions Stop$_i$ and Recover$_i$. A process i is *alive* (resp. *stopped*) in a given state if in that state we have $Status_i =$ **alive** (resp. $Status_i =$ **stopped**). A process i is alive (resp. stopped) in a given execution fragment, if it is alive (resp. stopped) in all the states of the execution fragment.

Between a failure and a recovery a process does not lose its state. We remark that PAXOS needs only a small amount of stable storage; however, for simplicity, we assume that the entire state of a process is in a stable storage.

Channels. We consider unreliable channels that can lose and duplicate messages. Reordering of messages is allowed and it is not considered a failure. Timing failures are possible. Figure 1 shows the signature[3] of a Clock GT automaton CHANNEL$_{i,j}$ which models the channel from process i to process j. Channel failures are formally modelled as input actions Lose$_{i,j}$ (which deletes one of the message currently in the channel), and Duplicate$_{i,j}$ (which duplicates one of the message currently in the channel).

System stabilization. In the introduction we have pointed out that PAXOS satisfies termination when the system stabilizes. The definition of "nice" execution fragment given below captures the requirements needed to guarantee termination.

---

[3] The code of this automaton, as well as the code of the other automata we will see later, are omitted from this extended abstract and are deferred to the full paper. The full code can be found in [4].

Signature of CHANNEL$_{i,j}$

Input:	Send$(m)_{i,j}$, Lose$_{i,j}$, Duplicate$_{i,j}$
Output:	Receive$(m)_{i,j}$
Time-passage:	$\nu(t)$

Fig. 1. Automaton CHANNEL$_{i,j}$. The code is deferred to the full paper.

Definition 3. Given a distributed system, we say that an execution fragment α is *stable* if every process is either alive or stopped in α, no Lose$_{i,j}$ and Duplicate$_{i,j}$ actions occur in α and α is regular.

Definition 4. Given a distributed system, we say that an execution fragment α is *nice* if α is a stable execution fragment and a majority of the processes are alive in α.

The next lemma provides a basic property of CHANNEL$_{i,j}$.

Lemma 5. *In a stable execution fragment α of CHANNEL$_{i,j}$ beginning in a reachable state s and lasting for more than d time, we have that (i) all messages that in state s are in the channel are delivered by time d, and (ii) any message sent in α is delivered within time d of the sending, provided that α lasts for more than d time from the sending of the message.*

3 The consensus problem

In this section we formally define the consensus problem (we remark that several variations of the definition of the consensus problem have been considered in the literature). Each process i in the network receives as input an initial value v, provided by an external agent by means of an action Init$(v)_i$. We denote by V the set of possible initial values and, given a particular execution α, we denote by V_α the subset of V consisting of those values actually used as initial values in α, that is, those values provided by Init$(v)_i$ actions.

To solve the consensus problem means to give an algorithm that, for any execution α, satisfies

- **Agreement:** No two processes output different values in α.
- **Validity:** Any output value in α belongs to V_α.

and, for any admissible infinite execution α, satisfies

- **Termination:** If $\alpha = \beta\gamma$ and γ is a nice execution fragment and for each process i alive in γ an Init$(v)_i$ action occurred in α, then any process alive in γ eventually outputs a value.

The PAXOS algorithm solves the consensus problem defined above.

4 A failure detector and a leader elector

In this section we provide a failure detector algorithm and then we use it to implement a leader election algorithm. The failure detector and the leader elector we implement here are both sloppy, meaning that they are guaranteed to give reliable information on the system only in a stable execution. However, this is enough for implementing PAXOS.

Signature of DETECTOR$_i$

Input:	Receive$(m)_{j,i}$, Stop$_i$, Recover$_i$
Internal:	Check$(j)_i$
Output:	InformStopped$(j)_i$, InformAlive$(j)_i$, Send$(m)_{i,j}$
Time-passage:	$\nu(t)$

Fig. 2. Automaton DETECTOR for process i. The code is deferred to the full paper.

A failure detector. Figure 2 shows the signature of Clock GTA DETECTOR$_i$, which detects failures. Automaton DETECTOR$_i$ works by having each process constantly sending "Alive" messages to each other process and checking that such messages are received from other processes. The strategy used by DETECTOR$_i$ is a straightforward one. For this reason it is very easy to implement. The failure detector so obtained is not reliable in the presence of failures (Stop$_i$, Lose$_{i,j}$, irregular executions). However, in a stable execution fragment, automaton DETECTOR$_i$ is guaranteed to provide reliable information on stopped and alive processes.

A leader elector. It is easy to use a failure detector to elect a leader: actions InformStopped$(j)_i$ and InformAlive$(j)_i$ are used to update the current set of alive processes and a common rule to elect the leader is used (the alive process with the biggest identifier is elected leader). Figure 3 shows the signature of automaton LEADERELECTOR$_i$. We denote with S_{LEA} the system consisting of DETECTOR$_i$ and LEADERELECTOR$_i$ automata for each process $i \in \mathcal{I}$ and CHANNEL$_{i,j}$ for each $i, j \in \mathcal{I}$. Processes have a state variable *Leader* that contains the identifier of the current leader. Formally we consider a process i to be *leader* if *Leader$_i$* $= i$. This definition allows multiple or no leaders. In a state s, there is a *unique leader* if and only if there exist an alive process i such that $s.Leader_i = i$ and for all other alive processes $j \neq i$ it holds that $s.Leader_j = i$. The following lemma holds.

Signature of LEADERELECTOR$_i$

Input:	InformStopped$(j)_i$, InformAlive$(j)_i$, Stop$_i$, Recover$_i$
Output:	Leader$_i$, NotLeader$_i$

Fig. 3. Automaton LEADERELECTOR for process i. The code is deferred to the full paper.

The following lemma holds.

Lemma 6. *If an execution fragment α of S_{LEA}, starting in a reachable state and lasting for more than $4\ell + 2d$, is stable, then by time $4\ell + 2d$, there is a state occurrence s such that in state s and in all the states after s there is a unique leader.*

5 The PAXOS algorithm

PAXOS was devised a very long time ago (the most accurate information dates it back to the beginning of this millennium) but its discovery, due to Lamport, dates back only to 1989 [8]. In this section we provide a new and detailed description of PAXOS.

The core part of the algorithm is BASICPAXOS$_i$. In BASICPAXOS$_i$ processes try to reach a decision by leading what we call a round. A process leading a round is the leader of that round. DETECTOR$_i$ and LEADERELECTOR$_i$ are used to elect leaders. STARTERALG$_i$ makes the current leader start new rounds if necessary. The description of BASICPAXOS$_i$ is further subdivided into three components, namely BPLEADER$_i$, BPAGENT$_i$ and BPSUCCESS$_i$. We will prove (Theorem 13) that the system S_{PAX} ensures agreement and validity, and (Theorem 18) that S_{PAX} guarantees also termination within $24\ell + 10n\ell + 13d$, when the system executes a nice execution fragment. It is worth to remark that some automata need to be able to measure the passage of time, while others do not. For the latter, time bounds are used only for the analysis.

5.1 Automaton BASICPAXOS

We begin with an overview, then provide the code and the analysis.

Overview. The basic idea, which is the heart of the algorithm, is to propose values until one of them is accepted by a majority of the processes; that value is the final output value. Any process may propose a value by initiating a *round* for that value. The process initiating a round is said to be the *leader* of that round while all processes (including the leader itself) are said to be *agents* for that round. Since different rounds may be carried out concurrently (several leaders may concurrently initiate rounds), we need to distinguish them. Every round has a unique identifier. A *round number* is a pair (x, i) where x is a nonnegative integer and i is a process identifier. The set of round numbers is denoted by $\mathcal{R}$. A total order on elements of $\mathcal{R}$ is defined by $(x, i) < (y, j)$ iff $x < y$ or, $x = y$ and $i < j$. If $r < r'$ we say that round r *precedes* round r'. We remark that the ordering on the round numbers is not related to the actual time when rounds are started, i.e., a round with a bigger round number can be conducted before a round with a smaller round number.

Informally, the steps for a round are the following.

1. To initiate a round, the leader sends a "Collect" message to all agents[4].
2. An agent that receives a message sent in step 1 from the leader of the round, responds with a "Last" message giving its own information about rounds previously conducted. It also commits to not accept any previous round. If the agents is already committed for a round with a bigger round number then it just sends an "OldRound" message.

---

[4] Thus it sends a message also to itself. This helps in that we do not have to specify different behaviors for a process according to the fact that it is both leader and agent or just an agent. We just need to specify the leader behavior and the agent behavior.

3. Once the leader has gathered more than $n/2$ "Last" messages, it decides, according to some rules, the value to propose for its round and sends to all agents a "Begin" message. The set of processes from which the leader gathers information is called the *info-quorum* of the round. In order for the leader to be able to choose a value for the round it is necessary that initial values be provided. If no initial value is provided the leader must wait for an initial value before proceeding with step 3.

4. An agent that receives a message sent in step 3 from the leader of the round, responds with an "Accept" message by accepting the value proposed in the current round. If the agent is committed for a round with a bigger number then it just sends an "OldRound" message.

5. If the leader gets "Accept" messages from a majority of agents, then the round is successful and the leader sets its own output value to the value proposed in the round. The set of agents that accepts the value proposed by the leader is called the *accepting-quorum*.

Since a successful round implies that the leader of the round reaches a decision, after a successful round the leader needs to broadcast the reached decision.

The most important issue is about the values that leaders propose for their rounds. Indeed, since the value of a successful round is the output value of some processes, we must guarantee that the values of successful rounds are all equal in order to satisfy the agreement condition of the consensus problem. Agreement is guaranteed by choosing the values of new rounds exploiting the information about previous rounds from at least a majority of the processes so that, for any two rounds there is at least one process that participated in both rounds. In more detail, the leader of a round chooses the value for the round in the following way. In step 1, the leader asks for information and in step 2 every agent responds with the number of the latest round in which it accepted the value and the accepted value (or with nil if the agent has not yet accepted a value). Once the leader gets such information from a majority of the processes, which is the info-quorum of the round, it chooses the value for its round to be equal to the value of the latest round among all those it has heard from the agents in the info-quorum or with its initial value if all processes in the info-quorum were not involved in any previous round. Moreover, in order to keep consistency, if an agent tells the leader of a round r that the last accepted round is round r', $r' < r$, then implicitly the agent commits itself to not accept any other round r'', $r' < r'' < r$.

To end up with a decision value, rounds must be started until at least one is successful. BASICPAXOS$_i$ guarantees agreement and validity, however, it is necessary to make BASICPAXOS$_i$ start rounds to get termination. We deal with this problem in section 5.3.

The code. In order to describe BASICPAXOS$_i$ we provide three automata. One is called BPLEADER$_i$ and models the "leader" behavior of the process, another one is called BPAGENT$_i$ and models the "agent" behavior of the process and the third one is called BPSUCCESS$_i$ and it simply broadcasts a reached decision (this can be thought of as part of the leader behavior, though we have separated it since it is not part of a round). Automaton BASICPAXOS$_i$ is simply the composition of

---

Signature of BPLEADER$_i$

Input:	Receive$(m)_{j,i}$, $m \in \{$"Last", "Accept", "Success", "OldRound"$\}$
	Init$(v)_i$, NewRound$_i$, Stop$_i$, Recover$_i$, Leader$_i$, NotLeader$_i$
Internal:	Collect$_i$, GatherLast$_i$, Continue$_i$ GatherAccept$_i$, GatherOldRound$_i$
Output:	Send$(m)_{i,j}$, $m \in \{$"Collect", "Begin"$\}$
	BeginCast$_i$, RndSuccess$(v)_i$

Fig. 4. Automaton BASICPAXOS for process i. The code is deferred to the full paper.

BPLEADER$_i$, BPAGENT$_i$ and BPSUCCESS$_i$. Our code is "tuned" to work efficiently when there are no failures. Indeed messages for a given round are sent only once, that is, no attempt is made to try to cope with loss of messages and responses are expected to be received within given time bounds (we actual deal with this in Section 5.3). Other strategies to try to conduct a successful round even in the presence of some failures could be used. For example, messages could be sent more than once (to cope with the loss of some messages) or a leader could wait more than the minimum required time before starting a new round and abandoning the current one (starting rounds is dealt with in Section 5.3). We remark that in practice it is efficient to cope with some failures by, for example, re-sending messages.

Signature of BPAGENT$_i$

Input:	Receive$(m)_{j,i}$, $m \in \{$"Collect", "Begin"$\}$
	Init$(v)_i$, Stop$_i$, Recover$_i$
Internal:	LastAccept$_i$, Accept$_i$
Output:	Send$(m)_{i,j}$, $m \in \{$"Last", "Accept", "OldRound"$\}$

Fig. 5. Automaton BPAGENT for process i. The code is deferred to the full paper.

Figures 4 and 5 show the signature of, respectively, BPLEADER$_i$ and BPAGENT$_i$. We remark that BPSUCCESS$_i$ simply takes care of broadcasting a reached decision.

Messages. In this paragraph we describe the messages used for communication between the leader and the agents. The description assumes that i is the leader.

1. "Collect" messages, $m = (r,$"Collect"$)_{i,j}$. Starts round r.
2. "Last" messages, $m = (r,$"Last"$,r',v)_{j,i}$. Provides the last round r' accepted by the agent, and its value v. If the agent did not accept any previous round, then v is either nil or the initial value of the agent and r' is $(0,j)$.
3. "Begin" messages, $m = (r,$"Begin"$,v)_{i,j}$. Announces the value v of round r.
4. "Accept" messages, $m = (r,$"Accept"$)_{j,i}$. The agent accepts the value and commits for round r.
5. "Success" messages, $m = ($"Success"$,v)_{i,j}$. Announces the decision v.
6. "Ack" messages, $m =($"Ack"$)_{j,i}$. The agent received the decision.

7. "OldRound" messages, $m = (r,\text{"OldRound"},r')$. The agent is committed for round $r' > r$.

Partial Correctness. Let us define the system S_{BPX} to be the composition of system S_{LEA} and an automaton BASICPAXOS$_i$ for each process $i \in \mathcal{I}$. In this section we prove the partial correctness of S_{BPX}: in any execution of the system S_{BPX} agreement and validity are guaranteed. For these proofs, we augment the algorithm with a collection $\mathcal{H}$ of history variables. Each variable in $\mathcal{H}$ is an array indexed by the round number. For every round number r a history variable contains some information about round r. In particular the set $\mathcal{H}$ consists of:

Hleader$(r) \in \mathcal{I} \cup$ nil, initially nil (the leader of round r).
Hvalue$(r) \in V \cup$ nil, initially nil (the value for round r).
Hfrom$(r) \in \mathcal{R} \cup$ nil, initially nil (the round from which **Hvalue**(r) is taken).
Hinfquo(r), subset of $\mathcal{I}$, initially $\{\}$ (the info-quorum of round r).
Haccquo(r), subset of $\mathcal{I}$, initially $\{\}$ (the accepting-quorum of round r).
Hreject(r), subset of $\mathcal{I}$, initially $\{\}$ (processes committed to reject round r).

Next we give some definitions that we use in the proofs.

Definition 7. In any state of the system S_{BPX}, a round r is said to be *dead* if $|\text{Hreject}(r)| \geq n/2$.

That is, a round r is dead if at least $n/2$ of the processes are rejecting it. This implies that if a round r is dead, there cannot be a majority of the processes accepting it, thus round r cannot be successful. We denote by $\mathcal{R}_V$ the set of rounds for which the value has been chosen. Next we formally define the concept of *anchored* round which is crucial to the proofs.

Definition 8. A round $r \in \mathcal{R}_V$ is said to be *anchored* if for every round $r' \in \mathcal{R}_V$, such that $r' < r$, either round r' is dead or **Hvalue**$(r') = $ **Hvalue**(r).

Next we prove that S_{BPX} guarantees agreement. The key invariant used in the proof is the following.

Invariant 9. *In any state of an execution of S_{BPX}, any non-dead round $r \in \mathcal{R}_V$ is anchored.*

To prove it we use a sequence of auxiliary invariants. In the following we provide the crucial ones.

Invariant 10. *In any state s of an execution of S_{BPX}, if message $(r,\text{"Last"},r'',v)_{j,i}$ is in CHANNEL$_{j,i}$, then $j \in \text{Hreject}(r')$, for all r' such that $r'' < r' < r$.*

Invariant 11. *In any state of an execution of S_{BPX}, if $j \in \text{Hinfquo}(r)$ then $\forall r'$ such that $\text{Hfrom}(r) < r' < r$, we have that $j \in \text{Hreject}(r')$.*

Validity is easier to prove since values for new rounds come from either initial values or values of previous rounds.

Invariant 12. *In any state of an execution α of S_{BPX}, for any $r \in \mathcal{R}_V$ we have that $\text{Hvalue}(r) \in V_\alpha$.*

The next theorem follows from Invariants 9 and 12.

Theorem 13. *In any execution of the system S_{BPX}, agreement and validity are satisfied.*

5.2 Analysis

In this section we analyze the performance of S_{BPX}. Before turning our attention to the time analysis, let us give the following lemma which provides a bound on the number of messages sent in any round.

Lemma 14. *If an execution fragment of the system S_{BPX}, starting in a reachable state, is stable then at most $4n$ messages are sent in a round.*

Next we consider the time analysis. We remark that in order for the leader to execute step 3, i.e., action BeginCast$_i$, it is necessary that an initial value be provided. If the leader does not have an initial value and no agent sends a value in a "Last" message, the leader needs to wait for the execution of the Init$(v)_i$ to set a value to propose in the round. Clearly the time analysis depends on the time of occurrence of the Init$(v)_i$. For simplicity we assume that an initial value is provided to every process at the beginning of the computation.

We remark that a leader reaches a decision when it conducts a successful round. Formally, a round is successful when action RndSuccess$_i$ is executed.

Lemma 15. *Suppose that for an execution fragment α of the system S_{BPX}, starting in a reachable state s in which no decision has been reached yet, it holds that: (i) α is stable; (ii) in α there exists a unique leader, say process i; (iii) α lasts for more than $7\ell + 4n\ell + 4d$ time; (iv) process i is conducting round r, for some round number r; (v) round r is successful. Then we have that action RndSuccess$_i$ is performed by time $7\ell + 4n\ell + 4d$ from the beginning of α.*

Lemma 16. *If an execution fragment α of the system S_{BPX}, starting in a reachable state and lasting for more than $3\ell + 2n\ell + 2d$ time, is stable and there is a unique leader which has decided before the beginning of α, then by time $3\ell + 2n\ell + 2d$, every alive process has decided, the leader knows that every alive process has decided and at most $2n$ messages are sent.*

Lemmas 14,15 and 16, state that if in a stable execution a successful round is conducted, then it takes a linear amount of time and a linear number of messages to reach consensus. However it is possible that, due to committed agents, even if the system executes nicely from some point in time on, no successful round is conducted and to have a successful round a new round must be started. We take care of this problem in the next section.

5.3 Starting rounds

Figure 6 shows the signature of Clock GT automaton STARTERALG$_i$. This automaton checks if an ongoing round has been successful within the expected time bound. By Lemma 15, if action RndSuccess$_i$ does not happen within time $7\ell + 4n\ell + 4d$ from the start of the round, then the round may not achieve success and a new round has to be started. This is done by action CheckRndSuccess$_i$. When, in a nice execution fragment, a second round has been started, there is nothing that can prevent the success of the new round. Indeed in the newly started round processes are not committed for higher numbered rounds since during the first round they inform the leader of the round number for which they are committed and the leader, when starting a new round, always uses a round number greater than any round number ever seen.

Signature of STARTERALG$_i$

Input:	Leader$_i$, NotLeader$_i$, BeginCast$_i$, RndSuccess$_i$, Stop$_i$, Recover$_i$
Internal:	CheckRndSuccess$_i$
Output:	NewRound$_i$
Time-passage:	$\nu(t)$

Fig. 6. Automaton STARTERALG for process i. The code is deferred to the full paper.

Correctness and analysis. Let S_{PAX} be the system obtained by composing system S_{BPX} with one automaton STARTERALG$_i$ for each process $i \in \mathcal{I}$. Since this system contains as a subsystem the system S_{BPX} then it guarantees agreement and correctness. However, in a long enough nice execution of S_{PAX} termination is achieved, too.

Lemma 17. *Suppose that for an execution fragment α of S_{PAX}, starting in a reachable state s, it holds that (i) α is nice; (ii) there is a unique leader, say process i; (iii) α lasts for more than $16\ell + 8n\ell + 9d$ time. Then by time $16\ell + 8n\ell + 9d$ the leader i has reached a decision.*

Notice that if the execution is stable for enough time, then the leader election will eventually come up with only one leader (see Lemma 6). Thus we have the following theorem.

Theorem 18. *Let α be a nice execution fragment of S_{PAX} starting in a reachable state and lasting for more than $24\ell + 10n\ell + 13d$. Then the leader i executes $Decide(v')_i$ by time $21\ell + 8n\ell + 11d$ from the beginning of α and at most $8n$ messages are sent. Moreover by time $24\ell + 10n\ell + 13d$ from the beginning of α any alive process j executes $Decide(v')_j$ and at most $2n$ additional messages are sent.*

A recover may cause a delay. Indeed if the recovered process becomes leader, it will start new rounds, possibly preventing the old round from success.

6 The MULTIPAXOS algorithm

The PAXOS algorithm allows processes to reach consensus on one value. We consider now the situation in which consensus has to be reached on a sequence of values; more precisely, for each integer k, processes need to reach consensus on the k-th value (as long as there are initial values for the k-th consensus problem).

Clearly we can use an instance of PAXOS for each integer k, so that the k-th instance is used to agree on the k-th value. Few modifications to the code provided in the previous section are needed. Since we need an instance of PAXOS to agree on the k-th value, we need for each integer k an instance of the BASICPAXOS$_i$ and STARTERALG$_i$ automata. To distinguish instances of BASICPAXOS$_i$ we use an additional parameter that specifies the ordinal number of the instance. So, we have BASICPAXOS$(1)_i$, BASICPAXOS$(2)_i$, BASICPAXOS$(3)_i$, etc., where BASICPAXOS$(k)_i$ is used to agree on the k-th value. This additional parameter will be present in each action. For instance, the Init$(v)_i$ action becomes Init$(k, v)_i$ in BASICPAXOS$(k)_i$. Similar modifications are needed for all the other actions. The STARTERALG; automaton has to be modified in a similar way. Theorem 18 can be restated for each instance of PAXOS.

Application to data replication. Providing distributed and concurrent access to data objects is an important issue in distributed computing. The simplest implementation maintains the object at a single process which is accessed by multiple clients. However this approach does not scale well as the number of clients increases and it is not fault-tolerant. Data replication allows faster access and provides fault tolerance by replicating the data object at several processes.

It is possible to use MULTIPAXOS to design a data replication algorithm that guarantees sequential consistency and provides the same fault tolerance properties of MULTIPAXOS. The resulting algorithm lies between the majority voting and the primary copy replication techniques. It is similar to voting schemes since it uses majorities to achieve consistency and it is similar to primary copy techniques since a unique leader is required to achieve termination. Using MULTIPAXOS gives much flexibility. For instance, it is not a disaster when there are two or more "primary" copies. This can only slow down the computation, but never results in inconsistencies. The high fault tolerance of MULTIPAXOS results in a highly fault tolerant data replication algorithm, i.e., process stop and recovery, loss, duplication and reordering of messages, timing failures are tolerated. However liveness is not guaranteed: it is possible that a requested operation is never installed.

We can use MULTIPAXOS in the following way. Each process in the system maintains a copy of the data object. When client i requests an update operation, process i proposes that operation in an instance of MULTIPAXOS. When an update operation is the output value of an instance of MULTIPAXOS and the previous update has been applied, a process updates its local copy and the process that received the request for the update gives back a report to its client. A read request can be immediately satisfied returning the current state of the local copy.

7 Concluding remarks

This paper introduces a special type of general timed automaton, called the *Clock GTA*, suitable for describing partially synchronous systems subject to timing failures. It can be used for practical time performance analysis based on the stabilization of the physical system. Using the Clock GTA, Lamport's PAXOS algorithm is modelled, verified and analyzed. Future work may encompass on one hand the use of the Clock GTA for modelling other algorithms that work in partially synchronous systems subject to timing failures, and on the other hand improvements and implementation of PAXOS.

References

1. T.D. Chandra, V. Hadzilacos, S. Toueg, The weakest failure detector for solving consensus, in *Proceedings of the 11th Annual ACM Symposium on Principles of Distributed Computing*, pages 147–158, Vancouver, British Columbia, Canada, August 1992.
2. T.D. Chandra, S. Toueg, Unreliable failure detector for asynchronous distributed systems, *Journal of the ACM*, Vol. 43 (2), pp. 225–267. A preliminary version appeared in the *Proceedings of the 10th Annual ACM Symposium on Principles of Distributed Computing*, pages 325–340, August 1991.
3. F. Cristian and C. Fetzer, The timed asynchronous system model, Dept. of Computer Science, UCSD, La Jolla, CA. Technical Report CSE97-519.
4. R. De Prisco, Revisiting the Paxos algorithm, M.S. Thesis, Massachusetts Institute of Technology, Laboratory for Computer Science, Cambridge, MA, June 1997. Technical Report MIT-LCS-TR-717, Lab. for Computer Science, MIT, Cambridge, MA, USA, June 1997.
5. C. Dwork, N. Lynch, L. Stockmeyer, Consensus in the presence of partial synchrony, *J. of the ACM*, vol. 35 (2), pp. 288–323, April 1988.
6. A. Fekete, N. Lynch, A. Shvartsman, Specifying and using a partitionable group communication service, to appear in *Proceedings of the 16th Annual ACM Symposium on Principles of Distributed Computing*, August 1997.
7. M.J. Fischer, The consensus problem in unreliable distributed systems (a brief survey). Rep. YALEU/DSC/RR-273. Dept. of Computer Science, Yale Univ., New Have, Conn., June 1983.
8. L. Lamport, The part-time parliament, Research Report 49, Digital Equipment Corporation Systems Research Center, Palo Alto, CA, September 1989.
9. B. Lampson, How to build a highly available system using consensus, in Proceedings of the 10th International Workshop on Distributed Algorithms WDAG 96, Bologna, Italy, pages 1–15, 1996.
10. B. Liskov, B. Oki, Viewstamped replication: A new primary copy method to support highly-available distributed systems, in *Proceedings of the 7th Annual ACM Symposium on Principles of Distributed Computing*, pages 8–17, August 1988.
11. N. Lynch, Distributed Algorithms, Morgan Kaufmann Publishers, San Francisco, 1996.
12. N. Lynch, F. Vaandrager, Forward and backward simulations for timing-based systems. in *Real-Time: Theory in Practice*, Vol. 600 of *Lecture Notes in Computer Science*, Springer-Verlag, pp. 397–446, 1992.
13. N. Lynch, F. Vaandrager, Forward and backward simulations—Part II: Timing-based systems. Technical Memo MIT-LCS-TM-487.b, Lab. for Computer Science, MIT, Cambridge, MA, USA, April 1993.
14. N. Lynch, F. Vaandrager. Actions transducers and timed automata. Technical Memo MIT-LCS-TM-480.b, Lab. for Computer Science, MIT, Cambridge, MA, USA, October 1994.
15. B. Oki, Viewstamped replication for highly-available distributed systems, Ph.D. Thesis, Laboratory for Computer Science, Massachusetts Institute of Technology, Cambridge, MA 02139, 1988.
16. B. Patt-Shamir, A theory of clock synchronization, Ph.D. Thesis, Laboratory for Computer Science, Massachusetts Institute of Technology, Cambridge, MA 02139, October 1994.
17. D. Skeen, Nonblocking Commit Protocols, Proceedings of the ACM SIGMOD International Conference on Management of Data, pp. 133–142, May 1981.

Heartbeat: A Timeout-Free Failure Detector for Quiescent Reliable Communication*

Marcos Kawazoe Aguilera   Wei Chen   Sam Toueg

Cornell University, Computer Science Department, Ithaca NY 14853-7501, USA
aguilera,weichen,sam@cs.cornell.edu

Abstract. We study the problem of achieving reliable communication with *quiescent* algorithms (i.e., algorithms that eventually stop sending messages) in asynchronous systems with process crashes and lossy links. We first show that it is impossible to solve this problem without failure detectors. We then show how to solve it using a new failure detector, called *heartbeat*. In contrast to previous failure detectors that have been used to circumvent impossibility results, the heartbeat failure detector *is* implementable, and its implementation does *not* use timeouts. These results have wide applicability: they can be used to transform many existing algorithms that tolerate only process crashes into quiescent algorithms that tolerate both process crashes and message losses. This can be applied to consensus, atomic broadcast, k-set agreement, atomic commitment, etc.

The heartbeat failure detector is novel: besides being implementable without timeouts, it does not output lists of suspects as typical failure detectors do. If we restrict failure detectors to output only lists of suspects, quiescent reliable communication requires $\Diamond \mathcal{P}$ [2], which is not implementable. Combined with the results of this paper, this shows that traditional failure detectors that output only lists of suspects have fundamental limitations.

1 Motivation

This paper introduces *heartbeat*, a failure detector that can be implemented without timeouts, and shows how it can be used to solve the problem of *quiescent* reliable communication in asynchronous message-passing systems with process crashes and lossy links.

To illustrate this problem consider a system of two processes, a sender s and a receiver r, connected by an asynchronous bidirectional link. Process s wishes to send some message m to r. Suppose first that no process may crash, but the link between s and r may lose messages (in both directions). If we put no restrictions on message losses it is obviously impossible to ensure that r receives m. An assumption commonly made to circumvent this problem is that the link is *fair*: if a message is sent infinitely often then it is received infinitely often.

With such a link, s could repeatedly send copies of m forever, and r is guaranteed to eventually receive m. This is impractical, since s never stops sending messages. The obvious fix is the following protocol: (a) s sends a copy of m repeatedly until it receives $ack(m)$ from r, and (b) upon each receipt of m, r sends $ack(m)$ back to s. Note that this protocol is *quiescent*: eventually no process sends or receives messages.

---

* Research partially supported by NSF grant CCR-9402896, by ARPA/ONR grant N00014-96-1-1014, and by an Olin Fellowship.

The situation changes if, in addition to message losses, process crashes may also occur. The protocol above still works, but it is not quiescent anymore: for example, if r crashes before sending $ack(m)$, then s will send copies of m forever. Is there a *quiescent* protocol ensuring that if neither s nor r crashes then r eventually receives m? It turns out that the answer is no, even if one assumes that the link can only lose a finite number of messages.

Since process crashes and message losses are common types of failures, this negative result is an obstacle to the design of fault-tolerant distributed systems. In this paper, we explore the use of *unreliable failure detectors* to circumvent this obstacle. Roughly speaking, unreliable failure detectors provide (possibly erroneous) hints on the operational status of processes. Each process can query a local failure detector module that provides some information about which processes have crashed. This information is typically given in the form of a list of *suspects*. In general, failure detectors can make mistakes: a process that has crashed is not necessarily suspected and a process may be suspected even though it has not crashed. Moreover, the local lists of suspects dynamically change and lists of different processes do not have to agree (or even eventually agree). Introduced in [12], the abstraction of unreliable failure detectors has been used to solve several important problems such as consensus, atomic broadcast, group membership, non-blocking atomic commitment, and leader election [5, 15, 20, 24, 27].

Our goal is to use unreliable failure detectors to achieve quiescence, but before we do so we must address the following important question. Note that any reasonable implementation of a failure detector in a message-passing system is itself *not* quiescent: a process being monitored by a failure detector must periodically send a message to indicate that it is still alive, and it must do so forever (if it stops sending messages it cannot be distinguished from a process that has crashed). Given that failure detectors are not quiescent, does it still make sense to use them as a tool to achieve quiescent applications (such as quiescent reliable broadcast, consensus, or group membership)?

The answer is yes, for two reasons. First, a failure detector is intended to be a basic system service that is *shared* by many applications during the lifetime of the system, and so its cost is amortized over all these applications. Second, failure detection is a service that needs to be active forever — and so it is natural that it sends messages forever. In contrast, many applications (such as a single RPC call or the reliable broadcast of a single message) should not send messages forever, i.e., they should be quiescent. Thus, there is no conflict between the goal of achieving quiescent applications and the use of a (non-quiescent) failure detection service as a tool to achieve this goal.

How can we use an unreliable failure detector to achieve quiescent reliable communication in the presence of process and link failures? Consider the *Eventually Perfect* failure detector $\Diamond\mathcal{P}$ [12]. Intuitively, $\Diamond\mathcal{P}$ satisfies the following two properties: (a) if a process crashes then there is a time after which it is permanently suspected, and (b) if a process does not crash then there is a time after which it is never suspected. Using $\Diamond\mathcal{P}$, the following obvious algorithm solves our sender/receiver example: (a) while s has not received $ack(m)$ from r, it periodically does the following: s queries $\Diamond\mathcal{P}$ and sends a copy of m to r if r is not currently suspected; (b) upon each receipt of m, r sends $ack(m)$ back to s. Note that this algorithm is *quiescent*: eventually no process sends or receives messages.

In [2], Aguilera *et al.* show that among all failure detectors that output lists of suspects, $\Diamond\mathcal{P}$ is the *weakest* one that can be used to solve the above problem. Unfortunately, $\Diamond\mathcal{P}$ is not implementable in asynchronous systems with process crashes (this would violate a known impossibility result [18, 12]). Thus, at a first glance, it seems that achieving quiescent reliable communication requires a failure detector that cannot be implemented. In this paper we show that this is not so.

2 The Heartbeat Failure Detector

We will show that quiescent reliable communication can be achieved with a failure detector that *can be implemented without timeouts* in systems with process crashes and lossy links. This failure detector, called *heartbeat* and denoted $\mathcal{HB}$, is very simple. Roughly speaking, the failure detector module of $\mathcal{HB}$ at a process p outputs a vector of counters, one for each neighbor q of p. If neighbor q does not crash, its counter increases with no bound. If q crashes, its counter eventually stops increasing. The basic idea behind an implementation of $\mathcal{HB}$ is the obvious one: each process periodically sends an *I-am-alive* message (a "heartbeat") and every process receiving a heartbeat increases the corresponding counter.[2]

Note that $\mathcal{HB}$ does *not* use timeouts on the heartbeats of a process in order to determine whether this process has failed or not. $\mathcal{HB}$ just counts the *total number of heartbeats* received from each process, and outputs these "raw" counters without any further processing or interpretation.

Thus, $\mathcal{HB}$ should not be confused with existing implementations of failure detectors (some of which, such as those in Ensemble and Phoenix, have modules that are also called *heartbeat* [28, 10]). Even though existing failure detectors are also based on the repeated sending of a heartbeat, *they use timeouts* on heartbeats in order to derive lists of processes considered to be up or down; applications can only see these lists. In contrast, $\mathcal{HB}$ simply counts heartbeats, and shows these counts to applications.

A remark is now in order regarding the practicality of $\mathcal{HB}$. As we mentioned above, $\mathcal{HB}$ outputs a vector of unbounded counters. In practice, these unbounded counters are not a problem for the following reasons. First, they are in *local memory* and not in messages — our $\mathcal{HB}$ implementations use bounded messages (which are actually quite short). Second, if we bound each local counter to 64 bits, and assume a rate of one heartbeat per nanosecond, which is orders of magnitude higher than currently used in practice, then $\mathcal{HB}$ will work for more than 500 years.

$\mathcal{HB}$ can be used to solve the problem of quiescent reliable communication and it is implementable, but its counters are unbounded. Can we solve this problem using a failure detector that is both implementable and has bounded output? [2] proves that the answer is *no*: The weakest failure detector *with bounded output* that can be used to solve quiescent reliable communication is $\Diamond P$.

Thus, the difference between $\mathcal{HB}$, whose output is unbounded, and existing failure detectors, whose output is bounded, is more than "skin deep". The results in this paper combined with those of [2], show that failure detectors with bounded output (including those that output lists of processes) are restricted in power and/or applicability.

3 Outline of the Results

We focus on two types of reliable communication mechanisms: *quasi reliable send and receive*, and *reliable broadcast*. Roughly speaking, a pair of send/receive primitives is quasi reliable if it satisfies the following property: if processes s and r are *correct* (i.e., they do not crash), then r receives a message from s exactly as many times as s sent that message to r. Reliable broadcast [22] ensures that if a correct process broadcasts a

---

[2] As we will see, however, in some types of networks the actual implementation is not entirely trivial.

message m then all correct processes deliver m; moreover, all correct processes deliver the same set of messages.

We first show that there is no quiescent implementation of quasi reliable send/receive or of reliable broadcast in a network with process crashes and message losses. This holds even if we assume that links can lose only a finite number of messages.

We then show how to use failure detectors to circumvent the above impossibility result. We describe failure detector $\mathcal{HB}$, and show that it is strong enough to achieve quiescent reliable communication, but weak enough to be implementable, in each one of the following two types of communication networks. In both types of networks, we assume that each correct process is connected to every other correct process through a *fair* path, i.e., a path containing only fair links and correct processes.[3] In the first type, all links are bidirectional and fair (Fig. 1a). In the second one, some links are unidirectional, and some links have no restrictions on message losses, i.e., they are not fair (Fig. 1b). Examples of such networks are unidirectional rings that intersect.

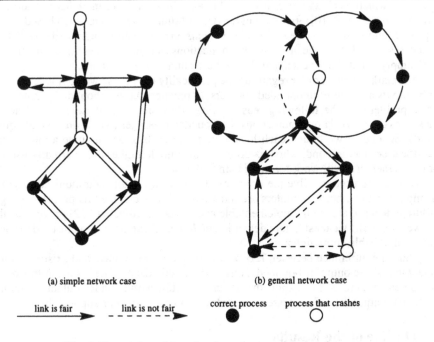

(a) simple network case   (b) general network case

link is fair   link is not fair   correct process   process that crashes

Fig. 1. Examples of the simple and general network cases

For each network type, we first describe quiescent protocols that use $\mathcal{HB}$ to solve quasi reliable send/receive and reliable broadcast, and then show how to implement $\mathcal{HB}$. For the first type of networks, a common one in practice, the implementation of $\mathcal{HB}$ and the reliable communication protocols are very simple and efficient. The algorithms for the second type are significantly more complex.

---

[3] This assumption precludes permanent network partitioning.

We then explain how $\mathcal{HB}$ can be used to easily transform many existing algorithms that tolerate process crashes into quiescent algorithms that tolerate both process crashes and message losses (fair links). This transformation can be applied to the algorithms for consensus in [4, 8, 9, 12, 14, 17, 26], for atomic broadcast in [12], for k-set agreement in [13], for atomic commitment in [20], for approximate agreement in [16], etc.

Finally, we show that $\mathcal{HB}$ can be used to extend the work in [6] to obtain the following result. Let P be a problem. Suppose P is correct-restricted (i.e., its specification refers only to the behavior of correct processes) or a majority of processes are correct. If P is solvable with a quiescent protocol that tolerates only process crashes, then P is also solvable with a quiescent protocol that tolerates process crashes and message losses.[4]

To summarize, the main contributions of this paper are:

1. This is the first work that explores the use of unreliable failure detectors to achieve *quiescent* reliable communication in the presence of process crashes and lossy links — a problem that cannot be solved without failure detection.
2. We describe a simple and *implementable* failure detector $\mathcal{HB}$ that can be used to solve this problem.
3. $\mathcal{HB}$ can be used to extend existing algorithms for many fundamental problems (e.g., consensus, atomic broadcast, k-set agreement, atomic commitment, approximate agreement) to tolerate message losses. It can also be used to extend the results of [6].
4. $\mathcal{HB}$ is novel: it is implementable without timeouts, and it does not output lists of suspects as typical failure detectors do [5, 12, 20, 21, 24, 27]. The results of this paper, combined with those in [2], show that lists of suspects is not always the best failure detector output.[5]

Reliable communication is a fundamental problem that has been extensively studied, especially in the context of data link protocols (see Chapter 22 of [25] for a compendium). Our work differs from previous results by focusing on the use of unreliable failure detectors to achieve quiescent reliable communication in the presence of process crashes and link failures. The work by Basu *et al.* in [6] is the closest to ours, but their protocols do not use failure detectors and are not quiescent. In Section 10, we use $\mathcal{HB}$ to extend the results of [6] and obtain quiescent protocols.

The paper is organized as follows. Our model is given in Section 4. Section 5 defines the reliable communication primitives that we focus on. In Section 6, we show that, without failure detectors, quiescent reliable communication is impossible. To overcome this problem, we define heartbeat failure detectors in Section 7, we show how to use them to achieve quiescent reliable communication in Section 8, and show how to implement them in Section 9. In Section 10, we explain how to use heartbeat failure detectors to extend several previous results. In Section 11, we mention a generalization of our results for the case where the network may partition. A brief discussion of protocol quiescence versus protocol termination concludes the paper.

All proofs are omitted here due to space limitations. They are provided in [1].

4 Model

We consider asynchronous message-passing distributed systems in which there are no timing assumptions. In particular, we make no assumptions on the time it takes to deliver a message, or on relative process speeds. Processes can communicate with each other by

---

[4] The link failure model in [6] is slightly different from the one used here (cf. Section 10).

[5] This was anticipated in [11].

sending messages through the network. We do not assume that the network is completely connected or that the links are bidirectional. The system can experience both process failures and link failures. Processes can fail by crashing, and links can fail by dropping messages.

To simplify the presentation of our model, we assume the existence of a discrete global clock. This is merely a fictional device: the processes do not have access to it. We take the range $\mathcal{T}$ of the clock's ticks to be the set of natural numbers.

4.1 Processes and Process Failures

The system consists of a set of n processes, $\Pi = \{1, \ldots, n\}$. Processes can fail by *crashing*, i.e., by prematurely halting. A *failure pattern* F is a function from $\mathcal{T}$ to 2^{Π}, where $F(t)$ denotes the set of processes that have crashed through time t. Once a process crashes, it does not "recover", i.e., $\forall t : F(t) \subseteq F(t+1)$. We define $crashed(F) = \bigcup_{t \in \mathcal{T}} F(t)$ and $correct(F) = \Pi - crashed(F)$. If $p \in crashed(F)$ we say p *crashes (or is faulty) in* F and if $p \in correct(F)$ we say p is *correct in* F.

4.2 Links and Link Failures

Some pairs of processes in the network are connected through unidirectional links. If there is a link from process p to process q, we denote this link by $p \rightarrow q$, and if, in addition, $q \neq p$ we say that q is a *neighbor* of p. The set of neighbors of p is denoted by $neighbor(p)$.

With every link $p \rightarrow q$ we associate two primitives: $\mathsf{send}_{p,q}(m)$ and $\mathsf{receive}_{q,p}(m)$. We say that process p *sends message m to process q* if p invokes $\mathsf{send}_{p,q}(m)$. We assume that if p is correct, it eventually returns from this invocation. We allow process p to send the same message m more than once through the same link. We say that process q *receives message m from process p* if q returns from the execution of $\mathsf{receive}_{q,p}(m)$. We describe a link $p \rightarrow q$ by the properties that its $\mathsf{send}_{p,q}$ and $\mathsf{receive}_{q,p}$ primitives satisfy. We assume that links do not create or duplicate messages, i.e., every link $p \rightarrow q$ in the network satisfies:

- *Uniform Integrity*: For all $k \geq 1$, if q receives m from p exactly k times by time t, then p sent m to q at least k times before time t.

A lossy link can fail by dropping messages. A link $p \rightarrow q$ is *fair* if $\mathsf{send}_{p,q}$ and $\mathsf{receive}_{q,p}$ satisfy Uniform Integrity and:

- *Fairness*: If q is correct and p sends m to q an infinite number of times, then q receives m from p an infinite number of times.

4.3 Network Connectivity

A path $(p_1, \ldots, p_k)$ is *fair* if processes $p_1, \ldots, p_k$ are correct and links $p_1 \rightarrow p_2, \ldots, p_{k-1} \rightarrow p_k$ are fair. We assume that every pair of distinct correct processes is connected through a fair path.

4.4 Failure Detectors

Each process has access to a local failure detector module that provides (possibly incorrect) information about the failure pattern that occurs in an execution. A process can query its local failure detector module at any time. A *failure detector history* H *with range* $\mathcal{R}$ is a function from $\Pi \times \mathcal{T}$ to $\mathcal{R}$. $H(p, t)$ is the output value of the failure detector module of process p at time t. A *failure detector* $\mathcal{D}$ is a function that maps each failure pattern F to a *set* of failure detector histories with range $\mathcal{R}_\mathcal{D}$ (where $\mathcal{R}_\mathcal{D}$ denotes the range of failure detector outputs of $\mathcal{D}$). $\mathcal{D}(F)$ denotes the set of possible failure detector histories permitted by $\mathcal{D}$ for the failure pattern F. Note that the output of a failure detector depends *only* on the failure pattern F. Thus, it does not depend on the behavior of applications.

Let $\mathcal{C}$ be a class of failure detectors. An algorithm solves a problem using $\mathcal{C}$ if it can solve this problem using any $\mathcal{D} \in \mathcal{C}$. An algorithm implements $\mathcal{C}$ if it implements some $\mathcal{D} \in \mathcal{C}$.

5 Quiescent Reliable Communication

In this paper, we consider quasi reliable send and receive and reliable broadcast, because these communication primitives are sufficient to solve many problems (see Section 10.1). The full version of this paper [1] also considers stronger types of communication primitives, namely, reliable send and receive, and uniform reliable broadcast.

5.1 Quasi Reliable Send and Receive

Consider any two distinct processes s and r. We define *quasi reliable send and receive from s to r* in terms of two primitives, send$_{s,r}$ and receive$_{r,s}$, that must satisfy Uniform Integrity and the following property:

- *Quasi No Loss*[6]: For all $k \geq 1$, if both s and r are correct, and s sends m to r exactly k times by time t, then r eventually receives m from s at least k times.

Intuitively, Quasi No Loss together with Uniform Integrity implies that if s and r are correct, then r receives m from s exactly as many times as s sends m to r.

We want to implement quasi reliable send/receive primitives using the (lossy) send/receive primitives that are provided by the network. In order to differentiate between these two, the first set of primitives is henceforth denoted by SEND/RECEIVE, and the second one, by send/receive. Informally, an implementation of SEND$_{s,r}$ and RECEIVE$_{r,s}$ is *quiescent* if it sends only a finite number of messages when SEND$_{s,r}$ is invoked a finite number of times.[7]

5.2 Reliable Broadcast

Reliable broadcast [9] is defined in terms of two primitives: broadcast(m) and deliver(m). We say that process p *broadcasts message* m if p invokes broadcast(m). We assume that every broadcast message m includes the following fields: the identity of its sender, denoted $sender(m)$, and a sequence number, denoted $seq(m)$. These fields make every message unique. We say that q *delivers message* m if q returns from the invocation of deliver(m). Primitives broadcast and deliver satisfy the following properties[22]:

---

[6] A stronger property, called *No Loss*, is used to define reliable send and receive [1].

[7] A quiescent implementation is allowed to send a finite number of messages even if no SEND$_{s,r}$ is invoked at all (e.g., some messages may be sent as part of an "initialization phase").

- *Validity*: If a correct process broadcasts a message m, then it eventually delivers m.
- *Agreement*: If a correct process delivers a message m, then all correct processes eventually deliver m.
- *Uniform Integrity*: For every message m, every process delivers m at most once, and only if m was previously broadcast by $sender(m)$.

We want to implement reliable broadcast using the (lossy) send and receive primitives that are provided by the network. Informally, an implementation of reliable broadcast is *quiescent* if it sends only a finite number of messages when broadcast is invoked a finite number of times.

5.3 Relating Reliable Broadcast and Quasi Reliable Send and Receive

From a quiescent implementation of quasi reliable send and receive one can easily obtain a quiescent implementation of reliable broadcast, and vice versa:

Remark 1 *From any quiescent implementation of reliable broadcast, we can obtain a quiescent implementation of the quasi reliable primitives* SEND$_{p,q}$ *and* RECEIVE$_{q,p}$ *for every pair of processes p and q.*

Remark 2 *Suppose that every pair of correct processes is connected through a path of correct processes. If we have a quiescent implementation of quasi reliable primitives* SEND$_{p,q}$ *and* RECEIVE$_{q,p}$ *for all processes p and q* $\in$ *neighbor(p), then we can obtain a quiescent implementation of reliable broadcast.*

6 Impossibility of Quiescent Reliable Communication

Quiescent reliable communication cannot be achieved in a network with process crashes and message losses. This holds even if the network is completely connected and only a finite number of messages can be lost.

Theorem 1. *Consider a network where every pair of processes is connected by a fair link and at most one process may crash. Let s and r be any two distinct processes. There is no quiescent implementation of quasi reliable send and receive from s to r. This holds even if we assume that only a finite number of messages can be lost.*

Corollary 2. *There is no quiescent implementation of reliable broadcast in a network where a process may crash and links may lose a finite number of messages.*

7 Definition of $\mathcal{HB}$

A *heartbeat failure detector* $\mathcal{D}$ has the following features. The output of $\mathcal{D}$ at each process p is a list $(p_1, n_1), (p_2, n_2), \ldots, (p_k, n_k)$, where $p_1, p_2, \ldots, p_k$ are the neighbors of p, and each n_j is a nonnegative integer. Intuitively, n_j increases while p_j has not crashed, and stops increasing if p_j crashes. We say that n_j is *the heartbeat value of* p_j *at* p. The output of $\mathcal{D}$ at p at time t, namely $H(p, t)$, will be regarded as a vector indexed by the set $\{p_1, p_2, \ldots, p_k\}$. Thus, $H(p, t)[p_j]$ is n_j. The *heartbeat sequence of* p_j *at* p is the sequence of the heartbeat values of p_j at p as time increases. $\mathcal{D}$ satisfies the following properties:

- $\mathcal{HB}$-*Completeness*: At each correct process, the heartbeat sequence of every faulty neighbor is bounded:

$$\forall F, \forall H \in \mathcal{D}(F), \forall p \in correct(F), \forall q \in crashed(F) \cap neighbor(p),$$
$$\exists K \in \mathbb{N}, \forall t \in \mathcal{T} : H(p,t)[q] \leq K$$

- $\mathcal{HB}$-*Accuracy*:
  - At each process, the heartbeat sequence of every neighbor is nondecreasing:

  $$\forall F, \forall H \in \mathcal{D}(F), \forall p \in \Pi, \forall q \in neighbor(p), \forall t \in \mathcal{T} : H(p,t)[q] \leq H(p,t+1)[q]$$

  - At each correct process, the heartbeat sequence of every correct neighbor is unbounded:

  $$\forall F, \forall H \in \mathcal{D}(F), \forall p \in correct(F), \forall q \in correct(F) \cap neighbor(p),$$
  $$\forall K \in \mathbb{N}, \exists t \in \mathcal{T} : H(p,t)[q] > K$$

The class of all heartbeat failure detectors is denoted $\mathcal{HB}$. By a slight abuse of notation, we sometimes use $\mathcal{HB}$ to refer to an arbitrary member of that class.

It is easy to generalize the definition of $\mathcal{HB}$ so that the failure detector module at each process p outputs the heartbeat of *every process in the system* [3], rather than just the heartbeats of the neighbors of p, but we do not need this generality here.

8 Quiescent Reliable Communication Using $\mathcal{HB}$

The communication networks that we consider are not necessarily completely connected, but we assume that every pair of correct processes is connected through a fair path. We first consider a simple type of such networks, in which every link is assumed to be bidirectional[8] and fair (Fig. 1a). This assumption, a common one in practice, allows us to give efficient and simple algorithms. We then drop this assumption and treat a more general type of networks, in which some links may be unidirectional and/or not fair (Fig. 1b). For both network types, we give quiescent reliable communication algorithms that use $\mathcal{HB}$. Our algorithms have the following feature: processes do not need to know the entire network topology or the number of processes in the system; they only need to know the identity of their neighbors.

In our algorithms, $\mathcal{D}_p$ denotes the current output of the failure detector $\mathcal{D}$ at process p.

8.1 The Simple Network Case

We assume that all links in the network are bidirectional and fair (Fig. 1a). In this case, the algorithms are very simple. We first give a quiescent implementation of quasi reliable SEND$_{s,r}$ and RECEIVE$_{r,s}$ for the case $r \in neighbor(s)$. For s to SEND a message m to r, it repeatedly sends m to r every time the heartbeat of r increases, until s receives $ack(m)$ from r. Process r RECEIVEs m from s the first time it receives m from s, and r sends $ack(m)$ to s every time it receives m from s.

From this implementation, and Remark 2, we can obtain a quiescent implementation of reliable broadcast. Then, from Remark 1, we can obtain a quiescent implementation of quasi reliable send and receive for every pair of processes.

---

[8] In our model, this means that link $p \rightarrow q$ is in the network if and only if link $q \rightarrow p$ is in the network. In other words, $q \in neighbor(p)$ if and only if $p \in neighbor(q)$.

8.2 The General Network Case

In this case (Fig. 1b), some links may be unidirectional, e.g., the network may contain several unidirectional rings that intersect with each other. Moreover, some links may not be fair (and processes do not know which ones are fair).

Achieving quiescent reliable communication in this type of network is significantly more complex than before. For instance, suppose that we seek a quiescent implementation of quasi reliable send and receive. In order for the sender s to SEND a message m to the receiver r, it has to use a diffusion mechanism, even if r is a neighbor of s (since the link $s \rightarrow r$ may not be fair). Because of intermittent message losses, this diffusion mechanism needs to ensure that m is repeatedly sent over fair links. But when should this repeated send stop? One possibility is to use an acknowledgement mechanism. Unfortunately, the link in the reverse direction may not be fair (or may not even be part of the network), and so the acknowledgement itself has to be "reliably" diffused — a chicken and egg problem.

Figure 2 shows a quiescent implementation of reliable broadcast (by Remark 1 it can be used to obtain quasi reliable send and receive between every pair of processes). For each message m that is broadcast, each process p maintains a variable $got_p[m]$ containing a set of processes. Intuitively, a process q is in $got_p[m]$ if p has evidence that q has delivered m. In order to broadcast a message m, p first delivers m; then p initializes variable $got_p[m]$ to $\{p\}$ and forks task $diffuse(m)$; finally p returns from the invocation of broadcast(m). The task $diffuse(m)$ at p runs in the background. In this task, p periodically checks if, for some neighbor $q \notin got_p[m]$, the heartbeat of q at p has increased, and if so, p sends a message containing m to *all* neighbors whose heartbeat increased — even to those who are already in $got_p[m]$.[9] The task terminates when all neighbors of p are contained in $got_p[m]$.

All messages sent by the algorithm are of the form $(m, got\_msg, path)$ where got_msg is a set of processes and $path$ is a sequence of processes. Upon the receipt of such a message, process p first checks if it has already delivered m and, if not, it delivers m and forks task $diffuse(m)$. Then p adds the contents of got_msg to $got_p[m]$ and appends itself to $path$. Finally, p forwards the new message $(m, got\_msg, path)$ to all its neighbors that appear at most once in $path$.

The code consisting of lines 19 through 27 is executed atomically.[10] Each concurrent execution of the *diffuse* task (lines 9 to 17) has its own copy of all the local variables in this task.

Theorem 3. *For the general network case, the algorithm in Fig. 2 is a quiescent implementation of reliable broadcast that uses $\mathcal{HB}$.*

Corollary 4. *In the general network case, quasi reliable send and receive between every pair of processes can be implemented with a quiescent algorithm that uses $\mathcal{HB}$.*

9 Implementations of $\mathcal{HB}$

We now give implementations of $\mathcal{HB}$ for the two types of communication networks that we considered in the previous sections. These implementations do not use timeouts.

---

[9] It may appear that p does not need to send this message to processes in $got_p[m]$, since they already got it! With this "optimization" the algorithm is no longer quiescent.

[10] A process p executes a region of code atomically if at any time there is at most one thread of p in this region.

```
1    For every process p:
2
3        To execute broadcast(m):
4            deliver(m)
5            got[m] ← {p}
6            fork task diffuse(m)
7            return
8
9        task diffuse(m):
10           for all q ∈ neighbor(p) do prev_hb[q] ← −1
11           repeat periodically
12               hb ← D_p                           { query the heartbeat failure detector }
13               if for some q ∈ neighbor(p), q ∉ got[m] and prev_hb[q] < hb[q] then
14                   for all q ∈ neighbor(p) such that prev_hb[q] < hb[q] do
15                       send_{p,q}(m, got[m], p)
16                   prev_hb ← hb
17           until neighbor(p) ⊆ got[m]
18
19       upon receive_{p,q}(m, got_msg, path) do
20           if p has not previously executed deliver(m) then
21               deliver(m)
22               got[m] ← {p}
23               fork task diffuse(m)
24           got[m] ← got[m] ∪ got_msg
25           path ← path · p
26           for all q such that q ∈ neighbor(p) and q appears at most once in path do
27               send_{p,q}(m, got[m], path)
```

Fig. 2. General network case — quiescent implementation of broadcast and deliver using $\mathcal{HB}$

9.1 The Simple Network Case

We assume all links in the network are bidirectional and fair (Fig. 1a). In this case, the implementation is obvious. Each process periodically sends a HEARTBEAT message to all its neighbors; upon the receipt of such a message from process q, p increases the heartbeat value of q.

9.2 The General Network Case

In this case some links are unidirectional and/or not fair (Fig. 1b). The implementation is more complex than before because each HEARTBEAT has to be diffused, and this introduces the following problem: when a process p receives a HEARTBEAT message it has to relay it even if this is not the first time p receives such a message. This is because this message could be a new "heartbeat" from the originating process. But this could also be an "old" heartbeat that cycled around the network and came back, and p must avoid relaying such heartbeats.

The implementation is given in Fig. 3. Every process p executes two concurrent tasks. In the first task, p periodically sends message (HEARTBEAT, p) to all its neighbors. The second task handles the receipt of messages of the form (HEARTBEAT, *path*). Upon the receipt of such message from process q, p increases the heartbeat values of all its neighbors that appear in *path*. Then p appends itself to *path* and forwards message (HEARTBEAT, *path*) to all its neighbors that do not appear in *path*.

```
1    For every process p:
2
3        Initialization:
4            for all q ∈ neighbor(p) do 𝒟ₚ[q] ← 0
5
6        cobegin
7        || Task 1:
8            repeat periodically
9                for all q ∈ neighbor(p) do send_{p,q}(HEARTBEAT, p)
10
11       || Task 2:
12           upon receive_{p,q}(HEARTBEAT, path) do
13               for all q such that q ∈ neighbor(p) and q appears in path do
14                   𝒟ₚ[q] ← 𝒟ₚ[q] + 1
15               path ← path · p
16               for all q such that q ∈ neighbor(p) and q does not appear in path do
17                   send_{p,q}(HEARTBEAT, path)
18       coend
```

Fig. 3. General network case — implementation of $\mathcal{HB}$

Theorem 5. *For the general network case, the algorithm in Fig. 3 implements* $\mathcal{HB}$.

10 Using $\mathcal{HB}$ to Extend Previous Work

$\mathcal{HB}$ can be used to extend previous work in order to solve problems with algorithms that are both quiescent and tolerant of process crashes and messages losses.

10.1 Extending Existing Algorithms to Tolerate Link Failures

$\mathcal{HB}$ can be used to transform many existing algorithms that tolerate process crashes into quiescent algorithms that tolerate both process crashes and message losses. For example, consider the randomized consensus algorithms of [8, 14, 17, 26], the failure-detector based ones of [4, 12], the probabilistic one of [9], and the algorithms for atomic broadcast in [12], k-set agreement in [13], atomic commitment in [20], and approximate agreement in [16]. All these algorithms tolerate process crashes. Moreover, it is easy to verify that the only communication primitives that they actually need are quasi reliable send and receive, and/or reliable broadcast. Thus, in systems where $\mathcal{HB}$ is available, all these algorithms can be made to tolerate both process crashes and message losses (with fair links) by simply plugging in the quiescent communication primitives given in Section 8. The resulting algorithms tolerate message losses and are quiescent.

10.2 Extending Results of [BCBT96]

Another way to solve problems with quiescent algorithms that tolerate both process crashes and message losses is obtained by extending the results of [6]. That work addresses the following question: given a problem that can be solved in a system where the only possible failures are process crashes, is the problem still solvable if links can also fail by losing messages? One of the models of lossy links considered in [6] is called *fair lossy*. Roughly speaking, a fair lossy link $p \to q$ satisfies the following property: If p sends an infinite number of messages to q and q is correct, then q receives an infinite number of messages from p. Fair lossy and fair links differ in a subtle way. For instance, if process p sends the infinite sequence of distinct messages $m_1, m_2, m_3, \ldots$ to q and $p \to q$ is fair lossy, then q is guaranteed to receive an infinite subsequence, whereas if $p \to q$ is fair, q may receive nothing (because each distinct message is sent only once). On the other hand, if p sends the infinite sequence $m_1, m_2, m_1, m_2, \ldots$ and $p \to q$ is fair lossy, q may never receive a copy of m_2 (while it receives m_1 infinitely often), whereas if $p \to q$ is fair, q is guaranteed to receive an infinite number of copies of both m_1 and m_2.[11]

[6] establishes the following result: any problem P that can be solved in systems with process crashes can also be solved in systems with process crashes and fair lossy links, provided P is *correct-restricted*[12] or a majority of processes are correct. For each of these two cases, [6] shows how to transform any algorithm that solves P in a system with process crashes, into one that solves P in a system with process crashes and fair lossy links. The algorithms that result from these transformations, however, are not quiescent: each transformation requires processes to repeatedly send messages forever.

Given $\mathcal{HB}$, we can modify the transformations in [6] to ensure that if the original algorithm is quiescent then so is the transformed one. Roughly speaking, the modification consists of (1) adding message acknowledgements; (2) suppressing the sending of a message from p to q if either (a) p has received an acknowledgement for that message from q, or (b) the heartbeat of q has not increased since the last time p sent a message to q; and (3) modifying the meaning of the operation "append $Queue_1$ to $Queue_2$" so that only the elements in $Queue_1$ that are not in $Queue_2$ are actually appended to $Queue_2$. The results in [6], combined with the above modification, show that if a problem P can be solved with a quiescent algorithm in a system with crash failures only, and either P is correct-restricted or a majority of processes are correct, then P is solvable with a quiescent algorithm that uses $\mathcal{HB}$ in a system with crash failures and fair lossy links.

11 Generalization to Networks that Partition

In this paper, we assumed that every pair of correct processes are reachable from each other through fair paths. In [3], we drop this assumption and consider the more general problem of quiescent reliable communication in networks that may partition. In particular, we (a) generalize the definitions of quasi reliable send and receive and of reliable broadcast, (b) generalize the definition of the heartbeat failure detector and implement it in networks that may partition, and (c) show that this failure detector can be used to achieve quiescent reliable communication in such networks. In [3] we also

---

[11] In [6], message piggybacking is used to overcome message losses. To avoid this piggybacking, in this paper we adopted the model of fair links: message losses can now be overcome by separately sending each message repeatedly.

[12] Intuitively, a problem P is correct-restricted if its specification does not refer to the behavior of faulty processes [7, 19].

consider the problem of consensus for networks that may partition, and we use $\mathcal{HB}$ to solve this problem with a quiescent protocol (we also use a generalization of the *Eventually Strong* failure detector [12]).

12 Quiescence versus Termination

In this paper we considered communication protocols that tolerate process crashes and message losses, and focused on achieving quiescence. What about achieving termination? A *terminating* protocol guarantees that every process eventually reaches a halting state from which it cannot take further actions. A terminating protocol is obviously quiescent, but the converse is not necessarily true. For example, consider the protocol described at the beginning of Section 1. In this protocol, (a) s sends a copy of m repeatedly until it receives $ack(m)$ from r, and then it halts; and (b) upon each receipt of m, r sends $ack(m)$ back to s. In the absence of process crashes this protocol is quiescent. However, the protocol is not terminating because r never halts: r remains (forever) ready to reply to the receipt of a possible message from s.

Can we use $\mathcal{HB}$ to obtain reliable communication protocols that are *terminating*? The answer is no, *even for systems with no process crashes*. This follows from the result in [23] which shows that in a system with message losses (fair links) and no process crashes there is no terminating protocol that guarantees knowledge gain.

Acknowledgments We are grateful to Anindya Basu, Bernadette Charron-Bost, and Vassos Hadzilacos for having provided extensive comments that improved the presentation of this paper. We would also like to thank Tushar Deepak Chandra for suggesting the name Heartbeat.

References

1. M. K. Aguilera, W. Chen, and S. Toueg. Heartbeat: a timeout-free failure detector for quiescent reliable communication. Technical Report 97-1631, Department of Computer Science, Cornell University, May 1997.

2. M. K. Aguilera, W. Chen, and S. Toueg. On the weakest failure detector for quiescent reliable communication. Technical report, Department of Computer Science, Cornell University, July 1997.

3. M. K. Aguilera, W. Chen, and S. Toueg. Quiescent reliable communication and quiescent consensus in partitionable networks. Technical Report 97-1632, Department of Computer Science, Cornell University, June 1997.

4. M. K. Aguilera and S. Toueg. Randomization and failure detection: a hybrid approach to solve consensus. In *Proceedings of the 10th International Workshop on Distributed Algorithms*, Lecture Notes on Computer Science, pages 29–39. Springer-Verlag, Oct. 1996.

5. Ö. Babaoğlu, R. Davoli, and A. Montresor. Partitionable group membership: specification and algorithms. Technical Report UBLCS-97-1, Dept. of Computer Science, University of Bologna, Bologna, Italy, January 1997.

6. A. Basu, B. Charron-Bost, and S. Toueg. Simulating reliable links with unreliable links in the presence of process crashes. In *Proceedings of the 10th International Workshop on Distributed Algorithms*, Lecture Notes on Computer Science, pages 105–122. Springer-Verlag, Oct. 1996.

7. R. Bazzi and G. Neiger. Simulating crash failures with many faulty processors. In A. Segal and S. Zaks, editors, *Proceedings of the 6th International Workshop on Distributed Algorithms*, volume 647 of *Lecture Notes on Computer Science*, pages 166–184. Springer-Verlag, 1992.

8. M. Ben-Or. Another advantage of free choice: Completely asynchronous agreement protocols. In *Proceedings of the 2nd ACM Symposium on Principles of Distributed Computing*, pages 27–30, Aug. 1983.

9. G. Bracha and S. Toueg. Asynchronous consensus and broadcast protocols. *J. ACM*, 32(4):824–840, Oct. 1985.

10. T. D. Chandra, April 1997. Private Communication.

11. T. D. Chandra, V. Hadzilacos, and S. Toueg. The weakest failure detector for solving consensus. *Journal of the ACM*, 43(4):685–722, July 1996.

12. T. D. Chandra and S. Toueg. Unreliable failure detectors for reliable distributed systems. *Journal of the ACM*, 43(2):225–267, March 1996.

13. S. Chaudhuri. More *choices* allow more *faults*: Set consensus problems in totally asynchronous systems. *Information and Computation*, 105(1):132–158, July 1993.

14. B. Chor, M. Merritt, and D. B. Shmoys. Simple constant-time consensus protocols in realistic failure models. *Journal of the ACM*, 36(3):591–614, 1989.

15. D. Dolev, R. Friedman, I. Keidar, and D. Malkhi. Failure detectors in omission failure environments. Technical Report 96-1608, Department of Computer Science, Cornell University, Ithaca, New York, 1996.

16. D. Dolev, N. A. Lynch, S. S. Pinter, E. W. Stark, and W. E. Weihl. Reaching approximate agreement in the presence of faults. *J. ACM*, 33(3):499–516, July 1986.

17. P. Feldman and S. Micali. An optimal algorithm for synchronous Byzantine agreement. Technical Report MIT/LCS/TM-425, Laboratory for Computer Science, Massachusetts Institute of Technology, June 1990.

18. M. J. Fischer, N. A. Lynch, and M. S. Paterson. Impossibility of distributed consensus with one faulty process. *J. ACM*, 32(2):374–382, Apr. 1985.

19. A. Gopal. *Fault-Tolerant Broadcasts and Multicasts: The Problem of Inconsistency and Contamination*. PhD thesis, Cornell University, Jan. 1992.

20. R. Guerraoui. Revisiting the relationship between non-blocking atomic commitment and consensus. In *Proceedings of the 9th International Workshop on Distributed Algorithms*, pages 87–100, Le Mont-St-Michel, France, 1995. Springer Verlag, LNCS 972.

21. R. Guerraoui, M. Larrea, and A. Schiper. Non blocking atomic commitment with an unreliable failure detector. In *Proceedings of the 14th IEEE Symposium on Reliable Distributed Systems*, pages 13–15, 1995.

22. V. Hadzilacos and S. Toueg. A modular approach to fault-tolerant broadcasts and related problems. Technical Report 94-1425, Department of Computer Science, Cornell University, Ithaca, New York, May 1994.

23. R. Koo and S. Toueg. Effects of message loss on the termination of distributed protocols. *Inf. Process. Lett.*, 27(4):181–188, Apr. 1988.

24. W.-K. Lo and V. Hadzilacos. Using failure detectors to solve consensus in asynchronous shared-memory systems. In *Proceedings of the 8th International Workshop on Distributed Algorithms*, pages 280–295, Terschelling, The Netherlands, 1994.

25. N. A. Lynch. *Distributed Algorithms*. Morgan Kaufmann Publishers, Inc., 1996.

26. M. Rabin. Randomized Byzantine generals. In *Proceedings of the 24th Symposium on Foundations of Computer Science*, pages 403–409. IEEE Computer Society Press, Nov. 1983.

27. L. S. Sabel and K. Marzullo. Election vs. consensus in asynchronous systems. Technical Report 95-1488, Department of Computer Science, Cornell University, Ithaca, New York, Febrary 1995.

28. R. van Renesse, April 1997. Private Communication.

Genuine Atomic Multicast

Rachid Guerraoui   André Schiper

Département d'Informatique
Ecole Polytechnique Fédérale de Lausanne
1015 Lausanne, Switzerland

Abstract. This paper addresses the problem of atomic *multicasting* messages in asynchronous systems with unreliable failure detection. First, we give a characterisation of the notion of algorithms *tolerating unreliable failure detection*. Second, we give a characterisation of the notion of *genuine atomic multicast*. This characterisation leads to a better understanding of the difference between atomic multicast and atomic broadcast, and to a clear distinction between genuine atomic multicast algorithms and non-genuine atomic multicast algorithms. Third, we show that in a system with at least three processes, the genuine atomic multicast problem cannot be solved with unreliable failure detection, if at least one process may crash. We mention however two ways of circumventing this impossibility result.

1   Introduction

The motivation of this work was to better understand the characteristics of the atomic multicast problem, and in particular to find out whether, as for consensus and atomic broadcast problems [1], the atomic multicast problem can be solved with unreliable failure detectors.

1.1   Atomic multicast versus atomic broadcast

An *atomic broadcast* primitive enables to send messages to all the processes in a system, with the guarantee that all correct processes (those that do not crash) agree on the *sequence* of messages they deliver. This primitive provides the agreement both on (1) the *set* of messages delivered, and (2) the *order* according to which the messages are delivered. Contrary to a broadcast that is targeted to the set of all the processes in a system, a *multicast* can be targeted exclusively to a subset of the processes. Apart from this, similarly to atomic broadcast, atomic multicast ensures that (1) the correct addresses of every message agree either to deliver or not the message, and (2) no two correct processes deliver any two messages in different order.

1.2   Genuine multicast vs feigned multicast

At first glance, it might seem that atomic broadcast and atomic multicast are similar problems, as each algorithm that solves one of these problems, can be transformed to solve the other problem. Indeed, let Ω denote the set of all the processes in the system, and let $\mathsf{Dst}(m) \subset \Omega$ denote the subset of the processes to which the message m is multicast. Firstly, by defining $\mathsf{Dst}(m) = \Omega$ for every message m, an atomic multicast algorithm can directly be used to implement an atomic broadcast algorithm. Secondly, a naive atomic multicast algorithm can be obtained from any atomic broadcast algorithm as follows: consider a message m to be multicast to $\mathsf{Dst}(m)$: (1) m is broadcast, together with the information $\mathsf{Dst}(m)$, to all the processes in Ω; (2) a process $p_i \in \Omega$ only delivers m if $p_i \in \mathsf{Dst}(m)$. The above transformation, of atomic broadcast into atomic multicast, leads however to a *feigned* multicast algorithm, because for $\mathsf{Dst}(m) \subset \Omega$, all the processes in the system are involved in the algorithm, *even those that are not concerned with the message m*, i.e., a multicast to a small subset turns out to be as costly as a broadcast (to all).

We require from a *genuine* multicast algorithm that it satisfies a specific *minimality* property. Roughly speaking, this property reflects the scalability of the algorithm, by requiring that only the sender and the addresses of a message be involved in the protocol needed to deliver the message. The naive implementation above using atomic broadcast does obviously not satisfy the minimality property, as every process in the system, even if not concerned by a message, is involved in the protocol needed to deliver the message.

1.3 Impossibility result

We consider in this paper a distributed system with process crash failures, reliable channels but unreliable failure detection (one can never know whether a process has crashed or not). We show that, in a system with at least three processes, among which one can crash, there exists no genuine atomic multicast algorithm tolerating unreliable failure detection. This impossibility result explains why, among the atomic multicast algorithms proposed in the literature, those that turn out to be genuine are either not fault-tolerant or are based on reliable failure detection ([2, 5]). A corollary of this result is that genuine atomic multicast is strictly harder than atomic broadcast, as the latter can be solved with unreliable failure detection [1].

Our impossibility result is somehow frustrating because the minimality property that makes an atomic multicast algorithm scalable (and hence well suited for large scale distributed systems), is precisely the property that makes the problem impossible to solve with unreliable failure detection (which is the typical case in large scale systems). We point out two ways of circumventing our impossibility result: (1) by weakening the definition of atomic multicast, and (2) by considering a stronger system model where messages are always multicast to sets of process groups (rather than to sets of individual processes).

The rest of the paper is organized as follows. Section 2 presents the system model. Section 3 characterizes algorithms that tolerate unreliable failure detection. Section 4 defines the notion of *genuine atomic multicast*. Section 5 gives an intuitive idea of the impossibility result and Section 6 presents its proof. Section 7 discusses two ways of circumventing this impossibility result and Section 8 summarises the contributions of the paper.

2 Model

Our model of asynchronous computation with failure detection is similar to the one described in [1]. In the following, we recall some definitions that are needed to prove our result.

2.1 Processes and Failures

A discrete global clock is assumed, and Φ, the range of the clock's ticks, is the set of natural numbers. Processes do not have access to the global clock. The distributed system consists of a set Ω of processes. Processes fail by *crashing*, and failures are permanent. A correct process is a process that does not crash. A *failure pattern* is a function F from Φ to 2^{Ω}, where $F(t)$ denotes the set of processes that have crashed through time t. We assume, as in [1], that in any failure pattern, there is at least one correct process. A *failure detector history* is a function from $\Omega \times \Phi$ to 2^{Ω}, where $H(p,t)$ denotes the set of processes suspected by process p at time t. A *failure detector* is a function $\mathcal{D}$ that maps each failure pattern F to a set of failure detector histories.

2.2 Algorithms

An *algorithm* is a collection A of n deterministic automata $A(p)$ (one per process p). In each step of an algorithm A, a process p performs atomically the following actions: (1) p receives a message from q, or a "null" message λ; (2) p queries and receives a value d from its failure detector module (d is said to be *seen* by p); (3) p changes its state and sends a message (possibly null) to some process. This third action is performed according to (a) the automaton $A(p)$, (b) the state of p at the beginning of the step, (c) the message received in action 1, and (d) the value d seen by p in action 2. The message received by a process is chosen non-deterministically among the messages in the message buffer destined to p, and the null message λ. A *configuration* is a pair (I, M) where I is a function mapping each process p to its local state, and M is a set of messages currently in the message buffer. A configuration (I, M) is an initial configuration if $M = \emptyset$. A step of an algorithm A is a tuple $e = (p, m, d, A)$, uniquely defined by the algorithm A, the identity of the process p that takes the step, the message m received by p, and the failure detector value d seen by p during the step. A step $e = (p, m, d, A)$ is *applicable to a configuration* (I, M) if and only if $m \in M \cup \{\lambda\}$. The *unique* configuration that results from applying e to $C = (I, M)$, is noted $e(C)$.

2.3   Schedules and runs

A *schedule* of an algorithm A is a (possibly infinite) sequence $S = S[1]; S[2]; \ldots$
$S[k]; \ldots$ of steps of A. A schedule S is applicable to a configuration C if (1) S is
the empty schedule, or (2) $S[1]$ is applicable to C, $S[2]$ is applicable to $S[1](C)$,
etc. Given any schedule S, we note $P(S)$ the set of the processes that have at
least one step in S.

A *partial run* of A using a failure detector $\mathcal{D}$, is a tuple $R =< F, H, C, S, T >$
where, F is a failure pattern, H is a failure detector history and $H \in \mathcal{D}(F)$, C
is an initial configuration of A, T is a finite sequence of increasing time values,
and S is a finite schedule of A such that: (1) $|S| = |T|$, (2) S is applicable to
C, and (3) for all $i \leq |S|$ where $S[i] = (p, m, d, A)$, we have $p \notin F(T[i])$ and
$d = H(p, T[i])$.

A *run* of an algorithm A using a failure detector $\mathcal{D}$, is a tuple
$R =< F, H, C, S, T >$ where F is a failure pattern, H is a failure detector history
and $H \in \mathcal{D}(F)$, C is an initial configuration of A, S is an infinite schedule of
A, T is an infinite sequence of increasing time values, and in addition to the
conditions above of a partial run ((1), (2) and (3)), the two following conditions
are satisfied: (4) every correct process takes an infinite number of steps, (5) every
message sent to a correct process q is eventually received by q.

Let $R =< F, H, C, S, T >$ be a partial run of some algorithm A. We say that
$R' =< F', H', C', S', T' >$ is *an extension of R*, if R' is either a run or a partial
run of A, and $F' = F$, $H' = H$, $C' = C$, $\forall i$ s.t. $T[1] \leq i \leq T[|T|]$, $S'[i] = S[i]$,
$T'[i] = T[i]$.

3   On the use of unreliable failure detectors

3.1   Failure detector properties

Failure detectors are abstractly characterized by completeness and accuracy
properties. The following *strong completeness* property was introduced in [1]:
eventually every process that crashes is permanently suspected by every correct
process. The following accuracy properties were defined in [1]: (1) *strong accuracy*: no process is suspected before it crashes; (2) *weak accuracy*: some correct
process is never suspected; (3) *eventual strong accuracy*: eventually no correct
process is suspected by any correct process, and (4) *eventual weak accuracy*:
eventually some correct process is never suspected by any correct process. A
failure detector class is a set of failure detectors defined by some accuracy and
some completeness property. An algorithm A is said to solve a problem P with
a failure detector class $\mathcal{C}$, if A solves P using any failure detector of class $\mathcal{C}$.
Figure 1 shows some of the notations of the failure detector classes introduced
in [1].

Among failure detectors, some never make any false failure detection. These
are failure detectors of class $\mathcal{P}$ (defined by *strong completeness* and *strong accuracy* properties). If a failure detector of class $\mathcal{P}$ suspects some process q, then
q must have crashed. Such failure detectors are said to be *reliable*. Intuitively,

Completeness	Accuracy			
	Strong	Weak	$\Diamond$Strong	$\Diamond$Weak
Strong	P (Perfect)	S (Strong)	$\Diamond P$	$\Diamond S$

Fig. 1. Failure detector classes

an unreliable failure detector is a failure detector which does not distinguish a crashed process from a correct one. Except class $\mathcal{P}$, all failure detector classes in Figure 1 contain unreliable failure detectors. In the following, we define what it means for an algorithm to tolerate unreliable failure detection.

3.2 Algorithms tolerating unreliable failure detection

Intuitively, an algorithm that uses an unreliable failure detector can never know whether a process has crashed or not. Hence, such algorithm *tolerates* unreliable failure detection. We characterise such algorithms with the following property. We say that an algorithm A using a failure detector D, *tolerates* unreliable failure detection if A satisfies the following property.

- **Unreliable failure detection tolerance.** *For every failure pattern F_1 where q crashes, for every a partial run $R_1 = < F_1, H_1, C, S, T >$ of A, there is a failure pattern F_1', which is similar to F_1 except that q is correct in F_1', and a failure detector history $H_1' \in \mathcal{D}(F_1')$, such that $R_1' = < F_1', H_1', C, S, T >$ is also a partial run of A.*

If a process q is suspected of having crashed, the A algorithm cannot distinguish the situation where q has indeed crashed (failure pattern F_1), from the situation where q has not crashed (failure pattern F_1'). Any algorithm that solves a problem with failure detector classes $\mathcal{S}$, $\Diamond\mathcal{S}$ or $\Diamond\mathcal{P}$ (Figure 1) tolerates unreliable failure detection (i.e., satisfies the unreliable failure detection property above).

4 Definition of genuine atomic multicast

4.1 On *multicast* and *delivery*

We assume here that the state of each process contains, among other things, an output buffer, named *multicast-buffer*, and an input buffer, named *delivery-buffer*. Each of these buffers contain a (possibly empty) set of messages. A process p_i is said to *multicast* a message m, if p_i puts m in its *multicast-buffer*. A process p_j is said to *deliver* a message m, if p_j puts m in its *delivery-buffer*. Every message m is uniquely identified, and it contains the identity of the process that multicasts m, noted Snd(m), as well as the set of processes to which m is multicast, noted Dst(m). It is important to notice here the distinction between the *receive* event and the *deliver* event. As we will see below, atomic multicast is defined on the *deliver* event (see Figure 2).

For any initial state of a process p_i, we assume that the *delivery-buffer* of p_i is empty. For simplicity of presentation, and without loss of generality, we assume that all messages multicast by p_i in some run R, are in the *multicast-buffer* of p_i in the initial state of R.

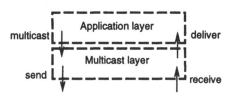

Fig. 2. send-receive vs multicast-deliver

4.2 Reliable multicast

An algorithm A is a *reliable multicast* algorithm, if for any run of A, the following properties are satisfied [4]:

- **Validity:** If a correct process multicasts a message m, then some correct process in Dst(m) eventually delivers m.

- **Agreement:** If a correct process delivers a message m, then every correct process in Dst(m) eventually delivers m.

4.3 Atomic multicast

An *atomic multicast* algorithm A is a reliable multicast algorithm, such that for any run of A, the following additional property is satisfied:

- **Pairwise Total Order:** If correct processes p and q deliver messages m and m', then p delivers m before m' if and only if q delivers m before m'. [1]

4.4 Genuine atomic multicast

A *genuine atomic multicast* algorithm A is an atomic multicast algorithm, such that for any run R of A, the following additional property is satisfied:

---

[1] In Section 6, we will come back to alternative definitions of atomic multicast, as presented in [4].

– **Minimality:** For any process $p \in \Omega$, unless a message m is multicast in R, and $p \in \mathsf{Dst}(m) \cup \{\mathsf{Snd}(m)\}$ (i.e., p is either the process that multicasts m, or one of the addresses of m), p does not send or receive any (non null) message in R.

The minimality property reflects the scalability of a genuine multicast algorithm. It is important to notice that this property applies to the atomic multicast algorithm layer and not to the underlying network. Typically, nothing would prevent the underlying network from making a message m transit through nodes (routers) whose processes are not the addresses of the message m (this would not violate our minimality property). The routing issue is related to the network topology, and not to the minimality property of a genuine multicast algorithm.

4.5 Genuine atomic multicast and failure detection

The following algorithm is a simple example of a genuine atomic multicast algorithm. The principle of this algorithm, generally attributed to Skeen, is the following. When a process p multicasts a message m to $\mathsf{Dst}(m)$, p sends the message to every member of $\mathsf{Dst}(m)$. Every process $q \in \mathsf{Dst}(m)$ that receives m, stores m in a *pending buffer*, and sends back to p, a timestamp $ts_q(receive(m))$ corresponding to q's current logical clock [6]. Process p then collects the timestamps from all the processes in $\mathsf{Dst}(m)$, defines a sequence number $sn(m)$ as the maximum of the timestamps, and sends $sn(m)$ to every member of $\mathsf{Dst}(m)$. Every process $q \in \mathsf{Dst}(m)$ delivers m when there is no message $m' \neq m$ in q's pending buffer for which $ts_q(receive(m')) < sn(m)$.

This algorithm is an atomic multicast algorithm, and it is a *genuine multicast* as only the sender p and the members of $\mathsf{Dst}(m)$ take part in the protocol needed to deliver m. The algorithm does not however tolerate even a single crash failure: if one process in $\mathsf{Dst}(m)$ crashes while p is waiting for the timestamps, the algorithm blocks. The algorithm can easily be transformed to tolerate failures, but would require reliable failure detection. In the following, we address the following question: can we find a genuine atomic multicast algorithm that tolerates unreliable failure detection ?

In a system with one process ($|\Omega| = 1$), genuine atomic multicast is trivially implemented using reliable channels (whatever the failure detection is). In a system with two processes ($|\Omega| = 2$), genuine atomic multicast can be implemented with reliable channels and atomic broadcast (hence with unreliable failure detection, see [1]) as follows: whenever a message is multicast to one process, send it on the reliable channel, and whenever a message is multicast to two processes, use atomic broadcast. In the next sections, we assume a system with at least three processes ($|\Omega| > 2$) among which one can crash, and we show that there exists no genuine multicast algorithm that tolerates unreliable failure detection.

5 The impossibility result: sketch

We give here an overview of the result and an intuitive idea of its proof. The complete proof is given in Section 6.

5.1 Atomic multicast versus atomic broadcast

In [1], Chandra and Toueg have shown that in a system Ω, (1) atomic broadcast can be solved with any failure detector of class $\Diamond \mathcal{P}$ iff a majority of processes in Ω are correct, and (2) atomic broadcast can be solved with any failure detector of class $\mathcal{S}$ if at least some process in Ω is correct.

One can intuitively see that these results do not apply to genuine atomic multicast. Consider result (1) and a subset Π of Ω within which the assumption of a majority of correct processes does not hold. In executions where messages are only multicast by processes of Π to Π, solving the genuine atomic multicast problem turns out to solve the atomic broadcast problem inside Π, which is impossible (as the assumption of a majority of correct processes does not hold in Π). Consider now result (2). If the failure detector in Ω is of class $\mathcal{S}$, it guarantees *weak accuracy*, i.e., some correct process p is not suspected by any process. In fact, this process p is actually the process that enables to ensure the total order property of atomic broadcast [1]. Consider a subset Π of Ω within which the assumption of *weak accuracy* does not hold, i.e., the process p is outside Π. In executions where messages are only multicast by processes of Π to Π, p will not be allowed to participate in the protocol, and hence no total order will be reached.

In the following, not only we formally confirm that results (1) and (2) do not apply to the genuine atomic multicast problem, but furthermore, we show that no algorithm tolerating unreliable failure detection solves the genuine atomic multicast problem (in a system with three processes, among which one can crash).

5.2 Overview of the proof

Assume (by contradiction) that there is some genuine atomic multicast tolerating unreliable failure detection. Consider a message m multicast to a destination set $\mathrm{Dst}(m)$, a message m' multicast to a destination set $\mathrm{Dst}(m')$, and assume $\mathrm{Dst}(m) \cap \mathrm{Dst}(m') = \{q_1, q_2\}$. We build the proof by showing that we can build a partial run R in which no process crashes, but where the processes of $\mathrm{Dst}(m)$ think that q_2 has crashed and then they deliver m (1), whereas the processes of $\mathrm{Dst}(m')$ think that q_1 has crashed and then they deliver m' (2). As a consequence, q_1 delivers m and not m', whereas q_2 delivers m' and not m, violating the properties of atomic multicast (3). In the following, we give an intuitive idea of how such a run R is built. The scenario is illustrated for $\mathrm{Dst}(m) = \{r_1, p_1, q_1, q_2\}$ and $\mathrm{Dst}(m') = \{q_1, q_2, p_2, r_2\}$.

(1) Building a partial run where q_2 does not deliver m. Consider the case where all the processes of $\mathrm{Dst}(m)$ are correct, except q_2 which initially crashes. By

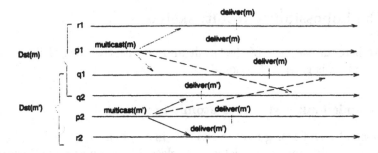

Fig. 3. In Run R, q_1 delivers m and not m', whereas q_2 delivers m' and not m.

the validity property of atomic multicast, there is a partial run R_1 where, except q_2, the processes of Dst(m) (among which q_1) deliver m (see Fig. 4). Consider now a partial run R_1' similar to R_1, except that q_2 is correct (e.g., q_2 is just extremely slow). Since the failure detection is unreliable, the processes cannot distinguish run R_1 from run R_1' (Sect. 2.5.). Hence, in R_1', all the processes of Dst(m), except q_2, deliver m (see Fig. 4).

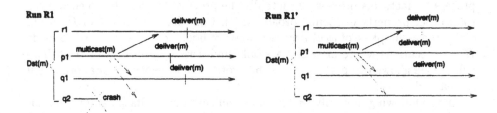

Fig. 4. In runs R_1 and R_1', all but q_2 deliver m.

(2) Building a partial run where q_1 does not deliver m'. Consider now the case where all the processes of Dst(m') are correct, except q_1 which initially crashes. There is a partial run R_2 where, except q_1, the processes of Dst(m') (among which q_2) deliver m' (Fig. 5). Consider a partial run R_2' similar to R_2, except that q_1 is correct. In R_2', all the processes of Dst(m'), except q_1, deliver m' (Fig. 5).

(3) Composing the partial runs. We build a partial run R (Fig. 3), by composing R_1' and R_2', in such a way that in R, q_1 delivers m without delivering m', and q_2 delivers m' without delivering m: a contradiction with atomic multicast.

6   The impossibility result: proof

In the following, we state the lemmas that are used in the proof, and we formally state the impossibility result.

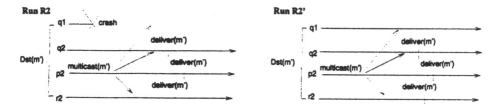

Fig. 5. In runs R_2 and R'_2, all but q_1 deliver m'.

6.1 On validity and minimality

Lemma 1 below characterises algorithms that satisfy the validity and minimality properties of atomic multicast. Roughly speaking, this lemma states that any genuine atomic multicast algorithm allows partial runs such as R_1 in Figure 4, and R_2 in Figure 5.

Lemma 1. *Let A be any genuine atomic multicast algorithm using any failure detector $\mathcal{D}$. Let C be any initial configuration where exactly one message m is multicast by some process $p \in \mathsf{Dst}(m)$. Let $q \neq p$ be any process in $\mathsf{Dst}(m)$. Let F be any failure pattern where q initially crashes and all other processes are correct. For any failure detector history $H \in F(\mathcal{D})$, there is a partial run of A, $R =< F, H, C, S, T >$ such that, every process $r \in \mathsf{Dst}(m) - \{q\}$ delivers m, and no process $s \notin \mathsf{Dst}(m) - \{q\}$ takes any step in R.*

PROOF: In F, all processes are correct except q. By the validity property of atomic multicast, for any failure detector history $H \in F(\mathcal{D})$, there is a partial run $\overline{R} =< F, H, C, \overline{S}, \overline{T} >$ of A, where every process in $\mathsf{Dst}(m) - \{q\}$ delivers m. As q has initially crashed then it has not taken any step. By the minimality property of genuine atomic multicast, in $\overline{S}$ no process $s \notin \mathsf{Dst}(m)$ has sent or received any non null message.

Let S be the restriction of $\overline{S}$ to the events taken by the processes of $\mathsf{Dst}(m)$ (i.e S is obtained by removing from $\overline{S}$ the events taken by the processes that are not in $\mathsf{Dst}(m)$). Let $\overline{T}$ be the sequence of times corresponding to the events taken in $\overline{S}$ by the processes in $\mathsf{Dst}(m)$. As $\overline{S}$ is applicable to C, then S is also applicable to C. The partial run $R =< F, H, C, S, T >$ is thus a partial run of A and, in R, (1) every process $r \in \mathsf{Dst}(m) - \{q\}$ delivers m, and (2) no process $s \notin \mathsf{Dst}(m) - \{q\}$ takes any step in R. □

6.2 On concatenation of runs

Lemma 2 below states that we can build a partial run out of two different partial runs, as long as both partial runs involve disjoint subsets of processes, and have the same failure pattern and failure detector history. Roughly speaking, this lemma states that we can build a partial run, such as R in Figure 3, out of two partial runs such as R'_1 and R'_2 (Fig. 4 and Fig. 5).

Notation. We consider below partial runs of the form $R_\alpha =< F, H, (I_\alpha[0], M_\alpha[0]), S_\alpha, T_\alpha >$; (I_α, M_α) denotes the sequence of configurations of R_α; $(I_\alpha[0], \emptyset)$ denotes an initial configuration (i.e., a set of initial states and an empty set of messages); $S_\alpha[1](I_\alpha[0], \emptyset) = (I_\alpha[1], M_\alpha[1])$, $S_\alpha[2](I_\alpha[1], M_\alpha[1])$ $= (I_\alpha[2], M_\alpha[2])$, etc; $P(S_\alpha)$ denotes the set of processes that have at least one step in S_α, and $I_\alpha|_{P(S_\alpha)}$ denotes the set of initial states of the processes in $P(S_\alpha)$. Given S_α (resp. T_α) and S_β (resp. T_β) two finite event sequences (resp. time sequences), we note $S_\alpha.S_\beta$ (resp. $T_\alpha.T_\beta$) the concatenation of S_α with S_β (resp. of T_α with T_β).

Lemma 2. *Let* $R_\alpha =< F, H, (I_\alpha[0], \emptyset), S_\alpha, T_\alpha >$ *and* $R_\beta =< F, H, (I_\beta[0], \emptyset), S_\beta, T_\beta >$ *be any two partial runs of any algorithm A. If* $P(S_\alpha) \cap P(S_\beta) = \emptyset$ *and* $T_\alpha[\|T_\alpha\|] < T_\beta[1]$ *then* $R =< F, H, (I_\alpha|_{P(S_\alpha)} \cup I_\beta|_{P(S_\beta)}, \emptyset), S_\alpha.S_\beta, T_\alpha.T_\beta >$ *is a partial run of A.*

PROOF: Let (I_α, M_α) be the sequence of configurations of R_α and (I_β, M_β) the sequence of configurations of R_β. As R_α is a partial run of A, then S_α is applicable to $(I_\alpha[0], \emptyset)$. As no process in $P(S_\beta)$ takes any step in S_α, and S_α is applicable to $(I_\alpha[0], \emptyset)$, then S_α is also applicable to $(I_\alpha|_{P(S_\alpha)} \cup I_\beta|_{P(S_\beta)}, \emptyset)$. As no process of $P(S_\beta)$ takes any step in S_α, then $S_\alpha.S_\beta[\|S_\alpha\|]|_{P(S_\beta)} = I_\beta|_{P(S_\beta)}$, i.e., , the processes of $P(S_\beta)$ keep the same state after S_α. As S_β is applicable to $(I_\beta, \emptyset)$, then S_β is also applicable to $(I_\alpha|_{P(S_\alpha)} \cup I_\beta|_{P(S_\beta)}, \emptyset)$. Hence, R is a partial run of A. $\square$

6.3 On agreement and pairwise total order

Lemma 3 below characterises algorithms that satisfy the agreement and pairwise total order properties. Roughly speaking, this lemma states that a partial run such as R in Figure 3, is not acceptable for any atomic multicast algorithm.

Lemma 3. *Let A be any atomic multicast algorithm. Let R be any partial run of A where two messages m and m' are multicast. For any two correct processes* $q_1, q_2 \in Dst(m) \cap Dst(m')$, *if there is a time* t_1 *at which* q_1 *has delivered m but not m', then there is no time* $t_2 > t_1$ *such that at* t_2, q_2 *has delivered m' but not m.*

PROOF: (BY CONTRADICTION) Assume that there is a time t_1 at which q_1 has delivered m but not m', and a time $t_2 > t_1$ at which q_2 has delivered m' but not m. Let R_∞ be any run which is an extension of R. By the agreement property of atomic multicast, as q_1 and q_2 are correct, then, in R_∞, eventually q_1 delivers m', and eventually q_2 delivers m_1. Hence, in R_∞, there is a time at which q_1 and q_2 have delivered both m and m', but in a different order: in contradiction with the pairwise total order property. $\square$

6.4 The result

Proposition 1 below states our impossibility result. To prove this result, we show that by using the characterisation of an algorithm tolerating unreliable failure detection (Sect. 3.2), and by combining Lemma 1 and Lemma 2 above, we build a partial run such as R in Figure 3, in contradiction with Lemma 3.

Proposition 1. *In a system with at least three processes among which one can crash, there exists no genuine multicast algorithm tolerating unreliable failure detection.*

PROOF: (BY CONTRADICTION) Consider p, q_1 and q_2, three processes in the system. Assume a genuine atomic multicast algorithm A tolerating unreliable failure detection. Let m be a message multicast by some process in $\mathsf{Dst}(m)$, m' a message multicast by some process in $\mathsf{Dst}(m')$, and $\mathsf{Dst}(m) \cap \mathsf{Dst}(m') = \{q_1, q_2\}$.

Let $(I_1[0], \emptyset)$ be some initial configuration where only the message m is multicast. Let F_1 be a failure pattern where q_2 initially crashes and all other processes are correct, and $H_1 \in \mathcal{D}(F_1)$. By Lemma 1, there is a partial run of A, $R_1 =< F_1, H_1, (I_1[0], \emptyset), S_1, T_1 >$ such that the processes in $\mathsf{Dst}(m) - \{q_2\}$ deliver m, and no process outside $\mathsf{Dst}(m) - \{q_2\}$ takes any step. Hence in R_1, q_1 delivers m whereas q_2 does not.

Let $(I_2[0], \emptyset)$ be some initial configuration where only the message m' is multicast. Let F_2 be a failure pattern where q_1 initially crashes and all other processes are correct, and $H_2 \in \mathcal{D}(F_2)$. By Lemma 1, there is a partial run of A, $R_2 =< F_2, H_2, (I_2[0], \emptyset), S_2, T_2 >$ such that, the processes in $\mathsf{Dst}(m) - \{q_1\}$ deliver m', and no process outside $\mathsf{Dst}(m) - \{q_1\}$ takes any step. Hence in R_2, q_2 delivers m' whereas q_2 does not.

Let F be the failure pattern where all processes are correct. As we assume an algorithm that tolerate unreliable failure detection, there is a failure detector history $H_1' \in \mathcal{D}(F)$ and a failure detector history $H_2' \in \mathcal{D}(F)$, such that $R_1' =< F, H_1', (I_1[0], \emptyset), S_1, T_1 >$ and $R_2' =< F, H_2', (I_2[0], \emptyset), S_2, T_2 >$ are partial runs of A.

Let T_2' be the time sequence defined as follows: $|T_2'| = |T_2|$, and $\forall i$ s.t. $1 \leq i \leq |T_2'|$, $T_2'[i] = T_2[i] + T_1[|T_1|]$, i.e., , T_2' is the time sequence with the same length as T_2, but which starts immediately after T_1.

Let H be the failure detector history defined as follows: $\forall p \in \Omega$, $\forall t$ s.t. $1 \leq t \leq T_1[|T_1|]$, $H(p, t) = H_1(p, t)$, $\forall t$ s.t. $T_1[|T_1|] < t \leq T_2'[|T_2'|]$, $H(p, t) = H_2(p, t)$, $\forall t$ s.t. $T_2'[|T_2'|] < t$, $H(p, t) = \emptyset$, i.e., , H is similar to H_1 until the end of $T_1[|T_1|]$, H is similar to H_2 from $T_1[|T_1|]$ to $T_2'[|T_2'|]$, then from $T_2'[|T_2'|]$ on, no process is ever suspected in H. In H, p is never suspected, and there is a time after which no process is suspected. Therefore $H \in \mathcal{D}(F)$.

Consider $R_\alpha =< F, H, (I_1[0], \emptyset), S_1, T_1 >$ derived from R_1', and $R_\beta =< F, H, (I_2[0], \emptyset), S_2, T_2' >$ derived from R_2'. As R_1' and R_2' are partial runs of A, then R_α and R_β are also partial runs of A. Furthermore, as $\mathsf{Dst}(m) \cap \mathsf{Dst}(m') = \{q_1, q_2\}$, $P(S_1) = \mathsf{Dst}(m) - \{q_2\}$, and $P(S_2) = \mathsf{Dst}(m') - \{q_1\}$, we have $P(S_1) \cap P(S_2) = \emptyset$. As we also have $T_1[|T_1|] < T_2'[1]$, by Lemma 2, $R =< F, H, (I_1[0]|_{P(S_1)} \cup I_2[0]|_{P(S_2)}, \emptyset), S_1.S_2, T_1.T_2' >$, is also a partial run of A.

In R, q_1 delivers m but not m' whereas q_2 delivers m' but not m, and $q_1, q_2 \in \mathsf{Dst}(m) \cap \mathsf{Dst}(m')$: in contradiction with Lemma 3. $\qquad \square$

A simple corollary of our result is that no algorithm using failure detector classes S or $\diamond P$ can solve the genuine atomic multicast problem. As atomic broadcast was shown to be solvable with those classes [1], a consequence of our result is that genuine atomic multicast is strictly harder than atomic broadcast (and hence strictly harder than consensus, as consensus and atomic broadcast are equivalent problems [1]).

7 Circumventing the impossibility result

7.1 Weakening the definition of atomic multicast

Our impossibility result also applies to stronger definitions of atomic multicast presented in [4]. Among these definitions are those which consider *uniform* versions of the agreement and pairwise total order properties, or which consider the *global total order* property. There is however a property, called *local total order*, that is weaker than the pairwise total order property we have considered. The local total order property ensures that messages sent to the same destination set are totally ordered, but no guarantee is however provided for messages in intersecting sets. With this definition, atomic multicast and atomic broadcast are equivalent problems, and thus all results on solving atomic broadcast with unreliable failure detection also apply to atomic multicast. In fact, our definition of atomic multicast is, among those defined in [4], the weakest for which the impossibility result holds. This is exactly why we have considered that definition to state our result.

7.2 Atomic multicast to multiple groups

According to our model, a process can multicast a message m to any subset of processes. In [3], we restrict this model by considering multicasts to subsets of process groups (rather than to subsets of individual processes), and we present an algorithm based on (1) unreliable failure detectors of class $\diamond S$, (2) the assumptions that there is a majority of correct processes within each group, and (3) causally ordered messages. This model actually corresponds to the practical situations where processes are used to manage replicated objects, and each group of processes represents a logical replica.

8 Summary

This paper has three contributions. First, we define what it means for an algorithm to tolerate unreliable failure detection. Second, we characterise the notion of genuine atomic multicast. This leads to a better understanding of the difference between atomic multicast and atomic broadcast, and we can distinguish between genuine atomic multicast algorithms, and feigned genuine atomic multicast algorithms.

Third, we show that genuine atomic multicast cannot be solved with an algorithm that tolerates unreliable failure detection, in a system with at least three processes among which one can crash. As atomic broadcast can be solved with unreliable failure detection, the impossibility result means that genuine atomic multicast is strictly harder than atomic broadcast. We mention two ways of circumventing our impossibility result: (1) by weakening the definition of atomic multicast, and (2) by strengthening the underlying system model.

Acknowledgement

We are very grateful to Vassos Hadzilacos and Bernadette Charron-Bost for their helpful comments on earlier drafts of this paper.

References

1. T. Chandra and S. Toueg. Unreliable failure detectors for reliable distributed systems. Journal of the ACM, 43(2), pages 225-267, 1996.
2. H. Garcia Molina and A. Spauster. Ordered and Reliable Multicast Communication. ACM Transactions on Computer Systems, 9(3), pages 242-271, August 1991.
3. R. Guerraoui and A. Schiper. Total Order Multicast to Multiple Groups. Proceedings of the 17th IEEE Int. Conf. on Distributed Computing Systems, Baltimore, pages: 578-585, May 1997.
4. V. Hadzilacos and S. Toueg. Fault-Tolerant Broadcasts and Related Problems. In Distributed Systems, Sape Mullender Editor, ACM Press Publisher, pages 97-145, 1993.
5. X. Jia. A Total Ordering Multicast Protocol Using Propagation Trees. IEEE Transactions on Parallel and Distributed Systems, 6(6), pages 617-627, June 1995.
6. L. Lamport. Time, Clocks, and the Ordering of Events in a Distributed System. Communications of the ACM, 21(7), pages 558-565, July 1978.

Low-Overhead Time-Triggered
Group Membership*

Shmuel Katz[1,2], Pat Lincoln[1], and John Rushby[1]

[1] Computer Science Laboratory, SRI International, Menlo Park, CA 94025 USA
email: {lincoln, rushby}@csl.sri.com
[2] Computer Science Department, The Technion, Haifa, Israel
email: katz@cs.technion.ac.il

Keywords: time-triggered protocol, group membership, synchronous algorithms, fault tolerance, formal modeling

Abstract. A group membership protocol is presented and proven correct for a synchronous time-triggered model of computation with processors in a ring that broadcast in turn. The protocol, derived from one used for critical control functions in automobiles, accepts a very restrictive fault model to achieve low overhead and requires only one bit of membership information piggybacked on regular broadcasts. Given its strong fault model, the protocol guarantees that a faulty processor will be promptly diagnosed and removed from the agreed group of processors, and will also diagnose itself as faulty. The protocol is correct under a fault-arrival assumption that new faults arrive at least $n+1$ time units apart, when there are n processors. Exploiting this assumption leads to unusual real-time reasoning in the correctness proof.

1 Introduction and Motivation

Group membership has become an important abstraction in providing fault-tolerant services for distributed systems [2]. As in any protocol for group membership, the one presented here allows nonfaulty processors to agree on the membership, and to exclude apparently faulty ones. Because of the strong fault model used, the protocol we consider has the additional desirable properties that the nonfaulty processors agree on the membership at *every* synchronous step, only faulty ones will be removed from the membership, and removal will be prompt. Moreover, a processor with a fault will also diagnose itself promptly.

This protocol for group membership is appropriate for bandwidth-constrained broadcast networks because it requires only one acknowledgment bit to be piggybacked onto existing regularly scheduled broadcasts. The protocol is derived

---

* This work was supported by Arpa through USAF Electronic Systems Center Contract F19628-96-C-0006, by the Air Force Office of Scientific Research, Air Force Materiel Command, USAF, under contract F49620-95-C0044, and by the National Science Foundation under contract CCR-9509931.

from one in a tightly integrated protocol architecture for automobile control [8]. Our contribution is to isolate this group membership protocol (which has not been described explicitly in previous papers), to abstract it from other elements of the integrated protocol, to give a precise formulation of its fault model, and to provide a systematic proof of its correctness. The argument for correctness is interesting and surprisingly intricate because the paucity of information carried in each individual broadcast requires inferences to be made over *sequences* of broadcasts; this, in turn, requires the statement of correctness to be strengthened significantly in order to obtain one that is inductive.

1.1 Background

Algorithms for industrial applications are optimized to deliver maximum utility from minimum resources. These optimizations pose interesting problems in protocol design and analysis that differ from those traditionally considered in the algorithms literature. For example, industrial algorithms for distributed consensus are less concerned with asymptotic reductions in the number of rounds than in maximizing the number of faults that can be tolerated with a small fixed number of rounds (generally two). This leads, for example, to "hybrid" fault models and associated algorithms that permit finer distinctions among faults than purely Byzantine fault models and provide strictly superior fault tolerance [4, 9, 11, 13, 15].

The starting point for the algorithm considered here is the time-triggered protocol (TTP) of Kopetz and Grunsteidl [8]. This protocol is intended for the control of critical functions in automobiles, where communications bandwidth is severely limited, some functions (e.g., ignition timing) require service at very high rates and with great temporal precision, and many functions (e.g., brake-by-wire, steer-by-wire) are safety critical [6]. For these reasons, TTP (and protocols for similar applications, such as ARINC 659 which provides the safety-critical backplane for the top-level avionics functions of the Boeing 777 [1]) are highly integrated, and services such as clock-synchronization, reliable broadcast, group membership, and primary-backup shadowing are combined with the basic data-communication service rather than layered. This allows high-quality services to be provided with very high performance at low overhead (for example, ARINC 659 achieves clock synchronization to within two bit-times at 30 MHz). These protocols also separate fault-tolerance for common cases from those for more severe ones. For example, the group membership protocol of TTP assumes only a single transmit or receive fault (and those faults are themselves narrowly defined) within any two rounds, with more severe fault modes and higher fault arrival rates being handled by a "blackout" operating mode. Empirical data supports these design decisions [8].

Bandwidth is a precious commodity in applications of the family of protocols we study here. Practical considerations such as cost of copper wire, likelihood of failures of interconnects, and lack of skilled maintenance drive designers to focus on simple and cheap hardware interconnect technology such as twisted pair. Extra runs of wire back and forth around a vehicle for redundancy and extra bandwidth are perceived to be too costly. Wireless communication is viewed as impractical due to the extreme interference expected in the environment. Thus relatively low bandwidth is one of the critical concerns of the designers of these protocols. Even an extra bit per message is considered significant in this domain.

The design constraints on a group membership protocol for an application such as TTP are that it should provide timely and accurate identification and exclusion of faulty processors with minimum overhead. The integrated nature of the protocol means that rather than interpose special "group membership packets" into the communications stream, it should piggyback what it needs for group membership onto the regular data packets. One way to do this is for each processor to append its assessment of the current membership to each packet that it sends. Under suitable assumptions, a protocol can be based on this approach [7], but it is clearly expensive—requiring n bits of membership data appended to each broadcast, for an n processor system (n is 10–20 for these applications). Later descriptions of TTP show only two bits being used for this purpose (actually, they show four, but that appears to be due to the fact that the buses are paired) [8], but the membership protocol is not described. In the following sections, we present a protocol that satisfies these constraints, using only one bit per broadcast, and analyze its properties.

In the following section the model, including its fault assumptions, is first described independently of the group membership problem. Then the assumptions that involve group membership are given, and the kind of reasoning needed for proving correctness is described. The detailed protocol is seen in Section 3 while the proof of correctness is given in Section 4. In the final sections we present a justification for the $n + 1$ limit on fault arrivals, sketch extensions to allow repaired processors to rejoin the group, and briefly describe our use of formal analysis with the Murϕ state exploration system.

The paper shows that a level of abstraction familiar to researchers in distributed programming can be used to isolate and reason about one of a suite of protocols that are combined at the implementation level for efficiency reasons. The separation leads to fault assumptions that seem strong, but are complemented by other assumptions and interleaved protocols.

2 The Model

There are n processors (numbered $0, \ldots, n - 1$) arranged in a logical ring and attached to a broadcast bus. Execution is synchronous, with a notional *time* variable increased by one at each step; this, in turn, defines a *slot* in the range $0, \ldots, (n-1)$ as *time* mod n. Nonfaulty processors broadcast whenever it is their slot.

The goal of group membership is to maintain a consistent record of those processors that appear able to communicate reliably and to execute the protocol. A group membership protocol need not tolerate all the types of faults that may afflict the system of which it is a part: other protocols, logically both "above" and "below" group membership, handle some types of faults. In TTP, for example, replication of the broadcast buses, and strong CRCs (checksums), effectively eliminate message corruption and reduce message loss to a very low level. Clock synchronization ensures that all nonfaulty processors share a common notion of time, and "bus guardians" with independent knowledge of the broadcast schedule prevent faulty processors from speaking out of turn. State-machine replication [14] or pairwise comparison is used to mask or to detect processor faults. These considerations (and empirical measurements) justify considering only two types of faults in the context assumed here.

Send fault: a processor fails to broadcast when its slot is reached.
Receive fault: a processor fails to receive a broadcast.

As noted above, other types of faults can be ignored because they are separately detected by other elements of the total protocol suite and then manifest themselves as either send or receive faults. For example, a transient internal data fault can lead to a processor shutting down and thus exhibiting a send fault when its slot is next reached.

Observe that a send fault can only occur to a processor when it is in the broadcast slot, and a receive fault can only occur to a processor different from the broadcaster. Notice, too, that messages cannot be corrupted, and that a send fault is consistent: *no* processor receives a message from a send-faulty broadcaster. Faults are intermittent: a faulty processor may operate correctly in some steps and manifest its fault in others. A processor is nonfaulty until it manifests a fault, thereafter it is considered faulty; a processor is *actively* faulty at a step if it manifests its fault at that step. That is, a processor is actively send-faulty at a step if it is expected to broadcast but fails to do so; it is actively receive-faulty at a step if it fails to receive the broadcast from a nonfaulty broadcaster.

Two additional assumptions are crucial to the correctness of our protocol, and are justified by the division between a "blackout" operating mode (not considered here) for coping with massive or clustered failures, and the "normal" mode (implemented by the mechanisms described here) that is required to cope only with relatively sparse fault arrivals.

Fault arrival rate: only one nonfaulty processor becomes faulty in any $n + 1$ consecutive slots.
Minimum nonfaulty processors: there are always at least two nonfaulty processors.

The fault model described so far is independent of the problem of group membership. Now we turn to the aspects needed to specify and describe the group membership protocol.

- Each processor has a *local membership set*, that initially contains all processors.
- Processor q is *expected* (to broadcast) by processor p if the current slot is q, and p's local membership set contains q.

A processor will normally broadcast in its slot; it can never broadcast out-of-turn, but it may fail to broadcast in its slot for two reasons:

- It suffers a send fault in that slot,
- It has diagnosed that it suffered an earlier (send or receive) fault and remains silent to inform other processors of that fact.

Using the assumptions and definitions of this model, it is now possible to summarize the requirements specification for the group membership protocol. The required safety property is that the local membership sets of nonfaulty processors are identical in every step, and contain all nonfaulty processors. Additionally, a progress property is needed to exclude trivial solutions: a faulty processor will be removed from the local membership sets of nonfaulty processors no later than the step following its next broadcast slot.[3] Our protocol also ensures that a faulty processor will eventually remove itself from its own membership set (self-diagnosis).

When a processor does broadcast, it appends an "ack" bit to whatever data constitutes the broadcast. This bit indicates whether or not that processor retained the previous expected broadcaster in its membership set. By observing the presence or absence of expected broadcasts, and by comparing the ack bits of received broadcasts to their own observations, processors are able to diagnose their own and other processors' faults and to maintain consistent membership sets.

Non-receipt of an expected broadcast can leave ambiguous the question of whether the transmitter or receiver is faulty. The report (encoded in the ack bit) from the next expected processor is needed to resolve this ambiguity; this report must be reliable, so we will need to show that the next expected processor must be nonfaulty in this case. This does not follow trivially from the fault arrival rate assumption because, for example, the initial non-receipt of a broadcast could be due to that broadcaster falling silent after self-diagnosing a much earlier receive fault. We will need to establish that the diagnosis of faults is sufficiently prompt that it combines with the fault arrival rate assumption to guarantee that the next expected broadcaster cannot be faulty in these circumstances. Thus certain progress properties cannot be separated from the basic agreement properties in the correctness proof.

3 The Protocol

Processors follow a simple fixed procedure: if it is processor p's slot, and p is in its own local membership set, then p attempts to broadcast. (If p is nonfaulty or receive-faulty, it succeeds; if send-faulty, it does not, but is unaware of the fault.) The broadcast includes one bit of state information defined below: the **ack** bit

---

[3] Technically, the real-time requirement seen here is a safety property and not a progress (or liveness) property in the sense of [10]. However, it does serve to guarantee that needed steps occur and so we refer to it informally as a progress property.

of the broadcaster. Each other processor updates its own local membership set by applying certain rules (described below) to the bit received (or not) from the expected broadcaster. The rules allow each processor to retain or remove either the expected broadcaster or itself from its local membership set, but it will not change its record of membership for any other processor.

Each processor p uses the global variable **time**, a local constant **slot**, and local variables **membership** and **ack**.

- The global variable **time** is an abstraction justified by clock synchronization among local clocks. As noted in the introduction, clock synchronization is assumed to be part of the complete protocol suite along with group membership, and guarantees that all processors agree on the (discrete) value of **time**.
- **slot** is a natural number in the range $0 \ldots n - 1$ that records the position of p with respect to other processors in the order of broadcast. This value is fixed and unique for each processor.
- **membership** is the set of processors in p's current view of the group.
- **ack** is a boolean recording whether p received the previous expected broadcast and agreed with the **ack** bit carried in that broadcast. As will be seen shortly, this means that the **ack** bit is true iff p has retained the previous expected broadcaster in its membership, or p was that broadcaster.

We use $\text{ack}(p)$ to indicate the **ack** bit of processor p, and $\text{slot}(p)$ to indicate its slot value. Initially, each processor's **membership** contains all other processors, its **ack** is *true*, the global **time** is some initial value (perhaps 0), and each processor is nonfaulty.

The protocol proceeds by discrete time steps; at each step, one processor may broadcast. That broadcaster is the processor b for which $\text{slot}(b) = \text{time} \bmod n$. The broadcast contains the broadcaster's **ack** bit, plus any data that may be needed for other purposes. The broadcast will be attempted only if b is in its own membership set, and will succeed only if b is not actively send-faulty in that step.

The protocol is described by specifying how each processor p updates its local variables **membership** and **ack** in terms of their previous values, the receipt or non-receipt of an expected broadcast, and the value of the **ack** bit carried in that broadcast.

We first define the auxiliary predicate $arrived(b, p)$ as *true* in a step if and only if processor p receives a broadcast from b, and b is the expected broadcaster in that step. This predicate can be considered local to p because that processor can sense the non-receipt of a broadcast.

- For each processor p, if the current broadcaster b is not an element of p's **membership**, none of the local variables are changed.
- If p is the broadcaster b and is in its own **membership** set, it broadcasts $\text{ack}(b)$ and then updates $\text{ack}(b)$ to *true*.

- Otherwise, when p is not the broadcaster b, each field of p is updated as follows (notice that $\mathbf{ack}(p)$ is a local variable of p, and that $\mathbf{ack}(b)$ is provided in the broadcast received from b).
  - Updated **membership:** same as previous **membership** except possibly for p and b.
    * p is excluded in two cases:
        (a) (NOT $arrived(b,p)$) AND NOT $\mathbf{ack}(p)$, or
        (b) $arrived(b,p)$ AND $\mathbf{ack}(b)$ AND NOT $\mathbf{ack}(p)$.
    * b is excluded in the two cases:
        (c) NOT $arrived(b,p)$, or
        (d) $\mathbf{ack}(p)$ AND NOT $\mathbf{ack}(b)$.
  - Updated **ack:** set to $arrived(b,p)$ AND ($\mathbf{ack}(b)$ OR NOT $\mathbf{ack}(p)$).
    Observe that the updated value of $\mathbf{ack}(p)$ is *true* iff p retains b in its local membership (i.e., it is the negation of the disjunction of (c) and (d)). We say that the broadcast by b is *acceptable* to p if the updated value of $\mathbf{ack}(p)$ is *true*.

Thus, p removes itself if (a) two consecutive expected broadcasts are unacceptable, or (b) it considers the previous broadcast unacceptable, but b considers it acceptable. Moreover, p removes b if (c) no broadcast is received or (d) p considers the previous expected broadcast acceptable, while b does not.

The broadcaster always assumes that its broadcast was correctly received even when that was not the case, and thus it sets its **ack** bit to *true*. For other processors, the **ack** bit will be *true* in the following step exactly when the broadcast arrives and either the broadcaster views the previous expected broadcast as acceptable, or the receiver does not.

4 Proof of Correctness

The key safety property of a group membership protocol is agreement: all the membership sets of nonfaulty processors should be identical. Furthermore, all nonfaulty processors should be included in that common membership set. These properties are proved in Theorem 1. The progress property that all faulty processors are promptly diagnosed and removed from the common membership set is proved in Theorem 2, but much of the justification is already present in the invariant required to establish Theorem 1. A corollary is that the common membership set contains at most one faulty processor. In addition, faulty processors are able to diagnose themselves, and do so promptly; this is proved in Theorem 3. These three theorems correspond to the requirements stated in Section 2.

Theorem 1 (Agreement). The local membership sets of all nonfaulty processors are always identical (and are called the *agreed set*) and contain all nonfaulty processors.

This theorem is proved by induction on **time**, but its statement must first be strengthened to yield an assertion that is inductive. In addition to claiming agreement among all nonfaulty processors, and that all nonfaulty processors are included in the agreed membership set, we must claim that all nonfaulty processors have the same values for the **ack** bits at each step, that these bits indeed reflect the intended meaning, and some additional facts about the diagnosis of earlier errors. These are needed to guarantee that in steps in which a fault has been detected, but not yet accurately ascribed, the next expected broadcaster will be nonfaulty and will resolve the uncertainty.

The invariant has the following conjuncts.

(1) All nonfaulty processors have the same local **membership** sets.
(2) All nonfaulty processors are in their own local **membership** sets.
(3) All nonfaulty processors have the same value for **ack**.
(4) For each processor p, **ack**(p) is true iff in the most recent previous step in which p expected a broadcast from a processor b, either p was b, or $arrived(b,p) \wedge (\textbf{ack}(b) \vee \neg\textbf{ack}(p))$ in that step.
(5) If a processor p became faulty less than n steps ago and q is a nonfaulty processor, either p is the present broadcaster or the present broadcaster is in p's local membership set iff it is in q's.
(6) If a receive fault occurred to processor p less than n steps ago, then either p is not the broadcaster or **ack**(p) is *false* while all nonfaulty q have **ack**$(q) =$ *true*, or p is not in its local membership set.
(7) If in the previous step b is in the broadcaster slot, p is a nonfaulty processor, and $arrived(b,p)$ does not hold, then b is faulty in the current step.
(8) If the broadcaster b is expected by a nonfaulty processor, then b is either nonfaulty, or became faulty less than n steps ago.

Note that since all nonfaulty processors have identical membership sets and agree on which slot has been reached, they also agree on which processor is the next expected broadcaster. Moreover, by (5), processors that became faulty less than n slots ago agree with the nonfaulty ones on whether the present slot is expected to broadcast. The conjunct (5) is needed to show that newly faulty processors still agree with nonfaulty ones on the next expected broadcaster until they are diagnosed both by others and by themselves.

Conjuncts (7) and (8) are needed to guarantee that no fault has occurred to the processor in an expected slot following one that is newly silent. As mentioned earlier, the prompt diagnosis of receive faults seen in (6) is needed to prove (8). The fault arrival rate assumption thus links the seemingly independent questions of how soon a fault is followed by a (possibly ambiguous) indication that *some* fault has occurred, and how soon after that another fault can occur.

An important feature of the protocol is used in the proof and will be called the *restricted-change* lemma: if a change is made in the local membership set of p relative to the previous step, it is either in the membership of p itself, or in the membership of the broadcaster in the previous step. This can be seen easily in the description of the protocol. Another useful property that can be seen directly in the description of the protocol is that $arrived(b,p)$ will be *true* precisely when $b = p$ or (b is not actively send-faulty, b is in its own membership, p is not actively receive-faulty, and both b and p are in p's membership).

The conjuncts (4) and (7) simply record the intended meanings of **ack** bits and the non-receipt of a broadcast, and follow directly from the assignments to **ack** and the definition of *arrived*, respectively. We show the inductive argument for (5), (6), and (8) separately, and then return to (1), (2), and (3).

Lemma [for conjunct (5)]: If the invariant has been true so far, conjunct (5) will be true of the next step. That is, if in the next step p became faulty less than n steps ago, and q is nonfaulty, then either p is the broadcaster in that step, or the broadcaster is in p's local membership set iff it is in q's.

Proof: Let r denote the broadcaster in the next step. If $p = r$, the lemma holds. Otherwise, $n - 1$ steps ago r was in p's membership iff it was in q's, because both p and q were then nonfaulty and agreed on their membership sets. In all steps since then and up until the next step, r is not the broadcaster and is not p, and thus its membership in p's local membership set is not changed, by the restricted-change lemma. If $q \neq r$, the same reasoning holds for q and r, and we are done. If $q = r$, by the inductive hypothesis, n steps ago the local membership sets of q and p both contained q (when both were nonfaulty), and q still contains itself, since it is nonfaulty in all steps up to the next step, while q is in the membership set of p by reasoning as before. $\square$

Lemma [for conjunct (6)]: If the invariant has been true so far, conjunct (6) will be true of the next step. That is, in the next step, if a receive fault occurred to processor p less than n time ago, then either p is not the broadcaster or **ack**(p) is *false* while all nonfaulty q have **ack**$(q) = true$, or p is not in its local membership set.

Proof: If in the next step p did not become faulty less than n steps earlier, or p is not the broadcaster, the assertion is true. Otherwise, since p became faulty less than n steps earlier, and is now the broadcaster, it was not the broadcaster since it became faulty. Thus until the next step (inclusive) the broadcaster in each step was in p's local membership set if and only if it was in q's, for any nonfaulty q, by (5). If in all previous steps after p became receive-faulty, p and any nonfaulty q did not have the broadcaster at each step in their membership sets, then the **ack** bit of p is *false*. This is true because it was set to *false* in the step it became receive-faulty (by definition of **ack** and a receive fault) and has not been changed since (again, using the definition of **ack** for nonexpected slots). Similarly, for all nonfaulty q in this case, their **ack** bit is *true*: it was set to *true* when p became receive-faulty (since they all did receive a broadcast from a nonfaulty processor with which they had the same **ack** bit) and has not been changed since. Thus the assertion holds in this case.

If there was a step since p became receive-faulty, but earlier than the next step in which p and any nonfaulty q had the broadcaster r in their local membership sets, then that r must be nonfaulty: by the fault arrival assumption it is not a previously nonfaulty one that is newly send-faulty or receive-faulty within the last n time units (because p has become faulty within the last n), and by the inductive hypothesis, if it had become receive or send-faulty more than n units ago, it would already have been diagnosed in its previous broadcast slot or earlier and thus would not be expected. (Actually, by (6) in the step after its broadcast following its becoming faulty, it would not be in the local membership set of any nonfaulty process.)

So r is nonfaulty and thus will have $\mathbf{ack}(r)$ *true* in its broadcast. If p did not receive that broadcast, then it did not receive two consecutive expected broadcasts and thus removed itself by rule (a). If p did receive the broadcast, it removed itself by rule (b) because it received $\mathbf{ack}(r)$ as *true* while $\mathbf{ack}(p)$ was *false*. Thus in the present step, p is not in its own local membership, as required by the assertion. □

Lemma [for conjunct (8)]: If the invariant has been true so far, conjunct (8) is true in the next step. That is, if the broadcaster in that step p is expected by a nonfaulty processor q, then p is either nonfaulty or became faulty less than n steps ago.

Proof: By contradiction. Consider a situation where broadcaster p is expected by nonfaulty processors q, but p became faulty at least n steps earlier. Then there is an earlier step in which p is the broadcaster, and it became faulty less than n steps earlier. By conjunct (6), if it became receive-faulty, then it will not be in the membership set of any nonfaulty processor in the step following its broadcast (using the conditions for removing a broadcaster), contradicting the fact that it is expected now. If it became send-faulty, it also is not in the membership of any nonfaulty processor in the following step, by rule (c), again contradicting the hypothesis. □

Theorem 1 follows easily from the following claim.

Claim. The conjuncts (1)–(8) are an invariant.

The Proof is by induction.

Basis: All processors are nonfaulty initially and are in all local membership sets, the $\mathbf{ack}$ bits agree, and there have been no faults.

Inductive step: Conjuncts (5), (6), and (8) have already been proved, while (4) and (7) are simple inductions using the definitions of the terms. Here we show the remaining conjuncts (1)–(3): membership sets of nonfaulty processors agree, they contain the nonfaulty processors, and the $\mathbf{ack}$ bits of nonfaulty processors agree.

Assume the invariant is satisfied in all steps up to and including the m'th step (that can be identified with the value of **time** in the state). Consider the $m + 1$'st. If the processor at slot $(m \bmod n)$ is not a member of the agreed set, nothing changes in step $m + 1$ except the update of **time**, and the result follows.

Otherwise, the processor at slot $(m \bmod n)$ is in the agreed set and is expected by nonfaulty processors. If it is nonfaulty, it will broadcast, be received by all nonfaulty processors, and be maintained in their local membership set (the broadcast and local **ack** bits agree by the inductive hypothesis). It also retains itself in its local membership set. All nonfaulty processors will set **ack** to *true* in the next step. No nonfaulty processor will remove itself. This is true because: condition (a) does not hold, since a nonfaulty processor will broadcast and the message is expected and thus is received; condition (b) does not hold because the agreed sets were the same in all previous stages, as were the **ack** bits. Thus all nonfaulty processors still have the same local membership sets and **ack** bits, and include themselves in their local membership sets.

If the processor b at slot (m mod n) is in the agreed set but has a send fault or has detected its own receive fault and removed itself from its local membership set, no nonfaulty processor p will receive b even though it was expected (i.e., $arrived(b, p)$ is *false*), and all will mark it as absent in step $m + 1$ by rule (c) and will set **ack** to *false* in that step. No nonfaulty processors will remove themselves in this case: since $arrived(b, p)$ is *false*, condition (b) is irrelevant, and (a) also does not hold, because the neighbors in expected slots around the silent processor must be nonfaulty, by the fault model and the conjuncts (7) and (8). In particular, the broadcast in the most recent expected slot before b was from a nonfaulty processor and thus must have arrived at p and had an **ack** bit that agreed with that of all nonfaulty recipients (by the inductive hypothesis). Therefore the **ack**(p) bit in step m is *true* by conjunct (4). Thus in step $m + 1$ the local membership sets and the **ack** bits of those nonfaulty processors remain identical, and no nonfaulty processor removes itself.

If the processor b in the broadcast slot is in the agreed set and in its local membership set (and thus is expected by nonfaulty processors) but is receive-faulty, then by conjunct (8) the receive fault occurred within the last n steps, and by conjunct (6), b will broadcast **ack**(b) as *false*, while nonfaulty processors p have **ack**$(p) = true$. Thus when the new broadcast occurs, all nonfaulty processors will remove the receive-faulty broadcaster by rule (d), and also set **ack** to *false*. In this case too, no nonfaulty processor will remove itself from its local membership set: since $arrived(b, p)$ is *true*, condition (a) is irrelevant, and condition (b) does not hold since the broadcaster had a *false* **ack** bit when it broadcast. □

Most of the justification for prompt diagnosis and removal of faulty processors was provided in the proof of the invariant above. We have:

Theorem 2 (Prompt Removal). A faulty processor is removed from the membership sets of nonfaulty processors in the step following its first broadcast slot while faulty.

Proof: As proved in conjunct (6) of the invariant, if a processor p becomes receive-faulty, then in its next broadcast either **ack**(p) is *false*, while **ack**(q) is *true* for nonfaulty processors q, or p is not in its local membership set. In the former case, p will be removed from the local membership set of q by rule (d) and in the latter case $arrived(p, q)$ is *false* so that p is removed by rule (c). If p becomes send-faulty, again $arrived(p, q)$ is *false*, so p is removed by rule (c). □

Corollary (One Faulty Member). In any step the agreed group contains at most one faulty processor.

Proof: Immediate from Theorem 2 and the fault arrival rate assumption. □

As part of the proof of the invariant needed for Theorem 1, in conjunct(6), we showed that a processor that is not the next expected broadcaster after becoming receive-faulty will remove itself from its local membership set. Here we show that any faulty processor, including send-faulty ones and those that became receive-faulty just before broadcasting, will remove themselves from their local membership sets.

Theorem 3 (Rapid Self-Diagnosis). A newly faulty processor will remove itself from its local membership set (and thereby diagnose itself) when the slots of at most two nonfaulty processors have been passed.

Proof: If a processor p becomes send-faulty, all nonfaulty processors will set their **ack** bits to *false* in the step following that processor's slot, since the slot is expected and no message is received. Similarly, if p just became receive-faulty in the expected broadcast before its slot, it will broadcast **ack** as *false*, while the nonfaulty processors have **ack** = *true*, and thus will set their **ack** bits to *false*. In either case, p will set its **ack** bit to *true* in the step after it broadcasts. Until its own or the previous broadcast, p was nonfaulty, and thus its local membership set agreed with all other nonfaulty processors. By the invariant of Theorem 1, no nonfaulty processor will remove itself due to the new fault, thus the next expected slot of the nonfaulty processors is the same as the next expected slot of the faulty one. By the fault arrival assumption, the next expected slot must be nonfaulty, since it cannot be newly faulty, and by the invariant it cannot be an undiagnosed old fault. Thus the newly faulty processor p will receive **ack** = *false* in the message from the next expected slot, disagree with the broadcaster, and set its own **ack** bit to *false*. Since all nonfaulty processors receive that broadcast and agree with its **ack** bit, p will receive **ack** as *true* in the expected slot after that (using the fact that there are at least two nonfaulty processors within the group). At that point, the faulty processor p will remove itself from its local membership set, using (b).

If a processor p becomes receive-faulty in its transition to the next step, but p is not the next expected broadcaster, it will remove the broadcaster from its local membership set, but otherwise has the same local membership sets and next expected slot as the nonfaulty ones. It will also set **ack**(p) to *false*. Again by the fault model, the next expected broadcaster must be nonfaulty, will broadcast **ack** as *true*, and the receive-faulty processor p will remove itself using (b). □

5 Discussion and Conclusions

The fault arrival rate we assume in our fault model is at most one new faulty processor in any consecutive $n+1$ slots. This is clearly tight, since if n were used in place of $n + 1$, the algorithm fails. Consider a scenario with a receive fault of the processor just before the broadcaster, followed n steps later by a send fault of that same broadcaster. Since the receive-faulty processor will self-diagnose and fall silent in its slot just before the subsequent send fault, all nonfaulty processors will not receive two consecutive expected broadcasts. They will all then incorrectly remove themselves from their local membership sets.

The requirement of two nonfaulty processors is also tight: if there are two processors remaining in the group and one of them becomes faulty, then there is no longer any possibility of distinguishing between a send and a receive fault. In either case, a broadcast is not received by the other processor, each will ultimately remove the other from its local membership set, and neither will ever self-diagnose.

We have described and proved correct a protocol for synchronous group membership that, driven by practical considerations, trades a very restrictive fault model in return for very low communications overhead—just one bit per message. Despite the paucity of information carried by each message, the protocol allows rapid and accurate identification and elimination of faulty processors. The reasoning that supports this claim, however, requires inferences to be made over *sequences* of messages; this, in turn, requires the statement of correctness to be strengthened significantly in order to obtain one that is inductive and requires a surprisingly intricate proof with extensive case-analysis. We found determination of an adequately strong (and true!) invariant, and development of the corresponding proof, to be quite challenging, and turned to formal techniques for assistance. We used the Murϕ state-exploration system [3] to examine instances of the protocol for the purposes of debugging the protocol, its fault model and its assumptions, and also to check candidate invariants. Using Murϕ, we were able to exhaustively check the behaviors of a ring of six processors with up to three faults. This required some tens of minutes (on a Sparc 20) and 100 MB of memory and entailed exploration of almost two million states. We are currently formalizing the general case and subjecting our proof of correctness to mechanical checking using the PVS verification system [12].

For the future, we are interested in systematic techniques for deriving strengthened invariants of the kind needed here, and for generating the proof of correctness. Some of the reasoning resembles that seen in the backward reasoning of precedence properties in temporal logic [10].

The group membership protocol presented here has no provision for readmitting previously-faulty processors that now appear to be working correctly again. Simple extensions, such as allowing a repaired processor to just "speak up" when its slot comes by, are inadequate. (A processor that has a receive fault just as the new member speaks up will not be aware of the fact and its local membership set will diverge from that of the other processors; a second fault can then provoke catastrophic failure of the entire system.) We are aware of solutions that do work, at the cost of strong assumptions on the fault-detection capability of the CRCs appended to each message, and plan to subject these to formal examination. TTP encodes its "critical state" in its CRC calculation, and the ack bit of our abstract protocol is in fact encoded implicitly in the CRC and recovered by recalculation of the CRC for each of the two possible values represented by that bit.

We are also eager to explore more of the highly optimized and integrated algorithms seen in industrial protocols for safety-critical distributed systems, such as TTP and ARINC 659. For example, the restrictive fault model used for our group membership protocol is partly justified by the existence of a blackout operating mode to deal with more severe, or clustered, faults. An interesting challenge for the future is to establish the fault coverage of this combination, and the correctness of the transitions between different operating modes in the presence of faults.

References

Papers by SRI authors are generally available from http://www.csl.sri.com/fm.html.

[1] *ARINC Specification 659: Backplane Data Bus.* Aeronautical Radio, Inc, Annapolis, MD, December 1993. Prepared by the Airlines Electronic Engineering Committee.

[2] Flaviu Cristian. Reaching agreement on processor-group membership in synchronous distributed systems. *Distributed Systems*, 4:175–187, 1991.

[3] David L. Dill. The Murφ verification system. In Rajeev Alur and Thomas A. Henzinger, editors, *Computer-Aided Verification, CAV '96*, volume 1102 of *Lecture Notes in Computer Science*, pages 390–393, New Brunswick, NJ, July/August 1996. Springer-Verlag.

[4] Li Gong, Patrick Lincoln, and John Rushby. Byzantine agreement with authentication: Observations and applications in tolerating hybrid and link faults. In *Dependable Computing for Critical Applications—5*, pages 79–90, Champaign, IL, September 1995. IFIP WG 10.4, preliminary proceedings; final proceedings to be published by IEEE.

[5] *Fault Tolerant Computing Symposium 25: Highlights from 25 Years*, Pasadena, CA, June 1995. IEEE Computer Society.

[6] H. Kopetz. Automotive electronics—present state and future prospects. In *Fault Tolerant Computing Symposium 25: Special Issue*, pages 66–75, Pasadena, CA, June 1995. IEEE Computer Society.

[7] H. Kopetz, G. Grünsteidl, and J. Reisinger. Fault-tolerant membership service in a synchronous distributed real-time system. In A. Avižienis and J. C. Laprie, editors, *Dependable Computing for Critical Applications*, volume 4 of *Dependable Computing and Fault-Tolerant Systems*, pages 411–429, Santa Barbara, CA, August 1989. Springer-Verlag, Vienna, Austria.

[8] Hermann Kopetz and Günter Grünsteidl. TTP—a protocol for fault-tolerant real-time systems. *IEEE Computer*, 27(1):14–23, January 1994.

[9] Patrick Lincoln and John Rushby. A formally verified algorithm for interactive consistency under a hybrid fault model. In *Fault Tolerant Computing Symposium 23*, pages 402–411, Toulouse, France, June 1993. IEEE Computer Society. Reprinted in [5, pp. 438–447].

[10] Z. Manna and A. Pnueli. *Temporal Verification of Reactive Systems: Safety*. Springer-Verlag, 1995.

[11] Fred J. Meyer and Dhiraj K. Pradhan. Consensus with dual failure modes. *IEEE Transactions on Parallel and Distributed Systems*, 2(2):214–222, April 1991.

[12] Sam Owre, John Rushby, Natarajan Shankar, and Friedrich von Henke. Formal verification for fault-tolerant architectures: Prolegomena to the design of PVS. *IEEE Transactions on Software Engineering*, 21(2):107–125, February 1995.

[13] John Rushby. A formally verified algorithm for clock synchronization under a hybrid fault model. In *Thirteenth ACM Symposium on Principles of Distributed Computing*, pages 304–313, Los Angeles, CA, August 1994. Association for Computing Machinery.

[14] Fred B. Schneider. Implementing fault-tolerant services using the state machine approach: A tutorial. *ACM Computing Surveys*, 22(4):299–319, December 1990.

[15] Philip Thambidurai and You-Keun Park. Interactive consistency with multiple failure modes. In *7th Symposium on Reliable Distributed Systems*, pages 93–100, Columbus, OH, October 1988. IEEE Computer Society.

The views and conclusions contained herein are those of the authors and should not be interpreted as necessarily representing the official policies or endorsements, either expressed or implied, of the Air Force Office of Scientific Research or the U.S. Government.

Virtual Precedence in Asynchronous Systems: Concept and Applications

Jean-Michel Hélary, Achour Mostéfaoui, and Michel Raynal

IRISA - Campus de Beaulieu, 35042 Rennes Cedex, France,
{helary,mostefaoui,raynal}@irisa.fr

Abstract. This paper introduces the *Virtual Precedence* (VP) property. An interval-based abstraction of a computation satisfies the VP property if it is possible to timestamp its intervals in a consistent way (i.e., time does not decrease inside a process and increases after communication). A very general protocol $\mathcal{P}$ that builds abstractions satisfying the VP property is proposed. It is shown that the VP property encompasses logical clocks systems and communication-induced checkpointing protocols. A new and efficient protocol which ensures no local checkpoint is useless is derived from $\mathcal{P}$. This protocol compares very favorably with existing protocols that solve the same problem. This shows that, due the generality of its approach, a theory (namely, here VP) can give efficient solutions to practical problems (here the prevention of useless checkpoints).

Keywords: Causality, Partial Order, Virtual Precedence, Logical Clocks, Checkpointing.

1 Introduction

Context, Statement of the Problem and Results. Without entering into a philosophical debate and roughly speaking, causality means first that the future can influence neither the past nor the present and second that the present is determined by the past. Causality plays a fundamental role when designing or analyzing distributed computations. A lot of causality-based protocols have been designed to solve specific problems encountered in distributed systems (resource allocation, detection of stable and unstable properties, checkpointing, etc.).

A distributed computation is usually modeled as a partially ordered set of (send, deliver and internal) events [4]. We consider in this paper a higher observation level in which each process of a distributed computation is perceived as a sequence of intervals, an *interval* being a set of consecutive events produced by a process. Intervals are defined by an *abstraction* of the computation. Moreover an abstraction associates with each computation a graph, called *A-graph*.

This paper addresses one of the many aspects of causality when considering an observation level defined by intervals; we call it *Virtual Precedence*. A main question is then: "Given an abstraction A of a distributed computation, does A allow a consistent timestamping of intervals?" (Intuitively "consistent" means that the "time" must not decrease inside a process and must eventually increase after communication).

The first two sections of the paper introduce the Virtual Precedence concept. Section 2 defines intervals and abstractions, and Section 3.1 provides a formal definition of Virtual Precedence. Section 3.2 gives a characterization of Virtual Precedence in terms of A-graphs. Then Section 3.3 presents a set of properties that are sufficient for a timestamping mechanism to ensure that interval timestamps satisfy Virtual Precedence. Finally Section 3.4 defines a very general protocol $\mathcal{P}$ that, given a distributed computation, builds abstractions satisfying Virtual Precedence.

Where these Results are Useful. Virtual Precedence has a lot of application domains (e.g., observation and monitoring of distributed applications). Section 4 investigates two of them.

- *Better understanding of the deep structure of existing protocols.* Section 4.2 illustrates this point with timestamping protocols. When considering the abstraction A_0 that associates an interval with each event, the resulting A-graph associated with a computation reduces to Lamport's partial order and protocol $\mathcal{P}$ can be instantiated to obtain classical timestamping protocols [3,4,6]. So, the protocol $\mathcal{P}$ provides us with a general framework that gives a deeper insight into a family of basic distributed protocols.

- *Design of new protocols.* This point (and again the previous one) is illustrated in Section 4.1 with checkpointing protocols. Uncoordinated checkpointing protocols are prone to the domino effect. In order to prevent this undesirable effect, these protocols can be augmented with a communication-induced checkpointing protocol. Upon the occurrence of a communication event and according to some condition, such a protocol may force a process to take an additional checkpoint in order no local checkpoint be useless (useless local checkpoints are the cause of the domino effect). Checkpointing protocols belonging to this family have already been published in the literature [2,7,11]. Section 4.1 shows that they are particular instances of the general protocol $\mathcal{P}$. Moreover, a new communication-induced checkpointing protocol, more efficient than the other protocols of this family, is obtained as a particular instance of $\mathcal{P}$. This demonstrates that a theoretic approach can have a positive impact on solutions of practical problems.

2 Abstractions of a Distributed Computation

2.1 Distributed Computations

A distributed program consists of a collection of sequential processes, denoted $P_1, P_2, \ldots, P_n$ ($n > 1$), that can communicate only by exchanging messages on communication channels. Processes have no access to a shared memory nor to a global clock. Communication delays are arbitrary.

A process can execute internal, send and delivery statements (we suppose a process does not send messages to itself). An internal statement does not involve communication. When a process P_i executes the statement *"send(m,P_j)"*, it puts the message m into the channel from P_i to P_j. When P_i executes the statement *"deliver(m)"*, it is blocked until at least one message directed to P_i has arrived; then a message is withdrawn from one of its input channels and delivered to P_i. Executions of internal, send and delivery statements are modeled by internal, send and delivery events.

Execution of a process P_i produces a sequence of events $h_i = e_{i,1} \ldots e_{i,z} \ldots$ This sequence is called the *history* of P_i; it can be finite or infinite. Events of h_i are enumerated according to the total order in which they are produced by P_i. Let H be the set of all events produced by the set of processes. A distributed computation is modeled by the partially ordered set $\widehat{H} = (H, \overset{hb}{\rightarrow})$, where $\overset{hb}{\rightarrow}$ denotes the well-known Lamport's *happened-before* relation [4]. As they are not relevant from the point of view of process interaction, internal events are no longer considered in the rest of the paper.

2.2 Abstraction of a Distributed Computation

Intervals An *interval* of process P_i is a set of consecutive events of h_i. An interval-based *abstraction A* partitions each process history h_i into a sequence of intervals $I_{i,1} \ldots I_{i,x} I_{i,x+1} \ldots$ More precisely:

- $\forall i, \forall e_{i,z} \in h_i : \exists x : e_{i,z} \in I_{i,x}$ (Every event belongs to an interval).
- $\forall i, \forall x > 0 : |I_{i,x}| \geq 1$ (Every interval contains at least one event).
- $\forall i : e_{i,z} \in I_{i,x} \wedge e_{i,t} \in I_{i,y} \wedge x < y \Rightarrow z < t$ (An event belongs to a single interval).

Figures 1.a.1, 1.a.2 and 1.a.3 depict three abstractions A_1, A_2 and A_3 of a same computation $\widehat{H}$. A rectangular box represents an interval.

A-graph An abstraction A of a distributed computation $\widehat{H}$ associates a directed graph (called *A-graph*) with this computation. This A-graph is defined in the following way:

- Vertices: the set of all intervals $I_{i,x}$.
- Edges: there is an edge $I_{j,y} \rightarrow I_{i,x}$ if:
  - either $j = i$ and $y = x - 1$ (such an edge is called *local* edge).
  - or there is a message m such that *send(m)*$\in I_{j,y}$ and *deliver(m)*$\in I_{i,x}$ (such an edge is called *communication* edge).

Figures 1.b.1, 1.b.2 and 1.b.3 depict the A-graphs defined by abstractions A_1, A_2 and A_3 of computation $\widehat{H}$. It is important to note that an A-graph may have cycles; this depends on the corresponding abstraction. Moreover, abstractions of different computations can produce the same A-graph. Let us also note that the A-graph produced by the trivial abstraction A_0 in which every interval exactly corresponds to a single event (actually, there is no abstraction) is the Lamport's partial order associated with the computation.

173

Notations. In the rest of the paper we use the following notations.

- $(S, \preceq)$ denotes a lattice with an infinite number of elements. $\bot$ and $\top$ denote the *least* element and the *greatest* element of $(S, \preceq)$, respectively. $a \prec b$ means $(a \preceq b) \wedge (a \neq b)$.
- $[a, b]$ denotes the sub-lattice of $(S, \preceq)$ whose least and greatest elements are a and b, respectively.
- $[a, b[$ denotes the sub-lattice of $(S, \preceq)$ including all elements x such that $a \preceq x \prec b$.
- Let X be a subset of $(S, \preceq)$. glb (X) denotes the *greatest lower bound* of X, and lub (X) denotes the *least upper bound* of X.
- For any $a \neq \bot, \top$: $a + \varepsilon$ denotes a value such that $(a \prec a + \varepsilon) \wedge (a + \varepsilon \neq \top)$. By convention, $\bot + \varepsilon = \bot$ and $\top + \varepsilon = \top$ ($\top$ and $\bot$ are absorbent values).

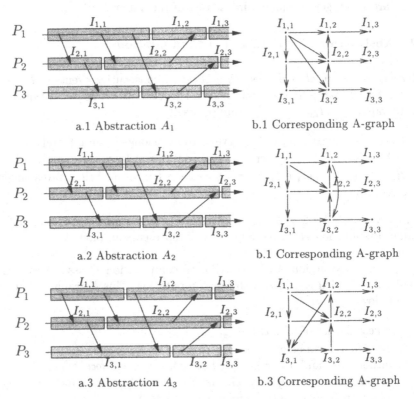

Fig. 1. Three Abstractions of the Same Computation

3 Virtual Precedence

3.1 Underlying Idea

Consider an abstraction A of a distributed computation $\widehat{H}$. Intuitively, A satisfies the *virtual precedence* (VP) property if it is possible to associate with each interval a value belonging to S, called its *timestamp*, in such a way that the ordering on intervals induced by their timestamps is compatible with the A-graph relation. For example, when considering the trivial abstraction A_0, Lamport's scalar clocks [4] or Fidge-Mattern's vector clocks [3,6] define a timestamping of events and messages, consistent with the causality relation (i.e., with the A_0-graph relation). For a more sophisticated abstraction A, the VP property ensures that there exists a mechanism that timestamps intervals and messages in such a way that, if we re-order all communication events of a given interval $I_{i,x}$ according to the timestamps of their messages, then (1) all *deliver* events precede all *send* events and, (2) the timestamp $f_{i,x}$ of $I_{i,x}$ is greater than or equal to the timestamps of delivered messages and lower than or equal to the timestamps of sent messages. This is illustrated in Figure 2 (where $S = I\!N$ the set of natural integers, an arrow denoting a message and the associated integer denoting its timestamp) and explains the name "Virtual Precedence". VP can be seen as a consistent re-ordering of communication events.

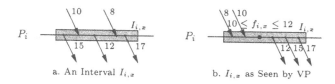

a. An Interval $I_{i,x}$ b. $I_{i,x}$ as Seen by VP

Fig. 2. What Is Virtual Precedence

3.2 Definition and Characterization

Definition 1. An abstraction A of a distributed computation $\widehat{H}$ satisfies the VP property if it exists a function f from the vertices of the A-graph into a lattice $(S, \preceq)$ such that ($f_{i,x}$ denotes the value of $f(I_{i,x})$):

(F1) $I_{j,y} \to I_{i,x} \Rightarrow f_{j,y} \preceq f_{i,x}$
(F2) $j \neq i \wedge I_{j,y} \to I_{i,x} \wedge \exists I_{i,x+1} \Rightarrow f_{j,y} \prec f_{i,x+1}$

Such a function f is called *timestamping* function. (F1) indicates that timestamps cannot decrease along a path of the A-graph, while (F2) indicates that they must increase after communication[1].

Albeit we limit our study of the VP property to the message passing computational model, the reader can see that the previous definition and its characterization given below are not limited to this model: an edge from an interval $I_{j,y}$ to another interval $I_{i,x}$ could also represent a write-read relation, a request-response relation, etc.[2]

---

[1] From timestamps point of view, (F1) can be seen as a *safety* requirement, while (F2) can be seen as a *liveness* requirement.

[2] [1] presents one of the very early works on abstractions in distributed computations. In this work, consistency requires cycle-freeness.

The following theorem gives a characterization of the VP property in terms of the A-graph defined by an abstraction A (this characterization will be used in Section 4).

Theorem 2. *An abstraction A of a distributed computation $\widehat{H}$ satisfies the VP property iff the corresponding A-graph has no cycle including a local edge.*

Proof

Necessity. Let f be a timestamping function of the A-graph and suppose that the A-graph has a cycle including a local edge $I_{i,x} \to I_{i,x+1}$. So, there is a path μ from $I_{i,x+1}$ to $I_{i,x}$. Since there is no local edge from $I_{i,x+1}$ to $I_{i,s}$ with $s \leq x$, μ has communication edges; let $I_{j,y} \to I_{i,s}, s \leq x$, be the last of these communication edges. We have: $f_{i,x+1} \preceq f_{j,y} \preceq f_{i,s} \prec f_{i,s+1} \preceq f_{i,x+1}$. A contradiction.

Sufficiency. Suppose the A-graph has no cycle including a local edge. Let $C(I_{i,x})$ denote the strongly connected component[3] to which vertex $I_{i,x}$ belongs. Consider the reduced graph A_R, the vertices of which are the strongly connected components of A and where an edge $C \to C'$ exists if and only if $C \neq C'$ and $\exists I_{i,x} \in C, \exists I_{j,y} \in C' : I_{i,x} \to I_{j,y}$. As A_R is acyclic it exists a function f_R with values in a lattice $(S, \preceq)$ such that $C \to C' \Rightarrow f_R(C) \prec f_R(C')$.

Define the function f from the vertices of the A-graph in S in the following way: $\forall I_{i,x} : f_{i,x} = f_R(C(I_{i,x}))$. Clearly, for each edge $I_{j,y} \to I_{i,x}$, we have:

- f satisfies (F1).
  -If $I_{j,y} \to I_{i,x}$ belongs to a cycle then $C(I_{j,y}) = C(I_{i,x})$ and consequently $f_{j,y} = f_{i,x}$, from which (F1) follows.
  - If $I_{j,y} \to I_{i,x}$ does not belong to a cycle then $C(I_{j,y}) \to C(I_{i,x})$ and consequently $f_{j,y} \prec f_{i,x}$, from which (F1) follows.
- f satisfies (F2). As by assumption no local edge $I_{i,x} \to I_{i,x+1}$ belongs to a cycle, we have $f_R(C(I_{i,x})) \prec f_R(C(I_{i,x+1}))$ and consequently $f_{i,x} \prec f_{i,x+1}$. If, additionally, there is a communication edge $I_{j,y} \to I_{i,x}$, we have: $f_{j,y} \preceq f_{i,x}$ (as (F1) is satisfied). So $f_{j,y} \prec f_{i,x+1}$, from which (F2) follows.

Thus A satisfies the VP property. $\square_{Theorem\ 2}$

3.3 How to timestamp Messages to Ensure the VP Property

This section displays properties that are sufficient for a timestamping protocol to implement abstractions satisfying the VP property. This protocol associates a timestamp $f_{i,x}$ with each interval $I_{i,x}$ and a timestamp $m.t \in S$ with each message m. Let $ts\_sent_{i,x}, ts\_rec_{i,x}, min\_sent_{i,x}$ and $max\_rec_{i,x}$ be the four following values:

$ts\_sent_{i,x} = \{m.t | send(m) \in I_{i,x}\}$.
$ts\_rec_{i,x} = \{m.t | deliver(m) \in I_{i,x}\}$.
$min\_sent_{i,x} = \mathsf{glb}\ (ts\_sent_{i,x})$ if $ts\_sent_{i,x} \neq \emptyset$, $\top$ else.
$max\_rec_{i,x} = \mathsf{lub}\ (ts\_rec_{i,x})$ if $ts\_rec_{i,x} \neq \emptyset$, $\bot$ else.
Let us consider the four following predicates:

---

[3] Two vertices x and y belong to the same strongly connected component if and only if $x = y$ or x and y belong to a same cycle.

(P1) $max\_rec_{i,x} \preceq f_{i,x}$ (P2) $f_{i,x} \preceq min\_sent_{i,x}$

(P3) $f_{i,x} \preceq f_{i,x+1}$ (P4) $\forall m.t \in ts\_rec_{i,x} : m.t \prec f_{i,x+1}$

Theorem 3. *Let A be an abstraction of $\widehat{H}$. $I_{i,x}$ denotes an interval defined by A, and $f_{i,x}$ denotes its timestamp.*

i) Let $\mathcal{F}$ be a protocol that associates a timestamp with each interval defined by A and each message. If $\mathcal{F}$ satisfies predicates (P1) to (P4), then A satisfies the VP property.

ii) If A satisfies the VP property, then it exists a protocol $\mathcal{F}$ that timestamps intervals and messages in such a way that (P1)-(P4) are satisfied.

Proof

i). if $i \neq j$ and $I_{j,y} \rightarrow I_{i,x}$ then there is a message m sent in $I_{j,y}$ and delivered in $I_{i,x}$. It follows from the definitions of $min\_sent_{j,y}$ and $max\_rec_{i,x}$ that: $min\_sent_{j,y} \preceq m.t \preceq max\_rec_{i,x}$ (1).

- (F1) is satisfied. If $I_{j,y}$ is $I_{i,x-1}$, then (F1) follows from (P3). If $j \neq i$ then by applying (P2) to $I_{j,y}$, (1) and then (P1) to $I_{i,x}$, we get: $f_{j,y} \preceq min\_sent_{j,y} \preceq m.t \preceq max\_rec_{i,x} \preceq f_{i,x}$.
- (F2) is satisfied. If $j \neq i \wedge I_{j,y} \rightarrow I_{i,x} \wedge \exists I_{i,x+1}$ then (F2) follows from (P2) applied to $I_{j,y}$, (1) and (P4), i.e., from: $f_{j,y} \preceq min\_sent_{j,y} \preceq m.t \prec f_{i,x+1}$.

ii). Let f be a function that satisfies (F1) and (F2). $\forall\ I_{j,y}$ and any message m sent in $I_{j,y}$ let $m.t = f_{j,y}$.

- (P3) follows from (F1) by taking $i = j$.

  (P2) follows from the definition of timestamp values.
- If $I_{j,y} \rightarrow I_{i,x}$ and $i \neq j$ there is a message m sent in $I_{j,y}$ and delivered in $I_{i,x}$ and we get:

  - from the definition of $m.t$ and (F1): $m.t = f_{j,y} \preceq f_{i,x}$, from which, by considering all messages m received in $I_{i,x}$, (P1) follows.

  - from the definition of $m.t$ and (F2): $m.t = f_{j,y} \prec f_{i,x+1}$, from which, by considering all messages m received in $I_{i,x}$, (P4) follows.

$\square_{Theorem\ 3}$

3.4   A General Protocol Ensuring the VP Property

The following protocol $\mathcal{P}$ executed by each process P_i constructs an abstraction of a distributed computation $\widehat{H}$, that satisfies the VP property, by associating timestamps with messages and intervals. Each interval is timestamped when it terminates. The protocol $\mathcal{P}$, described in Figure 3, is based on theorem 3, i.e., it maintains invariant predicates (P1)-(P4). In order to be as general as possible, some assignments of variables and parameters state only a subset from which the value to assign must be extracted. A particular rule to select a value from the corresponding subset gives a particular instance of $\mathcal{P}$ (see Section 4).

A process P_i starts a new interval either independently of the protocol (i.e., due to a purely local decision) or forced by the protocol. In both cases, when

P_i executes *new_interval* (line 16), it determines a timestamp $f_{i,x}$ for the terminating interval $I_{i,x}$ (lines 17-18).

If we have $\mathsf{lub}\,(\{f_{i,x-1}, max\_rec_{i,x-1} + \varepsilon, max\_rec_{i,x}\}) \preceq f_{i,x}$, then (P1), (P3) and (P4) are satisfied. Moreover, if $f_{i,x} \preceq min\_sent_{i,x}$ then (P2) is satisfied. The protocol consists in maintaining the following relation (P) invariant:

$$(P) \qquad \mathsf{lub}\,(\{f_{i,x-1}, max\_rec_{i,x-1} + \varepsilon, max\_rec_{i,x}\}) \preceq min\_sent_{i,x}$$

This is achieved by introducing three control variables, namely, MIN_SENT_i, MAX_REc_i and T_i, and by managing them appropriately.

Variables Meaning

• MIN_SENT_i and MAX_REc_i. These variables are used to compute $MIN\_SENT_{i,x}$ (line 3) and $max\_rec_{i,x}$ (line 10), respectively. According to their definitions, they are initialized to $\top$ and $\bot$, respectively, each time a new interval starts (lines 21 and 22).

• T_i. This variable measures progression of P_i. It is initialized to an arbitrary value distinct from $\bot$ and $\top$.

In order the previous predicate (P) be satisfied, the protocol maintains invariant the following relation:
(R) $\forall\, i$, $\forall\, x$, at any point of interval $I_{i,x}$: $\mathsf{lub}\,(\{f_{i,x-1}, max\_rec_{i,x-1} + \varepsilon, MAX\_REc_i\}) \preceq T_i \preceq MIN\_SENT_i$.
By using the notation $\alpha_{i,x-1} = \mathsf{lub}\,(\{f_{i,x-1}, max\_rec_{i,x-1} + \varepsilon\})$ it can be rewritten shortly as (note that $\alpha_{i,x-1}$ is a constant that P_i can use when executing $I_{i,x}$):
(R) $\forall\, i$, $\forall\, x$, at any point of interval $I_{i,x}$: $\mathsf{lub}\,(\{\alpha_{i,x-1}, MAX\_REc_i\}) \preceq T_i \preceq MIN\_SENT_i$.
Note that (R) is initially true by assuming $f_{i,0}$ and $max\_rec_{i,0}$ equal to $\bot$ (i.e., $\alpha_{i,0} = \bot$).

Variables Management

• When, after the termination of $I_{i,x}$, P_i starts a new interval $I_{i,x+1}$ (lines 17-23) it sets T_i to a value belonging to the interval $[\,\mathsf{lub}\,(\{f_{i,x}, MAX\_REc_i + \varepsilon\}), \top[= [\alpha_{i,x}, \top[$ (line 20). So, when $I_{i,x+1}$ starts (i.e., after the reinitialization of MIN_SENT_i to $\top$ (line 21) and MAX_REc_i to $\bot$ (line 22)), we have $\mathsf{lub}\,(\{\alpha_{i,x}, MAX\_REc_i\}) = \alpha_{i,x} \preceq T_i \preceq MIN\_SENT_i$, i.e., (R) is satisfied.
• When P_i sends a message m, this message is timestamped with a value $m.t$ belonging to $[T_i, \top[$ (line 2). This ensures that $T_i \preceq MIN\_SENT_i$ during interval $I_{i,x}$, and consequently $T_i \preceq min\_sent_{i,x}$ at the end of interval $I_{i,x}$.
• The core of the protocol lies in message reception. When m, timestamped $m.t$, arrives at P_i, the protocol forces P_i to terminate the current interval $I_{i,x}$ if the relation $max\_rec_{i,x} \preceq min\_sent_{i,x}$ (i.e., (P1) and (P2)) is about to be violated (lines 7-9). This relation (perceived as $\neg(m.t \preceq MIN\_SENT_i)$) is

the limit beyond which VP is no more satisfied. Let us note that parameters $param_1$ and $param_2$ allow the protocol to force termination of intervals even if the previous relation is not about to be violated: the number of forced interval terminations depends on the values selected for $param_1$ and $param_2$. The least constraining case is obtained when the extreme values $param_1 = m.t$ and $param_2 = MIN\_SENT_i$ are chosen. On the contrary, the extreme values $param_1 = \top$ and $param_2 = \bot$ force a new interval to be started before each message delivery. Finally, when m is delivered, MAX_REc_i is updated (line 10); T_i is also updated to the value $\mathsf{lub}\ (\{T_i, MAX\_REc_i\})$ (line 11). This update keeps (R) invariant as shown by the analyze of the two possible cases:

1. A new interval $I_{i,x+1}$ has been started at line 9. As shown above, before line 10 we have $\alpha_{i,x} \preceq T_i$ and thus, before line 11 we have $\mathsf{lub}\ (\{\alpha_{i,x}, MAX\_REc_i\}) \preceq \mathsf{lub}\ (\{T_i, MAX\_REc_i\})$. It follows that we have $\mathsf{lub}\ (\{\alpha_{i,x}, MAX\_REc_i\}) \preceq T_i \preceq MIN\_SENT_i = \top$ after line 11.

2. A new interval $I_{i,x+1}$ is not started at line 9. Thus, before line 10 we have $param_1 \preceq param_2$, which implies that $m.t \preceq MIN\_SENT_i$. Also, before line 10, (R) holds, i.e., $\mathsf{lub}\ (\{\alpha_{i,x-1}, MAX\_REc_i\}) \preceq T_i \preceq MIN\_SENT_i$; in particular, $\alpha_{i,x-1} \preceq T_i$. As $\alpha_{i,x-1}$ is constant during $I_{i,x}$ and T_i can only increase, it follows that $\alpha_{i,x-1} \preceq T_i$ remains true after line 10. Moreover, after line 11 we have $MAX\_REc_i \preceq T_i$ and $\mathsf{lub}\ (\{\alpha_{i,x-1}, MAX\_REc_i\}) \preceq T_i$. Similarly, before line 10 we have $MAX\_REc_i \preceq MIN\_SENT_i$, thus $\mathsf{lub}\ (\{MAX\_REc_i, m.t\}) \preceq MIN\_SENT_i$ which becomes, after line 10, $MAX\_REc_i \preceq MIN\_SENT_i$. But, before line 11 we have $\mathsf{lub}\ (\{MAX\_REc_i, T_i\}) \preceq MIN\_SENT_i$, and so, after line 11, we have $T_i \preceq MIN\_SENT_i$. Thus, (R) remains true after line 11.

To ensure that any interval $I_{i,x}(x > 0)$ includes at least one communication event, the boolean variable $New\_Interval\_Enabled$ (initialized to *false* and updated at lines 5, 13 and 23) is used. If P_i has produced events since the end of the previous interval $I_{i,x-1}$, it can terminate $I_{i,x}$ and start $I_{i,x+1}$ (line 16). P_i's desire to start a new interval is not defined by $\mathcal{P}$; it is the overlying application that triggers line 14 according to the problem it solves.

4 Applications

By appropriately defining the lattice $(S, \preceq)$, the condition ruling P_i's desire to start a new interval, and the rules used to select values for $m.t, param_1, param_2$ and $f_{i,x}$, we get particular instances of the protocol $\mathcal{P}$. As indicated in the Introduction, we consider two domains of applications: the design of communication-induced checkpointing protocols and the derivation of timestamping protocols from $\mathcal{P}$. In the following, we consider the two following particular lattices:

1. $\mathcal{N}$, such that $S = \mathbb{N} \cup \{\bot, \top\}$ with $\bot = -\infty$, $\top = +\infty$ and $\preceq$ is the usual order $\leq$.

```
(1)   When P_i sends m to P_j begin
(2)       let m.t be a value ∈ [T_i, ⊤[;
(3)       MIN_SENT_i := glb ({MIN_SENT_i, m.t});
(4)       send(m, m.t) to P_j;
(5)       New_Interval_Enabled := true; end

(6)   When P_i receives (m, m.t) begin
(7)       let param_1 be a value ∈ [m.t, ⊤];
(8)       let param_2 be a value ∈ [⊥, MIN_SENT_i];
(9)       if ¬(param_1 ≼ param_2) then new_interval endif;
(10)      MAX_REc_i := lub ({MAX_REc_i, m.t});
(11)      T_i := lub ({T_i, MAX_REc_i});
(12)      deliver m;
(13)      New_Interval_Enabled := true; end

(14)  When P_i desires to start an interval
(15)      if New_Interval_Enabled then new_interval endif;

(16)  Procedure new_interval is begin
(17)      let f_{i,x} be a value ∈ [T_i, ⊤[ ∩ ]⊥, MIN_SENT_i];
(18)      % f_{i,x} is the timestamp of the terminated interval I_{i,x}. %
(19)      % A new interval I_{i,x+1} is started. %
(20)      T_i := a value ∈ [ lub ({f_{i,x}, MAX_REc_i + ε}), ⊤[;
(21)      MIN_SENT_i := ⊤;
(22)      MAX_REc_i := ⊥;
(23)      New_Interval_Enabled := false; end
```

Fig. 3. A General Protocol $\mathcal{P}$ that Ensures the VP Property

2. $\mathcal{N}^n$, such that $S = I\!N^n \cup \{\bot, \top\}$ with $\bot = (-\infty, \ldots, -\infty)$, $\top = (+\infty, \ldots, +\infty)$, and $V \preceq V' \Leftrightarrow (\forall i : V[i] \leq V'[i]))$. In this lattice, 1_i denote the n-dimensional vector defined as $1_i[i] = 1$ and $\forall j \neq i \ 1_i[j] = 0$.

4.1 Preventing Useless Checkpoints

A local checkpoint is a snapshot of a local state of a process and a consistent global checkpoint is a set of local states, one from each process, such that no message sent by a process after its local checkpoint is received by another process before its local checkpoint. The computation of consistent global checkpoints is an important task when one is interested in designing or implementing systems that have to ensure dependability of the applications they run. Many protocols have been proposed to determine the way to select local checkpoints in order to form consistent global checkpoints [2]. Let us note that, if local checkpoints are taken independently, there is a risk that no consistent global checkpoint can ever be formed (this is the well-known *unbounded domino effect*, that can occur during rollback-recovery [8]). A local checkpoint that does not belong to any consistent global checkpoint is called *useless* [7]. Useless checkpoints are the cause of domino effect.

Let us consider an abstraction A_{ckpt} that defines an interval as the set of events produced by a process between two successive local checkpoints. Let

$C_{i,x}$ be the local checkpoint of P_i that corresponds to the local state reached after the last event of $I_{i,x}$. With these correspondences, the A-graph defined by A_{ckpt} reduces to the R-graph frequently encountered in the checkpointing literature [2,11]. In such a context, the fundamental result on the occurrence of useless checkpoints, formalized and stated for the first time in [7], has been formulated in terms of R-graph as: *A checkpoint $C_{i,x}$ is useless iff $C_{i,x+1} \rightarrow C_{i,x}$* [11]. Since this situation exactly corresponds to the occurrence of a cycle including local edges in the R-graph, this can be re-stated in our approach as *No local checkpoint is useless iff A_{ckpt} satisfies the VP property.*

To prevent useless checkpoints (and thus the domino effect), a kind of coordination in the determination of local checkpoints is required. In the approach called *communication-induced checkpointing*, processes select local checkpoints independently (basic checkpoints) and a protocol requires them to take additional local checkpoints (forced checkpoints) such that no checkpoint be useless; forced checkpoints are taken according to some predicate tested each time a message is received. Distinct definitions for this predicate give rise to distinct protocols. It is very important to note that the less forced local checkpoints are taken, the more efficient is the resulting protocol (to our knowledge, [5] proposes the most efficient protocol of this class). We show that these protocols can be derived from particular instances of the general protocol $\mathcal{P}$ introduced in Section 3.4. Moreover, we derive from $\mathcal{P}$ a new communication-induced checkpointing protocol more efficient than all existing ones.

Instantiation $\mathcal{P}_1'$. The family $\mathcal{P}_1'$ of communication induced checkpointing protocols is obtained from $\mathcal{P}$ by applying the following rules (The resulting instantiation is described at Figure 4):

(S1) Each process P_i triggers line 14 each time it takes a basic checkpoint
(S2) at line 2, for $m.t \in [T_i, \top[$, select $m.t = T_i$
(S3) at line 7, for $param_1 \in [m.t, \top]$, select $param_1 = m.t$
(S4) at line 8, for $param_2 \in [\bot, MIN\_SENT_i]$, select $param_2 = MIN\_SENT_i$
(S5) at line 17, for $f_{i,x} \in [T_i, \top[\ \cap \ ]\bot, MIN\_SENT_i]$, select $f_{i,x} = T_i$
(S6) at line 20, $T_i \in [$ lub $(\{f_{i,x}, MAX\_REc_i + \varepsilon\}), \top[,$
do the assignment $T_i := $ lub $(\{f_{i,x}, MAX\_REc_i + \varepsilon\})$

The choice of a particular lattice $(S, \preceq)$ gives rise to a particular communication-induced checkpointing protocol. As before, we consider two choices.

A new protocol (HMR). Taking the lattice $\mathcal{N}$ with $\varepsilon = 1$ and $(\forall i)$ T_i initialized to 0, results in a *new* protocol which ensures that no checkpoint is useless. This protocol has a low cost as it requires that application messages piggyback only one integer.

Wang's FDAS protocol. Taking the lattice $\mathcal{N}^n$ with $\varepsilon = 1_i$ and $(\forall i)$ T_i initialized to $(0, \dots, 0)$, we get the FDAS protocol introduced by Wang [11].

This protocol requires each message to carry an $O(n)$ size vector of integers. It is important to note that FDAS has been designed to ensure *RD-Trackability* [11], a property on local checkpoints stronger than the absence of useless checkpoints.

When P_i **sends** m **to** P_j **begin**
    $m.t := T_i$;
    $MIN\_SENT_i := \text{glb}(\{MIN\_SENT_i, m.t\})$;
    send$(m, m.t)$ **to** P_j;
    $New\_Checkpoint\_Enabled := true$; **end**

  When P_i **receives** $(m, m.t)$ **begin**
(9)   **if** $\neg(m.t \preceq MIN\_SENT_i)$ **then** *new_checkpoint* % *forced* % **endif**;
    $MAX\_REc_i := \text{lub}(\{MAX\_REc_i, m.t\})$;
    $T_i := \text{lub}(\{T_i, MAX\_REc_i\})$;
    deliver m;
    $New\_Checkpoint\_Enabled := true$; **end**

When P_i *desires to take a basic checkpoint*
    if $New\_Checkpoint\_Enabled$ **then**
        take a new checkpoint $C_{i,x}$;
        new_checkpoint **endif**;

Procedure *new_checkpoint* **is begin**
    $f_{i,x} := T_i$;
    % $f_{i,x}$ *is the timestamp of* $C_{i,x}$. *A new interval* $I_{i,x+1}$ *is started* %
    $T_i := \text{lub}(\{f_{i,x}, MAX\_REc_i + \varepsilon\})$;
    $MIN\_SENT_i := \top$;
    $MAX\_REc_i := \bot$;
    $New\_Checkpoint\_Enabled := false$;
end

Fig. 4. A Family $\mathcal{P}_1{}'$ of Checkpointing Protocols

If the aim is *only* that no local checkpoint be useless, then FDAS reveals to be less efficient than HMR. This is due to the following observation. With $\mathcal{N}$ and $\varepsilon = 1$, the value of $m.t$ counts the number of local checkpoints belonging to the longest causal path ending at $send(m)$ [9]. With $\mathcal{N}^n$ and $\varepsilon = 1_i$ for P_i, $m.t[k]$ counts the number of local checkpoints taken by P_k and belonging to the causal past of event $send(m)$ [3,6]. Let us consider a message m received by a process P_i. When the lattice is $\mathcal{N}$ (and $\varepsilon = 1$), if $m.t > T_i$ (i.e., the test of line 9 is true and a forced checkpoint is taken) then we can conclude that at least one process P_k has started an interval not previously known by P_i. In the same situation[4], when the lattice is $\mathcal{N}^n$ (and $\varepsilon = 1_i$ for P_i), we have necessarily : $\exists k : m.t[k] > T_i[k]$, which implies that the test of line 9 is also true. It follows that each time the test of line 9 is true when taking $\mathcal{N}$ and $\varepsilon = 1$ (HMR protocol) it is also true when taking $\mathcal{N}^n$ and $\varepsilon = 1_i$ for each P_i

---

[4] The one characterized by the sentence "at least one process P_k has started an interval not previously known by P_i".

(FDAS protocol). The reader can observe that the converse is not necessarily true. It follows that HMR is more efficient.

Instantiation P_2'. Consider the following variant P_2' of P_1' in which (S3) is replaced by:

(S3')   at line 7, for $param_1 \in [m.t, \top]$, select $param_1 = \top$

In P_2' the test of line 9, namely $\neg(param_1 \preceq param_2)$, becomes $\neg(\top \preceq MIN\_SENT_i)$. As MIN_SENT_i is initialized to $\top$ at the beginning of each interval, it follows that P_2' ensures that in each interval no *deliver* event follows a *send* event.

Let us compare P_1' and P_2' for a given lattice $(S, \preceq)$. As, when a message m is received, we have $m.t \prec \top$, it follows that if the test at line 9 in P_1' ($\neg(m.t \preceq MIN\_SENT_i)$) is satisfied[5], then it is also satisfied in P_2' ($\neg(\top \preceq MIN\_SENT_i)$). So, P_1' is more efficient than P_2'. Note that P_2' reduces to the well-known Russell's checkpointing protocol [10].

Instantiation P_3'. Both FDAS and HMR do not force a process P_i to take an additional local checkpoint as long as P_i has not sent a message since the beginning of the current interval. This is due to the fact that MIN_SENT_i is initialized to $\top$ when an interval starts and so the test $\neg(m.t \preceq MIN\_SENT_i)$ is false until a message is sent. More conservative protocols can be obtained by considering an instantiation P_3' of P, similar to P_1' but where (S4) is replaced by:

(S4')   at line 8, for $param_2 \in [\bot, MIN\_SENT_i]$, select $param_2 = T_i$

As $T_i \preceq MIN\_SENT_i$ is always true, we have: $\neg(m.t \preceq MIN\_SENT_i) \Rightarrow \neg(m.t \preceq T_i)$. It follows that at line 9 (S4') induces more forced checkpoints than (S4).

When choosing the lattice $\mathcal{N}$ with $\varepsilon = 1$ and $(\forall i)$ T_i initialized to 0, we get the MS protocol proposed by Manivannan and Singhal [5]. As indicated previously, to our knowledge, this was the most efficient communication-induced checkpointing protocol avoiding useless checkpoints. As (S4') is more constraining than (S4), the new protocol HMR compares favorably with MS.

So, the new HMR protocol, deduced from a theoretical approach, reveals to be more efficient than already known communication-induced checkpointing protocols whose aim is to prevent the occurrence of useless checkpoints.

4.2   Logical Clocks

Let us consider the trivial abstraction A_0 (introduced in Section 3.1) in which each event constitutes a new interval[6]. As the A-graph associated by A_0 with any computation $\widehat{H}$ has no cycle, it follows that A_0 satisfies the VP property.

---

[5] And consequently a forced local checkpoint is taken.

[6] As indicated in Section 2.1, we consider only communication events, namely, *send* and *deliver*. The following instantiations of P can easily be adapted to include *internal* events.

This subsection shows that a family of logical clocks protocols can be derived from a particular instance $\mathcal{P}''$ of the general protocol $\mathcal{P}$ described in Section 3.4. Let the instance $\mathcal{P}''$ of $\mathcal{P}$ be defined by the following rules:

(S1) each P_i associates an interval $I_{i,x}$ with each of its events e

(S2) at line 2, for $m.t \in [T_i, \top[$, select $m.t = T_i + \varepsilon$

(S3) at line 7, for $param_1 \in [m.t, \top]$, select $param_1 = m.t$

(S4) at line 8, for $param_2 \in [\bot, MIN\_SENT_i]$, select $param_2 = MIN\_SENT_i$

(S5) at line 17, for $f_{i,x} \in [T_i, \top[\; \cap \;]\bot, MIN\_SENT_i]$, select $f_{i,x} = T_i + \varepsilon$

(S6) at line 20, for $T_i \in [$ lub $(\{f_{i,x}, MAX\_REc_i + \varepsilon\}), \top[$,
   do the assignment $T_i :=$ lub $(\{f_{i,x}, MAX\_REc_i + \varepsilon\})$

Due to (S1), it follows that $\mathcal{P}''$ can be rewritten from $\mathcal{P}$, by suppressing lines 14-15 and by replacing lines 5 and 13 by copies of lines 17-22. Consider now the two cases $e = send(m)$ and $e = deliver(m)$.

- $I_{i,x} = \{deliver(m)\}$. As indicated, the behavior of $\mathcal{P}''$ is defined by lines 6-12 followed by a copy of lines 17-21. During this interval $I_{i,x}$, we have $MIN\_SENT_i = \top$. Moreover, due to (S3) and (S4), we have $param_1 = m.t$ and $param_2 = \top$, from which it follows that the test at line 9 is false at each message reception. Consequently, lines 7-9 can be suppressed from $\mathcal{P}''$. As during $I_{i,x}$, MAX_REc_i takes a single value, namely $m.t$, this variable can also be suppressed and replaced by $m.t$. From (S5), it follows that at line 17, we get the following timestamp for $I_{i,x}$: $f_{i,x} = T_i + \varepsilon$, and , due to (S6), at line 20, we get $T_i :=$ lub $(\{f_{i,x}, m.t + \varepsilon\})$.

- $I_{i,x} = \{send(m)\}$. In that case, the behavior of $\mathcal{P}''$ is defined by lines 1-4 followed by a copy of lines 17-21. During this interval $I_{i,x}$, we have $MAX\_REc_i = \bot$. As, due to (S2), $m.t = T_i + \varepsilon$, we get $MIN\_SENT_i = T_i + \varepsilon$ (line 3) and, due to (S5), at line 17, we select $f_{i,x} = T_i + \varepsilon$. It follows that MIN_SENT_i can be suppressed from $\mathcal{P}''$. Finally, at line 20, due to (S6) and to $MAX\_REc_i = \bot$, we get $T_i := m.t$ (i.e., $T_i + \varepsilon$).

The rules (S1)-(S6) make possible to suppress variables MIN_SENT_i and MAX_REc_i. The resulting protocol $\mathcal{P}''$ is described in Figure 5. Then according to the lattice $(S, \preceq)$ we select, a particular logical clock protocol is obtained. Choosing the lattice $\mathcal{N}$ with $\varepsilon = 1$ and $(\forall i)$ T_i initialized to 0, results in a classical scalar clock protocol [4]. Choosing the lattice $\mathcal{N}^n$ with, for each process P_i, $\varepsilon = 1_i$ and T_i initialized to $(0, \ldots, 0)$, results in a classical vector clock protocol [3,6]. Other timestamping protocols [9] can be obtained in the same way.

5 Conclusion

This paper has introduced the *Virtual Precedence* (VP) property. An interval-based abstraction of a computation satisfies the VP property if it is possible to timestamp its intervals in a consistent way (i.e., time does not decrease inside a process and increases after communication). A very general protocol

```
When P_i sends m to P_j              When P_i receives (m, m.t)
   begin                                begin
      let m.t = T_i + ε;                   deliver m;
      send(m, m.t) to P_j;                 T_i := lub ({T_i, m.t}) + ε;
      T_i := m.t;                       end
   end
```

Fig. 5. A Family $\mathcal{P}''$ of Logical Clock Protocols

$\mathcal{P}$ that builds abstractions satisfying the VP property has been proposed. It has been shown that the VP property encompasses logical clocks systems and communication-induced checkpointing protocols. A new and efficient protocol which ensures no local checkpoint is useless has been derived from $\mathcal{P}$. This protocol compares very favorably with existing protocols that solve the same problem. This shows that, due the generality of its approach, a theory (namely, here VP) can give efficient solutions to practical problems (here the prevention of useless checkpoints). Our current effort focuses on other applications of the VP theory such as logically instantaneous communications, deadlock detection and unstable properties detection.

References

1. Best, E. and Randell, B. A Formal Model of Atomicity in Asynchronous Systems, *Acta Informatica*, Vol. 16:93-124, 1981.
2. Elnozahy, E.N., Johnson, D.B. and Wang, Y.M. A Survey of Rollback-Recovery Protocols in Message-Passing Systems, *Technical Report* CMU-CS-96-181, Carnegie-Mellon University, 1996.
3. Fidge C.J. Logical Time in Distributed Computing Systems. *IEEE Computer*, 24(8):11-76, 1991.
4. Lamport, L. Time, Clocks and the Ordering of Events in a Distributed System, *Communications of the ACM*, 21(7):558-565, 1978.
5. Manivannan, D. and Singhal, M. A Low Overhead Recovery Technique Using Quasi-Synchronous Checkpointing. *Proc. of the 16th Int. Conf. on Distributed Computing Systems*, pp. 100-107, Hong-Kong, May 1996.
6. Mattern, F. Virtual Time and Global States of Distributed Systems. In Cosnard et al., Eds, *Proc. of the Int. Workshop on Parallel and Distributed Algorithms*, France, 1988, pp. 215-226, Elsevier Science Publishers, North Holland, 1989.
7. Netzer, R.H.B. and Xu, J. Necessary and Sufficient Conditions for Consistent Global Snapshots, *IEEE Trans. on Par. and Dist. Sys.*, 6(2):165-169, 1995.
8. Randell, B. System Structure for Software Fault-Tolerance, *IEEE Transactions on Software Engineering*, SE1(2):220-232, 1975.
9. Raynal, M. and Singhal, M. Logical Time: Capturing Causality in Distributed Systems. *IEEE Computer*, 29(2):49-56, February 1996.
10. Russell, D.L. State Restoration in Systems of Communicating Processes, *IEEE Trans. on Soft. Eng.*, SE6(2):183-194, 1980.
11. Wang, Y.M. Consistent Global Checkpoints That Contain a Given Set of Local Checkpoints, *IEEE Transactions on Computers*, 46(4), April 1997.

Detecting Global Predicates in Distributed Systems with Clocks

Scott D. Stoller*

Dept. of Computer Science, Indiana University, Bloomington, IN 47405, USA

Abstract. This paper proposes a framework for predicate detection in systems of processes with approximately-synchronized real-time clocks. Timestamps from these clocks are used to define two orderings on events: "definitely occurred before" and "possibly occurred before". These orderings lead naturally to definitions of 3 distinct *detection modalities*, *i.e.*, 3 meanings of "predicate Φ held during a computation", namely: $\mathbf{Poss_T}\,\Phi$ ("Φ possibly held"), $\mathbf{Def_T}\,\Phi$ ("Φ definitely held"), and $\mathbf{Inst}\,\Phi$ ("Φ definitely held at a specific instant"). This paper defines these modalities and gives efficient algorithms for detecting them; the algorithms are based on algorithms of Cooper and Marzullo, Garg and Waldecker, and Fromentin and Raynal.

Keywords: global predicate detection, consistent global states, partially-synchronous systems, distributed debugging, real-time monitoring

1 Introduction

A *history* of a distributed system can be modeled as a sequence of events in their order of occurrence. Since execution of a particular sequence of events leaves the system in a well-defined global state, a history uniquely determines a sequence of global states through which the system has passed. Unfortunately, in a distributed system without perfect synchronization, it is, in general, impossible for a process to determine the order in which events on different processors actually occurred. Therefore, no process can determine unambiguously the sequence of global states through which the system passed. This leads to an obvious difficulty for detecting whether a global state predicate (hereafter simply called a "predicate").

Cooper and Marzullo proposed a solution for asynchronous distributed systems [CM91]. Their solution involves two modalities, which we denote by **Poss** (read "possibly") and **Def** (read "definitely"). These modalities are based on logical time [Lam78] as embodied in the *happened-before* relation $\xrightarrow{e}_{hb}$, a partial ordering[2] of events that reflects causal dependencies. Happened-before is not a total order, so it does not uniquely determine the history, but it does restrict the possibilities. Given a predicate Φ, a computation satisfies **Poss** Φ iff there is *some* interleaving of events that is consistent with happened-before and in which the system passes through a global state satisfying Φ. A computation satisfies **Def** Φ iff for *every* interleaving of events that is consistent with happened-before, the system passes through a global state satisfying Φ.

---

* Email: *stoller@cs.indiana.edu*. Web: *http://www.cs.indiana.edu/~stoller/*
[2] In this paper, all partial orderings are irreflexive unless specified otherwise.

Cooper and Marzullo's definitions of these modalities established an important conceptual framework for predicate detection in asynchronous systems, which has been the basis for considerable research [DJR93, GW94, CBDGF95, JMN95, SS95, GW96]. In practice, though, detection of **Poss** or **Def** suffers from two significant burdens. First, most of the detection algorithms require that each process maintain a vector clock; this imposes computational overhead of $O(N)$ arithmetic operations per "tick" (of the vector clock) and requires that a vector timestamp with $O(N)$ components be attached to each message, where N is the number of processes in the system. Second, detecting **Poss** Φ or **Def** Φ can be computationally expensive: the worst-case time complexity is $\Omega(E^N)$, where E is the maximum number of events executed by each process.

This paper proposes a framework for predicate detection in systems with approximately-synchronized real-time clocks. Timestamps from these clocks can be used to define two orderings on events: $\xrightarrow{e}$ (read "definitely occurred before") and $\xrightarrow{e}$ (read "possibly occurred before"). By (roughly speaking) substituting each of these orderings for happened-before in the definitions of **Poss** and **Def**, we obtain definitions of four new modalities. The two modalities based on $\xrightarrow{e}$ are closely analogous to **Poss** and **Def**, so we denote them by **Poss**$_T$ and **Def**$_T$ (the "T" stands for "timed"). We obtain algorithms for detecting **Poss**$_T$ and **Def**$_T$ by adapting (and, as we do so, optimizing) algorithms of Cooper and Marzullo [CM91] and Garg and Waldecker [GW94, GW96]. Modalities based on $\xrightarrow{e}$ are quite different, because $\xrightarrow{e}$ (unlike $\xrightarrow{e}_{hb}$ and $\xrightarrow{e}$) is not a partial ordering. In fact, $\xrightarrow{e}$ yields a degenerate case, in which the analogues of **Poss** and **Def** are equivalent. We show that this single modality, which we denote by **Inst**, is closely related to Fromentin and Raynal's concept of **Properly** [FR94, FR95], and we adapt for detecting **Inst** an algorithm of theirs for detecting **Properly**.

Our detection framework is applicable to a wide range of systems, since it does not require that clocks be synchronized to within a fixed bound. We assume each event is time-stamped with a time interval, with the interpretation: when that event occurred, the value of every (relevant) clock in the system was in that interval. Implementing such timestamps is straightforward assuming the underlying clock synchronization mechanism provides bounds on the offsets between clocks (the *offset* between two clocks (at some instant) is the difference in their values). For example, such information can be obtained from NTP [Mil95] or the Distributed Time Service in OSF DCE [Tan95].

The quality of clock synchronization affects $\xrightarrow{e}$ and $\xrightarrow{e}$ and therefore affects the results of detection. For example, consider **Inst** Φ. Informally, a computation satisfies **Inst** Φ iff the timestamps imply that there was an instant during the computation when predicate Φ held, *i.e.*, iff there is some collection of local states that form a global state satisfying Φ and that, based on the timestamps, definitely overlapped in time. Suppose Φ actually holds in a global state g that persists for time δ. Whether **Inst** Φ holds depends on the quality of synchronization. Roughly, if the clock offsets are known to be smaller than δ, then **Inst** Φ holds; otherwise, there is in some cases no way to determine whether the local states in g actually overlapped in time, so **Inst** Φ might not hold.

The quality of clock synchronization affects also the cost of detection. For example, consider $\textbf{Poss}_T\ \varPhi$. Informally, a computation satisfies $\textbf{Poss}_T\ \varPhi$ iff there is some collection of local states that form a global state satisfying $\varPhi$ and that, based on the timestamps, possibly overlapped in time. The larger the bounds on the offsets between clocks, the more combinations of local states possibly overlap. In general, $\varPhi$ must be evaluated in each such combination of local states. Thus, the larger the bounds on the offsets, the more expensive the detection. If the bounds on the offsets are comparable to or smaller than the mean interval between events that potentially truthify or falsify $\varPhi$, then the number of global states that must be checked is comparable to the number of global states that the system actually passed through during execution, which is $O(NE)$. In contrast, the number of global states considered in the asynchronous case is $O(E^N)$.

We expect the above condition on the bounds on the offsets to hold in many systems. In most local-area distributed systems, protocols like NTP can efficiently maintain synchronization of clocks to within a few milliseconds [Mil95]. Even in extremely wide-area distributed systems like the Internet, clock synchronization can usually be maintained to within a few tens of milliseconds [Mil91]. The detection framework and algorithms proposed here are designed to provide a basis for monitoring and debugging applications in such systems.

2 Background

A *local computation*—that is, a computation of a single process—is represented as a sequence of local states and events; thus, a local computation has the form

$$e_1,\ s_1,\ e_2,\ s_2,\ e_3,\ s_3,\ \ldots \tag{1}$$

where the e_α are events, and the s_α are local states. For a local state s, $S(s)$ and $T(s)$ denote the start event and terminal event, respectively, of s. For example, in (1), $S(s_2)$ is e_2, and $T(s_2)$ is e_3.

A *computation* of a distributed system is a collection of local computations, one per process; we represent such a collection as a function from process names to local computations. We use integers $1, 2, \ldots, N$ as process names. Variables i and j always range over process names. We use $Ev(c)$ and $St(c)$ to denote the sets of all events and all local states, respectively, in a computation c. For convenience, we assume all events and local states in a computation are distinct. For a local state s, $pr(s)$ denotes the process that passes through s. For an event e, $pr(e)$ denotes the process on which e occurs. A *global state* of a distributed system is a collection of local states, one per process, represented as a function from process names to local states. The set of global states of a computation c is denoted $GS(c)$; thus, g is in $GS(c)$ iff for each process i, $g(i)$ is a local state in $c(i)$. We define a reflexive partial ordering $\preceq_G$ on global states by:

$$g \preceq_G g' \triangleq (\forall i : g(i) = g'(i) \lor (g(i) \text{ occurs before } g(i'))). \tag{2}$$

Each event e has a timestamp $C(e)$, which is an interval with lower endpoint $C_1(e)$ and upper endpoint $C_2(e)$, with the interpretation: when e occurred, every clock in the system had a value between $C_1(e)$ and $C_2(e)$. We require that the clock synchronization algorithm never decrease the value of a clock. This ensures:

SC1 For every event e, $C_1(e) \le C_2(e)$.

SC2 For every event e with an immediately succeeding event e' on the same process, $C_1(e) \le C_1(e')$ and $C_2(e) \le C_2(e')$.

3 Generic Theory of Consistent Global States

Predicate detection in asynchronous systems is based on the notion of consistent global states (CGSs) [BM93]. Informally, a global state is consistent if it could have occurred during the computation. Recall that an *ideal* of a partial order $\langle S, \prec \rangle$ is a set $I \subseteq S$ such that $(\forall x \in I : \forall y \in S : y \prec x \Rightarrow y \in I)$. Ideals of $\langle Ev(c), \xrightarrow{e}_{hb} \rangle$ are usually called *consistent cuts*. Recall that for any partial order, the set of its ideals ordered by inclusion $(\subseteq)$ forms a lattice [DJR93]. Furthermore, the lattice of CGSs ordered by $\preceq_G$ is isomorphic to the lattice of consistent cuts [SM94, BM93]. This isomorphism has an important consequence for detection algorithms; specifically, it implies that a minimal increase with respect to $\preceq_G$ corresponds to advancing one process by one event, and hence that the lattice of CGSs can be explored by repeatedly advancing one process by one event. This principle underlies detection algorithms of Cooper and Marzullo [CM91] and Garg and Waldecker [GW94, GW96].

In this section, we show that the above theory is not specific to the happened-before relation but rather applies to any partial ordering $\xrightarrow{e}$ on events, provided $\xrightarrow{e}$ is *process-wise-total*, i.e., for any two events e and e' on the same process, if e occurred before e', then $e \xrightarrow{e} e'$. This generalization underlies the detection algorithms in Sections 4 and 5.

Definition of CGSs. Let c be a computation, and let $\xrightarrow{e}$ be a relation on $Ev(c)$. We define a relation $\xrightarrow{s}$ on $St(c)$, with the informal interpretation: $s \xrightarrow{s} s'$ if s ends before s' starts. Formally,

$$s \xrightarrow{s} s' \triangleq \begin{cases} S(s) \xrightarrow{e} S(s') & \text{if } pr(s) = pr(s') \\ T(s) \xrightarrow{e} S(s') & \text{if } pr(s) \ne pr(s'). \end{cases} \tag{3}$$

Two local states are *concurrent* if they are not related by $\xrightarrow{s}$. A global state is *consistent* if its constituent local states are pairwise concurrent. Thus, the set of CGSs of computation c with respect to $\xrightarrow{e}$ is

$$CGS^{\xrightarrow{e}}(c) = \{g \in GS(c) \mid \forall i, j : i \ne j \Rightarrow \neg(g(i) \xrightarrow{s} g(j))\}. \tag{4}$$

Note that $CGS^{\xrightarrow{e}_{hb}}$ is the usual notion of CGSs.

Generic Definitions of **Poss** *and* **Def**. The detection modalities **Poss** and **Def** for asynchronous systems are defined in terms of the lattice of CGSs induced by happened-before. We generalize them as follows.

Poss: A computation c satisfies **Poss**$^{\xrightarrow{e}} \Phi$ iff $CGS^{\xrightarrow{e}}(c)$ contains a global state satisfying Φ.

Def$\overset{e}{\hookrightarrow}$ is defined in terms of paths. A *path* of a partial order $\langle S, \preceq \rangle$ is a sequence[3] σ of distinct elements of S such that $\sigma[1]$ and $\sigma[|\sigma|]$ are minimal and maximal, respectively, with respect to $\preceq$ and such that for all $\alpha < |\sigma|$, $\sigma[\alpha+1]$ is an immediate successor[4] of $\sigma[\alpha]$. Informally, each path in $\langle CGS \overset{e}{\hookrightarrow} (c), \preceq_G \rangle$ corresponds to an order in which the events in the computation could have occurred.

Def: A computation c satisfies **Def**$\overset{e}{\hookrightarrow} \Phi$ iff every path of $\langle CGS \overset{e}{\hookrightarrow} (c), \preceq_G \rangle$ contains a global state satisfying Φ.

CGSs and Ideals. When $\overset{e}{\hookrightarrow}$ is a process-wise-total partial ordering of events, there is a natural correspondence between $CGS \overset{e}{\hookrightarrow}$ and ideals of $\langle Ev(c), \overset{e}{\hookrightarrow} \rangle$. One can think of an ideal I as the set of events that have occurred. Executing set I of events leaves each process i in the local state immediately following the last event of process i in I. Thus, ideal I corresponds to the global state g such that for all i, $S(g(i))$ is the maximal element of $\{e \in I \mid pr(e) = i\}$. This correspondence is an isomorphism.

Theorem 1. *For any process-wise-total partial ordering $\overset{e}{\hookrightarrow}$ on $Ev(c)$, the partial order $\langle CGS \overset{e}{\hookrightarrow}(c), \preceq_G \rangle$ is a lattice and is isomorphic to the lattice of ideals of $\langle Ev(c), \overset{e}{\hookrightarrow} \rangle$.*

Proof. This is true for the same reasons as in the standard theory based on happened-before [SM94, BM93, DJR93]. The proof is straightforward. □

The following corollary underlies the detection algorithms in Sections 4 and 5.

Corollary 2. *If global state g' is an immediate successor of g in $\langle CGS(c), \preceq_G \rangle$, then the ideal corresponding to g' contains exactly one more event than the ideal corresponding to g.*

Proof. This follows from Theorem 1 and the fact that if one ideal of a partial order is an immediate successor of another ideal of that partial order, then those two ideals differ by exactly one element. □

4 Detection Based on a Strong Event Ordering: Poss$_T$ and Def$_T$

We instantiate the generic theory in Section 3 with a specific partial ordering $\overset{e}{\twoheadrightarrow}$ ("definitely occurred before"), defined by:

$$e \overset{e}{\twoheadrightarrow} e' \overset{\Delta}{=} \begin{cases} e \text{ occurs before } e' & \text{if } pr(e) = pr(e') \\ C_2(e) < C_1(e') & \text{if } pr(e) \neq pr(e'). \end{cases} \qquad (5)$$

---

[3] We use 1-based indexing for sequences.

[4] For a reflexive or irreflexive partial order $\langle S, \prec \rangle$ and elements $x \in S$ and $y \in S$, y is an *immediate successor* of x iff $x \neq y \land x \prec y \land \neg(\exists z \in S \setminus \{x, y\} : x \prec z \land z \prec y)$.

This ordering cannot be defined solely in terms of the real-time timestamps, since SC1 and SC2 allow consecutive events on a process to have identical timestamps. We solve this problem by assuming that when a process records the real-time timestamp for an event, it records a sequence number $L(e)$ (starting with zero) as well; thus, for events e and e' with $pr(e) = pr(e')$, $e \xrightarrow{e} e'$ iff $L(e) < L(e')$.

Theorem 3. *For any computation c, $\xrightarrow{e}$ is a process-wise-total partial ordering on $Ev(c)$.*

Proof. See Appendix. $\qquad\square$

By the discussion in Section 3, $\xrightarrow{e}$ induces an ordering $\xrightarrow{s}$ on local states, a notion $CGS^{\xrightarrow{e}}$ of CGSs, and detection modalities $\mathbf{Poss}^{\xrightarrow{e}}$ and $\mathbf{Def}^{\xrightarrow{e}}$, which we denote by $\mathbf{Poss_T}$ and $\mathbf{Def_T}$, respectively. If $g \in CGS^{\xrightarrow{e}}(c)$, then the local states in g possibly overlapped in time.

We consider in this paper only detection algorithms with a passive monitor. In such algorithms, each process in the original system sends its timestamped local states to a new process, called the *monitor*. More specifically, for each process, when an event terminating the current local state s occurs, the process sends to the monitor a message containing s and the timestamps $C(S(s))$ and $C(T(s))$.[5]

We consider only *on-line* detection, in which the monitor detects the property as soon as possible. Algorithms for *off-line* detection, in which the monitor waits until the computation has terminated and all local states have arrived before checking whether the property is satisfied, can be obtained as special cases. We consider first general algorithms for $\mathbf{Poss_T}$ and $\mathbf{Def_T}$ and then more efficient algorithms that work only for predicates of a certain form.

4.1 General Algorithms for $\mathbf{Poss_T}$ and $\mathbf{Def_T}$

The algorithms in [CM91, MN91] can be adapted to explore lattice $\langle CGS^{\xrightarrow{e}}(c), \preceq_G \rangle$ by (roughly) replacing each condition of the form $e \xrightarrow{e}_{hb} e'$ with $e \xrightarrow{e} e'$. Following [CM91, MN91], we give algorithms in which the monitor constructs one level of the lattice of CGSs at a time. The *level* of a global state g is $\sum_{i=1}^{N} L(S(g(i)))$. Level ℓ of the lattice of CGSs contains the CGSs with level ℓ. Constructing one level of the lattice at a time is unnecessary and sometimes delays detection of a property; this construction is used only to simplify the presentation.

The algorithm used by the monitor to detect $\mathbf{Poss_T}\,\Phi$ is given in Figure 1. To enumerate the states in the next level of the lattice (line 7 of the algorithm),

---

[5] Several straightforward optimizations are possible. For example, each message might describe only the differences between consecutive reported local states, rather than repeating the entire local state. Also, except for the initial local state, it suffices to include with local state s only the timestamp $C(T(s))$, since $C(S(s))$ was sent in the previous message to the monitor. Also, for a given predicate Φ, events that cannot possibly truthify or falsify Φ can be ignored.

the monitor considers each state g in *last* and each process i, and checks whether the next local state s of process i (*i.e.*, the immediate successor on process i of $g(i)$) is concurrent with the local states in g of all the other processes. (The monitor cannot complete construction of the next level until the next local state of each process has arrived.) If so, the monitor adds $g[i \mapsto s]$ to the set *current*, where for a function f and an element x in the domain of f, $f[x \mapsto c]$ is the function that maps x to c and that agrees with f on all arguments except x. Cooper and Marzullo's algorithm for detecting **Def** can be adapted in a similar way to detect **Def$_T$**.

$lvl := 0$;
wait until at least one local state has been received from each process;
current := the global state of level 0;
while no state in *current* satisfies Φ
    last := *current*;
    $lvl := lvl + 1$;
    current := consistent global states of level lvl reachable from a state in *last*
endwhile;
report **Poss$_T$** Φ

Fig. 1. Algorithm for detecting **Poss$_T$** Φ.

Recall that a process sends a local state to the monitor when that local state ends. This is natural (because $\overset{s}{\rightarrow}$ depends on when local states end) but can delay detection. One approach to bounding and reducing this delay is for a process that has not reported an event to the monitor recently to send a message to the monitor to report that it is still in the same local state (as if the process were reporting that it just executed a "skip" event). Another approach (described in [MN91]) requires knowledge of a bound on message latency: the monitor can use its own local clock and this bound to determine a lower bound on the ending time of the last local state it received from a process.

The time complexity of these algorithms depends on the rate at which events occur relative to the bounds on clock offsets. To simplify the complexity analysis, suppose the offset between two clocks is known to be always at most $\epsilon/2$, so for every event e, $C_2(e) - C_1(e) < \epsilon$. Suppose also that the interval between consecutive events at a process is always at least τ. For each CGS g, the algorithm takes constant time to evaluate Φ and $O(N)$ time to find all of the immediate successors of g in the lattice. If $\tau > \epsilon$, then there are $O(3^N E)$ CGSs, so the worst-case time complexity is $O(3^N NE)$, where E is the maximum number of events executed by any process. If $\tau \leq \epsilon$, then each local state appears in at most $O((\lceil \frac{2\epsilon + \tau}{\tau} \rceil + 1)^{N-1})$ CGSs, so the worst-case time complexity is $O((\lceil \frac{2\epsilon}{\tau} \rceil + 2)^{N-1} NE)$. In both cases, the worst-case time complexity is linear in E, which is normally much larger than N; in contrast, the worst-case time complexity of general algorithms for detecting **Poss** and **Def** is $\Omega(E^N)$.

4.2 Algorithms for Poss$_T$ and Def$_T$ for Restricted Predicates

Garg and Waldecker [GW94, GW96] have developed efficient algorithms for detecting **Poss** Φ and **Def** Φ for conjunctive predicates Φ. A predicate is *conjunctive* if it is a conjunction of predicates that each depend on the local state of one process. Their algorithms can be adapted in a straightforward way to detect **Poss**$_T$ and **Def**$_T$, by (roughly) replacing comparisons based on happened-before with comparisons based on $\stackrel{e}{\rightarrow}$. This yields detection algorithms with worst-case time complexity $O(N^2 E)$. The worst-case time complexity of both algorithms can be reduced to $O((N \log N)E)$ by exploiting the total ordering on numbers. We briefly review Garg and Waldecker's algorithm for detecting **Poss** Φ for conjunctive predicates and then describe the optimized algorithm for detecting **Poss**$_T$ for such predicates.

Suppose the global predicate of interest is $\Phi = \bigwedge_{i=1}^{N} \phi_i$, where ϕ_i depends on the local state of process i. In Garg and Waldecker's algorithm, each process i sends to the monitor timestamped local states satisfying ϕ_i; local states not satisfying ϕ_i are not reported. For each process i, the monitor maintains a queue q_i and adds each timestamped local state received from process i to the end of q_i. Let head(q) denote the head of a non-empty queue q. If for some i and j, head(q_i) $\stackrel{e}{\rightarrow}_{hb}$ head(q_j), then head(q_i) is removed from q_i. The heads of the queues are repeatedly compared in this way and (when appropriate) removed, until the heads of the non-empty queues are (pairwise) concurrent. Then, if all the queues are non-empty, then the heads of the queues form a CGS satisfying Φ, so the property has been detected; if some queue is empty, then the monitor waits to receive more local states. The worst-case time complexity is $O(N^2 E)$, because there are $O(NE)$ local states, and each time a local state is removed from q_i, the new head of q_i is compared with the heads of the other $O(N)$ queues.

For detection of **Poss**$_T$ $\bigwedge_{i=1}^{N} \phi_i$, the number of comparisons can be reduced as follows. Expanding the definition of $CGS^{\stackrel{e}{\rightarrow}}(c)$, $g \in GS(c)$ is consistent iff

$$(\forall i, j : i \neq j \;\Rightarrow\; C_2(T(g(i))) \geq C_1(S(g(j)))). \tag{6}$$

Using the fact that for all i, $C_2(T(\text{head}(g(i)))) \geq C_1(S(\text{head}(g(i))))$, which follows from SC1 and SC2, one can show that (6) is equivalent to

$$\min_i (C_2(T(\text{head}(g(i))))) \geq \max_i (C_1(S(\text{head}(g(i))))). \tag{7}$$

To evaluate (7) efficiently, we maintain two priority queues p_1 and p_2, whose contents are determined by the invariants:

I1: For each process i such that q_i is non-empty, p_1 contains a record with key $C_1(S(\text{head}(q_i)))$ and satellite data i. p_1 contains no other records.

I2: For each process i such that q_i is non-empty, p_2 contains a record with key $C_2(T(\text{head}(q_i)))$ and satellite data $\langle i, ptr \rangle$, where ptr is a pointer to the record with satellite data i in p_1. p_2 contains no other records.

Recall that the operations on a priority queue p include getMin(p), which returns a record $\langle k, d \rangle$ with key k and satellite data d such that k is the minimal value of the key, and extractMin(p), which removes and returns such a record [CLR90]. We also use priority queues with operations based on maximal key values. Thus, (7) is equivalent to

$$\text{key}(\text{getMin}(p_2)) \geq \text{key}(\text{getMax}(p_1)), \tag{8}$$

where key($\langle k, d \rangle$) = k. The negation of (8) is used in the **while** loop in Figure 2 to check whether a CGS has been found. Recall that an operation on a priority queue containing n records takes $O(\log n)$ time. A constant number of such operations are performed for each local state, so the worst-case time complexity of the algorithm in Figure 2 is $O((N \log N)E)$. Note that the time complexity is independent of the rate of events and the quality of clock synchronization.

The algorithm in [GW96] for detecting **Def** Φ for conjunctive Φ can be adapted in a similar way to detect **Def$_T$** Φ for such predicates.

```
On receiving x from process i:
    append(q_i, x);
    if head(q_i) = x then
        add records for i to p_1 and p_2;
        while ¬empty(p_1) ∧ key(getMin(p_2)) < key(getMax(p_1))
            ⟨k, ⟨i, ptr⟩⟩ := extractMin(p_2);
            remove record for i from p_1;
            removeHead(q_i);
            if ¬empty(q_i) then
                add records for i to p_1 and p_2;
            endif
        endwhile
        if (∀i : ¬empty(q_i)) then
            report Poss_T Φ and exit
        endif
    endif
```

Fig. 2. Algorithm for detecting **Poss$_T$** Φ for Φ a conjunction of local predicates.

5 Detection Based on a Weak Event Ordering: Inst

This section considers the ordering "possibly occurred before", defined by:

$$e \xrightarrow{e} e' \triangleq \begin{cases} e \text{ occurs before } e' & \text{if } pr(e) = pr(e') \\ C_1(e) \leq C_2(e') & \text{if } pr(e) \neq pr(e'). \end{cases} \tag{9}$$

Using (3), this induces a relation $\xrightarrow{s}$ on local states, with the interpretation: $s \xrightarrow{s} s'$ if s possibly ended before s' started. Two local states are *strongly concurrent* if they are not related by $\xrightarrow{s}$; such local states must overlap in time. The set $CGS^{\xrightarrow{e}}$ is defined by (4). We call elements of $CGS^{\xrightarrow{e}}$ *strongly consistent* global states (SCGSs).

Poss$^{\xrightarrow{e}}$ and **Def**$^{\xrightarrow{e}}$ are equivalent, *i.e.*, for all computations c and predicates Φ, c satisfies **Poss**$^{\xrightarrow{e}}$ Φ iff c satisfies **Def**$^{\xrightarrow{e}}$ Φ. This equivalence is an easy corollary of the following theorem.

Theorem 4. $\langle CGS^{\stackrel{e}{\rightarrow}}(c), \preceq_G \rangle$ *is a total order (and therefore a lattice).*

Proof. See Appendix. □

We define **Inst** (read "instantaneously") to denote this modality (*i.e.*, **Poss**$^{\stackrel{e}{\rightarrow}}$ and **Def**$^{\stackrel{e}{\rightarrow}}$). Informally, a computation satisfies **Inst** Φ if there is a global state g satisfying Φ and such that the system definitely passes through g during the computation. Theorem 1 does not apply to $\stackrel{e}{\rightarrow}$, because:

Theorem 5. $\stackrel{e}{\rightarrow}$ *is not a partial ordering.*

Proof. See Appendix. □

Since Theorem 1 does not apply, it is not surprising that a minimal increase in $\langle CGS^{\stackrel{e}{\rightarrow}}(c), \preceq_G \rangle$ does not necessarily correspond to advancing one process by one event (it is easy to construct examples of this). Consequently, the algorithms in Section 4 cannot be easily adapted to detect **Inst**. Our algorithm for detecting **Inst** is based on Fromentin and Raynal's algorithm for detecting **Properly** (read "properly") in asynchronous systems [FR94, FR95]. The definition of **Properly**, generalized to an arbitrary ordering on events, is:

Properly: A computation c satisfies **Properly**$^{\stackrel{e}{\hookrightarrow}}$ Φ iff there is a global state satisfying Φ and contained in every path of $\langle CGS^{\stackrel{e}{\hookrightarrow}}(c), \preceq_G \rangle$.

Theorem 6. Properly$^{\stackrel{e}{\rightarrow}}$ *is equivalent to* **Inst**.

Proof. See Appendix. □

As Theorem 6 suggests, Fromentin and Raynal's algorithm for detecting **Properly**$^{\stackrel{e}{\rightarrow}hb}$ can be adapted in a straightforward way to detect **Inst**. This yields an algorithm with worst-case time complexity $O(N^3 E)$. Optimizations similar to those presented in Section 4.2 are possible here as well. Expanding the definition of $CGS^{\stackrel{e}{\rightarrow}}(c)$, a global state g is strongly consistent iff

$$(\forall i, j : i \neq j \Rightarrow C_1(T(g(i))) > C_2(S(g(j)))). \tag{10}$$

To check this condition efficiently, we introduce priority queues p_1 and p_2, whose contents are determined by the following invariants:

J1: for each process i such that q_i is non-empty, p_1 contains a record with key $C_1(T(\text{head}(q_i)))$ and satellite data $\langle i, ptr \rangle$, where ptr is a pointer to the record with satellite data i in p_2. p_1 contains no other records.

J2: for each process i such that q_i is non-empty, p_2 contains a record with key $C_2(S(\text{head}(q_i)))$ and satellite data i. p_2 contains no other records.

The goal is to define a condition $SC(p_1, p_2)$ that tests whether the heads of the non-empty queues are (pairwise) strongly concurrent. Based on (10), a first attempt is empty$(p_1) \vee$ key$(\text{getMin}(p_1)) >$ key$(\text{getMax}(p_2))$. However, this condition is not correct when for some i, $C_1(T(g(i))) < C_2(S(g(i)))$. Taking this possibility into account, we obtain

$$SC(p_1, p_2) \triangleq \text{empty}(p_1) \vee \text{key}(\text{getMin}(p_1)) > \text{key}(\text{getMax}(p_2))$$
$$\vee \left(\pi_1(\text{data}(\text{getMin}(p_1))) = \text{data}(\text{getMax}(p_2)) \wedge \text{countMax}(p_2) = 1\right),$$
$$(11)$$

where $\text{countMax}(p)$ is the number of records containing the maximal value of the key in priority queue p, and where $\text{data}(\langle k, d \rangle) = d$ and $\pi_1(\langle i, ptr \rangle) = i$. Thus, the following procedure makeSC ("make Strongly Concurrent") loops until the heads of the non-empty queues are strongly concurrent:

```
procedure makeSC()
    while ¬SC(p₁, p₂)
        ⟨k, i⟩ := extractMin(p₁);
        remove record for i from p₂;
        removeHead(qᵢ);
        if ¬empty(qᵢ) then
            add records for i to p₁ and p₂;
        endif
    endwhile
```

The optimized algorithm for detecting **Inst** appears in Figure 3, where $\text{head2}(q)$ returns the second element of a queue q. When a SCGS g is found, if g does not satisfy Φ, then the algorithm starts searching for the next SCGS by advancing some process j such that this advance yields a CGS (*i.e.*, an element of $CGS^{\stackrel{e}{\rightarrow}}$). If at first no process can be so advanced (*e.g.*, if each queue q_i contains only one element), then the algorithm waits for more local states to be reported. It follows from the definitions of $CGS^{\stackrel{e}{\rightarrow}}$ and $CGS^{\stackrel{e}{\rightarrow}}$ that if some process can be so advanced, then a process j such that $C_1(S(\text{head2}(q_j)))$ is minimal can be so advanced. Thus, by maintaining a priority queue p_3 with key $C_1(S(\text{head2}(q_i)))$, a candidate process to advance can be found in constant time. We can determine in constant time whether advancing this candidate yields a CGS, using a test similar to (8), but with p_1 and p_2 replaced with appropriate priority queues. This requires maintaining an additional priority queue.

We analyze the worst-case time complexity of this algorithm by summing the times spent inside and outside of makeSC. Each iteration of the **while** loop in makeSC takes $O(\log N)$ time (because each operation on priority queues takes $O(\log N)$ time) and removes one local state. The computation contains $O(NE)$ local states, so the total time spent inside makeSC is $O((N \log N)E)$. The total time spent in the code outside makeSC is also $O((N \log N)E)$, since there are $O(NE)$ SCGSs (this is a corollary of Theorem 6), and each local state is considered at most once and at constant cost in the **wait** statement. Thus, the worst-case time complexity of the algorithm is $O((N \log N)E)$.

6 Sample Application: Debugging Coherence Protocols

Coherence of shared data is a central issue in many distributed systems, such as distributed file systems, distributed shared memory, and distributed databases. A typical invariant maintained by a coherence protocol is: if one machine has a copy of a data item in write mode, then no other machine has a valid copy of that

On receiving x from process i:
 append(q_i, x);
 if head$(q_i) = x$ then
  add records for i to p_1 and p_2;
  found := true;
  while *found*
   makeSC();
   if $(\exists i : \text{empty}(q_i))$ then
    found := false
   else (* found a SCGS *)
    $g :=$ the global state $(\lambda i.\,\text{head}(q_i))$;
    if g satisfies Φ then
     report **Inst** Φ and exit
    else
     wait until there exists j such that $g[j \mapsto \text{head2}(q_j)]$ is in $CGS \overset{e}{\rightarrow}(c)$;
     remove records for j from p_1 and p_2;
     removeHead(q_j);
     add records for j to p_1 and p_2
    endif
   endif
  endwhile
 endif

Fig. 3. Algorithm for detecting **Inst** Φ.

data item. Let *cohrnt* denote this predicate. As part of testing and debugging a coherence protocol, one might issue a warning if **Poss**$_T\ \neg cohrnt$ is detected and report an error if **Def**$_T\ \neg cohrnt$ is detected. A computationally cheaper but less informative alternative is to monitor only **Inst** $\neg cohrnt$ and report an error if it is detected. In either case, if on-line detection would cause an unacceptable probe effect, then the probe effect can be reduced by logging timestamped local states locally and using the detection algorithms off-line.

A detection algorithm based on happened-before could be used instead, if the system can be modified to maintain vector clocks (or is unusual and maintains them already). However, if the coherence protocol uses timers—for example, if leases are used instead of locks—then time acts as a hidden channel [BM93] (*i.e.*, a means of communication other than messages), so detection based on happened-before might yield less precise results. For example, expiration of a lease and granting of another lease to a different machine need not be related by happened-before, so **Poss** $\neg cohrnt$ may be detected, even though coherence was maintained and **Poss**$_T\ \neg cohrnt$ would not be detected.

7 Related and Future Work

Marzullo and Neiger [MN91] define two detection modalities for partially-synchronous systems. In the notation of this paper, those modalities are **Poss**$^{\overset{e}{\rightarrow}}{}_{MN}$ and **Def**$^{\overset{e}{\rightarrow}}{}_{MN}$, where

$$e \overset{e}{\rightarrow}_{MN} e' \overset{\Delta}{=} e \overset{e}{\rightarrow} e' \vee e \overset{e}{\rightarrow}_{hb} e'. \tag{12}$$

Combining logical and real-time orderings in this way exploits more information about the computation but requires that the system maintain vector clocks. In [MN91], there is no discussion of an event ordering analogous to $\overset{e}{\to}$ or a modality analogous to **Inst**. Also, [MN91] considers only systems in which all clocks are always synchronized within a fixed offset ϵ, while our framework accommodates varying quality of synchronization.

Veríssimo [Ver93] discusses the uncertainty in event orderings caused by the granularity[6] and imperfect synchronization of digital real-time clocks, analyzes the conditions under which this uncertainty is significant for an application, and describes a synchronization technique, suitable for certain applications, that masks this uncertainty. However, [Ver93] does not aim for a general approach to detecting global predicates in the presence of this uncertainty.

This paper proposes a foundation for detection of global predicate in systems with approximately-synchronized real-time clocks. One direction for future work is to implement and gain experience with the detection algorithms. Another is to study efficient detection of global predicates that depend explicitly on time.

References

[BM93]   Ö. Babaoğlu and K. Marzullo. Consistent global states of distributed systems: Fundamental concepts and mechanisms. In Sape Mullender, editor, *Distributed Systems*, ch. 5, pages 97–145. Addison Wesley, 2nd ed., 1993.

[CBDGF95] B. Charron-Bost, C. Delporte-Gallet, and H. Fauconnier. Local and temporal predicates in distributed systems. *ACM Trans. on Programming Languages and Systems*, 17(1):157–179, January 1995.

[CLR90]   T. Cormen, C. Leiserson, and R. Rivest. *Introduction to Algorithms*. MIT Press and McGraw-Hill, 1990.

[CM91]   R. Cooper and K. Marzullo. Consistent detection of global predicates. In *Proc. ACM/ONR Workshop on Parallel and Distributed Debugging*, 1991. Appeared as ACM SIGPLAN Notices 26(12):167-174, December 1991.

[DJR93]   C. Diehl, C. Jard, and J.-X. Rampon. Reachability analysis on distributed executions. In J.-P. Jouannaud and M.-C. Gaudel, editors, *TAPSOFT '93: Theory and Practice of Software Development*, vol. 668 of *Lecture Notes in Computer Science*, pages 629–643. Springer, 1993.

[FR94]   E. Fromentin and M. Raynal. Inevitable global states: a concept to detect unstable properties of distributed computations in an observer independent way. In *Proc. 6th IEEE Symposium on Parallel and Distributed Processing*, 1994.

[FR95]   E. Fromentin and M. Raynal. Characterizing and detecting the set of global states seen by all observers of a distributed computation. In *Proc. IEEE 15th Int'l. Conference on Distributed Computing Systems*, 1995.

[GW94]   V. K. Garg and B. Waldecker. Detection of weak unstable predicates in distributed programs. *IEEE Trans. on Parallel and Distributed Systems*, 5(3):299–307, 1994.

---

[6] Our framework accommodates the granularity of digital clocks by using $\leq$ instead of $<$ in SC1 and SC2.

[GW96]   V. K. Garg and B. Waldecker. Detection of strong unstable predicates in distributed programs. *IEEE Trans. on Parallel and Distributed Systems*, 7(12):1323–1333, 1996.

[JMN95]   R. Jegou, R. Medina, and L. Nourine. Linear space algorithm for on-line detection of global predicates. In J. Desel, editor, *Proc. Int'l. Workshop on Structures in Concurrency Theory (STRICT '95)*. Springer, 1995.

[Lam78]   L. Lamport. Time, clocks, and the ordering of events in a distributed system. *Communications of the ACM*, 21(7):558–564, 1978.

[Mil91]   D. L. Mills. Internet time synchronization: the Network Time Protocol. *IEEE Trans. Communications*, 39(10):1482–1493, October 1991.

[Mil95]   D. L. Mills. Improved algorithms for synchronizing computer network clocks. *IEEE/ACM Transactions on Networking*, 3(3):245–254, June 1995.

[MN91]   K. Marzullo and G. Neiger. Detection of global state predicates. In *Proc. 5th Int'l. Workshop on Distributed Algorithms (WDAG '91)*, vol. 579 of *Lecture Notes in Computer Science*, pages 254–272. Springer, 1991.

[SM94]   R. Schwarz and F. Mattern. Detecting causal relationships in distributed computations: In search of the holy grail. *Distributed Computing*, 7(3):149–174, 1994.

[SS95]   S. D. Stoller and F. B. Schneider. Faster possibility detection by combining two approaches. In J.-M. Hélary and M. Raynal, editors, *Proc. 9th Int'l. Workshop on Distributed Algorithms (WDAG '95)*, vol. 972 of *Lecture Notes in Computer Science*, pages 318–332. Springer, 1995.

[Tan95]   A. S. Tanenbaum. *Distributed Operating Systems*. Prentice–Hall, 1995.

[Ver93]   P. Veríssimo. Real-time communication. In Sape Mullender, editor, *Distributed Systems*, ch. 17, pages 447–490. Addison Wesley, 2nd ed., 1993.

Appendix

Proof of Theorem 3. It follows immediately from the definitions that $\xrightarrow{e}$ is process-wise-total. We need to show that $\xrightarrow{e}$ is irreflexive, acyclic, and transitive. Irreflexivity is obvious. For transitivity, we suppose $e \xrightarrow{e} e'$ and $e' \xrightarrow{e} e''$, and show $e \xrightarrow{e} e''$. First consider the case $pr(e) = pr(e'')$. If $pr(e') = pr(e)$, then the desired result follows from transitivity of "occurred before". Of $pr(e') \neq pr(e)$, then using SC1, the hypothesis $e \xrightarrow{e} e'$, SC1 again, and finally the hypothesis $e' \xrightarrow{e} e''$, we have the chain of inequalities $C_1(e) \leq C_2(e) < C_1(e') \leq C_2(e') < C_1(e'')$, so $C_1(e) < C_1(e'')$, so by SC2, e occurred before e''. Next consider the case $pr(e) \neq pr(e'')$. Note that $\neg(pr(e) = pr(e') \wedge pr(e') = pr(e''))$. If $pr(e) \neq pr(e')$, then it is easy to show that $C_2(e) < C_1(e') \leq C_1(e'')$, so $C_2(e) < C_1(e'')$, as desired. If $pr(e') \neq pr(e'')$, then it is easy to show that $C_2(e) \leq C_2(e') < C_1(e'')$, so $C_2(e) < C_1(e'')$, as desired.

Given transitivity, to conclude acyclicity, it suffices to show that there are no cycles of size 2. We suppose $e \xrightarrow{e} e'$ and $e' \xrightarrow{e} e$, and derive a contradiction. If $pr(e) = pr(e')$, then the fact that "occurred before" is a total order on the events of each process yields the desired contradiction. If $pr(e) \neq pr(e')$, then using SC1, the hypothesis $e \xrightarrow{e} e'$, SC1 again, and finally the hypothesis $e' \xrightarrow{e} e$, we obtain the chain of inequalities $C_1(e) \leq C_2(e) < C_1(e') \leq C_2(e') < C_1(e)$, which implies $C_1(e) < C_1(e)$, a contradiction. $\square$

Proof of Theorem 4. Suppose not, *i.e.*, suppose there exist a computation c, global states g and g' in $CGS^{\overset{e}{\rightarrow}}(c)$, and processes i and j such that $g(i) \overset{e}{\rightarrow} g'(i)$ and $g'(j) \overset{e}{\rightarrow} g(j)$. By definition of $CGS^{\overset{e}{\rightarrow}}(c)$, $\neg(g(i) \overset{e}{\rightarrow} g(j))$, so $C_2(S(g(j))) < C_1(T(g(i)))$. By hypothesis, $g(i) \overset{e}{\rightarrow} g'(i)$, so $C_1(T(g(i))) < C_2(S(g'(i)))$, so by transitivity, $C_2(S(g(j))) < C_2(S(g'(i)))$. By definition of $CGS^{\overset{e}{\rightarrow}}(c)$, $\neg(g'(j) \overset{e}{\rightarrow} g'(i))$, so $C_2(S(g'(i))) < C_1(T(g'(j)))$, so by transitivity, $C_2(S(g(j))) < C_1(T(g'(j)))$. By hypothesis, $g'(j) \overset{e}{\rightarrow} g(j)$, so $C_1(T(g'(j))) < C_2(S(g(j)))$, so by transitivity, $C_2(S(g(j))) < C_2(S(g(j)))$, which is a contradiction. □

Proof sketch of Theorem 5. Consider an computation in which, at approximately the same time, event e_1 occurs on process 1 and events e_2 and e_2' occur in rapid succession on process 2. If $C_2(e_1) - C_1(e_1)$, $C_2(e_2) - C_1(e_2)$, and $C_2(e_2') - C_1(e_2')$ are large relative to the separation (in time) between these events, then none of the actual orderings between e_1 and e_2 or between e_1 and e_2' can be determined from the timestamps, so $e_2' \overset{e}{\rightarrow} e_1$ and $e_1 \overset{e}{\rightarrow} e_2$. Since also $e_2 \overset{e}{\rightarrow} e_2'$, $\overset{e}{\rightarrow}$ contains a cycle and therefore is not a partial ordering.

Proof of Theorem 6. It suffices to show that a global state g is in $CGS^{\overset{e}{\rightarrow}}(c)$ iff it is contained in every maximal path of $CGS^{\overset{e}{\rightarrow}}(c)$. The proof of this is based on a result of Fromentin and Raynal. Recast in our notation, Theorem IGS of [FR94] (or Theorem C of [FR95]) states that a global state g is contained in every maximal path of $\langle CGS^{\overset{e}{\rightarrow}hb}(c), \preceq_G \rangle$ iff $(\forall i, j : S(g(i)) \overset{e}{\rightarrow}_{hb} T(g(j)) \vee g(i) = last(c(i)))$, where *last* returns the last element of a sequence. A closely analogous proof shows that a global state g is contained in every maximal path of $\langle CGS^{\overset{e}{\rightarrow}}(c), \preceq_G \rangle$ iff $(\forall i, j : S(g(i)) \overset{e}{\rightarrow} T(g(j)))$, which by definition of $\overset{e}{\rightarrow}$ is equivalent to

$$(\forall i, j : i \neq j \Rightarrow C_2(S(g(i))) < C_1(T(g(j)))). \tag{13}$$

The only significant difference involves the treatment of the last local state of each process. Informally, the disjunct $g(i) = last(c(i))$ is needed in Fromentin and Raynal's analysis based on happened-before because, by a peculiarity of the definitions, the global state f containing the last local state of each process appears in every maximal path of $\langle CGS^{\overset{e}{\rightarrow}hb}(c), \preceq_G \rangle$, even though the system might not have passed through g_f in real-time, since the processes might have terminated at different times. This peculiarity is absent from our analysis based on real-time timestamps—specifically, g_f appears in every maximal path of $\langle CGS^{\overset{e}{\rightarrow}}(c), \preceq_G \rangle$ iff the system necessarily passed through g_f in real-time—so (13) does not need a disjunct dealing specially with the last local state of each process. Expanding the definition of $CGS^{\overset{e}{\rightarrow}}(c)$ and simplifying yields (13). □

Fault Tolerance Bounds for Memory Consistency*

Jerry James and Ambuj K. Singh

Department of Computer Science
University of California at Santa Barbara

Abstract. We analyze the achievable fault tolerances of shared memory consistency conditions in the form of t-resilience, the ability to withstand up to t node failures. We derive tight bounds for linearizability, sequential consistency, processor consistency, and some weaker memories in totally asynchronous systems, in which failed and slow nodes cannot be distinguished. For linearizability, we show that neither the read nor the write operation can tolerate more failures than a minority of the nodes. For sequential consistency, processor consistency, and related conditions, we show that one operation can be wait-free and the other cannot tolerate more failures than a minority of the nodes. Several weaker conditions can have both operations wait-free.

1 Introduction

The programming of distributed systems is complex, due to the nondeterministic nature of such systems. In the message passing paradigm, the programmer has low-level control, but must explicitly manage shared data. The shared memory paradigm is attractive since it hides the details of such management, making both local and remote data available through read and write operations. When a shared memory abstraction is built on top of a message passing system, it is called *Distributed Shared Memory* [21] (DSM). A DSM system provides a contract to the programmer in the form of a *consistency condition*. Two well-known consistency conditions are *linearizability* [16, 19] and *sequential consistency* [18], which guarantee that the DSM behaves like a single physical memory module with no cache. However, such strong shared memories can have a significant negative impact on the performance of applications, and can limit the scalability of a system [5]. Weaker conditions have been defined in an attempt to ameliorate such effects, such as release consistency [12], causal memory [2], pipelined RAM [23], and mixed consistency [1].

The capabilities and characteristics of the various memory consistency conditions has been a fruitful topic of study. Both qualitative and quantitative comparisons have been carried out. A qualitative comparison differentiates memories by the kinds of problems they can solve, or the properties that any implementation of some consistency condition must have. A quantitative comparison shows the complexity of solving various tasks with different kinds of memory, or the complexity of any implementation of some consistency condition.

* This work was supported in part by NSF grants CCR92–21657 and CCR95–05807.

Condition	Read	Write	Acquire	Release
Linearizability	$\lceil \frac{N}{2} \rceil - 1$	$\lceil \frac{N}{2} \rceil - 1$		
Sequential &	$\lceil \frac{N}{2} \rceil - 1$	$N - 1$		
Processor Consistency	$N - 1$	$\lceil \frac{N}{2} \rceil - 1$		
Release	$N - 1$	$N - 1$	$\lceil \frac{N}{2} \rceil - 1$	$N - 1$
Consistency	$N - 1$	$N - 1$	$N - 1$	$\lceil \frac{N}{2} \rceil - 1$
Mixed, Coherence, etc.	$N - 1$	$N - 1$		

Table 1. Maximum resilience of operations

This paper examines the achievable fault tolerances of various kinds of shared memory. It does so in the context of a totally asynchronous message passing system, where message delays are not known a priori. In such a system, failed processors are indistinguishable from slow processors; in particular, we assume the absence of a failure detector [8] or membership service [9]. Algorithms designed for such a model are able to continue processing while fault detection and recovery take place, rather than waiting until such actions have completed. They are also more tolerant of temporary fluctuations in network speeds than algorithms designed to assume synchrony.

If all operations were required to be equally resilient, linearizability would be indistinguishable from sequential consistency. For that reason, we analyze the maximum resilience of the read and the write operations separately. In some cases, there is a tradeoff—increasing the resilience of one operation decreases the resilience of the other. This implies that it may be possible in practice to make critical or oft-used operations more resilient at the expense of other operations.

For linearizability, we show that both the read and the write operation can tolerate the failure of only a minority of the nodes. For sequential consistency, processor consistency, and some related kinds of memory, one of the operations can tolerate the failure of only a minority of the nodes, and the other can be wait-free. Many weak memories have fully wait-free implementations, some of which have been published previously. The results are summarized in Table 1. We show the bounds are tight by presenting algorithms that achieve them.

The rest of the paper is organized as follows. We survey related work in Sect. 1.1. In Sect. 1.2 we define the basic concepts. We analyze linearizability in Sect. 2. In Sect. 3, we analyze sequential consistency using a general theorem that also applies to other conditions. We close with some concluding remarks.

1.1 Related Work

We build on the results of [20], which shows that neither operation can be wait-free in any implementation of linearizability over a totally asynchronous system. It also shows that a sequentially consistent implementation cannot have both the read and the write operation be wait-free. We strengthen these bounds to those shown in Table 1.

Malki et al. [25] study the *Dynamic Uniformity* problem. Whenever any node in a particular group takes an action from some set A, all other nodes in the group must eventually take that same action, even if the first node subsequently fails. Nodes can leave and join the group during the computation. The authors show that D-Uniformity is solvable if a majority of the processes do not crash; that is, they give a ($\lceil \frac{N}{2} \rceil - 1$)-resilient solution to the problem. Thus, D-Uniformity is a strictly easier problem than Consensus. They also show that if a serial ordering constraint is added, any solution must be 0-resilient. Some of the problems we consider are similar, but there is no dynamic group membership. We show that the sequential consistency and linearizability problems, which impose a serial ordering constraint, have ($\lceil \frac{N}{2} \rceil - 1$)-resilient solutions.

Mavronicolas and Roth [26] give two implementations of linearizable shared memory for a partially synchronous system. In such a system, all message latencies are in the range $[d-u, d]$ for known constants d (delay) and u (uncertainty), $0 \leq u < d$. Like us, they consider read and write operations separately, so that one operation can be optimized in cases where it is used more frequently. They derive lower bounds on the response time of sequentially consistent and linearizable DSMs in terms of d and u. Our results are for a totally asynchronous system, in which u and d are unknown.

Attiya and Welch [5] compared linearizability and sequential consistency, and found that sequential consistency can be implemented more efficiently in a partially synchronous setting. In particular, they showed that either the read or the write operation of sequential consistency must suffer at least one network latency, and both operations of linearizability must do so. In the synchronous case, both conditions can have one instantaneous operation and one that suffers a network latency. Our proofs use a similar technique, but we work in a totally asynchronous setting.

Kosa [17] compares the costs of linearizability, sequential consistency, and hybrid consistency of ADTs in terms of worst-case time complexity. In addition to the consistency condition, two factors were considered: the synchrony of the system (synchronous or partially synchronous); and the algebraic properties of a given ADT. As in our analysis, Kosa found that a tradeoff occurs; improving one operation may require making other operations worse. The author also showed that hybrid consistency does not necessarily perform better than sequential consistency for arbitrary types.

Friedman [11] gave implementations of hybrid consistency with synchronization operations, in addition to the usual read and write operations. He derived lower bounds on the time required to implement several synchronization operations in a partially asynchronous setting when $d = u$ (i.e., message delays are in the range $[0, d]$). The bounds apply to weak consistency, so the lower bounds apply to all strictly stronger conditions, such as hybrid consistency. The implementations given in the text rely on atomic broadcast, which we cannot use since it has only 0-resilient implementations in totally asynchronous systems.

1.2 Definitions

A *distributed system* is a set of N nodes that communicate by sending messages over a point-to-point network. We assume a totally asynchronous network, in which message latencies are unknown. Each node has a fixed ID in the range $[1 \ldots N]$. A user program P_i executes on each node i and generates read and write requests. Each node also executes a DSM implementation M_i that responds to those requests. The execution of an operation may cause M_i to perform local actions, send messages, receive messages, and wait for an event (in no particular order). M_i may perform such actions before returning a response to the user program P_i, or it may return a response while concurrently taking such actions. The reception of a message may also cause such actions to take place.

The DSM implementations M_i cooperate to provide the shared memory abstraction. Such a memory consists of a finite set of *shared variables*. The DSM interface consists of a read operation and a write operation. Each operation invocation acts on a particular shared variable and has an associated value. We write $W_i(x)v$ to indicate a write by node i of value v into shared variable x. We write $R_i(x)v$ to indicate a read by node i returning value v from shared variable x. Each operation consists of two events: an *invocation* event by the user program P_i, and a *response* event by M_i. A *local history* H_i consists of the sequence of events at the program-DSM interface on node i. A history H of a DSM system is a collection $\{H_1, \ldots, H_N\}$ of local histories on each node. In this paper, we only consider histories in which the user program on each node has at most one pending operation at a time. This restriction can be lifted at the expense of some additional complexity in the proofs.

Let $ops(H)$ represent the set of operations in history H. Let $op_1 \longrightarrow op_2$ indicate that the return event of op_1 precedes the invocation event of op_2 in H. The relation $\longrightarrow$ is easily shown to be an irreflexive partial order. Since each node has at most one outstanding operation at a time, the operations invoked by node i are totally ordered by $\longrightarrow$. Let $\overset{i}{\longrightarrow}$ be the local (total) order on the operations at node i. A *linearization* of H is a total order $\overset{L}{\longrightarrow}$ on $ops(H)$ such that the sequential read/write semantics are preserved, and $op_1 \longrightarrow op_2 \Rightarrow op_1 \overset{L}{\longrightarrow} op_2$. A *serialization* of H is a total order $\overset{S}{\longrightarrow}$ on $ops(H)$ such that the sequential read/write semantics are preserved, and $(\exists i :: op_1 \overset{i}{\longrightarrow} op_2) \Rightarrow op_1 \overset{S}{\longrightarrow} op_2$. Note that any linearization of H is also a serialization of H.

In this paper, we investigate fault-tolerance in the form of *t-resilience*, the ability to withstand t node failures. The notion of t-resilience has been defined in terms of consensus protocols [10], asynchronous tasks [6, 15], and shared objects [7, 24]. We say that an operation is t-resilient if it can complete (i.e., not block) in spite of t node failures. An $(N-1)$-resilient operation is *wait-free* [14]; that is, it can complete without the assistance of any other node.

2 Linearizability

A DSM implementation guarantees linearizability if a linearization exists for every history of the system. Linearizability is a *local property* [16]; if each individual object in a system is linearizable, then the entire system is linearizable. Due to this property, a collection of individually linearizable variables forms a linearizable shared memory.

Neither the read nor the write operation can be wait-free, or $(N-1)$-resilient, as shown in [20]. This is proved by showing that two concurrent wait-free operations can execute with no messages received at any node, making it impossible to determine the global time ordering of the operations. We strengthen this result by showing that neither operation can be $\lceil \frac{N}{2} \rceil$-resilient. We do so by extending the proof of [20] to sets of $\lfloor \frac{N}{2} \rfloor$ nodes. We will refer to a set of nodes G as a *group* of nodes. When we say that some message crosses the boundary of group G, we mean that the sender is in G and the receiver is not in G or vice versa. We begin with a lemma that simplifies the proof of the main theorem.

Lemma 1. *Given:*

1. *a DSM implementation with a t-resilient operation op;*
2. *a history H;*
3. *a node i which does not have any outstanding operations in H; and*
4. *a group G of at least $N - t$ nodes such that $i \in G$,*

it is possible to extend H to history $H; H'$ such that:

a. *H' consists of a completed op operation by node i; and*
b. *no message crossing the boundary of G is received during the extension H'.*

Proof. Since node i does not have any outstanding operations, it can invoke operation op after H. Since op is t-resilient, it can complete without communicating with t of the nodes. Hence, communicating with some group G of $N - t$ nodes (including itself) is sufficient for i to complete op. Since the network is asynchronous, we can suppose that messages from G to nodes outside of G are delayed until after H', and likewise for messages from outside of G to nodes in G. This gives the desired extension H'. □

Theorem 2. *In a DSM implementation guaranteeing linearizability, the write operation is at most $(\lceil \frac{N}{2} \rceil - 1)$-resilient.*

Proof. By contradiction. Assume a linearizable DSM implementation with a variable x over at least 2 nodes with a t-resilient write operation, $t \geq \lceil \frac{N}{2} \rceil$. Let G_1 and G_2 be disjoint groups of $\lfloor \frac{N}{2} \rfloor$ nodes apiece; i.e., both groups have at least $N - t$ nodes. Consider a history H_1 in which program P_1 invokes a write operation W_1 to set x to 1, and after the completion of W_1, program P_2 invokes and completes a write operation W_2 to set x to 2. Since the write operations are t-resilient, because of Lemma 1, we can delay the reception of all messages that cross group boundaries (if any) until after the completion of W_2. Next, program P_1 invokes a read operation R. In order to ensure linearizability, R must return the more recent value, that is, 2.

Now consider a history H_2 in which the order of W_1 and W_2 are reversed. All messages that cross group boundaries (if any) are again delayed until the completion of the second write operation, W_1. All message receptions at P_1 are identical in the two histories H_1 and H_2, namely, those messages associated with W_1, followed by any messages associated with W_2. Therefore, read operation R cannot distinguish between the two histories and returns the value 2 as in H_1. But this violates linearizability, since 1 is now the more recent value. □

The upper bound for the read operation is somewhat more difficult to prove since reads are commutative. To derive a similar contradiction, there has to be a concurrent writer so that two $\lceil \frac{N}{2} \rceil$-resilient read operations return the new value first and the old value second. When there are an odd number of nodes, the proof is simpler, since the writer need not be in a group with either reader. However, with an even number of nodes, the writer must be in a group with one of the readers. We then have to show that the writer cannot interfere.

The intuitive idea is that the single writing node attempts to write a value and two other nodes read repeatedly. Because of linearizability, each reader eventually returns the new value. Because of asynchrony, the decision to return the new value is made independently in each of two groups of $\lfloor \frac{N}{2} \rfloor$ nodes. This leads to the possibility that one group will decide to return the new value, and a subsequent read by the other group will return the old value, compromising linearizability. If the writer attempts to interfere by not responding to the reader in such a way as to allow it to make progress, we show that the read operation can be blocked. This violates the supposed t-resilience of the read operation.

Theorem 3. *In a DSM implementation guaranteeing linearizability on at least 3 nodes, the read operation is at most $(\lceil \frac{N}{2} \rceil - 1)$-resilient.*

Proof. By contradiction. Assume a linearizable DSM implementation with a variable x over at least 3 nodes and a t-resilient read operation, $t \geq \lceil \frac{N}{2} \rceil$. Let G_1 and G_2 be disjoint groups of $\lfloor \frac{N}{2} \rfloor$ nodes apiece; i.e., both groups have at least $N - t$ nodes. Let $1 \in G_1$, $2 \in G_2$, and $3 \notin G_2$ be 3 nodes. Consider a history H_1 in which x is initially zero. Let P_3 invoke a write operation W to change the value of x to one. Let P_1 and P_2 repeatedly invoke read operations on x. For generality, we allow DSM implementations at the reader nodes (1 and 2) to send messages and do local computations between read operations. For the write operation W to complete, these DSM implementations may also need to receive messages. So, between consecutive read operations at nodes 1 and 2, we allow an arbitrary finite sequence of events of the DSM implementation. In history H_1, the nodes execute in a round robin manner, beginning with node 1, then node 2, then node 3. During their turn, nodes 2 and 3 extend the history by completing a read operation while communicating with only the nodes in groups G_1 and G_2, respectively. Each then executes a finite sequence of events. By Lemma 1, the extensions of the history by a complete read operation are made with messages received only within the respective group. Note that, when N is even, $P_3 \in G_1$. In that case, it may not be the case that P_1 can complete a read operation by communicating only with the nodes in G_1, as P_3 has a pending write. We assume, for the moment, that P_1 can complete a read operation by communicating only with nodes in G_1, and show below that this must be the case.

During its turn, node 3 takes a single step: sending a message, receiving a message, or a local event. The write operation W eventually completes in H_1. Let it do so after n steps. Divide the history into $n + 1$ rounds. The kth round ($k \leq n$) consists of:

- a read operation R_k, and a finite sequence of events x_k at node 1;

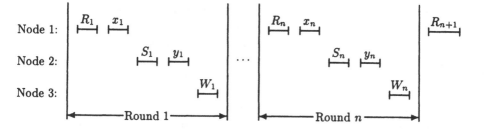

Fig. 1. Constructed history H_1

- a read operation S_k, and a finite sequence of events y_k at node 2;
- a single step w_k of write operation W at node 3.

The sequences x_k and y_k may be empty. Finally, extend the n rounds by considering one last read operation R_{n+1} of node 1. Because of Lemma 1, we can make the following restrictions on message receptions:

P1 Any message sent by a member of G_1 during round k as part of read operation R_k is not received by any member of G_2 until after the end of round k.

P2 Any message sent by a member of G_2 during round k as part of read operation S_k is not received by any member of G_1 until after the completion of R_{k+1}.

The history H_1 is shown pictorially in Figure 1.

Consider the sequence of values returned by the read operations R_1, S_1, R_2, S_2, ..., R_n, S_n, R_{n+1}. Because of linearizability:

- read operations R_1, S_1 complete prior to W and hence return the old value, zero;
- read operation R_{n+1} begins after W and hence returns the new value, one; and
- all read operations that follow a read operation returning the new value also return the new value.

So there exists a pair of consecutive read operations U and V such that U returns the old value and V returns the new value. Because of the interleaving of the read operations in H_1, there are two cases to consider. (Note that $0 < k \leq n$ in both cases.)

Case 1: $(U, V) = (R_k, S_k)$. That is, in history H_1, read operation R_k returns the old value and read operation S_k returns the new value. Consider the prefix h_1 of history H_1 up to read operation S_k. Then $h_1 = h_2; R_k; x_k; S_k$ for some prefix h_2. Because of restriction P1 above, no message sent from G_1 after the beginning of R_k is received until after the completion of S_k.

Therefore, it is possible to reorder S_k before R_k and x_k and still have a legal history, $h_3 = h_2; S_k; R_k; x_k$. Here, read operation S_k returns the new value and a subsequent read operation, R_k, returns the old value. This violates linearizability as follows. Complete the write operation in h_3, and suppose that this results in history h_4. For h_4 to be linearizable, we have to find a total ordering that preserves the partial ordering on operations in h_4, and that orders S_k *before* R_k. However, the total ordering also has to satisfy the read/write semantics of shared memory and has to order W after R_k and before S_k. This implies ordering R_k *before* S_k, a contradiction.

Case 2: $(U, V) = (S_k, R_{k+1})$. Here we begin with the prefix $h_1 = h_2; S_k; y_k; w_k;$ R_{k+1}, reorder R_{k+1} prior to S_k on account of P2 above, and obtain a contradiction with history $h_3 = h_2; R_{k+1}; S_k; y_k; w_k$.

Our remaining proof obligation is to show that P_1 can complete a read operation by communicating only with the nodes in G_1, even when $W \in G_1$. Suppose not. We know from [20] that the read operation cannot be wait-free, or $(N-1)$-resilient. Then it is t-resilient, with $ceil(N/2) \le t < N - 1$. When P_1 invokes a read operation R, there is some set of $t + 1$ nodes whose failure causes R to block. Let that set consist of a single node, node 2, and a set F of t nodes. (Note that, since $t + 1 < N$, node 1 is distinct from node 2 and F.)

Consider the history H_2 in which the group G contains all nodes not in F. Suppose that the entire set F fails, after which P_1 invokes a read operation, and P_2 simultaneously invokes a write operation. Since $|F| > \lceil \frac{N}{2} \rceil - 1$, by Theorem 2, the write operation is blocked. The remaining nodes consist only of the $N - t$ nodes in G, just enough for a read operation to complete. However, we supposed that a read operation cannot complete by communicating with only the nodes in its group when one of those nodes has an incomplete write operation. Hence, operation R is blocked, even though only t nodes failed. Since we supposed that the read operation was t-resilient, we have derived a contradiction. $\square$

Theorem 3 does not hold on implementations with only 2 nodes. In that case, it is possible to show that the read operation can be wait-free, although the write operation must be 0-resilient by Theorem 2. Next we show that the bounds of theorems 2 and 3 are tight, by exhibiting an implementation that achieves those bounds.

Theorem 4. *There exists an implementation of linearizability with $(\lceil \frac{N}{2} \rceil - 1)$-resilient read and write operations.*

Proof. Attiya et al. [4] give a construction for a 1-writer multi-reader atomic register on a totally asynchronous system. This register has the property that both the read and the write operation are $(\lceil \frac{N}{2} \rceil - 1)$-resilient. Li et al. [22] give a construction of a multi-writer multi-reader atomic register from 1-writer multi-reader atomic registers[1]. This construction has the property that it is

---

[1] The main construction is from 1-writer 1-reader registers to multi-writer multi-reader registers; the construction we use is a projection onto the simpler problem.

wait-free with respect to the underlying 1-writer register construction. That is, implementation of both the read and write operations consists of a series of operations on 1-writer registers, with no explicit waits. Composing the above two protocols yields an implementation of a multi-writer multi-reader atomic register on a totally asynchronous distributed system with ($\lceil \frac{N}{2} \rceil - 1$)-resilient read and write operations. Since linearizability is a local property, a collection of such registers constitutes a linearizable shared memory. □

The constructions in both [4] and [22] are bounded. A straightforward composition requires $O(N^4)$ space on each node; each read or write operation results in the sending of $O(N^3)$ messages, each of size $O(N^3)$, in $O(N)$ messaging rounds. The message bound can be improved at the expense of greater memory usage by substituting Attiya's new construction of a 1-writer multi-reader atomic register [3].

3 Sequential Consistency

A DSM implementation guarantees sequential consistency if a serialization exists for every history of the system. In [20] it is shown that for any implementation of sequential consistency, the read and write operations cannot both be wait-free, or $(N - 1)$-resilient. If both operations are wait-free, then two nodes can each complete a read and a write without receiving any messages from the other. This fact is used to show that such an implementation cannot avoid non-sequential behavior. We strengthen that result by extending the proof of [20] to sets of $\lfloor \frac{N}{2} \rfloor$ nodes. We show that one operation can be no more than ($\lceil \frac{N}{2} \rceil - 1$)-resilient, but that the other operation can be wait-free. In the full paper, we show that processor consistency has the same fault tolerance bounds. Thus, while processor consistency may have more efficient implementations, it provides no fault tolerance benefits over sequential consistency in totally asynchronous systems.

We begin with a simple result that implies the upper bounds for both sequential consistency and processor consistency. This result is founded on a simple assumption which holds for all of the commonly used consistency conditions: if H is inconsistent with respect to consistency condition C, then for all histories H' with H a subhistory of H', H' is also inconsistent with respect to C. We note that for some forms of DSM, nodes cannot issue a stream of operations without coordinating with other nodes. In particular, we are concerned with cases in which two nodes each issue a stream of operations without communicating, either directly or indirectly. We calls such streams of instructions *local sequences*. The following lemma almost immediately implies the upper bound for both sequential consistency and processor consistency.

Lemma 5. *Let I be an implementation of any consistency condition C that meets the assumption above. Let H be a history consisting of two local sequences, s_1 and s_2, executed on two distinct nodes. If H is inconsistent with respect to C, then either the read operation or the write operation of I is at most ($\lceil \frac{N}{2} \rceil - 1$)-resilient.*

$$n_1 : \boxed{W(x)1} \ \boxed{R(y)0}$$

$$n_2 : \boxed{W(y)1} \ \boxed{R(x)0}$$

Fig. 2. Non-sequential history

Proof. By contradiction. Suppose that both the read and the write operation of I are $\lceil \frac{N}{2} \rceil$-resilient. Let G_1 and G_2 be disjoint sets of $\lfloor \frac{N}{2} \rfloor$ nodes apiece. Let $n_1 \in G_1$ and $n_2 \in G_2$ be distinct nodes. Then n_1 can execute s_1 while communicating with only the nodes in G_1 and n_2 can execute s_2 while communicating with only the nodes in G_2. Messages from n_1 to nodes in G_2 are delayed until after the completion of H, and likewise for messages from n_2 to nodes in G_1. Thus H is a possible history of I, contrary to the assumption that I implements C. □

We now give tight bounds for sequential consistency, using this lemma. The results for processor consistency are identical, and are presented in the full paper.

Theorem 6. *In a DSM implementation guaranteeing sequential consistency with at least two shared variables, either the read operation or the write operation is at most $(\lceil \frac{N}{2} \rceil - 1)$-resilient.*

Proof. Suppose shared variables x and y are initially zero. Consider the history of Fig. 2, consisting of two local sequences. It is not sequentially consistent; otherwise at least one read operation would return 1. The theorem follows by Lemma 5. □

Theorem 6 does not hold for implementations of sequential consistency with one shared variable. In that case, sequential consistency collapses to the weaker condition of cache consistency or coherence [13]. As we show in the full paper, cache consistency has an implementation in which both operations are wait-free.

We now show that the upper bound for sequential consistency is tight, by demonstrating two implementations. Each has one wait-free operation and one $(\lceil \frac{N}{2} \rceil - 1)$-resilient operation. They are similar to the Atomic Broadcast-based "fast read" and "fast write" implementations of Attiya and Welch [5]. However, since any solution to Atomic Broadcast must be 0-resilient, we cannot use it. Our solutions employ an $O(N)$-round algorithm for the resilient operation. Thus, although we have shown that resilient solutions exist, our solution is very inefficient. Whether a more efficient solution exists is an open problem.

The first implementation, SC_{FR} (for "Sequential Consistency–Fast Read") has a $(\lceil \frac{N}{2} \rceil - 1)$-resilient write operation and a wait-free read operation. The implementation uses unbounded sequence numbers, but it should be straightforward to transform it into a bounded timestamp system. Pseudocode for SC_{FR} is given in Figs. 3 and 4. This pseudocode is executed on node i of a distributed system. It uses a point-to-point Send function to send messages between nodes. For simplicity, we assume that Send provides reliable, FIFO delivery of messages.

We also use a Broadcast function, which is simply $N - 1$ repetitions of Send. Nodes can fail in the middle of a Broadcast, resulting in some nodes receiving the message and some not receiving it.

The next macro takes an integer, x, as its argument. It returns the lowest number $y > x$ such that $y \pmod{N} = i-1$. Hence, the values produced by next on distinct nodes are disjoint. Variables of type Val are ordered by timestamp (field t). We define a partial order on variables of type View:

Definition 7. Let u and v be two variables of type View. Then $u < v$ iff $(\forall x :: u[x] < v[x])$. Also, $u = v$ iff $(\forall x :: u[x] = v[x])$.

A View is a view of the shared memory contents. That is, it is an assignment of values to shared variables. When a Read operation is invoked, it simply returns the value found in the current view.

Write operations are diffused across the system. The algorithm does not necessarily order every pair of writes; doing so amounts to Atomic Broadcast, which has only 0-resilient solutions. Competing write operations are simply incorporated in to the same view, causing them to appear simultaneously on every node. In case two or more writes to the same variable appear in such a set, the sequence numbers are used to determine which comes last. Each writing node sets up a target view, containing its current view plus its write operation. It then propagates this view across the system. As it learns about new writes, it incorporates them into its current attempt and propagates the new view. If at any time it learns that some node has accepted a view containing its original target view, it adopts that view as well and terminates the write operation.

This algorithm has several sources of unboundedness. First, it is not clear that the while loop in the Write function ever terminates. In the full paper, we show that any execution of Write terminates after $O(N)$ iterations of the loop. Second, the *Final* set of final views grows without bound. It is possible to limit its size, through garbage collection. For simplicity, we omit such considerations here. Finally, the sequence numbers grow without bound. Transformations to a bounded timestamp system are possible, but again are omitted for simplicity.

Lemma 8. *Any history of implementation SC_{FR} is sequentially consistent.*

Proof. Let H be any history of SC_{FR}. Then:

1. Let u and v be elements of any *Final* set. Then either $u \leq v$ or $v \leq u$.
   (a) Elements of *Final* are created locally by an uninterrupted execution of Write (i.e., *ws* is not set to *DONE*), or by the arrival of a message sent from an uninterrupted Write.
   (b) Each uninterrupted Write ends in a round in which a majority of the nodes agree that the view is comparable to all other views (i.e., it holds either a subset or a superset of the writes in all other views).
   (c) Since u and v both received agreement from a majority of the nodes, they received agreement from at least one common node, j.
   (d) Node j received the query corresponding to either u or v first, say u. Then it stored u in *Cur* before sending back an acknowledgment.

macro $next(x) = (\lfloor \frac{x-i}{N} \rfloor + 1) \times N + i$

type   **Val** =record v : **Word**;
                              t : **Integer**;
             end;
        View = array$[1 \dots M]$ of **Val**;
        WriteState = $\{NONE, WRITE, DONE\}$;
        MsgType = $\{RESOLVE, FINAL, ACK\}$;

var Mem : array$[1 \dots M]$ of **Word**;
        Cur, New : array$[1 \dots N]$ of **View**;
        $Final$: set of **View**;
        $Target$: **View**;
        ws : **WriteState**;
        $acks, round$: **Integer**

initially $(\forall x :: Mem[x] = 0) \wedge (\forall j, x :: Cur[p, x] = \langle i, -1 \rangle \wedge New[p, x] = \langle i, -1 \rangle)$
        $\wedge\ Final = \emptyset \wedge ws = NONE \wedge round = 0$

function $Read(x$: **Var**$)$ returns **Word**
begin
    return $Mem[x]$;
end

function $Write(x$: **Var**$, v$: **Word**$)$
begin
    $ws := WRITE$;
    $\forall y :: Target[y] := \max_j(Cur[j, y])$;
    $Target[x] := \langle v, next(Target[x].t) \rangle$;
    $\forall j :: New[j] := Target$;
    while $(\exists j :: (Cur[i] \not\succeq New[j]) \wedge ws = WRITE)$ do
        $\forall x :: Cur[i, x] := \max_j(New[j, x])$;
        $\forall j :: New[j] := Cur[i]$;
        $acks := 1$;
        Broadcast$(RESOLVE, i, round, Cur[i])$;
        await$(acks > \lfloor \frac{N}{2} \rfloor \vee ws = DONE)$;
        $round := round + 1$;
    od
    $Final := Final \cup \{Cur[i]\}$;
    Broadcast$(FINAL, i, -1, Cur[i])$;
    $\forall x :: Mem[x] := Cur[i, x].v$;   /* Atomic action */
    $ws := NONE$;
end

Fig. 3. SC_{FR} for node i: Part 1

(e) Hence, v must be comparable to u, since j acknowledged v as well.

2. The contents of Mem always correspond to either the initial state or an element of $Final$. Since Mem is only altered in **Write** and **MessageHandler**, each time to the contents of an element of $Final$, the statement follows.

3. The elements of *Final* define a partial order S on all the operations of H.

```
function MessageHandler(mt : MsgType, j : Node, rnd : Integer, vw : View)
var finalvw : View
begin
    case mt = RESOLVE :
        if (∀l :: Cur[l] ≤ vw ∨ vw ≤ Cur[l]) then
            finalvw := vw;
        else if (∃v ∈ Final :: v ≥ vw) then
            finalvw := v;
        else
            ∀x :: finalvw[x] := maxₗ(Cur[l, x]);
        fi;
        Send(ACK, i, rnd, finalvw);
        Cur[j] := finalvw;
    case mt = FINAL :
        Final, Cur[j] := Final ∪ vw, vw;
        if (ws = WRITE ∧ vw > Target) then
            Cur[i], ws := vw, DONE;
        else if (ws = NONE ∧ vw > Cur[j]) then
            Cur[i] := vw;
            ∀x :: Mem[x] := vw[x].v;   /* Atomic action */
        fi
    case mt = ACK :
        if (rnd = round) then
            acks, New[j] := acks + 1, vw;
        fi
end
```

Fig. 4. SC_{FR} for node i: Part 2

(a) Since there is a total order on the elements of *Final* (1), define a partial order on the writes based on the first element of *Final* in which they appear.

(b) Add the reads to the partial order by the element of *Final* that was current when the read occurred.

(c) Note that the current element of *Final* cannot go backwards in the *Final* order, due to checking that the view is greater than the current one before adopting it.

4. Strengthen S to form a total order S' on the operations of H by placing incomparable elements in timestamp order. Then S' is a serialization of H.

(a) The return values of the reads are consistent with S due to the way we placed them in (3).

(b) The program order is preserved since the current view never goes backwards in *Final*.

(c) Each block of writes between successive elements of *Final* corresponds to writes seen simultaneously everywhere. Thus, we can place them in timestamp order in S, and it will be consistent with all local histories.

□

It is clear that the read operation is wait-free. A simple analysis of the write operation shows that each iteration of the while loop involves communication with at least $\lfloor \frac{N}{2} \rfloor + 1$ nodes (including itself), allowing it to tolerate the failure of $\lceil \frac{N}{2} \rceil - 1$ nodes.

The fast write implementation, SC_{FW}, is almost identical to the fast read implementation. In this case, we make the view consistent just before doing a read operation, rather than while doing a write operation. Most of the program text and proofs are identical; they are contained in the full paper. The above prove the following:

Theorem 9. *There exist implementations of sequential consistency with one $(\lceil \frac{N}{2} \rceil - 1)$-resilient operation and one wait-free operation.*

4 Conclusion

We have shown that, in a totally asynchronous system, any implementation of linearizability has read and write operations that are less than $\lceil \frac{N}{2} \rceil$-resilient. We showed that consistency conditions for which two *local sequences* (uncoordinated sequences of operations) are inconsistent must have at least one operation that is less than $\lceil \frac{N}{2} \rceil$-resilient. We used this result to show that any implementation of sequential consistency has at least one operation that is less than $\lceil \frac{N}{2} \rceil$-resilient. In the full paper, we use the same result to show that processor consistency has the same bounds as sequential consistency. We also analyze release consistency in the full paper, and show that one synchronization operation must be less than $\lceil \frac{N}{2} \rceil$-resilient, and the other operations can be wait-free. We show that many forms of weak memory, such as mixed consistency and cache consistency (or coherence), have fully wait-free implementations. All bounds are shown to be tight by exhibiting implementations that achieve them.

References

1. AGRAWAL, D., CHOY, M., LEONG, H. V., AND SINGH, A. K. Mixed consistency: A model for parallel programming. In *PODC '94* (Los Angeles, CA, USA, 14–17 Aug. 1994), pp. 101–10.
2. AHAMAD, M., NEIGER, G., BURNS, J. E., KOHLI, P., AND HUTTO, P. W. Causal memory: Definitions, implementation and programming. *Distributed Computing 9*, 1 (Aug. 1995), 37–49.
3. ATTIYA, H. Efficient and robust sharing of memory in message-passing systems. In *WDAG '96* (Bologna, Italy, 9–11 Oct. 1996), Ö. Babaoglu and K. Marzullo, Eds., vol. 1151 of *Lecture Notes in Computer Science*, Springer-Verlag, pp. 56–70.
4. ATTIYA, H., BAR-NOY, A., AND DOLEV, D. Sharing memory robustly in message-passing systems. *J. ACM 42*, 1 (Jan. 1995), 124–42.
5. ATTIYA, H., AND WELCH, J. L. Sequential consistency versus linearizability. *ACM Trans. Comput. Syst. 12*, 2 (May 1994), 91–122.
6. BOROWSKY, E., AND GAFNI, E. Generalized FLP impossibility result for t-resilient asynchronous computations (extended abstract). In *STOC '93* (San Diego, CA, USA, 16–18 May 1993), pp. 91–100.

7. CHANDRA, T., HADZILACOS, V., JAYANTI, P., AND TOUEG, S. Wait-freedom vs. t-resiliency and the robustness of wait-free hierarchies. In *PODC '94* (Los Angeles, CA, USA, 14–17 Aug. 1994), pp. 334–43.

8. CHANDRA, T. D., AND TOUEG, S. Unreliable failure detectors for reliable distributed systems. *J. ACM 43*, 2 (Mar. 1996), 225–67.

9. CRISTIAN, F. Reaching agreement on processor group membership in synchronous distributed systems. *Distributed Computing 4*, 4 (Apr. 1991), 175–87.

10. DOLEV, D., DWORK, C., AND STOCKMEYER, L. On the minimal synchronism needed for distributed consensus. *J. ACM 34*, 1 (Jan. 1987), 77–97.

11. FRIEDMAN, R. Implementing hybrid consistency with high-level synchronization operations. *Distributed Computing 9*, 3 (Dec. 1995), 119–29.

12. GHARACHORLOO, K., LENOSKI, D., LAUDON, J., GIBBONS, P., GUPTA, A., AND HENNESSY, J. Memory consistency and event ordering in scalable shared-memory multiprocessors. In *ISCA '90* (Seattle, WA, USA, 28–31 May 1990), pp. 15–26. Revised in Stanford CSL Technical Report 93–568.

13. GOODMAN, J. R. Cache consistency and sequential consistency. Tech. Rep. 1006, Computer Sciences Department, University of Wisconsin-Madison, Feb. 1991.

14. HERLIHY, M. P. Wait-free synchronization. *ACM Trans. Program. Lang. Syst. 13*, 1 (Jan. 1991), 124–49.

15. HERLIHY, M. P., AND SHAVIT, N. The asynchronous computability theorem for t-resilient tasks. In *STOC '93* (San Diego, CA, USA, 16–18 May 1993), pp. 111–20.

16. HERLIHY, M. P., AND WING, J. M. Linearizability: A correctness condition for concurrent objects. *ACM Trans. Program. Lang. Syst. 12*, 3 (July 1990), 463–92.

17. KOSA, M. J. Making operations of concurrent data types fast. In *PODC '94* (Los Angeles, CA, USA, 14–17 Aug. 1994), pp. 32–41.

18. LAMPORT, L. How to make a multiprocessor computer that correctly executes multiprocess programs. *IEEE Trans. Comput. 28*, 9 (Sept. 1979), 690–1.

19. LAMPORT, L. On interprocess communication, parts I and II. *Distributed Computing 1*, 2 (Apr. 1986), 77–101.

20. LENCEVICIUS, R., AND SINGH, A. K. Latency bounds for memory consistency. Submitted for publication, 1997.

21. LI, K., AND HUDAK, P. Memory coherence in shared virtual memory systems. *ACM Trans. Comput. Syst. 7*, 4 (Nov. 1989), 321–59.

22. LI, M., TROMP, J., AND VITÁNYI, P. M. B. How to share concurrent wait-free variables. *J. ACM 43*, 4 (July 1996), 723–46.

23. LIPTON, R. J., AND SANDBERG, J. S. PRAM: A scalable shared memory. Tech. Rep. CS-TR–180–88, Department of Computer Science, Princeton University, Sept. 1988.

24. LO, W.-K. More on t-resilience vs. wait-freedom. In *PODC '95* (Ottawa, Ontario, Canada, 20–23 Aug. 1995), pp. 110–19.

25. MALKI, D., BIRMAN, K., RICCIARDI, A., AND SCHIPER, A. Uniform actions in asynchronous distributed systems. In *PODC '94* (Los Angeles, CA, USA, 14–17 Aug. 1994), pp. 274–83.

26. MAVRONICOLAS, M., AND ROTH, D. Efficient, strongly consistent implementations of shared memory (extended abstract). In *WDAG '92* (Haifa, Israel, 2–4 Nov. 1992), A. Segall and S. Zaks, Eds., vol. 647 of *Lecture Notes in Computer Science*, Springer-Verlag, pp. 346–61.

Precedence-Based Memory Models

Victor Luchangco[*]

M.I.T.

Abstract. This paper presents a general framework for understanding *precedence-based memory models*, which are generalizations of standard multiprocessor models. Precedence-based models need not mention processes explicitly, and can express any conditions that rely only on some operations being required to precede other operations. We define a generalized notion of *sequential consistency* and *per-location sequential consistency* in this framework, and we analyze the Backer algorithm used in the Cilk system [3], showing that it implements per-location sequential consistency. We also give conditions under which client processes cannot distinguish a per-location sequentially consistent memory from a sequentially consistent one.

1 Introduction

As distributed systems become ubiquitous, it becomes increasingly important to develop convenient ways to program these systems. Ideally, programs should express naturally the programmer's intention, and be easy to understand and reason about carefully. They should also be able to be implemented efficiently on multiprocessor systems, exploiting locality, re-ordering, and other techniques that mask disk and communication latency, to deliver high performance.

One common approach is to provide the processes with shared memory, which appears as though it is maintained by a single process. This provides programmers with relatively simple and intuitive semantics, called sequential consistency [11]. Unfortunately, maintaining such guarantees is expensive, even impossible on some systems. Thus, some systems are willing to tolerate some inconsistency in order to improve performance.

In order to reason about these systems, many weaker memory models have been proposed, such as processor consistency [9], release consistency [7], location consistency [6], scope consistency [10], eventual-serializability [5], dag-consistency [3], and others (see [1]). Unfortunately, these models are defined using different formalisms, and some of them do not even have formal definitions, making it hard to compare them rigorously.

Another drawback of sequential consistency and most of the models mentioned above is that the programmer must explicitly indicate which process issues each operation. Thus they cannot model systems such as Cilk [4, 13], which do not make processes directly accessible to the programmer.

---

[*] Supported by AFOSR-ONR contract F49640-94-1-0199, by ARPA contracts N00014-92-J-4033 and F19628-95-C-0118, and by NSF grant 9225124-CCR.

This paper presents a general framework for understanding *precedence-based memory models*, which are generalizations of standard multiprocessor models. Precedence-based models allow clients to issue operations concurrently, specifying dependencies on other operations, but not exclusivity requirements. They need not mention processes explicitly, and can express any conditions that rely only on some operations being required to precede other operations. We believe this captures an interesting set of memory models that can be understood in a unified framework. This work is intended to provide structure to the field of modelling distributed memories, allowing us to categorize and compare models more easily, and also prove some general properties about them.

The memory may represent any deterministic serial data type with a generic set of operators, $\mathcal{O}$. However, to model distributed memories, operations are allowed to be concurrent, and may even be re-ordered by the system. The degree to which this is allowed defines the memory model. In the pure precedence-based memories described here, each operation can specify a set of operations that must precede it, thus defining a partial order of the requested operations.

In this framework, we define a generalized version of sequential consistency, and also *per-location sequential consistency*, which is similar to cache coherence in systems with caching. We demonstrate conditions under which the two are equivalent.

An important part of this work involves carefully specifying the serial semantics of the data, identifying characteristics that are important when concurrent operations are introduced. We consider how restrictions on the clients, or on the types of operations that can be applied to the data, can be used to guarantee greater consistency.

To demonstrate the utility of this framework, we formally specify and analyze the Backer algorithm used in the Cilk system [3], and we show that it implements per-location sequential consistency for read/write memories.

The rest of the paper is organized as follows: Section 2 defines some conventions used throughout the paper and Section 3 describes the formal model. Section 4 characterizes the serial semantics of the data. The general framework for precedence-based memories is presented in Section 5, and sequential consistency and per-location sequential consistency are defined in Section 6. Section 7 describes the Backer algorithm, and sketches the idea of its proof. Finally, Section 8 discusses related work and future directions for research.

2 Mathematical Conventions

We denote a sequence by $\langle a, b, c, \ldots \rangle$, and the empty sequence by ϵ. S^* denotes the set of finite sequences of a set S, and $S^+ = S^* - \{\epsilon\}$. The concatentation of sequences α and β is denoted by $\alpha \cdot \beta$. This notation is overloaded for adding a single element to a sequence, i.e., $e \cdot \alpha = \langle e \rangle \cdot \alpha$ and $\alpha \cdot e = \alpha \cdot \langle e \rangle$. We denote the ith element of α by α_i. The *restriction* $\alpha|_S$ of a sequence α to a set S is the subsequence of α consisting of all the elements of S in α. A sequence α is an *interleaving* of two sequences β and β' if β and β' are disjoint subsequences of α that together contain all the elements of α.

We denote the image of a set $S \subseteq A$ under $f : A \to B$ by $f(S) = \{f(a) : a \in S\}$, and the image of a sequence $\alpha \in A^*$ under f by $f(\alpha)$, i.e., $f(\alpha)_i = f(\alpha_i)$ for all i. We use 2^S to denote the power set of S. A partial function from A to B is denoted $f : A \to B_\perp$, where $B_\perp$ is the *lifted set* $B \cup \{\perp\}$. $\perp$ is not contained in non-lifted sets and indicates that the function is not defined at a value.

A *partial order* is any binary relation that is transitive and anti-symmetric; it need not be reflexive nor irreflexive. Two partial orders $\prec_1$ and $\prec_2$ are *consistent* if they do not order any two elements differently, i.e., for all distinct e, e', either $e \not\prec_1 e'$ or $e' \not\prec_2 e$. A partial order $\prec_1$ *includes* $\prec_2$ if $\prec_2 \subseteq \prec_1$. We use $\prec_1 \vee \prec_2$ to denote the transitive closure of the union of $\prec_1$ and $\prec_2$.

Theorem 1. $\prec_1 \vee \prec_2$ *is a partial order if and only if* $\prec_1$ *and* $\prec_2$ *are consistent.*

A *serialization* of a set S is a sequence that contains each element uniquely. A serialization α of S defines a total order $\prec_\alpha$ of S where $\alpha_i \prec_\alpha \alpha_j$ if $i \leq j$. It also partially orders any superset of S, where elements of S are ordered by $\prec_\alpha$ and all other elements are not ordered with respect to any elements. A serialization α is *consistent with* a partial order if $\prec_\alpha$ is, and it *includes* the partial order if $\prec_\alpha$ does.

3 Formal Model

We use a slight simplification of the I/O automaton of Lynch and Tuttle [12], ignoring the aspects related to liveness. An *non-live I/O automaton* A consists of:

- three disjoint sets of actions: $in(A)$, $out(A)$, and $int(A)$;
- a set $states(A)$ of states;
- a nonempty subset $start(A)$ of start states;
- a set $steps(A) \subseteq states(A) \times acts(A) \times states(A)$ of steps such that there exists $(s, \pi, s') \in steps(A)$ for all $s \in states(A)$, $\pi \in in(A)$.

We call the actions in $in(A)$, $out(A)$, and $int(A)$ the *input*, *output*, and *internal* actions respectively. The input and output actions are also called *external actions*, and the set of external actions is denoted by $ext(A)$. We denote the set of all actions of A by $acts(A) = in(A) \cup out(A) \cup int(A)$. We write $s \xrightarrow{\pi}_A s'$ or just $s \xrightarrow{\pi} s'$ as shorthand for $(s, \pi, s') \in steps(A)$.

An *execution fragment* $s_0, \pi_1, s_1, \pi_2, s_2, \ldots$ is a finite or infinite sequence of alternating states and actions such that $s_{i-1} \xrightarrow{\pi_i} s_i$ for all i. An *execution* is an execution fragment with $s_0 \in start(A)$. We denote the set of executions of A by $execs(A)$. A state is *reachable* in A if it appears in any execution of A. An *invariant* of A is a predicate that is true of every reachable state of A.

The *external image* of an execution fragment α is the subsequence $\alpha|_{ext(A)}$ of its external actions. A *trace* of A is the external image of an execution, and the set of traces is denoted by $traces(\alpha)$.

We often want to specify a distributed system by specifying the components that constitute the system. The entire system is then described by an automaton which is the *composition* of the automata describing the components. Informally, composition identifies actions with the same name at different component automata. Thus, when an action is executed, it is executed by all components with that action. The new automaton has the actions of all its components. There are some restrictions on the automata to be composed so that the composition makes sense. In particular, internal actions cannot be shared, and an action can be the output action of at most one component, and for technical reasons, actions cannot be shared by infinitely many components.

Formally, for any index set I, a set $\{A_i\}_{i \in I}$ of automata is *compatible* if $int(A_i) \cap acts(A_j) = \emptyset$ and $out(A_i) \cap out(A_j) = \emptyset$ for all $i, j \in I$ such that $i \neq j$, and no action is in $acts(A_i)$ for infinitely many $i \in I$. The *composition* $A = \Pi_{i \in I} A_i$ of a compatible set $\{A_i\}_{i \in I}$ of automata has the following components:

- $in(A) = \bigcup_{i \in I} in(A_i) - \bigcup_{i \in I} out(A_i)$
  $out(A) = \bigcup_{i \in I} out(A_i)$
  $int(A) = \bigcup_{i \in I} int(A_i)$
- $states(A) = \Pi_{i \in I} states(A_i)$
- $start(A) = \Pi_{i \in I} start(A_i)$
- $steps(A) = \{(s, \pi, s') : s_i \xrightarrow{\pi}_{A_i} s_i' \text{ or } \pi \notin acts(A_i) \wedge s_i = s_i' \text{ for all } i \in I\}$

We denote the composition of two compatible automata A and B by $A \circ B$.

For any $\alpha \in execs(\Pi_{i \in I} A_i)$, the *projection* $\alpha|_{A_i}$ onto A_i is the sequence α' consisting of alternating states and actions of A_i such that $\alpha'|_{acts(A_i)} = \alpha|_{acts(A_i)}$ and the states of α' are the ith component of the states in α preceding the actions in α'. Intuitively, the projection of α onto A_i is how α appears to A_i. For any $\beta \in traces(\Pi_{i \in I} A_i)$, its *projection* $\beta|_{A_i}$ onto A_i is the restriction $\beta|_{acts(A_i)}$ to the actions of A_i. We also write $execs(\Pi_{i \in I} A_i)|_{A_i}$ and $traces(\Pi_{i \in I} A_i)|_{A_i}$ for the sets of projections onto A_i of executions and traces of $\Pi_{i \in I} A_i$.

I/O automata can be used as specifications as well as implementations. We say that an automaton A *implements* another automaton B, and write $A \subseteq B$, if $in(A) = in(B)$, $out(A) = out(B)$, and $traces(A) \subseteq traces(B)$. We say that A and B are *equivalent*, and write $A \equiv B$, if they implement each other.

Theorem 2. *If $A_i \subseteq B_i$ for all $i \in I$ then $\Pi_{i \in I} A_i \subseteq \Pi_{i \in I} B_i$.*

A standard way to show that one automaton implements another is to use *simulations*, which establish a correspondence between the states of the two automata. Formally, if A and B are automata with $in(A) = in(B)$ and $out(A) = out(B)$ then a *simulation* from A to B is a relation f between $states(A)$ and $states(B)$ such that:

- If $s \in start(A)$ then there exists some $u \in start(B)$ such that $f(s, u)$.
- For reachable states s and u of A and B, if $f(s, u)$ and $s \xrightarrow{\pi}_A s'$, then there exists some u' such that $f(s', u')$ and there is some execution fragment of B from u to u' with the same external image as π.

Theorem 3. *If there is a simulation from A to B then $A \subseteq B$.*

4 Serial Data Type

This section introduces the formal framework to specify the serial semantics of shared objects. This is similar to the definitions of Lynch [12].

A *serial data type* $\mathcal{D}$ consists of a set Σ of states, an initial state $\hat{\sigma} \in \Sigma$, a set $\mathcal{O}$ of operators, a set $\mathcal{R}$ of possible return values, and two functions, $\tau_\Sigma : \Sigma \times \mathcal{O} \to \Sigma$ and $\tau_\mathcal{R} : \Sigma \times \mathcal{O} \to \mathcal{R}$, which define the state transitions and return values of each operator. As a shorthand, we write $\tau(\sigma, o) = (\tau_\Sigma(\sigma, o), \tau_\mathcal{R}(\sigma, o))$. We define the functions $\tau_\Sigma^* : \Sigma \times \mathcal{O}^* \to \Sigma$ and $\tau_\mathcal{R}^+ : \Sigma \times \mathcal{O}^+ \to \mathcal{R}$ to yield the final state and return value of a sequence of operators applied in order. Formally, $\tau_\Sigma^*(\sigma, \epsilon) = \sigma$, $\tau_\Sigma^*(\sigma, \alpha \cdot o) = \tau_\Sigma(\tau_\Sigma^*(\sigma, \alpha), o)$, and $\tau_\mathcal{R}^+(\sigma, \alpha \cdot o) = \tau_\mathcal{R}(\tau_\Sigma^*(\sigma, \alpha), o)$.

Example 1. A read/write register with values V and initial value v_0 has $\Sigma = V$, $\hat{\sigma} = v_0$, $\mathcal{O} = \{read\} \cup \{write(v) : v \in V\}$, $\mathcal{R} = V \cup \{ack\}$, and τ such that $\tau(v, read) = (v, v)$ and $\tau(v, write(v')) = (v', ack)$.

We now make several definitions that are useful in the analysis later with concurrent accesses to the data. We say that an operator o is *oblivious* to an operator o' that does not affect its return value, i.e., $\tau_\mathcal{R}^+(\sigma, \langle o', o \rangle) = \tau_\mathcal{R}(\sigma, o)$ for all $\sigma \in \Sigma$. Two operators o and o' *commute* if the final state does not depend on the order in which they are applied, i.e., $\tau_\Sigma^*(\sigma, \langle o, o' \rangle) = \tau_\Sigma^*(\sigma, \langle o', o \rangle)$ for all $\sigma \in \Sigma$. Two sequences of operators commute if every operator of one commutes with every operator of the other. Two operators are *independent* if they commute and are oblivious to each other.

Example 2. For a read/write register, the *write* operators are oblivious to all operators, and the *read* operator commutes with all operators and is independent of itself.

The following lemma establishes some simple but useful results:

Lemma 4. *For all $o \in \mathcal{O}$ and $\alpha, \alpha' \in \mathcal{O}^*$:*

- *if o is oblivious to every operator in α then $\tau_\mathcal{R}^+(\sigma, \alpha \cdot o) = \tau_\mathcal{R}(\sigma, o)$.*
- *if o commutes with every operator in α then $\tau_\Sigma^*(\sigma, \alpha \cdot o) = \tau_\Sigma^*(\sigma, o \cdot \alpha)$.*
- *if α and α' commute then $\tau_\Sigma^*(\sigma, \beta) = \tau_\Sigma^*(\sigma, \alpha \cdot \alpha')$ for all $\sigma \in \Sigma$ and all interleavings β of α and α'.*

Some data objects may be viewed as a collection of "independent" objects, treated as a whole for convenience. Each component object may be considered to be at a different location. We formalize this intuition as follows:

Given a set $\mathcal{L}$ of locations, $f : \mathcal{O} \to \mathcal{L}$ is a *location partition* if operators mapped to different elements are independent, i.e., for all $o, o' \in \mathcal{O}$, if $f(o) \neq f(o')$ then o and o' are independent. Often, we use *loc* for location partitions. and write $o.loc$ instead of $loc(o)$. We say that $(\mathcal{D}, loc)$ is *location-based* if *loc* is a location partition. We say that o is performed at location $o.loc$. For $\alpha \in \mathcal{O}^*$ and $l \in \mathcal{L}$, we denote by $\alpha|_l$ the subsequence of α consisting of all operators performed at l. Similarly, if $S \subseteq \mathcal{O}$, we denote by $S|_l$ the subset of operators in S performed at l.

Lemma 5. *If $(\mathcal{D}, loc)$ is location-based then $\tau_{\mathcal{R}}^+(\sigma, \alpha \cdot o) = \tau_{\mathcal{R}}^+(\sigma, \alpha|_l \cdot o)$, where $l = o.loc$.*

Alternatively, the data type of such an object may be viewed as a composition of simpler data types. The full version of this paper includes a formal definition of composition for data types, but this is omitted here due to space limitations.

Example 3. A read/write memory with addresses A and values V is the composition of read/write registers with values V indexed by A. Specifically, $\Sigma = \Pi_{a \in A} V$, $\hat\sigma = (v_0)_{a \in A}$, $\mathcal{O} = \{read(a) : a \in A\} \cup \{write(a, v) : a \in A, v \in V\}$, $\mathcal{R} = V \cup \{ack\}$, and τ such that $\tau((v_{a'})_{a' \in A}, read(a)) = ((v_{a'})_{a' \in A}, v_a)$, and $\tau((v_{a'})_{a' \in A}, write(a, v)) = ((v'_{a'})_{a' \in A}, ack)$, where $v'_a = v$ and $v'_{a'} = v_{a'}$ for $a' \neq a$. An operator is said to be performed at its address.

Every *write* operator is oblivious to all operators, every *read* operator commutes with all operators and is independent of all *read* operators. Operators performed at different addresses are independent, so the function that maps each operator to its address is a location partition.

5 Precedence-Based Memories

This section lays out the basic framework for precedence-based memories, defining the interface between the memory which maintains the data object and the clients that wish to access it. We define the interface in a centralized fashion, with one automaton for the clients, and one for the memory. This allows us to formulate restrictions on the clients and memory as abstractly as possible, and to model systems which have nonlocal dependencies, or even systems with no explicit notion of processes. Although actual system implementations will typically have clients running on several processors, and a distributed implementation of the memory, these are merely particular implementations of these abstract automata. Processes and processors are not explicit in our abstract formulation.

5.1 Some Notation and Conventions

We assume that the memory is maintaining data of type $\mathcal{D}$. Memory operations consist of a request by the client to apply a data operator and a response by the memory system with the return value. To distinguish different requests of the same data operator, operations are tagged with identifiers from a set $\mathcal{I}$. No identifier may be used in more than one request. A request also specifies a set of identifiers of operations on which the requested operation depends, i.e., the operations that must precede it. To simplify notation, we denote an operation by its identifier, and assume there is a function $op : \mathcal{I} - \mathcal{O}$ that maps each identifier to its associated operator, and that this function is statically determined.

If α is a sequence of unique identifiers containing id then $retval(id, \alpha) = \tau_{\mathcal{R}}^+(\hat\sigma, op(\alpha'))$, where α' is the prefix of α ending with id. This function gives the return value of an operation given the sequence of operations performed.

If $(\mathcal{D}, loc)$ is location-based then for $l \in \mathcal{L}$, $\alpha \in \mathcal{I}^*$, and $S \subseteq \mathcal{I}$, we use $S|_l = \{id \in S : op(id).loc = l\}$ and $\alpha|_l = \alpha|_{\mathcal{I}|_l}$. The following lemmas express some simple results for operations on location-based data:

Lemma 6. *For $l \in \mathcal{L}$, $\alpha \in \mathcal{I}^*$, $op(\alpha)|_l = op(\alpha|_l)$*

Lemma 7. *For $\alpha \in \mathcal{I}^*$ and id in α, $retval(id, \alpha) = retval(id, \alpha|_{op(id).loc})$.*

5.2 Clients

We introduce a generic automaton which expresses the well-formedness requirements on the clients accessing the memory. Informally, these requirements are that identifiers are unique and that operations depend only on operations that have already been requested. This prevents cyclic dependencies. We also maintain some useful bookkeeping variables.

Note that this one automaton models all the clients together. This allows us to specify more general and abstract programming systems which may not have any explicit notion of processes, such as the Cilk system [4, 13]. This is important because the specification of practical programming systems is an active area of research. Systems in which the process that issues each request is explicit can easily be modelled in this framework by incorporating the process identifier into the operation identifier, or even the operator.

Generic Clients Automaton: $\mathcal{GC}(\mathcal{O}, \mathcal{I})$

State

    Used: a set of identifiers, initially empty.

    $prev : \mathcal{I} \rightarrow 2^{\mathcal{I}}\bot$; identifiers of client-specified preceding operations, initially all $\bot$.

Actions

    Output *request(id, prev)*
        Pre: $id \notin Used$
            $prev \subseteq Used$
        Eff: $Used \leftarrow Used \cup \{id\}$
            $prev(id) \leftarrow prev$

    Input *response(id, v)*
        Eff: None

Since $\mathcal{O}$ and $\mathcal{I}$ are fixed, we usually drop them from the notation. A *clients automaton* is any automaton that implements $\mathcal{GC}$. We assume that every clients automaton has these state variables, and updates them in exactly this fashion.[1] It is easy to see that *Used* is redundant since $Used = \{id : prev(id) \neq \bot\}$. We derive from *prev* a partial order $\prec_c$ that is the reflexive and transitive closure of $\{(id, id') : id \in prev(id')\}$. We say that *id* and *id'* are *concurrent* in a state if they are not ordered by $\prec_c$.

---

[1] In fact, because they are only updated deterministically by external actions, the value of these variables in any reachable state can be determined from the trace leading to that state. These variables are useful for analysis, but a real implementation need not maintain them.

This generic automaton specifies a very large class of automata which can meaningfully interact with precedence-based memories. It is helpful to distinguish families of automata within this class about which we may be able to say more. In particular, it is useful to note clients that, when composed with a weak memory consistency model, behave as though they were composed with a sequentially consistent memory.

If $\mathcal{L}$ is a set of locations, then we say that a clients automaton C respects $f : \mathcal{I} \rightarrow \mathcal{L}$ if in every reachable state of C, for all concurrent operations id and id', we have $f(id) \neq f(id')$, i.e., C does not issue concurrent operations to the same location. If $f : \mathcal{O} \rightarrow \mathcal{L}$, we say that a client respects f if it respects $op \circ f$.

We are interested in the clients that respect location partitions. In particular, if $(\mathcal{D}, loc)$ is location-based then clients that respect loc will exhibit the same behaviors when composed with per-location sequentially consistent memory as when composed with globally sequentially consistent memory, as defined later in this paper.

5.3 Generic Precedence-Based Memory Automaton

We now present automaton for a generic precedence-based memory, without any restrictions on the return values of operations. This automaton maintains some data structures that are useful for understanding precedence-based memory, and provide notation and a framework with which to understand the various memory models. The only restrictions this automaton places on the behaviors arise from the order specified by the client.

Generic Precedence-Based Memory Automaton: $\mathcal{GPBM}(\mathcal{D}, \mathcal{I})$

State

$prev : \mathcal{I} \rightarrow 2^{\mathcal{I}}{}_{\perp}$; client-specified preceding operations, initially all $\perp$.
$pending \subseteq \mathcal{I}$; operations that still need a response, initially empty.
$done \subseteq \mathcal{I}$; operations that have been "done", initially empty.
$return\text{-}value : \mathcal{I} \rightarrow \mathcal{R}_{\perp}$; the return value for each operation, initially all $\perp$.

Actions

Input $request(id, prev)$
    Eff: $pending \leftarrow pending \cup \{id\}$
        $prev(id) \leftarrow prev$

Internal $do\text{-}operation(id, v)$
    Pre: $id \in pending - done$
        $prev(id) \subseteq done$
    Eff: $done \leftarrow done \cup \{id\}$
        $return\text{-}value(id) \leftarrow v$

Output $response(id, v)$
    Pre: $id \in pending$
        $v = return\text{-}value(id)$
    Eff: $pending \leftarrow pending - \{id\}$

Since $\mathcal{D}$ and $\mathcal{I}$ are fixed, we usually drop them from the notation. A *memory automaton* is any automaton that implements $\mathcal{GPBM}$. We assume that every memory automaton has the *prev* and *pending* state variables, and updates them exactly as above.[2] We define $\prec_c$ and *concurrent* as we did for clients automata.[3]

Invariant 8. *For $\mathcal{GPBM}$:*

- $id \in pending \implies prev(id) \neq \perp$
- $id \in done \implies prev(id) \neq \perp \wedge prev(id) \subseteq done$
- $return\text{-}value(id) \neq \perp \implies id \in done$
- $id \in done \wedge id' \prec_c id \implies id' \in done$

5.4   The Generic Precedence-Based System

Lemma 9. *$\mathcal{GPBM}$ and $\mathcal{GC}$ are compatible.*

Invariant 10. *For $\mathcal{GPBM} \circ \mathcal{GC}$: $\mathcal{GPBM}.prev = \mathcal{GC}.prev$.*

Because of this invariant, we do not need to distinguish the *prev* variables, nor $\prec_c$ and *concurrent* which are derived from *prev*, of the memory and clients automata. This is true for any memory automaton M and clients automaton C.

6   Sequential Consistency

6.1   Global Sequential Consistency

In this section, we introduce a notion of sequential consistency generalized for arbitrary precedence-based memories. We specify this by an automaton, which rules out behaviors where operations predict what operations will be requested in the future. We present this automaton as an enhancement of the generic memory automaton. We include below only the *do-operation* action; the *request* and *response* actions are unchanged.

Lemma 11. $gSC(\mathcal{D}, \mathcal{I}) \subseteq \mathcal{GPBM}(\mathcal{D}, \mathcal{I})$

Proof. The trivial relation which relates states with exactly the same state components is a simulation because *request* and *response* are identical in the two automata, and *do-operation*(id, v, α) in gSC simulates *do-operation*(id, v) in $\mathcal{GPBM}$.

Invariant 12. *For gSC: There is a serialization α of done consistent with $\prec_c$ such that $retval(id, \alpha) = return\text{-}value(id)$ for all $id \in done$.*

Proof. The serialization of the last *do-operation* action satisfies these conditions.

---

[2] As with clients automata, since these are updated deterministically by external actions, they are determined by the trace.

[3] Although *Used* is not a state variable of $\mathcal{GPBM}$, it can be derived from *prev* or (as noted) from the trace.

Global Sequential Consistency Automaton: $gSC(\mathcal{D}, \mathcal{I})$

Actions (changes from $\mathcal{GPBM}$)

> Internal *do-operation*(id, v, α)
> Pre: $id \in pending - done$
> $prev(id) \subseteq done$
> α is a serialization of $done \cup \{id\}$ consistent with $\prec_c$
> $\forall id' \in done, retval(id', \alpha) = return\text{-}value(id')$
> $retval(id, \alpha) = v$
> Eff: As before

6.2 Per-Location Sequential Consistency

For this section, we assume that $(\mathcal{D}, loc)$ is location-based. Intuitively, a per-location sequentially consistent memory maintains global sequential consistency among operations at the same location, but makes no guarantees for operations at different locations. This is similar to the coherence condition for cached systems. As before, we present this automaton as an enhancement of $\mathcal{GPBM}$, but notice the similarity to gSC.

Per-Location Sequential Consistency Automaton: $plSC(\mathcal{D}, loc, \mathcal{I})$

Actions (changes from $\mathcal{GPBM}$)

> Internal *do-operation*(id, v, α)
> Pre: $id \in pending - done$
> $prev(id) \subseteq done$
> α is a serialization of $done|_{op(id).loc} \cup \{id\}$ consistent with $\prec_c$
> $\forall id' \in done|_{op(id).loc}, retval(id', \alpha) = return\text{-}value(id')$
> $retval(id, \alpha) = v$
> Eff: As before

Per-location sequential consistency can also be viewed, perhaps more naturally, as a composition of sequentially consistent memory locations. Intuitively, each operation gets "sent" to its location. To maintain the client-specified precedence, however, locations need to be informed of the existence and relative order in this precedence relation of operations at other locations. Thus, we can imagine that each operation gets "done" at its location, but a dummy operation with its identifier gets "sent" to all the other locations, so they can maintain the precedence relation.

6.3 Comparing gSC and $plSC$

Intuitively, we can see that gSC is stronger than $plSC$. It is also intuitive, but less obvious, that if the clients always explicitly order operations done at different locations, then they will not be able to distinguish the two types of memory. The following theorems formalize this intuition.

Theorem 13. $gSC(\mathcal{D}, \mathcal{I}) \subseteq plSC(\mathcal{D}. loc. \mathcal{I})$

Proof. The trival relation which relates states with the same state components is a simulation because the *request* and *response* actions are identical, and *do-operation*(id, v, α) in gSC simulates *do-operation*$(id, v, \alpha|_{op(id).loc})$ in $plSC$. This last condition follows since any partial order consistent with α is consistent with $\alpha|_l$, and $retval(id', \alpha|_l) = retval(id', \alpha)$ for all id', where $l = op(id').loc$.

Theorem 14. *If* C *respects* loc *then* $plSC(\mathcal{D}, loc, \mathcal{I}) \circ C \subseteq gSC(\mathcal{D}, \mathcal{I}) \circ C$.

Proof. (Sketch) Notice that because C respects *loc*, all operations on the same location are totally ordered by $\prec_c$. This means that for each location $l \in \mathcal{L}$, there is a unique serialization of the operations at l that is consistent with *prev*. Thus, this must be a subsequence of any serialization of *done* in gSC. Since operators are oblivious to operators at different locations, the return values are determined by this subsequence, and these are the values that must be recorded in *return-value*.

7 Generic Backer Automaton

We now specify and analyze the Backer algorithm of [3]. The algorithm implements a per-location sequentially consistent read/write memory on a multiprocessor system with a cache for each process and a shared "backing store". Operations may depend explicitly on operations done at other processors. The coherence strategy is simple: An operation cannot be done unless all the operations it depends on are done at the same processor, or they have been committed to the backing store. In addition, a *read* or a *noop* must make sure the value is not in the cache if any operation it depends on is done by a different processor. That way, it will not be keeping a stale value. A processor may also flush the value back at any time, and may load the value whenever its own cache copy is not dirty. There are separate internal actions for the various types of operations, instead of a single *do-operation* action.

Because a read/write memory is a collection of read/write registers, it is sufficient to demonstrate that *Backer* implements gSC for a single register. This automaton models a set $\mathcal{P}$ of processors, each of which maintains a cache copy of a read/write register with values V, and, like gSC and $plSC$, is written as an enhancement of $\mathcal{GPBM}$. To analyze this automaton and show it is correct, we need to augment it with some auxiliary variables. We also combine the *read*, *write* and *noop* actions into a single *do-operation* action.

In order to prove that *Backer* implements gSC, we need several invariants. We consider the major invariants and steps in the proof.

First, we notice that the *opseqs* are just serializations of the operations at each processor, or that have been committed.

Invariant 15. *For Backer:*

- *$opseq(p)$ is a serialization of uncommitted(p)*
- *$opseq(\mathcal{B})$ is a serialization of done $- \bigcup_{p \in \mathcal{P}}$ uncommitted(p)*

Backer

Additional State Variables

$val : \mathcal{P} \to V_\perp$; initially all $\perp$
$val(\mathcal{B}) :\to V$; initially v_0
$dirty : \mathcal{P} \to Bool$; initially all *true*
$uncommitted : \mathcal{P} \to 2^{\mathcal{I}}$; initially all empty.

$proc : \mathcal{I} \to \mathcal{P}$; initially all $\perp$
$lastop : \mathcal{P} \to \mathcal{I}_\perp$; initially all $\perp$
$opseq : \mathcal{P} \to \mathcal{I}^*$; initially all ϵ
$opseq(\mathcal{B}) :\to \mathcal{I}^*$; initially ϵ

Actions

Internal *do-operation*(id, p)
  Pre: $id \in pending - done$
     $prev(id) \subseteq done$
     $val(p) = \perp \wedge \forall id' \in prev(id), id' \notin uncommitted(proc(id'))$
       or $\forall id' \in prev(id), proc(id') = p$
  Eff: $proc(id) \leftarrow p$
     if $op(id) = read$ then
       if $val(p) = \perp$ then $val(p) \leftarrow val(\mathcal{B})$
       $return\text{-}value(id) \leftarrow val(p)$
       if $opseq(p) \neq \epsilon$ then append id to $opseq(p)$
       if $lastop(p) = \perp$ then append id to $opseq(\mathcal{B})$
       if $opseq(p) = \epsilon \wedge lastop(p) \neq \perp$ then
          insert id after $lastop(p)$ in $opseq(\mathcal{B})$
       $lastop(p) \leftarrow id$
     if $op(id) = write(v)$ then
       $val(p) \leftarrow v$
       $dirty(p) \leftarrow true$
       $return\text{-}value(id) \leftarrow ack$
       append id to $opseq(p)$
       $lastop(p) \leftarrow id$
     if $op(id) = noop$ then
       $return\text{-}value(id) \leftarrow ack$
       if $opseq(p) \neq \epsilon$ then append id to $opseq(p)$
       if $lastop(p) = \perp$ then append id to $opseq(\mathcal{B})$
       if $opseq(p) = \epsilon \wedge lastop(p) \neq \perp$ then
          insert id after $lastop(p)$ in $opseq(\mathcal{B})$
       if $lastop(p) \neq \perp$ then $lastop(p) \leftarrow id$
     if $dirty(p)$ then $uncommitted(p) \leftarrow uncommitted(p) \cup \{id\}$
     $done \leftarrow done \cup \{id\}$

Internal *flush*(p)
  Pre: None
  Eff: if $dirty(p)$ then
       $val(\mathcal{B}) \leftarrow val(p)$
       $dirty(p) \leftarrow false$
       $uncommitted(p) \leftarrow \emptyset$
       append $opseq(p)$ to $opseq(\mathcal{B})$
       $opseq(p) \leftarrow \epsilon$
     $val(p) \leftarrow \perp$
     $lastop(p) \leftarrow \perp$

Internal *load*(p)
  Pre: $\neg dirty(p)$
  Eff: $val(p) \leftarrow val(\mathcal{B})$
     $lastop(p) \leftarrow$ the last element of $opseq(\mathcal{B})$

Proof. (Sketch) By induction on the length of an execution. Notice that *uncommitted(p)* and *opseq(p)* are modified together since $dirty(p) \iff opseq(p) \neq \epsilon$.

We now define *Opseq* to be the set of sequences that are *opseq(B)* followed by the concatenation of *opseq(p)* for all $p \in \mathcal{P}$ in any order. (This is a derived state variable.) We will show that every serialization in *Opseq* is a possible serialization for all the operations in *done* that is consistent with the specified dependencies and the returned values.

Invariant 16. *For Backer: For all $\alpha \in Opseq$, α is a serialization of done.*

Define a partial order $\prec_B$ such that $id \prec_B id'$ if $id \prec_\alpha id'$ for all $\alpha \in Opseq$. We show that $\prec_B$ includes $\prec_c$ for the operations in *done*.

Lemma 17. *For any reachable state s of Backer, if $s \overset{\pi}{\longrightarrow} s'$ then $\prec_B$ in s' includes $\prec_B$ in s.*

Invariant 18. *For Backer: If $proc(id) = p$ and $lastop(p) \neq \perp$ then $id \prec_B lastop(p)$.*

Invariant 19. *For Backer: For all $id, id' \in done$, if $id' \in prev(id)$ then $id' \prec_B id$.*

Invariant 20. *For Backer: For all $\alpha \in Opseq$, α is consistent with $\prec_c$.*

Proof. Since $\alpha \in Opseq$, α is a serialization of *done* that includes $\prec_B$. Using the previous invariant, we can show that for all $id, id' \in done$, if $id \prec_c id'$ then $id \prec_B id'$, and thus $id \prec_\alpha id'$, so $id' \not\prec_\alpha id$.

We now show that the serializations in *Opseq* are consistent with the values returned. To do so, we define a function $assocval : \mathcal{I} \times \mathcal{I}^*$ as follows: If α is a sequence of unique identifiers containing id then $assocval(id, \alpha) = v$ if $op(id) = write(v)$ or $op(id) \in \{read, noop\}$ and either id is the first element of α and $v = v_0$ or $v = assocval(id', \alpha)$ where id' is the immediate predecessor of id in α. Another way of saying this is that $assocval(id, \alpha)$ is the value written immediately before id in α, or v_0 if there are no writes precede id in α.

First, we note that for any $id \in done$ and $\alpha \in Opseq$, *assocval* depends only on the particular *opseq* that contains *id*.

Invariant 21. *For Backer: For all $\alpha \in Opseq$, $id \in done$:*

- *If $id \in uncommitted(p)$ then $assocval(id, \alpha) = assocval(id, opseq(p))$*
- *If $id \in done - \bigcup_{p \in \mathcal{P}} uncommitted(p)$ then $assocval(id, \alpha) = assocval(id, opseq(B))$*

Proof. (Sketch) This follows because the first element of *opseq(p)* is always a *write* if $opseq(p) \neq \epsilon$.

The next two invariants say that *assocval* gives the value that would be read by a *read* operation.

Invariant 22. *For Backer: If $opseq(p) \neq \epsilon$ then $lastop(p)$ is the last element of $opseq(p)$ and $val(p) = assocval(lastop(p), opseq(p))$.*

Invariant 23. *For Backer: If opseq($\mathcal{B}$) $\neq \epsilon$ then val($\mathcal{B}$) = assocval(id, opseq($\mathcal{B}$)), where id is the last element of opseq($\mathcal{B}$).*

Thus, the value returned by any *read* is the value of *assocval* for that operation for any $\alpha \in Opseq$:

Invariant 24. *For Backer: For all id $\in$ done such that op(id) = read, return-value(id) = assocval(id, α) for all $\alpha \in Opseq$.*

Theorem 25. *Backer $\subseteq$ gSC*

Proof. (Sketch) The trivial relation between states with identical *prev*, *pending*, *done*, and *return-value* state components is a simulation. To see this, notice that this is okay for the start states. The *request* and *response* actions simulate the same actions in *gSC*, and the *do-operation*(id, p) action simulates *do-operation*(id, v, α), where $\alpha \in Opseq$ and $v = retval(id, \alpha)$. The *flush* and *load* actions correspond to no action in *gSC*. We know that the *do-operation*(id, v, α) action is enabled by the invariants. It is easy to check that the correspondence is maintained in the post-states of the two steps.

8 Discussion

We have presented a unified framework for understanding precedence-based memory models, which we hope can serve as a foundation to understanding more general memories. Because this framework is completely formal, we can prove the correctness of algorithms, and make rigorous comparisons between various proposed models. We believe that the careful definition and characterization of the serial semantics of data will also be helpful in understanding memory, and how algorithms can exploit specific classes of data, particular read/write memories.

Many people have proposed different memory models (see [1] for an overview), but only a few have proposed a unified framework that can be used to compare different models. Gibbons and Merritt [8] present a framework to specify non-blocking shared memories, and they do so at roughly the same level as we do. Attiya, et al [2] present a higher level framework which also considers the control operations in programs. However, both still model processes explicitly, and thus would not be able to model the Cilk system, for example. Furthermore, while it is important to be able to reason about programs eventually, rather than simply the sequence of operations actually requested of the memory, this requires some assumptions about the expressiveness of the programming language, and this is still an area of active research.

This work continues in the direction of Fekete, et al [5] and Blumofe, et al [3] in allowing memory models without explicit processes, but can still express models with explicit processes. It is not intended to express all memory models, however, since this task has proven to be very difficult. Rather, it is intended as a first step in trying to understand the essential properties of memory models in a coherent framework.

One direction that we believe will be very helpful to explore is how exclusivity requirements, such as mutual exclusion, or read/write locks, can be incorporated into this framework. A more modest goal would be to characterize different synchronization primitives in this framework. and whether the various primitives being proposed by be handled within this framework, or if they have some additional exclusivity requirements.

References

1. S. Adve and K. Gharachorloo. Shared memory consistency models: A tutorial. Technical Report 9512, Rice University, Sept. 1995.
2. H. Attiya, S. Chaudhuri, R. Friedman, and J. Welch. Shared memory consistency conditions for non-sequential execution: Definitions and programming strategies. In *Proc. of the Fifth ACM Symp. on Parallel Algorithms and Architectures*, June 1993.
3. R. D. Blumofe, M. Frigo, C. F. Joerg, C. E. Leiserson, and K. H. Randall. Dag-consistent distributed shared memory. In *Proc. of the 10th Int'l Parallel Processing Symp.*, Honolulu, Hawaii, Apr. 1996.
4. R. D. Blumofe, C. F. Joerg, B. C. Kuszmaul, C. E. Leiserson, K. H. Randall, and Y. Zhou. Cilk: An efficient multithreaded runtime system. In *Proc. of the Fifth ACM SIGPLAN Symp. on Principles and Practice of Parallel Programming (PPoPP)*, pages 207–216, Santa Barbara, California, July 1995.
5. A. Fekete, D. Gupta, V. Luchangco, N. Lynch, and A. Shvartsman. Eventually-serializable data services. In *Proc. of the 15th ACM Symp. on Principles of Distributed Computing*, pages 300–309, May 1996.
6. G. R. Gao and V. Sarkar. Location consistency: Stepping beyond the barriers of memory coherence and serializability. Technical Report 78, McGill University, ACAPS Laboratory, Dec. 1993.
7. K. Gharachorloo, D. Lenoski, J. Laudon, P. Gibbons, A. Gupta, and J. Hennessy. Memory consistency and event ordering in scalable shared-memory multiprocessors. In *Proc. of the 17th Int'l Symp. on Computer Architecture*, pages 15–26, Seattle, Washington, June 1990.
8. P. Gibbons and M. Merritt. Specifying nonblocking shared memories. In *Proc. of the Fourth ACM Symp. on Parallel Algorithms and Architectures*, June 1992.
9. J. R. Goodman. Cache consistency and sequential consistency. Technical Report 61, IEEE Scalable Coherent Interface (SCI) Working Group, Mar. 1989.
10. L. Iftode, J. P. Singh, and K. Li. Scope consistency: A bridge between release consistency and entry consistency. In *Proc. of the Eighth ACM Symp. on Parallel Algorithms and Architectures*, June 1996.
11. L. Lamport. How to make a multiprocessor computer that correctly executes multiprocess programs. *IEEE Transactions on Computers*, C-28(9):690–691, Sept. 1979.
12. N. A. Lynch. *Distributed Algorithms*. Morgan Kaufmann Publishers, San Francisco, Calif., 1996.
13. Supercomputing Technologies Group. *Cilk 4.0 Reference Manual*. MIT Laboratory for Computer Science, 545 Technology Square, Cambridge, Massachusetts 02139, June 1996.

Strong Interaction Fairness in a Fully Distributed System with Unbounded Speed Variability*

Yuh-Jzer Joung[1] and Jen-Yi Liao[2]

[1] Dept. of Information Management, National Taiwan University, Taipei, Taiwan
[2] Dept. of Electrical Engineering, National Taiwan University, Taipei, Taiwan

Abstract. We present two randomized algorithms, one for message passing and the other for shared memory, that, with probability 1, schedule multiparty interactions in a strongly fair manner. Both algorithms improve upon a previous result by Joung and Smolka (proposed in a shared memory model) in the following two aspects: First, processes' speeds as well as the communication delay need not be bounded by any predetermined constant. Secondly, our algorithms are *fully distributed* in the sense that no centralized mechanism is used for the scheduling. In the shared memory model this means that no global variable can be shared among processes for writing.

1 Introduction

Since Hoare introduced his prominent and now widespread language CSP [12], *interactions* and *nondeterminism* have become two fundamental features in many programming languages for distributed computing (e.g., Ada [31], Script [9], Action Systems [2], IP [8], and DisCo [14, 13]) and algebraic models of concurrency (e.g., CCS [21], SCCS [20], LOTOS [5], π-calculus [22, 23]). Interactions serve as a synchronization and communication mechanism: the participating processes of an interaction must synchronize before embarking on any data transmission. Nondeterminism allows a process to choose one interaction to execute, from a set of potential interactions it has specified.

For example, consider a replica system consisting of two client processes C_1 and C_2, and two replica managers M_1 and M_2. The two clients C_1 and C_2 interact with the managers M_1 and M_2 respectively to access the database. Moreover, from time to time the two managers interact with each other to update their replica data (see Figure 1). The system can be described by the following program written in CSP's style except that input/output commands are now replaced by interactions:

$$C_i, i = 1, 2 :: * [\quad access_i \longrightarrow local\text{-}computing;]$$

$$M_i :: * [\quad access_i \longrightarrow local\text{-}computing;$$
$$\square \quad gossip \longrightarrow local\text{-}computing;]$$

---

* This research was supported by the National Science Council, Taipei, Taiwan, under Grants NSC 84-2213-E-002-005, NSC 85-2213-E-002-059, and NSC 86-2213-E-002-053

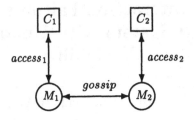

Fig. 1. A replica system.

In the program $access_i$ represents the interaction between C_i and M_i, and $gossip$ is the interaction between M_1 and M_2. Like CSP's input/output guards, interactions can also serve as guards in an alternative/repetitive command, and an interaction guard can be executed only if its participating processes are all ready for the interaction. So the replica manager M_1 can either establish an interaction with its client C_1, or an interaction with its peer M_2; and if both targets are ready, then the choice is nondeterministic. Interactions and nondeterminism therefore provide a higher level of abstraction by hiding execution-dependent synchronization activities into the implementation level.

Intuitively, since a process may be ready for more than one interaction at a time, the implementation of interaction guards must guarantee a certain level of fairness to avoid a prejudicial scheduling that favors a particular process or interaction. For example, the notion of *weak interaction fairness (WIF)* is usually imposed to ensure that an interaction that is continuously enabled will eventually be executed. (An interaction is *enabled* if its participants are all ready for the interaction, and is *disabled* otherwise.) To illustrate, the following execution of the replica program does not satisfy WIF, as interaction $access_2$ is continuously enabled forever but is never executed:

- All four processes are ready for interaction initially, and then the following scenario is repeated forever:
  - C_1 and M_1 establish $access_1$;
  - C_1 and M_1 exit $access_1$ and then respectively become ready again.

WIF has been widely implemented in CSP-like biparty interactions [6, 28, 26, 4, 30], as well as in the more general form of interactions where an arbitrary number of processes may be involved in a single interaction, i.e., a *multiparty interaction*[1] [25, 3, 24, 19, 16].

Although WIF can ensure some form of liveness, it is sometimes too weak to be useful. For example, the following execution of the replica program satisfies WIF but the two managers M_1 and M_2 never establish an interaction, regardless of the infinitely many opportunities they have:

---

[1] Multiparty interactions provide a higher level of abstraction than biparty interactions as they allow interactions in some applications to be naturally represented as an atomic unit. For example, the natural unit of process interactions in the famous Dining Philosophers problem involves a philosopher and its neighboring chopsticks, i.e., a three-party interaction. More examples can be found in [8], and a taxonomy of programming languages offering linguistic support for multiparty interaction is presented in [17].

- All four processes are ready for interaction initially, and then the following scenario is repeated forever:
  - C_1 and M_1 establish $access_1$;
  - C_2 and M_2 establish $access_2$;
  - the four processes respectively leave their interactions and become ready again.

On the other hand, the above execution can be prevented if the implementation were to satisfy *strong interaction fairness (SIF)*, meaning that an interaction that is infinitely often enabled be executed infinitely often. SIF is much stronger than most known fairness notions (including WIF) [1], and therefore induces more liveness properties. Unfortunately, given that (1) a process decides autonomously when it will be ready for interaction, and (2) a process's readiness for interaction can be known by another only through communications, and the time it takes two processes to communicate is nonnegligible, SIF cannot be implemented by any deterministic algorithm [29, 15].

To cope with the impossibility phenomenon, Joung and Smolka [18] propose a randomized algorithm for scheduling multiparty interactions that guarantees SIF with probability 1. That is, if an interaction is enabled infinitely often, then the probability is 1 that it will be executed infinitely often. The algorithm is an extension of Francez and Rodeh's randomized algorithm for CSP-like biparty interactions [10] to the multiparty case. Francez and Rodeh were able to claim only weak interaction fairness, and only under the limiting assumption that the communication delay (as well as the process speed) is negligible compared to Δ—a parameter used by each process to determine how long it should wait for its partner to respond to its request for interaction before it withdraws the request.[2] Joung and Smolka remove the negligible delay assumption, but they require the delay be bounded by some constant ξ_{max} so that Δ can then be appropriately determined.[3] Given that the algorithm's time complexity is in linear proportion to Δ, the performance may be significantly decreased if the average communication delay is much less than the upper bound ξ_{max}.

Moreover, like Francez and Rodeh's algorithm, Joung and Smolka's algorithm is presented in a shared memory model where the participating processes of an interaction communicate by reading from and writing to a common variable. Within the realm of shared memory, we are usually seeking for what is referred to in the literature as a *fully distributed* algorithm [11], meaning that there is no global variables shared among the processes; instead, each process has its own set of variables upon which it can read and write, but other processes can only read the variables without modifying them. In this regard Joung and Smolka's algorithm can only be considered as "semi-distributed" because it allows a set of processes to write to a common variable.

The main contribution of this paper is two randomized algorithms for the interaction scheduling problem, one for shared memory models and the other

---

[2] A similar parameter is used in Reif and Spirakis's randomized algorithm [27] to time-out a process's request, albeit the parameter there is more deliberately calculated to meet the real-time response requirement. Like Francez and Rodeh's algorithm, however, Reif and Spirakis's algorithm is proposed only for biparty interactions, and guarantees WIF with probability 1.

[3] As noted in [18], the impossibility result for SIF holds as well even if the communication delay is bounded.

for the message-passing paradigm. Like Joung and Smolka's algorithm, our algorithms are presented for a multiparty setting. However, we do not assume any upper bound on process speed. Instead, we allow a process's Δ parameter to be dynamically adjusted according to other processes' speeds. Therefore the system's performance is determined by the actual speeds of the processes, not by a worst case scenario of the system. We show that so long as processes do not hang (a process *hangs* if it stops executing its actions, or there exist an infinite sequence of actions such that the time it takes to execute each action is strictly increasing forever), our algorithms guarantee SIF with probability 1. Moreover, our algorithms are fully distributed as each process can only modify its own variables. They are also *symmetric* in the sense that all processes execute the same code, and no unique identifiers are used to distinguish processes. Symmetry is particular useful if we will to extend the algorithms to an environment where processes can be dynamically created and destroyed.

To help understanding our algorithms and to fulfill the space restriction, we have chosen to present here our message passing algorithm; the full paper will present both algorithms. The algorithm based on message passing is simpler because a communication imposes a causal ordering between the initiator (usually the information provider) and its target (the information recipient), and the **send** and **receive** commands in the message passing paradigm implicitly assumes this causal ordering in their executions. By contrast, a more sophisticated technique is required in a fully distributed shared memory model to ensure that two asynchronous processes engaged in a communication are appropriately synchronized so that the information provider will not overwrite the information before the other process has observed the content. Both algorithms share the same idea in the dynamic adjustment of the Δ-parameter.

The rest of the paper is organized as follows. Section 2 presents the multiparty interaction scheduling problem. Section 3 presents the message-passing algorithm and analyzes its correctness. Concluding remarks are offered in Section 4.

2   The Problem

We assume a fixed set of sequential processes $p_1, \ldots, p_n$ which interact by engaging in multiparty interactions $X_1, \ldots, X_m$. Each multiparty interaction X_i involves a fixed set of processes $P(X_i)$. Initially, each process in the system is in its *local computing phase* which does not involve any interaction with other processes. From time to time, a process becomes ready for a set of potential interactions of which it is a member. After executing any one of them the process returns to its local computing phase.

Assume that a process starting an interaction will not complete the interaction until all other participants have started the interaction. Assume further that a process will eventually complete an interaction if all other participants have started the interaction. The *multiparty interaction scheduling* problem is to devise an algorithm to schedule interactions satisfying the following requirements:

Synchronization: If a process p_i starts X, then all other processes in $P(X)$ will eventually start X. Note that by the above two assumptions that a process will not complete an interaction until all other participants have started the interaction, and that a process will eventually complete an interaction if all other participants have started the interaction, the synchronization requirement implies that when a process starts X, all participants of X will eventually complete an instance of X.

Exclusion: A process can execute only one interaction at a time. That is, no two ongoing interactions share a common process.

Strong Interaction Fairness: If an interaction is enabled infinitely often, then it will be executed infinitely often. An interaction is *enabled* if its participants are all ready for the interaction, and becomes *disabled* when some of the them starts an interaction.

3 A Message-Passing Solution

3.1 The Algorithm

We now present our solution for the multiparty interaction scheduling problem in the message-passing paradigm. To help understanding our algorithm, we present it in two stages. The first stage concerns the overall structure of the algorithm, which works only if processes' speeds are bounded. The restriction is then lifted in the second stage.

In the first stage, each process p_i is associated with a unique token T_i. When p_i is ready for interaction, it randomly chooses one interaction X from the set of potential interactions it is willing to execute, and informs each process in $P(X)$ of p_i's interest in executing X. To do so, p_i makes $|P(X)|$ copies of T_i, tags them with "X", and sends one copy to each participant of X (including p_i itself). When all of the recipients have acknowledged the reception of T_i, p_i waits for Δ time, hoping that every other process in $P(X)$ will also send p_i a copy of their tokens in this time interval.

If for each $p_j \in P(X)$, p_i does receive a copy of T_j, and each copy is tagged with "X", then p_i has successfully observed the establishment of X (because the processes in $P(X)$ all agree to execute X). Then p_i changes the tag of each T_j it possesses to "*success*". When Δ expires, p_i retrieves its tokens from each $p_j \in P(X)$ and then starts X.

If before Δ expires p_i cannot receive $|P(X)|$ copies of tokens tagged with "X", then p_i also retrieves its tokens by sending each p_j a message *request*. When the tokens are returned, p_i checks if any one of them is tagged with "*success*". If so, then the process returning that token has observed the establishment of X. So p_i also starts X. If none of the tokens is tagged with "*success*", then p_i must give up X, discard all duplicated copies of T_i, and return to the beginning of this procedure to attempt another interaction.

The algorithm to be executed by each p_i is given in Figure 2 as a CSP-like repetitive command consisting of guarded commands. Each guarded command is of the form "b; *message* $\longrightarrow S$." A guarded command can be executed only if it is *enabled*, i.e., its boolean guard b evaluates to true and the specified message has arrived. Both the boolean guard and the message guard are optional. The execution receives the message and then the command(s) S is executed. If there is more than one enabled guarded command, then one of them is chosen for execution, and the choice is nondeterministic. We do, however, require that a guarded command which is continuously enabled be executed eventually.

```
1       *[ ¬ready  ⟶  do local computations; ready := true;
2       □  ready ∧ ¬commit ∧ attempt = nil ⟶
3              randomly select an interaction X for which pᵢ is ready;
4              attempt := X;
5              send a copy of Tᵢ tagged with "X" to each pⱼ ∈ P(X);
6              wait until each pⱼ ∈ P(X) acknowledges the reception;
7              init_ck := clock(pᵢ); /* start timing Δ */
8       □  receive Tⱼ from pⱼ ⟶
9              add Tⱼ to token_pool;
10             send an acknowledgment to pⱼ;
11             ∀pⱼ ∈ P(attempt) : Tⱼ ∈ token_pool ∧ tag(Tⱼ) = attempt ⟶
12                     for each such Tⱼ, tag(Tⱼ) := "success";
13      □  receive request from pⱼ ⟶
14             remove Tⱼ from token_pool and send it back to pⱼ;
15      □  clock(pᵢ) − init_ck ≥ Δ ⟶ /* Δ expires */
16             send each pⱼ ∈ P(attempt) a message request;
17             wait until each pⱼ returns its copy of Tᵢ;
18             if any returned Tᵢ is tagged with success
19                     then commit := true;
20                     else attempt := nil;
21             delete the returned tokens;
22             init_ck := ∞;
23      □  commit ⟶
24             execute attempt;
25             attempt := nil;
26             commit := false;
27             ready := false;  ]
```

Fig. 2. The first stage of the algorithm.

The variables local to each p_i are given as follows:

- *ready*: a boolean flag which is set true when p_i is ready for interaction, and is set false when p_i has executed some interaction.
- *attempt*: the interaction that p_i randomly chooses to attempt; it is set *nil* if there is none.
- *commit*: a boolean flag indicating if p_i has committed to any interaction.
- *token_pool*: set of tokens received by p_i.
- T_i: p_i's token. Function $tag(T_i)$ retrieves the tag associated with T_i.
- *init_ck*: a temporary variable for p_i to record the time at which it starts waiting for a Δ-interval before it determines whether or not its chosen interaction is established.

Moreover, each process p_i is equipped with a clock, and $clock(p_i)$ returns the content of the clock when the function is executed. We assume that processes' clocks tick at the same rate. Section 4 discusses how this assumption can be lifted from the algorithm.

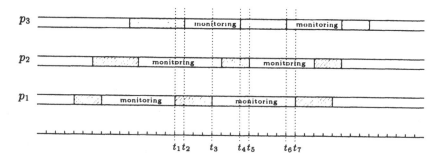

Fig. 3. A scenario of three processes executing the algorithm. Each non-shaded interval represents the time during which a process is monitoring an interaction.

From the above description, it is not difficult to see that the algorithm satisfies the synchronization requirement of the multiparty interaction scheduling problem. This is because a process can start an interaction X only if it has received a copy of it's token tagged with "*success*". Since only the process p_k which possesses a set of tokens $\{T_j \,|\, p_j \in P(X), tag(T_j) = \text{``}X\text{''}\}$ can change the tags to "*success*", when a process p_j finds that the token returned by p_k is tagged with "*success*", all other processes in $P(X)$ will also find that their tokens are tagged with "*success*" when they retrieve the tokens from p_k, and so will all start X. Moreover, the exclusion requirement is easily satisfied because a process attempts one interaction at a time.

Fairness property depends on an appropriate choice of Δ, however. To see this, assume that interaction X involves p_1, p_2, and p_3, which are all ready for X. We say that a process is *monitoring* X if it, after choosing X, has set up *init_ck* (line 7 of Figure 2) and is waiting for its Δ-interval to expire (i.e., to execute line 15). Consider the scenario depicted in Figure 3. In this figure, each non-shaded interval represents the time during which a process is monitoring an interaction. A shaded interval then amounts to the maximum time a process can spend from the time it has executed line 15 until the time it loops back to line 7 to set a new *init_ck* to monitor another interaction. According to this scenario, p_1 is monitoring some interaction from t_3 to t_7. During this interval, p_2 and p_3 will also start monitoring some interaction (at t_5 and t_6, respectively). If the three processes monitor the same interaction, say X, then by t_5 p_1 will have received p_2's token tagged with X, and by t_6 p_1 will also have received p_3's token with the same tag.[4] So by t_6 p_1 will have collected all three process's tokens tagged with "X" (p_1's own token is received prior to t_3). So each process, when receives its own token returned by p_1, will start X.

On the other hand, if a process does not stay long enough in monitoring an interaction, then no interaction may be established among processes even if their random choices coincide. For example, consider the same scenario shown in Figure 3. At time t_1 p_1 has collected tokens from p_1 and p_2 (assuming that they both choose the same interaction X to monitor). Suppose p_3 also chooses

---

[4] Recall that p_2's token sent to p_1 is acknowledged by p_1, and p_2 will not start monitoring an interaction until its tokens are received by all receivers.

X to monitor at t_2. However, p_3's token is not guaranteed to arrive at p_1 before t_1, and so p_1 may give up X at t_1 when its Δ-interval expires.

From the above discussion it can be seen that if there exists a time instance at which all processes in $P(X)$ are monitoring X, then X will be established after the processes finish up the monitorings. Moreover, suppose that the maximum possible interval during which p_i is ready for interaction but is not monitoring any interaction (i.e., the maximum possible length of a shaded interval in Figure 3) is less than η_i. When the set $P(X)$ of processes are all ready for interaction, if each p_i's Δ satisfies the condition $\Delta \geq \sum_{p_k \in P(X) - \{p_i\}} \eta_k$, then there exists a time instance t at which the processes in $P(X)$ are all monitoring interactions. By the algorithm, the interactions they are monitoring are determined by the random draws performed prior to the monitorings. So when the processes of $P(X)$ are all monitoring interactions, the probability that X will be established after the monitorings is given by the probability that a set of random draws, one by each process in $P(X)$, yield the same outcome X. The *Law of Large Numbers* in probability theory (see, for example, [7]) then tells us that if there are infinitely many points at which all processes in $P(X)$ are monitoring interactions, then the probability is 1 that they will monitor the same interaction X infinitely often, and so with probability 1 they will establish X infinitely often.

So fairness of the algorithm relies on the assumption that the length of the interval during which p_k is ready for interaction but is not monitoring any interaction (henceforth referred to as a "non-monitoring window", see Section 3.2) is bounded by some η_k so that another process's Δ can be determined accordingly. Note that the condition $\Delta \geq \sum_{p_k \in P(X) - \{p_i\}} \eta_k$ for p_i implies that the Δ values chosen by processes need not be the same. Moreover, a temporary short Δ can at most cause a process to miss a rendezvous, but cannot cause the algorithm to err.

Based on these observations, in the second stage of the algorithm we remove the bounded speed assumption by letting processes communicate with each other about the length of their previous non-monitoring windows. Processes then use this information to adjust their next Δ-intervals. So long as processes do not hang and every message will eventually be delivered, the dynamic adjustment of processes' Δ-intervals guarantees that when the participants of X are all ready for X, eventually their Δ-intervals will be adjusted to meet the rendezvous requirement (i.e., they will all monitor interactions at the same time). The chance that they will establish X is then determined by their random draws. In this regard we need not assume any upper bound on process speed and the communication delay; the algorithm will adapt itself to the run time environment.

So we can modify the algorithm as that shown in Figure 4, which adds the following time variables to each p_i:

- η: recording the duration from the time p_i previously stopped monitoring interaction to the time p_i starts monitoring interaction.
- *init_η*: a temporary variable for p_i to record the time at which it starts to measure η.
- $E[1..n]$: $E[j]$ records the maximum value of p_j's η sent by p_j.

We shall refer to the algorithm as TB (for Token-Based).

In the algorithm p_i measures its η by lines 15.1 and 7.1. When p_i has sent out its token to p_j (line 5), p_j acknowledges the reception by sending its η to p_i

```
1       *[ ¬ready ⟶ do local computations; ready := true;
2       □  ready ∧ ¬commit ∧ attempt = nil ⟶
3                 randomly select an interaction X for which pᵢ is ready;
4                 attempt := X;
5                 send a copy of Tᵢ tagged with "X" to each pⱼ ∈ P(X);
6                 wait until each pⱼ ∈ P(X) acknowledges the reception;
6.1               let ηⱼ be the timestamp in pⱼ's acknowledgment;
6.2               ∀pⱼ ∈ P(X) − {pᵢ} : E[j] := max(E[j], ηⱼ);
7                 init_ck := clock(pᵢ); /* start timing Δ */
                  /* start monitoring interaction */
7.1               η := clock(pᵢ) − init_η; /* record a new η */
8       □  receive Tⱼ from pⱼ ⟶
9                 add Tⱼ to token_pool;
10'               send an acknowledgment with timestamp η to pⱼ;
11                ∀pⱼ ∈ P(attempt) : Tⱼ ∈ token_pool ∧ tag(Tⱼ) = attempt ⟶
12                          for each such Tⱼ, tag(Tⱼ) := success;
13      □  receive request from pⱼ ⟶
14                remove Tⱼ from token_pool and send it back to pⱼ;
15'     □  clock(pᵢ) − init_ck ≥ ∑_{pⱼ ∈ P(attempt)−{pᵢ}} E[j] ⟶ /* Δ expires */
15.1              init_η := clock(pᵢ); /* start measuring η */
                  /* stop monitoring interaction */
16                send each pⱼ ∈ P(attempt) a request;
17                wait until each pⱼ returns its copy of Tᵢ;
18                if any returned Tᵢ is tagged with success
19                          then commit := true;
20                          else attempt := nil;
21                delete the returned tokens;
22                init_ck := ∞;
23      □  commit ⟶
24                execute attempt;
25                attempt := nil;
26                commit := false;
26.1              /* reset time variables */
26.2              ∀j : E[j] := 0;
26.3              init_η := ∞; /* reset init_η */
27                ready := false; ]
```

Fig. 4. Algorithm TB.

(line 10'). Then p_i adjusts its $E[j]$ to the larger value of $E[j]$ and p_j's new η. These $E[j]$'s are used in line 15' to time-out p_i's Δ-interval.

Clearly, the system's performance depends on the lengths of Δ-intervals the processes choose, which in turn depend on the values of $E[j]$'s. To avoid that the system gets slower and slower due to some abnormal speed retardation, each $E[j]$ is reset to zero (line 26.2) after p_i has executed some interaction. Note that since a temporary short Δ-interval cannot cause the algorithm to err, $E[j]$ can also be reset to any value, e.g., an estimated average value of p_j's η if such value is available.

3.2 Analysis of Algorithm TB

In this section we prove that TB satisfies the synchronization and exclusion requirements of the multiparty interaction scheduling problem, and, with probability 1, is strong interaction fair.

Definitions. We assume a discrete global time axis where, to an external observer, the events of the system are totally ordered. Moreover, we assume that for any given time instances $t_0, t_1, \ldots$ on this axis, the usual less-than relation over these instances are well-founded. That is, for any given two time instances t_i and t_j, there are only a finite number of points $t_{i_1}, t_{i_2}, \ldots, t_{i_k}$ on the global time axis such that $t_i < t_{i_1} < t_{i_2} < \ldots < t_{i_k} < t_j$. Accordingly, the phrase "there are infinitely many time instances" refers to the interval $[0, \infty)$.

Recall that in algorithm TB a process p_i, after sending out its tokens to the processes in $P(X)$, must wait for a Δ-interval before it determines whether to start X or give up X. We say that p_i *starts monitoring* X if it has executed line 7 of the algorithm to time its Δ. It *stops monitoring* X when line 15.1 is executed. Let t_1 and t_2, respectively, be the time at which these two events occur. The semi-closed interval $[t_1, t_2)$ is a *monitoring window* of p_i, and p_i is monitoring X in this window. Suppose that X fails to be established in this monitoring window, then p_i must start another monitoring window. Therefore, from the time (say t_0) p_i becomes ready for interaction until the time (say t_l) p_i stops monitoring some interaction that is successfully established, the interval $[t_0, t_l)$ contains a sequence of monitoring windows $[t_1, t_2), [t_3, t_4), \ldots, [t_{l-1}, t_l)$. The interspersed intervals $[t_0, t_1), [t_2, t_3), \ldots, [t_{l-2}, t_{l-1})$ are called *non-monitoring windows*. The length of a window is the difference of the two ends in the interval. The monitoring window of p_i at time t refers to the monitoring window $[t_s, t_f)$ of p_i (if any) such that $t_s \leq t < t_f$.

Note that if p_i is monitoring X, then every process in $P(X)$ must hold a copy of T_i with a tag "X". Moreover, recall that a process records the length of a non-monitoring window by variable η. Since a process records an η value only *after* it has started monitoring an interaction (line 7.1), the recorded value is slightly larger than the actual length. This is crucial to the correctness of Lemma 5.

If p_i is monitoring X at time t, then the choice of X must be the result of some random draw performed by p_i before t. Let D_{t,p_i} denote the event of this random draw, and we stipulate that D_{t,p_i} is undefined if p_i is not in a monitoring window at t. Set $D_{t,P(X)} = \{D_{t,p} \mid p \in P(X) \text{ and } D_{t,p} \text{ is defined}\}$ then consists of the random draws performed by processes in $P(X)$. We use $v(D_{t,p_i})$ to denote the outcome of the random draw D_{t,p_i}. The probability that $v(D_{t,p_i}) = X$ is denoted by $\psi_{p_i,X}$, which is assumed to be independent of t.

Properties of TB That Hold with Certainty. We now analyze the correctness of TB. We begin with the synchronization property. For this, it is useful to distinguish between an interaction (a static entity) and an instance of an interaction (a dynamic entity): when an interaction X is established, an instance of X is executed.

Theorem 1 (Synchronization). *If a process starts a new instance of X, then all other processes in $P(X)$ will eventually start the instance of X.*

Proof. A process starts an instance of X only if it has sent a copy of its token tagged with "X" to some p_j, and the token is returned with a tag "success". Since only the process which holds the set of tokens $\{T_j \mid p_j \in P(X), tag(T_j) = "X"\}$ can change the tags to "success", and since a process will not give up its attempt to establish X until its tokens are returned, when a process attempting X retrieves a token tagged with "success", all other processes in $P(X)$ will also obtain a token tagged with "success" when they retrieve their tokens. The theorem therefore follows. □

Theorem 2 (Exclusion). *No two interactions start simultaneously if they have a common member.*

Proof. This follows from the fact that a process attempts one interaction at a time. □

Properties of TB That Hold with Probability 1. We move on to prove that TB is strong interaction fair.

Lemma 3. *Suppose that starting from t, for each $p_i \in P(X)$ all p_i's non-monitoring windows have length less than $\eta_i^{\max}$ for some arbitrary constant $\eta_i^{\max}$. Suppose further that all p_i's monitoring windows have length greater than or equal to $\Theta - \eta_i^{\max}$, where $\Theta = \sum_{p_i \in P(X)} \eta_i^{\max}$. Then, if X is continuously enabled in $[t, t + \Theta]$, there exists a time instance $t \leq t' < t + \Theta$ such that D_{t,p_i} is defined for every $p_i \in P(X)$.*

Proof. This requires a careful timing analysis of the processes; details to be given in the full paper. □

Lemma 4. *If $|D_{t,P(X)}| = |P(X)|$ and all the random draws in $D_{t,P(X)}$ yield the same outcome X, then an instance of X will be started when the monitoring windows of the processes in $P(X)$ at time t expire.*

Proof. Since $\forall p_i \in P(X) : v(D_{t,p_i}) = X$, each p_i must be monitoring X at time t. So at time t each p_i has collected every other process's token tagged with "X", and has changed all the tags to "success". Hence, every process in $P(X)$ will start X when it retrieves its tokens after its monitoring window at time t expires. □

The following lemma requires some assumption on the faultless behavior of the system. We assume that if the communication link remains connected, then every message sent by a process will eventually reach its destination. Moreover, if processes do not hang, then they remain active (that is, every process will eventually execute its next action unless the action is a message reception and no message specified in the command has been sent to the process), and starting from any point the time it takes a process to execute an action will eventually be bounded.

Lemma 5 (Weak Interaction Fairness). *Assume that processes do not hang and the communication link remains connected. Then, if X is enabled at time t, the probability is 1 that X will be disabled in some finite time.*

Proof. We show that the probability is 0 that X is continuously enabled from t onward till forever. Observe that since the communication link remains connected and processes remain active, and since every continuously enabled guarded command will eventually be executed, by the algorithm a process will not be blocked from executing its next action indefinitely. So the time it takes for each process to measure an η value (i.e., the time between the execution of line 15.1 and line 7.1) is finite. Moreover, the fact that processes do not hang also ensures that starting from any point all possible η values measured by a process will eventually be bounded by some constant c. The well-founded ordering of events on the time axis ensures that a process may at most measure a finite number of distinct η values less than c.

Recall that the length of a monitoring window for p_i to monitor X is determined by the value $\sum_{p_j \in P(X)-\{p_i\}} E[j]$, where $E[j]$ is the maximum of p_j's previous η values collected between the time p_i becomes ready for interaction until the time p_i starts the monitoring window. Moreover, every time when p_i chooses to attempt X, it will learn all other participants' current η values when they acknowledge the reception of p_i's tokens (see lines 6-6.2 of TB.) Since if p_i is continuously ready it will attempt interactions infinitely often, by the Law of Large Numbers (Theorem 6 will explain this law in more detail), with probability 1 p_i will attempt X infinitely often. So if X is continuously enabled forever, then by the previous observations on η values there must exist some t_0 such that from t_0 onward for every $p_i \in P(X)$, p_i's new η value is no greater than some η_i^{max}, and p_i's value of $\sum_{p_j \in P(X)-\{p_i\}} E[j]$ is equal to $\sum_{p_j \in P(X)-\{p_i\}} \eta_j^{max}$. Since the actual length of p_i's monitoring window is no less than[5] $\sum_{p_j \in P(X)-\{p_i\}} E[j]$, it follows that the length of p_i's monitoring window is no less than $\sum_{p_j \in P(X)-\{p_i\}} \eta_j^{max}$.

Let $\Theta = \sum_{p_i \in P(X)} \eta_i^{max}$. Consider the intervals $w_j = [t_0 + (j-1) \times \Theta, t_0 + j \times \Theta]$, $j > 0$. Given that from t_0 onward each p_i's monitoring window is no less than $\Theta - \eta_i^{max}$, and that the actual length of p_i's non-monitoring window is less than the η value (which shall be no greater than η_i^{max}) measured by

---

[5] The length may be greater than $\sum_{p_j \in P(X)-\{p_i\}} E[j]$ because the condition that the length of p_i's monitoring window equals to $\sum_{p_j \in P(X)-\{p_i\}} E[j]$ only causes the guarded command in line 15' to be enabled; it is not necessarily executed right away.

the algorithm, Lemma 3 guarantees that in each w_j there exists some t_j such that $|D_{t_j,P(X)}| = |P(X)|$. Let μ denote the probability that X remains enabled starting from t up to the point the random draws in $D_{t_1,P(X)}$ are to be made. If the random draws in $D_{t_1,P(X)}$ yield the same outcome X, then by Lemma 4 X will be disabled after the monitoring windows of the processes in $P(X)$ at time t_1 expire. Even if the random draws do not yield the same outcome, some process of X may still establish another interaction X' if its random draw coincides with other processes' random draws. So the probability that the random draws in $D_{t_1,P(X)}$ do not cause X to be disabled is no greater than $\mu \cdot (1 - \psi_X)$, where ψ_X is the probability that the random draws in $D_{t_1,P(X)}$ yield the same outcome X.

Similarly, the probability that X remains enabled (up to time t_3) after the set of random draws $D_{t_2,P(X)}$ is no greater than $\mu \cdot (1 - \psi_X)^2$. In general, the probability that X remains continuously enabled from t to t_{j+1} is no greater than $\mu \cdot (1 - \psi_X)^j$. As j tends to infinity, $\mu \cdot (1 - \psi_X)^j$ tends to 0. So the probability that X remains enabled forever is 0. □

Theorem 6 (Strong Interaction Fairness). *Assume (A1) that processes do not hang and the communication link remains connected, and (A2) that a process's transition to a state ready for interaction does not depend on the random draws performed by other processes. Then, if an interaction X is enabled infinitely often, with probability 1 the interaction will be executed infinitely often.*

Proof: By Lemma 5 and the fact that there are only a finite number of processes in the system, we may assume that there are infinitely many t_i's and t_i''s, $i \geq 0$, $t_i < t_i' < t_{i+1}$, such that X becomes enabled at t_i, and then is disabled at t_i' because some process $p \in P(X)$ executes some interaction at t_i'.

Let D_i be the last random draw performed by p before it executes some interaction at t_i'. By assumption A2, D_i is independent of the enabledness of X at t_{i+1}. Hence $D_1, D_2, \ldots$ is a sequence of mutually independent random variables whose outcomes do not depend on the premise that X is enabled infinitely often at $t_0, t_1, t_2 \ldots$. Without loss of generality assume that p is ready for the same set X of interactions at each t_i. Let $\psi_{p,X}$ be the non-zero probability that X is chosen from X in a random draw. Then for every D_i the probability that $v(D_i) = X$ is $\psi_{p,X}$.

Define random variable E_i to be 1 if $v(D_i) = X$, and 0 otherwise. Then $E_i = 1$ also has the probability $\psi_{p,X}$. By the *Law of Large Numbers* in probability theory (see, for example, [7]), for any given ϵ we have

$$\lim_{n \to \infty} P\left(\left| \frac{\sum_{1 \leq i \leq n} E_i}{n} - \psi_{p,X} \right| \leq \epsilon \right) = 1$$

That is, when n tends to infinity, the probability is 1 that $\dfrac{\sum_{1 \leq i \leq n} E_i}{n}$ tends to $\psi_{p,X}$. Therefore, with probability 1 the set $\{i \mid E_i = 1, i \geq 1\}$ is infinite. Hence, with probability 1 there are infinitely many i's such that the random draws D_i yield the same outcome X. Since the interaction p will execute at t_i' is determined by D_i, with probability 1 X is executed infinitely often. □

Like the algorithm presented in [18], a conspiracy against strong interaction fairness can be devised if Assumption A2 is dropped from Theorem 6. To see this, consider a system of two processes p_1 and p_2, and three interactions X_1, X_2, and X_{12}, where $P(X_1) = \{p_1\}$, $P(X_2) = \{p_2\}$, and $P(X_{12}) = \{p_1, p_2\}$. Assume that p_1 is ready for both X_1 and X_{12}. So it will toss a coin to choose one to attempt. The malicious p_2 could stay in its local computing phase until p_1 has randomly selected X_1; then p_2 becomes ready for X_2 and X_{12} before p_1 executes X_1. Since p_1's attempt to execute X_1 will succeed once it selects X_1, X_{12} will not be executed this time. However, X_{12} is enabled as soon as p_2 becomes ready. Similarly, p_1 could also stay in its local computing phase until p_2's random draw yields X_2. So if this scenario is repeated ad infinitum, then the resulting computation would not be strong interaction fair.

Due to the space limitation, the time complexity of TB will be analyzed in the full paper.

4 Concluding Remarks

In algorithm TB a process p_i attempting to establish X adjusts its Δ based on the length of non-monitoring windows sent by the other processes in $P(X)$. Suppose for each $p_j \in P(X)$, the maximum length of p_j's non-monitoring window known by p_i is less than η_j. As we have shown, the necessary condition for TB to satisfy the fairness requirement is that $\Delta \geq \sum_{p_j \in P(X) - \{p_i\}} \eta_j$. Since Δ and each η_j are measured by different processes using their own clocks, in the algorithm we have assumed that processes' clocks tick at the same rate. Clearly, if the clocks may move at different rate, then the condition $\Delta \geq \sum_{p_j \in P(X) - \{p_i\}} \eta_j$ (where the interpretation of Δ and η_j are w.r.t. a universal clock) may no longer be satisfied. However, if the relative clock speed between p_i and p_j is known, then p_i can time η_j by the drift rate to compensate its interpretation of η_j. If such a factor is not available, then, since a temporary choice of a short Δ cannot cause the algorithm to err, p_i can incrementally enlarge its Δ so that eventually the condition $\Delta \geq \sum_{p_j \in P(X) - \{p_i\}} \eta_j$ will be met.

Acknowledgments. We thank an anonymous WDAG'97 referee for providing very useful comments on the presentation of the paper.

References

1. K.R. Apt, N. Francez, and S. Katz. Appraising fairness in languages for distributed programming. *Distributed Computing*, 2(4):226–241, 1988.
2. R.J.R. Back and R. Kurki-Suonio. Distributed cooperation with action systems. *ACM TOPLAS*, 10(4):513–554, October 1988.
3. R. Bagrodia. Process synchronization: Design and performance evaluation of distributed algorithms. *IEEE TSE*, SE-15(9):1053–1065, September 1989.
4. R. Bagrodia. Synchronization of asynchronous processes in CSP. *ACM TOPLAS*, 11(4):585–597, October 1989.
5. T. Bolognesi and E. Brinksma. Introduction to the ISO specification language LOTOS. *Computer Networks and ISDN Systems*, 14:25–59, 1987.
6. G.N. Buckley and A. Silberschatz. An effective implementation for the generalized input-output construct of CSP. *ACM TOPLAS*, 5(2):223–235, April 1983.

7. K.L. Chung. *A Course in Probability Theory*. A Series of Monographs and Textbooks. Academic Press, second edition, 1974.
8. N. Francez and I.R. Forman. *Interacting Processes: A Multiparty Approach to Coordinated Distributed Programming*. Addison Wesley, 1995.
9. N. Francez, B. Hailpern, and G. Taubenfeld. Script: A communication abstraction mechanism. *Science of Computer Programming*, 6(1):35–88, January 1986.
10. N. Francez and M. Rodeh. A distributed abstract data type implemented by a probabilistic communication scheme. Technical Report TR-80, IBM Israel Scientific Center, April 1980. A preliminary version appeared in the *Proceedings of the 21st FOCS*, pages 373–379, 1980.
11. D. Harel. *Algorithmics: The Spirit of Computing*. Addison-Wesley, 1987.
12. C.A.R. Hoare. Communicating sequential processes. *CACM*, 21(8):666–677, August 1978.
13. H.-M. Järvinen and R. Kurki-Suonio. DisCo specification language: Marriage of actions and objects. In *Proceedings of the 11th ICDCS*, pages 142–151, 1991.
14. H.-M. Järvinen, R. Kurki-Suonio, M. Sakkinen, and K. Systä. Object-oriented specification of reactive systems. In *Proceedings of the 12th Int'l Conf. on Software Engineering*, pages 63–71, 1990.
15. Y.-J. Joung. Characterizing fairness implementability for multiparty interaction. In *Proceedings of the 23rd ICALP, LNCS 1099*, pages 110–121, 1996.
16. Y.-J. Joung and S.A. Smolka. Coordinating first-order multiparty interactions. *ACM TOPLAS*, 16(3):954–985, May 1994.
17. Y.-J. Joung and S.A. Smolka. A comprehensive study of the complexity of multiparty interaction. *JACM*, 43(1):75–115, January 1996.
18. Y.-J. Joung and S.A. Smolka. Strong interaction fairness via randomization. In *Proceedings of the 16th ICDCS*, pages 475–483, 1996.
19. D. Kumar. An implementation of N-party synchronization using tokens. In *Proceedings of the 10th ICDCS*, pages 320–327, 1990.
20. R. Milner. Calculi for synchrony and asynchrony. *Theoretical Computer Science*, 25:267–310, 1983.
21. R. Milner. *Communication and Concurrency*. Prentice Hall, 1989.
22. R. Milner, J. Parrow, and D. Walker. A calculus of mobile processes, I. *Information and Computation*, 100(1):1–40, September 1992.
23. R. Milner, J. Parrow, and D. Walker. A calculus of mobile processes, II. *Information and Computation*, 100(1):41–77, September 1992.
24. M.H. Park and M. Kim. A distributed synchronization scheme for fair multi-process handshakes. *IPL*, 34:131–138, April 1990.
25. S. Ramesh. A new and efficient implementation of multiprocess synchronization. In *Proceedings Conference on PARLE, LNCS 259*, pages 387–401, 1987.
26. S. Ramesh. A new efficient implementation of CSP with output guards. In *Proceedings of the 7th ICDCS*, pages 266–273, 1987.
27. J.H. Reif and P.G. Spirakis. Real time synchronization of interprocess communications. *ACM TOPLAS*, 6(2):215–238, April 1984.
28. P.A. Sistla. Distributed algorithms for ensuring fair interprocess communications. In *Proceedings of the 3rd ACM PODC*, pages 266–277, 1984.
29. Y.-K. Tsay and R.L. Bagrodia. Some impossibility results in interprocess synchronization. *Distributed Computing*, 6(4):221–231, 1993.
30. Y.-K. Tsay and R.L. Bagrodia. Fault-tolerant algorithms for fair interprocess synchronization. *IEEE TPDS*, 5(7):737–748, June 1994.
31. U.S. Department of Defense. *Reference Manual for the Ada Programming Language*. ANSI/MIL-STD-1815A. U.S. Government Printing Office, 1983.

Reliable Communication over Partially Authenticated Networks

Amos Beimel[1] and Matthew Franklin[2]

[1] DIMACS, Rutgers University, Piscataway, NJ. E-mail: beimel@dimacs.rutgers.edu.
[2] AT&T Labs — Research, Florham Park, NJ. E-mail: franklin@research.att.com.

Abstract. Reliable communication between parties in a network is a basic requirement for executing any protocol. In this work, we consider the effect on reliable communication when some pairs of parties have common authentication keys. The pairs sharing keys define a natural "authentication graph", which may be quite different from the "communication graph" of the network. We characterize when reliable communication is possible in terms of these two graphs, focusing on the very strong setting of a Byzantine adversary with unlimited computational resources.

1 Introduction

Suppose that some processors are connected by a network of reliable channels. All of the processors cooperate to execute some protocol, but some of them are maliciously faulty. Dolev [4] proved that if there are t faulty processors, then every pair of processors can communicate reliably if and only if the network is $(2t+1)$-connected. What happens if we want to tolerate more faulty processors? Adding more reliable channels is costly. We suggest a simpler solution, let some pairs of processors (other than the pairs connected by channels) share authentication keys, i.e., the means to identify messages from the other. We show how to extend the authentication capabilities of a distributed environment through interaction and enable reliable communication.

We consider two versions of this problem: "single-pair" and "all-pairs". For single-pair reliable communication, we specify the sender and receiver, and want to succeed against any coalition of at most t faulty processors. For all-pairs reliable communication, we want to succeed for any sender, any receiver, and any coalition of at most t faulty processors. The network of channels defines a natural "communication graph", with an edge between two vertices for every channel between two processors. The pairs of parties sharing authentication keys define a natural "authentication graph", with an edge between two vertices for every shared key. Success for all-pairs reliable communication depends in a natural way on the connectivity of these graphs. The necessary and sufficient condition is that the communication graph is $(t+1)$-connected and the union of the two graphs is $(2t+1)$-connected.

It can be proved that if single-pair reliable communication from a to b is possible then the communication graph is $(t+1)$-connected between a and b, and the union of the two graphs is $(2t + 1)$-connected between a and b. On the other hand, if the graph is $(t + 1)$-connected between a and b, and the union of the two graphs is $(2t + 1)$-connected (not just $(2t + 1)$-connected between a and b) then reliable communication from a to b is possible. However, neither of these conditions gives an exact characterization for single-pair reliable communication. For example, in all three graphs in Fig. 2, vertex a can transmit a message reliably to b (as an exercise the reader can try and find protocols for these graphs). To develop the characterization for the single-pair reliable communication, we found it useful to consider (and fully characterize) a third version of the problem: "single-pair fault-restricted" reliable communication. In this version, we specify the sender and receiver, and two sets T_0, T_1 such that one of them is guaranteed to contain all of the faulty processors. The characterization depends critically on a recursively defined graph which includes all of the communication graph and some of the authentication graph.

For both all-pairs and single-pair, we can show that the possibility of reliable communication implies the possibility of reliable *and private* communication (that is, the faulty processors do not learn any information about the transmitted message). This generalizes results of Rabin and Ben-Or [7] and Dolev et al. [5], who considered this setting without any authentication keys. Furthermore, as shown by Ben-Or et al. [1] and Chaum et al. [3], all-pairs reliable and private communication implies the possibility of secure multiparty computation (when less than a third of the parties are maliciously faulty).

Organization: In Section 2, we describe our model, and supply background definitions. In Section 3, we characterize the all-pairs reliable communication problem. In Section 4, we characterize the single-pair fault-restricted reliable communication problem. In Section 5, we characterize the single-pair reliable communication problem. In Section 6, we deal with private communication. Due to space limits, some of the proofs are omitted from this extended abstract.

2 Preliminaries

We first describe the model. There are n parties connected by a network. We describe the network by an undirected graph $G = \langle V, E \rangle$, where V is the set of parties in the network (i.e., $|V| = n$), and E is the communication channels. That is, there is an edge $\langle u, v \rangle$ in G if and only if there is a communication channel between u and v. We assume that these communication channels are reliable: the set $V \setminus \{u, v\}$ cannot change a message sent on the edge $\langle u, v \rangle$ or insert a message on the channel. We assume that some pairs of parties share authentication keys (to be discussed latter). We describe which pairs of parties have a common authentication key by a graph $G_A = \langle V, E_A \rangle$. That is, u and v have a common key, denoted by $k_{u,v}$, if and only if $\langle u, v \rangle \in E_A$. These keys are chosen according to some known probability distribution, and every set of vertices has no information on the keys of disjoint edges (except for their a-priori probability distribution).

We consider protocols for message transmission, in which a transmitter $a \in V$ wants to transmit a message m to a receiver $b \in V$. We assume that the system is synchronous. That is, a protocol proceeds in rounds; at the beginning of each round each party $v \in V$ sends messages to some of his neighbors in the graph G. These messages get to the neighbors before the beginning of the next round. The protocol specifies which messages each party sends to his neighbors in each round. The messages sent by a party $v \in V$ depend on a local random input held by v, the keys v holds (specified in G_A), the messages v got in previous rounds, and the number of the round. The messages that the transmitter sends can also depend on the message m. We assume that all parties in the system know the topology of the graphs G and G_A. Furthermore, all the parties in the system know in which round party a starts to transmit a message to party b.

During the execution there might be Byzantine attacks (also known as "active attacks"). An adversary, with an unlimited power, controls a subset T of the parties. The adversary knows the protocol, the distribution under which the authentication keys where chosen, and the topology of the network (i.e., G and G_A). During an execution of the protocol, the adversary can choose T dynamically. The inclusion of a party can be done any time before, during, or after the execution of the protocol. For every party in T, the adversary knows all the messages received by that party, its random inputs, and its keys. From the moment a party is included into T, the adversary determines the messages this party sends thereafter (possibly deviating from the protocol specification in an arbitrary manner).

Definition 1. Let $a, b \in V$ be a transmitter and a receiver, and $\mathcal{B}$ be a collection of subsets of $V \setminus \{a, b\}$. We say that a message transmission protocol is $(\mathcal{B}, \epsilon)$-*reliable* if, when the adversary can control any set in $\mathcal{B}$, for every message m the probability that b accepts the message m, given that a transmitted m, is at least $1 - \epsilon$, where the probability is over the random inputs of the parties, the distribution of the authentication keys, and the random input of the adversary.

If b does not accept the message transmitted by a then b might accept an incorrect message without knowing it. We say that the protocol is *perfectly detecting* if b never accepts an incorrect message (however b might not accept any message). A message transmission is (t, ϵ)-reliable if it is $(\mathcal{ACL}_t, \epsilon)$-reliable, where $\mathcal{ACL}_t = \{T \subseteq V \setminus \{a, b\} : |T| \leq t\}$.

Next, we briefly define authentication schemes; the reader is referred to [8] for more details. Let K be a finite set, called the set of keys. An authentication scheme is a pair $\langle \text{AUTH}, \mu \rangle$, where $\text{AUTH} : \{0, 1\}^* \times K \to \{0, 1\}^*$ is a function, and μ is a probability distribution on the set of keys, K. Assume that a pair of parties, Alice and Bob, share a common key $k \in_\mu K$. If Alice wants to authenticate a message m, she computes the value $\alpha = \text{AUTH}(m, k)$ and sends to Bob the message m together with α. When Bob receives a pair m, α, he verifies that the authentication is correct by computing the value $\text{AUTH}(m, k)$ and comparing it to α. If they are equal then Bob assumes that the message was transmitted by Alice. The scheme is secure if Eve, knowing $\langle \text{AUTH}, \mu \rangle$ but not

k, cannot generate a pair which Bob accepts. Formally, the scheme $\langle \text{AUTH}, \mu \rangle$ is called an (ℓ, ϵ)-authentication scheme if every probabilistic algorithm that sees any ℓ pairs, $\langle m_1, \text{AUTH}(m_1, k) \rangle, \langle m_2, \text{AUTH}(m_2, k) \rangle, \ldots, \langle m_\ell, \text{AUTH}(m_\ell, k) \rangle$, cannot generate, with probability greater than ϵ, a pair m, α, such that $m \neq m_i$ for every i, and $\alpha = \text{AUTH}(m, k)$, where the probability is over the distribution of the authentication keys, and the random input of the probabilistic algorithm.

The reliability of a network is closely related to its connectivity. In this work we consider *vertex* connectivity of *undirected* graphs. A path P passes through a set T if there is a vertex $u \in T$ in the path. Otherwise, we say that P misses T. A set $T \subseteq V \setminus \{u, v\}$ is called a (u, v)-separating set if *every* path between u and v passes through at least one vertex in T. A graph $G = \langle V, E \rangle$ is $(t + 1, u, v)$-connected if there is no (u, v)-separating set of size at most t. A graph G is t-connected if it is (t, u, v)-connected for every pair of vertices in the graph. Menger [6] proved that a graph G is (t, u, v)-connected if and only if $\langle u, v \rangle \in E$ or there exists t vertex disjoint paths between u and v. Notice that if there is an edge between u and v then the graph is (t, u, v)-connected for every t and there is no (u, v)-separating set.

3 All-Pairs Reliable Communication

In this section we characterize when reliable transmission between every pair of parties is possible. We prove that, when some pairs of parties share authentication keys, reliable transmission is possible if and only if the communication graph is $(t + 1)$-connected and the union of the communication and authentication graphs is $(2t + 1)$-connected.

3.1 Sufficiency

Theorem 2. *If the graph G is $(t+1)$-connected and the graph $G \cup G_A$ is $(2t+1)$-connected, then for every $\epsilon > 0$ there is an efficient protocol for (t, ϵ)-reliable message transmission between any pair of parties which uses a $(1, \epsilon/(2nt))$-authentication scheme. Furthermore, the protocol is perfectly detecting.*

We start with a subprotocol for sending messages reliably on edges in G_A.

Lemma 3. *For every edge $\langle u, v \rangle \in G_A$, there exists a subprotocol for $(t, \frac{\epsilon}{2n})$-reliably sending a message from u to v. Furthermore, this subprotocol is perfectly detecting.*

Proof. The subprotocol is as follows. Vertex u authenticates the message with the key $k_{u,v}$ using a $(1, \frac{\epsilon}{2nt})$ authentication scheme and sends it to v on $t + 1$ disjoint paths in G. If v receives an authenticated message m on any one of the $t + 1$ paths, and if no message other than m arrives authenticated on any other path, than v accepts m as the received message. Otherwise, v accepts nothing.

Since there are at most t Byzantine vertices, v will receive the right authenticated message on at least one path. Thus v will receive the correct message whenever v does not receive a different authenticated message on another path (and receive nothing otherwise, thus proving that the protocol is perfectly detecting). The probability that the adversary can cause v to receive a different authenticated message on another path is bounded by t times the probability of the adversary forging a single authenticated message, i.e., $t\frac{\epsilon}{2nt} = \frac{\epsilon}{2n}$. $\square$

We can now state the protocol for reliable message transmission. When a transmitter wants to transmit a message to a receiver, it sends the message on $2t + 1$ disjoint paths in the graph $G \cup G_A$. That is, the transmitter sends the message to the first vertices in the paths, and each intermediate vertex propagates the messages to the next vertex on the path until it reaches the receiver. To propagate a message on an edge from G_A we use the subprotocol from Lemma 3. If a propagation on an edge from G_A fails, then no messages is propagated to the receiver on this path (at least not by honest parties). The receiver accepts a message if it is received on at least $t + 1$ of the $2t + 1$ paths. Otherwise, the receiver accepts nothing. We complete the proof of Theorem 2 by proving that this protocol is reliable. It can be proved that this protocol is perfectly detecting. We omit the proof from this extended abstract.

Lemma 4. *This protocol achieves (t, ϵ)-reliable message transmission between any pair of parties.*

Proof. If the adversary has not disrupted one of the subprotocols for sending a message on an edge in G_A, then the correct message is received on at least $t + 1$ paths. Each vertex, except for the transmitter and receiver, appears at most once on at most one of the $2t + 1$ paths. There are at most $2n$ edges on the union of all the paths. Thus there are at most $2n$ executions of the subprotocol for sending a message on an edge in G_A. The probability that the adversary can disrupt at least one of these executions is bounded by $2n$ times the probability that the adversary can disrupt a single execution, i.e., $2n\frac{\epsilon}{2n} = \epsilon$. $\square$

3.2 Necessity

The next theorem states that if the sufficient condition does not hold then reliable message transmission is not possible, i.e. it is also a necessary condition. The result does not assume how the common keys are used. That is, even if the keys in G_A are used for purposes other than authentication (e.g., for encryption) then reliable message transmission is not possible. Furthermore, the result does not assume any limit on the size of the keys. The proof is similar to the proof that without keys $2t + 1$ connectivity is necessary [5]. The (simple) proof of Lemma 5 is omitted from this extended abstract.

Lemma 5. *If G is not $(t+1)$-connected and $\epsilon < 1/2$, then there exists a sender and receiver for which (t, ϵ)-reliable transmission is not possible.*

Lemma 6. *Suppose that G is $(t + 1)$-connected but $G \cup G_A$ is not $(2t + 1)$-connected. Then there exists vertices a, b and subsets of vertices T_0, T_1 of size* *t such that for every pair of messages m_0, m_1 the receiver b cannot distinguish whether the set T_0 is Byzantine and the message transmitted by a is m_0 or the set T_1 is Byzantine and the message transmitted by a is m_1.*

Proof. Since $G \cup G_A$ is not $(2t+1)$-connected there exists vertices a, b and an (a, b)-separating set T of size at most $2t$ in $G \cup G_A$. Define B to be the set of vertices which have a path to b in $G \cup G_A$ that misses T (i.e., $v \in B$ if T is not a (v, b)-separating set in $G \cup G_A$). Define A to be $V \setminus (B \cup T)$. Finally, let T_0, T_1 be an arbitrary partition of T into two disjoint sets of size at most t. Notice that there are no edges between A and B since T is a separating set in $G \cup G_A$.

Fix two messages $m_0 \neq m_1$ arbitrarily, and define two executions 0 and 1 as follows. In execution $i \in \{0, 1\}$, the Byzantine set is T_i, the message m_i is transmitted by a, the random inputs of the vertices in $A \cup T_1$ are $\{r_u^i : u \in A \cup T_1\}$, and the authentication keys of pairs in $A \cup T$ are $\{k_{u,v}^i : u, v \in A \cup T, \langle u, v \rangle \in E_A\}$. The behavior of the Byzantine set T_i in execution i is to send no messages whatsoever to $A \cup T_{\bar{i}}$, and to send to B exactly the same messages that are sent to B by the (honest) T_i in execution $\bar{i}$.

In order for the Byzantine T_i to behave as specified in execution i, the adversary needs to simulate the behavior of $A \cup T_i$ for execution $\bar{i}$. We show how this can be done. The adversary simulates, round by round, the behavior of the vertices in $A \cup T_i$ for execution $\bar{i}$, using $\{r_u^{\bar{i}} : u \in A \cup T_i\}$ as the random inputs for $A \cup T_i$, and $\{k_{u,v}^{\bar{i}} : u, v \in A \cup T, \langle u, v \rangle \in E_A\}$ as the authentication keys for pairs of parties in $A \cup T$. At the beginning of each round, each simulated party has a history of messages that it got in the simulation of the previous rounds, its simulated local random input, and its simulated keys. The simulated party sends during the simulation the same messages that the honest party would send in the original protocol in the same state. The simulated messages that T_i sends to B are really sent by the parties. All other messages are used only to update the history for the next round. The messages which are added to the history of each simulated vertex are the real messages that are sent by the parties in B and the simulated messages that are sent by the vertices in $A \cup T_i$. No messages from $T_{\bar{i}}$ are added to the history. These two executions are described in Fig. 1.

The history of messages of each simulated vertex in execution i is the same as the history of the vertex in execution $\bar{i}$. Therefore, the messages sent by T_0 and T_1 to members of B in both executions are exactly the same. Thus the parties in B cannot distinguish whether the set T_0 is Byzantine and the message transmitted by a is m_0, or the set T_1 is Byzantine and the message transmitted by a is m_1. Since $b \in B$, the receiver b cannot distinguish these cases either. $\square$

Theorem 7. *If (t, ϵ)-reliable transmission is possible between any pair of parties with $\epsilon < 1/2$, then the graph G is $(t+1)$-connected and the graph $G \cup G_A$ is $(2t+1)$-connected.*

Proof. Consider all the pairs of the above executions, where the random inputs $\{r_u^0 : u \in A \cup T_1\}$, $\{r_u^1 : u \in A \cup T_0\}$, and keys $\{k_{u,v}^0 : u, v \in A \cup T, \langle u, v \rangle \in E_A\}$,

	First execution	Second execution
Byzantine set	T_0	T_1
Real execution of A		
Real message	m_0	m_1
Random inputs	$\left\{r_u^0 : u \in A \cup T_1\right\}$	$\left\{r_u^1 : u \in A \cup T_0\right\}$
Keys of $A \cup T$	$\left\{k_{u,v}^0 : u,v \in A \cup T, \langle u,v \rangle \in E_A\right\}$	$\left\{k_{u,v}^1 : u,v \in A \cup T, \langle u,v \rangle \in E_A\right\}$
Behavior	T_0 sends no messages to $A \cup T_1$	T_1 sends no messages to $A \cup T_0$
Simulation of A by the Byzantine set		
Simulated message	m_1	m_0
Random inputs	$\left\{r_u^1 : u \in A \cup T_0\right\}$	$\left\{r_u^0 : u \in A \cup T_1\right\}$
Keys of $A \cup T$	$\left\{k_{u,v}^1 : u,v \in A \cup T, \langle u,v \rangle \in E_A\right\}$	$\left\{k_{u,v}^0 : u,v \in A \cup T, \langle u,v \rangle \in E_A\right\}$
Behavior	T_1 sends no messages to $A \cup T_0$	T_0 sends no messages to $A \cup T_1$

Fig. 1. The two executions that confuse b

$\left\{k_{u,v}^1 : u,v \in A \cup T, \langle u,v \rangle \in E_A\right\}$ range over all their possible values. In each pair of executions, whenever b is correct in one execution it errs in the second. Thus, in any strategy by b for choosing whether to receive m_0 or m_1 there is some i such that when m_i is transmitted, the receiver accepts m_i with probability at most $1/2$.

Consider the following adversary. The adversary chooses T_i as the Byzantine set, chooses the random local inputs for the parties in $A \cup T_0$, and chooses keys for pairs of parties in $A \cup T$ according to the same distribution that the real keys are distributed. (The adversary does not try to guess the actual keys and random inputs that parties in $A \cup T$ have, but only chooses them from the same distribution which they are chosen in the real execution.) The adversary simulates the parties in A with $m_{\bar{i}}$, the keys and the local random inputs it chose. When a transmits the message m_i, the receiver b errs with probability at least half. Thus, every scheme has reliability of at least $1/2$. □

4 Single-Pair Fault-Restricted Reliable Communication

We now prove a characterization of single-pair fault-restricted reliable communication. That is, the sender a transmits a message to the receiver b when one of two given sets T_0, T_1 is guaranteed to contain all of the faulty processors. The proof of sufficiency is constructive, i.e., we present a protocol that achieves reliable communication whenever it is possible.

4.1 Ideas of the Protocol

In this section we informally present the ideas of the protocol, and try to motivate the definition of a graph G^* which is used in the characterization. We sketch a series of protocols, relying on increasingly weaker assumptions, and ending with our actual protocol. For simplicity, let us assume that the adversary can never authenticate false messages unless it holds the authentication key (ignoring for the moment the negligible probability that this assumption is violated).

First Protocol: The first protocol assumes that $\langle a, b \rangle \in G_A$, i.e., a and b share an authentication key $k_{a,b}$. The transmitter a authenticates the message m by computing $\alpha = \text{AUTH}(m, k_{a,b})$. If neither T_0 nor T_1 separates a, b in G, then there is one path from a to b that misses T_0 and another path that misses T_1. If a sends m, α on both of these paths, then b succeeds by accepting any message that arrives with the proper authentication. Suppose that T_1 separates a and b in G while T_0 does not. When a sends m, α on a path that misses T_0, one of two things will happen. Either b receives m, α on this path and the transmission succeeds, or b learns that T_1 is Byzantine. In this case we say that T_1 has "disabled" the edge $\langle a, b \rangle$. We shall see shortly how this information helps the receiver.

Second Protocol: The second protocol does not assume that $\langle a, b \rangle \in G_A$. Consider the graph G' obtained from $G \cup G_A$ by removing all authentication edges $\langle u, v \rangle$ such that T_0 is a (u, v)-separating set in G. (Thus, T_0 cannot disable any edge in G'.) Assume that G' contains a path that misses $T_0 \cup T_1$ (e.g, Graph 1 in Fig. 2). The transmitter a sends the message on this path, where for each edge $\langle u, v \rangle \in G_A$ the First Protocol is used (i.e., an authenticated message is sent on a path in G that misses T_0). We further assume that there is a path in G that misses T_1 (but might pass through T_0). The transmitter sends the message on this path as well.

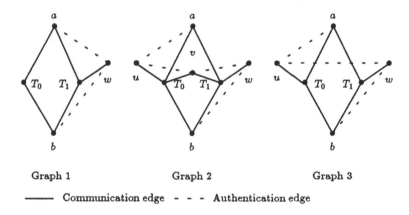

Graph 1   Graph 2   Graph 3

——— Communication edge   - - - Authentication edge

Fig. 2. Examples of graphs in which a can reliably transmit a message to b.

If at the end of the execution of the protocol the receiver b has received a message on the path in G' that misses $T_0 \cup T_1$ then this is the message transmitted by a (since neither T_0 nor T_1 can change this message). If b has not received a message on this path then the message received on the path in G that misses T_1 is the message sent by a (since only T_1 can disable the edges on the first path). To summarize, the idea of the Second Protocol was to get information on the Byzantine set from the fact that the message was not received on a certain path. That is, either the Byzantine set does not disable the edge and the receiver learns the message which was transmitted, or the Byzantine set can disable an edge

$\langle u, v \rangle \in E_A$ and the receiver learns which set is Byzantine. If the receiver knows which set is Byzantine then it can learn the messages that was transmitted.

Third Protocol: In an execution of a protocol the receiver can learn not only that a message was not received on some path, but also which edge was disabled on the path. This information can help the receiver; for example, in Graph 2, described in Fig. 2, if the receiver knows that v did not get a message from u then T_0 must be Byzantine, and the message received on the path a, T_1, b is the message transmitted by a.

In the third protocol vertices that should receive a message on an authentication edge report to b if they have not received such a message. Consider the graph G'' obtained from $G \cup G_A$ by removing all authentication edges $\langle u, v \rangle$ such that each of T_0 and T_1 is a (u, v)-separating set in G. Assume that this graph contains a path P that misses $T_0 \cup T_1$. The transmitter a sends the message on this path, where for each edge $\langle u, v \rangle \in G_A$ on the path, u sends the authenticated messages $\langle m, \text{AUTH}(m, k_{u,v}) \rangle$ on a path P in G that either misses T_0 or misses T_1 (such path exists). This path is defined by the protocol, and the receiver b knows it. We assume that each vertex on this path knows when the protocol has started. For every edge $\langle u, v \rangle \in E_A$ on this path, if v does not receive an authenticated message from u, it sends an alert message "v has not received a message from u" to b. This message is propagated to b on P in the same way as the regular message. As in the Second Protocol, if b received a message on this path then it accepts the message. Otherwise, since the path P misses $T_0 \cup T_1$, there must be an authentication edge on the path that was disabled. In this case, b receives an alert message "v has not received a message from u". The receiver b knows an $i \in \{0, 1\}$ such that u sent an authenticated message to v on a path in G that misses T_i. Thus, b deduces that $T_{\bar{i}}$ is Byzantine. If, in addition to sending the message on P, the transmitter a sends the message on a path in G that misses T_0 and on a path that misses T_1, then b accepts the message received on the path that misses $T_{\bar{i}}$.

Final Protocol: The additional idea in this protocol is that if every T_i that can disable an edge is caught, then this edge can be considered as a reliable edge. That is, when checking if another authentication edge is reliable we use the edges of G as well as those authentication edges which we already established as reliable.

4.2 Characterization of Single-Pair Fault-Restricted Communication

The intuition behind the definition of the graph G^* is that it contains all the edges that cannot be disabled without b learning which set disabled them. We formally define G^*, and from G^* the notion of a "confusing pair":

Definition 8. Let $a, b \in V$ be the transmitter and receiver, and $T_0, T_1 \subseteq V \setminus \{a, b\}$ be a pair of sets. For any $v \in V$, let $[v]$ denote the connected component in $G \setminus (T_0 \cup T_1)$ that contains v. Let $E_1 \subseteq E_2 \subseteq \ldots$ be a sequence of subsets of authentication edges, such that $\langle u, v \rangle \in E_i$ whenever the following is true:

1. $u, v \notin T_0 \cup T_1$.
2. The vertex v is in the connected component of b in the graph $\langle V \setminus (T_0 \cup T_1), E \cup E_{i-1}\rangle$. That is, $v \in [b] \cup \{[u'] : \langle u', v'\rangle \in E_{i-1}\}$
3. At most one of T_0 or T_1 is a (u, v)-separating set in $G \cup E_{i-1}$.

If $E_{k+1} = E_k$ then $G^* = \langle V, E^*\rangle = \langle V, E \cup E_k\rangle$.

For example, consider Graph 3 described in Fig. 2. We first add the edge $\langle w, b\rangle$ since T_0 is not a separating set in G. Now, the set T_1 is not a (u, w)-separating set in the current graph and therefore $\langle u, w\rangle$ is added, and finally $\langle s, u\rangle$ is added. Thus, the Final protocol succeeds in this graph. However, $\langle u, v\rangle$ does not belong to G'' and the Third protocol fails in Graph 3. For every G and G_A it can be shown that $E_{k+1} = E_k$ for every $k \geq n$.

Definition 9. Let $T_0, T_1 \subseteq V \setminus \{a, b\}$. The sets T_0 and T_1 are an a, b-*confusing pair* if

1. Either T_0 or T_1 is an (a, b)-separating set in G, or
2. The set $T_0 \cup T_1$ is an (a, b)-separating set in G^*

Given these definitions, our characterization can now be stated formally. The proof of Theorem 11 is omitted from this extended abstract.

Theorem 10. *Let $T_0, T_1 \subseteq V \setminus \{a, b\}$ such that $\langle T_0, T_1\rangle$ is not a confusing pair. Then, for every $\epsilon > 0$, there is a protocol for $(\{T_0, T_1\}, \epsilon)$-reliable message transmission from a to b.*

Theorem 11. *If $\langle T_0, T_1\rangle$ is a confusing pair then $(\{T_0, T_1\}, \epsilon)$-reliable message transmission between a and b is not possible with $\epsilon < 1/2$.*

4.3 Protocol for Proving Sufficiency

First we present Protocol SEND, described in Fig. 3, which sends a message along a path in G^*. In this protocol either v accepts the message sent by u or the receiver b learns which set is Byzantine. For this protocol we need the following notation. The *level* of an edge $\langle u, v\rangle \in G^*$ is the minimum j such that $\langle u, v\rangle \in E_j$ (if $\langle u, v\rangle \in E$ then its level is 0). The level of a path is the maximum level of an edge on a path. For every $\langle u, v\rangle \in E_j \setminus E$ we fix a path between u and v in G^*, denoted by PATH(u, v), such that the level of the path is less than the level of the edge and the path either misses T_0 or misses T_1. (By Definition 8 such path exists.) Furthermore, for every v that is adjacent to an authentication edge $\langle u, v\rangle$ in G^*, define PATH(v, b) as a fixed path with minimum level among all the paths from u to b in G^* which miss $T_0 \cup T_1$. Again by Definition 8 such path exists, and its level is at most the level of $\langle u, v\rangle$. If the level of every path from v to b in G^* is at least the level of $\langle u, v\rangle$ (thus, u was added to the connected component of b in the graph $\langle V \setminus (T_0 \cup T_1), E \cup E_{i-1}\rangle$ before v) then PATH$(v, b) \stackrel{\text{def}}{=} v \circ \text{PATH}(u, b)$

PROCEDURE SEND(m, P, Destb)

PARAMETERS:

m – a message

$P = v_0, v_1, \ldots, v_\ell$ – a path in G^*

Destb – Boolean variable, TRUE if destination of the message is b

$m_0 \leftarrow m$

FOR $i = 0$ TO $\ell - 1$ DO   (* v_i propagates the message to v_{i+1} *)

IF $\langle v_i, v_{i+1} \rangle \in E$ THEN v_i sends m_i to v_{i+1} on this edge.

OTHERWISE, $\langle v_i, v_{i+1} \rangle \in E_A$:

  1. v_i executes SEND($\langle m_i, \text{AUTH}(m_i, k_{v_i, v_{i+1}}) \rangle$, PATH($v_i, v_{i+1}$), FALSE)
     (* This is an internal call *)
  2. IF v_{i+1} received $\langle \hat{m}, \hat{\alpha} \rangle$ such that $\hat{\alpha} \neq \text{AUTH}(\hat{m}, k_{v_i, v_{i+1}})$
     THEN $m_{i+1} \leftarrow$ "v_{i+1} has not accepted a message from v_i".
     OTHERWISE, $m_{i+1} \leftarrow$ "v_{i+1} has accepted $\hat{m}$ from v_i".
  3. IF (Destb = FALSE) THEN v_{i+1} executes (in parallel)
     SEND("alert, m_{i+1}", PATH(v_{i+1}, b), TRUE).
     (* This is an alert call *)

Fig. 3. A procedure to send a message on a path in G^*.

(where ∘ is concatenation of paths). All the parties in V know PATH(u, v) and this is part of the specification of the protocol.

In Protocol SEND, described in Fig. 3, there are two recursive calls to SEND. The call at line (1) is part of the propagation of the message on P and is called an internal call. The call at line (3) informs the receiver b whether v_{i+1} has accepted a message. It can be executed in parallel to the rest of the protocol and is called an alert call. In Fig. 4 we describe Protocol TRANSMIT in which a to transmits a message to b.

PROTOCOL TRANSMIT(m)

The transmitter a executes SEND to b three times:

  SEND(m, P_0, TRUE) – P_0 is a path from a to b in G which misses T_0.
  SEND(m, P_1, TRUE) – P_1 is a path from a to b in G which misses T_1.
  SEND(m, PATH(a, b), TRUE)

IF the receiver b has received a message on PATH(a, b) THEN b accepts it.

  OTHERWISE, b learns that T_i is Byzantine for some $i \in \{0, 1\}$.
      b accepts the message received on P_i.

Fig. 4. A procedure to transmit a message from a to b.

4.4 Proof of Sufficiency

We first establish that the execution of SEND(m, PATH(u, v), Destb) always terminates, although it might take as many as n^n rounds.

Lemma 12. *Let j be the level of* PATH(u, v). *The execution of the procedure* SEND$(m, \text{PATH}(u, v), Destb)$ *terminates after at most* $O(n^j)$ *rounds.*

Proof. The proof is by induction on the level of PATH(u, v). The alert recursive calls are executed in parallel to the rest of the execution. Thus, the number of rounds in which the protocol terminates is the sum of the number of rounds of each internal recursive call and the maximum number of rounds required for an alert recursive call. The level of every path in a recursive internal call is at most $j - 1$, where j is the level of PATH(u, v). Thus, by the induction hypothesis, each recursive internal call takes n^{j-1} rounds, and the execution of PATH(u, v) terminates after at most $n \cdot n^{j-1} = n^j$ rounds (since the length of PATH(u, v) in G^* is at most n).

Now examine the time required for each alert call for an authentication edge $\langle v_i, v_{i+1} \rangle$ in PATH(u, v). If the level of PATH(v_{i+1}, b) is at most $j - 1$ then the message is propagated to b after at most n^{j-1} rounds. Otherwise, PATH$(v_{i+1}, b) = v_{i+1} \circ \text{PATH}(v_i, b)$, thus, v_i will get the message (on PATH(v_{i+1}, v_i)) after at most n^{j-1} rounds, and the message is propagated to b after at n^{j-1} additional rounds. We conclude that all messages sent in the execution of PATH(u, v) (caused by internal and alert recursive calls) are performed at most $O(n^j)$ rounds after the execution has started. □

We next prove that in the execution of Protocol SEND either the correct message is accepted, or b can identify the Byzantine set. Intuitively, if b has not received the message on PATH(v, b) then there was at least one authentication edge $\langle u, v \rangle$ that was disabled. Consider the first such edge. Then b should receive a message saying that "v has not accepted a message from u". From all previous edges b should receive a message saying that the message was received. The receiver b know that PATH(u, v) misses T_i, and thus T_i^- must be Byzantine.

Lemma 13. *Assume that v executes* SEND$(m, \text{PATH}(v, b), \text{TRUE})$, *where m is either an alert message or a regular message. If the adversary has not authenticated any message without having the authentication key, then either b accepts the message sent by v or b can identify which set is Byzantine.*

Proof. We prove by induction on the level of PATH(v, b), that if b does not receive a message on the path then b can identify the Byzantine set. If the level of PATH(v, b) is zero then this is a path in G that misses all possible Byzantine parties in $T_0 \cup T_1$, thus b receives the message m on this path.

Now, let PATH(v, b) be a path of level $j > 0$. Since alert messages are only sent during recursive calls (when Destb = FALSE) then if an alert message is sent on PATH(v_{i+1}, b) then the level of PATH(v_{i+1}, b) is at most $j - 1$. If b does not receive an alert message then, by the induction hypothesis, b can identify the Byzantine set. Thus, we assume that b receives all alert messages.

Consider all the alert messages that the receiver b received during the execution of SEND$(m, \text{PATH}(v, b), \text{TRUE})$ (excluding the alert messages resulting from alert recursive calls). By the induction hypothesis, if b receives some alert message from a vertex v_{i+1} then this is the message sent by v_{i+1}. By Definition 8, for every authentication edge $\langle v_i, v_{i+1} \rangle \in G^*$, we have that $v_i, v_{i+1} \notin T_0 \cup T_1$. Thus, an alert message claims that "v_{i+1} has accepted a message from v_i" if and only if v_{i+1} has really accepted a message from v_i.

Assume that all alert messages that b received are of the type "v has accepted a message from u". Then no authentication edge was disabled during the recursive calls and the only authentication edges that were disabled are on $\text{PATH}(v, b)$. In this case the message that b receives on $\text{PATH}(v, b)$ is "v_{i+1} has not accepted a message from v_i" for some v_i, v_{i+1} on $\text{PATH}(v, b)$, and this message can be trusted. There is only one set that hits $\text{PATH}(v_i, v_{i+1})$ and b learns that this set must be Byzantine. Otherwise, let $\langle v_i, v_{i+1} \rangle$ be the first edge for which b receives an alert message claiming that "v_{i+1} has not accepted a message from v_i". No edge used in the recursive call during the execution of $\text{SEND}(m, \text{PATH}(v_i, v_{i+1}), \text{FALSE})$ was disabled, and the edge $\langle v_i, v_{i+1} \rangle$ was disabled by a vertex on $\text{PATH}(v_i, v_{i+1})$ which did not propagate the message it got. Again, there is only one set that hits $\text{PATH}(v_i, v_{i+1})$ and b learns that this set must be Byzantine. $\square$

Proof. (Theorem 10) The protocol described in Fig. 4 suffices. First notice that by Definition 9 the paths P_0, P_1 and $\text{PATH}(a, b)$ exist. By Lemma 13, if the adversary has not authenticated a false message, b receives the message transmitted by a. Let ℓ be the maximum number of times that any single authentication key is used, and let k be the total number of times that all of the authentication keys are used; by Lemma 12 both of these values are well-defined. Then, using an $(\ell, \epsilon/k)$-authentication scheme will ensure that the probability that the adversary has authenticated a false message is at most ϵ. $\square$

5 Single-Pair Reliable Communication

In this section we consider (t, ϵ)-reliable transmission between a given pair of parties a and b. Using the fault-restricted characterization from the preceding section, we can prove the following:

Theorem 14. *There is a (t, ϵ)-reliable protocol in which a can transmit a message to b if and only if G is $(t+1, a, b)$-connected and for every $T_0, T_1 \subseteq V \setminus \{a, b\}$ such that $|T_0|, |T_1| = t$, the set $T_0 \cup T_1$ is not an (a, b)-separating set in G^*.*

Lemma 15. *If for every pair of sets $\langle T_0, T_1 \rangle$, where $|T_0|, |T_1| = t$ and $T_0, T_1 \subseteq V \setminus \{a, b\}$, the transmitter a can $(\{T_0, T_1\}, \epsilon)$-reliably transmit a message to b, then there is a $(t, \epsilon \cdot \binom{n}{t})$-reliable protocol in which a transmits a message to b.*

Proof. For every pair of sets of size t, $\langle T_0, T_1 \rangle$, the transmitter executes the $(\{T_0, T_1\}, \epsilon)$ reliable protocol. (Since the Byzantine set is not necessarily contained in T_0 or in T_1, the receiver b might not accept any message in the execution.) The receiver accepts a message m' such that there is a set T of size t, for which b accepts the message m in the $(\{T, T_1\}, \epsilon)$ reliable protocol for every T_1.

Let T_0 be a set of size t that contains all Byzantine parties in the execution. The probability that one of the $(\{T_0, T_1\}, \epsilon)$ reliable protocols has failed is at most $\epsilon \cdot \binom{n}{t}$. If non of these executions has failed then the combined protocol succeeds. For every T_1, the receiver b receives the message m in the protocol for $\langle T_0, T_1 \rangle$. Assume that there is a set T_0' such that the receiver b receives the same message m' in the protocol for $\langle T_0', T_1 \rangle$ for every T_1. In particular b receives the message m' in the protocol for $\langle T_0, T_0' \rangle$, and $m = m'$. □

Proof. (Theorem 14) If G is not $(t+1, a, b)$-connected or there are sets $T_0, T_1 \subset V \setminus \{a, b\}$ such that $|T_0|, |T_1| = t$ and the set $T_0 \cup T_1$ is an (a, b)-separating set in G^*, then by Theorem 11 the receiver a cannot transmit a message to b with reliability less than $1/2$. On the other hand, if the conditions of the theorem hold then by Lemma 15 and Theorem 11 a can transmit a message to b. □

6 Privacy from Reliability

In this section we consider private and reliable communication, i.e., the adversary should not learn any information about the transmitted message. For this, we have to assume that the reliable channels are private: the set $V \setminus \{u, v\}$ has no information on the messages sent on the channel $\langle u, v \rangle$. We show that for both all-pairs and single-pair, the sufficiency condition for reliable communication is also a sufficient condition for reliable communication with privacy. In this section, we sketch the argument for the all-pairs version; the single-pair case is similar.

For any sender a and receiver b, the sufficiency condition for the all-pairs version (Theorem 2) implies that there are $t + 1$ disjoint paths from a to b, and that a and b can communicate reliably without privacy. We next present the outline of the protocol for private message transmission. The transmitter a first sends a different random one-time pad on each path to b. Using reliable non-private communication, and a randomized authentication procedure, a and b determine which pads have been received correctly by Bob. The transmitter a then encrypts the message using the sum of the pads that pass the test, and sends this encryption to b reliably and non-privately. We use universal hashing [2, 9] for the randomized authentication procedure, and perform all arithmetic in a large finite field $\mathbf{F}$. We describe the exact protocol in Fig. 4.

We first argue that this protocol is reliable with high probability. If both of the reliable non-private transmissions are successful, then $r_j^a, s_j^a = r_j^b, s_j^b$ for all $1 \le j \le t+1$, and $G^a, z^a = G^b, z^b$. Then the probability that $c_j^a \ne c_j^b$ for any given $j \in G^a$ is at most $\frac{1}{\#\mathbf{F}}$, since it can only happen when $r_j^a = (d_j^b - d_j^a)(c_j^a - c_j^b)^{-1}$. But $m^a = m^b$ unless $c_j^a \ne c_j^b$ for some $j \in G^a$. If each reliable non-private transmission fails with probability $\epsilon/3$, then this protocol fails to be reliable with probability at most $\frac{2\epsilon}{3} + \frac{t+1}{\#\mathbf{F}} \le \epsilon$, where $\#\mathbf{F} > 3n/\epsilon$ is the number of elements in $\mathbf{F}$.

We argue that the protocol is private with high probability. The adversary's only source of information about m^a is z^a. It suffices to show that the adversary has no information about $c_{j^*}^a$ for some $j^* \in G^a$. There exists a path j^* with no faults on it, i.e., $c_{j^*}^a, d_{j^*}^a. = c_{j^*}^b, d_{j^*}^b.$. If the reliable non-private transmission from b to a succeeds, then $j^* \in G^a$. The adversary's only source of information about

---

PROTOCOL PRIVATE-TRANSMISSION

- Along each disjoint path j, $1 \leq j \leq t+1$, the transmitter a sends to b the values $c_j^a, d_j^a \in_R \mathbf{F}^2$.
- Let c_j^b, d_j^b be what b receives on path j, $1 \leq j \leq t+1$.
- Using the reliable non-private communication protocol, b sends to a the values r_j^b, s_j^b, $1 \leq j \leq t+1$, where $r_j^b \in_R \mathbf{F}$ and $s_j^b = r_j^b c_j^b + d_j^b$.
- Let r_j^a, s_j^a, $1 \leq j \leq t+1$, be what a receives.
- Using the reliable non-private communication protocol, a sends to b the values G^a, z^a, where $G^a = \{j : s_j^a = r_j^a c_j^a + d_j^a\}$ and $z^a = m^a + \sum_{j \in G^a} c_j^a$.
- Let G^b, z^b be what b receives.
- b computes $m^b = z^b - \sum_{j \in G^b} c_j^b$.

Fig. 5. A protocol for private transmission of a message

c_{j*}^a is r_j^a, s_j^a, from which all possible values of c_{j*}^a are equally likely. Notice that privacy may be threatened when the reliable non-private transmission from b to a fails. A partial disruption of this transmission (while otherwise following the protocol honestly) could cause G^a to contain only paths on which there is a fault. This could allow the adversary to learn c_j^a for every $j \in G^a$, and hence determine m^a from z^a. However, if the reliable transmission protocol is perfectly detecting then Protocol PRIVATE-TRANSMISSION is perfectly private. To conclude :

Theorem 16. *Let G be a graph describing a network of reliable and private channels. If the graph G is $(t+1)$-connected and the graph $G \cup G_A$ is $(2t+1)$-connected, then for every $\epsilon > 0$ there is an efficient protocol for (t, ϵ)-reliable and perfectly private message transmission between any pair of parties which uses a $(2, \epsilon/(6nt))$-authentication scheme.*

References

1. M. Ben-Or, S. Goldwasser, and A. Wigderson. Completeness theorems for noncryptographic fault-tolerant distributed computations. In *20th STOC*, pp. 1–10, 1988.
2. J. Carter and M. Wegman. Universal classes of hash functions. *J. of Computer and System Sciences*, 18:143–154, 1979.
3. D. Chaum, C. Crepau, and I. Damgard. Multiparty unconditionally secure protocols. In *Proc. of the 20th STOC*, pages 11–19, 1988.
4. D. Dolev. The Byzantine generals strike again. *J. of Algorithms*, 3:14–30, 1982.
5. D. Dolev, C. Dwork, O. Waarts, and M. Yung. Perfectly secure message transmission. *J. of the ACM*, 40(1):17–47, 1993.
6. K. Menger. Allgemeinen kurventheorie. *Fund. Math.*, 10:96–115, 1927.
7. T. Rabin and M. Ben-Or. Verifiable secret sharing and multiparty protocols with honest majority. In *Proc. of the 20st STOC*, pages 73–85, 1989.
8. G. J. Simmons. A survey of information authentication. In G. J. Simmons, editor, *Contemporary Cryptology, The Science of Information Integrity*, pages 441–497. IEEE Press, 1992.
9. M. Wegman and J. Carter. New hash functions and their use in authentication and set equality. *J. of Computer and System Sciences*, 22:265–279, 1981.

Self-Stabilizing Depth-First Token Passing on Rooted Networks

Colette Johnen[1] Gianluigi Alari[2] Joffroy Beauquier[1] and Ajoy K. Datta[3]

[1] L.R.I., C.N.R.S. URA 410, Université de Paris-Sud, France
[2] Unité d'Informatique, Université catholique de Louvain, Belgium
[3] Department of Computer Science, University of Nevada Las Vegas

Abstract. We present a deterministic distributed depth-first token passing protocol on a rooted network. This protocol does not use either the processor identifiers or the size of the network, but assumes the existence of a distinguished processor, called the root of the network. The protocol is self-stabilizing, meaning that starting from an arbitrary state (in response to an arbitrary perturbation modifying the memory state), it is guaranteed to reach a state with no more than one token in the network. The protocol implements a strictly fair token circulation— during a round, every processor obtains the token exactly once. The proposed protocol has extremely small memory requirement—only $O(1)$ bits of memory per incident network link.

Keywords: Mutual exclusion, self-stabilization, spanning tree, token passing.

1 Introduction

Robustness is one of the most important requirements of modern distributed systems. Various types of faults are likely to occur at various parts of the system. These systems go through the transient states because they are exposed to constant change of their environment. The concept of self-stabilization [7] is the most general technique to design a system to tolerate arbitrary transient faults. A self-stabilizing system, regardless of the initial states of the processors and initial messages in the links, is guaranteed to converge to the intended behavior in finite time.

The token circulation problem is similar to the mutual exclusion problem. A solution to the problem of mutual exclusion on a (uni-directional) ring is to implement a token circulating from one processor to the next in one direction; the token moves around the ring and a processor having the token is granted access to the shared resource and may execute the code in the critical section.

Related Work. Dijkstra introduced the property of self-stabilization in distributed systems by applying it to algorithms for mutual exclusion on a ring [7]. Several self-stabilizing token passing algorithms for different topologies have been proposed in the literature [20]: Dijkstra [7, 8], Burns and Pachl [6], Flatebo and Datta [10], and Flatebo, Datta, and Schoone [11] for a ring; Brown, Gouda, and

Wu [5] and Ghosh [12] for a linear array of processors, Kruijer [19] for tree network, and Tchuente [21] on general networks. Recently, Huang and Chen [14] presented a token circulation protocol for a connected network in non-deterministic depth-first-search order. A memory-efficient token passing protocol on general network is presented in [17]. In [15], a randomized uniform self stabilizing mutual exclusion (USSME) protocol is presented on general network where each processor has an infinite number of states; in the same paper, Israeli and Jalfon proved that the solution is optimal for the USSME problem.

Afek, Kutten and Yung [2] presented a self-stabilizing algorithm that elects a leader and builds a spanning tree on general network using processor ids. Dolev, Israeli, and Moran [9] designed a self-stabilizing DFS tree generation algorithm on a rooted network assuming only read/write atomicity. Afek and Bremler [1] presented a self-stabilizing algorithm that elects a leader and builds a spanning tree on a unidirectional network processor ids. A self-stabilizing BFS spanning tree construction algorithm on a rooted network which requires only $O(1)$ bits of memory per link is presented by Johnen, in [18]. In [9], Dolev, Israeli and Moran gave a self-stabilzing mutual exclusion protocol on a tree network and showed how to compose their mutual exclusion protocol with a self-stabilzing spanning tree generation algorithm to derive a self-stabilzing mutual exclusion protocol on a general network.

All the deterministic solutions to the token passing problem mentioned above are not uniform (there is a distinguished processor whose code is different from the code of other processors in the network or each processor has a identifier). This feature is undesirable in a fault-tolerant distributed system, but Dijkstra noticed in [8] that, there is no uniform deterministic self-stabilizing ring with a composite number of processors. Burns and Pachl [6] showed that there is a uniform self-stabilizing ring for every prime $n \geq 3$.

One of the important performance issues of self-stabilizing algorithms is the memory requirement per processor. The previous solutions to the token circulation problem on general networks have a space complexity of $O(\log n)$, where n is the number of processors. In these protocols, each processor maintains its *distance* to the distinguished processor. Awerbuch and Ostrovsky [3] proposed a $O(\log^* n)$ algorithm by using a data structure to maintain the *distance* variables in a distributed manner. Itkis and Levin [16] introduced another data structure based on Thue-Morse sequence and presented a $O(1)$ bits per link solution.

Contributions. In this paper, we present a self-stabilizing depth-first token circulation scheme on a general network with a distinguished root, called Algorithm $\mathcal{TP}$. One of the desirable features of the protocols written on large distributed systems is that they should not depend on the global properties, such as, network size, which can change over time. Algorithm $\mathcal{TP}$ has this feature and requires $O(1)$ bits of memory per link. When the network size changes, the Algorithm $\mathcal{TP}$ does not need to be modified. The code at a processor needs to be modified only when the degree of the processor changes (a locally checkable property). Our algorithm uses neither the *distance* variable nor any special data structure to achieve the $O(1)$ bits per link memory requirement. Algorithm $\mathcal{TP}$ also implements a strictly fair circulation of token.

The algorithm presented in [17] has the same space complexity. But, in this algorithm, a processor uses the knowledge of the state of the neighbors of its neighbors. Since the algorithm assumes the atomic execution of the actions, this requirement makes the atomic step bigger: in one atomic step, a processor reads the state of its neighbors, the neighbors of its neighbors, and finally changes its own state. In Algorithm $\mathcal{TP}$, a processor only reads the state of its neighbors in an atomic step. Thus, Algorithm $\mathcal{TP}$ has a smaller atomicity degree than the algorithm in [17].

2 Preliminaries

In this section, we define the distributed systems and programs considered in this paper, and state what it means for a protocol to be self-stabilizing. Then, we present the statement of the token passing problem and its properties.

2.1 Self-Stabilizing System

System. Let $\mathcal{DS} = (PR, M)$ be a *distributed system*, where PR is a set of processors and M is a set of bidirectional communication links. We will denote the processors by $i :: i \in \{1..n\}$ and the root processor by r. A communication link (i, j) exists iff i and j are neighbors. Each processor i maintains its set of neighbors, denoted as $N.i$. Every processor owns a shared register (defined in the following paragraph). The processors may only communicate with their neighbors using the shared registers.

Programs. Each processor executes a program and the processors execute their programs asynchronously. The program consists of a set of variables and a finite set of actions. The processors have two types of variables: *local variables* and *field variables*. The field variables are part of the shared register which is used to communicate with the neighbors. The local variables defined in the program of processor i are used strictly locally, meaning that they cannot be accessed by the neighbors of i. A processor can only write to its own shared register and can only read shared registers owned by the neighboring processors. So, the field variables of i can be accessed by i and its neighbors. The program of each processor consists of a finite set of actions. Each action is uniquely identified by a label and is of the following form:

$$< label >:: < guard > \longrightarrow < statement >$$

The guard of an action in the program of i is a boolean expression involving the local variables of i, and the field variables of i and its neighbors. The statement of an action of i updates zero or more local variables and field variables of i. An action can be executed only if its guard evaluates to true. We assume that the actions are atomically executed: the evaluation of a guard and the execution of the corresponding statement of an action, if executed, are done in one atomic step. The atomic execution of an action of i is called a *step* of i; this is known as the *distributed daemon* [4].

The *state* of a processor is defined by the values of its field variables. The *state* of a system is a product of the states of all processors ($\in PR$). In the sequel, we refer to the state of a processor and of a system as a *local state* and a *global state*, respectively. A *computation* of a protocol $\mathcal{P}$ is a *fair, maximal* sequence of global states $\Phi = (\delta_1, \delta_2, \ldots)$ such that for $i = 1, 2, \ldots$, the global state δ_{i+1} is reached from δ_i by a single *computation step*. During a computation step, one or more processors execute a step and a processor may take at most one step. *Fairness* of the sequence means that if any action in $\mathcal{P}$ is continuously enabled along the sequence, it is eventually chosen for execution. *Maximality* means that the sequence is either infinite, or it is finite and no action of $\mathcal{P}$ is enabled in the final global state. All computations considered in this paper are assumed to be fair and maximal.

Let $\mathcal{L}$ be a global state predicate of a protocol $\mathcal{P}$ specified with respect to the problem specification SP that $\mathcal{P}$ implements. $\mathcal{L}$ holds at all global states reached by the computations of $\mathcal{P}$ that meet SP. Thus, $\mathcal{L}$ characterizes the set of all global states reached in the "correct" computations of $\mathcal{P}$. The predicate $\mathcal{L}$ is called a *legitimacy predicate* or an *invariant* of $\mathcal{P}$.

The protocol $\mathcal{P}$ is *self-stabilizing* for the specification SP if (i) every computation of $\mathcal{P}$ starting from a global state where $\mathcal{L}$ holds preserves $\mathcal{L}$ (**closure**), and (ii) starting from any arbitrary global state, every computation of $\mathcal{P}$ reaches a global state where $\mathcal{L}$ holds (**convergence**).

2.2 Specification of the Token Passing Protocol

The legitimacy predicate $\mathcal{L}_{TP}$ of our token passing protocol is any global state such that (i) no two processors have simultaneous token access at any time (called the **Single Token** property), and (ii) for each computation that starts in such a global state, during a token circulation round, each processor obtains the token exactly once (called the **Strict Fairness** property).

We also require our solution to the token passing problem to be **self-stabilizing**.

3 Token Passing Protocol

In this section, we propose a self-stabilizing depth-first token circulation algorithm. We first present the general approach to the solution, followed by the definition of the local and field variables at each processor. Finally, we present the actions of the algorithm formally.

3.1 Idea of the Solution

The proposed algorithm has two major tasks: to circulate the token in the network in a deterministic depth-first order and to handle the abnormal situations (illegal states) due to the unpredictable initial states and transient errors. The actions of the program for the token circulation are formally presented in Section 3.3 and the actions for the error handling processor are given in Section 3.4.

The root r (in the sequel referred to as the *legal root*) initiates a depth-first *circulation round* with a color of 1 or 3. We will refer to the *circulation round* as *cround*, and the color used in a circulation round as *r_color*. The circulation rounds with the colors of 1 and 3 are referred to as $cround_1$ and $cround_3$, respectively. Once the system is stabilized, in one *cround*, the token traverses every processor in the network in the depth-first order. The branches created due to the traversal of the token are called the *depth-first branches*.

In the beginning of a *cround*, the processor r holds the token and r is the leaf of the depth-first branch. The leaf (in this case r) chooses one of the neighbors i as a child and passes the token to i. So, i is the leaf now. After i uses the token (or exits the critical section), i selects one of its neighbors j who did not get the token yet. So, the token traversal procedure extends the branch originating at r. This continues until a leaf is unable to find any unvisited neighbor. At this time, the leaf drops the token, allowing its parent to remove this branch, to create another depth-first branch (to choose another child), and to pass the token to an unvisited neighbor (the child). If the parent cannot find an unvisited neighbor, the branch is shrunk. This token traversal continues until the branch is reduced to r, i.e, all processors of the network have been visited during this *cround*. This completes the *cround*. r now initiates another *cround* with the other color and the token traversal is repeated.

The system has an unpredictable initial state—illegal branches or cycles can may exist initially. There are mainly two error handling tasks: one to remove the illegal branches and the other to eliminate the cycles. Our approach to handling the illegal branches (which are not cycles and are not rooted to the legal root) is similar to the ideas in [14] and [17], and is formally presented in Section 3.4. The illegal roots detect their abnormal situation and change their status to E. The E status is propagated to their leaves, these E status leaves are de-linked from their parents, and finally, these detached processors are recovered (changing their status to Ok).

The cycle elimination strategy is similar to the one proposed in [17]. Typically, a *distance* variable is used for this purpose. But, we do not want to use such variables. The basic idea is to detect the cycle by a processor which does not belong to the cycle. The coloring scheme (discussed in detail in Section 3.2) is designed such that during $cround_1$ ($cround_3$), no processor should have a color of 3 (1). Therefore, if in $cround_1$ ($cround_3$), the processor having the token i has a 3-colored (1-colored) neighbor j, j is faulty (j may be inside a cycle). The leaf i chooses j as the child. The faulty processor j detects that it has two parents and changes its status to $E + +$. All descendents of j change their status to E, Then the parent of the faulty processor inside the cycle drops its faulty child and breaks the cycle. As, the processors inside a cycle cannot change their color, all cycles are eventually destroyed.

3.2 Basic Structures

In this section, we define the field variables of the register and local variables at each processor.

The field variables are denoted as $field\_name.processor\_id$. For example, $D.i$ refers to the field D of processor i. If a field variable $D.i$ points to a processor j (a neighbor of i), then $D.D.i$ refers to the field D of $D.i$, i.e., $D.D.i = j$.

The field variables of processor i are defined as follows:

- $D.i$:: The child pointer. It points to one of its neighbors or contains $NULL$, i.e., $D.i \in N.i$ or $D.i = NULL$. If $D.i = NULL$, then $D.D.i = NULL$.

- $S.i$:: The status. It contains a value in $\{Ok, E, E + +\}$. Once the system stabilizes, all processors have the Ok status. The E and $E + +$ status are used during the error recovering processor and explained in the following sections.

- $C.i$:: The color. It takes value in $\{0, 1, 2, 3\}$. All arithmetic operations ($+$ and $-$) on C are $modulo$ 4. The legal root r initiates depth-first token circulation rounds $cround_1$ and $cround_3$ alternately (see Section 3.1). Once the system stabilized, all processors except the leaf, in the current depth-first branch, have an odd color (1 or 3) corresponding to r_color. Other processors have an even color. The processors who are yet received the token during this circulation round are colored $r\_color - 1$. The processors who received the token, but are not in the depth-first branch (the branch expands and shrinks as explained in Section 3.1) are colored $r\_color + 1$. The idea of using a 4-state variable is an extension of the ideas in [7, 12] on a general graph.

Before evaluating their guards, the processors read the shared registers of their neighbors and update their local variables. The local variables of i are defined below:

- P_i:: The set of parents of i. Ideally, a processor should have at most one parent. But, due to the faults, a processor may have more than one parent. The parent-child relations satisfy $j \in P_i \Leftrightarrow D.j = i$.

- NP_i:: The number of parents of $i = |P_i|$.

In the next two sections, we present the actions of the Algorithm $\mathcal{T}P$. Our protocol consists of fourteen actions: TC1-TC4, IB1-IB5, CE1-CE4, and ER1.

3.3 Token Circulation

Figure 1 shows the circulation of a token starting from the legal root. The legal root r initiates a circulation round ($cround_3$ in the figure) by executing the action TC2. The token moves from r (previous leaf) to its first child which is now the leaf. Thus, the tree expands following a branch. The leaf uses the token, but cannot find a first child to pass the token to. So, it drops the token by action

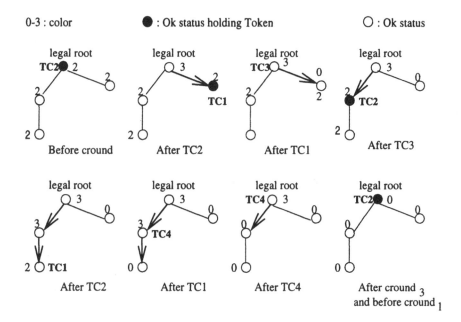

Fig. 1. Token Circulation.

TC1. The legal root now finds another suitable unvisited child which can receive the token (action TC3). This child becomes the new leaf. If the current leaf has used the token and an unvisited processor does not exist, the branch is shrunk by the action TC4. When the branch is completely destroyed (e.g. the round is over), the legal root (r) has the token and it starts another *round* ($cround_1$ in Figure 1).

The actions for the token circulation use the following definitions:

- $EvenColor(i) \equiv (C.i = 0) \vee (C.i = 2)$
- $OddColor(i) \equiv (C.i = 1) \vee (C.i = 3)$
- $GoodLeaf(i) \equiv (D.i = NULL) \wedge (S.i = Ok) \wedge EvenColor(i)$
- $Token(i) \equiv GoodLeaf(i) \wedge ((i = r) \vee ((i \neq r) \wedge (NP_i = 1) \wedge (\exists j \in P_i :: (C.i = C.j - 1))))$
  The legal root r holds the token iff $GoodLeaf(r)$ holds. Processor $i \neq r$ holds a token iff $GoodLeaf(i)$ holds and its color is its parent's color minus 1. i may enter the critical section iff $Token(i)$ holds.
- $Anomalous(i, k) \equiv (k \in N.i) \wedge (k \neq r) \wedge (C.k = C.i + 3)$
  The processor i has a neighbor k which has an "unexpected" color with respect to i. The unexpected color is $C.i + 3$.
- $FirstChild(i, k) \equiv Token(i) \wedge (k \in N.i) \wedge (k \neq r) \wedge (S.k = S.i) \wedge (C.k = C.i) \wedge (\forall j \in N.i :: \neg Anomalous(i, j))$

Processor i holds the token, in i's neighborhood there is no processor with an "unexpected color", and i has a neighbor k which could be a potential child.

- $DeadEnd(i) \equiv Token(i) \wedge (\forall j \in N.i :: \neg Anomalous(i, j) \wedge \neg FirstChild(i, j))$
  Processor i does not have any neighbor which can be a possible $FirstChild$.

- $ChildDone(i) \equiv (D.i \neq NULL) \wedge (S.i = Ok) \wedge OddColor(i) \wedge (C.i = C.D.i - 1)$
  Processor i has a child k who has used the token and is a leaf.

- $NVChild(i, k) \equiv (k \in N.i) \wedge (k \neq r) \wedge (S.k = Ok) \wedge (C.k = C.i - 1)$
  Processor i has a neighbor k who can be a possible child. k did not get the token yet in this $cround$.

- $NewChild(i, k) \equiv ChildDone(i) \wedge NVChild(i, k)$
  Processor i selects k as the next child.

- $Backtrack(i) \equiv ChildDone(i) \wedge (\forall j \in N.i : \neg NVChild(i, j))$
  Processor i does not have any neighbor which can be a possible child.

The actions of the program for token circulation at processor i are defined in Figure 2.

TC1:: $DeadEnd(i) \longrightarrow C.i = C.i + 2$
TC2:: $FirstChild(i, k) \longrightarrow C.i = C.i + 1; \ D.i = k$
TC3:: $NewChild(i, k) \longrightarrow D.i = k$
TC4:: $Backtrack(i) \longrightarrow D.i = NULL; \ C.i = C.i+$

Fig. 2. Actions for Token Circulation.

When a processor may enter the critical section (holds the Token predicate), it satisfies the guard of TC1 or TC2.

3.4 Error Handling

A distributed system has an unpredictable initial state where the D pointers may point to any neighbors or $NULL$. Thus, illegal branches or cycles may exist in the initial state. In this section, we present two error handling tasks: one to eliminate the illegal branches and the other to remove the cycles of D pointers. The actions defined in the following sections together with those defined in the previous section (Section 3.3) complete our solution to the Algorithm $\mathcal{TP}$.

Elimination of Illegal Branches We use the following definitions in the actions to eliminate the illegal branches:

- $BadShape(i) \equiv ((D.i \neq NULL) \wedge (S.i = Ok) \wedge EvenColor(i)) \vee$
  $((D.i = NULL) \wedge (S.i = Ok) \wedge OddColor(i)) \vee$
  $((D.i = NULL) \wedge (S.i = E + +))$

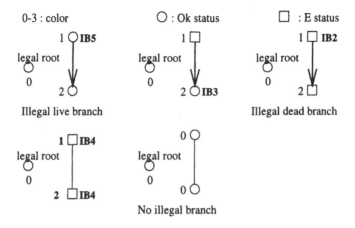

Fig. 3. Elimination of An Illegal Root and Illegal Branch

- $FastBacktrack(i) \equiv (D.i \neq NULL) \wedge (D.D.i = NULL) \wedge (S.D.i \neq Ok)$
  Processor i has a child whose status is *not Ok* and is a leaf.
- $Detached(i) \equiv (D.i = NULL \wedge (NP_i = 0)$
  Processor i has no child and no parent.
- $IllegalRoot(i) \equiv (i \neq r) \wedge (D.i \neq NULL) \wedge (NP_i = 0)$
  Processor i is the root of a branch, but is not the legal root r.
- $IllegalParent(i) \equiv (S.i = Ok) \wedge (\exists k \in N.i :: ((D.k = i) \wedge (S.k \neq Ok)))$
  The status of i's parent is not Ok.

The actions to eliminate the illegal roots and branches at processor i are defined in Figure 4.

IB1:: $BadShape(i)$	$\longrightarrow$	$D.i = NULL;\ S.i = E$
IB2:: $FastBacktrack(i)$	$\longrightarrow$	$D.i = NULL;\ S.i = E$
IB3:: $IllegalParent(i)$	$\longrightarrow$	$S.i = E$
IB4:: $Detached(i) \wedge (S.i \neq Ok)$	$\longrightarrow$	$S.i = Ok;\ C.i = 0$
IB5:: $IllegalRoot(i) \wedge (S.i \neq E)$	$\longrightarrow$	$S.i = E$

Fig. 4. Actions to Eliminate the Illegal Roots and Illegal Branches.

Processor i which is in *BadShape* but not in status E executes action IB1, changes its status to E and de-links itself from its child. Processor i's status is changed to Ok later by executing actions IB2, IB3, and IB4.

Figure 3 shows an example of eliminating an illegal root and an illegal branch. An illegal root executes action IB5 and changes its status to E. The E status propagates from a processor to its child by executing action IB3. A processor de-links an erroneous child that is a leaf (with status E) by executing action IB2. Thus, child get detached. The Erroneous detached processors are recovered by action IB4 by changing their status to Ok.

Elimination of Cycles The actions of the program to eliminate the cycles of D pointers are given in Figure 6 and are illustrated using an example in Figure 5. Processor i detects an anomalous processor k and becomes its new parent (action CE1). A processor having several parents and a child (thus, may be inside a cycle) changes its status to $E + +$ (action CE2).

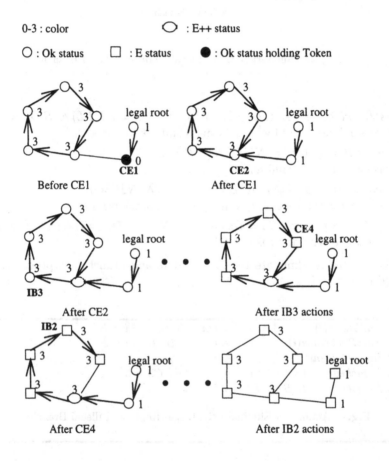

Fig. 5. Elimination of Cycles.

The E status is assigned to a processor having several parents but no child (action CE3). The E status propagates to the descendants of the anomalous processor by repeated execution of action IB3. Then the parent of the anomalous processor (that is inside the cycle) executes action CE4 and breaks the cycle. Action IB2 is repeatedly executed until all the D pointers in the previous cycle are reset to $NULL$. Thus, all processors become detached. Finally, as explained in Figure 3, these detached processors are recovered by executing the action IB4 repeatedly.

CE1:: $Token(i) \wedge Anomalous(i, k)$ $\longrightarrow D.i = k;\ C.i = C.i + 1$
CE2:: $(D.i \neq NULL) \wedge (S.i \neq E + +) \wedge (NP_i \geq 2 \longrightarrow S.i = E + +$
CE3:: $(D.i = NULL) \wedge (S.i \neq E) \wedge (NP_i \geq 2)$ $\longrightarrow S.i = E$
CE4:: $(S.i \neq Ok) \wedge (S.D.i = E + +)$ $\longrightarrow D.i = NULL;\ S.i = E$

Fig. 6. Actions to Eliminate Cycles.

Miscellaneous Error Handling If processor i's D pointer points to the root r, then i removes that link (action ER1) because the root cannot have a parent.

- **ER1::** $D.i = r \longrightarrow D.i = NULL$

4 Outline of the Correctness of the Token Passing Protocol

In this section, we present only the main results and the ideas of proving them. A few short proofs are given in the appendix.

Definition 1 Attractor. A global state predicate B of a protocol $\mathcal{P}$ is called an attractor for another global state predicate A of $\mathcal{P}$, if (i) B is closed in $\mathcal{P}$, i.e., once B holds in an arbitrary system computation in $\mathcal{P}$, it continues to hold subsequently, and (ii) upon starting at an arbitrary state in A, the system is guaranteed to reach a global state in B. We denote this relation as $B \triangleleft A$.

The notation $\delta \vdash p$ means that the global state δ satisfies predicate p.

We apply the convergence stair method [13] to prove our protocol. We exhibit a finite sequence of state predicates $A_0, A_1, \ldots, A_m$, of Algorithm $\mathcal{TP}$ such that (i) $A_0 \equiv true$ (meaning any arbitrary state); (ii) $(A_m \equiv L_{TP}) \vee (A_m \vdash L_{TP})$; (iii) $\forall j : 0 \leq j < m :: A_{j+1} \triangleleft A_j$.

First, we prove that all maximal computations are infinite. We partition the global states into two sets depending on whether there exists a leaf or not. If there exists no leaf processor, then the legal root has a parent (ER1 is enabled), or there is an infinite path rooted at r (i.e., a processor inside this path has two parents). A processor in the path can execute CE2, CE4, or IB2 action. If there exists a leaf, then the leaf or its parent can execute one of the actions.

Theorem 2. *In any global state, at least one action of Protocol $\mathcal{T}P$ at a processor is enabled.*

The following two theorems easily follow from the actions of $\mathcal{T}P$.

Theorem 3. $A_1 \equiv NP_r = 0.$ $A_1 \vartriangleleft A_0.$

Theorem 4. $A_2 \equiv A_1 \wedge (\forall i : i \in \{1, n\} :: \neg BadShape(i)).$ $A_2 \vartriangleleft A_1.$

A branch not rooted at r and whose leaf is in Ok status, is called an *illegal and live branch*. This kind of branch may expand because the processors in this branch may execute the token circulation actions. We need to prove that all illegal and live branches will eventually be destroyed. One complication in the process of removing these branches is that new illegal and live branches may be created.

A new illegal and live branch is created when all parents of a processor i simultaneously execute CE4—i becomes the root of the new illegal branch. After the execution of CE4 by a parent j of i, j becomes a dead leaf, and the branch containing j and i is now a dead branch. If i is inside a dead branch, after the execution of CE4 by all parents of i, i is a root of a dead branch (there is not creation of a new illegal branch). If i is in several illegal and live branches, after the execution of CE4 by i's parents, all theses branches are now dead. Thus, the illegal branch rooted at i replaces several illegal branches. If i is in only one illegal and live branch, then i has $E + +$ status and has only one parent. Such a situation may exist initially, or may happen if i had several parents and has already lost at least one parent (by a previous execution of CE4 by a parent of i): during the computation, several illegal and live branches are replaced by only one. Thus, only a finite number of illegal live branches may be created (this number depends on the initial global state). Then, by fair scheduling of IB3 and IB5, the illegal and live branches are converted to dead branches.

Theorem 5. $A_3 \equiv A_2 \wedge$ *(there exists no illegal and live branch).* $A_3 \vartriangleleft A_2.$

In A_3, there is at most one live leaf which is inside the legal branch. Thus, only one of the actions TC1, TC2, TC3, TC4, or CE1 is enabled at only one processor i (the leaf of the legal branch or its parent).

We call a legal branch *color consistent* if it is dead or all processors in it (except the leaf) are colored r_color. Once $Token(r)$ holds true, the legal branch is color consistent and stays color consistent. We can prove that all maximal computations contain an infinite number of states where $Token(r)$ holds. Let Φ be a computation with a finite number of states where $Token(r)$ holds. In A_3, after the execution of CE1, the legal branch ends in a cycle or a dead leaf. Then the legal branch will eventually destroy itself and $Token(r)$ will hold. Thus, Φ does not contain any execution of CE1. Eventually, along Φ, only the token circulation actions are executed infinitely many times. If Φ does not contain the execution of TC4 in r, then Φ is finite. After the execution of TC4, the system reaches a state where $Token(r)$ holds.

Theorem 6. *In A_3, all computations contain an infinite number of states where $Token(r)$ holds.*

Theorem 7. $A_4 \equiv A_3 \wedge$ *(the legal branch is color consistent).* $A_4 \lhd A_3$.

If the legal branch is not color consistent, then a cycle may be created. The live leaf of the legal branch may execute CE1 and choose a child which is in the legal branch and which is not colored r_color, creating a cycle. Therefore, if there is at least an illegal, live branch, or if the legal branch is color inconsistent. then a cycle can be created. But, in A_4, no cycle is created.

We need to prove that the cycles are eventually destroyed. We consider a computation Φ where some processors are in some cycles. Let $\mathcal{N}_\Phi$ denote the non-empty set of processors which are in a cycle in any state in Φ. We denote the distance between i and r as Dis_i, and the minimal distance between r and a processor in $\mathcal{N}_\Phi$ by Dis_Φ. The processors in $\mathcal{N}_\Phi$ are in *strict cycles*. A cycle is called a *strict cycle* if every processor in the cycle has only one parent and is not in $E++$ status. By fair scheduling of CE2, IB3, and CE4, the cycles which are not strict cycles, will eventually become dead branches. Let $Dis_\Phi = Dis_i + 1$ and i has a neighbor $k \in \mathcal{N}_\Phi$. By induction on the distance between i and r, we prove that Φ contains an infinite number of states where $Token(i)$ holds. If $Token(i)$ holds, either $C.i = C.k + 1$ or $C.i = Ck + 3$. If $C.i = C.k + 1$, then the next time $Token(i)$ holds, i's color will become $C.k + 3$. The reason is that, in the meantime, i has executed $TC1$ or a sequence $TC2TC3^nTC4$, and k did not change its color. If $Token(i)$ holds and $C.i = C.k + 3$, then CE1 is enabled at i. CE1 is the only action that can be executed in the protocol. After CE1 is executed at i, k is no longer inside a strict cycle.

Theorem 8. $A_5 \equiv A_4 \wedge (\forall i : i \in \{1, n\} :: \neg StrictCycle(i))$. $A_5 \lhd A_4$.

The cycles which are not strict cycles will become dead branches. The dead branches will destroy themselves by fair scheduling of IB2.

Theorem 9. $A_6 \equiv A_5 \wedge (\forall i : i \in \{1, n\} :: i$ *is inside the legal branch or* $Detached(i)$ *holds).* $A_6 \lhd A_5$.

The detached processors that do not have the Ok status will recover (change to Ok status) by executing IB4.

Theorem 10. $A_7 \equiv A_6 \wedge (\forall i : i \in \{1, n\} :: S.i = Ok \wedge NP_i \leq 1)$. $A_7 \lhd A_6$.

In A_7, (i) only the token circulation actions are enabled, (ii) only one processor may execute one action (at any time, at most one processor may enter the critical section), (iii) there is no cycle and no illegal branch, and (iv) all processors are in Ok status.

Let δ_0 be the global state where all processors are detached and are $0\_colored$, and δ_2 be the global state where all processors are detached and are $2\_colored$. At the end of a *cround*, more processors will be colored r_color. Thus, in any computation in A_7, δ_0 or δ_2 will be eventually reached.

Theorem 11. $A_8 \equiv$ *(set of global states that are reached during a computation step starting at δ_0 or at δ_2). $A_8 \triangleleft A_7$.*

Starting from δ_0 or δ_2, in one *cround*, all processors get the token exactly once, and at the end of the *cround*, the current state becomes δ_0 or δ_2. Thus, Protocol $\mathcal{TP}$ provides a strictly fair token circulating in the network after the system is stabilized.

Theorem 12. $A_8 \vdash L_{TP}$.

5 Conclusion

We proposed a depth-first (strictly fair) token circulation protocol on rooted networks. The previous solutions for token circulation, except [17], on general network topology have a space complexity of $O(\log n)$, where n is the number of processors, because each processor stores its distance to the legal root. In Algorithm $\mathcal{TP}$, the distance variable is not used. The cycles are detected by processors who are not in the cycles. The size of variable D (child) of i is $O(\log \Delta_i)$ where Δ_i is the degree of i. The variables C (color) and S (status) are of constant size—4 bits total. The local variable NP (number of parents) takes $O(\log \Delta_i)$ space. The other local variable P (parents list) requires one bit per communication link. Thus, the space complexity of Algorithm $\mathcal{TP}$ is $O(1)$ per communication link.

References

1. Y. Afek and A. Bremler, "Self-Stabilizing Unidirectional Network Algorithms by Power-Supply," *Sixth ACM-SIAM Symposium on Discrete Algorithms (SODA)*, San Francisco, California, 1997.
2. Y. Afek, S. Kutten and M. Yung, "Memory-Efficient Self-Stabilizing Protocols for General Networks," *Proc. 4th Int. Workshop on Distributed Algorithm*, LNCS 486, Springer-Verlag, pages 15-28, 1990.
3. B. Awerbuch and R Ostrovsky, "Memory-efficient and self-stabilizing network reset," *Symposium on Principles of Distributed Computing*, Los Angeles, California, pages 254-263, 1994.
4. J. Burns, M. Gouda, and R. Miller, "On Relaxing Interleaving Assumptions," *Proceedings of the MCC Workshop on Self-Stabilization*, Austin, Texas, November 1989.
5. G. Brown, M. Gouda, and M. Wu, "Token Systems that Self-Stabilize," *IEEE Transactions on Computers*, Vol. 38, No. 6, pages 845-852, June 1989.
6. Burns J. and Pachl J. "Uniform Self-Stabilizing Rings," *ACM Transactions on Programming Language and Systems*, Vol. 11, No. 2, pages 330-344, 1989.
7. E. W. Dijkstra, "Self-Stabilizing Systems in Spite of Distributed Control," *Communications of the ACM 17*, pages 643-644, 1974.
8. E. W. Dijkstra, "Self-Stabilization in Spite of Distributed Control," in *Selected writings on computing: a personal perspective*, Springer-Verlag, Berlin, pages 41-46, 1982.

9. S. Dolev, A. Israeli, and S. Moran, "Self-Stabilization of Dynamic Systems Assuming only Read/Write Atomicity," *Proceedings of the 9th Annual ACM Symposium on Principles of Distributed Computing*, Quebec City, Canada, 1990, pages 103-117; also *Distributed Computing* Vol. 7, pages 3-16, 1993.

10. M. Flatebo and A. K. Datta, "Two-State Self-Stabilizing Algorithms for Token Rings," *IEEE Transactions on Software Engineering*, pages 500-504, June 1994.

11. M. Flatebo, A. K. Datta, and A. A. Schoone, "Self-Stabilizing Multi-Token Rings," *Distributed Computing*, Vol. 8, pages 133-142, 1995.

12. S. Ghosh, "An Alternate Solution to a Problem on Self-Stabilization," *ACM Transactions on Programming Languages and Systems*, Vol. 15, No. 4, pages 735-742, September 1993.

13. M.G. Gouda and N. Multari, "Stabilizing Communication Protocols," *IEEE Transactions on Computing*, Vol. 40, No. 4, pages 448-458, 1991.

14. S. Huang and N. Chen, "Self-Stabilizing Depth-First Token Circulation on Networks," *Distributed Computing*, Vol. 7, pages 61-66, 1993.

15. A. Israeli and M. Jalfon, "Token Management Schemes and random walks yiels self stabilizing mutual exclusion," *Symposium on Principles of Distributed Computing*, pages 119-131, 1990,

16. G. Itkis and L. Levin, "Fast and lean self-stabilizing asynchronous protocols," *35th Symposium on Foundations of Computer Science*, Santa Fe, New Mexico, pages 226-239, 1994.

17. C. Johnen and J. Beauquier, "Space-Efficient Distributed Self-Stabilizing Depth-First Token Circulation," *Proceedings of the 2nd Workshop on Self-Stabilizing Systems*, Las Vegas, Nevada, pages 4.1-4.15, 1995.

18. C. Johnen, "Memory Efficient, Self-Stabilizing algorithm to construct BFS spanning trees," *Proceeding 16th Principles of Distributed Computing*, August 1997.

19. H.S.M. Kruijer, "Self-stabilizing (in spite of distributed control) in tree-structured systems," *Information Processing Letters*, vol 29, pages 91-95, 1979,

20. M. Schneider, "Self-Stabilization," *ACM Computing Surveys*, Vol. 25, No. 1, pages 45-67, March 1993.

21. M. Tchuente, "Sur l'auto-stabilisation dans un reseau d'ordinateurs," *RAIRO Informatique Theorique 15*, No. 1, pages 47-66, 1981.

Secure Distributed Storage and Retrieval

Juan A. Garay   Rosario Gennaro   Charanjit Jutla   Tal Rabin

IBM T.J. Watson Research Center, PO Box 704, Yorktown Heights, NY 10598, USA

Abstract. In his well-known Information Dispersal Algorithm paper, Rabin showed a way to distribute information among n processors in such a way that recovery of the information is possible in the presence of up to t inactive processors. An enhanced mechanism to enable construction in the presence of malicious faults, which can intentionally modify their shares of the information, was later presented by Krawczyk. Yet, this method assumed that the malicious faults occur only at reconstruction time.

In this paper we address the more general problem of secure storage and retrieval of information (SSRI), and guarantee that also the process of storing the information is correct even when some of the processors fail. Our protocols achieve this while maintaining the (asymptotical) space optimality of the above methods.

We also consider SSRI with the added requirement of *confidentiality*, by which no party except for the rightful owner of the information is able to learn anything about it. This is achieved through novel applications of cryptographic techniques, such as the distributed generation of receipts, distributed key management via threshold cryptography, and "blinding."

An interesting byproduct of our scheme is the construction of a secret sharing scheme with shorter shares size in the amortized sense. An immediate practical application of our work is a system for the secure deposit of sensitive data.

1 Introduction

The notion of *information dispersal* was introduced by Rabin [26] in his well-known Information Dispersal Algorithm (IDA). The basic approach taken in IDA is to distribute the information being stored, F, among n active processors, in such a way that the retrieval of F is possible even in the presence of up to t failed (inactive) processors. The salient point was to achieve this goal while incurring a small overhead in needed memory. And indeed Rabin's result is space optimal. Retrieval of F is possible from $n-t$ pieces, where each piece is of length $\frac{|F|}{n-t}$.

In addition to its optimal space complexity, the IDA technique has very attractive properties as it permits any party in the system to retrieve the distributed information (by communicating with the piece holders); it does not require a central authority; it is symmetric with respect to all participants; and no secret cryptographic keys are involved. However, this combination of very desirable properties is achieved at the expense of limiting the kind of faults against which the algorithm is robust, namely, by assuming that available pieces are always unmodified.

An enhanced mechanism to reconstruct the information when more general faults occur was presented by Krawczyk [21], who called this problem–and its solution–the *Secure Information Dispersal* problem/algorithm (SIDA). This mechanism is able to tolerate malicious parties that can intentionally modify their shares of the information, and is also space optimal (asymptotically). In a nutshell, SIDA makes use of a cryptographic tool called *distributed fingerprints*, which basically consists of each processor's share being hashed—the *fingerprints*, and then distributing this value among all processors using the coding function of an error correcting code that is able to reconstruct from altered pieces (e.g., Reed-Solomon [1]). This way, the correct processors are able to reconstruct the fingerprints using the code's decoding function, check whether pieces of the file were correctly returned, and finally reconstruct F from the correct pieces using the IDA algorithm.

OUR CONTRIBUTIONS. A shortcoming of these methods is that they assume that the faults only occur at reconstruction time, after the dispersal of the shares has been properly done. In this paper we address the more general problem of secure storage and retrieval of information (SSRI), and also guarantee that the process of storing the information is correct even when some of the processors fail. We consider the scenario in which a user interacts with the storage system by depositing a file and receiving a proof (in the form of a *receipt*) that the deposit was correctly executed. For efficiency reasons we require the distributed nature of the system to be *transparent* to the user, who will interact with a single distinguished processor which we call the *gateway* [1]. This adds the extra technical difficulty of designing the protocol in a way that the gateway is not a single point of failure.

First we concern ourselves only with the **integrity** of the information. We introduce simple protocols that extend the above methods to enable storage in the presence of malicious faults, while maintaining the (asymptotical) space optimality of the above methods. Namely, each share is of size $\frac{|F|}{n-t}$ plus a small quantity which does not depend on the size of the file (but on n and a security parameter). Our storage protocol is designed so that some form of consistency is maintained among the processors without incurring the cost of (potentially expensive) agreement protocols. Another important technical element of the storage protocol is the generation of receipts for the deposit of files through the application of distributed digital signatures. It will be guaranteed that a receipt is issued only when the correct information has been stored.

We also consider SSRI with the added requirement of **confidentiality** of information, i.e., that any collusion of up to t processors (except ones including the rightful owner of the information) should not be able to learn anything about the information. Confidentiality of information is easily achieved by encryption. Yet, this in return poses the problem of *key management*, that is, the safe deposit—in the same storage system—of the cryptographic key used to encrypt the file that is deposited. Under this scheme, how would the user retrieve his file confiden-

---

[1] Note that this distinguished processor does not need to be the same for all users.

tially? Remember that he is communicating with the system through a single gateway, which means that if only known techniques of secret sharing reconstruction were used [28, 7], then the gateway would know all the information available to the user. One novel component of our confidentiality protocol for the solution of the above problem, is its distributed key management. This is achieved via the application of a combination of threshold cryptography (see Section 2.1), and blinding [5] techniques.

The contributions of this paper can be summarized as follows:

- We consider the more general problem of information storage and retrieval, guaranteeing that also the process of storing the information is secure in the presence of (maliciously) failing processors. Our solutions have an (asymptotically) optimal blow-up factor, and tolerate up to $t < n/2$ malicious processors.
- Novel applications of cryptographic techniques: the generation of receipts through distributed digital signatures, distributed key management via threshold cryptography, and blinding (together with threshold cryptography) in the context of decryptions rather than signatures.
- An interesting by-product of our constructions is a secret sharing scheme which achieves shorter size shares (in the amortized sense) than the one of [22].

Due to space limitation, in this extended abstract we only present general correctness arguments and proof sketches.

2 Model, Definitions, and System Considerations

We start by describing an abstraction of the distributed system we consider. We consider a communication network with two classes of entities: the *users*, denoted $U_1, U_2, \cdots, U_m$, and the *servers*, denoted $V_1, \cdots, V_n$. We will sometimes refer to the servers collectively as V. It is among the servers that the distributed storage of the information takes place. We model the communication among the servers by a completely connected graph of authenticated links; for the purpose of this paper we also assume a point-to-point communication link between each of the users and every server. (What we have in mind is Web implementations of our design. In such environments, authenticated communication can be realized through, e.g., SSL [20]. Similarly, point-to-point communication can be realized in various ways, and not necessarily through a direct connection.)

For efficiency's sake, in our protocols the users will interact with a single, not necessarily the same, distinguished server, called the *gateway* (GW). However, our design shall be *uniform*, in the sense that all servers are able to perform the same distribution and recovery functions.

We assume the availability of a global clock, which allows the network computation to evolve as a series of *rounds*. (Again, this is for simplicity of exposition, as the only thing we need is a reliable time-out mechanism, and a means to guarantee the *freshness* of authentication. Possible realizations of the latter are via secure time stamps, or just *nonces*. See, e.g., [6].)

It is assumed that at any time during the life of the system, at most t of the n servers can malfunction, possibly in malicious ways. (This reflects the security concern we concentrate on in this paper, that of *break-ins*.) Further, we assume that the faulty servers can even collude and act in concert in order to disrupt the computation—e.g., in a plain spoiling manner; try to prevent the storage or reconstruction of a file; or learn some information (e.g., a key) which a user wants to keep private. We also assume that $n > 2t$.

The definition and following paragraph are taken from [21]. Reconstruction is possible in information dispersal methods because some redundancy is added to the n pieces into which the original information is partitioned. The amount of redundancy in an information dispersal method is typically measured by the following parameter.

Definition 1. The *blow-up factor* (or just *blow-up*) of an information dispersal scheme is the ratio between the total size of the information being dispersed and the size of the original information. (By total size we mean the sum of sizes of all distributed pieces.)

The blow-up of the methods of [26, 21] is $\frac{n}{n-t}$ ($+o(1)$ in the case of [21]), which is clearly optimal if only $n-t$ pieces are to be used for reconstruction. Our methods also maintain this bound. We remark that reconstruction of information is also possible through error correcting codes. However, the inherent blow-up factor deteriorates to $\frac{n}{n-2t}$ in this case (see [1, 21]).

We now turn to describe the various cryptographic mechanisms that our protocols will make use of.

2.1 Cryptographic Terminology and Tools

The cryptographic primitives used in the protocols are summarized in the Appendix. All the users have two pairs of public/secret keys. (For simplicity, we will assume that the servers also act as the *certification authority* (*CA*), so that no third party needs to be involved in the transactions in order to verify the validity of the public keys.) One key pair $(\mathrm{PK}_{U,s}, \mathrm{SK}_{U,s})$ is used for authentication ("signing") purposes (This is a natural assumption, as all browsers provide this function in some form or another.) The other key pair $(\mathrm{PK}_U, \mathrm{SK}_U)$ is used for public-key encryption/decryption operation. The encryption function is *randomized*: E, invoked upon message m will use, to compute its output, some randomizer, so that each encryption is different from previous ones.

The privacy requirement of SSRI with confidentiality poses the question of key management, i.e., the safe deposit of the keys used to encrypt the file. This requires the user U to maintain SK_U in a safe manner as loss of this key would cause losing all encrypted data. For this reason we store SK_U at the servers in a distributed (shared) fashion. (See Section 4.1.)

Conversely the authentication key $\mathrm{SK}_{U,s}$ can be kept by the user (ideally in her smartcard or alternatively managed by her application, e.g. browser). If this key is compromised then the user can easily revoke it and get a new one.

The following two subsections describe two major tools that we use in our protocols.

Threshold Cryptography. The security of cryptographic protocols relies mainly on the security of the secret keys used in these protocols. Security means that these keys should be kept secret from unauthorized parties, but at the same time should always be available to the legitimate users.

Threshold cryptography is the name given to a body of techniques that help in achieving the above goals. In a nutshell suppose you have a key K which is used in the computation of some cryptographic function F on a message m, denote the result with $F_K(m)$. Examples of this include $F_K(m)$ to be a signature of m under key K, or a decryption of m under that key.

In a threshold cryptography scheme the key K is shared among a set of players $P_1, \ldots, P_n$ using a (t, n) *secret sharing* scheme [28]. Let K_i be the share given to player P_i. [2] Recall that by the definition of (t, n) secret sharing, we know that t shares give no information about K, but $t+1$ shares allow reconstruction of the key K. The main goal of the threshold cryptography technique is to compute F_K without ever reconstructing the key K, but rather using it implicitly when the function F_K needs to be computed.

In the following we will use this terminology. Let the n servers $V_1, \ldots, V_n$ hold shares $sk_1, \ldots, sk_n$ respectively of a secret key SK which is the inverse of a public key PK.

A distributed threshold decryption protocol for $V_1, \ldots, V_n$ is a protocol that takes as input a ciphertext c which has been encrypted with PK (i.e., $c = E_{PK}(m)$ for some message m), and outputs m.

A distributed threshold signature protocol for $V_1, \ldots, V_n$ is a protocol that takes as input a message m and outputs a signature σ for m under SK.

The above protocols must be secure, i.e., they must reveal no information about the secret key SK. A threshold cryptography protocol is called t-*robust* if it also tolerates t malicious faults.

Using threshold cryptography increases the secrecy of the key since now an attacker has to break into $t + 1$ servers in order to find out the value of K. Also, the basic approach increases the availability of the key in the presence of so-called fail-stop faults (crashes); indeed, there is a need only for $t + 1$ servers to be functioning in order to be able to compute the function F_K, meaning that one can tolerate up to $n - t - 1$ crashes.

Threshold cryptography was originated in works by Desmedt [10], Boyd [2], Croft and Harris [CH89], and Desmedt and Frankel [12]. A survey of threshold cryptography techniques can be found in [11]. Protocols for discrete log-based threshold cryptosystems can be found in [2, 8, 12, 18, 24, 16]. Protocols for RSA-based threshold cryptosystems include [9, 13, 15, 17].

---

[2] There are two kinds of protocols for key generation: with or without a *dealer*. In a protocol with a dealer, it is assumed a trusted entity that produces the secret key K (with possibly an associated public-key K^{-1}), and then shares the key among the players. The dealer then "self-destroys." Notice that this assumes some trust in this entity since it knows the key in its entirety for a period of time. In a protocol without a dealer, the players themselves run a distributed protocol with some random inputs. This results in player P_i holding a share K_i of a secret key K.

Blinding. The cryptographic technique called "blinding" [5] can be explained as follows. Suppose that a server holds a secret key SK that allows him to compute a cryptographic function F_{SK} (once again, think of F as a signature or a decryption algorithm). Assume also that the matching public key PK is known, which allows the computation of the inverse function $F_{PK} = F_{SK}^{-1}$.

Consider the following problem. A user wants to obtain the result of $F_{SK}(m)$ but without telling the server the value m on which he wants the function to be computed. If the functions F_{PK} and F_{SK} are homomorphic, i.e., $F(ab) = F(a)F(b)$, then the problem has a solution.

The user generates a random string r, computes the value $s = F_{PK}(r)$ using the public key PK and presents the server with the value ms which is random and thus gives no information about m. The server returns the value $F_{SK}(ms)$ which, by the homomorphic properties of F_{SK}, is equal to $F_{SK}(m)F_{SK}(s) = F_{SK}(m)F_{SK}(F_{PK}(r)) = F_{SK}(m) \cdot r$. Thus, if the user divides the returned result by r he obtains the desired output.

A novelty of our scheme is the way we use blinding. Traditionally this technique was introduced to obtain signatures on messages that the server would not know [5]. This was in turn used to produce untraceable electronic cash. We use blinding in the context of decryptions rather than signatures in order to enhance the security of our distributed key management. The use of blinding will protect the privacy of the user's information against all servers (in particular the "gateway" GW—see Section 3), hence eliminating any single point of privacy failure from the system.

3 Integrity Only

We now present (a high-level description of) our protocols for integrity only. The protocols extend the methods of [26, 21] for integrity to achieve SSRI while maintaining (asymptotically) the space optimality. Namely, each share of the file F deposited at each server is of size $\frac{|F|}{n-t}$ plus a small quantity which does not depend on the size of the file. We distinguish the following three transactions in SSRI for integrity:

Deposit: User U contacts the gateway GW, deposits file F, and gets a receipt.
Dispersal: The actual information dispersal takes place among the servers V_j.
Retrieval: The user contacts GW to get F back.

Deposit. We require that the two following conditions be satisfied regarding Deposit:

- **Deposit Validity:** If a user U receives a receipt for file F, then all the correct servers have a copy of the file.
- **Deposit Consistency:** If a correct server stores F (actually, its share), then all correct servers do.

Figure 1 shows a skeleton of the (fault-free) flow of the protocol for Deposit.

For the purpose of this abstract, we leave aside all kinds of optimization issues, such as reducing the number of "echo" messages, reducing their size (e.g.,

- **Fields:**

F	User's file to be deposited at the servers.

- **Protocol Flows:**

$$\text{DReq} \quad : \quad U \xrightarrow{\quad F, S_{U,s}(F) \quad} GW$$

$$\text{DExec1} : \quad GW \xrightarrow{\quad F, S_{U,s}(F) \quad} V_j, \ \forall j$$

$$\text{DExec2} : V_j, \ \forall j \xrightarrow{\quad F, S_{U,s}(F) \quad} V_j, \ \forall j$$

$$\text{DExec3} : \quad GW \xleftarrow{\quad \sigma_{V_j}(U, F) \quad} V_j \text{ from DExec1}$$

$$\text{Receipt} : \quad U \xleftarrow{\quad S_{V_1,\cdots,V_n}(U, F) \quad} GW$$

Fig. 1. Sketch of Deposit Protocol.

only re-transmit the file when necessary, send its hash instead), arranging fields so that cryptographic operations do not have to be computed twice, the use of "nonces," or transaction id's in order to prevent so-called "re-play" attacks, etc.

For the issuance of the receipt, the servers implement a $(t + 1)$-threshold signature (cf. Section 2.1), meaning that at least $t + 1$ servers have to participate in the signing, and that the faulty servers by themselves cannot generate a correct signature.

We now describe the protocol in more detail. In Deposit Request, the user contacts GW and submits the file she wants to deposit, together with her signature on the file under her private authentication key. The user keeps a hash of the file $\mathcal{H}(F)$ for future control. In Execution, the GW forwards the request from the previous flow to the remaining servers. Every server receiving a (valid) message from GW "echoes" this message request to every other server. Servers receiving at least one valid message store F as a valid request from user U. Servers receiving the DExec1 message from GW use their share of the secret key to generate a partial signature on F and U, and send this message to GW. Servers not receiving a DExec1 message from GW do not participate. In Receipt, the GW computes the distributed digital signature on F and U, and sends it to the user. Should the user not receive a receipt from GW, she tries again a different server (as, by assumption, only a fraction of the servers can malfunction, and the design of the servers is uniform, it is guaranteed that the user will eventually contact a correct server).

We now provide some justification for the correctness of the Deposit protocol.

Lemma 2. *Protocol* Deposit *is correct, that is, it satisfies both* Deposit Validity *and* Consistency *conditions.*

Proof Sketch. The user's signature on the file under her secret signing key guarantees the authenticity of a user request. The protocol's liveness is immediate: if GW is correct, then all the correct servers get its message, reply with a partial signature under their share of the private key, and a correct receipt is generated by GW and sent to the user.

Otherwise, GW may exhibit different kinds of faulty behavior. One possibility is that GW does not forward any messages to the other servers. This is coped with by having the user try other servers (details not shown). If GW does not forward the user request to any of the correct servers, then the faulty servers (GW plus $t - 1$ other servers) are not able to generate a valid receipt. On the other hand, if GW forwards the user request to at least one correct server, then this server will echo the request to all servers (DExec2), who will verify the user's signature and accept the request as a valid one (Consistency). This server will also send its partial signature to the GW. If the GW generates a valid receipt then we have Validity; otherwise, the user will try again (a different GW). □

We remark that there is a "denial of service" attack, in which the correct servers are forced to save a file(s) multiple times without a receipt being generated. This situation, however, is easily detectable. We defer the detailed steps to cope with this problem to the full version of the paper.

Dispersal. The sketch for the second transaction, Dispersal, is shown in Figure 2.

- **Fields:**

F	User file to be dispersed among servers $V_i, 1 \leq i \leq n$.
F_i	Portion of the file dispersed at server V_i.
$\mathcal{H}(F_i)$	Hash of F_i.

- **Protocol Steps:**

  Each server V_i, $1 \leq i \leq n$, does:

  $\forall j,\ 1 \leq j \leq n$, compute $F_j = F \cdot T_j$ (IDA);
  $\forall j,\ 1 \leq j \leq n$, compute $\mathcal{H}(F_j)$;
  save F_i and $\mathcal{H}(F_j)$, $1 \leq j \leq n$.

Fig. 2. Dispersal Protocol.

We assume that the starting point for Dispersal is a consistency situation, outcome of Deposit. Namely, every correct server has a copy of the user's file F. There is no communication involved during this transaction. Instead, every correct server computes everybody's share of F using IDA and the corresponding hashes of the pieces, and saves its own share of the file and *all* the hashes.

The storage required by this method is as follows. Each server is saving its portion of the file $|F_i|$, plus all the hashes $\mathcal{H}(F_j)$, $1 \le j \le n$. Thus, the space required at each server is $|F_j| + n\,|\mathcal{H}(F_j)|$. We note that $|\mathcal{H}(F_j)|$ is independent of the size of F, and small (e.g., 160 bits), becoming less significant as the size of the file increases. In contrast, [21] suggests to share the hashes of the pieces themselves using Reed-Solomon codes. The space required by that method is $|F_i| + \frac{n}{n-2t}\,|\mathcal{H}(F_j)|$. Thus, our approach is slightly less storage-efficient, but with the advantage of avoiding the complexity of the coding plus the communication. (Also note that for values of realistic implementations—e.g., $n = 5$ and $t = 2$— the storage requirements would be identical.)

Retrieval. In this transaction, the user contacts GW to get the file she deposited back.

- **Retrieval Correctness:** Valid requests for retrieval will go through, i.e., the legitimate user will be able to receive the file. Moreover, it is impossible for a party other than the rightful owner of the file to retrieve it.

After the file has been delivered back to the user, the servers might discard the file, or move their shares of the file to off-line storage. Since GW might be faulty, we additionally require that the following two conditions be satisfied:

- **Off-line Storage Validity:** If the GW is correct, then all the correct servers move their shares of the file to off-line storage.
- **Off-line Storage Consistency:** If a correct server V_i moves its share F_i to off-line storage, then all the correct servers do.

The protocol for the Retrieval transaction is shown in Figure 3.

In Retrieval Request, the user contacts the GW to get the file back. She sends information identifying the deposit that is signed under her authentication key, which convinces the servers of the authenticity of the request.[3] In Execution, GW forwards the user's request to all servers. Every server V_j receiving the request sends to GW its share F_j of the file, together with the hashes of all the shares $\mathcal{H}(F_i), 1 \le i \le n$. GW establishes what hashes are valid by computing majority, and discards those shares of the file whose hash does not evaluate to the computed one. Finally, the GW reconstructs the file using the remaining shares using IDA. In Delivery GW sends the file to the user. Upon receiving the file F, the user computes $\mathcal{H}(F)$ and verifies that it matches the hash that she stored during DReq in Figure 1. If so, she sends a conformity message to

---

[3] Again, more is needed than shown—e.g., a transaction id—in order to prevent so-called "re-play" attacks, but we ignore this problem for the purpose of this abstract.

- **Fields:**

F_j	Portion of the file stored in server V_j.
$\mathcal{H}(F_j)$	Hash of F_j.
H	Hashes of all F_i's stored at each server, i.e., $\mathcal{H}(F_i), 1 \leq i \leq n$.

- **Protocol Flows:**

$$\text{RReq} \quad : \quad U \xrightarrow{\mathcal{H}(F), S_{U,s}(F)} \text{GW}$$

$$\text{RExec1} : \quad \text{GW} \xrightarrow{\mathcal{H}(F), S_{U,s}(F)} V_j, \forall j$$

$$\text{RExec2} : \quad \text{GW} \xleftarrow{F_j, H} V_j, \forall j$$

GW computes:

$\forall j, \ \mathcal{H}(F_j) = $ majority of received $\mathcal{H}(F_j)$;

G : set of good indices; $G = \emptyset$;

$\forall j,$ if F_j evaluates to $\mathcal{H}(F_j)$ then $G = G \cup \{j\}$;

$F = \sum_{i \in G} F_i \cdot T_i^{-1}$ (reconstruct with IDA)

$$\text{Delivery} : \quad U \xleftarrow{F} \text{GW}$$

$$\text{RAck1} \quad : \quad U \xrightarrow{\text{'OK'}, S_{U,s}(\text{'OK'}, F)} \text{GW}$$

$$\text{RAck2} \quad : \quad \text{GW} \xrightarrow{\text{'OK'}, S_{U,s}(\text{'OK'}, F)} V_j, \forall j$$

$$\text{RAck3} \quad : V_j \text{ from RAck2} \xrightarrow{\text{'OK'}, S_{U,s}(\text{'OK'}, F)} V_j, \forall j$$

Fig. 3. Retrieval Protocol.

the GW, who forwards the 'OK' message to all servers. Servers receiving the message from GW echo it to all servers.

Lemma 3. *The protocol of Figure 3 is a correct retrieval protocol for* SSRI.

Proof Sketch. As before, if GW is faulty several scenarios might occur. If the user does not hear from the GW it contacts other servers. If GW does not forward the request to any of the correct servers, then it will not be able to reconstruct the file: at least a majority of (good) shares are needed. The user sends an acknowledgment upon receiving the file. If GW forwards the message to at least one correct server, then the echo (RAck3) guarantees that every correct server will move its share to off-line storage (Off-line Storage Consistency). □

Lemmas 2 and 3, together with the arguments of the Dispersal subsection allow us to corroborate our claims of an integrity SSRI system with an asymptotically optimal blow-up. We now turn to the added requirement of confidentiality of the information.

4 Integrity plus Confidentiality

In this function, the user is also interested in keeping the contents of the file private. The requirements for the confidentiality function consist of the Validity and Consistency conditions of the integrity-only solution of Section 3, plus a **Privacy** one.

- **Privacy:** It is not possible for *any* coalition of up to t servers (even those including GW), to learn anything about the contents of the file.

The privacy requirement poses the question of key management, that is, the safe deposit of the keys used to encrypt the file. The simplest solution requires each user U to have a public key for encryption, say PK_U, and the corresponding private key SK_U. This requires the user U to maintain SK_U in a safe manner, just as he is maintaining the authentication private key $SK_{U,s}$. To deposit a file F with confidentiality, the user would generate a key (say a DES key) FK, encrypt the file F with FK, encrypt the key FK with the public key PK_U, and deposit both the encrypted file and the encrypted key $E_U(FK)$. The retrieval procedure is just the reverse.

However, it may be impractical or insecure to require that the user maintain the key SK_U. In the case of a smartcard implementation, the smartcard which maintains such keys securely may be limited in memory. In a software-only solution, it would be ill-advised to keep SK_U at the user's, as if this key is compromised, then the secrecy of all the data will be lost. On the other hand, just maintaining the authentication key presents less of a problem, as authenticity can be regained through a combination of on-line and out-of-band steps. Also, the user application (e.g., a browser) may only provide an authentication key.

In the following we show how SK_U can be kept shared among the servers. This improves the security of SK_U and it also provides a key recovery function for emergency situations. The file DES key FK will be retrieved by the user (or transferred to another user) without even the gateway server GW getting any knowledge about FK. To this end we use "blinding" in a novel way.

4.1 Confidentiality via Distributed Key Management and Blinding

In our design we require that the user's private key SK_U be kept shared among the servers, as described in section 2.1.

We will be adding confidentiality on top of the integrity-only solution of Section 3, so we now assume that in the Deposit protocol of Section 3, the file F is really the encrypted file $e_{FK}(F)$, along with the encrypted key $E_U(FK)$. (In the Dispersal protocol, however, it might be more time efficient to keep the encrypted key as it is at each server V_i.) Thus, one consequence of the above is that at deposit time GW does not gain any information about F or FK.

At retrieval time, the GW requests each server to send it not only the portions of the encrypted file (and hashes), but also the partial decryptions of $E_U(FK)$ using a threshold decryption protocol (see Section 2.1). However, this would allow the gateway to reconstruct the complete decryption of $E_U(FK)$, i.e., the file key FK. In our protocol we use a "blinding" technique (see Section 2.1) in order to prevent this. Namely, only the authorized user will be able to reconstruct FK.

The protocol for Retrieval with Confidentiality is shown in Figure 4.

- **Fields:**

r	Blinding factor: random number chosen by user U
b	$E_U(r)$.
F_i	Portion of the file dispersed at server V_i.
H	Hashes of all F_i's stored at each server, i.e., $\mathcal{H}(F_i), 1 \le i \le n$.
d_i	Server V_i's share of the decryption exponent, i.e., SK_U.
P_i	Partial decryption from V_i of $E_U(FK \cdot r)$.
P	$P = (FK \cdot r)$.

- **Protocol Flows:**

$$
\begin{array}{llll}
\text{CReq} & : & U \xrightarrow{\mathcal{H}(F), b, S_{U,s}(b, F)} GW \\
\text{CExec1} & : & GW \xrightarrow{\mathcal{H}(F), b, S_{U,s}(b, F)} V_i, \forall i \\
\text{CExec2} & : & GW \xleftarrow{F_i, H, P_i} V_i \\
\text{Delivery} & : & U \xleftarrow{e_{PK}(F), P} GW \\
\text{CAck} & : & \text{(As in Figure 3.)}
\end{array}
$$

Fig. 4. Retrieval Protocol with Confidentiality.

OUTLINE. The user U generates a retrieval request by generating a random integer r. It then saves r securely, though temporarily. The number r is intended to act as a *blinding* factor. She then computes $b = E_U(r)$ (if we are using RSA then $b = r^3 \bmod N$.) She then signs b and the name of the file she is requesting under her signing key, and sends to the GW. The GW forwards this request to each of the servers V_i. The servers check that the user signing this request has permission to access this file. If so, server V_i generates P_i a partial decryption of $E_U(FK) \cdot b = E_U(FK \cdot r)$ (assuming some homomorphic property of E, as in the case of RSA). If we are using a threshold RSA cryptosystem then simply $P_i = (\mathbf{E}_U(\text{FK}) \cdot b)^{d_i} \bmod N$, where d_i is the share of SK_U held by server V_i. Each server V_i then sends F_i, the hashes $\mathcal{H}(F_j), 1 \leq j \leq n$, and P_i to the GW. As in protocol Retrieval before, the GW computes $e_{\text{FK}}(F)$ using the hashes and the F_i's received (not shown). It also computes the value $P = \text{FK} \cdot r$ from the partial decryptions P_i. The GW now sends the encrypted file and the blinded key $P = (\text{FK} \cdot r)$ to user U. The user obtains the file key FK by factoring out r, and acknowledges receipt of the file.

Lemma 4. *Protocol* Retrieval *in Figure 4 is correct, i.e., it satisfies the* Retrieval Correctness *and* Privacy *conditions.*

Proof Sketch. Retrieval Correctness is an immediate consequence of the integrity-only protocol of Section 3. The Privacy condition can be argued as follows. Note that at no time the full key SK_U is reconstructed. Also, we assume that the threshold decryption protocol used by the servers is secure, so it reveals no information other than the plaintext being decrypted, in this case $P = \text{FK} \cdot r$, to coalitions of size smaller than t. GW is the only party who gets to see $P = \text{FK} \cdot r$, but this is a randomly distributed value which gives no information about FK. The same measures that are used in the integrity-only solution against possible denial of service caused by a faulty GW are applied in this case too. □

5 Applications: Secret Sharing made Shorter

An application of our result which is interesting in its own is an improvement on the size of the shares for computationally-secure secret sharing protocols [22]. Recall that in a (threshold) secret sharing protocol a dealer shares a secret s among n servers so that t servers cannot reconstruct it, but $t + 1$ can.

It is a well known fact that for an information theoretically secure secret sharing protocol (i.e., one in which t shares give no information about the secret even when infinite computing time is given), the size of the shares must be at least the size of the secret. In [22] Krawczyk shows that if one relaxes the notion to one of "computationally secure," then it is possible to obtain shares of size $\frac{|s|}{t+1} + \ell$ where ℓ depends only on a security parameter. His idea goes as follows:

- Choose a key K for a symmetric encryption scheme e of length ℓ.
- Encrypt the secret to be shared; let $\sigma = \mathbf{e}_K(s)$.
- Use IDA [26] to "share" σ among the servers so that $t+1$ shares are enough to reconstruct σ; let σ_i be the share given to the ith server.
- Share K with an information theoretically secure scheme as in [28]; let K_i be the share given to the ith server.

By the IDA bound we know that $|\sigma_i| = \frac{|\sigma|}{t+1}$. Clearly $|\sigma| = |s|$ and $|K_i| = \ell$, hence the stated bound.

Our SSRI protocol with confidentiality can be thought as a computationally secure secret sharing scheme. In it we have the servers sharing a secret key SK_V for an asymmetric encryption function $\mathbf{E}$. Let sk_{V_i} be the share of SK_V held by the ith server. The user who deposits a file can be thought of as a dealer sharing a secret s according to the following steps:

- Choose a key K of length ℓ for a symmetric encryption scheme e.
- Encrypt the secret s; let $\sigma = e_K(s)$. Encrypt the key with the public key PK_V of the servers; let $\tau = E_V(K)$.
- Use IDA [26] to "share" σ and τ among the servers so that $t+1$ shares are enough to reconstruct σ; let σ_i and τ_i be the shares given to the ith server.

Let m be the length of the keys used by E, i.e., $m = |SK_V|$. Typically we have $m > \ell$. We can assume that $|\tau| = m$, thus each server keeps only a share of size $\frac{|s|+m}{t+1}$ which is asymptotically shorter than in [22]. One also has to take into account the m bits used to represent sk_{V_i}. But notice that sk_{V_i} can be used for several sharings (as it is the case in our SSRI scenario). So we do far better than in [22]—in the amortized sense.

Acknowledgements The authors are thankful to Hugo Krawczyk for his many useful comments.

References

1. Blahut R., *Theory and Practice of Error Control Codes*, Addison-Wesley, 1984.
2. C. Boyd. Digital Multisignatures. In H. Baker and F. Piper, editors, *Cryptography and Coding*, pages 241–246. Claredon Press, 1986.
3. Bellare M., Canetti R. and Krawczyk H., "Keying Hash Functions for Message Authentication," *Proc. Advances in Cryptology – CRYPTO '96*, LNCS Vol. 1109, Springer-Verlag, pp. 1–15, 1996.
4. Berlekamp E. and Welch L., "Error Correction of Algebraic Block Codes," US Patent 4,633,470.
5. D. Chaum, "Blind signatures for untraceable payments," *Proc. CRYPTO 82*, pp. 199-203, 1983.
6. P. Chen, J. Garay, A. Herzberg, and H. Krawczyk. "Design and Implementation of Modular Key Management Protocol and IP Secure Tunnel," *Proc. USENIX Security '95*, Salt Lake City, Utah, June 1995.
7. Chor, B., Goldwasser, S., Micali, S., and Awerbuch, B., "Verifiable Secret Sharing and Achieving Simultaneity in the Presence of Faults," *Proc. 26th Annual IEEE Symposium on the Foundations of Computer Science*, pp. 383-395, 1985.
8. M. Cerecedo, T. Matsumoto, and H. Imai. Efficient and Secure Multiparty Generation of Digital Signatures Based on Discrete Logarithms. *IEICE Trans. Fundamentals*, E76-A(4):532-545, April 1993. US Patent 4,633,470.
[CH89] R. A. Croft and S. P. Harris. Public-key cryptography and re-usable shared secrets. In H. Baker and F. Piper, editors, *Cryptography and Coding*, pages 189–201. Claredon Press, 1989.
9. A. De Santis, Y. Desmedt, Y. Frankel, and M. Yung. How to share a function securely. In *Proc. 26th ACM Symp. on Theory of Computing*, pages 522–533, Santa Fe, 1994. IEEE.
10. Y. Desmedt. Society and group oriented cryptography: A new concept. In Carl Pomerance, editor, *Proc. CRYPTO 87*, pages 120–127. Springer-Verlag, 1988. Lecture Notes in Computer Science No. 293.
11. Y.G. Desmedt. Threshold cryptography. *European Transactions on Telecommunications*, 5(4):449–457, July 1994.
12. Y. Desmedt and Y. Frankel. Threshold cryptosystems. In G. Brassard, editor, *Proc. CRYPTO 89*, pages 307–315. Springer-Verlag, 1990. Lecture Notes in Computer Science No. 435.
13. Y. Desmedt and Y. Frankel. Shared generation of authenticators and signatures. In J. Feigenbaum, editor, *Proc. CRYPTO 91*, pages 457–469. Springer, 1992. Lecture Notes in Computer Science No. 576.
14. "Entrust–Enterprise-Wide Encryption and Digital Signatures," System Overview and Installation Guide.
15. Y. Frankel, P. Gemmell, and M. Yung. Witness-based Cryptographic Program Checking and Robust Function Sharing. In *Proceedings of the ACM Symposium on Theory of Computing*, 1996.
16. R. Gennaro, S. Jarecki, H. Krawczyk, and T. Rabin. Robust Threshold DSS Signatures. In *Advances in Cryptology-EUROCRYPT'96*, Lecture Notes in Computer Science vol.1070, Springer-Verlag, 1996.

17. R. Gennaro, S. Jarecki, H. Krawczyk, and T. Rabin. Robust and Efficient Sharing of RSA Functions. In *Advances in Cryptology—CRYPTO'96*, Lecture Notes in Computer Science vol.1109, pp.157–172, Springer-Verlag, 1996.

18. L. Harn. Group oriented (t, n) digital signature scheme. *IEE Proc.-Comput.Digit.Tech*, 141(5), Sept 1994.

19. T. Hardjono and J. Seberry, "Strongboxes for Electronic Commerece," *Proc. 2nd USENIX WOrkshop on Electronic Commerece*, pp. 135-145, Oakland, CA, November 1996.

20. Hickman, K. E. B. Secure Socket Library. *Netscape Communications Corp.*, Feb. 9th, 1995. <http://www.mcom.com/info/SSL.html>.

21. Krawczyk H., "Distributed Fingerprints and Secure Information Dispersal," *Proc. 20th Annual ACM Symp. on Principles of Distributed Computing*, pp. 207-218, Ithaca, NY, 1993.

22. Krawczyk H., "Secret sharing made short," *Advances in Cryptology—Crypto '93*, Lecture Notes in Computer Science, pp.136–146, Springer-Verlag, 1993.

23. L. LAMPORT, R.E. SHOSTAK AND M. PEASE, *The Byzantine generals problem*, ACM Trans. Prog. Lang. and Systems, 4:3 (1982), pp. 382–401.

24. C. Park, and K. Kurosawa. New ElGamal Type Threshold Digital Signature Scheme. *IEICE Trans. Fundamentals*, E79-A(1):86–93, January 1996.

25. Preparata F.P., "Holographic Dispersal and Recovery of Information", *IEEE Trans. on Information Theory*, IT-35, No. 5, pp. 1123-1124, 1989,

26. Rabin M., "Efficient Dispersal of Information for Security, Load Balancing, and Fault Tolerance," *Journal of the ACM*, Vol. 36(2), pp. 335-348, 1989.

27. Rivest R., Shamir, A. and L. Adleman, "A Method for Obtaining Digital Signatures and Public-Key Cryptosystems," *Communications of the ACM*, Vol. 21, pp. 120-126, 1978.

28. Shamir, A., "How to Share a Secret," *Communications of the ACM*, Vol. 22, pp. 612-613, 1979.

Cryptographic Primitives

Keys:

PK_U, SK_U Public and secret keys of user/party U.

$CERT_U$ Public key certificate of user U, issued by a certification authority CA. (e.g., the servers themselves). We assume it includes U, PK_U and CA's signature on PK_U.

$PK_{U,s}, SK_{U,s}$ Public and secret "signing" keys of user/party U.

sk_{V_i} Server V_i's share of secret key SK_V.

Cryptographic primitives:

$\mathcal{H}(\cdot)$ A strong collision-resistant one-way hash function. Think of $\mathcal{H}(\cdot)$ as returning "random" values.

E_U Public key encryption using PK_U.

$S_U(\cdot)$ Digital signature with respect to SK_U. Note the signature of message m does NOT include m. We assume the signature function hashes the message before signing.

$S_{V_1,\cdots,V_n}(\cdot)$ Distributed digital signature with respect to keys $sk_{V_1}, \cdots, sk_{V_n}$.

$\sigma_{V_i}(\cdot)$ Partial digital signature with respect to sk_{V_i}

e_K Symmetric key-based encryption algorithm, taking key K and a plaintext, and producing the ciphertext.

mac_K Symmetric key-based signature, or message authentication code (MAC), taking key K and a plaintext, and returning a short tag. (Examples include block ciphers, e.g., DES in CBC-MAC mode, or key-ed cryptographic hash functions, e.g., key-ed MD5, HMAC [3].)

f_K A pseudorandom function with index K.[4] (The above examples of MAC functions are also believed to be pseudorandom functions.)

$RS(\cdot)$ Reed-Solomon code.

---

[4] Roughly speaking, pseudorandom functions are characterized by the pseudorandomness of their output, namely, each bit in the output of the function is unpredictable if K is unknown.

Optimal Wait-Free Clock Synchronization Protocol on a Shared-Memory Multi-processor System

Michiko Inoue, Sen Moriya, Toshimitsu Masuzawa* and Hideo Fujiwara
{kounoe, sen-m, masuzawa, fujiwara}@is.aist-nara.ac.jp

Graduate School of Information Science,
Nara Institute of Science and Technology (NAIST)
Ikoma, Nara 630-01, JAPAN

Abstract. We consider wait-free clock synchronization protocols on an in-phase shared-memory multi-processor system. A wait-free clock synchronization protocol guarantees that, for a fixed k, local clocks of processors which have been working consecutively for at least k pulses are synchronized. Such k is called synchronization time. The best previous result with regard to the synchronization time is $O(n^2)$, where n is the number of processors. In this paper, we present a wait-free synchronization protocol with synchronization time $O(n)$, and also show that this synchronization time is asymptotically optimal.

Keywords. clock-synchronization, shared-memory multi-processor system, wait-freedom, fault-tolerance, napping fault.

1 Introduction

Implementing a common clock that tolerates faults is one of the most important problems on multi-processor systems. One simple way to implement a common clock is to provide a single clock that is connected to all the processors. However, such a centralized clock unit does not seem to be reliable. If a common clock is implemented by synchronizing individual clocks of individual processors, it may be able to tolerate wrong behaviors of individual clocks.

The fault-tolerant clock synchronization problem has been investigated for various system setting and for various fault models. It was first considered on message-passing systems, where the target fault models are *Byzantine* faults[1, 2, 3, 4, 5], *authenticated Byzantine* faults[6], or both *transient* and Byzantine faults[7]. The problem was also considered on the system where processors communicate with neighbors on the communication graph through shared registers. On such a system, *self-stabilizing* clock synchronization protocols[8, 9], which are resilient to transient faults, or self-stabilizing protocols which are also resilient to permanent faults(ex. *crash* faults, or Byzantine faults) are considered[10, 11].

* Research supported in part by the Scientific Research Grant-in-Aid from Ministry of Education, Science and Culture of Japan, and the Telecommunications Advancement Foundation's Research Grant.

Recently, Dolev and Welch [12] presented a highly resilient view of the fault-tolerant clock synchronization problem for a *shared memory multi-processor system*. They considered *napping faults* of processors. A napping fault of a processor is a fault such that a processor stops operation and then resumes (with or) without recognizing that a fault has occured. They introduced a *wait-free clock synchronization protocol*, which does not only tolerate any number of processors' napping faults, but also has the following good features: The non-faulty processors' clocks are unaffected by the failures, and processors that have ceased being faulty can rejoin the system and become synchronized. More precisely, the protocol guarantees that, for some fixed k, once a processor P has been working correctly for at least k pulses, then as long as P continues to work correctly, (1) P does not adjust its clock, and (2) P's clock agrees with the clock of every other processor that has been also working correctly for at least k pulses. Such k is called *synchronization time*.

Dolev and Welch[12] considered an *in-phase system* where all processors share a common clock pulse, and also considered an *out-of-phase* system where each processor has its own clock pulse. For the in-phase system, they presented three protocols, one is for a *global-read/modify/write* atomicity model and two are for a *nonglobal-read/modify/write* atomicity model. Each shared register is a *single-writer multi-reader* register, that is, only one processor, called *owner*, can write to it. In the global-read/modify/write atomicity model, a processor can read all the shared registers in the system in one pulse, while it can read shared registers owned by a single processor in the nonglobal-read/modify/write atomicity model. The presented protocols for the nonglobal-read/modify/write atomicity model were a wait-free clock synchronization protocol with synchronization time $O(n^2)$ and a wait-free and self-stabilizing clock synchronization protocol with synchronization time $O(n^3)$ (n : the number of processors). Papatriantafilou and Tsigas [13] improved the wait-free and self-stabilizing one. They presented a wait-free and self-stabilizing protocol with synchronization time $O(n^2)$.

In this paper, we restrict our attention on the in-phase system, wait-freedom and nonglobal-read/modify/write atomicity. We present a wait-free (and not self-stabilizing) clock synchronization protocol with synchronization time $10n$, and also show that its synchronization time is asymptotically optimal.

The remainder of the paper is organized as follows. In the next section, we define the model and a wait-free clock synchronization protocol. We present a wait-free clock synchronization protocol in Section 3. Section 4 shows a lower bound result. In the conclusions appear in Section 5, we mention that our protocol improve the previous results with regard to not only the synchronization time but also the total running time required for synchronization.

2 Definitions

We consider an *in-phase shared memory multi-processor system* which consists of n processors $P_0, P_1, \cdots P_{n-1}$ and multiple registers shared by all the processors. Processors communicate each other only through the registers. We use single-writer multi-reader registers, for each of which, only one processor, called *owner*, can write to it and all processors can read from it. Each processor is modeled as a state machine. A processor changes its state by taking a *step*. In one step, a processor P in state s (1) reads some registers owned by a single processor indicated in s, and (2)changes its state and writes to its own registers. In the system, all processors share a common clock pulse, and it drives each processor to take a step. We consider the following *napping faults* of processors. A napping fault of a processor is a fault such that it stops operation for an arbitrary time interval and then resumes (with or) without recognizing that a fault has occured. We formalize behavior of such a system.

A *configuration* of a system is a tuple of all processors' states and all registers' values. An *execution* of a system is a sequence $E = c_0, \pi_1, c_1, \cdots$, where each c_t $(t \geq 0)$ is a configuration and each π_t $(t \geq 1)$ is a set of processors. The initial configuration c_0 consists of initial states of all processors and initial values of all registers. An execution E may be infinitely long, and E ends with a configuration if finite. Each π_t represents a set of processors each of which takes a step on receiving the tth pulse. Each processor in π_t takes a step based on c_{t-1}, and the configuration changes to c_t. We call the global time when the tth pulse occurs time t, and call a configuration c_t a configuration at time t. If a processor P is not in π_t, we say that P takes *a nap* at time t. Such P does nothing at time t, therefore its state and the values of its own registers are identical in c_{t-1} and c_t.

A *protocol* specifies a behavior of each processor. Each processor uses some variables in the protocols. The variables whose values are written to the shared registers are called *global variables*, and the other variables are called *local variables*. Let $P.x$ denote a variable x of a processor P. For an execution $E = c_0, \pi_1, c_1, \cdots$, let $P.x(c_t)$ denote a value of $P.x$ in a configuration c_t. If there is no ambiguousness, we write just $P.x(t)$. For a fixed execution $E = c_0, \pi_1, c_1, \cdots$, let $work(P, t)$ denote the length of time duration in which P has been working correctly until t, that is, $work(P, t) = max\{len | P \in \bigcap_{t-(len-1) \leq t' \leq t} \pi_{t'}\}$ (for completeness, we define $work(P, t) = 0$ if $P \notin \pi_t$).

Now we define the problem. Each processor has a global variable *Clock*. A protocol is a *wait-free clock synchronization protocol with synchronization time* k, where k is a positive integer, if every execution of the system specified by the protocol satisfies the following two conditions.

Adjustment: For any $t > 0$ and any processor P_i, if $work(P_i, t) > k$ then $P_i.Clock(t) = P_i.Clock(t-1) + 1$.

Agreement: For any $t > 0$ and any processors P_i and P_j, if $work(P_i, t) \geq k$ and $work(P_j, t) \geq k$ then $P_i.Clock(t) = P_j.Clock(t)$.

3 Protocol

3.1 Outline

We present a wait-free clock synchronization protocol with synchronization time $O(n)$ (main program in Fig.1 and procedures in Fig.2). In the protocol described

```
1     global variable
2         Clock;
3         Count; (initially 0)
4         Work_count; (initially 0)
5         Gen; (initially 1)
6         Invalid_j; (j = 0..n − 1, initially 0)
7         Mode; (initially "adjusting")
8     local variable
9         cur; (initially 0)
10        last_count_j; (j = 0..n − 1, initially 0)
11        last_gen_j; (j = 0..n − 1, initially 0)
12        last_my_count_j; (j = 0..n − 1, initially 0)
13        next, sync, pos, key[0..n − 1], list[0..n − 1];

14    repeat forever do on receipt of a pulse
15        read global variables of P_cur;
16        if (check_nap) then
17            partial_reset; /* by naps */
18        else if Mode = "adjusting" then adjust;
19        else /* adjusted mode */
20            Clock := Clock + 1; next := cur + 1(mod n);
21        last_count_cur := P_cur.Count;
22        last_gen_cur := P_cur.Gen,;
23        last_my_count_cur := Count;
24        cur := next;
25        Count := Count + 1; Work_count := Work_count + 1;
26    end
```

Fig. 1. Protocol (main program for P_i).

here, to distinguish global variables and local variables, we use global variable names starting from capital letters (ex. $Clock$), and local variable names starting from small letters (ex. $next$).

In the protocol, P_i has two modes, an *adjusting* mode, and an *adjusted* mode. In each step, P_i first reads global variables of P_{cur} (line 15), where a variable cur represents a processor id whose global variables P_i reads in the current step. Then P_i checks naps of P_i (line 16, procedure *check_nap*). If P_i detects its nap, it resets some of its variables (line 17, procedure *partial_reset*). Otherwise, if P_i is in the *adjusting* mode, it tries to adjust its clock (line 18, procedure *adjust*). If P_i is in the *adjusted* mode, it increases its clock value by exactly one in a step (line 20). At the end of a step, P_i stores some of values of P_{cur}'s global variables, decides next cur, and updates some of its global variables (lines 21–25). In the following explanation, a *generation* of P_i is a maximal time interval in which P_i executes *partial_reset* only at the end of the interval if executes.

First, we explain how to check naps (a procedure *check_nap*). In *check_nap*, P_i checks naps of P_i itself and P_{cur}. P_i uses its global variables $Count$, Gen, and $Invalid_{cur}$. A variable $Count$ denotes the number of steps from the initial state,

```
27    procedure check_nap;
28       diff := (Count − last_my_count_cur) − (P_cur.Count − last_count_cur);
29       if diff > 0
30         and P_cur.Gen = last_gen_cur then
31            Invalid_cur := P_cur.Gen;
32       if Work_count ≥ n
33         and (diff < 0 or P_cur.Invalid_i ≥ Gen)
34            then return true;
35         return false;
36    end procedure;

37    procedure partial_reset;
38       next := 0; Mode := "adjusting";
39       Gen := Gen + 1;
40       Work_count := −1; /* becomes 0 at line 25 */
41    end procedure;

42    procedure check_adjusted;
43       if list[pos] = i then
44            Mode := "adjusted"; next := 0;
45       else
46            next := list[pos];
47    end procedure;

48    procedure adjust;
49       if 0 ≤ Work_count ≤ 4n − 1 then
50         if 3n ≤ Work_count then
51            if Invalid_cur < P_cur.Gen then
52              key[cur] := (P_cur.Work_count − Work_count, cur);
53            else key[cur] := (−1, cur);
54         next := cur + 1(mod n);
55         if Work_count = 4n − 1 then
56         list := sort ids in the descending order of key;
57         sync := 0; pos := 0; check_adjusted;
58       else if 4n ≤ Work_count:
59         if Invalid_cur = P_cur.Gen or P_cur.Work_count < Work_count then
60              pos := pos + 1; check_adjusted;
61              Clock := Clock + 1;
62         else if P_cur.Mode = "adjusted" then
63            if sync = 1 and Clock ≠ P_cur.Clock then
64                 partial_reset; /* by naps */
65            else
66                 Clock := P_cur.Clock + 1; sync := 1;
67                 pos := pos + 1; check_adjusted;
68         if Work_count = 5n − 1 and Mode = "adjusting"
69            then partial_reset; /* by overtime */
70    end procedure;
```

Fig. 2. Protocol (procedures for P_i).

and *Gen* denotes a generation number of P_i, which increases by one in every generation. If $P_{cur}.Count$ increased more than P_i's since P_i read P_{cur}'s variables last, P_i learns that P_i has taken a nap. If $P_i.Count$ increased more, P_i learns that P_{cur} has taken a nap. In this case, if P_{cur} has not detected its nap, that is, if P_{cur} has not executed *partial_reset* after the last read (line 30), P_i writes the generation number of P_{cur} to $Invalid_{cur}$ so that P_{cur} can notice its nap when P_{cur} reads P_i's variables. If P_i detects its nap directly or indirectly, *check_nap* returns *true* to execute *partial_reset*. However, once P_i takes a nap, P_i may detect its nap in continuous $n - 1$ steps. To avoid redundant executions of *partial_reset*, P_i executes *partial_reset* at most once in continuous $n - 1$ steps. For this purpose, P_i uses a variable *Work_count* which represents the number of steps P_i takes in the current generation. A procedure *check_nap* returns *true* only if *Work_count* is more than or equal to n (line 32). Note that this checking mechanism does not detect naps completely. For example, if P_i and P_{cur} take naps the same times, either processor may not detect the naps.

Next, we explain how to adjust P_i's clock in the *adjusting* mode (a procedure *adjust*). The key idea for improving the synchronization time is that the processor trying to adjust its clock refers to only the processors that have been working correctly longer than it. The processor can adjust its clock without referring the processors that have been working correctly shorter, since it does not refer them but will be referred by them later. In the *adjusting* mode, P_i tries to synchronize its clock with the *adjusted* clocks of all processors with greater *Work_count* than P_i, where the adjusted clock of a processor P_j means the clock after P_j enters the *adjusted* mode. In the protocol, P_i may repeatedly read P_j's clock twice or more until P_j enters the *adjusted* mode. To avoid a deadlock, P_i synchronizes its clock with other processors in the descending order of *Work_counts* (breaking tie by processor *ids*).

A processor P_i in the *adjusting* mode behaves as follows. First, P_i reads global variables of all processors in the cyclic order of processor ids for four cycles, and then reads in the descending order of *Work_counts* which P_i read in the fourth cycle. In the fourth cycle, P_i stores the relative value of *Work_count* of P_j and P_i to *key[j]* for each j ($0 \le j \le n - 1$). However, if P_i has detected P_j's nap in P_j's current generation, P_i stores the value -1 instead. P_i sorts processor ids in the descending order of *key* at the end of the fourth cycle, and stores it to a local variable *list* (line 56). We need the first three cycles to guarantee that P_i can enter the *adjusted* mode within the next n steps succeeding the fourth cycle if P_i works correctly in the current generation (See correctness proof for details). Once *Work_count* becomes $4n$, P_i reads the variables of processors in the order of $P_i.list$. When P_i reads the variables of P_j, P_i synchronizes its clock with P_j only if the following three conditions hold: (a) P_i does not detect P_j's nap(line 59), (b) P_j is in the *adjusted* mode (line 62), and (c) P_j's clock agrees with other processors with which P_i has already synchronized its clock (line 63). If P_j is in the *adjusting* mode (line 62), P_i reads the same variables of P_j in the next step. P_i enters the *adjusted* mode, if P_i synchronized its clock with all the processors that have greater *Work_count*. However, if P_i cannot enter the *adjusted* mode within n steps, P_i executes *partial_reset*, and starts an adjustment of its clock from $Work\_count = 0$ again. This is the case where P_i actually takes a nap but does not detect it. We call a partial reset in this case, a *partial reset by overtime* (line 69), and call the other cases *partial reset by naps* (lines 17 and 64).

3.2 Correctness

Now we show the correctness of the protocol. We show two conditions **Adjustment** and **Agreement** hold for any execution $E = c_0, \pi_1, c_1, \cdots$. We first consider the case where P_i starts an adjustment of its clock at t, and then works correctly for at least $5n$ pulses without executing *partial_reset* by naps. In this case, we show that P_i enters the *adjusted* mode within $5n$ steps from starting the adjustment (Lemmas 1 and 2). Next we consider the general case. Lemmas 4 and 5 show that if two processors in the *adjusted* mode have been working correctly sufficient long, their clocks agree. This is holds even if the processors actually took naps but have not detected the naps. Lemma 6 shows that a processor detects its nap within $5n$ steps if the processor detects the nap. From these lemmas, we show that if processors work correctly sufficient long, they do not execute *partial_reset*, therefore, they enter the *adjusted* mode and their clocks agree. That is, two conditions **Adjustment** and **Agreement** hold.

We define a relation $(a_1, a_2) \prec (b_1, b_2)$ on pairs as $a_1 < b_1$, or $a_1 = b_1$ and $a_2 > b_2$, and define $(a_1, a_2) \preceq (b_1, b_2)$ as $(a_1, a_2) \prec (b_1, b_2)$ or $(a_1, a_2) = (b_1, b_2)$. We also use "$<$" to denote the order $a_1 < b_1$, or $a_1 = b_1$ and $a_2 < b_2$.

Lemma 1. Let P_{j_1}, P_{j_2} and P_{j_3} be processors that are working correctly and do not execute *partial_reset* in an interval $[t + n, t + 4n - 1]$, and let t^1, t^2 and t^3 be times when P_{j_1}, P_{j_2} and P_{j_3} sort their *lists*, respectively. If $(t^1, j_1) \preceq (t^2, j_2)$, $(t^2, j_2) \prec (t^3, j_3)$, $t + 3n \leq t^1$, and $t^3 \leq t + 4n - 1$ hold, and P_{j_2} precedes P_{j_3} in $P_{j_3}.list(t^3)$, then the processors preceding P_{j_1} in $P_{j_1}.list(t^1)$ precede P_{j_2} or succeed P_{j_3} in $P_{j_3}.list(t^3)$.

Proof. Let P_m be any processor that precedes P_{j_1} in $P_{j_1}.list(t^1)$. P_{j_1} reads P_m's variables at $t^1 - n + m + 1$ and sets $P_{j_1}.key[m]$. Let (x, m) be a value of this $P_{j_1}.key[m]$. Since P_m precedes P_{j_1} in $P_{j_1}.list(t^1)$, $(x, m) > (0, j_1)$ holds. On the other hand, P_{j_3} reads P_m's variables at $t^3 - n + m + 1$ and sets $P_{j_3}.key[m]$. Before then, P_{j_3} reads P_m's variables at $t^3 - 2n + m + 1$, and $t^3 - 2n + m + 1 < t^1 - n + m + 1 \leq t^3 - n + m + 1$ holds. In the interval $[t^3 - 2n + m + 1, t^3 - n + m + 1]$, P_{j_3} is working correctly, therefore, if P_m takes a nap in this interval P_{j_3} can detect it at $t^3 - n + m + 1$. Therefore, if the first term of the $P_{j_3}.key[m]$ is positive or zero, it must be $x + t^3 - t^1$. This implies that $P_{j_3}.key[m] = (x + t^3 - t^1, m) > (t^3 - t^1, j_1) > (t^3 - t^2, j_2) = P_{j_3}.key[j_2]$, or $P_{j_3}.key[m] < (0, j_3) = P_{j_3}.key[j_3]$ hold. That is, P_m precedes P_{j_2} or succeed P_{j_3} in $P_{j_3}.list(t^3)$. □

The next lemma shows that a processor P_i which is working correctly for at least $5n$ pulses from starting adjustment without executing *partial_reset* by naps enters the *adjusted* mode. That is, we show P_i enters *adjusted* mode without executing *partial_reset* by overtime.

We show the lemma by the following strategy. Let $\alpha(P_i, g)$ be the number of steps P_i takes after $P_i.Work\_count$ became $4n$ until entering the *adjusted* mode or executing *partial_reset* in the generation g. In the next lemma, we count $\bar{\alpha} = \alpha(P_i, P_i.Gen(t))$ in the case where P_i is working correctly in the interval $[t, t+5n-1]$ without executing *partial_reset* by naps. If $\bar{\alpha}$ is less than n, it implies that P_i does not execute *partial_reset* by overtime in this interval, and P_i is in the *adjusted* mode at $t + 5n - 1$. We count $\bar{\alpha}$ recursively. Let P_j be the last processor that P_i reads its variables continuously twice or more in the interval $[t+4n, t+4n+\bar{\alpha}-1]$, and let $s+1$ be a time when P_i reads P_j's variables in the last time in this interval. Then, $\bar{\alpha}$ is represented as the sum of the lengths of $[t+4n, s]$ and $[s+1, t+4n+\bar{\alpha}-1]$. The length of $[t+4n, s]$ is counted as the number of steps P_j takes after $t + 4n$ until entering the *adjusted* mode or executing *partial_reset*. Since P_i reads variables of distinct processors in $[s + 1, t + 4n + \bar{\alpha} - 1]$, We can relate distinct processors with times in $[s + 1, t + 4n + \bar{\alpha} - 1]$, and can relate processors with times in $[t + 4n, s]$ recursively. If distinct processors are related with times in $[t + 4n, t + 4n + \bar{\alpha} - 1]$ and P_i itself is not related with any time, it implies that $\bar{\alpha}$ is less than n.

Lemma 2. Let t be the time when P_i starts an adjustment of its clock, that is, $P_i.Work\_count(t - 1) = 0$. If $work(P_i, t + 5n - 1) \geq 5n$ and P_i does not execute *partial_reset* by naps in the interval $[t, t + 5n - 1]$ then $P_i.Mode(t + 5n - 1) = $ "*adjusted*" holds.

Proof. We consider $\bar{\alpha} = \alpha(P_i, P_i.Gen(t))$. If P_i executes *partial_reset* by overtime in the generation $P_i.Gen(t)$, it occurs at $t + 5n - 1$, therefore, $\bar{\alpha} = n$ holds. We define a sequence $(dest_{t+4n}, reader_{t+4n}), \cdots, (dest_{t+4n+\bar{\alpha}-1}, reader_{t+4n+\bar{\alpha}-1})$ of pairs of processors, where $dest_s$ is a processor such that $reader_s$ reads its global variables at time s $(t + 4n \leq s \leq t + 4n + \bar{\alpha} - 1)$ (Fig.3). In the sequence defined below, all $dest_s$ are distinct and P_i does not appear as any $dest_s$. This implies that $\bar{\alpha} \leq n - 1$, therefore, P_i enters the *adjusted* mode before $t + 5n - 1$ and does not execute *partial_reset* until $t + 5n - 1$. Therefore, $P_i.Mode(t + 5n - 1) = $ "*adjusted*" holds. We define $reader_s$ from $s = t + 4n + \bar{\alpha} - 1$. For each s, $dest_s$ is defined as $reader_s.cur(s - 1)$.

- First, $reader_{t+4n+\bar{\alpha}-1} = P_i$.
- For any s $(t + 4n \leq s < t + 4n + \bar{\alpha} - 1)$,
  - If $reader_{s+1}$ reads global variables of different processors at s and $s + 1$, that is,
    $reader_{s+1}.cur(s) \neq reader_{s+1}.cur(s-1)$ holds, then $reader_s = reader_{s+1}$.
  - If $reader_{s+1}.cur(s) = reader_{s+1}.cur(s-1)$ holds, then $reader_s = dest_{s+1}$.

For the sequence $dlist = (dest_{t+4n}, dest_{t+4n+1}, \cdots, dest_{t+4n+\bar{\alpha}-1})$, consider the sublists $dlist_1, dlist_2, \cdots, dlist_h$ obtained by partitioning $dlist$ to maximum subsequences with the same reader. To show the lemma, it is sufficient to show that P_i does not appear in any $dlist_x$, all $dest_s$ in each $dlist_x$ $(1 \leq x \leq h)$ are distinct, and any two distinct $dlist_x$ and $dlist_y$ are disjoint. Let $reader\_id(x)$ and $head(x)$ denote an id of the reader processor and the first element of $dlist_x$,

processor

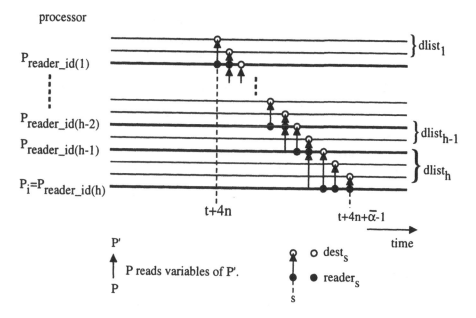

Fig. 3. A sequence $(dest_{t+4n}, reader_{t+4n}), \cdots, (dest_{t+4n+\bar{\alpha}-1}, reader_{t+4n\bar{\alpha}-1})$.

respectively. Let $last\_time(x)$ denote the time such that the last element of $dlist_x$ is $dest_{last\_time(x)}$, and $sort\_time(x)$ denote the time when $P_{reader\_id(x)}$ sorts its list in the same generation as $last\_time(x) - 1$ if exists.

The reader of $dlist_h$ is P_i, $dlist_h$ consists of $head(h)$ and the processors succeed $head(h)$ and precede P_i in $P_i.list$, and $sort\_time(h) = t + 4n - 1$ hold. If $h = 1$, clearly, the lemma holds. If $h \neq 1$, P_i reads $head(h)(= P_{reader\_id(h-1)})$ at $last\_time(h-1)$ and $last\_time(h-1) + 1$. This implies that $P_{reader\_id(h-1)}$ is working correctly in the interval $[t+n, last\_time(h-1)-1]$, $t+3n \leq sort\_time(h-1)$ and $(sort\_time(h-1), reader\_id(h-1)) \prec (sort\_time(h), reader\_id(h))$ hold, and $P_{reader\_id(h-1)}$ is still in the *adjusting* mode at $last\_time(h-1)-1$. Therefore, $dlist_{h-1}$ also consists of $head(h-1)$ and the processors succeed $head(h-1)$ and precede $P_{reader\_id(h-1)}$ in $P_{reader\_id(h-1)}.list$.

In general, if $P_{reader\_id(x+1)}$ $(1 \leq x < h)$ is working correctly in the interval $[t + n, last\_time(x + 1) - 1]$, then $P_{reader\_id(x)}$ is also working correctly in $[t + n, last\_time(x) - 1]$ (P_i guarantees this for $[t + n, sort\_time(x) - n + i + 1]$, $P_{reader\_id(x+1)}$ guarantees this for $[t + 2n, last\_time(x) - 1]$, and $t + 2n \leq sort\_time(x) - n + i + 1$ holds.). We can see that $t + 3n \leq sort\_time(x)$ and $(sort\_time(x), reader\_id(x)) \prec (sort\_time(x + 1), reader\_id(x + 1))$ hold, and $dlist_x$ consists of $head(x)$ and the processors succeed $head(x)$ and precede $P_{reader\_id(x)}$ in $P_{reader\_id(x)}.list$. Therefore, for any x $(1 \leq x < h)$ and any y $(x < y \leq h)$, Lemma 1 holds for $P_{j_1} = P_{reader\_id(x)}$, $P_{j_2} = P_{reader\_id(y-1)}$ and $P_{j_3} = P_{reader\_id(y)}$. Therefore, $dlist_x$ is disjoint with any $dlist_y$ $(x < y \leq h)$.

Since $dlist_h$'s reader is P_i, from Lemma 1, P_i does not appear in any $dlist_x$. Moreover, each $dlist_x$ is a subsequence of $P_{reader\_id(x)}.list$, therefore, all $dest_s$ in each $dlist_x$ are distinct. Therefore, the Lemma holds. □

Now consider the general case. First consider how many steps a processor takes to read all processors' variables. Let $steps(P_i, t, t')$ denote the number of steps P_i takes in the interval $[t, t')$ $(t < t')$ $(steps(P_i, t, t') = 0$ if $t = t')$. For convenience, define $steps(P_i, t, t') = 0$ if $t = t'$ and $steps(P_i, t, t')$ as $-steps(P_i, t', t)$ if $t' < t$. This definition is convenient because $steps(P_i, t_1, t_2) + steps(P_i, t_2, t_3) = steps(P_i, t_1, t_3)$ holds for any t_1, t_2, and t_3.

Fact 3 *For a processor P_i and time t, let t' be time such that the interval $[t', t)$ is the minimal interval in which P_i reads all processors' variables.*

- *If $n \leq P_i.Work\_count(t-1) \leq 4n$ or*
  $5n + \alpha(P_i, P_i.Gen(t-1)) \leq P_i.Work\_count(t-1)$, then $steps(P_i, t', t) \leq n$.
- *If $4n < P_i.Work\_count(t-1) < 5n + \alpha(P_i, P_i.Gen(t-1))$,*
  then $steps(P_i, t', t) \leq 2n$.
- *If $P_i.Work\_count(t-1) < n$, then $steps(P_i, t', t) \leq 3n$.* □

Since the checking mechanism of naps in the protocol is not complete, there may exist the configuration where two processors P_i and P_j have sorted their lists but P_j succeeds P_i in $P_i.list$ and P_i succeeds P_j in $P_j.list$. This is the case where P_i or P_j actually took a nap before sorting, but none of two processors detect it. The next lemma show that such inconsistency are eliminated if both processors work correctly sufficiently long after sorting.

Lemma 4. Let P_i and P_j be different processors, and let t be time such that $P_i.Work\_count(t) \geq 4n$ and $P_j.Work\_count(t) \geq 4n$. Let $list_i$ and $list_j$ denote the values of $P_i.list$ and $P_j.list$ obtained by sorting in the generations $P_i.Gen(t)$ and $P_j.Gen(t)$, respectively. If $work(P_i, t) \geq 3n$, $work(P_j, t) \geq 3n$, then P_i precedes P_j in $list_j$ or P_j precedes P_i in $list_i$.

Proof. Let t_i and t_j be times when P_i and P_j sort in the generations $P_i.Gen(t)$ and $P_j.Gen(t)$, respectively.

- **Case** $max(t_i, t_j) \geq t - 2n$:
  Without loss of generality, assume that $(t_i, i) \prec (t_j, j)$ holds. In this case, $t - 3n + 1 \leq t_j - n + 1 < t_j \leq t$ holds. P_j is working correctly in the interval $[t_j - n + 1, t_j]$, and sets $P_j.key[i]$ at some time t' in this interval. Because of $(t_i, i) \prec (t_j, j)$, P_j finds $((P_i.Work\_count - P_j.Work\_count), i) > (0, j)$. Therefore, unless P_j has detected P_i's nap in this generation, P_i precedes P_j in $list_j$. Assume P_j has detected P_i's nap at t' or before. Since P_i is working correctly in the interval $[t - 3n + 1, t]$, P_i takes a nap before $t - 3n + 1$. Since $n \leq P_j.Work\_count(t - 2n - 1) \leq 4n$ and $steps(P_j, t - 3n + 1, t - 2n + 1) \geq n$, it follows from Fact3, P_j reads P_i's variables at some time t'' in the interval $[t - 3n + 1, t - 2n]$, and detects P_i's nap at t'' or before.

Since $P_i.Work\_count(t) \geq 4n$ and $steps(P_i, t-2n+1, t+1) \geq 2n$ hold, from Fact3, P_i reads P_j's variables in the interval $[t-2n+1, t]$. Since P_i has not detected its nap before t'', P_i detects it in the interval $[t'', t]$ and executes *partial_reset*. The length of $[t'', t]$ is $3n$ or less, therefore, $P_i.Work\_count(t) \leq 3n$. A contradiction.

– **Case** $max(t_i, t_j) < t - 2n$:
In this case, $steps(P_i, t_i, t+1) > 2n$ and $steps(P_j, t_j, t+1) > 2n$ hold, therefore, $P_i.Work\_count(t) \geq 6n$ and $P_j.Work\_count(t) \geq 6n$ hold. Because of $\alpha(P_i, P_i.Gen(t)) \leq n$ and $\alpha(P_j, P_j.Gen(t)) \leq n$, $P_i.Work\_count(t) \geq 5n + \alpha(P_i, P_i.Gen(t))$ and $P_j.Work\_count(t) \geq 5n + \alpha(P_j, P_j.Gen(t))$ hold. From Fact3, P_i (resp. P_j) reads P_j's (resp. P_i's) variables in the interval $[t-n+1, t]$. Since $t_i < t - 2n$ and $t_j < t - 2n$, P_i (resp. P_j) never detect P_j's (resp. P_i's) nap at t_i (resp. t_j) or before. Therefore, P_i sets $P_i.key[j] = ((P_j.Work\_count - P_i.Work\_count), j)$ at some time t_i' in the generation $P_i.Gen(t)$, and P_j sets $P_j.key[i] = ((P_i.Work\_count - P_j.Work\_count), i)$ at some time t_j' in the generation $P_j.Gen(t)$. If $P_i.key[j] > (0, i)$ or $P_j.key[i] > (0, j)$, the Lemma holds. Assume that $P_i.key[j] < (0, i)$ and $P_j.key[i] < (0, j)$ hold. Without loss of generality, assume that $i > j$ holds. Then, $P_j.Work\_count(t_i'-1) \leq P_i.Work\_count(t_i'-1)$ and $P_j.Work\_count(t_j'-1) > P_i.Work\_count(t_j' - 1)$. This implies $t_i' \neq t_j'$. Define $t^1 = min(t_i', t_j')$ and $t^2 = max(t_i', t_j')$, and let P^1 be P_i if $t_i' = t^1$, otherwise P_j, and let P^2 be the other processor. Then, $steps(P^1, t^1, t^2) < steps(P^2, t^1, t^2)$ holds. Let t^3 (resp. t^4) be time when P^1 (resp. P^2) reads P^2's (resp. P^1's) variables in the interval $[t-n+1, t]$. P^1 and P^2 never execute *partial_reset* in this interval, $steps(P^1, t^1, t^3) \geq steps(P^2, t^1, t^3)$ and $steps(P^2, t^2, t^4) \geq steps(P^1, t^2, t^4)$ hold. Because of $work(P^1, t) \geq 3n$ and $work(P^2, t) \geq 3n$, $steps(P^1, t^3, t^4) = steps(P^2, t^3, t^4)$ holds, therefore, the following holds.

$$steps(P^1, t^1, t^2)$$
$$= steps(P^1, t^1, t^3) + steps(P^1, t^3, t^4) - steps(P^1, t^2, t^4)$$
$$\geq steps(P^2, t^1, t^3) + steps(P^2, t^3, t^4) - steps(P^2, t^2, t^4)$$
$$= steps(P^2, t^1, t^2)$$

A contradiction. □

Now we show that if two processors in the *adjusted* mode work correctly sufficient long, their clocks agree.

Lemma 5. Let P_i and P_j be different processors, and let t be time such that $P_i.Mode(t) = $ "adjusted" and $P_j.Mode(t) = $ "adjusted". If $work(P_i, t) \geq 3n$ and $work(P_j, t) \geq 3n$, then $P_i.Clock(t) = P_j.Clock(t)$ holds.

Proof. Because of $P_i.Mode(t) = $ "adjusted" and $P_j.Mode(t) = $ "adjusted", $P_i.Work\_count(t) \geq 4n$ and $P_j.Work\_count(t) \geq 4n$ holds. From Lemma 4, P_j precedes P_i in $P_i.list(t)$ or P_i precedes P_j in $P_j.list(t)$. Without loss of generality, assume that P_j precedes P_i in $P_i.list(t)$. From the assumption, there exists time t' when P_i sets $P_i.Clock(t') = P_j.Clock(t' - 1) + 1$.

- **Case** $t' \geq t - 3n + 1$:
  P_i and P_j are working correctly and do not execute *partial_reset* in the interval $[t - 3n + 1, t]$, therefore, $P_i.Clock(t) = P_j.Clock(t)$ holds.
- **Case** $t' < t - 3n + 1$:
  Since $P_i.Work\_count(t' - 1) \geq 4n$ and $P_j.Work\_count(t' - 1) \geq 4n$ hold, $P_i.Work\_count(t) \geq 7n$ and $P_j.Work\_count(t) \geq 7n$ hold. From Fact3, P_i reads P_j's variables at some time t'' in $[t - 2n + 1, t - n]$ and in $[t - n + 1, t]$, and P_j reads P_i's variables in $[t - n + 1, t]$. Both P_i and P_j do not execute *partial_reset* in $[t - n + 1, t]$, therefore, P_i does not detect naps of either P_i or P_j at t''. That is, P_i finds $steps(P_i, t', t'') = steps(P_j, t', t'')$, therefore, $P_i.Clock(t'' - 1) = P_j.Clock(t'' - 1)$ holds. Since P_i and P_j are working correctly and do not execute *partial_reset* in the interval $[t'', t]$, $P_i.Clock(t) = P_j.Clock(t)$ holds. □

Next lemma considers how long it takes since a processor takes a nap until the processor detects the nap if it detects.

Lemma 6. If a processor P_i executes *partial_reset* by naps at time t, then $work(P_i, t) < 5n$ holds.

Proof. Let P_j be the processor whose variables P_i reads at t. Since P_i executes *partial_reset* by naps at t, the condition at lines 32–33 or the condition at line 63 holds. The condition at line 32–33 is a disjunction of two conditions (1) $P_i.Work\_count(t-1) \geq n$ and $P_i.diff(t-1) < 0$, and (2) $P_i.Work\_count(t-1) \geq n$ and $P_j.Invalid_i(t - 1) \geq P_i.Gen(t - 1)$.

- **Case** $P_i.Work\_count(t - 1) \geq n$ and $P_i.diff(t - 1) < 0$:
  Let t' be time when P_i reads P_j's variables in the last time before t. In this case, P_i takes a nap in the interval $[t' + 1, t - 1]$. $P_i.Work\_count(t - 1) \geq n$ implies $steps(P_i, t', t) \leq 2n$, therefore, $work(P_i, t) < 2n$ holds.
- **Case** $P_i.Work\_count(t - 1) \geq n$ and $P_j.Invalid_i(t - 1) \geq P_i.Gen(t - 1)$:
  There is time t_j ($< t$) when P_j detects P_i's nap and sets $P_j.Invalid_i = P_i.Gen(t - 1)$. Let t'_j be time when P_j reads P_i's variables in the last time before t_j. At t_j, P_j finds $steps(P_i, t'_j, t_j) < steps(P_j, t'_j, t_j)$. Since P_j does not read P_i's variables in $[t'_j + 1, t_j - 1]$, $steps(P_j, t'_j + 1, t_j) < 3n$ holds, therefore, $steps(P_j, t'_j, t_j) \leq 3n$ and $steps(P_i, t'_j, t_j) < 3n$ hold. Moreover, t is the first time when P_i reads P_j's variable after t_j and $P_i.Work\_count(t - 1) \geq n$, therefore, $steps(P_i, t_j + 1, t) \leq 2n$ and $steps(P_i, t'_j, t) < 5n$ hold. P_i take a nap at t'_j or after, therefore, $work(P_i, t) < 5n$ holds.
- **Case line 63:** From the protocol, $P_i.Clock(t - 1) \neq P_j.Clock(t - 1)$ holds, and there is a processor P_m with which P_i has synchronized its clock in this generation at some t', that is, $P_m.Mode(t' - 1) =$"adjusted" and P_i sets $P_i.Clock(t') = P_m.Clock(t' - 1) + 1$. Assume that $work(P_i, t) \geq 5n$, then P_i is working correctly in this generation and $t - n < t' < t$ holds. Let t^0 be time when $P_i.Work\_count(t^0) = 1$ in this generation. Since $4n \leq P_i.Work\_count(t - 1) < 5n$ and $work(P_i, t) \geq 5n$, P_i is working correctly in $[t^0, t]$ and $t_0 \leq t' - 4n < t - 4n$ holds. P_i reads variables of both P_m and P_j

in $[t_0, t_0 + n - 1]$ and P_i has not detect naps of P_m until t' and P_j until t, therefore, $work(P_m, t' - 1) \geq t' - t^0 + n \geq 3n$, $work(P_j, t' - 1) \geq 3n$ and $work(P_j, t - 1) > 3n$ hold.

If $P_j.Mode(t'-1) = $ "adjusted", from Lemma5, $P_m.Clock(t'-1) = P_j.Clock(t'-1)$ holds. Both P_i and P_j are working correctly in $[t', t-1]$, therefore, $P_i.Clock(t-1) = P_j.Clock(t-1)$ holds. A contradiction.

If $P_j.Mode(t'-1) = $ "adjusting", since P_i and P_j set their key at $t' - 2n$ $(> t - 3n)$ or after and P_i, P_j and P_m are working correctly in $[t' - 2n, t' - 1]$, $P_i.key[m](t-1) > P_i.key[j](t-1)$ implies that $P_j.key[m](t'-1) > P_j.key[j](t'-1)$. Therefore, P_m precedes P_j in $P_j.list$, then there exists some t'' $(t' - n < t'' < t)$ in the generation $P_j.Gen(t'-1)$ when P_j synchronizes its clock with P_m, that is, P_j sets $P_j.Clock(t'') = P_m.Clock(t'' - 1) + 1$. P_m is working correctly in $[t', t'' - 1]$ if $t' < t''$. Therefore, $P_i.Clock(t-1) = P_j.Clock(t-1)$ holds. A contradiction. $\square$

Lemma 7. (Adjustment) For any $t > 0$ and any processor P_i, if $work(P_i, t - 1) \geq 10n$ holds then $P_i.Mode(t-1) = $ "adjusted". In addition, if $work(P_i, t) > 10n$ holds then $P_i.Clock(t) = P_i.Clock(t-1) + 1$ holds.

Proof. Even if P_i executes *partial_reset* by naps or by overtime at some t' after the last nap, from Lemmas 2 and 6, $work(P_i, t') < 5n$ holds. Therefore, if $work(P_i, t - 1) \geq 10n$ holds, P_i does not execute any *partial_reset* in the interval $[t - 5n, t - 1]$, that is, $P_i.Work\_count(t-1) \geq 5n$ holds. Therefore, $P_i.Mode(t-1) = $ "adjusted" holds. In addition, if $work(P_i, t) > 10n$ holds, P_i takes a step at t in the *adjusted* mode. Therefore, $P_i.Clock(t) = P_i.Clock(t-1) + 1$ holds. $\square$

Lemma 8. (Agreement) For any $t > 0$ and any processors P_i and P_j, if $work(P_i, t) \geq 10n$ and $work(P_j, t) \geq 10n$ then $P_i.Clock(t) = P_j.Clock(t)$.

Proof. From Lemma 7, $P_i.Mode(t-1) = P_j.Mode(t-1) = $ "adjusted". From Lemma 5, $P_i.Clock(t-1) = P_j.Clock(t-1)$ holds. Both of P_i and P_j take a step at t in the *adjusted* mode, $P_i.Clock(t) = P_j.Clock(t)$ holds. $\square$

Theorem 9. The proposed protocol is a wait-free clock synchronization protocol with synchronization time $10n$. $\square$

4 Lower Bound

We show the proposed protocol is asymptotically optimal with regard to the synchronization time.

Theorem 10. There is no clock synchronization protocol with synchronization time $n - 2$ or less.

Proof. For contradiction, assume that there exists a clock synchronization protocol $\mathcal{A}$ with synchronization time k $(k \leq n - 2)$. We consider two executions $E = c_0, \pi_1, c_1, \cdots$ and $E' = c'_0, \pi'_1, c'_1, \cdots$ satisfying the following three conditions.

Condition 1 There exists a time t such that $c_0, \pi_1, c_1, \cdots, c_t$ and $c'_0, \pi'_1, c'_1, \cdots, c'_t$ are identical and $work(P, t) \geq k$ holds for every processor P for both E and E'.

Condition 2 For the execution E, $\pi_{t+1} = \pi_{t+2} = \cdots = \pi_{t+n-1} = \{P_0\}$ holds.

From **Agreement**, all clock values are identical in c_t and also in c'_t. Let $clock(t)$ denote this value. From **Adjustment**, $P_0.Clock(c_{t+n-2})(t) = clock(t) + n - 2$ holds. Since P_0 takes $n - 2$ steps in the interval $[t+1, t+n-2]$ in E, there exists a processor, say P_i $(i \neq 0)$, whose variables P_0 does not read in this interval.

Condition 3 For the execution E', $\pi'_{t+1} = \{P_i\}$ and $\pi'_{t+2} = \cdots = \pi'_{t+n-1} = \{P_0, P_i\}$ holds.

In this case, from **Adjustment**, $P_i.Clock(c'_{t+n-1}) = clock(t) + n - 1$ holds. In both E and E', processors other than P_0 and P_i take no step in $[t+1, t+n-1]$, therefore, P_0 behaves in the interval $[t+2, t+n-1]$ in E' in the exactly same way as P_0 behaves in the interval $[t+1, t+n-2]$ in E. Therefore, $P_0.Clock(c'_{t+n-1}) = P_0.Clock(c_{t+n-2}) = clock(t) + n - 2 = P_i.Clock(c'_{t+n-1}) - 1$ holds. However, since $work(P_0, t + n - 1) = n - 2 \geq k$ and $work(P_i, t + n - 1) \geq k$ hold for E', $P_0.Clock(c'_{t+n-1}) = P_i.Clock(c'_{t+n-1})$ should be hold from **Agreement**. A contradiction. □

5 Conclusions

In this paper, we have presented a wait-free clock synchronization protocol with synchronization time $10n$ on the in-phase shared memory multi-processor system, and also have shown the proposed protocol is asymptotically optimal with regard to the synchronization time.

To reduce synchronization time, one may think that our protocol requires more running time for one pulse than the previous protocols. Actually, a processor sorts n items in one step in our protocols. This needs $O(n \log n)$ running time for one pulse. In the previous best protocol [13], the synchronization time is $O(n^2)$, while it needs a constant running time for one pulse. Therefore, the total running time required for synchronization is $O(n^2)$, and it is better than our protocol. However, we can improve the total running time to $O(n \log n)$ by using *heap sort*. In the modified version, each processor inserts one key to a heap in each step in the case where $3n \leq Work\_count \leq 4n - 1$, and finds and removes the first key from the heap in each step after becoming $Work\_count = 4n$ until entering the *adjusted* mode or executing *partial_reset*. Moreover, the first n steps in the next generation is sufficient long to clear the heap space to reuse. In such a modified version, each processor needs $O(\log n)$ running time for one step, and the total running time required for synchronization is $O(n \log n)$. That is, this modified protocol improves the previous results with regard to the total running time required for synchronization.

One of the future works is investigating a *self-stabilizing and wait-free clock synchronization protocol* with synchronization time $O(n)$.

References

1. L. Lamport and P. Melliar-Smith: "Synchronizing clocks in the presence of faults", Journal of the ACM, **32**, 1, pp. 1–36 (1985).
2. S. Dolev, J. Halpern and H. Strong: "On the possibility and impossibility of achieving clock synchronization", Journal of Computer Systems Science, **32**, 2, pp. 230–250 (1986).
3. S. Mahaney and F. Schneider: "Inexact agreement: Accuracy, precision and graceful degradation", Proceedings of the 4th ACM Symposium on Principles of Distributed Computing, pp. 237–249 (1985).
4. T. Srikanth and S. Toueg: "Optimal clock synchronization", Journal of the ACM, **34**, 3, pp. 626–645 (1987).
5. J. Welch and N. Lynch: "A new fault-tolerant algorithm for clock synchronization", Information and Computation, **77**, 1, pp. 1–36 (1988).
6. J. Halpern, B. Simons, R. Strong and D. Dolev: "Fault-tolerant clock synchronization", Proceedings of the 3rd ACM Symposium on Principles of Distributed Computing, pp. 89–102 (1984).
7. S. Dolev and J.L.Welch: "Self-stabilizing clock synchronization in the presence of byzantine faults", Proceedings of the Second Workshop on Self-Stabilizing Systems, pp. 9.1–9.12 (1995).
8. M. Gouda and T. Herman: "Stabilizing unison", Information Processing Letters, **35**, pp. 171–175 (1990).
9. A. Arora, S. Dolev and M. Gouda: "Maintaining digital clocks in step", Parallel Processing Letters, **1**, 1, pp. 11– 8 (1991).
10. A. S. Gopal and K. J. Perry: "Unifying self-stabilization and fault-tolerance", Proceeding of the 12th ACM Symposium on Principles on Distributed Computing, pp. 195–206 (1993).
11. S. Dolev: "Possible and impossible self-stabilizing digital clock synchronization in general graphs", Technical Report TR 96-06, Department of Mathematics and Computer Science. Ben-Gurion University (1996).
12. S. Dolev and J. Welch: "Wait-free clock synchronization", Proceedings of the 12th ACM Symposium on Principles of Distributed Computing, pp. 97–108 (1993).
13. M. Papatriantafilou and P. Tsigas: "On self-stabilizing wait-free clock synchronization", Proceedings of the 4th Scandinavian Workshop on Algorithm Theory (LNCS 824), pp. 267–277 (1994).

Transparent Support for Wait-Free Transactions

Mark Moir*
Department of Computer Science
The University of Pittsburgh, Pittsburgh, PA 15260.

Abstract. This paper concerns software support for non-blocking transactions in shared-memory multiprocessors. We present mechanisms that convert sequential transactions into lock-free or wait-free ones. In contrast to some previous mechanisms, ours support transactions for which the set of memory locations accessed cannot be determined in advance. Our implementations automatically detect and resolve conflicts between concurrent transactions, and allow transactions that do not conflict to execute in parallel. The key to the efficiency of our wait-free implementation lies in using a lock-free (but not wait-free) multi-word compare-and-swap (MWCAS) operation. By introducing communication between a high-level helping mechanism and the lock-free MWCAS, we show that an expensive wait-free MWCAS is not necessary to ensure wait-freedom.

1 Introduction

The use of locking to coordinate accesses to shared data in multiprocessor applications has a number of associated pitfalls including a lack of concurrency, performance bottlenecks, convoying, priority inversion, deadlock, and susceptibility to faults and delays. As a result, there is increasing interest in non-blocking synchronization, and in particular, lock-free and wait-free implementations of shared objects. To ease the burden on programmers in using lock-free and wait-free shared objects, Herlihy proposed *universal constructions* [6]. A lock-free (wait-free) universal construction converts a sequential implementation of *any* shared object into a lock-free (wait-free) one. We present new lock-free and wait-free universal constructions, which we believe represent important progress towards the use of non-blocking shared object implementations. Our constructions implement arbitrary "transactions" that can also support multi-object operations.

Our new constructions are based on an efficient, "conditionally wait-free" implementation of the multi-word compare-and-swap (MWCAS) operation. A conditionally wait-free implementation is a lock-free implementation that provides a means for communicating with an external helping mechanism. This allows the helping mechanism to cancel MWCAS operations that are no longer required to complete. Conditionally wait-free implementations have advantages over both lock-free and wait-free ones. First, the only known wait-free implementation of MWCAS has substantial space requirements, and is not very efficient [2]. By dropping the wait-freedom requirement, significantly more efficient implementations can be derived [7, 10]. Unfortunately, however, lock-free MWCAS operations do not guarantee termination. Thus, they are not useful for wait-free implementations. The conditionally wait-free MWCAS operation presented in

---

* Work supported in part by an NSF CAREER Award, CCR 9702767.

this paper has only nominal overhead beyond that of a lock-free implementation, but guarantees termination if the invoking operation is completed by another process. This allows us to avoid the use of a costly wait-free MWCAS operation in our wait-free implementation by using a high-level helping mechanism to ensure termination of the MWCAS operation.

Our lock-free and wait-free transaction implementations provide the same interface to programmers; this interface provides the illusion of a large contiguous array, which contains all the data to be accessed by transactions. Programmers write sequential code for transactions that access this data, and are not required to reason about concurrency at all. Our constructions implement arbitrary lock-free and wait-free transactions, automatically detect and resolve conflicts between concurrent transactions, and allow transactions that do not conflict to execute in parallel. Both constructions have reasonable space requirements, and introduce little overhead in the absence of contention. Finally, the helping mechanism employed by our wait-free construction, as well as the mechanisms for detecting termination and communicating return values between processes, are much simpler than similar mechanisms employed by previous constructions.

We summarize related work in Section 2. In Section 3, we present our conditionally wait-free implementation of MWCAS. In Sections 4 and 5, respectively, we present our lock-free and wait-free transaction implementations. Finally, in Section 6, we conclude, and discuss future work. Due to space limitations, a formal treatment of our results is deferred to a full version of the paper.

2 Related Work

In Herlihy's constructions [6], operations copy the entire shared object, sometimes more than once. The space required for these copies, as well as the time spent copying, is prohibitive for larger objects. To address this problem, Herlihy also designed a universal construction for "large" objects. While this construction improves the copying and space overhead for some objects, it also requires significant creative effort on the part of the object programmer, provides only lock-free implementations, and results in no advantage for some commonly used objects. Furthermore, these constructions do not allow concurrent operations to execute in parallel. Below we briefly describe efforts to address these problems.

Barnes [5] recognizes the importance of allowing operations to execute in parallel where possible. He presents a mechanism in which an object is protected by a number of locks. Operations on the object acquire the locks associated with affected parts of the object in such a way that processes can "help" each other to perform operations and release locks. (A similar technique was proposed by Turek, Shasha, and Prakash [11].) This technique guarantees lock-freedom. Barnes's method accommodates "dynamic" transactions. (A transaction is *static* if the memory locations it accesses are known in advance, and *dynamic* otherwise.) Nonetheless, this method has several drawbacks. First, because user-supplied transactions are based on locks, the programmer must still be concerned with concurrency to some extent. Second, if a process p that is helping the operation of another process q encounters a lock that is held by a third process r, then p must help r before continuing to help q. This can give rise to long chains of useless helping. Finally, Barnes's method is not wait-free.

Shavit and Touitou [10] present a method called *software transactional memory* (STM). Their approach allows transactions to be executed in a lock-free (but not wait-free) manner, and also allows multiple transactions to execute in parallel, provided that they do not interfere with each other. This is achieved through the use of a technique that is similar to Barnes's technique: processes acquire locks associated with the memory locations to be updated, and a location that is locked by another process can be released by "helping" that process. A key difference between these two approaches is that STM avoids the use of a recursive helping policy by ensuring that a process helps only one other process before retrying. Shavit and Touitou present performance studies which suggest that this difference improves performance significantly. One limitation of STM (as presented in [10]) is that it does not support dynamic transactions. As a result, it is not well suited to implementing general shared objects. However, most synchronization primitives access a fixed set of locations, and can therefore be implemented using static transactions. (Israeli and Rappoport also presented lock-free constructions for multi-word synchronization primitives [7]; these constructions employ the costly recursive helping policy discussed above.)

Most previous wait-free universal constructions [1, 3, 6] implement only one object: in order to use them to implement multiple objects and to allow operations to access multiple objects atomically, the objects must be considered as a single object. None of these wait-free constructions allow concurrent operations to execute in parallel. Thus, considering multiple objects as one means that operations are executed sequentially, even if they access different objects. In [2], Anderson and Moir present a wait-free universal construction that allows operations to atomically access multiple objects, and allows operations that access disjoint sets of objects to execute in parallel. This is the first wait-free construction to exploit parallelism, but does not provide the desired functionality of general, wait-free transactions that can execute in parallel. This is because the objects to be accessed by these multi-object operations must be specified in advance; general implementations should not impose this restriction.

Finally, efforts have been made to provide wait-free constructions that avoid excessive copying overhead [1, 3], and that have time complexity that depends on contention, rather than on the number of processes [1, 4].[1] However, none of these constructions allow operations to execute in parallel.[2]

3 Conditionally Wait-Free MWCAS Implementation

In this section we describe our conditionally wait-free MWCAS operation, which is used by the lock-free and wait-free transaction implementations presented in the following two sections. A single-word compare-and-swap (CAS) operation takes three parameters: an address, an "old" value, and a "new" value. The CAS operation fails, returning false, if the old value differs from the current value stored at the specified address. Otherwise, the CAS succeeds, modifying the value at the specified address to the new value, and returns true. MWCAS

---

[1] The constructions presented in [4] are not strictly speaking wait-free: they are designed to tolerate $k-1$ failures, where k is a user-tunable parameter. While contention for the object remains below k, these constructions are effectively wait-free.

[2] Actually, the constructions in [3] do allow read-only operations to execute in parallel.

extends CAS in the natural way by accessing multiple addresses atomically. The parameters to MWCAS are the number of words, a list of addresses, a list of old values, and a list of new values. In order for MWCAS to succeed, *all* old values must equal the contents of the corresponding address. Our conditionally wait-free MWCAS implementation also accepts as parameters a procedure and parameters to that procedure. Our implementation invokes the given procedure with the given parameters periodically. If the procedure eventually returns true, then the MWCAS operation terminates (possibly returning "quit").[3] This allows our wait-free helping mechanism to determine which processes need help, and to inform processes that they have been helped.

Our MWCAS implementation is based on the wait-free implementation presented in [2]. However, because the implementation presented here is not required to be wait-free, it is significantly simpler and more efficient, and uses substantially less space than the implementation in [2]. The resulting implementation is quite similar to the STM implementation of Shavit and Touitou [10]. Specifically, in both implementations, a process first locks each of the words it accesses using load-linked (LL) and store-conditional (SC) instructions, and then, if successful, modifies each word in accordance with the implemented operation. If, in attempting to lock its words, a process p finds a word already locked by another process q, then p attempts to help q to complete its operation. In contrast to the implementations of [2, 5, 7], STM and the implementation presented here do not continue this helping recursively. That is, if p fails to complete q's operation because of another process r, then p does not start to help r, but instead causes q to start its operation again. This policy ensures that p helps only enough that a subsequent attempt of p's own operation can succeed. Shavit and Touitou call this approach *non-redundant helping*.

Despite these similarities, our implementation has several advantages over STM, especially when used in the transaction implementations presented in the next two sections. First, STM is intended for general, static, read-modify-write transactions — that is, transactions that access a predetermined set of memory locations, return the previous values of those locations, and write new values that are computed as a function of the old values. In contrast, our implementation is designed specifically for MWCAS. This simplification admits a number of optimizations in our implementation that are not possible with general transactions. For example, a MWCAS operation can immediately return false if it detects that one of the accessed words differs from the "old" value for that word.

The second advantage of our implementation over STM is that it provides a constant-time, wait-free read operation. If STM were used to implement MW-CAS, then, in order to obtain the current value of a word (to be used as the old value for that word in a subsequent MWCAS), a lock-free transaction would need to be invoked, possibly causing the reading process to help other processes.

Other advantages of our implementation involve the mechanisms that lock and unlock memory locations. First, when process p helps process q to acquire its locks in STM, p must ensure that all of q's words are locked, even if q has already locked most of them. In our implementation, process p can start from the word where it first encountered a conflict with q, rather than starting from the

---

[3] For convenience, we assume that if the procedure returns true, then subsequent invocations will also return true until the MWCAS returns. This assumption can easily be eliminated.

beginning. Also, in STM, unlocking the memory locations of process q involves resetting the locks for each of q's words. In our implementation, this is achieved simply by changing the status of process q from "lock" to "unlock".[4] This further reduces the work a process must do on behalf of another.

Our conditionally wait-free implementation of Read and MWCAS is presented in Figs. 1 and 2.[5] This implementation provides an array of M words, and supports a Read operation and a MWCAS operation of up to W words for N processes. As mentioned above, this implementation is largely based on the wait-free implementation presented in [2]. Due to space limitations, we therefore concentrate on the differences between these two implementations here, and defer a more detailed description to the full paper.

There are two differences in the way the MWCAS operation presented here is called. First, process p writes the parameters to its MWCAS operation into the shared variable $PAR[p]$ before calling MWCAS, rather than passing the parameters directly to MWCAS. This avoids unnecessary copying of the parameters. Second, the procedure and parameters used to allow communication with an external helping mechanism are passed directly to MWCAS. If the procedure eventually returns true when called with the provided parameters, then the MWCAS operation will terminate. (The only loops that potentially repeat forever call the quit procedure during every iteration (lines 3 and 48).)

Other differences arise from the relaxation of the wait-freedom requirement. First, in the implementation of [2], when a process p successfully locks a memory location, it potentially interferes with a lock attempt by another process — say q. Therefore, to ensure wait-freedom, p must detect this possibility and "help" q to complete its operation. To allow this interference to be detected, the implementation in [2] employs an access matrix (called AM). This matrix, which has one position for every process-memory location pair, imposes a significant space overhead. Moreover, in order to detect processes that concurrently access a memory location, a process must read all N matrix positions associated with that memory location. This checking dominates the work done by a process in an operation, even if no other process is executing. Because the wait-freedom requirement is relaxed here, the access matrix is no longer required. This results in substantial space savings as well as improved best-case performance. Most of the differences between the implementation presented here and the one in [2] are a result of these changes. Specifically, there is no longer any need for processes to record each word that they access, nor to help other processes with which they concurrently access words in common.

The final difference arises from the use of non-redundant helping (as introduced by Shavit and Touitou [10]). Using this helping policy, a process attempts to help only one process before retrying its own operation. To see how lock-freedom can be achieved despite this lack of additional helping, suppose that while helping process q, process p encounters a word locked by a third process r (line 8). In this case, process p causes process q to release all of its locks, and

---

[4] A technique similar to this one was first proposed by Israeli and Rappoport [7].

[5] This algorithm uses Load-Linked (LL), Validate (VL), and Store-Conditional (SC) instructions. We recently proposed a slight modification to the way these instructions are used in order to accommodate practical implementations of the ideal semantics of these instructions using limited forms commonly available in hardware [8]. These modifications are not reflected here, but are easily incorporated into this algorithm.

```
procedure Do_Locking(i: 0..N − 1;
                     index: −1..W − 1)
1:  nw := PAR[i].nw;
    for j := index + 1 to nw − 1 do
2:    done, addr := false, PAR[i].addr[j];
      while ¬done do
3:      if proc(parm) then
4:        if LL(&STAT[p]).stat = lock then
5:          SC(&STAT[p], (unlock, fail))
          fi; return
        fi;
6:      v := LL(&LOCK[addr]);
7:      if ¬VL(&STAT[i]) then return
        elseif v.owner = i then
          done := true
8:      elseif v.owner ≥ 0 ∧ STAT[v.owner]
                    ∈ {lock, modify} then
9:        if i = p then
            Help(v.owner, addr, v.index)
10:       else SC(&STAT[i], (unlock, retry));
            return
          fi
        else
11:       old := PAR[i].old[j];
12:       val := MEM[addr];
13:       if VL(&LOCK[addr]) then
14:         if val ≠ old then
              SC(&STAT[i], (unlock, fail));
              return
15:         elseif ¬VL(&STAT[i]) then
              return
16:         elseif SC(&LOCK[addr],
                          (i, j)) then
              done := true
            fi
          fi
        fi
      od
    od;
17: SC(&STAT[i], (modify, none));
    return
```

```
procedure Do_Modifying(i: 0..N − 1)
18: nw := PAR[i].nw;
    for j := 0 to nw − 1 do
19:   addr := PAR[i].addr[j];
20:   old := PAR[i].old[j];
21:   new := PAR[i].new[j];
22:   if old ≠ new ∧
            LL(&MEM[addr]) = old then
23:     if ¬VL(STAT[i]) then return fi;
24:     SC(&MEM[addr], new)
      fi
    od;
25: SC(&STAT[i], (unlock, succ));
    return

procedure Help(i: 0..N − 1;
              last_locked: −1..M − 1;
              index: −1..W − 1)
26: if (LL(STAT[i])).stat = lock then
27:   if index ≥ 0 ∧
            ¬VL(&LOCK[last_locked])
                        then return fi;
28:   Do_Locking(i, index)
    fi;
29: if (LL(STAT[i])).stat = modify then
      Do_Modifying(i)
    fi;
30: return

procedure Read(a: 0..M − 1)
                        returns valtype
31: val := MEM[a];
32: v := LL(&LOCK[a]);
33: if v.owner = −1 ∨
          LL(&STAT[v.owner]).stat ≠
                              modify then
      return val
    fi;
34: old := PAR[v.owner].old[v.index];
35: if ¬VL(&LOCK[a]) then return val fi;
36: if VL(&STAT[v.owner]) then
        return old else return val fi
```

Fig. 1. Conditionally wait-free MWCAS implementation for process p (part 1). Type and variable declarations are in Fig. 2.

311

type *valtype* = any type that fits into one machine word; *lock_type* = **record** *owner*: $-1..N-1$; *index*: $0..W-1$ **end**; *par_type* = **record** *nw*: $1..W$; *addr*: **array**$[0..W-1]$ **of** $0..M-1$; *old*, *new*: **array**$[0..W-1]$ **of** *valtype* **end**; *stat_type* = **record** *stat*: {*init*, *lock*, *modify*, *unlock*}; *flag*: {*succ*, *fail*, *retry*, *none*} **end**

shared variable *LOCK*: **array**$[0..M-1]$ **of** *lock_type* **init** $(-1,0)$; *STAT*: **array**$[0..N-1]$ **of** *stat_type* **init** (*init*, *succ*); *MEM*: **array**$[0..M-1]$ **of** *valtype* **init** initial values for implemented words; *PAR*: **array**$[0..N-1]$ **of** *par_type*

private variable *proc*: **boolean procedure**; *parm*: *parmtype*; *v*: *lock_type*; *val*, *old*, *new*: *valtype*; *st*: *stat_type*; *nw*: $1..W$; *j*: $0..W-1$; *done*: **boolean**; *addr*: $0..M-1$

procedure *MWCAS*(*quitproc*: **boolean procedure**; *quitparm*: *parmtype*) **returns** {*succ*, *fail*, *quit*}
37: *proc*, *parm* := *quitproc*, *quitparm*;
   repeat
38:   *LL*(&*STAT*[p]);
39:   *SC*(*STAT*[p], (*lock*, *none*));
      Help(p, -1, -1);
40:   *st* := *STAT*[p];
41:   *nw* := *PAR*[p].*nw*;
      for $j := 0$ **to** $nw - 1$ **do**
42:     *addr* := *PAR*[p].*addr*[*j*];
43:     *v* := *LL*(&*LOCK*[*addr*]);
44:     **if** *v.owner* $\in \{-1, p\}$ $\vee$
        STAT[*v.owner*] $\notin$ {*lock*, *modify*} **then**
45:       **if** $\neg$*SC*(&*LOCK*[*addr*], $(-1, 0)$) **then**
46:         **if** *LL*(&*LOCK*[*addr*]).*owner* = p **then**
47:           *SC*(&*LOCK*[*addr*], $(-1, 0)$)
          fi
        fi
      fi
      od;
48:   **if** *st.flag* $\neq$ *succ* $\wedge$ *proc*(*parm*) **then**
        st.flag := *quit*
      fi
   until *st.flag* $\neq$ *retry*;
49: *LL*(&*STAT*[p]);
50: *SC*(*STAT*[p], (*init*, *none*)); **return** *st.flag*

Fig. 2. Conditionally wait-free MWCAS implementation for process p (part 2).

to restart its operation from the beginning (line 10). Because each process locks its memory locations in increasing order, it is impossible for this interference to repeat cyclically. Therefore, the implementation is lock-free.

4 Lock-Free Transaction Implementation

In this section, we describe our lock-free transaction implementation. This implementation provides the transaction programmer with the illusion of a contiguous array, which contains all data to be accessed by transactions. Following the terminology of Shavit and Touitou [10], this array is referred to hereafter as the *transactional memory*. The transactional memory is in fact represented by a series of B blocks, each of which contains S words. (A similar approach was used in [3].) We assume that an upper bound T is known on the number of blocks that are modified by any transaction, and that there are N processes. Each process has T "copy blocks", which are used to replace modified array blocks.

Before presenting details of the implementation, we first consider an example that shows how our construction can be used to implement a FIFO queue. Fig. 3(a) shows the initial state of a transactional memory of four blocks, each of

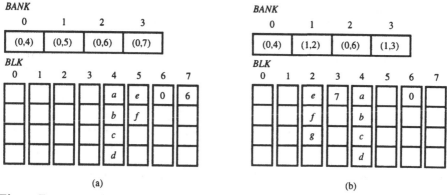

Fig. 3. Example data structures for implementing a FIFO queue. $B = 4$, $S = 4$, $N = 2$, $T = 2$. Queue elements are stored in the first two blocks of the implemented array, the head index is stored in the third block, and the tail index is stored in the fourth. (a) Initial state: implemented array is stored in blocks 4 through 7, so queue contains $\{a, b, c, d, e, f\}$. Process 0's copy blocks are 0 and 1, process 1's copy blocks are 2 and 3. (b) After *enqueue(g)* by process 1: queue contains $\{a, b, c, d, e, f, g\}$, process 0's copy blocks are 0 and 1, process 1's copy blocks are 5 and 7.

which contains four words (i.e., $B = 4$ and $S = 4$). In this example, $N = 2$ and $T = 2$ (because enqueue and dequeue operations modify at most two blocks). Queue elements are stored in the first two blocks of the transactional memory, the head index is stored in the third block, and the tail index is stored in the fourth. In the initial state, the queue contains $\{a, b, c, d, e, f\}$, process 0's copy blocks are 0 and 1, and process 1's copy blocks are 2 and 3. The *BANK* variable contains four words — one for each block of the transactional memory. Each word contains a version number and a block index. The block index indicates which block currently resides in the corresponding position of the transactional memory. Thus, in the example, blocks 4 through 7 are the initial blocks of the transactional memory. Fig. 3(b) shows the result of an *enqueue(g)* operation by process 1. Observe that the *BANK* variable has been modified so that process 1's previous copy blocks are now part of the transactional memory. Process 1 reclaims the displaced blocks (5 and 7) for use in subsequent transactions.

BANK is modified by means of a MWCAS operation. If a transaction modifies a block, then the MWCAS increments the version number for that block, as seen in Fig. 3(b). If a transaction reads from a block but does not modify it, then that block is included in the MWCAS operation, but the version number is not incremented. This approach ensures that if two transactions have a write conflict, then the MWCAS of one of them will fail, while still allowing transactions that do not modify common blocks to execute in parallel.[6]

To prepare for the MWCAS operation of a transaction, the invoking process executes the transaction while maintaining a logical view of the transactional memory; blocks that are currently part of the transactional memory are not modified. (Details are presented below.) After the transaction has been executed, the

---

[6] The version field theoretically grows without bound. In reality, it may eventually wrap around. Our construction is correct assuming no version counter wraps around during one transaction. A similar assumption is made and defended in [8].

parameters for the MWCAS are generated, and MWCAS is invoked. If the MW-CAS succeeds, then the transaction is completed. Otherwise, the transactional memory is not affected, and the transaction can be retried.

Our lock-free transaction implementation is shown in Fig. 4. Programmers call the *LF_Tran* procedure, passing a pointer to the transaction itself, as well as parameters to the transaction. Transaction programmers access the transactional memory using the *Tr_Read* and *Tr_Write* procedures. During the execution of a transaction, the invoking process maintains its logical view of the transactional memory using a balanced tree that contains indexes of blocks accessed so far by the transaction. This tree, pointed to by *view*, is set to *nil* at the beginning of the transaction (lines 27 and 28). Then, whenever *Tr_Read* or *Tr_Write* is invoked, the block containing the location to be accessed is determined, and the *inview* procedure is called to ensure that this block is in the process's logical view (lines 9 and 13). *inview* (lines 1 to 8) returns a pointer to the tree node containing that block, inserting a new node into the tree if necessary.[7] When a new node is inserted into the tree, its *dirty* bit is set to false (line 5), indicating that the locations in this block have not yet been modified by the transaction, and the *old* and *new* fields are set to the current value of the *BANK* entry for this block (lines 6 and 7). If a location in that block is subsequently modified, then *Tr_Write* creates a copy of the block (line 15), records this copy as part of the logical view (line 16), marks the block as dirty (line 17), and finally makes the requested modification to the copy, rather than to the block that is currently part of the transactional memory (line 19). *Tr_Write* also records the old block in *oldlst* so that it may be reclaimed later if necessary, and increments the count of dirty blocks (line 18).

The *TR_Read* operation determines which block in the logical view currently contains the memory location to be accessed (line 9), and returns the value in that block (line 12). Before returning control to the programmer-supplied transaction, however, *Tr_Read* first checks to see if the block being accessed has changed during the transaction. If so, the transaction is aborted and restarted (line 11). This check serves two purposes. First, if the check fails, then the MW-CAS operation is certain to fail, so there is no point in executing the rest of the transaction. Second, if this check were not performed, then it would be possible for the transaction to see an inconsistent view of the transactional memory. This potentially leads to an error that would not occur if the transaction were executed sequentially. Thus, this check helps us to achieve our goal of relieving the transaction programmer of any burden in reasoning about concurrency.

When the user-supplied transaction has completed, *genpars* is called (line 30) to generate the parameters for the MWCAS operation using the logical view generated by the transaction. The *genpars* procedure does an in-order traversal of the balanced tree *view*, writing the *old*, *new*, and *addr* fields of successive elements of the shared variable *PAR* as it goes. (Recall that a process is required to write its parameters into *PAR* before calling MWCAS.) Once the MWCAS parameters have been generated, *LF_Tran* checks each block accessed to see if it has been modified during the transaction (lines 31 through 33). If some block has been modified, then the transaction must restart, so there is no point in calling

---

[7] The *search* and *insert* procedures are for any balanced tree implementation. The *freetree* procedure called at line 27 is assumed to free all of the nodes in a balanced tree so that they may be used by subsequent calls to *insert*.

type *wordtype* = **record** *ver*: **integer**; *blk*: 0..$B+N*T-1$ **end**; *blktype* = **array**[0..$S-$
1] **of** *valtype*; *nodeptr* = **pointer to** *nodetype*; *nodetype* = **record** *left, right*: *nodeptr*;
blk: 0..$B-1$; *old, new*: *wordtype*; *dirty*: **boolean end**

shared variable *BLK*: **array**[0..$B+N*T-1$] **of** *blktype*; *BANK*: **array**[0..$B-1$] **of**
wordtype /* *BANK* is a B-word MWCAS memory (implemented by Figs. 1 and 2).*/

initially ($\forall n : 0 \leq n < B :: BANK[n] = (N*T+n, 0) \wedge BLK[N*T+n] = $ (nth
block of initial value))

private variable *copy, oldlst*: **array**[0..$T-1$] **of** 0..$B+N*T-1$; *i, cnt, dcnt*: 0..T;
blk: 0..$B-1$; *v*: *valtype*; *ret*: *valtype*; *ptr, view*: *nodeptr*

initially ($\forall n : 0 \leq n < T :: copy[n] = p*T+n$) $\wedge$ *view* = *nil*

procedure *inview*(*blk*: 0..$B-1$)
　　　　　　　　　　　　returns *nodeptr*
1: *ptr* := *search*(*view, blk*);
2: **if** *ptr* = *nil* **then**
3: 　　*ptr* := *insert*(*view, blk*);
4: 　　*ptr* → *blk* := *blk*;
5: 　　*ptr* → *dirty* := *false*;
6: 　　*ptr* → *old* := *Read*(*blk*);
7: 　　*ptr* → *new* := *ptr* → *old*
8: **fi**; **return** *ptr*

procedure *Tr_Read*(*addr*: 0..$B*S-1$)
　　　　　　　　　　　　returns *valtype*
9: *blk* := *addr* **div** *S*; *ptr* := *inview*(*blk*);
10:*v* := *BLK*[*ptr* → *new.blk*][*addr* **mod** *S*];
11:**if** *Read*(*blk*) ≠ *ptr* → *old* **then goto** 27
12:**else return** *v*
　　fi

procedure *Tr_Write*(*addr*: 0..$B*S-1$;
　　　　　　　　　　　　val: *valtype*)
13:*blk* := *addr* **div** *S*; *ptr* := *inview*(*blk*);
14:**if** ¬*ptr* → *dirty* **then**
15: 　*memcpy*(*BLK*[*copy*[*dcnt*]],
　　　　BLK[*ptr* → *old.blk*], *sizeof*(*blktype*));
16: 　*ptr* → *new* := (*ptr* → *old.ver* + 1,
　　　　　　　　　　　　copy[*dcnt*]);
17: 　*ptr* → *dirty* := *true*;
18: 　*oldlst*[*dcnt*], *dcnt* :=
　　　　　　　ptr → *old.blk*, *dcnt* + 1
　　fi;
19:*BLK*[*ptr* → *new.blk*][*addr* **mod** *S*] := *val*

procedure *genpars*(*ptr*: *nodetype*)
20:**if** *ptr* = *nil* **then return fi**;
21:*genpars*(*ptr* → *left*);
22:*PAR*[*p*].*old*[*cnt*] := *ptr* → *old*;
23:*PAR*[*p*].*new*[*cnt*] := *ptr* → *new*;
24:*PAR*[*p*].*addr*[*cnt*] := *ptr* → *blk*;
25:*cnt* := *cnt* + 1;
26:*genpars*(*ptr* → *left*)

procedure *LF_Tran*(*tran*: *trantype*;
　　　　　　　　　　　　pars: *partype*)
　　　　　　　　　　　　returns *valtype*
　　while *true* **do**
27: 　*freetree*(*view*);
28: 　*view, cnt, dcnt* := *nil*, 0, 0;
29: 　*ret* := *tran*(*pars*);
30: 　*genpars*(*view*);
31: 　**for** *i* := 0 **to** *cnt* − 1 **do**
32: 　　　**if** *Read*(*PAR*[*p*].*addr*[*i*]) ≠
　　　　　　　　PAR[*p*].*old*[*i*] **then**
33: 　　　　**goto** 27
　　　　fi
　　od;
34: 　**if** *dcnt* = 0 **then return** *ret* **fi**;
35: 　*PAR*[*p*].*nw* := *cnt*;
36: 　**if** *MWCAS*(*falsefunc, nil*) =
　　　　　　　　　　succ **then**
37: 　　**for** *i* := 0 **to** *dcnt* − 1 **do**
　　　　　copy[*i*] := *oldlst*[*i*]
　　　od;
38: 　　**return** *ret*
　　fi
　　od

Fig. 4. Lock-free transaction implementation for process p.

MWCAS. Also, if the transaction is read-only and none of the blocks it accesses have changed, then it can return immediately without executing a MWCAS operation (line 34). This not only makes the read-only transaction more efficient, but also prevents it from slowing down other transactions that do invoke the MWCAS operation. Lastly, the number of words for the MWCAS is set (line 35) and *MWCAS* is invoked (line 36). Because this is not a wait-free transaction implementation, a dummy function that always returns false is passed to *MWCAS*. If the MWCAS succeeds, then the invoking process reclaims the displaced blocks to be used later as copy blocks, and returns the value acquired from the transaction (lines 37 and 38). Otherwise, the transaction restarts. In this case, some other transaction succeeded, so the implementation is lock-free.

5 Wait-Free Transaction Implementation

In this section we describe our wait-free transaction implementation. The interface and basic structure of this implementation is similar to that of the lock-free implementation presented in Section 4. However, several changes have been made in order to achieve wait-freedom. First, two new words are added to the MWCAS operation that completes a transaction: the first records the return value of the transaction, and the second indicates that the transaction has been completed and ensures that the transaction is not subsequently re-executed. Second, we have added an "announce" array called *ANC* in which processes announce their transactions and parameters, so that other processes may help perform the transactions. Finally, we have introduced a *HELP* array, through which processes "request help" in order to ensure that their transactions eventually complete.

We now explain our wait-free transaction implementation, which is shown in Figs. 6 and 7,[8] in more detail. The *BANK* variable (the MWCAS memory) has $2N$ more locations than the corresponding variable in our lock-free implementation. The first B locations are used as in the lock-free implementation. The next N locations are used as return values for each process, and the last N locations are used as transaction counters for each process. Each time a transaction by process i is completed, the version field of word $B + N + i$ is incremented by one. This prevents a transaction from being executed twice, and also allows a process to easily detect that its transaction has been completed.

Fig. 5(a) shows the initial state of the *BANK* variable when implementing the FIFO queue considered in Fig. 3. (Recall that $N = 2$ in the example.) The first four locations are the same as in the previous example, except that each one contains a new field (explained below). The next two locations contain return values, and the last two contain transaction counters. (Initially, the return values are blank and the transaction counters are zero because no transaction has yet been executed.) Fig. 5(b) shows the result of executing an *enqueue*(g) operation by process 1. As before, process 1's copy blocks are now part of the transactional memory. Also, for reasons explained below, the blocks that were changed by process 1 have been tagged with process 1's id.

We have also introduced an N by N array *HELP*. If some process detects that process j interferes with an operation of process i, then $HELP[i, j]$ is used

---

[8] Type and variable declarations and procedures that are identical to the ones in the lock-free implementation are not repeated in this figure. Actually, the **goto** in *Tr_Read* branches to line 1 in the wait-free implementation.

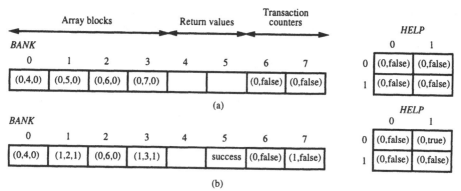

Fig. 5. Example data structures for implementing a wait-free FIFO queue (*BLK* not shown). (a) Initial state: no transactions have executed. (b) After *enqueue(g)* by process 1: process 1's return value is "success", process 1's transaction counter has increased, process 0 has detected interference from process 1 and has requested help.

to indicate that process j should eventually help process i. This "request for help" is generated by the *GetHelp* procedure in the case that a process detects a change to one of the memory locations accessed by the transaction it is executing. This could be the result of calling *GetHelp* from line 7 or line 23, or because the MWCAS operation called *Check*. (Observe that processes pass the *Check* procedure and the version number and invoking process of the current transaction to MWCAS (line 19).)

Every time a process completes a transaction of its own, it checks one process to see if it has requested help (see lines 37 and 38). Each process cycles through all processes in N transactions (lines 44 and 45). Thus, if process i requests help from process j, then process j will eventually attempt to help process i's transaction (assuming the transaction has not already been completed). Processes call *GetHelp* (line 23) each time they fail to complete a transaction, in order to detect a process that interfered and to request help from that process.

If the transaction of some process does not terminate, then eventually all processes will be trying to help that process, and one of them must succeed. Thus, each transaction eventually completes. To see that the invoking process terminates, observe that the loop at lines 1 to 24 terminates if the transaction being executed is completed by another process because of the check at line 1. Also, if the transaction being executed is completed by another process, then *Check* eventually returns true. Thus, because *MWCAS* is conditionally wait-free, it will eventually return. Therefore, the implementation in Fig. 7 is wait-free.

In the example of Fig. 5(b), process 0 has also attempted to perform an *enqueue* operation, but its MWCAS operation has failed because process 1's MWCAS succeeded. Therefore, process 0 has checked the locations accessed by its MWCAS operation (i.e., locations 1 and 3), and determined that process 1 caused its MWCAS to fail. Therefore, process 0 has requested help from process 1 by setting *HELP*[0, 1] to (0, *true*). Next time process 1 checks this location, it will determine whether process 0 still needs help with this transaction (line 38), and will help if necessary (line 43).

type *wordtype* = **record** *ver*: **integer**; *blk*: $0..B + N * T - 1$; *pid*: $0..N - 1$ **end**; *vertype* = **record** *ver*: **integer**; *active*: **boolean end**; *anctype* = **record** *tran*: *trantype*; *pars*: *partype* **end**

shared variable ANC: **array**$[0..N - 1]$ **of** *anctype*; BLK: **array**$[0..B + N * T - 1]$ **of** *blktype*; $HELP$: **array**$[0..N - 1, 0..N - 1]$ **of** *vertype*; $BANK$: **array**$[0..B - 1 + 2N]$ **of** *valtype* / * $B + 2N$-word MWCAS memory (implemented by Figs. 1 and 2). $BANK[0]$ to $BANK[B - 1]$ are treated as *wordtype*, $BANK[B]$ to $BANK[B + N - 1]$ as *valtype*, and $BANK[B + N]$ to $BANK[B + 2N - 1]$ as *vertype* */

initially $(\forall n : 0 \leq n < B :: BANK[n] = (0, N * T + n, 0) \wedge BLK[N * T + n] = ($nth block of initial value$)) \wedge (\forall m, n : 0 \leq m, n < N :: BANK[B + N + n] = (0, false) \wedge HELP[m, n] = (0, false))$

private var j: $0..N - 1$; *loop*: **boolean**; *myver*: **integer**; *ask*: *vertype*; *curr*: *wordtype*; *currtran*: *trantype*; *currpars*: *partype*

initially $(\forall n : 0 \leq n < T :: copy[n] = p * T + n) \wedge myver = 0 \wedge view = nil \wedge j = 0$

Fig. 6. Type and variable declarations for Fig. 7.

6 Concluding Remarks and Future Work

We have presented new mechanisms for converting sequential implementations of dynamic transactions into lock-free or wait-free implementations. These implementations automatically detect and resolve conflicts between concurrent operations, and allow operations that do not conflict to execute in parallel. Our implementations are based on a "conditionally wait-free" implementation of MW-CAS. This implementation does not incur the high overhead of existing wait-free MWCAS implementations. Nonetheless, it ensures wait-freedom by synchronizing with a higher-level helping mechanism.

Our wait-free helping mechanism is substantially simpler than the one employed in Herlihy's wait-free construction [6]. This simplification is achieved by taking advantage of the MWCAS operation to avoid potential race conditions, and hence the complicated techniques used by Herlihy for dealing with them. Our helping mechanism also differs from Herlihy's in that transactions are executed one at a time, rather than using Herlihy's "operation combining".

In most previous wait-free universal constructions, even the best-case time complexity depends on the number of processes, the object size, or both. We have attempted to optimize the best-case performance of transactions. To this end, we have tried to keep the overhead of helping processes and determining which processes to help to a minimum. This results in a higher worst-case time complexity. We are currently preparing to evaluate our mechanisms (and others) by simulation. By these studies, we hope to gain a better understanding of what synchronization techniques are appropriate in what settings, and also to characterize design tradeoffs such as the one mentioned above. We will also evaluate the effectiveness of various optimizations not included here.

Our implementations allow nonconflicting transactions to execute in parallel. This property was formalized by Israeli and Rappoport [7], who defined the notion of *disjoint access parallel* implementations. Roughly speaking, a disjoint access parallel implementation ensures that transactions that do not access com-

procedure $LF\_Tran(help: 0..N-1;$
$\qquad\qquad$ *ver:* **integer**;
$\qquad\qquad$ *tran:* *trantype*;
$\qquad\qquad$ *pars:* *partype*)
$\quad$ **while** *true* **do**
1: $\quad$ **if** $(Read(B+N+help)).ver \neq ver$ **then**
2: $\qquad$ **return**
$\quad$ **fi**;
3: $\quad$ *freetree(view)*;
4: $\quad$ *view, cnt, dcnt, loop* := *nil, 0, 0, false*;
5: $\quad$ *ret* := *tran(pars)*;
6: $\quad$ *genpars(view)*;
7: $\quad$ **if** $GetHelp(help, ver)$ **then goto** 1 **fi**;
8: $\quad$ **if** $dcnt = 0$ **then** $cnt := 0$ **fi**;
9: $\quad$ **for** $i := 0$ **to** $cnt - 1$ **do**
10: $\qquad$ **if** $PAR[p].old[i] \neq PAR[p].new[i]$ **then**
11: $\qquad\quad$ $PAR[p].new[i].pid := p$
$\qquad$ **fi**
$\quad$ **od**;
12: $\quad$ $PAR[p].addr[cnt] := B + help$;
13: $\quad$ $PAR[p].old[cnt] := Read(B + help)$;
14: $\quad$ $PAR[p].new[cnt] := ret$;
15: $\quad$ $PAR[p].addr[cnt + 1] := B + N + help$;
16: $\quad$ $PAR[p].old[cnt + 1] := (ver, false)$;
17: $\quad$ $PAR[p].new[cnt + 1] := (ver + 1, false)$;
18: $\quad$ $PAR[p].nw := cnt + 2$;
19: $\quad$ **case** $MWCAS(Check, (help, ver))$ **of**
20: $\quad$ *succ:* **for** $i := 0$ **to** $dcnt - 1$ **do**
21: $\qquad$ $copy[i] := oldlst[i]$
$\qquad$ **od**;
22: $\quad$ *fail:* **if** $dcnt \neq 0$ **then**
23: $\qquad$ $GetHelp(help, ver)$;
$\qquad$ $loop := true$
$\qquad$ **fi**
$\quad$ **esac**;
24: $\quad$ **if** $\neg loop$ **then return fi**
$\quad$ **od**

procedure $Check(proc: 0..N-1;$
$\qquad\qquad$ *ver:* **integer**)
$\qquad\qquad$ **returns boolean**
25: **if** $Read(B + N + proc).ver \neq ver$ **then**
$\quad$ **return** *true*
$\quad$ **fi**;
26: $GetHelp(proc, ver)$; **return** *false*

procedure $GetHelp(help: 0..N-1;$
$\qquad\qquad$ *ver:* **integer**)
$\qquad\qquad$ **returns boolean**
$\quad$ **for** $i := 0$ **to** $cnt - 1$ **do**
27: $\quad$ $curr := Read(PAR[p].addr[i])$;
28: $\quad$ **if** $curr \neq PAR[p].old[i]$ **then**
29: $\qquad$ **if** $LL(\&HELP[help, curr.pid])$
$\qquad\qquad\qquad$ $\neq (ver, true)$ **then**
30: $\qquad\quad$ **if** $Read(B + N + help).ver$
$\qquad\qquad\qquad$ $= ver$ **then**
31: $\qquad\qquad$ $SC(\&HELP[help, curr.pid])$,
$\qquad\qquad\qquad$ $(ver, true))$
$\qquad$ **fi**;
32: $\qquad$ **return** *true*
$\qquad$ **fi**
$\quad$ **fi**
$\quad$ **od**;
33: **return** *false*

procedure $WF\_Tran(tran: trantype;$
$\qquad\qquad$ *pars: partype*)
$\qquad\qquad$ **returns** *valtype*
34: $ANC[p].tran := tran$;
35: $ANC[p].pars := pars$;
36: $LF\_Tran(p, myver, tran, pars)$;
37: $ask := LL(Help[j, p])$;
38: **if** $ask.active$ **then**
39: $\quad$ $currtran := ANC[j].tran$;
40: $\quad$ $currpars := ANC[j].pars$;
41: $\quad$ **if** $Read(B + N + j).ver =$
$\qquad\qquad$ $ask.ver$ **then**
42: $\qquad$ **if** $SC(Help[j, p]$,
$\qquad\qquad\qquad$ $(0, false))$ **then**
43: $\qquad\quad$ $LF\_Tran(j, ask.ver$,
$\qquad\qquad\qquad$ $currtran, currpars)$
$\qquad$ **fi**
$\quad$ **fi**
$\quad$ **fi**;
44: $myver := myver + 1$;
$\quad$ $j := (j + 1) \bmod N$;
45: **if** $j = p$ **then**
$\quad$ $j := (j + 1) \bmod N$
$\quad$ **fi**;
46: **return** $Read(B + p)$

Fig. 7. Wait-free transaction implementation for process p.

mon data do not interfere with each other. Both our lock-free and our wait-free implementations are disjoint access parallel (assuming transactions that access disjoint parts of the transactional memory also access disjoint sets of blocks). However, our algorithms are somewhat complicated by our efforts to achieve this property. We believe that better performance might be achieved by foregoing this requirement, while still striving to ensure maximum concurrency and to avoid hot spots [9] arising from excessive contention for shared variables.

Our implementations allow transactions to execute in parallel even if they do access common parts of the transactional memory, provided the commonly accessed parts are not modified by the transactions. This is an important property, for example, when implementing a balanced tree, in which all operations access the root of the tree, but relatively few modify it. However, our MWCAS implementation does not allow read-only concurrency. Thus, while transactions that read common data can execute largely in parallel, it is still possible for their respective MWCAS operations to interfere with each other. It would be interesting to improve this by implementing a conditionally wait-free MWCAS operation that allows read-only concurrency. The requirements of such an operation are similar to those of a readers-writers protocol, in which multiple processes can read a location concurrently, but must not access that location concurrently with a process that writes it. We leave this as a topic for future research.

References

1. Y. Afek, D. Dauber, and D. Touitou, "Wait-free Made Fast", *Proceedings of the 27th Annual ACM Symposium on Theory of Computing*, 1995.
2. J. Anderson and M. Moir, "Universal Constructions for Multi-Object Operations", *Proceedings of the 14th Annual ACM Symposium on Principles of Distributed Computing*, 1995.
3. J. Anderson and M. Moir, "Universal Constructions for Large Objects", *Proceedings of the Ninth International Workshop on Distributed Algorithms*, 1995.
4. J. Anderson and M. Moir, "Using Local-Spin k-Exclusion Algorithms to Improve Wait-Free Object Implementations", to appear in Distributed Computing.
5. G. Barnes, "A Method for Implementing Lock-Free Shared Data Structures", *Proceedings of the Fifth Annual ACM Symposium on Parallel Algorithms and Architectures*, 1993.
6. M. Herlihy, "A Methodology for Implementing Highly Concurrent Data Objects", *ACM Transactions on Programming Languages and Systems*, 15(5), 1993.
7. A. Israeli and L. Rappoport, "Disjoint-Access-Parallel Implementations of Strong Shared Memory Primitives", *Proceedings of the 13th Annual ACM Symposium on Principles of Distributed Computing*, 1994.
8. M. Moir, "Practical Implementations of Synchronization Primitives", to appear in the 16th Annual ACM Symposium on Principles of Distributed Computing.
9. G. Pfister and V. Norton, "Hot Spot Contention and Combining in Multistage Interconnection Networks", *IEEE Transactions on Computing*, C-34, 10, 1985.
10. N. Shavit and D. Touitou, "Software Transactional Memory", *Proceedings of the 14th Annual ACM Symposium on Principles of Distributed Computing*, 1995.
11. J. Turek, D. Shasha, and S. Prakash, "Locking Without Blocking: Making Lock Based Concurrent Data Structure Algorithms Non-Blocking", *Proceedings of the 11th Symposium on Principles of Database Systems*, 1992.

On the Power of Multi-objects[*]

PRASAD JAYANTI and SANJAY KHANNA

Dartmouth College, 6211 Sudikoff Laboratory, Hanover, NH 03755-3510, USA

Abstract. In the standard "single-object" model of shared-memory computing, it is assumed that a process accesses at most one shared object in each of its steps. A (more powerful) variant is the "multi-object" model in which each process may access an arbitrary finite number of shared objects simultaneously in each atomic step. In this paper, we present results that relate the synchronization power of a type in the multi-object model to its synchronization power in the single-object model. Afek, Merritt, and Taubenfeld considered the case where one could access up to a given number of objects simultaneously as well as the case where one could access any finite number of objects simultaneously in a single atomic step. We consider only the case where one may access an arbitrary finite number of objects simultaneously.

Although the types fetch&add and swap have the same synchronization power in the single-object model, Afek, Merritt, and Taubenfeld showed that their synchronization powers differ in the multi-object model [AMT96]. We prove that this divergence phenomenon is exhibited *only* by types at levels 1 and 2; all higher level types have the same unbounded synchronization power in the multi-object model.

This paper identifies *all* possible relationships between a type's synchronization power in the single-object model and its synchronization power in the multi-object model, where as many objects of one type as required may be accessed in a single atomic step.

Keywords: shared objects, multi-objects, waitfree, implementation, object hierarchy

1 Introduction

A shared-memory system consists of asynchronous processes and typed shared objects. An execution of such a system is an interleaving of the steps of individual processes. In the commonly studied model, it is assumed that a process accesses at most one shared object in each of its steps. We call this the *single-object model*. A variant (and a more powerful) model is the *multi-object model* in which each process may access multiple shared objects *atomically* in each of its steps. Specifically, each step of a process P corresponds to the following sequence of actions, all of which occur together atomically: (i) based on its present state, P determines the number m of objects to access, the identities $O_1, \ldots, O_m$ of (distinct) objects to access, and the operations $oper_1, \ldots, oper_m$ to apply to

[*] Work supported by NSF grant CCR-9410421, and Dartmouth College Startup grant.

these objects, (ii) for all $1 \leq i \leq m$, P applies $oper_i$ on O_i and receives O_i's response res_i, and (iii) P makes a transition to a new state, where the new state depends on the responses $res_1, \ldots, res_m$ and the previous state of P. This model was studied earlier by Herlihy [Her91] and by Merritt and Taubenfeld [MT94] in the context of shared-memories that consisted only of registers, and was recently explored further by Afek, Merritt, and Taubenfeld [AMT96]. In this paper, we present results that relate the synchronization power of a type in the multi-object model to its synchronization power in the single-object model.

Let T^m denote a shared-memory consisting of infinitely many objects of type T such that in each of its steps a process may access any of at most m objects atomically. Let T^* denote a shared-memory consisting of infinitely many objects of type T such that in each of its steps a process may access any finite number of objects atomically. Since consensus is universal [Her91], the extent to which consensus is implementable in a shared-memory is a reasonable measure of the synchronization power of that shared-memory. Accordingly, as in [AMT96], we define $Con(T^m)$ as the maximum number of processes for which a consensus object can be implemented in shared-memory T^m; if there is no such maximum, $Con(T^m) = \infty$. $Con(T^*)$ is similarly defined. Notice that $Con(T^1)$, which we will simply write as $Con(T)$, denotes the synchronization power of T in the single-object model.

Afek, Merritt, and Taubenfeld observed the following "divergence phenomenon" as we shift from the single-object model to the multi-object model [AMT96]. Although the types fetch&add and swap have the same synchronization power in the single-object model ($Con(\text{fetch\&add}) = Con(\text{swap}) = 2$ [Her91]), their synchronization powers differ in the multi-object model: $Con(\text{fetch\&add}^*)$ is still 2 while $Con(\text{swap}^*)$ is ∞. Thus, the multi-object model enhances the power of swap, but not of fetch&add, despite the fact that the two types have the same power in the single-object model. The same divergence phenomenon also occurs for certain types at level 1.[2] Specifically, consider the type trivial which supports a single operation that always returns the same response. Clearly $Con(\text{trivial}) = 1$. It is well-known that $Con(\text{register})$ is also 1 [CIL94, DDS87, LA87, Her91]. Yet, $Con(\text{trivial}^*) = 1$ and $Con(\text{register}^*) = \infty$ [Her91].

The main result of this paper is that the divergence phenomenon described above is exhibited *only* by types at levels 1 and 2. Specifically, we prove that if $Con(T) \geq 3$, then $Con(T^*) = \infty$. In other words, the synchronization power of *all* types at levels 3 or higher is enhanced to the fullest degree by the multi-object model. Thus, it is not a coincidence that the types which appeared above in the examples of the divergence phenomenon — fetch&add, swap, trivial, and register — are at levels 1 or 2.

We also present the following results for types at levels 1 and 2. If $Con(T) = 1$, we show $Con(T^*) \in \{1, 2, \infty\}$. Further, we show that there are types in all of these three categories. If $Con(T) = 2$, we show $Con(T^*) \in \{2, \infty\}$. Further, there are types in both these categories, as was demonstrated in [AMT96] with fetch&add and swap.

---

[2] We refer to a type T as being at level k if $Con(T) = k$.

Figure 1 summarizes all possible ways in which $Con(T)$ and $Con(T^*)$ are related. There is an "X" in the table element at row labeled i and column labeled j if and only if there is a type T such that $Con(T) = i$ and $Con(T^*) = j$. The table also includes example types for the different possible relationships. Although [AMT96] studied the variation of synchronization power of a type as one may access up to m objects of a given type as well as when one may access as many objects as required, we consider only the latter case. As the table indicates, we present a complete picture of how the synchronization power of a type is affected by a shift from the single-object model, where one may access only one shared object in a single atomic step, to the multi-object model, where one may access as many shared objects as required in a single atomic step.

$Con(T)$	$Con(T^*)$		
	1	2	∞
1	X trivial	X blind-increment	X register [Her91]
2		X fetch&add [AMT96]	X swap [AMT96]
≥ 3			X

Fig. 1. All possible ways in which $Con(T)$ and $Con(T^*)$ are related

2 Preliminaries

The concepts in this section are not new and our treatment is therefore informal.

2.1 Definition of wait-free implementation and linearizability

An implementation of an object shared by processes $P_1, P_2, \ldots P_n$ is said to be wait-free if every process is able to complete its operation on the shared object regardless of the relative speeds of the other processes, or if the other processes have crashed.

An implementation of a shared object is said to be linearizable if every operation on the shared object appears to take place at some unique point between the start time of the operation and the completion time of the operation as described in [HW90]. The linearizability property also requires that the implementation of the object satisfies the sequential specifications of the object as though it had been accessed sequentially with the same operations in the order of the times at which the operations appear to have taken place as described above.

In this paper we assume that all implementations are wait-free and linearizable.

2.2   Definitions of n-consensus and n-IDconsensus

An object of type n-**consensus** can be accessed by at most n processes. Each process may invoke *propose 0* or *propose 1*. The sequential specification is as follows: all operations return the value first proposed.

An object of type n-**IDconsensus** can be accessed by at most n processes. Let $P_0, P_1, \ldots, P_{n-1}$ be the names of these processes. Process P_i may only invoke *propose i*. The sequential specification is as follows: all operations return the value first proposed.

Using a single n-IDconsensus object, $P_0, P_1, \ldots, P_{n-1}$ can determine a winner among them as follows: each P_i proposes i to the object; if the object's response is j, P_i regards P_j as the winner.

As in the above, we write the type names in the typewriter font. Thus, "**register**" denotes a type and "register" (in non-typewriter font) denotes an object.

2.3   Direct implementation

Let X and Y be types. X^m denotes a shared-memory system of infinitely many objects of type X, where a process may access at most m objects simultaneously in a single atomic step. X^* denotes a shared-memory system where a process may access any finite number of objects simultaneously in a single atomic step. Informally, X^m *implements* Y^n if there is a wait-free simulation of shared-memory Y^n using a finite number of objects of type X in shared-memory X^m. Each operation on the (implemented) shared-memory Y^n is simulated by executing (possibly many) operations on the shared-memory X^m.[3]

Afek, Merritt, and Taubenfeld introduced the notion of "direct implementation" [AMT96]. X^m *directly implements* Y^n if there is an implementation of Y^n from X^m such that the linearization of every operation op on the shared-memory Y^n can always be placed at the first access to X^m during the simulation of op [AMT96].

We write $X^m \rightarrow Y^n$ to denote that X^m implements Y^n and $X^m \xrightarrow{di} Y^n$ to denote that X^m directly implements Y^n.

The transitivity of $\xrightarrow{di}$ follows easily from definitions and is therefore stated below without proof.

Proposition 1. *The relation $\xrightarrow{di}$ is transitive: $X^m \xrightarrow{di} Y^n$ and $Y^n \xrightarrow{di} Z^p$ implies $X^m \xrightarrow{di} Z^p$.*

2.4   Previous results

Here we state previous results that will be used in this paper.

Theorem 2 [AMT96]. *Let X and Y be any types. $X^p \xrightarrow{di} Y^q$ implies $X^{pm} \xrightarrow{di} Y^{qm}$, for all $m > 0$.*

---

[3] Sometimes it is assumed that the implementation also has access to registers. We do not make such an assumption in this paper.

Theorem 3 [AMT96]. *Let X and Y be any types. $X^p \xrightarrow{di} Y$ implies $Con(X^{pq}) \geq Con(Y^q)$, for all $p, q > 0$.*

The following is a special case of a more general theorem from [AMT96].

Theorem 4 [AMT96]. $Con(\text{3-consensus}^m) \geq \sqrt{2m}$.

2.5 Key results

The following two lemmas and theorem are the key results in this paper. The first lemma is easy to verify. The theorem is proved in Section 3.4. The second lemma follows from the theorem because the types T^* and $(T^*)^*$ are the same.

Lemma 5. $Con(T^*) \geq Con(T)$

Theorem 6. $Con(T) \geq 3 \rightarrow Con(T^*) = \infty$

Lemma 7. $Con(T^*) \geq 3 \rightarrow Con(T^*) = \infty$

3 Multi-object theorem for types at level 3 or higher

In this section we prove that if $Con(T) \geq 3$, then $Con(T^*) = \infty$. Theorem 4 [AMT96] provides a simple [not direct] implementation for $\sqrt{2m}$-consensus from 3-consensus^m, but we provide a direct implementation of a similar result. In Section 3.2 we show that n-IDconsensus directly implements n-consensus, and in Section 3.3 we show that any type T that can implement 3-consensus may be used to directly implement 3-IDconsensus if up to two objects of type T maybe accessed simultaneously. Our result follows from the above results and the results of Afek, Merritt, and Taubenfeld stated above. We conclude in Section 3.4, and in Section 3.5, sketch an alternative proof for the same result. We begin with our notation for describing implementations of n-consensus and n-IDconsensus.

3.1 Notation for describing consensus implementations

Informally, the following two elements constitute an implementation of an n-consensus object $\mathcal{O}$, shared by processes $P_0, \ldots, P_{n-1}$, in shared memory T^k: (i) the objects $O_1, O_2, \ldots, O_m$ that $\mathcal{O}$ is implemented from, and (ii) the access procedures $\text{Propose}(P_i, v, \mathcal{O})$, for $i \in \{0, 1, \ldots, n-1\}$ and $v \in \{0, 1\}$. To apply a *propose* v operation on $\mathcal{O}$, P_i calls and executes the access procedure $\text{Propose}(P_i, v, \mathcal{O})$. The access procedure specifies how to simulate the operation on $\mathcal{O}$ by executing operations on $O_1, O_2, \ldots, O_m$, accessing at most k of these objects in any one step. The return value from the access procedure is deemed to be the response of $\mathcal{O}$ to P_i's operation. We refer to $O_1, O_2, \ldots, O_m$ as *base objects* of $\mathcal{O}$. The *space complexity* of the implementation is m, the number of base objects required in implementing $\mathcal{O}$.

Similarly, an implementation of an n-IDconsensus object $\mathcal{O}$, shared by processes $P_0, \ldots, P_{n-1}$, in shared memory T^k is constituted by: (i) the objects $O_1, O_2, \ldots, O_m$ that $\mathcal{O}$ is implemented from, and (ii) the access procedures $\texttt{Propose}(P_i, i, \mathcal{O})$, for $i \in \{0, 1, \ldots, n-1\}$ (recall that process P_i may only propose i on $\mathcal{O}$).

3.2 Directly implementing n-consensus from n-IDconsensus[2]

In this section, we show that n-**IDconsensus**[2] *directly* implements n-**consensus**. Let $\mathcal{O}$ denote the n-consensus object to be implemented. Let $P_0, \ldots, P_{n-1}$ denote the processes that share $\mathcal{O}$, and let v_i be the value that P_i wishes to propose to $\mathcal{O}$. For ease of exposition, we develop the implementation in steps. First we show a simple implementation of an n-consensus object from a single n-IDconsensus object and n registers. We then refine this implementation to eliminate the use of registers. The resulting implementation uses $2n + 1$ n-IDconsensus objects, but is still not a direct implementation. We then describe how to make it direct.

Here is the first implementation: each P_i first writes its proposal v_i in a register R_i and then performs IDconsensus with other processes by proposing i to an n-IDconsensus object $\mathcal{W}$. If P_k is the winner of this IDconsensus, then P_i returns the value in register R_k as the response of the implemented n-consensus object $\mathcal{O}$.

The next implementation, eliminating the use of registers, is in Figure 2. This implementation uses $2n + 1$ n-IDconsensus objects. The object named $\mathcal{W}$ serves the same purpose as before: to determine the identity of the process whose proposal is the winning proposal. The objects $O_{i,0}$ and $O_{i,1}$ help P_i communicate its proposal to other processes. Each P_i begins by proposing i to O_{i,v_i} (this corresponds to the step of writing v_i in R_i in the previous implementation). P_i then performs IDconsensus with other processes by proposing i to $\mathcal{W}$. Let $winner$ be the value returned by $\mathcal{W}$. If $winner = i$, then P_i is the winner and its proposal v_i is the winning proposal, so P_i returns v_i as the response of the implemented n-consensus object $\mathcal{O}$. Otherwise, P_i must learn P_{winner}'s proposal, which is the winning proposal. For this, P_i proposes i to $O_{winner,0}$. If $O_{winner,0}$ returns $winner$, then the proposal of P_{winner} must be 0, so P_i returns 0; otherwise the proposal of P_{winner} must be 1, so P_i returns 1. The correctness of this implementation is obvious. We thus have:

Lemma 8. n-IDconsensus $\rightarrow$ n-consensus.

The above implementation is not direct: P_i's operation on $\mathcal{O}$ is linearized at its access to $\mathcal{W}$ and *not* at its first access to a base object. We turn it into a direct implementation simply by requiring P_i to perform lines 1 and 2 in Figure 2 simultaneously, in one atomic action. This results in a direct implementation of n-consensus from n-IDconsensus[2]. We thus have:

Lemma 9. n-IDconsensus[2] $\xrightarrow{di}$ n-consensus.

$\mathcal{W}, \{O_{i,0}, O_{i,1} \mid 0 \leq i \leq n-1\}$: n-IDconsensus objects

Procedure Propose$(P_i, v_i, \mathcal{O})$ /* $v_i \in \{0,1\}$ */
    winner : integer local to P_i
begin
1.   Propose(P_i, i, O_{i,v_i})
2.   *winner* := Propose$(P_i, i, \mathcal{W})$
3.   **if** *winner* = i **then**
4.   **return** v_i
5.   **else if** Propose$(P_i, i, O_{winner,0})$ returns *winner*
6.   **return** 0
7.   **else return** 1
end

Fig. 2. Implementing n-consensus from n-IDconsensus

3.3 The main lemma

We prove that, for all T, if there is an implementation of 3-**consensus** from T, then there is a *direct* implementation, of twice the space complexity, of 3-**IDconsensus** from T^2, i.e. twice the number of base objects are required for the direct implementation.

Our design exploits the well-known bivalency argument due to Fischer, Lynch, and Paterson [FLP85]. Since bivalency arguments are standard, our definitions here are informal. Let $\mathcal{O}$, shared by P_0, P_1, and P_2, be a 3-consensus object implemented from objects $O_1, \ldots, O_m$ of type T. Let v_i denote P_i's proposal to $\mathcal{O}$. A *configuration* of $\mathcal{O}$ is a tuple consisting of the states of the three access procedures Propose$(P_i, v_i, \mathcal{O})$ ($i \in \{0,1,2\}$) and the states of objects $O_1, \ldots, O_m$. A configuration C is *v-valent* (for $v \in \{0,1\}$) if there is no execution from C in which $\bar{v}$ is decided upon by some P_i. In other words, once in configuration C, no matter how P_0, P_1, and P_2 are scheduled, no P_i returns $\bar{v}$. A configuration is *monovalent* if it is either 0-valent or 1-valent. A configuration is *bivalent* if it is not monovalent. If E is a finite execution of the implementation starting from configuration C, $E(C)$ denotes the configuration at the end of the execution E.

Lemma 10. $T \to 3$-**consensus** *implies* $T^2 \xrightarrow{di} 3$-**IDconsensus**.

Proof. Let $\mathcal{I}$ be an implementation of 3-**consensus** from T. Note that **IDconsensus** requires that process P_i may invoke only *propose i*. Let $\mathcal{O}$, shared by P_0, P_1, and P_2, be a 3-consensus object implemented using $\mathcal{I}$ from objects $O_1, \ldots, O_m$ of type T. Pick val_0, val_1, and val_2, the proposals of P_0, P_1, and P_2, respectively, so that C_0, the initial configuration of $\mathcal{O}$, is bivalent. (For instance, $val_0 = 0$ and $val_1 = val_2 = 1$ would be adequate.)

Let E be a finite execution from C_0 such that (1) $C_{crit} = E(C_0)$ is bivalent, and (2) For all P_i, if P_i takes a step from C_{crit}, the resulting configuration is monovalent. (If such E does not exist, it is easy to see that there is an infinite execution E' in which no process decides. Thus, some process takes infinitely many steps in E' without deciding, contradicting the wait-freedom property of the implementation of $\mathcal{O}$.) Let S_v be the set of P_i whose step from C_{crit} results in a v-valent configuration. Since C_{crit} is bivalent, neither S_0 nor S_1 is empty. Furthermore, $S_0 \cap S_1 = \emptyset$. Without loss of generality, let $S_0 = \{P_0\}$ and $S_1 = \{P_1, P_2\}$. Thus, if P_0 is the first to take a step from C_{crit}, then regardless of how P_0, P_1, and P_2 are scheduled subsequently, every P_i eventually decides 0. Similarly, if either of P_1 and P_2 is the first to take a step from C_{crit}, then regardless of how P_0, P_1, and P_2 are scheduled subsequently, every P_i eventually decides 1.

In the configuration C_{crit}, let σ_0, σ_1, and σ_2 denote the states of the access procedures $\texttt{Propose}(P_0, val_0, \mathcal{O})$, $\texttt{Propose}(P_1, val_1, \mathcal{O})$, and $\texttt{Propose}(P_2, val_2, \mathcal{O})$, respectively. Also let $\mu_1, \ldots, \mu_m$ denote the states of $O_1, \ldots, O_m$, respectively, in C_{crit}.

Given the above context, we are ready to describe the *direct* implementation of a 3-IDconsensus object $\mathcal{A}$, shared by processes Q_0, Q_1, and Q_2, from objects $O'_1, \ldots, O'_m, O''_1, \ldots, O''_m$ of type T. Each Q_i may access up to two base objects atomically in a single step.

The idea is to use the given implementation $\mathcal{I}$ to build two 3-consensus objects (from the available objects $O'_1, \ldots, O'_m, O''_1, \ldots, O''_m$), initialize both of them to C_{crit}, and require Q_0, Q_1, and Q_2 to access them in such a way that, if Q_i is the first to take a step, all of Q_0, Q_1, and Q_2 eventually return i. The details are as follows.

Using implementation $\mathcal{I}$ and the objects $O'_1, \ldots, O'_m$, implement a 3-consensus object $\mathcal{O}'$ that can be shared by P'_0, P'_1, and P'_2. Similarly, using implementation $\mathcal{I}$ and the objects $O''_1, \ldots, O''_m$, implement another 3-consensus object $\mathcal{O}''$ that can be shared by P''_0, P''_1, and P''_2.

Initialize each of $\mathcal{O}'$ and $\mathcal{O}''$ to C_{crit}; more specifically,

1. Since $\mathcal{O}'$ is implemented to be shared by P'_0, P'_1, and P'_2, it supports the three access procedures $\texttt{Propose}(P'_0, val_0, \mathcal{O}')$, $\texttt{Propose}(P'_1, val_1, \mathcal{O}')$, and $\texttt{Propose}(P'_2, val_2, \mathcal{O}')$. Initialize the states of these access procedures to σ_0, σ_1, and σ_2, respectively.
2. Initialize the states of objects $O'_1, \ldots, O'_m$ to $\mu_1, \ldots, \mu_m$, respectively.
3. Since $\mathcal{O}''$ is implemented to be shared by P''_0, P''_1, and P''_2, it supports the access procedures $\texttt{Propose}(P''_0, val_0, \mathcal{O}'')$, $\texttt{Propose}(P''_1, val_1, \mathcal{O}'')$, and $\texttt{Propose}(P''_2, val_2, \mathcal{O}'')$. Initialize the states of these three access procedures to σ_0, σ_1, and σ_2, respectively.
4. Initialize the states of objects $O''_1, \ldots, O''_m$ to $\mu_1, \ldots, \mu_m$, respectively.

Each Q_i executes two access procedures, one of $\mathcal{O}'$ and one of $\mathcal{O}''$. The exact mapping of which two access procedures Q_i executes is as follows: Process Q_0 executes procedures $\texttt{Propose}(P'_0, val_0, \mathcal{O}')$ and $\texttt{Propose}(P''_1, val_1, \mathcal{O}'')$;

Q_1 executes $\texttt{Propose}(P_1', val_1, \mathcal{O}')$ and $\texttt{Propose}(P_0'', val_0, \mathcal{O}'')$; and Q_2 executes $\texttt{Propose}(P_2', val_2, \mathcal{O}')$ and $\texttt{Propose}(P_2'', val_2, \mathcal{O}'')$. Each process executes its access procedures as follows. In its first step, each process executes the first step of *both* of its access procedures simultaneously (this is possible because in the implementation being designed a process is allowed to access up to two objects in one step). After its first step, each process executes any one of its access procedures to completion and then executes the other access procedure to completion. Once a process executes both its access procedures to completion, it knows the decision values d' and d'' returned by the 3-consensus objects $\mathcal{O}'$ and $\mathcal{O}''$, respectively.

The key observation is the following: If Q_i is the first process to take a step (among Q_0, Q_1, and Q_2), since the first step of Q_i corresponds to the first step of both of its access procedures, the decision values of both $\mathcal{O}'$ and $\mathcal{O}''$ become fixed at the end of Q_i's first step. Furthermore, given our mapping between processes and access procedures, we have the following obvious relationships: $(d', d'') = (0, 1)$ if and only if Q_0 is the first process to take a step, $(d', d'') = (1, 0)$ if and only if Q_1 is the first process to take a step, and $(d', d'') = (1, 1)$ if and only if Q_2 is the first process to take a step. (Notice that $(d', d'') = (0, 0)$ cannot occur.) Thus, from the values d' and d'', each Q_j determines the identity of the Q_i which took the very first step and returns i. This completes the proof of the lemma. ∎

Lemma 11. $T \to 3\text{-consensus}$ *implies* $T^4 \xrightarrow{di} 3\text{-consensus}$.

Proof. Suppose that $T \to 3\text{-consensus}$. By Lemma 10, $T^2 \xrightarrow{di} 3\text{-IDconsensus}$. By Theorem 2, $T^4 \xrightarrow{di} 3\text{-IDconsensus}^2$. This, together with Lemma 9 and the transitivity of $\xrightarrow{di}$ (Proposition 1), gives the lemma. ∎

3.4 Multi-object theorem for types at level 3 or higher

The next lemma states that if type T objects are strong enough to implement 3-consensus objects in the standard single-access model, then they are good for implementing n-consensus objects (for any n) provided that processes can access sufficiently many of them ($2n^2$, to be precise) in a single step.

Lemma 12. $Con(T) \geq 3$ *implies* $Con(T^{2n^2}) \geq n$.

Proof. $Con(T) \geq 3$
$\Rightarrow \quad T \to 3\text{-consensus}$
$\Rightarrow \quad T^4 \xrightarrow{di} 3\text{-consensus}$ $\qquad$ (by Lemma 11)
$\Rightarrow \quad \forall m > 0 : Con(T^{4m}) \geq Con(3\text{-consensus}^m)$ $\qquad$ (by Theorem 3)
$\Rightarrow \quad \forall m > 0 : Con(T^{4m}) \geq \sqrt{2m}$ $\qquad$ (by Theorem 4)
$\Rightarrow \quad Con(T^{2n^2}) \geq n$ $\qquad$ (letting $m = n^2/2$) ∎

Finally, we present the multi-object theorem for types at level 3 or higher. This theorem is immediate from the above lemma.

Theorem 13. $Con(T) \geq 3$ *implies* $Con(T^*) = \infty$.

3.5 Sketch of an alternative proof

In this section, we sketch an alternative proof of Theorem 13. Afek, Merritt, and Taubenfeld introduced a consensus object that also supports a read operation [AMT96]. Specifically, an object of type (f, r)-**consensus** can be accessed by f "proposer" processes and r "reader" processes. A proposer may only invoke *propose 0* or *propose 1*, and a reader may only invoke *read*. The sequential specification is as follows: if the first operation is *propose v*, all operations return v; if the first operation is a *read*, operations return arbitrary responses. A result in [AMT96] states that an n-consensus object, for any n, can be implemented using (f, r)-consensus objects if sufficiently many of them can be accessed simultaneously. Specifically:

Theorem 14 [AMT96]. (f, r)-**consensus**$^m \to n$-**consensus**, *where*
$n \leq \sqrt{mrf + f^2/4} + f/2$.

We can define the type (f, r)-**IDconsensus** and obtain a result analogous to Theorem 14. Specifically, an object of type (f, r)-**IDconsensus** can be accessed by at most f proposers, $P_0, P_1, \ldots, P_{f-1}$, and r readers. Proposer P_i may only invoke *propose i*, and a reader may only invoke *read*. The sequential specification is as follows: if the first operation is *propose i*, all operations return i; if the first operation is a *read*, operations return arbitrary responses. With minor modifications, the proof of Theorem 14 can be adapted to obtain the following result, an analog of Theorem 14 for IDconsensus:[4]

Theorem 15. (f, r)-**IDconsensus**$^m \to n$-**IDconsensus**, *where* $n \leq \sqrt{mrf + f^2/4} + f/2$.

If a type implements 3-**consensus**, using the familiar bivalency arguments it is fairly easy to show that T directly implements $(2, 1)$-**IDconsensus**. Thus:

Theorem 16. $T \to$ 3-**consensus** *implies* $T \xrightarrow{di} (2, 1)$-**IDconsensus**.

Now Theorem 13 can be proved as follows. Suppose that $T \to$ 3-**consensus**. By Theorem 16, $T \xrightarrow{di} (2, 1)$-**IDconsensus**. Letting $p = q = 1$ in Theorem 2, we

---

[4] The proof of Theorem 14 uses the following idea. To solve consensus, processes split themselves into two groups G_0 and G_1, processes in each G_i solve consensus recursively to obtain the consensus value v_i for the group, then the two groups compete with all processes in G_i proposing v_i, and finally every process adopts the value proposed by the winning group. For this idea to work in the proof of Theorem 15, which deals with IDconsensus instead of consensus, it should be possible for the processes in the losing group, say G_1, to determine the winner of the winning group, namely, G_0. If registers are available, processes in each group G_i can write the winner of G_i in some register $R(G_i)$ before competing with the other group $G_{\bar{i}}$. Thus, processes in G_1, the losing group, can easily determine the winner of the group G_0 by reading the register $R(G_0)$. Unfortunately, however, registers are not available — the only available objects are (f, r)-IDconsensus objects. We overcome this difficulty with a trick similar to the one used in Section 3.2, where we first presented a construction that uses registers and then showed how to eliminate registers.

obtain that $X \xrightarrow{di} Y$ implies $X^m \xrightarrow{di} Y^m$. Using this, we have $T^{n^2/2} \xrightarrow{di} (2,1)$-IDconsensus$^{n^2/2}$. By Theorem 15, $(2,1)$-IDconsensus$^{n^2/2} \rightarrow n$-IDconsensus. Thus, we have $T^{n^2/2} \rightarrow n$-IDconsensus. Since n-IDconsensus $\rightarrow n$-consensus (by Lemma 8), we have $T^{n^2/2} \rightarrow n$-consensus. Therefore, $Con(T^*) = \infty$. Hence Theorem 13.

4 Multi-object theorems for types at levels 1 and 2

In this section, we relate $Con(T)$ and $Con(T^*)$ when $Con(T)$ is 1 or 2. Specifically, if $Con(T) = 1$, we show that $Con(T^*) \in \{1, 2, \infty\}$, and exhibit types in all three of these categories. If $Con(T) = 2$, we show that $Con(T^*) \in \{2, \infty\}$; it was shown in [AMT96] that there are types in both these categories. The following lemma is useful in establishing some of these results.

Lemma 17. $Con(T^*) \geq 3$ implies $Con(T^*) = \infty$.

Proof. $Con(T^*) \geq 3$
$\Rightarrow$ $Con(T^m) \geq 3$ for some $m > 0$
$\Rightarrow$ $Con((T^m)^*) = \infty$ (by Theorem 13)
$\Rightarrow$ $Con(T^*) = \infty$
∎

Next we present the multi-object theorem for types at level 1.

Theorem 18.

1. $Con(T) = 1$ implies $Con(T^*) \in \{1, 2, \infty\}$.
2. There is a type T such that $Con(T) = 1$ and $Con(T^*) = 1$.
3. There is a type T such that $Con(T) = 1$ and $Con(T^*) = 2$.
4. There is a type T such that $Con(T) = 1$ and $Con(T^*) = \infty$ [Her91].

Proof. Part (1) follows directly from Lemma 17. For part (2), consider the type **trivial** which supports only a single operation that always returns the same response. Clearly, $Con(\textbf{trivial}) = 1$ and $Con(\textbf{trivial}^*) = 1$. For part (4), **register** is an example of a type T for which $Con(T) = 1$ [CIL94, DDS87, LA87, Her91] and $Con(T^*) = \infty$ [Her91]. We prove part (3) below.

Consider the **blind-increment** type that supports *read* and *blindInc* operations. The *read* operation returns the value of the object without affecting it. The *blindInc* operation increments the value and returns *ack*.

Claim 19. $Con(\textbf{blind-increment}) = 1$.

Proof. This claim is well-known and is immediate from the following three facts:

(i) **blind-increment** has a (trivial) implementation from **atomic-snapshot**,[5]

---

[5] Informally, an object of type **atomic-snapshot** stores a vector of n integers, where n is the number of processes that may access the object. Any process may perform a *read* operation, which simply returns the vector. Process P_i may perform a *write* (i, v) which changes the value of the ith element of the vector to v.

(ii) `atomic-snapshot` has an implementation from `register` [AAD+93, And93], and

(iii) `register` cannot implement 2-`consensus` [CIL94, DDS87, LA87, Her91]. ■

Claim 20. $Con(\texttt{blind-increment}^2) \geq 2$.

Proof. We can implement a 2-IDconsensus object, shared by processes P_0 and P_1, from two blind-increment objects O_0 and O_1, both initialized to 0, as follows. Process P_i both reads O_i and blind-increments $O_{\bar{i}}$ in the same step. If P_i reads 0, it is the winner, and so it returns i. Otherwise $P_{\bar{i}}$ is the winner, so it returns $\bar{i}$. It is easy to verify that this protocol is correct. From this and Lemma 8, we have the claim. ■

Claim 21. *For all $m > 0$, $Con(\texttt{blind-increment}^m) \leq 2$.*

Proof. The operations of `blind-increment` commute as described in [AMT96][6]. Therefore, by a result in [AMT96], $Con(\texttt{blind-increment}^m) \leq 2$. ■

By the above three claims, `blind-increment` is an example of a type T for which $Con(T) = 1$ and $Con(T^*) = 2$. This completes the proof of Theorem 18. Finally, we present the multi-object theorem for types at level 2.

Theorem 22.

1. $Con(T) = 2$ implies $Con(T^*) \in \{2, \infty\}$.
2. There is a type T such that $Con(T) = 2$ and $Con(T^*) = 2$ [Her91, AMT96].
3. There is a type T such that $Con(T) = 2$ and $Con(T^*) = \infty$ [Her91, AMT96].

Proof. Part (1) is immediate from Lemma 17 and the observation $Con(T^*) \geq Con(T)$. Parts (2) and (3) follow from the following known results: $Con(\texttt{fetch\&add}) = Con(\texttt{swap}) = 2$ [Her91], $Con(\texttt{fetch\&add}^*) = 2$ [AMT96] and $Con(\texttt{swap}^*) = \infty$ [AMT96]. ■

References

[AAD+93] Y. Afek, H. Attiya, D. Dolev, E. Gafni, M. Merritt, and N. Shavit. Atomic snapshots of shared memory. *Journal of the ACM*, 40(4):873–890, 1993.

[AMT96] Y. Afek, M. Merritt, and G. Taubenfeld. The power of multi-objects. In *Proceedings of the 15th Annual ACM Symposium on Principles of Distributed Computing*, May 1996.

[And93] J. Anderson. Composite registers. *Distributed Computing*, 6(3):141–154, 1993.

[CIL94] B. Chor, A. Israeli, and M. Li. Wait-free consensus using asynchronous hardware. *SIAM Journal on Computing*, 23(4):701–712, August 1994.

---

[6] The operations of an object commute if no process can determine the relative order of any two operations on the object in which it did not participate. The processes participating in the two operations may be able to find out the relative order by the values returned by each operation.

[DDS87] D. Dolev, C. Dwork, and L. Stockmeyer. On the minimal synchronism needed for distributed consensus. *Journal of the ACM*, 34(1):77–97, January 1987.

[FLP85] M. Fischer, N. Lynch, and M. Paterson. Impossibility of distributed consensus with one faulty process. *JACM*, 32(2):374–382, 1985.

[HW90] M.P. Herlihy and J.M. Wing. Linearizability: A Correctnes Condition for Concurrent Objects. *ACM TOPLAS*, 12(3):463–492, 1990.

[Her91] M.P. Herlihy. Wait-free synchronization. *ACM TOPLAS*, 13(1):124–149, 1991.

[LA87] M.C. Loui and H.H. Abu-Amara. Memory requirements for agreement among unreliable asynchronous processes. *Advances in computing research*, 4:163–183, 1987.

[MT94] M. Merritt and G. Taubenfeld. Atomic m-register operations. *Distributed Computing*, 7:213–221, 1994.

Author Index

Springer
and the
environment

At Springer we firmly believe that an international science publisher has a special obligation to the environment, and our corporate policies consistently reflect this conviction.

We also expect our business partners – paper mills, printers, packaging manufacturers, etc. – to commit themselves to using materials and production processes that do not harm the environment. The paper in this book is made from low- or no-chlorine pulp and is acid free, in conformance with international standards for paper permanency.

Springer

Lecture Notes in Computer Science

For information about Vols. 1–1238

please contact your bookseller or Springer-Verlag